D1626447

3584837500

University of Sti...

STUDIES IN IMPERIALISM

general editor John M. MacKenzie

When the 'Studies in Imperialism' series was founded
more than twenty years ago, emphasis was laid upon the
conviction that 'imperialism as a cultural phenomenon
had as significant an effect on the dominant as on the
subordinate societies'. With more than fifty books
published, this remains the prime concern of the series.
Cross-disciplinary work has indeed appeared covering the
full spectrum of cultural phenomena, as well as
examining aspects of gender and sex, frontiers and law,
science and the environment, language and literature,
migration and patriotic societies, and much else.
Moreover, the series has always wished to present
comparative work on European and American
imperialism, and particularly welcomes the submission
of books in these areas. The fascination with
imperialism, in all its aspects, shows no sign of abating,
and this series will continue to lead the way in
encouraging the widest possible range of studies in the
field. 'Studies in Imperialism' is fully organic in its
development, always seeking to be at the cutting edge,
responding to the latest interests of scholars and the
needs of this ever-expanding area of scholarship.

The French empire between the wars

MANCHESTER
1824

Manchester University Press

AVAILABLE IN THE SERIES

The French empire between the wars

IMPERIALISM, POLITICS AND SOCIETY

Martin Thomas

MANCHESTER UNIVERSITY PRESS

Manchester and New York

distributed exclusively in the USA by PALGRAVE

Copyright © Martin Thomas 2005

The right of Martin Thomas to be identified as the author of this work has been asserted by him in accordance with the Copyright, Designs and Patents Act 1988.

Published by MANCHESTER UNIVERSITY PRESS
OXFORD ROAD, MANCHESTER M13 9NR, UK
and ROOM 400, 175 FIFTH AVENUE, NEW YORK, NY 10010, USA
www.manchesteruniversitypress.co.uk

Distributed exclusively in the USA by
PALGRAVE, 175 FIFTH AVENUE, NEW YORK, NY 10010, USA

Distributed exclusively in Canada by
UBC PRESS, UNIVERSITY OF BRITISH COLUMBIA,
2029 WEST MALL, VANCOUVER, BC, CANADA V6T 1Z2

British Library Cataloguing-in-Publication Data
A catalogue record for this book is available from the British Library

Library of Congress Cataloging-in-Publication Data applied for

ISBN 0 7190 6518 6 hardback
EAN 978 0 7190 6518 7

First published 2005

14 13 12 11 10 09 08 07 06 05   10 9 8 7 6 5 4 3 2 1

Typeset in Kuenst
by Mudra Typesetters, Pondicherry, India
Printed in Great Britain
by CPI, Bath

CONTENTS

CONTENTS

LIST OF MAPS AND TABLES

Maps

Tables

GENERAL EDITOR'S INTRODUCTION

There is no doubt that in the present state of the historiography of imperialism there is a crying need for parallel and comparative studies. In the anglophone world there has been excessive concentration on the British empire, as has been reflected not only in the older and newer Cambridge and Oxford histories, but also in publishers' lists. Although there are of course major works on the French, Dutch, German and Italian empires in their native European languages, the sources available to the English-speaking student are much less rich. If this is true in general terms for these European empires, how much more is it true of the inter-war period, which has until recently tended to be a 'cinderella' era in imperial scholarship. So far as the French empire is concerned, there has been a notable quickening of interest, not least in the fields of popular culture, propaganda and administrative concerns.

This book constitutes a very welcome addition to the literature in English on French imperialism, especially valuable because it deals with the period between the two world wars of the twentieth century. It is also striking that the work picks up on so many valuable themes in the period. It has sometimes been argued that this period constitutes, against all the odds, something of a classic era in imperial rule. It was the time when the most strenuous efforts were made to integrate metropolitan and colonial economies. It was a period when administrative practice was most highly developed. And these were the years when empires, buffeted by world economic depression, apprehension at political and military developments in Europe and the Far East, as well as assaulted by revolt and intellectual disillusion at home and in the colonies, became most active in issuing propaganda and asserting the centrality of the imperial relationship through popular culture. In the French case, this was reflected in the extraordinary colonial exhibitions that took place in Marseilles in 1922 and in Paris in 1931 and 1937, among the grandest and most eclectic of their type.

Martin Thomas deals here with the multiple aspects of what he calls the period of 'consolidation and expansion', the emergence of colonial planning policies, the attempted integration of economies, the roles of urban growth and development, education and women's activities, as well as the quickening of both nationalist resistance and fears of international crisis. All these themes are illustrated by examples from North and West Africa, the Middle East and Indochina, and all contribute to the sense of the major paradox of the inter-war years. On the one hand, here was a sort of Golden Age, if regularly tarnished. On the other, here was the prelude to the major disruptions of the Second World War, with an empire divided in allegiance to Vichy or the Free French, and consequently to the acts of decolonisation forced upon the French state after the Second World War.

Obviously, the experience of the French empire stands alone, but the parallels with developments in the British, and perhaps other, empires (not least the American and the Japanese, as well as the European) are striking. The need for major studies of comparative imperialism can be fully realised only when histories of individual empires, particularly of the quality of this one, have been researched and published.

John M. MacKenzie

PREFACE AND ACKNOWLEDGEMENTS

Historians like to classify. But modern colonialism defies taxonomy. The 'French empire between the wars' is so gargantuan a subject – or rather, such an agglomeration of so many subjects – that it eludes codification. The history of empire is social history, economic history, international relations, military history, gender history, to name but a few of our discipline's favourite classifications. I have tried to embrace such eclecticism in this book. More than anything else, it is a study of the mechanics of empire governance: the administrations, coalitions, interest groups, committees and governments that shaped policy; the political movements, street demonstrators and anti-colonialists that opposed them. No phase of French colonialism, not least in the inter-war period, is reducible to a combination of high policy, local initiative and the clash of administrators and their, often resentful, colonial subjects. The complexion of the French empire was as much the product of impersonal forces, of accident and error, as it was of design. To convey this requires examining the social ramifications of colonial control: what the French presence actually meant to colonial populations compelled to pay unfamiliar taxes, to perform labour service, to fight France's wars and to adopt at least some of the trappings of French language and culture. Here, I confess, the conclusions are limited by the sources used. The chapters that follow are based on a combination of archival research and recent secondary literature. Many of these secondary sources draw on field study, colonial archives and oral testimony in former territories of the French empire. My own research has, however, been overwhelmingly concentrated in the ministries, archives and papers of France – the former colonial ruler.

Perhaps the most difficult challenge facing the historian of French colonialism is to bring those most directly touched by it out of the shadows. Few colonial people left paper records, wrote letters or passed through a formal educational system. Colonial subjects traverse the archival record in tax returns, police surveillance reports, court records, medical data and civil registers of births, marriages and deaths. Relatively few were given personal opportunity or public space to voice their true feelings about colonial rule, whether through open debate, political representation or oppositional activity. Freedom of expression was strictly limited; rights of association were often nugatory. The reader must decide whether a balance has been struck between the written sources of the colonisers and the more disparate and elusive histories of the indigenous peoples living under the French tricolour between 1918 and 1940. Any shortcomings in this respect are entirely my own.

By contrast, I owe a huge amount to grant-giving agencies, archivists and librarians that have facilitated my research. I gratefully acknowledge the financial support of the Leverhulme Trust, the British Academy, the Nuffield Foundation and the University of the West of England. In Paris, the personnel of the Service Historique de l'Armée de Terre at Vincennes, particularly Sébastian Laurent, Claire Sibille and the archive directors, facilitated access to private paper collections and reserved files. Their colleagues in the Service Historique de l'Armée de l'Air were equally supportive. The staff of the Archives Nationales, the Paris Prefecture of Police archives, the Foreign Ministry archive, and its near cousin in Nantes, provided much needed help on numerous occasions. Work at the colonial archives in Aix-en-Provence was made easier by the encyclopaedic knowledge of the archive staff and the good humour of the issue desk team. Madame Sylvie Caucanas and her colleagues at the Archives Départementales de l'Aude guided me through the Albert Sarraut papers. I am grateful to the Public Record Office (now National Archives), London, for the map reproductions. The Centre des Archives d'Outre-Mer kindly granted permission to reproduce the jacket poster, and the Archives Départementales de l'Aude provided reserved material from the Albert Sarraut papers. The archive and library staff of Stanford University's Hoover Institution helped me track down private papers and colonial press sources. Closer to home, the staff of the UWE St Matthias Library and Exeter University Library have been generous with their time and advice. The hospitality of Christine and André Frézal in Nantes, my sister Helen and her family in Carcassonne, Simon Kitson, Peter Jackson and Andrew Webster in Paris, and the Suzuki family in Los Altos, California, was very much appreciated.

A number of other friends and colleagues have made the research and writing of this book a real pleasure. Several among them read draft chapters, providing invaluable advice and sharp criticism along the way. Robert Aldrich kindly brought his unparalleled knowledge of French colonialism to bear, and brought several crucial sources to my attention. Bill Hoisington supported the project from its inception, and refined my views about the inter-war politics of French North Africa. Martin Alexander, Peter Jackson, William Keylor and Talbot Imlay navigated me through the difficult waters of inter-war international relations. Ruth Ginio and June Hannam helped me clarify ideas about women's lives under French colonial rule. Eric Jennings and Cliff Rosenberg generously shared their ideas and forthcoming work with me. The support of my former colleagues in Bristol, among them Kent Fedorowich, Glyn Stone and Philip Ollerenshaw, as well as my current colleagues in Exeter, enabled me to bring the book to fruition. Alison Welsby and Jonathan Bevan at Manchester University Press have been thoughtful and indulgent editors.

To Suzy, as usual, go my very greatest thanks – this one's for you.

A note on transliteration

The transliteration of local language terms in common parlance among French colonial officials presents considerable problems, compounded by the variations in spellings and pronunciations of a single language between differing overseas territories. French transliterations were themselves often based on the spoken or colloquial language of a particular colony or territory, Arabic in particular. I have tried to use the simplest, most readily understandable English transliterations of these terms, the meanings of which are outlined in the glossary.

LIST OF ABBREVIATIONS

Territories, parties and organisations

AEF   Afrique Equatoriale Française, the federation of French Equatorial Africa, comprised of French Congo, Oubangui-Chari, Gabon and Chad. The federal authorities in Brazzaville also administered the French Cameroon mandate after 1919.

AOF   Afrique Occidentale Française, the federation of French West Africa, comprised of Senegal, Mauritania, French Sudan, Niger, Ivory Coast (Côte d'Ivoire), Guinea, Dahomey and, between 1919 and 1932, Upper Volta (Haute-Volta). The federal authorities in Dakar also administered France's Togoland mandate after 1919.

CFAO   Compagnie Française de l'Afrique Occidentale, one of AOF's two main trading companies, along with the SCOA.

CGT   Confédération Générale du Travail, French trade union confederation, founded in 1895.

CGTA   Compagnie Générale des Transports en Afrique, the main private transport company in AEF.

CPDN   Comité Permanent de la Défense Nationale, Standing National Defence Committee, established 1936.

CSDN   Conseil Supérieur de la Défense Nationale, Supreme Council for National Defence.

ENA   Etoile Nord-Africaine, the North African Star, first Algerian nationalist party, led by Messali Hadj, founded in 1926.

HBMs   *Habitations à bon marché*, cheap multi-storey worker housing blocks.

ICP   Indochinese Communist Party, formed in 1930.

PCF   Parti Communiste Français, French Communist Party, established in 1920.

PPA   Parti Populaire Algérien, Algerian Popular Party: Messalist Algerian nationalist party, founded in 1937.

PPF   Parti Populaire Français, French Popular Party, fascistic party led by Jacques Doriot, established in 1937.

PSF   Parti Social Français, French Social Party, ultra-rightist party, heir to the Croix de Feu, established in 1937.

SCOA   Société Commerciale de l'Ouest Africain, the second of France's major trading companies in black Africa, along with the CFAO.

SFIO   Section Française de l'Internationale Ouvrière, unified French Socialist Party, founded in 1905.

VNQDD Viet Nam Quoc Dan Dong, Vietnam National Party, founded in 1927.

Archives

ADA	Archives Départementales de l'Aude, Carcassonne.
AN	Archives Nationales, Paris.
APP	Archives de la Préfecture de Police, Paris.
CADN	Centre des Archives Diplomatiques, Nantes.
CAOM	Centre des Archives d'Outre-Mer, Aix-en-Provence.
MAE	Ministère des Affaires Etrangères, Paris.
PRO	Public Record Office (National Archives), London.
SHA	Service Historique de l'Armée, Vincennes.
SHAA	Service Historique de l'Armée de l'Air, Vincennes.
SHM	Service Historique de la Marine, Vincennes.

Shorthand terms for ministries

Cabinet	An ambiguous term when used interchangeably in English and French. I have used 'Cabinet' in the English sense to mean all ministerial members of the Council of Ministers. In French, the term denotes the private office – or senior advisory team – of a Minister or colonial governor.
Grand Sarail	Beirut location of the Levant High Commission.
Hôtel Matignon	Prime Minister's residence.
Quai d'Orsay	French Foreign Ministry.
rue Oudinot	French Ministry of Colonies.
rue Saint Dominique	French War Ministry.

GLOSSARY OF TERMS

Armée d'Afrique	the army of French North Africa, including French cavalry units (*chasseurs d'Afrique*), North African cavalry units (*Spahis*), French infantry units (*Zouaves*), North African infantry (*tirailleurs*), units of Moroccan irregulars (*Goums*), and Foreign Legion regiments.
bey	reigning prince of the Husaynid dynasty in Tunisia, formerly subordinate to the Ottoman Sultan.
beylical	pertaining to the administration of Tunisia's monarch, or *bey*.
cadi (*qadi*)	a magistrate or judge of Shar'ia Law.
caïd	tribal representative or administrator.
Caliph	usually refers to the Moroccan or Ottoman Sultan as successor to the Prophet Mohammed.
caza	administrative districts in Lebanon and Syria.
cercle	colonial administrative district, headed by a French district officer.
la Coloniale	the French colonial army after 1900, apart from forces raised in French North Africa. Largely made up of professional metropolitan regiments (Coloniale Blanche) and colonial infantry regiments (*tirailleurs*).
colony	I have tried to limit use of the word 'colony' to those territories that were directly administered as colonies, as opposed to as protectorates or mandates. On occasion, however, I have used the term more generically to denote any of France's overseas dependencies, and to indicate that all were colonially subjugated.
commandant de cercle	French colonial district officer.
dahir	decree legislation passed by the Moroccan Sultanate.
dar al-Islam	the Islamic world.
Destour	the Arabic term for 'constitution', and the title adopted by the Tunisian Constitutionalist Party.
djemâa	village assembly in colonial Algeria.
effendiyya	educated urban middle class in Arab cities, often junior officials.
évolué	a colonial subject that had received a European-style

	education, often employed as a government clerk or junior official. *Évolués* were in the forefront of demands for citizenship.
fellah	peasant farmer.
goum	a small force of Moroccan irregular infantry, typically numbering 150–75 men.
habous	property or land bequeathed for a religious or charitable purpose.
harka	an organised military force.
Hijaz	the western region of the Arabian peninsula.
indigénat	colonial legislative code that empowered French regional officials to punish colonial subjects with fines or a short prison sentence without recourse to trial.
Istiqlal	Arabic for independence. A title adopted by nationalist parties in Syria and Morocco.
khalifa	a *caïd's* representative.
khammès	In French North Africa the term denotes a sharecropper, nominally allocated twenty per cent of the produce farmed in return for his labour.
khodja	a clerk. Typically refers to junior clerical staff in the French North African administration.
Ky	appellation for the Vietnamese territories of Tonkin (Bac Ky), Annam (Trung Ky) and Cochin-China (Nam Ky).
lang do	refers to the so-called 'red villages' loyal to the ICP during the Nghê Tinh revolt in 1930.
lazaretto	isolation hostel for bubonic plague victims.
Maghreb	collective term for the countries and region of North West Africa; used here to denote Morocco, Algeria and Tunisia.
makhzen	the collective term for the Moroccan government and its administrative services.
marabout	Muslim holy man, typically the local leader of a religious sanctuary, or *zawiya*.
medersa (*madrasa*)	a religious school of advanced Muslim learning, often linked to a mosque.
métis(se)	offspring of mixed-race parents.
métissage	miscegenation, or the interbreeding of people classified as members of different racial groups.
mukhtar	Muslim village headman.
natalité	the birth rate. Hence in post-First World War France

	pro-natalism denoted active political support for measures to increase the population.
navétanes	seasonal economic migrants from the French West African interior working in the Senegal peanut basin.
originaires	French African citizens born, or with parents born, in one of Senegal's 'original' Four Communes of Saint-Louis, Rufisque, Dakar and Gorée.
pasha	urban administrator of the Moroccan Sultanate.
prestation	a defined period (typically eight to ten days) of forced labour on designated colonial public works projects, usually road construction.
Sahel	In Arabic, literally 'shore': denotes the regions immediately south of the Sahara.
sanjak	Ottoman administrative sub-district of a *vilayet*, hence 'the sanjak of Alexandretta' in French Syria.
Sharif	a leader directly descended from the Prophet Mohammed.
sheikh	the leader of a tribal fraction, a recognised elder, or the head of a religious institution such as a *zawiya*.
spahi	French North African cavalry of the Armée d'Afrique.
Sufism	Islamic mysticism, often associated with a revered saint.
tariqa	a Muslim religious brotherhood.
tirailleurs	literally, riflemen. Usually applied to Coloniale infantry, hence *tirailleurs sénégalais*, referring to West African infantry units.
ulama	a recognised Koranic teacher.
vilayet (in Turkish, *wilayet*)	Ottoman province.
zawiya	a Sufi Muslim religious institution, based around the tomb of a saint and sometimes including a school and/or hospice.

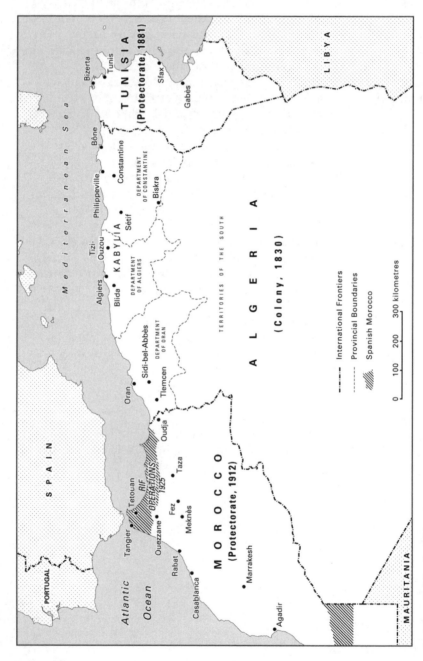

1 French North Africa

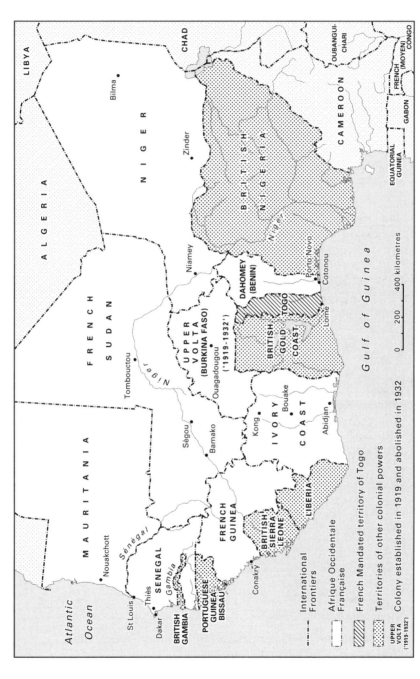

2 Affrique Occidentale Française (French West Africa, AOF)

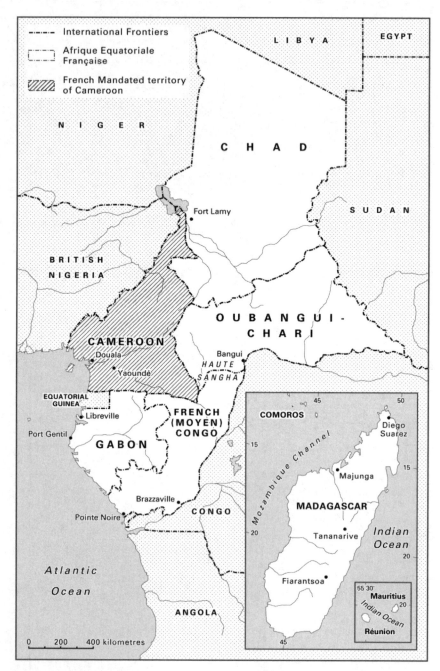

Legend:
- International Frontiers
- Afrique Equatoriale Française
- French Mandated territory of Cameroon

LIBYA

EGYPT

NIGER

CHAD

SUDAN

Fort Lamy

BRITISH NIGERIA

OUBANGUI-CHARI

CAMEROON

Douala

Yaoundé

Bangui

HAUTE SANGHA

EQUATORIAL GUINEA

Libreville

Port Gentil

FRENCH (MOYEN) CONGO

GABON

COMOROS

Diego Suarez

MADAGASCAR

Majunga

Tananarive

Fiarantsoa

Indian Ocean

Mozambique Channel

Brazzaville

Pointe Noire

CONGO

Atlantic Ocean

ANGOLA

55 30'
Mauritius
Indian Ocean
Réunion

0   200   400 kilometres

45   50   15   20

3   Afrique Equatoriale Française (French Equatorial Africa, AEF), Madagascar, Réunion and Mauritius

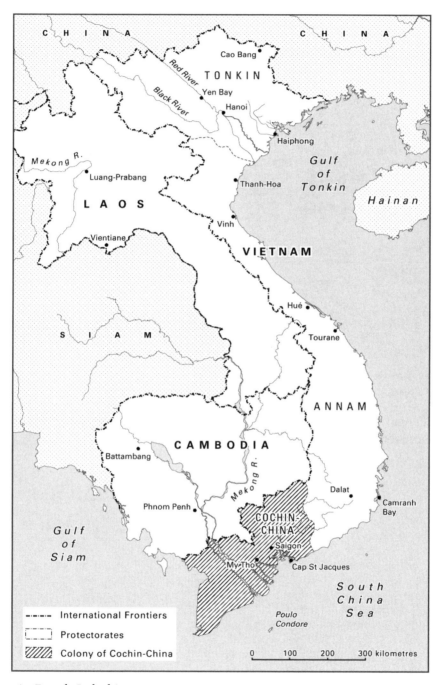

CHINA

CHINA

Cao Bang

TONKIN

Red River

Yen Bay

Black River

Hanoi

Haiphong

Gulf
of
Tonkin

Hainan

Mekong R.

Luang-Prabang

Thanh-Hoa

LAOS

VIETNAM

Vinh

Vientiane

S I A M

Hué

Tourane

ANNAM

CAMBODIA

Battambang

Mekong R.

Dalat

Phnom Penh

Camranh
Bay

COCHIN
CHINA

Gulf
of
Siam

Saigon

My-Tho

Cap St Jacques

South
China
Sea

Poulo
Condore

International Frontiers

Protectorates

Colony of Cochin-China

0   100   200   300 kilometres

4   French Indochina

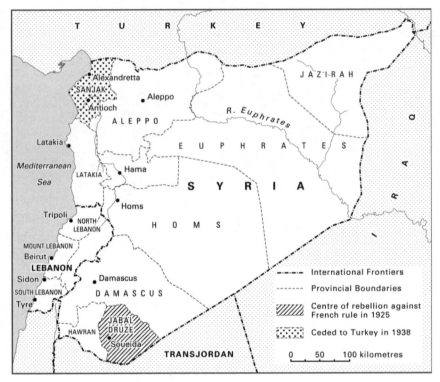

Map legend:

- ·–·–· International Frontiers
- - - - Provincial Boundaries
- Centre of rebellion against French rule in 1925
- Ceded to Turkey in 1938

0   50   100 kilometres

5   Syria and Lebanon

France's inter-war empire: a framework for analysis

An empire at peace?

In the twenty years between the end of the First World War and the start of the Second, the French overseas empire reached its greatest physical extent. By July 1920 France and its colonial empire comprised 12,540,000 km^2: nine per cent of the earth's landmass. Even after war losses were taken into account, the addition of new mandate territories formerly governed by Ottoman Turkey and Germany to France's overseas empire increased the global population living under French rule. By 1936, the year in which a left-liberal Popular Front government conceded the principle of national independence to the Syria and Lebanon mandates, the French tricolour flew over four per cent of the world's population – an estimated 86,110,000 people.[1] Geographically, the inter-war period marked the zenith of France's colonial power. Yet few contemporaries considered the 1920s and 1930s an age of 'high imperialism'. Scratch the surface, and one finds an altogether different picture. If anything, France's 'imperial trajectory' was downward. The French imperial system was more diffuse and unmanageable than ever.

Imperial decline became more widely anticipated as the material costs of colonial control surged ahead in the 1920s. The grand-sounding imperial federations – French West Africa (Afrique Occidentale Française, AOF), French Equatorial Africa (Afrique Equatoriale Française, AEF) and French Indochina (Indochine Française) – had limited bureaucratic and economic tangibility, still less basis in indigenous culture. The group of three French-controlled territories in the North West African Maghreb – Morocco, Algeria and Tunisia – were neither federated nor commonly administered. The older island territories, former slave colonies, penal settlements and trading stations had proportionately higher populations of French-speakers and imperial citizens. But they were not welded into a coherent administrative or cultural whole. Algeria, the main French territory of settlement, stood out precisely because it was the sole colony to which French emigrants had flocked in their hundreds of thousands. The 'Frenchness' of other colonial communities was measured less in terms of a settler presence than through visible signs of social change. Linguistic transformation, Catholic observance, urban design and the reordering of public space, the adoption of French property law, and mixed-race coupling, or *métissage*, were more frequently cited as indicators of the imperial presence than the growth of settler societies. Indeed, the culture wars between competing metropolitan and indigenous ways of life, language usage and religious practice were just as critical in the social history of colonised peoples as their armed resistance against the imperial power.

The French empire that emerged from the First World War is often portrayed as essentially consolidated. The messy work of colonial conquest was over. Subjugation of frontier populations continued at the imperial margins, but rarely drew headlines in the Paris press. France, like other victor powers, professed no interest in further territorial expansion. But it would hold what it had. After 1920 more complex, if less spectacular, problems of administrative practice, fiscal policy, commercial integration, urban planning and social provision were the stuff of colonial governance. These posed more testing challenges than military occupation. Yet the inter-war empire was neither pacified nor secure. Colonial domination faced unprecedented challenges from within and without – from marginalised and exploited colonial peoples, from critics of imperial practice across the French political spectrum, and from hostile nation states opposed to a French colonial presence in Africa and Asia.

The majority of the French nation were as indifferent to the manifest cruelties of colonial exploitation as to the professed benefits of an empire. Reflecting on his experiences in Madagascar and Indochina before the outbreak of the First World War, the writer and journalist Pierre Mille noted that a month in the colonies was sufficient to undermine any French person's interest in the rights of man. But, as Alec Hargreaves points out, Mille did not reject French colonialism. Rather he considered it an economic and political imperative to which metropolitan rules of behaviour and restraint simply could not apply. The business of empire imposed an authoritarian system of rule.[2] This was a price worth paying, owing to the benefits that accrued to France. Mille's brutal honesty was unusual, but French politicians without personal connections with imperial expansion shared his order of priorities. During the 1920s even the Socialist Party's critique of harsh colonial administration did not imply the progressive equalisation of rights between colonisers and colonised. The hierarchy of imperial rule necessarily meant that political offices were reserved to the colonial authorities and only gradually opened up to an educated indigenous elite, if at all.

The central contention of this book is that French colonial rule was in severe decline between the wars. Public taste for the exoticism of empire was not matched by any greater willingness to settle in the colonies, to spend on imperial products or to fight in defence of colonial territory. Public interest in empire was, at best spasmodic, despite repeated information campaigns, commercial initiatives and exhibitions of empire coordinated by members of the Ligue maritime et coloniale, post-First World War successor to the Parti colonial.[3] Arguments raged among the political elite in metropolitan France and inside colonial administrations over the nature, purpose and value of colonial possessions. But most governments of the inter-war years stifled, abandoned or ignored ambitious colonial projects to develop the empire's economic potential, to improve the living standards of subject populations or to concede political freedoms in dependent territories.

The sense of isolation and embattlement expressed by French settlers (colons) in Tonkin (northern Vietnam) for years after the formal creation of the Indochinese Union in 1887 reveals the disjuncture between metropolitan imperialists, local officials and agricultural settlers at the forefront of colonial consolidation.[4] The *Indochine française* described in official policy statements was an artificial construct, a concept with little basis in fact. Its supposed marriage of French administration and local tradition bore no correlation to the economic and cultural gulf separating French settlers from their Vietnamese, Cambodian and Laotian subordinates.[5] Disputes between imperial lobbyists, colonial bureaucrats and settlers took place beneath the horizon of government. Ministers rarely argued about imperial problems, except when major funding issues were at stake. 'The official mind of French imperialism, non-existent at the cabinet level, was weak and fragmented even at the ministerial level'.[6]

The armed services, where one might expect imperial pride to burn strongest, never concurred over their strategic responsibilities in the colonies. An integrated system of colonial defence planning was put in place only in 1938, following the disintegration of the French alliance system in Eastern Europe.[7] Prior to this, recurrent disputes over colonial garrisons, defensive works, stockpiles of equipment and military priorities concealed a deeper unresolved tension in French imperial defence. This boiled down to a single question: should the colonies contribute to France's continental security in Europe or should metropolitan France ensure the protection of all overseas possessions against any external threat? The general staff viewed this problem in Eurocentric terms, an understandable position after the experience of the Great War. But a more fundamental problem remained. Imperial defence was widely read as an unacceptable dissipation of resources rather than the management of a global security system.[8] Again, one confronts the underlying fact that empire was marginal to official minds, specifically, in this case, the planning establishment of the general staff and the metropolitan army. Admiral Raoul Castex, the first head of the Advanced Military Staff College in Paris, added discussion of the colonies' role in global strategy to officer training courses in the 1930s. But in the 1936–37 academic session, imperial strategy featured in only six per cent of the College curriculum.[9]

Whatever the arguments among senior military planners in France, political instability at the imperial periphery generated by indigenous resistance remained a constant preoccupation for the colonial authorities *in situ*. Some territories were never wholly 'pacified' in the inter-war period. Others that were supposedly brought under French political control were never entirely subjected to French legal regulation, social organisation or cultural norms. Colonial rule, always an incremental process, was never static. French domination might be consolidated in one region while it simultaneously disintegrated in another. The processes of imperial consolidation and colonial disintegration were not strictly sequential, but often went hand in hand. The French authorities faced Communist-led uprisings in the Vietnamese territories of Annam and Tonkin in 1930–31 at the very moment that France's largest-ever celebration of empire – the Vincennes colonial exhibition of 1931 – opened to the public. The Vincennes *exposition coloniale* became a marker for popular imperialism in inter-war France. But the Nghê Tinh Soviet movement of 1930–31 that marked the emergence of the Indochinese Communist Party (ICP) as the major anti-colonial force in Vietnamese politics suggests that celebrations of imperial achievement were premature.[10] The colonial presence was by no means uniform. Flying the imperial flag meant different things in different places. An isolated cantonal administrator in landlocked Oubangui-Chari in Afrique Equatoriale Française could spend weeks, even months, without meeting a French compatriot. His experience (such officials were invariably male) bore no comparison with regional administration in Algeria, where prefects of the colony's three departments presided over local bureaucracies several hundred strong by the late 1920s.[11]

Variations in administrators' experience were probably sharpest in French West Africa. In Senegal, the administrative and economic hub of AOF, the instruments of colonial authority were most firmly entrenched in the four coastal communes that were the sites of the first French mercantile ventures into sub-Saharan Africa. But a posting to the West African interior could put an official on the outer margins of the colonial frontier. Some inland territories defied French conquest. To the immediate north of Senegal, the desert expanses of southern Mauritania were 'conquered' by General Henri Gouraud in 1908, but the country's northern limits remained beyond French administrative reach for a further twenty years. It seems doubtful that Mauritania's largely nomadic population was ever bureaucratically, let alone culturally, integrated into the AOF federation.[12] There, and in numerous other overseas territories, indigenous tradition and customary law still regulated colonial subjects' daily lives. Elsewhere,

economic obligations to the colonial state were ignored, mediated or subverted by wily local auxiliaries selected to spread the word of the colonial
presence.[13] France's 'civilising mission' was exposed as vacuous hypocrisy
by the indigenous peoples that were its alleged beneficiaries. Put simply, in
much of the inter-war empire, French colonialism was barely tolerated.
Authority was generally imposed through coercion, whether actual or
implied, and yet it rested on indigenous intermediaries prepared to co-
operate with French officialdom to consolidate their wealth and status
within their own communities.

Colonial peoples participated in complex civil societies that antedated
French conquest. Within tribal, communal or urban locales many still found
space to regulate their own affairs, and thereby resist the encroachment of
colonial authority. At the macro-level of empire, however, French economic
policies, fiscal systems, labour service, military recruitment and legal
penalties imposed new constraints.[14] Administrators typically judged the
colonial system to be working well if taxes were collected, labour service
was performed and military conscription passed off without incident.[15]
When these obligations were challenged from below, the colonial authorities deployed additional police or troops from nearby territories to quell
dissent. State repression was at once a sign of strength and an admission
that the colonial state was failing.[16]

For the most part, reluctant acquiescence rather than obedient compliance signified the power relationship between indigenous subjects and
French rulers. The entire system could survive only as long as organised
mass opposition could be prevented. The impact of the global depression
in the early 1930s added to these stresses as French economic exploitation
of colonial populations intensified. By this point, new forms of organised
opposition to rule from Paris had emerged, from the French Caribbean to
North Africa, Syria, Madagascar and the territories of the Indochina federation. The colonial state was never monolithic nor an exclusively French
affair. Imperial rule was upheld by a series of complex power relationships
between officials, propertied elites, tribal leaders and differing ethnic communities. Distribution of authority was in constant flux, blurring the distinction between rulers and ruled. The bipolar paradigm of colonisers and
colonised is unsatisfactory because it ignores the changing boundaries of
power between colonial governments and indigenous populations. But the
first principle of such collaboration was submission to French authority.
At its core, colonialism was a system of racial oppression.

French debates over empire

The framework for analysis of French imperialism adopted here is based
on a model of a French 'imperial community': the network of politicians,

bureaucrats, colonial administrators, manufacturers, traders, media commentators, educators, missionaries, lobbyists and settlers that dominated the political discourse of empire after the First World War. By the 1920s this community was disunited and fractious. In broad terms, one may identify five long-term debates among this French imperial elite about the role and purpose of the colonial system they claimed to control.

These five debates – disputes might be a more accurate term – may be summarised as follows. First, the bureaucracy of colonial government was split between proponents of assimilation and advocates of associationism. In other words, divided between those who believed in the acculturation of colonial populations to French republican rights and values and those who favoured a less ambitious style of indirect rule that minimised change in the prevailing social order while denying political inclusion to most colonial subjects. Neither policy was adopted throughout the empire. Nor was either alternative consistently applied in individual colonies. But the interwar period is generally considered to have marked the ascendancy of associationist pragmatism in imperial administration. We should be wary of viewing these doctrinal arguments too rigidly. As Alice Conklin has argued, French imperial practice in the late Third Republic was the product of several paradoxes. These, in turn, arose from the nuances in colonial administrative and judicial methods born of adaptation to local conditions. A republican democracy withheld basic rights and freedoms from its overseas subjects, amplifying the exclusion of French women from the metropolitan electoral process by insisting that colonial peoples of both sexes were generally incapable of making informed political choices. A republican state founded on hostility to hereditary privilege relied on tribal chiefs and colonial monarchs to maintain order in vast swathes of the empire. Anticlerical republicans committed to secular education defended France's continued reliance on missionary educators in rudimentary colonial school systems. French liberals attached to individual freedom and equal access to justice accepted the use of forced labour and a separate legal code – the *indigénat* – for the vast majority of colonial subjects. These contradictions were the stuff of argument between supporters of associationism and their opponents. Yet, for all that, this political community of republican imperialists concurred that French colonialism could be a constructive force for progress.[17]

A second dispute hinged on the economics of colonial policy. The scale, viability and costs of colonial development schemes, and the expansion of colonial export markets, provoked bitter political arguments that cut across party lines. Political elites were reluctant to pay for the modern empire that they claimed France deserved. Much of the growth in colonial economies still depended on mercantilist intervention by trading companies, investment banks and settler co-operatives. Colonial administrations regulated these bodies at local level, just as central government shaped the macroeconomic environment in which they operated through tariffs, monetary policy and fiscal incentives. But the colonial state none the less relied on private enterprise to produce the wealth necessary to sustain the machinery of government. Corporations, banking houses and settler producers achieved profitability by the utmost exploitation of cheap colonial manpower rather than by the pursuit of long-term infrastructure development or market diversification. The short-termism characteristic of these economic policies drew frequent criticism in colonial capitals and in Paris, but at no stage was a state-led programme of colonial development implemented for the empire as whole.

The empire's contribution to French international power was a third problem that engaged colonial administrators, politicians, and the police and military agencies responsible for the apparatus of imperial security. The argument here resolved itself into one of net contributions. Should France contribute to the defence of its empire? Or should the colonies be responsible for funding their own defence? Politicians, generals and imperial lobbyists conceptualised the empire as a reservoir of men, women, raw materials and strategic assets that would add to French strength in a European war. But what about in peacetime? Should French resources be used to maximise the potential economic and military contribution that the empire could make to France? Or were French resources better expended in France itself? Here again, matters of grand strategy and imperial defence often boiled down to more prosaic problems of budgetary finance. In the longer term, the neglect of imperial defences was as significant as the neglect of indigenous pressure for reform. Indeed, the two would coalesce once the empire began to disintegrate into competing blocs during the Second World War.

The fourth dispute among the French imperial community was closely related to the third. It turned on what intelligence analysts term threat assessments. Before 1940 there was no consensus among the rulers of empire about the principal threat to colonial control. To an extent, this reflected the differing academic backgrounds of the French imperial community. For racial theorists, the social scientists of the Musée Social, and the Durkheimian sociologists that proliferated in the ranks of colonial bureaucracy between the wars, colonial peoples themselves were the 'enemy' of imperial stability. This enemy was variously constructed as a colonial proletariat, Islamic anti-Westernists, pro-Communist nationalists or quite simply the colonial 'crowd'. At a more emotive level, it was but a short step from the portrayal of colonial cultures as inferior to their presentation as an undifferentiated and inherently threatening 'Other'. There was no colonial social contract between rulers and ruled, just an unequal relationship in which the latter submitted to French domination. Inherently unstable, the colonial system placed enormous weight on the early identification of potential sources of disorder. It is hardly surprising, then, that arguments over internal sedition were so prevalent. The emergence of more pressing international threats to empire in the 1930s meshed with existing worries about revolutionaries within the colonies themselves. French diplomats, intelligence services, police agencies and the plethora of informants on which they relied, amassed evidence of global networks of Soviet, fascist and pan-Arab subversives united in their resolve to destroy the empire. By 1939 those sceptics in government inclined to dismiss such intelligence as far-fetched were drowned out by the clamour for heightened colonial surveillance and repression.

A more straightforward left–right split marked political discussion in France about the type of empire that France should construct. Year after year this fifth source of dispute hardly amounted to any debate at all. Party political priorities generally lay elsewhere. One may easily point to recurrent parliamentary, electoral and media treatment of colonial issues. It must be remembered, however, that only in times of acute imperial crisis, in 1924–25, in 1930–31, in 1936–37, and again in 1939, did these debates figure large in metropolitan political culture.

On one such occasion, during 1925–26, the conjunction of the Rif war in northern Morocco and a major rebellion in French Syria put colonial counter-insurgency on the front pages of the Paris press for the first time since the end of the First World War. The resultant political furore and media coverage only amplified the prevalent ignorance of colonial conditions. A spate of articles on the Rif war held a mirror to the party allegiance of press bosses, already sharpening their editorial knives after the election of a reformist centre-left coalition, the Cartel des Gauches. Copious newspaper coverage revealed little grasp of events on the ground, still less about the objectives of Riffian leader Abd el-Krim or the scale of the French military repression under way by October 1925. Instead, right-wing journalists exploited the opportunity presented to attack 'the Cartel's war'. Hostility to the government precluded an objective reading of the political situation and social conditions in Morocco and Syria. Readers were fed a diet of racial stereotypes and chauvinistic readings of recent history to explain inevitable French victory.[18] The pro-Cartel press and Communist publications were no better. The pro-government line of newspapers such as *L'Ere nouvelle* and *L'Oeuvre* precluded a balanced assessment of Abd el-Krim's demands. Even the Communist *L'Humanité* and *Corréspondance internationale* reduced the Riffians to two-dimensional heroes, bit players in an abstract revolutionary struggle against capitalist imperialism.[19]

The imperialism of the non-Communist left in France has been misleadingly termed 'humanist' in motivation, if not in practice. Drawing on a Jacobin tradition of republican statism, the liberal left was temperamentally inclined to favour assimilationist policies that would gradually integrate colonial populations with metropolitan France. The Socialist leadership was increasingly uncomfortable with the drift towards associationism in the 1920s. It did not, however, offer a clear alternative strategy before the Popular Front coalition began to take shape in 1935.[20] During a Party Congress in 1920 the formerly unified, and nominally Marxist, Socialist Party (Section Française de l'Internationale Ouvrière, SFIO) split between parliamentary socialists and their communist rivals. Henceforth, the executive committees of the rump Socialist Party shied away from detailed scrutiny of colonial policy at annual party conferences. Colonial issues did not figure large in the party press, or in the deliberations of Socialist Deputies in the Chamber of Deputies.

The French Communist Party (Parti Communiste Français, PCF) echoed the Socialists' inconsistency. Communist leaders never sustained a coherent anti-colonial position before the party was banned following the outbreak of war in September 1939. In the decade from 1924, the one acknowledged colonial 'expert' in the PCF leadership was Jacques Doriot, head of the PCF executive's Colonial Section and, from February 1931, Mayor of Saint-Denis – the Parisian citadel of proletarian militancy.[21] A capable polemicist, Doriot cut a lonely figure in his Leninist condemnation of French imperialism in parliament and the press. Having for years advocated co-operation with the Socialists against the growing fascist menace, the maverick Doriot was expelled from the PCF in June 1934, ironically just as Comintern opposition to collaboration with the non-Marxist left receded. The poles of his ideological gyroscope then reversed. After the election of the Popular Front, in July 1936 this former critic of imperialist exploitation reinvented himself as the ultra-rightist leader of a new grouping, the Parti Populaire Français, dedicated to the overthrow of the Republic and the eradication of Communism. Doriot's career path was unusual, but it reveals one constant: the rigidity of Communist Party loyalty to instruction from the Moscow Comintern. And throughout the Stalinist period the Soviet regime subordinated criticism of Western colonialism to the pursuit of Soviet interests in Europe. As a result, the Comintern's anti-colonialism was half-hearted at best. The French Communists were themselves divided across several fault-lines: between an internationalist hostility to colonialism and a residual republican universalism used to justify imperial control, and between willingness to foment worker militancy in colonial cities and fear that colonial unrest would privilege indigenous nationalists above their Communist rivals.

The left from time to time turned up the ideological heat of colonial debate in inter-war France, but it was generally those on the right who cooked up colonial policies. With the brief exception of the Popular Front interlude of centre-left government in 1936–37, the three main parliamentary parties

[9]

of the centre and right in France, the Radical-Socialists, the Democratic Alliance and the Republican Federation, filled the ministerial posts directly concerned with empire: Finance, Foreign Affairs, War, Navy, Interior, and, of course, Colonies. Here, too, there was less engagement with imperial questions than one might expect from governing parties with a stake in the world's second largest overseas empire. When it came to colonies, money mattered more than anything else. The French right was ostensibly imperialist, almost by instinct. But it was less so when it came to budgetary allocation, strategic policy formulation, and questions of colonial immigration.[22] The bourgeois male voters who sustained the centre-right in power for most of the inter-war period were not a constituency fired by imperial enthusiasm. Politicians of every stripe could count on minimal domestic pressure to reform the colonial system.

Ardent imperialism remained a minority concern, tacitly endorsed by the parliamentary right rather than loudly supported by it. If anything, the most thoroughly imperialist right-wing groups were the extraparliamentary, anti-republican leagues, above all the Croix de Feu (reinvented as the Parti Social Français in 1937.)[23] Ultra-rightist organisations drew thousands of colonial settlers into their ranks during the 1930s, especially in French North Africa. The Croix de Feu leader, Colonel François de La Rocque, even volunteered for service in Morocco in 1925, and was assigned a key role in gathering intelligence against Abd el-Krim's Riffian forces.[24] But the leagues were fundamentally hostile to any concept of a republican imperialism or a colonial system to which republican values were transmitted. As a result, the ultra-right, and the French right more generally, were increasingly out of step with a colonial system that required some measure of liberalisation if it was to survive.

None of these arguments was resolved before 1940. Instead, dispute over the complexion and purpose of colonies persisted. This helps account for the more bitter divisions that split the French empire during the Vichy years, and explains why the last French attempt to construct a 'colonial consensus' after 1945 was doomed to fail. The roots of decolonisation should be traced back much further than the fall of France in 1940. The widespread assumption that the Second World War marked a decisive watershed is convenient historical shorthand but a distortion of conditions in the pre-war empire. By 1920 the colonial system bore the seeds of its own destruction. The picture that emerges of the inter-war empire is a gaudy, violent affair – a garish scene of disparate skirmishes, recurrent uprisings, economic polarisation, urban segregation and nationalist dissent, rather than a soothing impressionist tableau of imperial unity. The watchwords of imperial policy making in France and its colonial capitals were economy, profit and control. Ironically, public indifference to empire allowed the ardent republican imperialists at the heart of the colonial system to delude the French nation into believing the myth of 'la plus grande France'.

A final question thus presents itself. Where does the inter-war empire fit into the long-running debates over the state of the French nation that went to war in 1939? In recent years, two distinct groups of historians have analysed the condition of France on the eve of war. On the one hand, historians of anti-republicanism, and more particularly of the ultra-rightist leagues, have refined the concept of a uniquely French fascism emerging in the context of worsening social division and widespread popular dis-enchantment with the institutions of republicanism.[25] On the other hand, historians of foreign policy and military strategy are divided between those who set France's preparations for war within a framework of national decline and those whose assessment of French international policy is more forgiving. For this latter group, France pursued a viable defensive strategy but could not ultimately withstand the onslaught of German power without a major land ally.[26]

These historians have, on occasion, incorporated empire within their arguments. For scholars of the ultra-right, Charles Maurras, the ideological demigod of Action Française, and Colonel de La Rocque garner most atten-tion. Maurras praised imperial settler communities as the embodiment of a lost patriotic virtue based on powerful masculinity, ardent Catholicism, and attachment to the soil. La Rocque found a receptive audience among the *petits commerçants* of Algiers and, above all, Oran. Croix de Feu organisers in Algeria and their local ultra-rightist rivals in Doriot's PPF even tapped into the residual antisemitism of the settler community and some elements of the wider Muslim population in a bid to mobilise mass support against the Popular Front.[27] Studies of these individuals, their fol-lowers and their ideas therefore acknowledge an imperial dimension to rightist anti-republicanism. Equally, scholars of French strategic planning admit that colonial possessions added a global aspect and a reservoir of resources to French foreign and military policy.

One issue that unites analysts of French ultra-rightism and France's preparations for war as well as scholars of antisemitism in France is the need to explain the apparent ease with which French society acquiesced in the transition from republican democracy to the authoritarianism of the Vichy state.[28] A parallel problem in French colonial history is to explain why in the early twentieth century republicans committed to universalist values of equality, liberty and inclusive citizenship became increasingly determined to cling on to empire, and to exclude colonial subjects from membership of the French *cité* – a term denoting the republican state.[29] Historians of French fascism and pre-war strategy also intersect over the problem of national power. The capacity of a nation state to dominate another society through colonial control marked the clearest expression of national dominance in the international system of the early twentieth century. As a result, imperial cohesion was a barometer of metropolitan power. That said, empire has remained tangential within most studies of France as an international actor. Is it useful to conceptualise reactionary settler conservatism as part of a broader anti-republicanism increasingly identifiable with the ultra-right? Should we interpret the divisions among the French imperial community as another facet of decadence in the Third Republic? Was the gradual erosion of colonial control indicative of French national decline?

Some of the chapters that follow revisit these questions. Certain chapters discuss the colonial empire as a whole, for instance examining the application of associationist colonial policy, the economic relationship between France and its colonies, the effects of Popular Front reforms in the late 1930s, and the empire contribution to French international strategy. Others use case studies – of the treatment of women in the colonies, of colonial education policy, of popular imperialism in France, of colonial disorder, and of anti-colonial nationalist groups in North Africa – to highlight changes in the French relationship with empire during the inter-war years. The composite picture that emerges shows the widening fissures in the French colonial edifice between 1919 and 1940. The imperialistic vision of an empire reborn after the shattering experience of the First World War was at odds with the impoverishment of colonial populations, the growth of organised anti-colonial nationalism, the failure of reform projects, and the stubborn refusal of the French population to view colonial issues as central to their lives.

Notes

1 ADA, Sarraut Papers, 12J162: Politique coloniale, 1920–35, 'Le problème colonial et la paix du monde', étude pour Albert Sarraut, Président du Conseil, sans date, 1936. The British empire comprised twenty-seven per cent of the world's surface in 1936.

2 Alec G. Hargreaves, *The Colonial Experience in French Fiction. A Study of Pierre Loti, Ernest Psichari and Pierre Mille* (London: Macmillan, 1981), 121–2.

3 Charles-Robert Ageron, 'Les colonies devant l'opinion publique française (1919–1939)', *Revue Française d'Histoire d'Outre-Mer*, 77:286 (1990), 31–73.

4 John F. Laffey, 'Imperialists divided. The views of Tonkin's colons before 1914', *Histoire Sociale/Social History*, 92 (1977), 92–113.

5 Nicola Cooper, *France in Indochina. Colonial Encounters* (Oxford: Berg, 2001), 2–3; the concept of *Indochine française* in the French colonial imagination is explored in Panivong Norindr, *Phantasmaic Indochina. French Colonial Ideology in Architecture, Film and Literature* (Durham NC: Duke University Press, 1996).

6 Quote from Christopher M. Andrew and A. S. Kanya-Forstner, 'France, Africa, and the First World War', *Journal of African History*, 19:1 (1978), 11.

7 SHM, 1BB2, C182/D1A/14, 'Défense des Colonies – instructions interministérielles', n.d. February 1938.

8 Martin Thomas, 'At the heart of things? French imperial defense planning in the late 1930s', *French Historical Studies*, 21:2 (1998), 325–61.

9 Marc Michel, 'La puissance par l'empire. Note sur la perception du facteur imperial dans

l'élaboration de la défense nationale (1936–1938)', *Revue Française d'Histoire d'Outre-Mer*, 69:254 (1982), 37.

10 Hunyh Kim Khánh, *Vietnamese Communism, 1925–1945* (Ithaca NY: Cornell University Press, 1982), 151–71; R. B. Smith, 'The foundation of the Indochinese Communist Party, 1929–1930', *Modern Asian Studies*, 32:4 (1998), 769–805.

11 Centre des Archives d'Outre-Mer (CAOM), Archives du Gouvernement Général d'Algérie (GGA), sous-série 9H: Surveillance des indigènes, 9H32, no. 18388, Constantine prefecture report to Algiers governor-general, 21 November 1928.

12 David Robinson, *Paths of Accommodation. Muslim Societies and French Colonial Authorities in Senegal and Mauritania, 1880–1920* (Athens OH: Ohio University Press, 2000), 58–9, 259 n. 4.

13 Emily Lynn Osborn, ' "Circle of iron". African colonial employees and the interpretation of colonial rule in French West Africa', *Journal of African History*, 44:1 (2003), 29–50.

14 Elizabeth Thompson discusses civil society in Syria and Lebanon, societies where the full impact of French colonialism was mitigated by the nature of the mandate system. See her *Colonial Citizens. Republican Rights, Paternal Privilege, and Gender in French Syria and Lebanon* (New York: Columbia University Press, 2000).

15 This point was made explicitly by the Dakar government-general in its annual report for 1924, the most prosperous year since the end of the First World War: CAOM, Archives de la Direction des Affaires Politiques (affpol), affpol/536, 'Rapport politique, année 1924', 28 September 1924.

16 See, for example, the instances of repression that followed the demobilisation of African troops after the First World War, recounted in chapter one.

17 Alice L. Conklin, 'Colonialism and human rights: a contradiction in terms? The case of France and West Africa, 1895–1914', *American Historical Review*, 103:2 (1998), 419–42.

18 Charles-Robert Ageron, 'La presse parisienne devant la guerre du Rif (avril 1925–mai 1926)', *Revue de l'Occident Musulman et de la Méditerranée* 24 (1977), 7–13.

19 Ageron, 'La presse parisienne', 13–22.

20 Michel Dreyfus, 'Pacifistes, socialistes et humanistes dans les années trente', *Revue d'Histoire Moderne et Contemporaine*, 35 (1988), 452–69; Manuela Semidei, 'Les Socialistes Français et le problème colonial entre les deux guerres (1919–1939)', *Revue Française de Science Politique*, 18:6 (1968), 1115–53.

21 Regarding Doriot, see Philippe Burrin, *La dérive fasciste : Doriot, Déat, Bergery 1933–1945* (Paris: Editions du Seuil, 1986); J-P. Brunet, *Jacques Doriot. Du communisme au fascisme* (Paris: Balland, 1986). Regarding Saint-Denis, see Tyler Stovall, *The Rise of the Paris Red Belt* (Berkeley CA: University of California Press, 1990).

22 Aviel Roshwald, 'Colonial dreams of the French right wing, 1881–1914', *Historian*, 57:1 (1994), 59–74; Michael J. Heffernan, 'The French right and the overseas empire', in Nicholas Atkin and Frank Tallett (eds), *The Right in France, 1789–1997* (London: I. B. Tauris, 1997), 89–113.

23 Robert Soucy, *French Fascism. The Second Wave, 1933–1939* (New Haven CT: Yale University Press, 1995), 83–4, 117, 255–6.

24 *Ibid.*, 106.

25 See, for example, Eugen Weber, *Action Française. Royalism and Reaction in Twentieth Century France* (Stanford CA: Stanford University Press, 1962); Jacques Prévotat, *Les Catholiques et l'Action Française 1988–1939* (Paris: Fayard, 2001); Zeev Sternhell, *Ni droite, ni gauche. L'idéologie fasciste en France* (Paris: Editions du Seuil, 1983); William D. Irvine, 'Fascism in France and the strange case of the Croix de Feu', *Journal of Modern History* 63:2 (1991), 271–95; Soucy, *French Fascism. The Second Wave, 1933–1939*; Kevin Passmore, *From Liberalism to Fascism. The Right in a French Province, 1928–1939* (Cambridge: Cambridge University Press, 1997). For excellent summaries of current debates about French fascism see Robert Paxton, 'The five stages of fascism', *Journal of Modern History*, 70:1 (1998), 1–23; Robert D. Zaretsky, 'Neither left, nor right, nor straight ahead. Recent books on fascism in France', *Journal of Modern History*, 73:1 (2001), 118–32.

26 The classic critique of French strategy is Jean-Baptiste Duroselle, *La Décadence. Politique étrangère de la France 1922–39* (Paris: Imprimerie Nationale, 1979). Anthony

Adamthwaite, *France and the Coming of the Second World War* (London: Frank Cass, 1977) was similarly critical. More sympathetic treatments include Robert J. Young, *In Command of France. French Foreign Policy and Military Planning, 1933–1939* (Cambridge MA: Harvard University Press, 1978); Robert Frankenstein, *Le Prix du réarmement français 1935–1939* (Paris: Publications de la Sorbonne, 1982); Martin S. Alexander, *The Republic in Danger. General Maurice Gamelin and the Politics of French Defence, 1933–1940* (Cambridge: Cambridge University Press, 1992); Michael Dockrill, *British Establishment Perspectives on France, 1936–1940* (London: Macmillan, 1999), Peter Jackson, *France and the Nazi Menace. Intelligence and Policy Making, 1933–1939* (Oxford: Oxford University Press, 2000); and Talbot Imlay, *Facing the Second World War. Strategy, Politics, and Economics in Britain and France, 1938–1940* (Oxford: Oxford University Press, 2003).

27 Soucy, *French Fascism. The Second Wave*, 133, 152–6; Irvine, 'Fascism in France', 292–3, also cited in Soucy, p. 156.

28 A key work that links antisemitism in the late Third Republic to events under Vichy is Vicki Caron's *Uneasy Asylum. France and the Jewish Refugee Crisis, 1933–1942* (Stanford CA: Stanford University Press, 1999). Another important book that connects tighter restriction on colonial immigrants and more restrictive citizenship rights in the late Third Republic with the subsequent policies of the Vichy state is Gérard Noiriel, *Les Origines républicaines de Vichy* (Paris: Hachette, 1999).

29 Siân Reynolds has addressed this issue in the context of gender and women's rights in inter-war France. See her *France between the Wars. Gender and Politics* (London: Routledge, 1996), 222–6.

PART I

The setting: politics and colonial administration after the First World War

CHAPTER ONE

Consolidation and expansion: the French empire after the First World War

The war and the peace: la plus grande France?

At the end of the First World War those in the French political community who thought about empire at all were sure it was a vital asset in a total war of mass armies, industrial mobilisation, civilian engagement, and global competition for strategic resources. The priority was to consolidate it, not to loosen the ties of French dominion.[1] In 1919 the French colonial project was incomplete. Territories such as Mauritania and Oubangui-Chari, nominally incorporated into the French African federations, remained unpacified.[2] The very meaning of that most misleading of terms, 'pacification', varied from place to place. In Morocco pacification denoted protracted military operations characterised by violent skirmishes, seizure of tribal pasturage, destruction of rural property, and mass killing of livestock prior to complex negotiations for the submission of a clan group.[3] In the Equatorial African interior the term sometimes connoted the insertion of a lone French official and a handful of locally recruited armed auxiliaries to administer a vast tract of territory otherwise untouched by the colonial presence.[4]

Further French expansion into African and Middle Eastern territory took place in conditions of profound societal dislocation. In 1918 famine gripped the cities of Syria and Lebanon. Senegal was ravaged by bubonic plague. The wartime collapse of grain distribution and poor harvests in 1919–20 compounded the impact of the Spanish influenza epidemic in French North Africa.[5] Colonial soldiers saw trench warfare.[6] Immigrant workers confronted racial violence on French city streets, employment discrimination, and casual racism on the factory floor.[7] Colonial conscripts aside, labourers from the colonies formed the second largest immigrant group in wartime France, outnumbered only by Spanish agricultural workers.[8] Official figures recorded the entry of 222,793 colonial labourers during the First World War, of which 78,556 Algerians, and 48,995 Indochinese made up the largest national groups.[9] War Ministry planners organised this civilian labour force on military lines. Rigid segregation of colonial munitions workers, labour battalions, mineworkers and farm labourers was defended as a means to protect an immigrant workforce unfamiliar with metropolitan life. If that were the case, it was singularly ineffective. During 1917–18 especially, incidents of assault against colonial labourers by French co-workers reached new heights. Few enjoyed any kind of union protection.[10] As Tyler Stovall puts it, 'This wartime experiment in multiculturalism was undertaken reluctantly, and essentially revoked within a year after the end of the conflict'. Government hostility to mixed-race relationships mirrored the anxiety expressed by colonial officials that immigrant workers' exposure to more equitable interracial contacts in France inverted the racial and gender hierarchies of colonial rule.[11] Between 1919 and 1921 most colonial war workers sent to serve in France in infantry regiments, labour service battalions, munitions factories and farms were abruptly dismissed and sent home, deeply affected by their wartime experiences. The colonies to which they returned were economically undeveloped and, for the most part, chronically poor.[12]

At one extreme were the colonies of French Equatorial Africa (AEF) – French (or Moyen/Middle) Congo, Gabon, Oubangui-Chari and Chad. The original network of military administration imposed during the French conquest persisted across much of this vast region. Rivers and waterways were the principal entry to the colonial interior in the absence of an integrated road network. The federal administration in Brazzaville still knew little about the subject populations it claimed to rule. The last pre-colonial census conducted in AEF during 1911 proved utterly unreliable, underestimating indigenous population levels by up to sixty per cent. In 1919 Gabon and Oubangui-Chari were linked with the outside world by a solitary telegraph station in their respective capitals, Libreville and Bangui. Malaria and sunstroke took a heavy toll of local administrators. Ecole coloniale graduates dreaded AEF as a last-ditch posting. Their lack of enthusiasm was understandable. In a staggering distortion of fact, a 1919 Foreign Ministry instruction booklet for new French arrivals warned that cannibalism was commonplace among tribal populations.[13]

At the other extreme, even the well established colonies of the overseas empire retained their 'new frontier' aspect after the First World War. During the 1920s, with the centenary of the 1830 Algerian conquest fast approaching, the imperialist lobby in Paris still represented French North Africa as a 'new world'. French Algeria was a great work still under construction, not a completed imperial project.[14] France itself was also rebuilt and extended after the war. In the newly recovered 'lost province' of Alsace, the process of demographic reintegration to France after almost fifty years of German administration was assisted by imperialist society lectures and exhibitions designed to foster local pride in the continuing colonial enterprise.[15] The French hexagon and the overseas empire were to be welded together as a new, more powerful polity.

Renewed emphasis on consolidation of control emerged before the guns fell silent in November 1918. Six months earlier, with the war on the western front far from over, a Ministry of Colonies study commission established to 'investigate issues raised by the war' published its findings on 'native policy' in a seventy-two-page report. The commission chair, Albert Duchêne, absolved the government of any need to extend additional rights to colonial subjects beyond the educated elite. French imperialism had served the interests of colonised peoples before the war, and would continue to do so after it.[16] The priority for many administrators was less to justify French rule to local populations than to convince the French people of the value of empire – a task that required even greater missionary zeal. Here, too, hopes were high. On 25 August 1918 Albert Sarraut, the long-serving federal governor-general of Indochina, soon to emerge as the strongest, most eloquent voice of French imperialism in the inter-war period, wrote to Minister of Colonies Louis Henry Simon in these terms:

> Each day my strong faith in the brilliant destiny of Indochina and its practical contribution to the economic and political needs of the mother country increases. As we wait for the whole of France to share this sentiment, developing a more passionate interest in the destiny of its most beautiful colony as it learns about Asia, I devote myself to inspiring the same great expectations in my colleagues.[17]

Official ebullience of this sort dominated colonial pronouncements in the National Assembly, in parliamentary commissions, in annual reports submitted by colonial governments, and in the metropolitan press. Little noticed at the time, a Supreme Allied Council commission at the Paris Peace Conference produced an aerial navigation convention on 13 October 1919 that regulated access to colonial air space. Signatory powers anticipated the development of commercial air traffic, colonial tourism, and enhanced communications between the imperial powers and their dependent territories. A colonial 'global village' was emerging.[18] But the day-to-day reportage of colonial administration immediately after the First World War was altogether less confident.

After the armistice there were more disquieting parallels with the situation in 1914 than ardent French imperialists cared to admit. The socio-political consequences of colonial conscription, little considered when the measure was introduced in 1912, were still poorly understood at war's end.[19] As Indochina's governor-general Sarraut strove to extend native representation in Cochin-China's Colonial Council to accommodate the growing urban bourgeoisie. The measure aroused fierce opposition among the settler community. But by 1918 a greater threat was the prospect that returning soldiers and war workers would demand equivalent political rights, thus expanding the indigenous electorate far beyond what Sarraut judged a tolerable level.[20] It seems unlikely that the Vietnamese recruited for service in labour battalions and infantry regiments, and their compatriots compelled to buy French war bonds and produce more rice for export, swallowed Sarraut's pronouncements as governor depicting the war effort as a fraternal Franco-Vietnamese partnership.[21] In April 1920 Indochina's federal authorities reported that colonial servicemen's families were exasperated with the meagre fifteen-franc monthly allowance they received from the army. Additional colonial levies could be raised to cover the shortage of metropolitan troops after the 1919 demobilisation only if servicemen's families received sufficient income to live on.[22] Yet the economic changes wrought in the Franco-colonial relationship by the war effort were subsumed by the government's more urgent priorities of domestic reconstruction. And the slaughter of the war left psychological scars that precluded enthusiastic popular engagement with imperial development. At least 1.3 million Frenchmen were killed during the war. In the first five months of the conflict, French losses averaged 2,000 per day. This grim daily statistic never fell below 400 throughout the war. The circles of mourning that embraced immediate family, more distant relatives, friends, neighbours, and local communities left no one untouched by the sense of loss, the reality of ambiguous victory.[23] Everyone in France who survived the war was changed by it. How did what Annette Becker terms the 'long-lasting and persistent state of shock' in post-war French society affect public attitudes to empire?[24] The question defies a simple answer. But the rediscovery of religious observance among some, the questioning of faith among others, the wave of commemorative ceremonies and public mourning to memorialise the war dead, the social and political alienation common among war veterans, and the governmental preoccupation with domestic economic recovery and European security all militated against stronger commitment to colonies. This was hardly surprising. France in 1919 was a nation transformed. In another sense, however, public and state neglect of colonial matters in the immediate aftermath of the war was part of the return to political normality.

Over the course of 1914–18 the upper tiers of colonial bureaucracy fell into line with Paris. Central government imposed its authority over recalcitrant imperial governors as colonial administration was harnessed to the primordial needs of France at war. In May 1914 Resident-general Louis Hubert Lyautey celebrated the military occupation of Taza, gateway to Morocco's eastern Rif. Control of Taza opened up overland communications with Algeria.[25] Weeks after the outbreak of war in Europe, he was instructed to evacuate French forces to the coast prior to their shipment back to France. Initially he did the reverse, keeping a limited reserve inland to protect pacified territory.[26] Lyautey's show of defiance was short-lived. Large-scale transfers of troops to the western front did occur. Between them the two North African protectorates of Morocco and Tunisia supplied some 84,000 soldiers and 64,000 war workers to France.[27] Withdrawal of military manpower threatened to undermine French authority, and compelled Lyautey to rely more heavily on tribal *caïds* to contain local dissent.[28] In December 1917 French governmental demands for additional Moroccan troops reached a new peak. Premier Georges Clemenceau instructed Lyautey to transfer six new battalions to the western front, and warned him against further expansion of French influence in the Moroccan interior. Nothing was to be done to inflame tribal opposition.[29] Deaf to Lyautey's complaints that the use of so many Moroccan soldiers would provoke public outcry, Clemenceau's repeated calls for more men confirmed a shift in the balance of power between French governments and their colonial proconsuls. The old days of frontier imperialism – unauthorised seizures of territory and creeping extension of colonial control – were gone.[30] In future, colonial officials would answer to Paris when imperial expansion provoked unrest. Yet the fact that such rebellion became more and not less likely after 1918 stemmed in part from the colonial expansion, settler violence, and aggressive land annexations of the pre-1914 period.

Loyalty proven? The recruitment of colonial troops

The satisfaction with which French ministers and colonial officials recalled the empire war effort in 1918–19 ignored the pervasive unease among French officialdom about colonial loyalty during the war, and the near panic among colonial governments about the demobilisation of conscripts after the conflict. After the desperate defence of the Marne, it became clear by October 1914 that France would impose heavy demands for military manpower on French North and West African territories rather than giving priority to civilian labour requirements as originally assumed in August.[31] Colonial conscription could be read two ways: as an empowerment of subjects afforded a lever to extract concessions from the metropolitan power, or as the ultimate proof of colonial subjugation. The treatment of colonial troops in France mirrored this tension. Throughout the war, West African infantrymen, the tirailleurs sénégalais,[32] were depicted in popular imagery from trench journalism to mass-produced postcards and advertising as physically powerful, sexually predatory, and inherently savage. Although white Coloniale officers were expected to channel their soldiers' aggression against the common enemy, 'uncivilised' behaviour – and particularly assaults on women – by colonial troops remained a constant topic of conversation in southern garrison towns and north-eastern *départements* bordering the western front.[33] The ferocious reputation of West and North African soldiers cemented this racialised stereotyping. So, too, did the vituperative German government propaganda during and after the war directed against 'the black shame' of colonial troops, first on European battlefields, and then as overseers of post-war Rhineland occupation.[34] These German complaints did not sway French military policy at the time but, as Jean-Yves Le Naour has shown, they did affect French use of colonial troops as occupation forces in the longer term.[35]

Another consideration came into play in October 1914: Ottoman Turkey entered the war alongside the Central Powers. The Maghreb administrations moved swiftly to contain popular disenchantment with a French war effort directed against a fellow Muslim state. Official anxiety on this score was less acute in Morocco, a state with its own Sultanate, than in Algeria, a former Ottoman territory with historic ties to the Turkish Caliphate. Additional press restrictions were imposed in Algiers and government statements emphasised French respect for the Turkish people, if not their leaders.[36] Evidence from Algeria of public sympathy for the Ottoman cause was ambivalent. In a crude assertion of colonial dominance, the Algiers authorities interned Islamic leaders who opposed the war in a prison constructed on the Kudyat Aty promontory just west of Constantine's city walls: a sacred site for the city's Muslims.[37] But in March 1916 the Quai d'Orsay advised the government that public opinion in France's Muslim territories was still broadly supportive of the allies. Military censors noted that, after a bitter Flanders winter, front-line colonial troops complained most about protracted absence from home. Even so, the Maghreb governments were relieved at news of the allied withdrawal from Gallipoli, which marked the temporary suspension of direct Franco-Turkish hostilities. The prospect of North African troops being called upon to kill fellow Muslims loyal to the Ottoman Caliph drew more adverse comment in Algeria and Tunisia than news of increasing losses at Verdun.[38]

By January 1915 the standing inter-ministerial committee on Muslim affairs had tightened its grip on the recruitment, transfer and repatriation of North African troops and workers. Wary of adverse public reaction, army recruiters in Algeria, where conscription applied, initially limited themselves to calling up between 1,500 and 2,000 men of the 1912–14 contingents. In fact from August 1914 to January 1915 volunteers came forward at a rate of 3,500 per month. By the start of the new year thirty-four battalions of Algerian riflemen and thirty-nine *spahi* cavalry squadrons had been raised. Even so, the inter-ministerial committee was unsettled by incoming reports from Algiers and Casablanca that returning Muslim troops invalided from the front claimed they had been used as cannon fodder ahead of French regiments. Committee members duly blocked further repatriations of disabled soldiers.[39] Increasing French demands for men and materials in early 1915 only added to these official anxieties in Algiers, Dakar, Hanoi and elsewhere. In AOF recruitment encountered fierce resistance. The call-up system assigned recruitment quotas to local chiefs, obliging them to supply a designated number of men to regimental recruiters. Wave after wave of French drafts disrupted the agricultural economy, undermined tribal hierarchies, and caused untold misery for African families. The Wolof and Sereer communities of Senegal were among those hardest hit by this insatiable demand for manpower. The traumatic exodus of men to Europe entered collective folk memory. Lasting recriminations arose over the recruiters' methods, the chiefs who helped them, and the families torn apart as painful choices were made over which young family members should be sent to serve.[40] Eventually, in October 1917, the new federal governor in Dakar, Joost Van Vollenhoven, convinced the War Ministry to suspend the West African recruitment quotas, but only after protracted uprisings in French Sudan (now Mali), Upper Volta (now Burkina Faso) and Dahomey (now Benin).[41] The respite was short-lived. In the following year Clemenceau initiated a fresh recruitment drive of unprecedented intensity, assisted by the promise of monetary incentives and future privileges to servicemen who completed their tour of duty.[42]

Metropolitan demand for empire troops to man the trenches extended to colonial officials as well. The war decimated the colonial service. At least twenty-five per cent of pre-war officials never returned to overseas postings after 1918.[43] As the battle of Verdun dragged on and the ill-fated Nivelle offensive was thrown back, by April 1917 the native affairs administrations in French Africa came close to breaking point. Even specialist tribal affairs officers were required to serve a year on the western front or in the Armée d'Orient operating from Salonika. The number of qualified Arab and African-language speakers fell sharply. A unique body of experience built up over years of contact with local tribes was lost.[44] In smaller colonies, the socio-economic impact of military service could be just as great. New Caledonia, for instance, supplied 2,160 soldiers, of whom 1,137 were colonial infantrymen. 541 New Caledonian troops were killed, of whom 374 were *indigènes*. Hardly noticed amidst the constant daily cycle of reported deaths, these losses destabilised economy and society in the French Pacific.[45]

By 1916 fear of rebellion shaped colonial recruitment policy. On 11 January 1916 Aristide Briand's government promised Maghrebi war veterans preferential access to public sector employment after the war in a bid to encourage more voluntary enlistment and so avert accusations of coercive pressure.[46] The measure had little impact. The pace of recruitment in Algeria slowed in 1917 after rebellion broke out in and around Batna in late 1916. By contrast, the use of West African colonial regiments as shock troops became increasingly prevalent in the later stages of the war, notwithstanding governor Van Vollenhoven's predictions that further call-ups would provoke revolt. Although corroborative evidence remains patchy, it seems fair to assume that most colonial recruits joined up under duress, or as a route out of grinding poverty.[47] By November 1918 French West Africa had provided some 134,000 recruits. If one takes the broader period, 1912–19, that figure rises to some 200,000 soldiers. Approximately 32,000 were killed. Yet French officials were less animated by these losses than by their ramifications on local opinion.[48]

In May 1918 interim governor-general Gabriel Angoulvant, an administrator known for his opposition to major reform, conceded that the African sacrifices on the western front made further concessions inevitable. After their years in France soldier returnees were 'transformed, decorated with medals, and full of pretensions justified by their services rendered and the blood spilt'.[49] Angoulvant was prepared to grant African ex-servicemen limited citizenship rights, but he was alarmed at the wider consequences for colonial control. Tribal chiefs that assisted French military recruiters did not expect those enlisted to return home with political rights comparable to their own. Former soldiers were bound to find readjustment to civilian life in rural society difficult, and probably unappealing. Urban populations were bound to grow, causing greater social marginalisation as economic migrants struggled to find work and housing. Job opportunities and wage rates were sure to disappoint ex-servicemen accustomed to regular army pay.[50]

The challenge facing the colonial authorities was to reintegrate a larger community of African citizen soldiers while keeping respect for chiefly authority and the colonial order intact. Hence, the singular feature of the colonial reforms contemplated in the immediate post-First World War years was their exclusivity. Concessions of citizenship, suffrage and access to junior administrative posts were all targeted at a male indigenous elite. The members of this group were identifiable by economic or educational background, tribal lineage, past performance of service to France, traces of French ancestry, or some combination of these factors. Reforms were designed to create loyal citizens with a personal investment in the colonial project. This held true whether consolidating an existing relationship with French authority, as in the case of tribal chiefs, or preventing alienation from it, as in the case of mixed-race *métis*, ex-servicemen, and the minority of French-educated colonial subjects.

Concessions to colonial ex-servicemen marked belated official recognition of the profound social changes wrought by protracted military service. On the one hand, young West African men, their families, even entire villages, abandoned their homes in areas of high-density recruitment and sought refuge in less affected areas or in accessible British colonies. On the other hand, in regions such as the upper Senegal valley, where local chiefs assumed substantial responsibility for filling recruitment quotas, men of slave origin were sought out in preference to free-born men and artisans.[51] As Martin Klein and François Manchuelle have shown, returning ex-servicemen of slave descent were understandably reluctant to return to their former lives at the bottom of the socio-economic ladder.[52] In Guinea, for example, an estimated 30,000 infantrymen were recruited to infantry regiments during 1914–18. French hopes that these ex-servicemen would form a distinct cadre of junior functionaries, culturally assimilated to French values and reconciled to the colonial order, clashed with the soldiers' experience of discriminatory treatment, dreadful service conditions and delayed demobilisation.[53] The majority of Guinean ex-servicemen returned from France with a keen sense of their political influence. Many resented the cantonal chiefs that had helped force them into uniform in the first place. Former soldiers played a leading role in violent industrial disputes, as well as more isolated assaults on chiefs and settler plantation bosses during 1919–20.[54]

In the upper Senegal valley, east of the colony's groundnut producing region, recruiters' early optimism about high rates of voluntary enlistment gave way to pervasive unease about the socio-economic dislocation caused by the incessant demand for military manpower. The first round of wartime recruitment in 1914 was facilitated by widespread famine throughout the West African Sahel at the southern margins of the Sahara.[55] In later years the picture across AOF was quite different. Between December 1915 and July 1916 thirteen companies of troops were assigned to contain unrest along the Niger River valley during the course of which sixty-eight soldiers were killed and 431 injured. Civilian casualties went unrecorded, but War Ministry figures detailed 204 villages destroyed in the course of these operations.[56]

The situation was no better in 1918. Public hostility to a heightened tax burden intensified during Clemenceau's conscription drive. In these conditions, the success achieved by the Senegalese Deputy Blaise Diagne, who toured AOF and AEF in support of government military demands, was remarkable.[57] The two federations produced 72,000 new recruits in the last year of the war, a testament to Diagne's influence and oratory but something that would return to haunt him when Diagne was accused by the *pan-noir* journal *les Continents* of wanton collaboration in forced recruitment.[58] But Senegalese troops demobilised in 1919 returned to a colony in crisis. In Dakar, Rufisque and the former administrative capital of Saint Louis, the beginning and end of the First World War were periods remembered for virulent outbreaks of bubonic plague. In the 1919 epidemic 712 people died of the disease in Dakar, 437 in Rufisque and 257 in Saint Louis.[59] In 1914 and again in 1919 the authorities' public health measures were sluggish, and often resisted by local communities in town and countryside. Urban clearance schemes and the practice of isolating suspected cases in 'lazaretto' quarantine hostels caused widespread public anger. In the worst affected rural areas of Senegal, French vaccination programmes and disposal of bodies ran roughshod over local customs, traditional medicine, religious observance and complex funeral rites.[60]

It was against this background of a severe health crisis that in 1919 Diagne joined French government spokesmen in promising additional rights and benefits to ex-servicemen. Diagne was no puppet. Thanks to his efforts, following a poorly attended parliamentary debate, on 4 January 1918 the National Assembly granted French citizenship to the *originaires* – the assimilated African inhabitants of Senegal's four *communes de plein exercice* (Saint Louis, Gorée, Dakar and Rufisque), the original centres of French colonisation in West Africa.[61] Once the war ended Diagne integrated his campaign for ex-servicemen's rights into a broader strategy to consolidate the authority of representative institutions in AOF. In 1919 his supporters in the Republican Socialist Party of Senegal swept to victory in local and mayoral elections held in the four communes. Settler interests that had previously dominated municipal institutions were marginalised. Diagne's attempt to widen access to citizenship beyond Senegal's four *originaire* communes brought him into conflict with Van Vollenhoven's designated successor as AOF governor-general, Martial Merlin, a senior career official of the old school. In an increasingly acrimonious personal dispute, Diagne worked behind the scenes in Dakar and Paris to have Merlin replaced by his secretary-general, Brunet. He eventually succeeded in 1923, engineering Merlin's replacement by Jules Carde.[62] Until his eviction in 1923 Merlin, in turn, resisted Diagne's efforts to extend the legal and electoral rights of the *originaires* to the wider population of Senegal.[63]

African war veterans were an important constituency in the emergent representative politics that Diagne strove to achieve.[64] Two wartime pledges to colonial servicemen had serious ramifications. Release from the *prestation* (a system of labour requisitioning that required colonial subjects to perform six to ten days of labour service per year on public works within the boundaries of their district administration), as well as exemption from the *indigénat* (the native legal code that allowed chiefs, *caïds*, and French cantonal administrators to impose arbitrary punishments) did not satisfy ex-servicemen's demands for higher social status. But they did undermine the power of native chiefs to impose their authority on disruptive former troops. In the inter-war period *commandants de cercle* and cantonal officials – more often than not, tribal headmen – calculated the exact *prestation* requirements for their *canton*. Work gangs of *prestataires* performing unpaid compulsory labour on roads, bridges and telegraphs symbolised colonial power and chiefs' authority over their local subordinates.[65] War veterans made bad *prestataires*. Soldiers' anger over their maltreatment by the French military authorities meshed with their resentment at the closed elitism of tribal chieftaincy.

Meanwhile, the battle of wills in Dakar continued. Faced with Merlin's skilful obstructionism and a loss of personal influence in Paris, Diagne gradually moderated his demands, focusing on extended rights for

Senegal's urban, educated elite.[66] The wider problem of reintegrating disgruntled African ex-servicemen remained. Colonial soldiers were acutely aware that the discriminatory treatment they experienced in combat conditions was replicated in the greater speed with which metropolitan regiments were demobilised, and in the more generous benefits accorded to French troops. From region to region, veteran returnees held the colonial authorities and local chieftaincies responsible for their plight. In 1919 attacks on tribal chiefs by former servicemen were reported in six cantons in French Guinea alone.[67]

In Madagascar the linkage between wartime military service and the post-war campaign for wider citizenship rights was equally strong. Post-war estimates of the number of Malagasy soldiers recruited between 1914 and 1918 ranged from the Ministry of Colonies' 1923 calculation of 41,355 to a figure of 45,865 published to coincide with the 1931 Colonial Exhibition. Most survived the war. Between 1919 and 1922 ex-servicemen formed the nucleus of the Ligue française pour l'accession des indigènes de Madagascar aux droits de citoyen (LFAIMDC), a citizenship pressure group that identified past service to France as the key criterion for naturalisation. The LFAIMDC was unusual in another respect: it was founded in Paris and represented an alliance between left-wing anti-colonialists and Malagasy immigrants opposed to French rule. Although short-lived, the LFAIMDC revealed how veterans' demands for greater rights could be subverted to fit a more radical anti-colonial agenda.[68]

The Supreme Defence Council (Conseil Supérieur de la Défense Nationale, CSDN), the government's senior military advisory committee, took a leading role in the post-war reassignment of colonial forces. The council warned in 1920 that an uprising in French North Africa was more probable than any external attack on the empire, hardly a remarkable prediction so soon after the defeat of the Central Powers. The French naval presence in the western Mediterranean secured the Maghreb against invasion. But Britain's capture of German Tanganyika during the First World War, the Spanish seizure of northern Morocco and the French conquest of Algeria proved how difficult it was to evict an invasion force once it acquired a coastal base through which supplies and reinforcements could flow. The council therefore recommended urgent improvements to communications links between the Maghreb territories, expansion of the garrison in North Africa, and greater use of aircraft to suppress rural disorder. In a sign of the times, CSDN members also suggested the creation of fortified regional armouries for use by settlers and loyal troops in the event of Muslim unrest.[69]

In January 1919 worsening disorder in Morocco, repeatedly predicted by Lyautey's Rabat administration during the previous eighteen months, served as a pretext to keep several Armée d'Afrique battalions in uniform.[70]

Moroccan and West African regiments were packed off to enforce the peace in the Rhineland, while in a tragicomic twist Foreign Legion units in North Africa received a large injection of mainly German recruits. On 19 December 1920 Lyautey's military cabinet finalised plans to use these Foreign Legion forces as the spearhead for the 'total pacification' of Morocco, a scheme thrown off course in 1921 by the further reinforcement of French occupation forces in the Rhine and Cilicia, immediately north of the Syrian frontier.[71]

In Indochina, too, the Hanoi government-general feared that the war would precipitate local disorder, less because of the social destabilisation caused by returning veterans than because of the heightened economic demands on Indochinese peasants and workers arising from the conflict.[72] Between 1914 and 1918 the Indochina federation contributed 43,000 troops to the metropolitan war effort, of whom 1,123 died. As was the case with Malagasy regiments, most Indochinese troops avoided the trenches until late 1917. Unit commanders did not rate their combat effectiveness highly. Vietnamese soldiers were judged incapable of withstanding low winter temperatures, and were typically deployed as labour battalions supporting front-line troops. But during 1918 Indochinese infantry battalions were mixed into metropolitan divisions. Others served in the Salonika campaign from May 1916 to January 1919.[73]

The politicisation of Indochina's war veterans was eclipsed by the administration's preoccupation with internal unrest. Anti-colonial violence in pre-war Indochina peaked in spring 1913 with a spate of bombings and assassinations. These attacks were orchestrated by Vietnamese secret societies that proliferated among well educated émigrés, many inspired by Sun Yat-Sen's Chinese revolution. Later wartime disorders were often provoked by local grievances and chronic economic hardship rather than revolutionary sedition. In October 1914 Mans tribesmen in Tonkin's mountainous upper Red River region attacked an infantry garrison and destroyed sections of the Yen Bay–Lao Kay railway in protest at the disruption of their aboriginal lifestyle. Urban unrest in Cochin-China in early 1916 provoked greater official concern. Over several weeks demonstrators ran riot in Saigon, culminating in an attempt to free secret society leaders from Saigon central prison on the night of 14 February 1916.[74] Local rebellion and prison unrest were inextricably linked, and frequently involved savage violence. Three weeks before the Saigon prison attack, a peasant mob broke into the Bien Hoa provincial prison, All the inmates were freed, and numerous guards murdered.[75] By 1918 the largest penitentiaries in Tonkin and Annam had been razed to the ground. As Peter Zinoman puts it, 'Prisoner revolts occurred so frequently that colonial officials came to view them as a routine by-product of the functioning of the prison system'.[76] So the concept of order in wartime Indochina was narrowly circumscribed. On 15 July 1917 the regional administrator of Nam Dinh province south of Haiphong congratulated the Tonkin administration on its prevention of rebellion over the preceding year. The population in the most northerly of the three Vietnamese *ky* seemed reconciled to the war, willing to make sacrifices for the war effort in recognition of the community of interest between France and Vietnam.[77] Within six weeks the largest anti-colonial revolt in Indochina during the war years broke out further north at the Thai Nguyen penitentiary.[78]

If anything, administrators' nervousness about unrest in Indochina increased after the armistice. On 15 December 1918 Governor-general Sarraut was shot, but not fatally wounded, at the Hanoi fair. The surprise was that his assailant was not a Vietnamese protester but a French building contractor dismissed by the Tonkin administration for shoddy workmanship.[79] Over the next twelve months French devaluation raised the exchange value of the Indochinese piastre from a wartime average of between 2.2 and 2.7 francs to 13 francs. Indochina's export industries went into sharp decline, and French demand for Indochinese rice collapsed. The cost of living increased dramatically. As the economic situation deteriorated, *sûreté* surveillance of potential dissent intensified.[80]

Policy making and popular expectation

Official anxieties about the colonial impact of the war did not resonate among the wider public in France. The city fathers of *belle époque* Paris had promoted the imperial connection through street names, architectural designs, monuments, museum displays and exhibitions.[81] But neither the capital's financial heart nor its industrial suburbs derived their lifeblood from colonial markets. On the eve of war French overseas investors were more animated by the threat to their holdings in Tsarist Russia than by the prospect of increased imperial trade once continental markets were closed off. Imperialist commitment remained the preserve of the Parti colonial. The various committees, dining clubs, chambers of commerce, press outlets, geographical and anthropological societies that together comprised this grouping – actually an umbrella organisation of pressure groups – coalesced in the first years of the Third Republic. During the 1870s professional geographers established links with provincial chambers of commerce in cities such as Bordeaux, Lyons and Marseilles eager to trade in nascent colonial markets. By the 1890s Parti colonial members had toeholds in key ministries, in parliamentary standing committees, and in the Paris press.[82] So strong was the identification between university geographers and imperial lobbyists in the early Third Republic that Michael Heffernan describes geography as the 'science of empire'. Its practitioners, much like their counterparts in the other 'new' disciplines of sociology, psychology and evolutionary biology, found much to study and admire in colonial territories. Leading Durkheimians, Social Darwinist theorists, political geographers and even Freudian psychologists provided an intellectual veneer to conceal the exploitative nature of French colonialism.[83] The two pre-eminent colonial conquistadors of the early twentieth century, General Joseph Gallieni, conqueror of Madagascar, and his deputy, the then Colonel, Lyautey, harnessed geographical societies and the Parti colonial's Madagascar Committee to promote the consolidation of French control on the island.[84]

Before 1914 Parti colonial lobbyists rarely faced organised domestic opposition. Imperial lobbyists worked within the political apparatus rather than outside it. Their regional committees, special interest groups and supportive members of the National Assembly influenced the decisions made in the policy directorates of the relevant ministries as well as the budgetary debates conducted in parliamentary commissions and at Cabinet level. The challenge facing the Parti colonial was to secure the resources necessary to run the empire and to expand it, rather than to persuade domestic sceptics that imperialism was worthwhile. Unabashed anti-colonialism was confined to the margins of French political life before 1914. The unified French Socialist Party, the Section Française de l'Internationale Ouvrière (SFIO) founded in 1905, and the League for the Rights of Man (Ligue des droits de l'homme), founded in June 1898 in response to the author Emile Zola's fraudulent conviction for libel at the height of the Dreyfus case, raised ethical objections to colonial militarism and human rights abuses.[85] But the liberal left shared the prevalent racialism of the day, and rarely questioned the right of advanced white nations to govern more 'backward' societies.[86] For the bulk of the socialist left, Catholic liberals, and rationalist intellectuals the challenge was to reconcile their humanist principles with their underlying acceptance of the economic and strategic utility of colonial territory.[87] Politicians argued far more about colonial costs than the ethics of imperialism. Advocates of empire fought their rhetorical battles to secure money and military manpower from unenthusiastic Deputies, cost-conscious bureaucrats, and a Eurocentric general staff. The apathy and continental fixations of the political community were more formidable obstacles than the eloquent, but isolated, voices of France's few anti-colonialists.

In 1915–16 Aristide Briand's government encouraged imperial lobbyists to formulate France's colonial war aims. Forty-five members of the Paris Geographical Society (PGS), the oldest and most erudite of France's geographical societies, were co-opted on to four investigative commissions set up for the purpose. Two of these sub-commissions delineated French claims to German colonial territory in Africa and to the Ottoman-controlled Levant. Germany's West African colonies of Togoland and Cameroon were captured between 1914 and 1916. Encircled by French and British colonial territory, Togoland capitulated on 26 August 1914. British forces entered the principal Cameroon cities of Douala and Yaoundé in early 1916, but then, on Foreign Secretary Lord Grey's instructions, 'casually' ceded control of most of the colony to the chief French negotiator, François Georges Picot in a partition agreement signed on 4 March.[88] The Africa sub-commission seized the opportunity presented by Britain's paramount concern for Nigerian security and its limited enthusiasm for additional obligations elsewhere.[89] Led by Auguste Terrier, secretary-general of the French African Committee, and Augustin Bernard, a vocal member of the PGS, the African sub-commission proposed the annexation of both German colonies. Members of another Parti colonial affiliate, the French Asia Committee, likewise dominated a parallel grouping, the Asia-Oceania sub-commission. Chaired by Robert de Caix, this sub-commission championed French control over a greater Syria comprising modern-day Syria, Lebanon and Palestine.[90] Once the war ended, however, the disparate elements of the Parti colonial struggled to remould state policy. Their shared enthusiasm for colonial expansion was dissipated by their competing regional and commercial interests in differing territories.[91] Merchants argued with industrialists, anthropologists with developers, and Africa enthusiasts with the 'Asiatiques' eager to consolidate the French presence in the Middle East and Indochina.

France's first post-war general elections took place in November 1919. They produced the 'sky-blue Chamber', an oblique reference to army uniform and the fact that a majority of parliamentarians were either war veterans or keen supporters of French military interests. Many were long-serving Parti colonial members. Fervently nationalistic, the 1919 Parliament sat until the election of Edouard Herriot's centre-left coalition, the *Cartel des gauches*, in May 1924.[92] Throughout the early 1920s then the right-wing 'National Bloc' held sway in the Chamber of Deputies. During May and June 1920 Alexandre Millerand's government finally defeated a rolling programme of industrial action that began in 1919 without acceding to trade unionists' demands. Government supporters were delighted, and proved equally intransigent in matters of colonial policy. These Deputies conflated nationalism and colonialism, seeing in empire another facet of French national greatness. Within a month of the 1919 elections the so-called 'colonial group', parliamentary arm of the more diffuse Parti colonial, emerged as the largest interest group in the National Assembly. Albert Sarraut, the prestigious former Governor of Indochina appointed Minister of Colonies in Millerand's first National Bloc coalition, became chief spokesman for the group's 190 members, which were, in turn, subdivided into study sections that defended particular imperial interests. They convened under the watchful eye of the group's six founders: former governors, propagandists, and the presidents of the Marseilles and Lyons Chambers of Commerce, cities with strong colonial connections.[93]

The parliamentary colonial group was backed by another new coalition of Parti colonial supporters, the colonial union, founded in Paris in 1920. The colonial union programme boiled down to a single objective: to make the National Assembly a truly imperialist Parliament. The colonial group inside the Chamber was a start, but would only prove itself when the government accepted the need for long-term colonial development, closer economic integration between France and its empire, and higher imperial defence spending. Meanwhile, it fell to the colonial union to spread the imperialist word in the corridors of power. As its founders put it, 'Parliament must finally *understand* the colonies, *protect* them, and *aid* them'.[94]

Sarraut was the foremost politician among this new generation of imperial lobbyists. His vision of colonial development (*mise en valeur*) as the cornerstone of France's post-war economic recovery drew cross-party backing in the parliamentary finance and commerce commissions, the decisive watchdog committees on issues of major public expenditure.[95] But he knew this was not enough. Economic modernisation of the empire required long-term state investment. In the early 1920s the ideological divisions in the French political community precluded the broad imperialist consensus necessary to ensure that successive governments of whatever political stripe paid the costs of colonial modernisation. Nevertheless, a meaningful development strategy could not be realised overnight or on the cheap. Sarraut's colonial modernisation programme, put before the Chamber of Deputies on 12 April 1921, envisaged spending commitments spread over fifteen years. The Ministry of Colonies assigned most funding to infrastructure development, focusing on the expansion of key colonial ports, exploitation of AEF and Cameroon's vast forestry and mineral resources, and major railway projects in French Africa, Madagascar and Indochina. A separate development scheme was proposed for the assimilated *anciennes colonies*, including a rail system in Réunion, completion of the Dakar–Saint Louis rail link, and the extension of the Antilles ports of Fort de France and Pointe-à-Pitre. Once he began drawing up the project in 1919, Sarraut warned his ministerial colleagues that overall costs might exceed 3 billion francs (at 1918 franc levels).[96] To him, colonial development was imperative. To more sceptical observers, *mise en valeur* was manna from heaven for a self-interested imperialist lobby out to line its pockets after the economic dislocation of the war years. Opponents of the scheme highlighted its concentration on transport, a reflection of the influence of yet another Parti colonial lobby group, the National Committee for African Railways, established in October 1918 by a consortium of thirty-four rail industry and mining company bosses and the presidents of eleven chambers of commerce in France and North Africa.[97]

Nor were all Parti colonial supporters happy with the thrust of colonial development. Indeed, long-term investment of this order demanded a shift in French imperialist thinking as fundamental as that required of the empire-sceptics. The allocation of over 600 million francs to AEF, a market dominated hitherto by concessionary companies and private sector investment, drew most adverse comment in France. When Sarraut presented the final 366 page Ministry of Colonies scheme to Parliament in April 1921 he stressed the strategic advantages and ethical imperative of colonial modernisation alongside the purely economic arguments for the expansion of Franco-imperial trade.[98] Some were clearly prepared to listen. By 1931 the second and more popular of Sarraut's books on colonial development, *Grandeur et servitude coloniales*, reached its tenth edition.[99] Even then the arcane, simplistic concept of a 'colonial pact' in which France conferred benevolent administration in exchange for colonial economic resources was more widely understood than Sarraut's insistence on the need for an empire-wide managed economy underpinned by public sector funding.[100] Ultimately, the 'sky-blue Chamber' disappointed its imperialist members. Colonial policy initiatives acquired a higher national profile, but they rarely made it unscathed through Parliament. Proponents of higher colonial spending were stymied by overwhelming Ministry of Finance opposition. Between 1919 and 1924 state funding for colonial projects slowed to a trickle.

What held true economically also held true politically. Only in exceptional circumstances – during the depression years or on the eve of war in 1939 – did the colonies figure large in French political calculations. In these, and in other cases, the dynamic was the same. The overseas empire was expected to contribute to the preservation of the French Republic. In its crudest form, republican imperialism was less a matter of the transmission of French political culture to the colonies than an expectation that these territories would serve the interests of the Third Republic itself. In the early 1930s, as France's economic troubles worsened and international tensions deepened, colonised peoples living under the tricolour faced more onerous obligations to France. Trade statistics, tax returns and army recruitment rolls tell only part of the story. As France sank into depression in 1932, increased colonial export quotas meant harsher working conditions, and extended recourse to forced labour. Intensified preparation for war with Germany and Italy from 1936 to 1939 prompted more coercive recruitment of colonial regiments and a renewed effort to conscript a mass colonial army. Colonial forces were not just called upon to repeat their First World War contribution to French defence. In terms of overall numbers and material supplies, they were expected to surpass it.[101] Economically and militarily, colonial subjects experienced empire as a heavier burden after 1918 than before.

Protracted national debate over Sarraut's development project proved one thing above all. The acid test of imperialist commitment in the 1920s was economic. In peacetime conditions empire would count for the mass of French workers and bourgeois investors only if colonial trade became indispensable to national prosperity. Advocates of colonial development knew that this implied more than a return to the pre-war certainties of captive colonial markets and primary products sold at rates advantageous to French consumers. Dumping of French manufactured goods in the colonies and cheap purchases of colonial commodities were no basis for a sustainable economic relationship. Only a long-term strategy of commercial diversification and market integration could make empire trade the cornerstone of France's industrial recovery after the destruction of the Great War. The obstacles to any such colonial 'new deal' were obvious.[102] As we have seen, massive state investment was needed to create the rudimentary commercial and transport infrastructure in the colonies essential to increased export traffic. This was only the start. Private investors had to be persuaded to follow the flag overseas. French shipbuilders required cash incentives to build a merchant fleet capable of handling the anticipated colonial cargoes. Colonial populations, many of which were scarcely part of a cash economy at all, had to become consumers of French imports. This, in turn, depended on growth in local employment markets and increasing use of wage labour. But perhaps the greatest challenge of all was to convince French industrial and agricultural producers that the colonies were an untapped reservoir of wealth rather than a source of unwelcome competition.

The apparatus of colonial government

The frequency with which Ministries, governors, military planners and regional officials imposed additional obligations on dependent populations reflected the multiple layers of colonial bureaucracy. Duplication of responsibility went unchecked for years. Lack of sustained government interest in imperial policy was reflected in the low official regard for the Ministry of Colonies and the colonial service more generally. In 1887 the under-secretary of state for the colonies, Eugène Etienne, finally established a Corps of Colonial Administrators with uniform entry standards and promotion structures to replace previous *ad hoc* recruitment of officials colony by colony. After the First World War the Corps of Colonial Administrators numbered little more than a thousand staff. A school *baccalauréat* was a requirement for entry; graduation from the Ecole coloniale – the colonial service training college set up by Etienne in 1889 –

was not. Indeed, the Ecole coloniale effectively closed down during the war and reopened its doors afterward only with difficulty. Admission to the colonial service promised fast-track promotion, but lacked kudos. William Cohen's pioneering research indicates that the colonial bureaucracy attracted larger numbers of bourgeois French applicants in the inter-war years, principally from Corsica and the coastal regions, the more so after the high-profile Vincennes Colonial Exhibition in 1931. And by 1939 the colonial service recruited over twenty per cent of its personnel from among the settler populations of the empire.[103]

The lack of *élan* attached to colonial policy making helps explain the condescending smiles in Parliament which greeted a Minister merely awarded 'the Colonies'. With few exceptions, appointment to the rue Oudinot, home of the Ministry of Colonies, was at best a consolation prize, at worst a humiliating demotion. Adolphe Messimy, a Parti colonial enthusiast renowned for his tenure at the War Ministry in the second Moroccan crisis, recalled his earlier selection to the Ministry of Colonies in March 1911 in these terms:

> Since time immemorial, this important portfolio was usually assigned any old how [*au petit bonheur*], after the division of the 'Big Ministries' between the outstanding Cabinet members. During the course of this 'tombola', by which each ministerial crisis was brought to an end, the Colonies was gener-ally awarded to the weakest person in the Cabinet team without regard for their competence.[104]

Messimy seized the chance to leave the rue Oudinot three months later, knowing he could advance imperial causes more effectively as Minister of War.

The Ministry of Colonies invariably fared badly in the inter-departmental competition for funds and influence. As France turned its attention to the Paris Peace Conference the rue Oudinot was still a backwater in the govern-mental establishment. Its institutional existence stretched back a mere twenty-five years to 1894. The Naval Ministry boasted a longer pedigree in the management of colonies, and the transfer of the central administration of empire from the navy to specialist civilian bureaucrats was a messy, protracted process. A junior colonial secretariat was created in 1881, but it was attached, first to the Department of Commerce, then briefly to the Naval Ministry, and finally to the renamed Department of Commerce and Industry in 1893. These twelve years of bureaucratic wrangling exposed deeper tensions between colonial governments dominated by career soldiers and the mercantilist economists at the Ministries of Commerce and Finance.[105]

In sum, next to more established Ministries, the rue Oudinot bureau-cracy was numerically small, under-resourced and little respected. Its task was made harder by the lack of agreement in government or among senior colonial officials about the optimum administrative apparatus for colonial rule. Colonial governments were fiercely protective of their jurisdictional autonomy. But the late nineteenth-century experiments with federal imperial systems, first in Indochina and then, at the turn of the century, in French West Africa, although by no means uncontested or uniformly applied, received strong support inside the Ministry of Colonies. The federal administrative structure in Dakar was mapped out between 1895 and 1904. Six years later, in 1910, French Equatorial Africa became the second sub-Saharan federation of African colonies.[106] Yet the idea that this vast region was systematically governed from its federal capital of Brazzaville was even more ludicrous than the suggestion that the federal bureaucracies in Hanoi and Dakar imposed a common pattern of authority throughout Indochina and AOF. In practice, a strong-willed governor-general was essential to hold together the disparate interests of lieutenant-governors, trading companies, settler groups and garrison commanders. On 22 January 1918, for example, Brazzaville governor-general Gabriel Louis Angoulvant took over the additional responsibilities of interim governor-general in French West Africa, pending the arrival of Martial Merlin, the designated appointee. During early 1918 Angoulvant, by then relocated to Dakar with his Brazzaville secretariat, ran AOF and AEF as a single autocratic regime.[107] The abstract bureaucratic neatness of these huge colonial collectives concealed the reality of a diffuse imperial system in which the division of fiscal, economic and political power between federal administration and individual colonial governments remained unclear.[108]

Far from streamlining government, the colonial federations generated additional layers of administrative control. During the 1920s the Senate finance commission, a vigilant watchdog of imperial spending, repeatedly questioned the worth of burgeoning colonial bureaucracy. Moreover, ostensibly federal systems belied the centralisation of colonial government, a problem acknowledged by Albert Sarraut as governor-general in Indochina as far back as 1911.[109] Notwithstanding the parliamentary grumbling, central administrative agencies grew apace after 1919, to the accompaniment of expensive and segregationist urban planning in colonial capitals from Rabat to Hanoi.[110]

The apparatus of colonial officialdom was reorganised by decree in September 1920 in order to provide overseas administrations better specialist advice. The Ministry of Colonies replicated the jurisdictional practice of the Foreign Ministry. Rue Oudinot staff, previously allocated to geographical sections with responsibility for particular colonies or regions, were reassigned to specialist divisions (*Directions*) for political affairs, economic and social policy, public works, military matters, health, and personnel. Between 1920 and 1940 four departmental bureaux operated at a broader level in the Ministry, drawing on specialist divisional advice as required. The deuxième bureau was by far the strongest,[111] supervising general policy, spending and administration, with the sole exception of the Indochina federation, preserve of the troisième bureau.

The 1920 decree did more than shift offices and labels. Under Sarraut's aegis, economic development acquired more importance alongside the expansion of colonial commerce and banking. Military organisation of the empire also drew unprecedented attention. Contested ministerial jurisdiction over colonial policy was always most intense in military affairs. In the eighteenth and nineteenth centuries navy marines played a leading role in colonial conquest. But in July 1900 the navy formally handed over responsibility to the War Ministry for standing French colonial forces: the troupes coloniales, more often designated La Coloniale.[112] It seemed logical for the War Ministry to administer professional colonial regiments (Coloniale blanche) and colonial infantry (tirailleurs) units.[113] With the exception of the wages and equipment of the Frenchmen who volunteered for service in Coloniale blanche units, the bulk of imperial defence expenditure was drawn from colonial budgets. After 1905 the federal administration in Dakar became the hub of this system, since AOF provided the largest number of Coloniale recruits.[114] In theory, from 1908 the Ministry of Colonies military services division oversaw this colonial defence spending. In practice, immediately before and during the First World War, the rue Oudinot struggled to meet rising War Ministry demands for men and material. The 1920 reforms were intended to redress the balance. The rue Oudinot's military section was subdivided into separate offices to supervise colonial defence spending, recruitment targets and defensive works. A Ministry of Colonies military inspectorate toured the empire's principal garrisons, ports and defensive installations. In an effort to bring military expenditure under control, from May 1923 the rue Oudinot economic division supervised all colonial defence planning outside French North Africa and the Middle East mandates.[115]

Military jurisdiction in these Arab territories was rather different. The standing military forces, the Armée d'Afrique (the army of French North Africa), the Armée du Levant (a mixture of North African and Coloniale units), and the Syrian gendarmerie, always remained under strict War Ministry control. Again this reflected the distinctive origins of colonial conquest. It was several decades after the 1830–31 landings before the army relinquished its grip over colonial administration in Algeria. The southern desert region and much of Algeria's rural interior remained under *de facto* military control after 1918. And in the Moroccan protectorate and the Levant mandates, military pacification and the containment of revolt placed the War Ministry at the heart of colonial administration throughout the inter-war period. North African regiments saw more active service in the twenty years separating the two world wars than any other units of the French professional army. Moreover, the administration of protectorates and mandates was theoretically the product of a diplomatic relationship between French representatives and an indigenous governing elite. It therefore fell to the Foreign Ministry to administer Morocco and Tunisia, and the Lebanon and Syria mandates. As a result, in much of France's Arab empire the Ministry of Colonies had no formal jurisdiction and little tangible influence. By contrast, in the older Far Eastern protectorates of Cambodia, Annam and Upper Laos the Ministry of Colonies acquired greater jurisdictional responsibility, these territories having been largely administered by the Naval Ministry in the late nineteenth century.

Two grandly named advisory committees stood at the apex of the restructured Ministry of Colonies: the Supreme Colonial Council (Conseil Supérieur des Colonies, CSC) and the Higher Colonial Council (Haut Conseil Colonial). Each was packed with former Ministers, ex-governors, career officials and outstanding Ecole coloniale (or 'Colo') graduates. In the event, these committees rarely convened in the early 1920s. The CSC was called into operation only in 1925, at which point it became obvious that it could function only when broken down into smaller, manageable sub-committees.[116] When Sarraut returned to government in November 1926 as Interior Minister in Raymond Poincaré's government, he established a permanent CSC secretariat and a specialist economic section. He hoped to mobilise the CSC in support of his cherished colonial development scheme by seeking its approval for short-term state investment more likely to secure parliamentary approval than any return to the more ambitious original *mise en valeur* plan.[117] Unfortunately for Sarraut, his ministerial colleagues showed little inclination to support him.

The Middle East and African mandates

In 1919–20 parliamentarians and press commentators were more animated by the prospect of imperial expansion than by the challenge of development in existing colonial territory. This marked a new departure. French attachment to Syria, Lebanon, the Cameroons and Togoland after 1920 stood in marked contrast to the limited governmental interest in Middle Eastern and African expansion during the First World War. As we have seen, Briand's ministers abdicated responsibility for colonial war aims in 1915–16. The Clemenceau government's commitment to mandate acquisition was fitful at best. Policy making was delegated to the imperialist lobby by default.

Parti colonial members eagerly filled the gap left for them by wartime Cabinets. Imperialist pressure groups, the French Geographical Society foremost among them, immediately urged Auguste Terrier's French Africa committee to 'think big'. It took up the challenge, resurrecting a scheme for the unification of West and Equatorial Africa through annexation of ex-German colonies and a series of territorial deals with allied colonial powers. During 1916–17 it garnered support from the federal administration in Dakar. AOF governors Gabriel Angoulvant and François-Joseph Clozel were drawn to schemes that promised to unify the Senegambia region. They dreamt of a once-and-for-all exchange of colonial territory. French-controlled Togo might be 'swapped' for British Gambia. In addition, Angoulvant pondered an approach to the Lisbon government to sell Portuguese Guinea. The two governors even hoped that the British might somehow be persuaded to cede control of Sierra Leone and southern Gold Coast to France. But a new West African scramble faded from view once Joost Van Vollenhoven took over as governor-general in 1917.[118] Attention shifted instead to the reconstruction of the Cameroon port and rail system, much of which was destroyed during the war. The repair of Douala's dock installations, dredging of the Wouri estuary that served the port, and rebuilding of the two railway lines that connected the coastal port network to the interior of the Cameroon became the dominant preoccupation in mandate administration during the early 1920s.[119]

Clashes of Franco-British imperial interest outside Africa caused greater long-term bitterness, or were left unresolved. The size and economic importance of the territories involved was not a reliable guide to the depth of animosity between the victorious colonial powers. The New Hebrides were a case in point. Before and after 1914–18 these Pacific islands were administered as a Franco-British condominium, an uneasy arrangement that reflected the mixed population of French and anglophone settlers, many from Australia.[120] In New Caledonia, only 400 km from the New Hebrides archipelago, settler landowners, corporate managers and the Nouméa Chamber of Commerce formed a loose coalition to push France's exclusive claim on the nearby islands.[121] In 1920 another Parti colonial group, the French Oceania committee chaired by former Minister of Colonies, Paul Froment-Guieysse, lambasted Foreign Minister Stephen Pichon's failure to advance French interests in the Pacific at the Paris Peace Conference. As a trained hydrographer, Froment-Guieysse recognised the archipelago's potential for development. His committee's anger increased as Australian immigrants acquired a hold over the New Hebrides agricultural economy.

In French Polynesia, too, the end of the war unleashed high hopes of territorial gains. On 22 September 1914 the Tahitian port of Papeete became one of the few French Pacific possessions to experience a German attack. Three German ships bombarded the port, sinking its solitary French naval vessel and setting fire to Papeete's central market.[122] By 1918 over a thousand Tahitian settlers and indigenous Polynesians had served in France, adding to settler demands for the annexation of German Samoa and a string of islands including Pitcairn, Easter Island and Clipperton. French acquisition of Samoa would provide a fillip to long-standing plans to develop Papeete as a major transit port between the Panama Canal, Australia, Hawaii and San Francisco. These schemes fell foul of rival British Dominion claims at the peace conference.[123] France's failure to acquire additional territory in the South Pacific belied its success in doing so in Africa. Even so, imperialists' resentment at supposedly missed opportunities to secure a bigger share of post-war colonial prizes surfaced time and again in the Supreme Colonial Council.[124]

Land redistribution in the Middle East was of a different order again, but was similarly neglected by central government. Briand famously gave free rein to the Beirut consul-general François Georges Picot, a Parti colonial activist and former deputy director of the Quai d'Orsay's Middle East division, to negotiate a division of Ottoman and African spoils with the British. The Ministry of Colonies did belatedly establish a study commission in October 1917 to codify colonial issues likely to arise at the end of the war. Predictably, the French Africa committee and its French Asia counterpart dominated commission sessions. Lacking Cabinet support, Louis Henry Simon, the minister responsible, left commission members to formulate policy alone, insisting that he would defer to their superior knowledge.[125] For all that, imperial expansion after 1918 was the swan song of the Parti colonial.[126]

The first meaningful French occupation of Syrian territory occurred in late October 1918 after Admiral Varney, commander of the French naval squadron off the Anatolian coast, won government approval for a landing of combined French and Armenian units at Alexandretta.[127] It was two further years before France cemented its grip on Syria and Lebanon. French forces fought their way into government in Damascus, deposing Emir Faisal's regime in July 1920 and suppressing the emergent mass engagement in Syrian national politics.[128] The three main Arab nationalist organisations in Faisal's republic – the Palestine Arab Club; the Syrian-run Arab Independence Party; and the al-'Ahd Officers' Association, dominated by Iraqis – were by then deeply split, a fact obscured by the regime's overthrow and the relocation of leading nationalists to Baghdad, Cairo and Jerusalem. But the inter-communal tensions engendered by the violence of the French take-over reverberated through the political life of the Levant mandates for the next twenty years.[129]

The Syrian and Lebanese mandates were governed through faltering partnerships. French rule in Syria was mediated by an Ottoman-educated political community of urban notables, professional politicians and leading families to the exclusion of a largely Sunni Muslim Arab majority that had found its political voice in opposition to Faisal's Hashemite government. In Lebanon the Maronite Christians of Mount Lebanon and Beirut accrued administrative power, as did leading members of local Jesuit and Lazarist orders, and the academic staff of the Catholic University of St Joseph.[130] In Faisal's Syria, women and men of the Arab lower orders accumulated a fund of political experience through their support of popularly based organisations such as the Arab National Committee and the Committees of National Defence that sprang up across Syria and the Biqa' valley. Popular opposition to external rule intensified in the months between the Mudros armistice with Turkey in October 1918 and the French take-over in July 1920. It was fuelled by the chronic social and economic disruption of the First World War, a huge influx of refugees to Damascus, Aleppo and Beirut, and the proliferation of Arab newspapers, coffee houses and theatres that followed the collapse of Ottoman rule.[131]

The predations of Cemal Pasha's Damascus-based Ottoman Fourth Army combined with a series of wartime harvest failures, recurrent epidemics and severe currency depreciation to bring the Syrian and Lebanese economy to its knees by 1918. The dominant collective memories of the First World War among the Levant population were famine, fear and loss. Cemal Pasha terrorised Arab opponents in Syria and Lebanon once he assumed emergency powers as military governor in May 1915 after Turkey's earlier defeat in the Egyptian campaign. Scores of public hangings of Arab and Maronite Christian leaders occurred in 1915–16. Up to 5,000 Syrian families were deported to Anatolia. Arab conscripts were posted to remote theatres of war, and Turkish was reintroduced as the sole language of instruction in Damascus.[132] To make matters worse, Mount Lebanon and Beirut were cut off by the Entente naval blockade of the eastern Mediterranean. In 1916 a second year of harvest failure provoked widespread starvation. The situation was little better in Syria, where food shortages, chronic price inflation, as well as Ottoman conscription and military requisitioning, contributed to mass hunger. Contemporary estimates of the civilian death toll in both countries ranged from 300,000 to 450,000.[133] Such profound social dislocation had lasting political effects. Mass political engagement in defiance of European imperialism and an imposed Hashemite authority dominated by Hijazi, Iraqi and Palestinian Arabs was an accomplished fact by the time the French mandate in Syria took shape. French troops seized control in Damascus and Aleppo in late July 1920 in the aftermath of popular Arab insurrections against Faisal's government.[134]

At the level of high politics, four events in rapid succession triggered the French take-over in Syria. First was the unwelcome selection in May 1919 of a US commission of inquiry to formulate recommendations for Syria's future administration. Appointed in fulfilment of Woodrow Wilson's wishes, and better known as the King–Crane Commission, the commission's presence in Syria widened the breach between French officials, Faisal's government and the Arab popular committees that dominated street politics in Damascus. The French studiously ignored the King–Crane Commission. Faisal's administration and the Arab Higher Committee tried to exploit it.[135] The second catalyst to decisive French intervention was the Anglo-French agreement forged between 13 and 15 September 1919 by which the British agreed to withdraw troops of General Sir Edmund Allenby's Egyptian Expeditionary Force from Syria. Lloyd George's government wanted units of Faisal's Arab army to replace the British garrisons in Damascus, Homs, Hama and Aleppo. Clemenceau refused. The French premier was conscious of declining British interest in Syria and poorly reconciled to Britain's control of the Mosul oilfield in northern Iraq. He was in no mood to compromise eventual French control over Damascus. The resultant probability of a far wider French military presence than Faisal had previously envisaged was a setback from which his administration never recovered.[136]

This second reverse for the Damascus government precipitated a third. Faisal's slim chances of building a solid foundation of popular support disappeared once news of the Anglo-French accord spread. The monthly British subsidies to Faisal's government were also reduced, leaving his regime poorly placed to combat the economic collapse in the Syrian interior and unable to buy off the leading sheikhs that helped enforce security in the countryside.[137] In consequence, Faisal was compelled to negotiate a settlement with Clemenceau in Paris signed on 6 January 1920.[138] The Clemenceau–Faisal agreement was nothing new; its terms were prefigured in Quai d'Orsay proposals in circulation since April 1919. But it was fundamentally contradictory. France recognised Syria's right to self-government and eventual independence. Faisal's government accepted exclusive French protection and political guidance. The contradiction in the accord mirrored Clemenceau's ambivalent attitude to Faisal, whom he regarded as inveterately francophobe and yet the sole figure capable of restraining militant Arab nationalists in Damascus.[139] The sting in the tail for both sides was the acceptance of a separate Lebanese state with a small Christian majority incorporating Mount Lebanon, the Biqa' valley, the Akkar, southern Lebanon and the coastal cities. A settlement that precluded a unified Greater Syria – la Syrie intégrale – stretching west to east from Beirut to Albukamal was consistent with Mount Lebanon's status as a Christian enclave, confirmed in the year following the massacres of Christians in 1860.[140] The abandonment of a Greater Syria project none the less antagonised Parti colonial lobbyists and Syrian nationalists alike.[141]

Frustration with Clemenceau's dilatory approach to Syria was strongest among National Bloc deputies, landslide victors of the November 1919 general election. Here was the fourth decisive event in the march towards a seizure of power in Syria. As we have seen, the National Bloc victory catapulted Parti colonial supporters to the heart of government. Flushed with electoral success, in the early months of 1920 French premier Millerand cut a powerful figure. His dominance in Cabinet was enhanced by his stewardship of the Foreign Ministry. Millerand and General Henri Gouraud, military commander in the Levant, worked together to achieve French suzerainty over Syria and Lebanon.[142] To some extent Millerand simply picked up where Stephen Pichon, his predecessor at the Quai d'Orsay, left off. Pichon had long pressed for French expansion in the Middle East, and was president of the Oriental Committee, mouthpiece of the Parti colonial on Syrian affairs. But the real power behind the throne was Robert de Caix, a veteran 'Asiatique' of the Parti colonial's Levant lobby groups. Throughout 1918–19 de Caix formulated the Quai d'Orsay's Syria policy, only to see his complex schema for an Anglo-French Middle East partition thrown off course by Clemenceau's willingness to bargain Levant interests for concessions to French security requirements in Europe.[143]

In October 1919 de Caix was appointed secretary-general in Gouraud's new Beirut administration. Following discussions in Paris with Lebanon's Maronite patriarch, Monsignor Elias Pierre Huwayyik, by this point even Clemenceau favoured 'Grand Liban' – a compact Lebanese state controlled by Beirut's Maronite Christian community.[144] Clemenceau's commitment to a French Syria was more doubtful, although his badgering of Faisal suggested otherwise. Frustrated by the outgoing premier's cavalier attitude, and painfully aware of French military weakness in Lebanon and Syria, from his new power base in Beirut de Caix exploited Millerand's enthusiasm for a French-controlled Syrian state to the full.

There were several pillars to Millerand's policy. The new prime minister accepted Oriental Committee arguments that the provisions of the January 1916 Sykes–Picot agreement guaranteed France undisputed political control over a large Syrian polity stretching from Cilicia in the north, along the Mediterranean coast southward to Acre and far inland toward Mosul. Millerand also considered it vital to match Britain's efforts to consolidate its grip on Palestine and Iraq. He wanted to exploit the window of opportunity presented by the Greco-Turkish conflict to establish control in northern Syria and, it was hoped, Cilicia, before the Kemalist government could respond. Finally, Millerand and his close adviser and old school friend, Foreign Ministry secretary-general Maurice Paléologue, were determined to bring Faisal's regime to heel. In the early months of 1920 the two Frenchmen sought to prevent Faisal's consolidation of a functioning Syrian state. Their task was facilitated by Syria's deepening economic crisis and the insolvency of the Damascus government. Faisal's introduction of new taxes, commercial tariffs and legal fees compounded popular hostility to his administration and exposed its limited authority beyond the Syrian capital.[145] Fearing the imminent confirmation of Faisal's position as Syrian head of state, in March and April 1920 the contest for power between Paris and Faisal's supporters in Damascus became a race. Faisal's ministers strove to make Syrian self-government a *fait accompli*. French conference diplomacy meanwhile laid the legal foundations for a take-over. This culminated in the San Remo conference agreement on 28 April allocating Syria and Lebanon to France as Type A mandates. Meanwhile, Gouraud's forces fought an undeclared war of bloody skirmishes and occasional massacres against Kemalist forces and Arab army irregulars.[146] As French losses mounted, Millerand concluded that Faisal was nothing more than a British stooge.[147]

The Millerand government's interpretation of French treaty rights, cultural interests and the country's rediscovered imperial destiny in the Levant precluded negotiation with any existing Arab authority in Damascus or elsewhere. Gouraud was an enthusiastic agent of this aggressive Middle Eastern imperialism. He saw little more than anti-French intrigue in the assertion of Arab cultural identity in Syria. The Levant army command ascribed regional disorder and attacks on French garrison forces in the Syrian interior to the malign influence of the Damascus government. With scant appreciation of the country's competing urban and tribal elites, Gouraud's senior staff depicted the Syrian capital as the source of all the opposition bedevilling a French take-over already legitimised by the victor powers.[148]

The imposition of French mandatory power culminated in a definitive showdown with Arab army units loyal to Faisal. There was little prospect that Arab forces could long resist the French. Faisal's government encountered formidable opposition to its extended conscription measures in May and June 1920, and the voluntary local militias favoured by the Syrian popular committees were no match for Gouraud's troops.[149] French commanders were more concerned that protracted instability in Syria would tempt the Turkish authorities to seize territory in Cilicia and northern Syria, including the Aleppo *vilayet* and the Alexandretta *sanjak*. In the spring of 1920 Gouraud's first priority was therefore military manpower. He sought and obtained twelve additional battalions of reinforcements – seasoned Senegalese riflemen fresh from the Rhine occupation, and Moroccan cavalry transferred from Constantinople. These forces were assigned to establish French control over the Syrian rail network, a vital prerequisite to any effective occupation of Rayak, Aleppo and Damascus itself. The general then cast around for alternative sources of local support. He established informal contacts with leading notables in Damascus and Syria's main provincial centres as well as prominent sheikhs and Bedouin chiefs in the Syrian interior.[150] Between them Millerand, de Caix and Gouraud laid the politico-military foundations for a French take-over that nullified Faisal's protracted efforts to carve himself a role as head of a Syrian mandate government.

In the Lebanon, Maronite Catholic supremacy could be reconciled with French imperial ambitions as long as the Lebanese withheld demands for independence. In Syria, by contrast, the Sunni majority rejected French authority.[151] French reliance on Maronite co-operation in Lebanon amounted to a system of 'political confessionalism' that made religious affiliation the primary marker of social exclusion.[152] France's choice of partners in Syria intensified not only inter-communal tension but class antagonisms and urban–rural divisions as well. French entry to Damascus on 25 July 1920 set the tone. Gouraud sent an ultimatum to Faisal's government on 14 July ordering it to surrender power to advancing French forces. But the general disregarded Faisal's acceptance of these terms on 19 July, arguing that the timetable for compliance had expired.[153] A brief but bloody battle with the remnants of the Syrian Arab army took place at Khan Maysalun west of Damascus on 24 July. Victorious French columns under Gouraud's assistant, General Goybet, took control of Damascus in the afternoon of the 25th, twenty-four hours after General de Lamothe established French authority in Aleppo.[154] Troops were posted at the main entry points to the capital, the railway station and government installations. The venal administration that replaced the Faisali regime immediately ratified a collective fine imposed on the population of Damascus in punishment for the harassment of French forces over the preceding year.[155]

Conclusion

It is unhelpful to state that the First World War transformed attitudes to empire in metropolitan France and in the colonies. Unhelpful because public opinion, and especially the views of disenfranchised colonial subjects denied basic freedom to associate or to speak freely, is exceptionally difficult to gauge. Unhelpful because there is little indication that French appreciation of the colonial contribution to the recent war effort precipitated much discussion about the nature of colonial domination itself. And unhelpful because the basic rules of that domination remained unchanged. The idealism stimulated in reaction to the war, the wave of revolutionary change across Europe, and the emergence of a strident, if ill defined, Arab nationalism in the Middle East, reverberated through the empire. But French governments and political parties did not envisage a fundamental transformation of colonial rule. The war conflated nationalist fervour with imperialist conviction; but French nationalism proved more enduring than imperialism in the 1920s.[156]

The cessation of hostilities did not signify the end of government concern over colonial troops and unrest in the empire. Even the most conservative officials saw a need to confer limited political rights on men compelled to serve France. But concessions were made through clenched teeth. In Algeria planned reforms were whittled away. In Indochina the new governor-general Maurice Long struggled to control the federation's budgetary deficit, and put the interests of settlers and French commercial interests above those of the mandarin elite and the wider population at large.[157] Meanwhile, just as colonial administrations in black Africa rediscovered their interest in reinforcing chiefly power as the mainstay of a conservative tribal elite, the return of ex-servicemen and the economic pressures and labour shortages built up during the war years threatened to undermine French policy.

As for the acquisition of additional territory in the Africa and, more especially, the Middle East, the new phase of French imperial expansion was no less brutal than the earlier era of colonial conquest. And, as we shall see in the next chapter, the administrative practices underlying French colonial governance after the First World War were also contested ground.

Notes

1 A. S. Kanya-Forstner, 'The war, imperialism and decolonization', in Jay Winter, Geoffrey Parker and Mary R. Hubeck (eds), *The Great War and the Twentieth Century* (New Haven CT: Yale University Press, 2000), 231–62.

2 SHA, 5H6/D6, André Maginot to Raymond Poincaré, 'Défense du Sahara', 17 December 1923; 6H124/D1: Oubangui-Chari – renseignements, 1899–1932.

3 Robin Bidwell, *Morocco under Colonial Rule. French Administration of Tribal Areas, 1912–1956* (London: Frank Cass, 1973), 13–15, 34–7; Moshe Gershovich, *French Military Rule in Morocco. Colonialism and its Consequences* (London: Frank Cass, 2000), 153–61. The residency declared Moroccan pacification over in 1934.

4 CAOM, Maurice Prouteaux papers, PA50/3/D12, no. 61, 'Rapport sur l'organisation du commandement indigène : subdivision du Baïbokoum', 23 February 1930.

5 Linda Schatkowski Schilcher, 'The famine of 1915–1918 in Greater Syria', in J. Spagnolo (ed.), *Problems of the Modern Middle East in Historical Perspective. Essays in Honour of Albert Hourani* (Reading MA: Ithaca Press, 1992), 229–58; Myron Echenberg, *Black Death, White Medicine. Bubonic Plague and the Politics of Public Health in Colonial Senegal, 1914–1945* (Oxford: James Currey, 2002), 184–9; John Ruedy, *Modern Algeria. The Origins and Development of a Nation* (Bloomington IN: Indiana University Press, 1992), 115.

6 Regarding the experiences of African colonial troops, see Marc Michel, *L'Appel à l'Afrique. Contributions et reactions à l'effort de guerre en AOF 1914–1919* (Paris: Publications de la Sorbonne, 1982); Joe Lunn, *Memoirs of the Maelstrom. A Senegalese Oral History of the First World War* (Portsmouth NH: Heinemann, 1999); Belkacem Recham, *Les Musulmans algériens dans l'armée française 1919–1945* (Paris: Editions l'Harmattan, 1996); Anthony Clayton, *France, Soldiers and Africa* (London: Brassey's, 1988); Gershovich, *French Military Rule*.

7 Tyler Stovall, 'Colour-blind France? Colonial workers during the First World War', *Race and Class*, 35:2 (1993), 35–55; and 'The color line behind the lines. Racial violence in France during the First World War', *American Historical Review*, 103:3 (1998), 739–69.

8 John Horne, 'Immigrant workers in France during World War I', *French Historical Studies*, 16:1 (1985), 59–60.

9 Stovall, 'The color line', 741–2. The figure of 222,793 included 36,941 Chinese, not technically colonial workers but administered in the same way.

10 Stovall, 'The color line', 748–60. Moroccans suffered the most assaults. Race riots occurred in Brest, Dijon and Le Havre over the summer of 1917.

11 Tyler Stovall, 'Love, labor, and race. Colonial men and women in France during the Great War', in Tyler Stovall and Georges Van Den Abbeele (eds), *French Civilization and its Discontents. Nationalism, Colonialism, Race* (Oxford: Lexington Books, 2003), 97–321, quote at 297.

12 Andrew and Kanya-Forstner, 'France, Africa, and the First World War', 11. The authors suggest that the First World War stimulated four key changes in France's relationship with its African empire: territorial expansion; African conscription; state interest in colonial development; and wider French public interest in the colonies.

13 SHA, 6H99/D1, Ministère des Affaires Etrangères, Mission Hugues Le Roux 1919 guidebook, *Gabon* (Paris: Imprimerie Jean Cusac, 1919); 6H124/D1, Mission Hugues Le Roux 1919 guidebook, *Oubangui-Chari* (Paris: Imprimerie Jean Cussac, 1919). The 1911 census for Oubangui-Chari recorded a population of 311,000. By 1919 the Foreign Ministry estimated Oubangui's population at 2.1 million.

14 See, for example, Stéphane Faye, *Le Nouveau Monde français. Maroc, Algérie, Tunisie* (Paris: Plon, 1924); Maréchal Franchet D'Esperey, *Une Oeuvre française. l'Algérie, Conférences organisés par la Société des anciens élèves de l'Ecole libre des sciences politiques* (Paris: Alcan, 1929).

15 Odile Goerg, 'The French provinces and "Greater France" ', in Tony Chafer and Amanda Sackur (eds), *Promoting the Colonial Idea. Propaganda and Visions of Empire in France* (London: Palgrave, 2002), 83, 96–7.

16 CAOM, affpol/859, Commission d'étude des questions coloniales posées par la Guerre, rapport II: 'La politique indigène de la France', 31 May 1918.

17 ADA, Sarraut papers, 12J280, personal letter to Minister of Colonies, 25 August 1918. Sarraut served two terms as governor-general, and became Minister of Colonies on 20 January 1920.

18 CAOM, affpol/C840/D1, 'Note par M. Bessou, Aéronautique coloniale – convention internationale', 13 October 1919.

19 Anne Summers and R. W. Johnson, 'World War I conscription and social change in Guinea', *Journal of African History*, 19:1 (1978), 25–7.

20 Hue-Tam Ho Tai, 'The politics of compromise. The Constitutionalist Party and the electoral reforms of 1922 in French Cochinchina', *Modern Asian Studies*, 18:3 (1984), 378–80.

21 David G. Marr, *Vietnamese Tradition on Trial, 1920–1945* (Berkeley CA: University of California Press, 1981), 5–6. David Marr's penetrating study of anti-colonial nationalism in inter-war Vietnam makes it clear that Sarraut was deluding himself.

22 SHA, 9N269/D2, no. 5347/B, Direction des troupes coloniales, 4e bureau, 'Note pour la Direction du Contrôle – budgets', 8 April 1920.

23 Leonard V. Smith, Stéphane Audoin-Ruzeau and Annette Becker, *France and the Great War, 1914–1918* (Cambridge: Cambridge University Press, 2003), 68–71. The term 'ambiguous victory' is theirs.

24 Annette Becker, *War and Faith. The Religious Imagination in France, 1914–1930* (Oxford: Berg, 1998), quote at p. 1, see also chapter 3.

25 Gershovich, *French Military Rule*, 100–1.

26 Bidwell, *Morocco*, 22, 33–47.

27 Gershovich, *French Military Rule*, 12.

28 Bidwell, *Morocco*, 78–9.

29 AN, 475AP Lyautey papers, 475AP107/D1, no. 2990–9/11, Clemenceau to Lyautey, 16 December 1917. Clemenceau was also War Minister at the time.

30 The young Lyautey was a past-master of such techniques, see Kim Munholland, 'Rival approaches to Morocco. Delcassé, Lyautey, and the Algerian–Moroccan border, 1903–1905', *French Historical Studies*, 5 (1968), 328–43.

31 *DDF*, 1914 (Paris: Imprimerie Nationale, 1999), no. 534, 'Procès-verbal, Séance de la Commission interministérielle des affaires musulmanes, 14 novembre 1914'.

32 The term tirailleurs sénégalais denoted infantrymen recruited throughout AOF, not only Senegal.

33 Annabelle Melzer, 'Spectacles and sexualities. The *mise en scène* of the Tirailleur Sénégalais on the western front, 1914–1920', in B. Melman (ed.), *Borderlines. Gender and Identities in War and Peace, 1870–1930* (London: Routledge, 1998), 213–44.

34 Keith L. Nelson, 'The "black horror on the Rhine". Race as a factor in post-World War I diplomacy', *Journal of Modern History*, 42:4 (1970), 606–27. German propaganda also focused on the threat of rape, and of mixed-race progeny, posed by colonial troops in the Rhineland, see Christian Koller, 'Race and gender stereotypes in the discussion on colonial

troops. A Franco-German comparison, 1914–1923', in Karen Hagemann and Stefanie Schüler-Springorum (eds), *Home/Front. The Military, War and Gender in Twentieth Century Germany* (Oxford: Berg, 2002), 134–57.

35 Jean-Yves Le Naour, *La Honte noire. L'Allemagne et les troupes coloniales françaises 1914–1945* (Paris: Hachette, 2003).

36 *DDF*, 1914, no. 461, Governor-general Lutaud (Algiers) to Théophile Delcassé, 2 November 1914; no. 521, Lyautey (Rabat) to Delcassé, 12 November 1914.

37 Allen Christelow, 'The mosque at the edge of the plaza. Islam in the Algerian colonial city', *Maghreb Review*, 25:3–4 (2000), 293–4, 298.

38 AN, Lyautey Papers, 475AP155/D1, Direction des affaires politiques et commerciales, 'Renseignements intéressant les populations musulmanes, 22–24 mars 1916'; 475AP155/D4, Foreign Minister Delcassé to Lyautey, forwards Cairo mission report 'La question du Khalifat', 3 January 1915; regarding Tunisian opinion see François Arnoulet, 'Les Tunisiens et la première guerre mondiale (1914–1918)', *Revue de l'Occident Musulman et de la Méditerranée* 38 (1985), 47–61.

39 *DDF*, 1915, I (Brussels: Peter Lang, 2002), no. 47, 'Procès-verbal de la Commission interministérielle des affaires musulmanes du 12 janvier 1915'. The German naval bombardment of Bône and Philippeville in early January was almost greeted with relief by Quai d'Orsay staff.

40 James F. Searing, 'Conversion to Islam. Military recruitment and generational conflict in a Sereer-Safèn village (Bandia), 1920–38', *Journal of African History*, 44:1 (2003), 80–2.

41 Alice L. Conklin, *A Mission to Civilize. The Republican Idea of Empire in France and West Africa, 1895–1930* (Stanford CA: Stanford University Press, 1997), 142–8.

42 *Ibid.*, 149–50.

43 Frederick Quinn, *The French Overseas Empire* (Westport CT: Praeger, 2000), 190.

44 MAE, série P: Tunisie 1917–29, vol. 245, 'Note au sujet du personnel des officiers de l'armée active des affaires indigènes de Tunisie', 15 June 1917.

45 E. Pelleray, 'La France en guerre', *L'Océanie Française*, 35:163 (August–October 1939), 61–4.

46 Byron D. Cannon, 'Irreconcilability of reconciliation. Employment of Algerian veterans under the Plan Jonnart, 1919–1926', *Maghreb Review*, 24:1–2 (1999), 43.

47 For discussion see Myron Echenberg, *Colonial Conscripts. The Tirailleurs Sénégalais in French West Africa, 1857–1960* (Portsmouth NH: Heinemann, 1990); Michel, *L'Appel à l'Afrique*; Christelow, 'The mosque at the edge of the plaza', 298.

48 Andrew and Kanya-Forstner, 'France, Africa, and the First World War', 15; Conklin, *A Mission to Civilize*, 143. For damning evidence of the use of tirailleurs sénégalais units as shock troops see Joe Lunn, ' "Les races guerrières". Racial preconceptions in the French military about West African soldiers during the First World War', *Journal of Contemporary History*, 34:4 (1999), 517–36. For detailed analysis of West African recruitment see Marc Michel, *L'Appel à l'Afrique*.

49 CAOM, AOF Fonds moderne, 17G40, Angoulvant circular, 4 May 1918.

50 *Journal Officiel de l'AOF*, no. 701, 11 May 1918.

51 *Ibid.*; François Manchuelle, 'Slavery, emancipation and labour migration in West Africa. The case of the Soninke', *Journal of African History*, 30:1 (1989), 101–2.

52 Martin Klein, *Slavery and Colonial Rule in French West Africa* (Cambridge: Cambridge University Press, 1998), 211–19; François Manchuelle, *Willing Migrants. Soninke Labor Diasporas, 1848–1960* (London: James Currey, 1997), chapter 6.

53 Many returning French veterans were also profoundly alienated from republican society in the inter-war period. For an introduction to their concerns see Antoine Prost, *Republican Identities in War and Peace. Representations of France in the 19th and 20th Centuries* (Oxford: Berg, 2002), 277–310.

54 Summers and Johnson, 'World War I conscription', 26–7. Guinean recruitment estimates vary from an official low of 20,000 to Marc Michel's 1973 calculation of 30,204, cited in Summers and Johnson, p. 25 n. 1.

55 Andrew F. Clark, 'Internal migrations and population movements in the Upper Senegal Valley (West Africa), 1890–1920', *Canadian Journal of African Studies*, 28:3 (1994), 413–14; Klein, *Slavery and Colonial Rule*, 210; The 1913–14 famine was very severe among the Soninke of upper Senegal, see Manchuelle, *Willing Migrants*, 148.

56 SHA, 5H6/D2, Pétain report, 'Troubles et soulevements intérieurs en Afrique Occidentale Française pendant la guerre 1914–1918', 26 March 1925.
57 G. Wesley Johnson, 'The impact of the Senegalese elite upon the French, 1900–1940', in G. Wesley Johnson (ed.), *Double Impact. France and Africa in the Age of Imperialism* (Westport CT: Greenwood Press, 1985), 162–3; James E. Genova, *Colonial Ambivalence, Cultural Authenticity, and the Limitations of Mimicry in French-Ruled West Africa, 1914–1956* (New York: Peter Lang, 2004), 35–9.
58 Marc Michel, 'La genèse du recrutement de 1918 en Afrique noire française', *Revue Française d'Histoire d'Outre-Mer*, 58 (1971), 437–43. Alice Conklin gives a figure of approximately 50,000 recruits in AOF during 1918: *Mission to Civilize*, 150; Alice L. Conklin, 'Who speaks for Africa? The René Maran–Blaise Diagne trial in 1920s Paris', in Sue Peabody and Tyler Stovall (eds), *The Color of Liberty. Histories of Race in France* (Durham NC: Duke University Press, 2003), 302–9.
59 Echenberg, *Black Death, White Medicine*, 184–9, 268, table A1.
60 *Ibid.*, 159–74, 190–1.
61 Catherine Coquery-Vidrovitch, 'Nationalité et citoyenneté en Afrique occidentale française. Originaires et citoyens dans le Sénégal colonial', *Journal of African History*, 42 (2001), 290. The outstanding study of Diagne is G. Wesley Johnson, *The Emergence of Black Politics in Senegal. The Struggle for Power in the Four Communes, 1900–1920* (Stanford CA: Stanford University Press, 1971).
62 ADA, Sarraut papers, 12J253. The file contains copies of Diagne–Merlin correspondence, January–August 1921. Both men gave Sarraut copies of their letters. See also Johnson, 'The impact of the Senegalese elite', 164.
63 George Wesley Johnson, 'The rivalry between Diagne and Merlin for political mastery of French West Africa', in Charles Becker, Saliou Mbaye and Ibrahima Thioub (eds), *AOF : Réalités et héritages. Sociétés ouest-africaines et ordre colonial, 1895–1960* I (Dakar: Direction des Archives du Sénégal, 1997), 303–14; Conklin, *Mission to Civilize*, 156–8; Genova, *Colonial Ambivalence*, 59–60.
64 CAOM, affpol/542/D8, Diagne letter to Sarraut, 8 July 1922. Diagne often clashed with the Dakar authorities regarding the jurisdiction of the AOF colonial council.
65 Dennis D. Cordell and Joel W. Gregory, 'Labour reservoirs and population. French colonial strategies in Koudougou, Upper Volta, 1914 to 1939', *Journal of African History*, 23 (1982), 213–14.
66 Johnson, 'The rivalry', 306–7, 313–14. By late 1923 Diagne's willingness to compromise with the colonial establishment and Bordeaux commercial interests in Senegal had weakened his power base in the four communes.
67 Summers and Johnson, 'World War I conscription', 28–33.
68 Solofo Randrianja, *Société et luttes anticoloniales à Madagascar 1896 à 1946* (Paris: Karthala, 2001), 163–9. The LFAIMDC disbanded in late 1922.
69 SHA, 2N243/D2, CSDN draft memo, 'Défense de l'Afrique du Nord', n.d. [1920].
70 AN, Lyautey Papers, 475AP107/D2, War Ministry to Lyautey, 24 January 1919.
71 *Ibid*, no. 5252/9/11, War Minister Flaminius Raiberti to Lyautey, 24 December 1920; no. 566/9/11, War Minister Louis Barthou to Lyautey, 8 February 1921.
72 CAOM, GGI, 64190, Résident Supérieur au Tonkin Bourcier Saint Chaffray, 'Rapport politique du 1er semester, 1919', 17 August 1919.
73 Emmanuel Bouhier, 'Les troupes coloniales d'Indochine en 1914–1918', in Claude Carlier and Guy Pedroncini (eds), *Les Troupes coloniales dans la Grande guerre* (Paris: Economica, 1997), 69–82.
74 ADA, Sarraut Papers, 12J301/*sûreté générale* dossier, 'L'agitation anti-française dans les pays Annamites de 1905 à 1918'. Tribal unrest, this time among the Méo community, flared up again in 1918–19, requiring the reinforcement of the Tonkin garrison, see Sarraut papers, 12J303, 'Rapport du Résident Supérieur au Tonkin sur le mouvement Méo de Lai-Châu et Sonla', 10 February 1919.
75 Peter Zinoman, *The Colonial Bastille. A History of Imprisonment in Vietnam, 1862–1940* (Berkeley CA: University of California Press, 2001), 157.
76 *Ibid*, 137.
77 CAOM, GGI, 64189, Resident (Nam-Dinh), annual report, 15 July 1917.

78 For details see Peter Zinoman's excellent *The Colonial Bastille*, 158–99.
79 'M. Albert Sarraut blessé', *La Dépêche de Toulouse*, 17 December 1918. Sarraut had not had a good year: months earlier he was hit by a car that dragged him 50 ft.
80 CAOM, GGI, 64190, Résident Supérieur au Tonkin, 'Rapport politique du 2ème semester, 1919', n.d. January 1920.
81 Robert Aldrich, 'Putting the colonies on the map. Colonial names in Paris streets', in Tony Chafer and Amanda Sackur, *Promoting the Colonial Idea: Propaganda and Visions of Empire in France* (London: Palgrave, 2002), 211–23. The 1900 Universal Exhibition in Paris had a section devoted to the colonial empire.
82 L. Abrams and D. J. Miller, 'Who were the French colonialists? A reassessment of the Parti colonial, 1890–1914', *Historical Journal*, 19:3 (1976), 685–725; Stuart Michael Persell, *The French Colonial Lobby, 1889–1938* (Stanford CA: Stanford University Press, 1983), 54–74.
83 The role of geographical and anthropological societies in promoting colonial expansion peaked before the First World War, see Michael Heffernan, 'The science of empire. The French geographical movement and the forms of French imperialism, 1870–1920', in Anne Godlewska and Neil Smith (eds), *Geography and Empire* (Oxford: Blackwell, 1994), 92–114; Susan Bayly, 'French anthropology and the Durkheimians in colonial Indochina', *Modern Asian Studies*, 34:3 (2000), 581–622; Jean-Loup Amselle and Emmanuelle Sibeud (eds), *Maurice Delafosse. Entre orientalisme et ethnographie: l'itinéraire d'un africaniste 1870–1926* (Paris: Maisonneuve & Larose, 1998). Michael Osborne's study of the Société Zoologique d'Acclimatation shows how one scientific society supported imperial conquest: Michael A. Osborne, *Nature, the Exotic, and the Science of French Colonialism* (Bloomington IN: Indiana University Press, 1994).
84 Pascal Venier, 'A campaign of colonial propaganda. Gallieni, Lyautey and the defence of the military regime in Madagascar, May 1899 to July 1900', in Chafer and Sackur, *Promoting the Colonial Idea*, 29–39.
85 During the 1920s the Ligue des droits de l'homme set up a Colonial Study Commission, divided into four regional sub-committees, to monitor conditions in the empire. Prominent sub-committee members included Blaise Diagne and future Minister of Colonies Marius Moutet, see ADA, Sarraut Papers, 12J301: Indochine: SR/Agitation anti-française, 1916–33.
86 Semidei, 'Les Socialistes français et le problème colonial', 1120–4; Jean-Pierre Biondi, *Les Anticolonialistes 1881–1962* (Paris: Robert Laffont, 1992), première partie; Jonathan Derrick, 'The dissenters. Anti colonialism in France, c. 1900–1940', in Chafer and Sackur, *Promoting the Colonial Idea*, 54–6.
87 Paul Clay Sorum, *Intellectuals and Decolonization in France* (Chapel Hill NC: University of North Carolina Press), 25–6.
88 Peter Yearwood, 'Great Britain and the repartition of Africa, 1914–1919', *Journal of Imperial and Commonwealth History*, 18:1 (1990), 323–4; and ' "In a casual way with a blue pencil". British policy and the partition of Kamerun, 1914–1919', *Canadian Journal of African Studies*, 27:2 (1993), 218–44.
89 Blaise Alfred Ngando, *La France au Cameroun 1916–1939. Colonialisme ou mission civilisatrice?* (Paris: Editions l'Harmattan, 2002), 79–80.
90 Heffernan, 'The science of empire', 108–11; Christoper M. Andrew and A. S. Kanya-Forstner, *France Overseas. The Great War and the Climax of French Imperial Expansion* (London: Thames & Hudson, 1981), 102–5.
91 Pierre Brocheux and Daniel Hémery, *Indochine, la colonisation ambiguë, 1858–1954*, 2nd edn (Paris: Editions La Découverte, 2001), 109.
92 Regarding Edouard Herriot's role as Radical Party leader in the 1924 election victory see Mildred Schlesinger, 'The Cartel des gauches: precursor to the Front populaire', *European Studies Review*, 8:2 (1978), 211–34.
93 Andrew and Kanya-Forstner, *France Overseas*, 209–12. The six Groupe colonial organisers were Albert Sarraut, Pierre Perreau-Pradier, Adrien Artaud (President of the Marseilles Chamber of Commerce), André Ballande (a Bordeaux shipbuilder with trading interests in New Caledonia), Auguste Isaac (president of the Lyons Chamber of Commerce) and Jules Siegfried (a business leader in Le Havre). Sarraut remained at the rue Oudinot in three successive Bloc National governments.

94 ADA, Sarraut Papers, 12J162/D2, Union Colonial statement, 'Considérations dont les représentants de l'Union pourraient s'inspirer', n.d. 1920 Original emphasis.
95 ADA, Sarraut papers, 12J163, 'Avis de la Commission du Commerce et de l'Industrie de la Chambre des Députés sur le projet de loi portant fixation d'un programme général de mise en valeur des colonies françaises', n.d. 1922.
96 ADA, Sarraut papers, 12J163, Sarraut note for Cabinet, n.d. 1919. Sarraut hoped to transform Dakar, Djibouti, Tamatave, Fort de France, Pointe-à-Pitre and Papeete into deep-water ports capable of handling much greater shipping volume.
97 ADA, Sarraut papers, 12J163, E. du Vivier de Streel to Sarraut, 5 February 1920; Comité national du rail africain: Conseil de patronage, 2ème liste, n.d. Committee members included A. V. Bernard, former Director of the Société Minière de l'Afrique Occidentale; General Nivelle, commander-in-chief in North Africa; G. Pascalis, president of the Paris Chamber of Commerce; the presidents of the Marseilles, Le Havre, Nancy, Casablanca, Rabat, Algiers, Bône, Constantine, Philippeville and Tunis chambers of commerce; the mayors of Bône and Oran; and Philippe Millet, chief colonial correspondent of *Le Temps*.
98 ADA, Sarraut papers, 12J163, no. 2449, Chambre des Députés, 12ème Législature, Session de 1921, annex au procès-verbal de la séance du 12 avril 1921, 'Projet de loi portant fixation d'un programme général de mise en valeur des colonies françaises'.
99 Albert Sarraut, *Grandeur et servitude coloniales* (Paris: Sagittaire, 1931).
100 ADA, Sarraut papers, 12J163, Sarraut note on *mise en valeur*, n.d. 1919.
101 As examples see SHA, 2N70/D3, CSDN memo, 'Le budget général de l'Afrique Occidentale Française pour l'exercice 1939', 2 February 1939; 2N66/D3, EMA-4, 'Contribution militaire de l'Algérie', 17 February 1939.
102 See Gilbert Meynier's contribution to Jacques Thobie, Gilbert Meynier, Catherine Coquery-Vidrovitch and Charles-Robert Ageron, *Histoire de la France coloniale 1914–1990* (Paris: Armand Colin, 1990), 133–63 *passim*.
103 William B. Cohen, 'The lure of empire. Why Frenchmen entered the colonial service', *Journal of Contemporary History*, 4:1 (1969), 103–16; Armelle Enders, 'L'Ecole nationale de la France d'Outre-Mer et la formation des administrateurs coloniaux', *Revue d'Histoire Moderne et Contemporaine*, 40:2 (1993), 274. The Ecole coloniale's reputation improved under Georges Hardy, appointed Head in 1927.
104 Adolphe Messimy, *Mes souvenirs* (Paris: Plon, 1937), 39.
105 The best work on the colonial service is William B. Cohen, *Rulers of Empire. The French Colonial Service in Africa* (Stanford CA: Stanford University Press, 1971).
106 Denise Bouche, *Histoire de la colonisation française* II, *Flux et reflux 1815–1962* (Paris: Fayard, 1991), 129–37.
107 *Journal Officiel de la République Française*, 25 February 1919.
108 Elizabeth Rabat's guide to French colonial archives describes the evolution of French colonial bureaucracy. See *Les Archives nationales. Etat général des fonds* III, *Marine et Outre-Mer* (Paris: Archives Nationales, 1980), 373–5.
109 CAOM, affpol/21, Senate Finance Commission budgetary report for 1932.
110 Janet L. Abu-Lughod, *Rabat. Urban Apartheid in Morocco* (Princeton NJ: Princeton University Press, 1980), chapter 8; Cooper, *France in Indochina*, chapter 3.
111 At the risk of befuddling the reader, the Ministry of Colonies deuxième bureau should not be confused with its more famous namesakes at the War Ministry and the Naval Ministry – the main military intelligence agencies in French government. By contrast, the Ministry of Colonies deuxième bureau was primarily concerned with day-to-day government of the empire. The point bears emphasis, as the term 'deuxième bureau' is often used generically as shorthand for 'military intelligence service'.
112 Jean-Charles Jauffret, 'La loi du 7 Juillet 1900 sur l'organisation des troupes coloniales. Un accroissement de la puissance?' in Pierre Milza and Raymond Poidevin (eds), *La Puissance française à la 'Belle Epoque'. Mythe ou réalite?* (Paris: Editions Complèxe, 1992), 51–62.
113 Clayton, *France, Soldiers and Africa*, 4–8.
114 Echenberg, *Colonial Conscripts*, 25–8.
115 Rabat, *Les Archives Nationales. Etat général des fonds* III, 499–501.
116 CAOM, affpol/852, Note on the CSC, n.d. December 1927.

117 ADA, Sarraut papers, 12J163, 'Programme de mise en valeur et d'intensification de la production coloniale', n.d. November 1926.
118 Yves Marguerat, 'À quoi rêvaient les gouverneurs-généraux? Les projets de "remembrement" de l'Afrique de l'ouest pendant la première guerre mondiale', in Becker et al., AOF : réalités et héritages I, 89–100.
119 ADA, Sarraut papers, 12J163, 'Note pour la Commission des finances du Sénat. Objet: Subvention de 2 millions au Cameroun pour les chemins de fer et le port', n.d.
120 Maurice Viollette, 'La crise du condominium aux Nouvelles-Hébrides', L'Océanie Française, 10:32 (1914), 34–7.
121 Jacques Feillet, 'La Nouvelle Calédonie, les Nouvelles Hébrides et l'après-guerre', L'Océanie Française, 14:46 (1918), 70–1; Robert Aldrich, The French Presence in the South Pacific (London: Macmillan, 1990), 263, 279–81.
122 Aldrich, The French Presence, 277.
123 Georges Froment-Guieysse, 'La Polynesie Française et l'après-guerre', L'Océanie Française, 14:46 (1918), 73–7. Regarding French involvement in the Panama Canal project see Aldrich, The French Presence, 243–7.
124 Lacave La Plagne, New Caledonia delegate on the CSC, 'L'Avenir de la Nouvelle-Calédonie', L'Océanie Française, 17:56 (1921), 26–7.
125 Andrew and Kanya-Forstner, France Overseas, 66, 144–7.
126 Persell, The French Colonial Lobby, 140–4.
127 SHAT, 7N4183/D1, Notes on Alexandretta for General Spears, 24 October 1918.
128 Eliezer Tauber, The Formation of Modern Syria and Iraq (London: Frank Cass, 1995), 24–31.
129 Philip S. Khoury, 'Factionalism among Syrian nationalists during the French mandate', International Journal of Middle East Studies, 13 (1981), 442–3.
130 In 1920 the combined population of Syria and Lebanon was somewhere between three and four million, of which about eighty-five per cent of Syrians were Muslim, and around fifty per cent of Lebanese. The remainder were largely Christian. Sunnis were the majority Muslim group. There was a strong Shi'ite presence in southern Lebanon, and two distinct concentrations of heterodox Muslim sects: almost 750,000 Alawites around Latakia in north-western Syria, and the Druzes concentrated in the Jabal Druze in southern Syria and Mount Lebanon, see Thompson, Colonial Citizens. 10–11. Regarding the Maronites, see David H. Kerr, 'The temporal authority of the Maronite patriarchate, 1920–1958. A study in the relationship of religious and secular power', Oxford University DPhil, 1973, 151. Regarding differing political groupings in Faisal's Syria see Tauber, The Formation of Modern Syria and Iraq.
131 James L. Gelvin, Divided Loyalties. Nationalism and Mass Politics in Syria at the Close of Empire (Berkeley CA: University of California Press, 1998), 14–15, 22–5.
132 Hasan Kayali, Arabs and Young Turks. Ottomanism, Arabism, and Islamism in the Ottoman Empire, 1908–1918 (Berkeley CA: University of California Press, 1997), 192–4.
133 Schilcher, 'The famine of 1915–1918 in Greater Syria', 229–58; Thompson, Colonial Citizens, 20–30.
134 Gelvin, Divided Loyalties, 97–137 passim.
135 Gérard D. Khoury, La France et l'Orient arabe. Naissance du Liban moderne 1914–1920 (Paris: Armand Colin, 1993), 37–9; Tauber, The Formation of Modern Syria and Iraq, 18–19; Gelvin, Divided Loyalties, 35. The American commissioners, Dr Henry King, a scion of the YMCA movement, and Charles Crane, a leading Chicago banker, faced an impossible task trying to reconcile all sides in Syria.
136 Matthew Hughes, Allenby and British Strategy in the Middle East, 1917–1919 (London: Frank Cass, 1999), 149–52; Malcolm Russell, The First Modern Arab State. Syria under Faysal, 1918–1920 (Minneapolis MN: Bibliotheca Islamica, 1985), 103–31; Andrew and Kanya-Forstner, France Overseas, 200–1; Edward P. Fitzgerald, 'France's Middle East ambitions, the Sykes–Picot negotiations, and the oilfields of Mosul, 1915–1918', Journal of Modern History, 66:4 (1994), 697–725.
137 Gelvin, Divided Loyalties, 88–9; Hughes, Allenby and British Strategy, 153–7.
138 For a blow-by-blow account of the negotiations between October 1919 and January

1920 see Khoury, *La France et l'Orient arabe*, 271–319. The provisional Clemenceau–Faisal agreement is reproduced at pp. 312–16.

139 SHAT, 6N194, tel. 30, Clemenceau to Gouraud (Beirut), 7 January 1920.

140 Regarding the administrative reorganisation of Mount Lebanon in 1861 see Kerr, 'The temporal authority', 64–71, and Ussama Makdisi, 'After 1860. Debating religion, reform, and nationalism in the Ottoman empire', *International Journal of Middle East Studies*, 33:3 (2002), 601–17. Regarding the 1920 allocation of territory see Caroline L. Gates, 'The historical role of political economy in the development of modern Lebanon. The state and the economy from colonialism to independence, 1939–1952', Oxford University DPhil, 1985, 23–5.

141 Andrew and Kanya-Forstner, *France Overseas*, 203–4.

142 Dan Eldar, 'France in Syria. The abolition of the Sharifian government, April–July 1920', *Middle Eastern Studies*, 29:3 (1993), 487–504.

143 Andrew and Kanya-Forstner, *France Overseas*, 28, 171–208 *passim*. The 'Asiatiques' referred to those Parti colonial members most interested in Indochina and, above all, the Levant. They were organised into several committees, the most influential being the Comité de l'Asie Française, the Comité de l'Orient and the Comité France–Syrie. The membership of these groups overlapped.

144 CADN, Fonds Beyrouth, Cabinet Politique, vol. 477/D1, 'Texte de la lettre de M. Clemenceau à S. B. Monsignor Hoyek du 10 novembre 1919'. Meir Zamir, *Lebanon's Quest. The Road to Statehood, 1926–1939* (London: I. B. Tauris, 2000), 120; Kerr, 'The temporal authority', 116–34. Meir Zamir, *The Formation of Modern Lebanon* (London: Croom Helm, 1978), 36–96 *passim*.

145 Gelvin, *Divided Loyalties*, 37.

146 *DDF*, 1920, I, no. 460, Millerand to Paul Cambon (London), 11 May 1920.

147 *DDF* 1920, II, docs 3 and 107, Millerand to Gouraud, 27 May and 13 June 1920.

148 SHAT, 6N194, tel. 11, Gouraud (Beirut) to Foreign Ministry, 4 January 1920.

149 Gelvin, *Divided Loyalties*, 45–6; Tauber, *The Formation of Modern Syria*, 213–17. Arab army units were poorly equipped, had little ammunition and suffered increasing desertion rates as the army payment system broke down.

150 *DDF*, 1920, II, docs 62 and 285, Gouraud to Millerand, 1 June and 2 August 1920.

151 Kerr, 'The temporal authority', 142–4.

152 Gates, 'The historical role of political economy', 26.

153 SHAT, 6N194, tel. 1429, Gouraud to Foreign Ministry, 24 July 1920.

154 Casualty figures in the battle of Maysalun vary, but Eliezer Tauber estimates that 1,200 to 1,500 Arabs died, see *The Formation of Modern Syria and Iraq*, 218.

155 SHAT, 6N194, tel. 1460, Gouraud to Foreign Ministry, 27 July 1920.

156 Andrew and Kanya-Forstner, *France Overseas*, 11–14, 23–6.

157 ADA, Sarraut papers, 12J280, Directeur du Cabinet Pierre Pasquier (Hué), personal note to Sarraut, 2 April 1923.

CHAPTER TWO

Colonial planning and administrative practice

The distinctive nature of French colonial administration, and its theoretical basis in republican thought is important, whether judged by the volume of official writings on the subject, or in terms of policy outcomes in the colonies. This chapter revisits debates over 'associationism' and 'assimilationism' in French colonial administration.[1] It suggests that neither idea was clearly demarcated or consistently enacted. In crude terms, assimilationism signified the adoption of French language, culture and modes of social organisation by colonial peoples who would be rewarded with French citizenship once fully assimilated. To put it in idealistic terms, the civilising mission, reinvented as gradual cultural transformation, would ultimately remould colonial subjects into fully fledged citizens of 'Greater Overseas France'. Associationism may conjure up images of British-style 'indirect rule' as developed by British administrators in the Indian princely states and, most famously, by Lord Lugard in Nigeria.[2] The key to indirect rule was to find indigenous intermediaries to uphold colonial authority. In similar fashion, French associationism cultivated local elites in order to indigenise the lower tiers of colonial administration. Tribal chiefs, Vietnamese mandarins and village headmen became adjuncts of the colonial state, retaining limited autonomy in matters of local justice, land disputes, tax collection and military recruitment. Its proponents regarded associationism as far more than a means to cut administrative costs. In the 1920s especially, it denoted a new-found respect for indigenous societies driven by the realisation that traditional hierarchies were the surest guarantee of social order. Colonial authority was, to a degree, mediated between rulers and ruled rather than vertically imposed. Aspects of indigenous civil society such as chiefly prerogative and traditional village councils were revalorised as pillars of community stability.[3]

Some advocates of associationism distorted the universalist values of French republicanism to justify a colonialism modelled on Social Darwinist race theory.[4] Colonial coercion was diametrically opposed to the egalitarianism

[54]

of 1789. But colonial officials tried to square this impossible circle by insti-
tutionalising an imperial system inspired by republican ideals of societal
structure.[5] In Indochina before 1914, for example, repression of Vietnamese
nationalist groups suggested that the requirements of colonial order would
triumph over the impulse to social reform.[6] This points to a more generic
conclusion: assimilationism and associationism threw up too many paradoxes to be articulated as distinct ideologies of colonialism. Rather, there
was an assimilationist approach to colonial governance and an associationist
alternative, in vogue after 1918. Supporters of each method spanned the
political spectrum.[7] In the 1930s proponents of a French imperial constitution, akin to the French union devised after the Second World War,
stressed that France lacked a coherent colonial administrative doctrine that
distinguished between nation and state, citizen and subject, theoretical
equality before the law and actual variations between French and colonial
judicial systems.[8]

Scholars of empire and postcolonialism have explained the gulf between
abstract principle and colonial reality in similar terms. In Alec Hargreaves's
words, 'In the overseas empire, the French commitment to assimilation
was always more rhetorical than real: few resources were devoted to the
"civilising mission," and the promise of political equality was perpetually
deferred, since it was fundamentally at odds with the whole colonial system'.[9] Or, as Elizabeth Ezra puts it: 'Although both assimilation and association were integral components of colonial rhetoric, the context of
subjugation that gave rise to them precluded their enactment in practice'.[10]

Belief in racial hierarchy underpinned French colonial policy. It is vital,
however, to distinguish between an emotive racism hostile to mixing
between ethnic groups and the pseudo-scientific racialism used to justify
colonial conquest in the nineteenth century. Racialist theorists such as
Count Joseph-Arthur de Gobineau and Edouard Drumont delineated a global
hierarchy of races. De Gobineau identified the French as members of a
superior Aryan race in his *Essay on the Inequality of Human races* (*Essai
sur l'inégalité des races humaines*, 1853–55). And Drumont took de
Gobineau's antisemitism a step further in his *Jewish France* (*La France
juive*), a poisonous 1886 diatribe against the Jews' alleged complicity in
everything from industrial capitalism to anticlericalism, Freemasonry, and
the suppression of workers' rights.[11] They then transposed their ideas to
French overseas territories.[12] These theorists saw colonial domination as
the inevitable consequence of France's superior racial stock rather than as
a triumph of republican political culture. By the 1890s the nationalist right
was also drawn to the concept of a 'true France' rooted, not in the values of
1789, but in peasant endeavour, social hierarchy and Catholic observance.
Imperialism acquired new respectability among this constituency as tangible proof of the virile qualities of the French race. By contrast, in the late

nineteenth century most colonial administrators defended the consolidation of French control in specifically republican terms. In the early Third Republic the centralisation of state power, the consequent reduction of regional autonomy and the gradual modernisation of the agricultural economy reduced the political gulf between Paris and the provinces. An equivalent impulse to centralise administrative power and promote market capitalism was integral to colonial governance. Whether articulated as republican imperialism or racial expansionism, colonial assimilation signified the adoption of a French model of social organisation. But racialist notions of ethnic hierarchy could just as easily justify associationist policies. If individual races were inherently unequal and different, then attempts by the colonised to emulate their rulers were bound to be limited. The egalitarian values of Jacobin republicanism could not be transposed to an authoritarian colonial system.[13]

Colonial rule and subjects' rights after the First World War

French legislators in the National Bloc governments of 1919–24 rejected any linkage between Wilsonian concepts of national self-determination and the need for colonial reform. But, its gender bias aside, the most striking omission from post-1919 reforms was any broad recognition of fundamental human rights. The very term was problematic, at variance with colonialism and yet cherished by the new generation of republican imperialists that came to prominence in the early twentieth century.[14] The individual liberties of colonial subjects (collectively termed *indigènes*) were nugatory. Freedom of expression, rights of association and assembly, equality before the law were all denied. Matters were somewhat different in the protectorates and mandated territories, where the survival of a functioning indigenous political system precluded untrammelled colonial rule. There was, for example, no separate native legal code, or *indigénat*, in Morocco, Tunisia, Syria or Lebanon. This was in contrast to nearby Algeria, a full colony, where the *indigénat* was first codified in 1881. It established separate criminal punishments and restricted Muslims' freedom of movement and labour. Without right of appeal, colonial subjects could be fined, interned, exiled, expelled from their homes or imprisoned at the stroke of a local official's pen.[15]

By 1914 the *indigénat* applied in most of French Africa, Madagascar and Indochina. In Algeria and the Muslim territories of AOF customary law was left intact in respect of marriage, inheritance and minor misdemeanours, but it was subordinated to French law in property disputes and criminal cases involving Muslims and settlers.[16] In the North African protectorates and the Levant mandates Muslim customary law also applied in most civil and family cases. Yet here, too, Muslims' legal protection and political liberties were eroded. French legal regulation took precedence in civil and criminal cases involving Europeans and Muslims.[17] In Morocco the Rabat residency also manipulated the legal codes applied to Arab and Berber Muslims – notoriously so with the May 1930 'Berber *dahir*' – to drive a wedge between the two communities.[18]

In Tunisia the formation of any political group, however defined by the residency, required state authorisation. French officials reserved the right to prohibit political and religious meetings, other than electoral gatherings and daily prayer services. Unauthorised assembly was punishable by a prison sentence, fines or internal exile. Tunisians suspected of sedition could be detained without trial, a measure copied from the Algerian *indigénat*. A January 1926 decree gave the Tunis authorities additional powers to ban meetings, arrest activists and close down newspapers for any expression of hostility to France, its protectorate or the Tunisian monarch, the Bey. The residency even invoked a royal edict of 1778 to expel French Communists from Tunisia without right of appeal. Before the Popular Front coalition took office in 1936 the only significant political liberty conceded was the right to form trade unions, a concession granted by Edouard Herriot's second ministry in November 1932.[19]

Colonial governments ruled by decree throughout the inter-war period. The broad thrust of constitutional reform at the apex of the colonial state was to widen admission to local consultative assemblies rather than to recognise individual freedoms at variance with colonial authoritarianism. These assemblies accrued powers of scrutiny over the budgetary expenditure of the colonial state, but they had no power to originate legislation, and no authority to contest laws promulgated in France or colonial governmental decrees. There was no functioning parliamentary system in any colonial territory. *Anciennes colonies* of the first French empire, such as Martinique, Guadeloupe, Saint-Pierre et Miquelon and Réunion were theoretically fully assimilated into the French body politic, electing parliamentary representatives to Paris. But, as in Algeria, France's largest 'assimilated' colony, local political power was largely confined to a collaborative elite.[20] Only the Middle East mandates of Syria and Lebanon conducted regular general elections to a national parliament, and for much of the late 1920s and early 1930s the Beirut high commission disrupted the Syrian parliamentary system by suspending the Damascus legislature entirely.

The membership and means of selection of consultative assemblies varied from territory to territory, but followed a common pattern. In those dependencies where vestiges of a pre-colonial administrative system survived, usually because their conquest had been regulated by treaty rather than outright annexation, a local elite retained limited powers of oversight over French policy. Such was typically the case in 'protectorate' regimes.

These included Morocco and Tunisia, Annam and Cambodia. In each of these states the pre-colonial monarchy remained *in situ*, as did the vestiges of the legal and bureaucratic systems through which these indigenous rulers had formerly governed. The administrative system was more complicated in Laos, which was divided between an Upper Laos protectorate, centred on the royal house at Luang Prabang, and Lower Laos, ruled directly by France from its administrative capital Vientiane.[21] French officials in most overseas territories were at pains to maintain a façade of partnership with the indigenous elite and local heads of state. Most of this was ceremonial. In practice, the writ of French authority in the protectorates was akin to that in neighbouring colonies. That said, neither economic exploitation, military exaction, nor annexation of land by French settlers went as far in the North African and Indochinese protectorates as in the colonies of Algeria and Cochin-China. In the final analysis, in the 1920s a monarchical, land-owning elite constituted a more effective barrier to colonial penetration than the direct resistance of peasant producers faced with dispossession.

In the colonies of Algeria, Cochin-China, black Africa and Madagascar, European settlers dominated the Consultative Assembly system. Frenchmen controlled most colonial assemblies, regional councils and municipal authorities. Their predominance was assured in a number of ways. Some assemblies were simply packed with settler representatives to the virtual exclusion of the local population. Most were selected by a discriminatory system of separate electoral rolls, dual electoral colleges and restrictive voting qualifications that were as effective as they were blatant. From Saigon to Algiers, the only way to infiltrate this system was to acquire French citizenship, a process that presupposed acceptance of colonial rule. Colonial subjects had to traverse numerous barriers to become an enfranchised French citizen. The most basic source of discrimination was gender: all voting colonial citizens were male. Language qualifications excluded the uneducated. It was insufficient to speak fluent French, one had to write it competently as well, a requirement that generally disbarred the minority that received colonial primary schooling. The only way round these restrictions was to serve the empire over a number of years. As we have seen, in the aftermath of the First World War ex-soldiers who completed their full service term were offered citizen status. Similar concessions were made to junior members of the colonial bureaucracy, such as clerks, policemen and village councillors. Decree legislation passed on 9 June 1922 increased the native electorate in Cochin-China from 1,800 to 20,000. This was the result of a long-running campaign of electoral reform to enfranchise co-operative members of the colony's professional and administrative classes championed by Albert Sarraut and his successors as governor.[22] In Algeria the children of these loyal servants were exempted from the *indigénat* legal code once they passed their French-language primary schools certificate. These concessions promoted intergenerational service to the colonial regime. They were not devised to widen access to basic education, which risked uncontrolled social mobility among the Muslim population.[23] In Muslim territories the majority of those eligible for citizenship chose not to pursue it because the rights and duties of the imperial citizen of the secular French republic demanded renunciation of their personal status as Muslims. Jacobin secularism thus provided a means to limit the numbers of indigenous males granted meaningful political rights. Between 1919 and 1939 the indigenous electorate ran to thousands but never to tens of thousands. From land ownership to politics and the law, the great majority of the Muslim population ranked not even as second-class citizens but merely as subjects denied influence, legal status or rights within the colonial system.

Local government institutions were most fully developed in Algeria's *communes de plein exercice*, so called because they were modelled on the French system of communal administration. These communes elected local councils and mayors with limited fiscal and judicial powers, although the franchise was weighted in favour of male settlers. Algeria's national electoral system was also blatantly discriminatory. The colony's three departments were administered by general councils and prefects each of which answered to an overwhelmingly settler electorate. In 1898 financial delegations were created with limited powers of budgetary oversight. Three distinct constituencies selected the membership of these delegations: *colon* farmers, city-dwelling settler taxpayers, and the Algerian citizen elite. Nominees from the general councils and the financial delegations sat alongside members of the governor-general's office in the Algerian supreme council, a purely advisory assembly before which governors could not be held accountable. In general, it fell to the governor's secretary-general to deal with the day-to-day concerns raised by the delegations. The governor rarely became involved until the annual budget vote loomed large.[24]

Between the wars a cross-section of liberal administrators and the French left found the contradiction of a repressive colonial system justified by republican ideals harder to ignore. Yet few of the leading lights of the non-Communist left rejected colonialism as incompatible with egalitarian, socialist values. Left-wingers in two SFIO factions, Jean Zyromski's Bataille socialiste and the Gauche révolutionnaire led by Marceau Pivert and Daniel Guérin, became increasingly outspoken in their attacks on colonialism. Guérin used the platform of the SFIO colonial commission to denounce French oppression and the Socialists' hypocrisy. In the early 1930s he also cultivated links with young colonial nationalists, notably the leaders of the Jeunes Marocains (Young Moroccans), Mohamed el-Ouezzani, Ahmed Balafrej and Omar Ben Abdeljalil.[25] As the Popular Front coalition took shape between 1934 and 1936 socialist anti-colonialism became more strongly identifiable with two dissident groups: Marcel Déat's 'planistes' that broke with the SFIO in November 1933 to form the short-lived Parti Socialiste de France, and the younger generation of Gauche révolutionnaire supporters drawn by the rhetoric of Trotskyite internationalism.[26] Leftist anti-colonialists like Guérin and Pivert were still outnumbered by a socialist mainstream personified by party leader Léon Blum, who saw justification in republican imperialism provided that it conferred tangible benefits and cultural improvement on colonial peoples.[27] Some in the Socialist Party went further. At the 1926 party congress in Clermont-Ferrand the president of the Martiniquan SFIO section, J. Lagrosillière, insisted that the Socialists stood for genuine assimilation. This was a distortion. Few Socialist Party members, or Communists for that matter, showed any sustained interest in colonial affairs.[28] Fewer still were committed to assimilationism. But imperial reformers of all hues shared a common trait: they denied that colonial administration was inherently unjust. These strands of liberal opinion converged in their efforts to reconcile the hierarchical, undemocratic nature of colonial government with the core republican ideals that supposedly informed the entire imperial project.[29]

A false dichotomy? Assimilation or association

Did assimilation imply that all colonial peoples could or should become French in every facet of their political, cultural and religious life? If not, then to which peoples should assimilation apply, and to what spheres of life should it be confined? State propaganda in the First World War portrayed France and the colonies as united in a common struggle. Combat, war work, convalescence, private loss and national victory were a shared imperial experience. The main 'beneficiaries' of assimilationism – educated colonial citizen évolués in Africa and Indochina – were anxious to stress this community of interest after 1918. For instance, Eric Jennings has shown how ex-servicemen and Guadeloupe's local elite incorporated their personal vision of 'Frenchness' as assimilated colonials into their campaign for the memorialisation of the island's war dead. Importing a war monument from France was more than an *ersatz* demonstration of loyalty; it signified assimilated Guadeloupians' identification with the mother country.[30]

In France, however, assimilationism fell out of favour before the armistice. War Ministry propaganda was assimilationist, but there was no political will to translate its ideals into policy.[31] The old obstacles remained. On what grounds – racial, economic or cultural – were colonial governments to determine which subject peoples could be assimilated? And what was the final objective – a real 'overseas France' or, as was always more

likely, the cultivation of a privileged francophone elite in colonial societies? The material costs of the educational projects and infrastructure improvements required to lend substance to assimilationist ideas would be
high. Who would pay for them, and for how long?

In 1922 Marcel Peyrouton visited French North Africa for the first time.
Peyrouton was then a fast rising colonial official, later to achieve notoriety
as Interior Minister under Vichy. His first experience of the Maghreb territories convinced him that the 'assimilationist mania' of previous years
should be avoided. Colonial administration should cultivate a capable indigenous elite, provide security for the masses and contain potential sources
of opposition. In short, only associationism was achievable.[32] In the following year a series of lectures on colonial administration at the Ecole libre
des sciences politiques in Paris brought together Ministry of Colonies
bureaucrats, Parti colonial activists and retired colonial service personnel.
Their original goal was to identify generic rules of administrative practice,
much as Peyrouton recommended. Ironically, the cumulative lesson of
these discussions was that the colonies would inevitably remain culturally
diverse, politically distinctive and economically diffuse. How could such a
heterogeneous group of territories form a unified empire? And how could
the French public be persuaded to cherish it? An answer seemed to lie in a
republican rhetoric that, by proclaiming the merits of associationism,
imperial economic growth, and strength in colonial diversity, would
educate politicians and public into the worth of what was variously
described as 'Greater France', 'total France' or 'the France of 100 million'.[33]

In the public mind, associationism was largely understood as a less
ambitious alternative to assimilation. For some officials, associationism
denoted the compromises with local elites necessary to make governance
and economic exploitation work. For others, associationism was a sin-
cerely held belief that colonial cultures, belief systems and economic practices should be respected. This was at once ethical and economical. These
attitudinal changes were clearest in AOF, where wartime dissent led
administrators in Dakar to rethink the assimilationism pursued by the
pre-war governors Ernest Roume and William Ponty.[34]

Associationism was more readily understood in economic terms. Its
accent on the preservation of hierarchical social structures required less
state investment than the creation of an assimilated colonial society. The
early colonial practitioners of associationist policy responded to the limited monetary means at their disposal, the more so after Parliament de-
creed in 1900 that colonies should be financially self-supporting. Schemes
to educate a Europeanised elite to serve in the junior ranks of the colonial
bureaucracy, the development of colonial wage economies that dramatically expanded the number of indigenous taxpayers and the drive to produce commodities for export all fitted the broader objective of a remunerative

empire. Albert Sarraut made this plain in his most famous work, *La Mise en valeur des colonies françaises*, published in 1923: 'As regards mass education, it is important to make economic utility the first considera-tion'. Sarraut's comment echoed associationist ideas refined in the 1890s. As proconsul in Madagascar General Joseph Gallieni famously coined the phrase 'the educational character of taxation'.[35] As the Malagasy were com-pelled to adopt capitalist modes of production, so they would acquire West-ern modes of thought. Gallieni's maxim justified economic exploitation but also reflected the associationist philosophy of social change within colonies as a consequence of imperial development rather than vice versa. By 1914 transmission of French cultural values was secondary to the effi-cient operation of an expanding colonial economy.

Sarraut and Gallieni were cost-conscious administrators, but they had far more lofty ideals. Gallieni, the lowborn general of impeccable republican credentials, was the most influential military theorist of late nineteenth-century imperialism. He devised the system of consolidating a local power base before pushing outward to establish wider colonial control, a method he famously likened to an 'oil stain'. And his exploitation of inter-communal rivalries in Indochina and Madagascar through his *politique des races* the better to entrench French authority became second nature to the gover-nors that followed him.[36]

More than any other senior politician, Albert Sarraut dug deep to find new ideological and material justification for French colonialism.[37] His 1921 colonial development scheme and support for limited enfranchise-ment of local elites echoed proposals put forward repeatedly in the 1890s.[38] In other respects, though, Sarraut's ideas signified a new departure.[39] He challenged the idea that colonies should fund their own modernisation, arguing that strategic investment was incumbent on any responsible colo-nial power. Empire could not stand by force alone.[40] The ethical impera-tive at the core of Sarraut's plan did not persuade his fellow parliamentarians. Debate over the associationist tenets of the Sarraut plan was eclipsed by arguments over its cost. As we saw in chapter one, the scheme never made it into law.[41]

Associationism and indigenous administration: Morocco and Indochina

A week after the armistice, on 18 November 1918 Resident-general Lyautey issued a manifesto of indirect rule in Morocco. In an administra-tive circular to his staff he stressed that France's wartime economic and manpower demands on Morocco had transformed the Franco-Moroccan relationship. The French now realised Morocco's vital importance to France's national salvation. Moroccans had, in turn, become partners in the French imperial venture. The guiding principle of indirect rule had been maintained throughout:

> The conception of the protectorate is that of a country retaining its own institutions, [and] governing and administering itself through its own authorities, all under the guiding hand of a European power, which . . . assumes responsibility for overseas representation, takes general charge of the administration of armed forces and finances and manages economic development. This conception is governed by the formula: *control*, as opposed to that of *direct administration*.[42]

To understand the significance of Lyautey's proclamation, a little must be said about the man. In William Hoisington's apt description, Lyautey was for the French 'the representative of "those things that were best" in their colonial experience'.[43] His early biographers interpreted Lyautey's early colonial career as a mere prelude to his crowning achievements as France's first resident-general in the Moroccan protectorate established in 1912. More recent historians assess Lyautey's imperial vision and his colonial practices more critically.[44] But Lyautey the man has always exerted as much fascination as Lyautey the proconsul. His military-aristocratic origins, his copious writings and his dandyish homosexuality (although this is generally assumed rather than proven) were clearly instrumental in Lyautey's belief in conservative elites, the importance of public service and the glorification of a masculine ideal of colonial sacrifice.[45]

Lyautey's commitment to associationist colonial policies gestated over almost three decades of military service in the empire after his first posting to Orléansville in Algeria in 1880.[46] By 1920 his personal letters sent from imperial postings in Indochina and Madagascar during the 1890s were in print. Lyautey pointed to his published correspondence as affirmation of his long-standing attachment to the precepts of indirect rule: respect for indigenous culture, co-operation with traditional elites, and the gradual introduction of French administration and cultural values.[47] But the theoretical roots of Lyautey's ideas were in French soil. His admiration for the style and methods of his mentor, Joseph Gallieni, in 1890s Indochina and Madagascar reflected Lyautey's underlying discontent with the cliquish self-absorption of the French officer corps, the democratisation of the Third Republic and the vulgarisation of French popular culture.[48] Lyautey's long-standing aversion to money-grubbing *grands colons* and the European settler proletariat in the major cities of Algeria and Morocco was not mere snobbery. It stemmed from the conviction that colonisation corrupted indigenous societies precisely because the colonisers were self-interested, uncultured and racist. Much of the unending violence of colonial Algeria stemmed from this craven submission to settler interest at the expense of the colony's Muslim culture. Lyautey's Morocco would not repeat the same mistakes.[49]

The problem was that even in Morocco associationist indirect rule was difficult to distinguish from unrestrained colonial power. During his term as resident-general between 1912 and 1925 Lyautey tried to integrate experienced Moroccan officials, judges, doctors, psychiatrists and other public sector professionals into the politico-administrative apparatus of a French-controlled *makhzen* (a term that denoted both the Sultan's government and the governing Muslim elite). Until the French arrival Morocco was, after all, a functioning state with a competent bureaucracy. Lyautey claimed that experienced *pashas* and *khalifas* would be called on once more to run Morocco's cities and towns, ensuring the provision of public services, tax collection and the maintenance of civil peace. Muslim judges (*cadis*) would try the majority of ordinary civil and criminal cases involving the indigenous population. Village headmen and traditional Muslim councils in the Moroccan interior would preserve rural order. These indigenous administrators would interact with French officials of the Contrôle civil, Lyautey's administrative cadre of Arab specialists, to modernise Moroccan society in conformity with local custom. Lyautey thus envisaged a new civil society built on Islamic tradition, *makhzen* administration and French cultural innovation.[50] Loyalty to the Sultan and the French residency would become synonymous once the protectorate was embedded in Moroccan culture. The entire system rested on efficient delegation of power. This, in turn, depended on the quality of intelligence supplied by the Arabic-speaking French officials on the spot. In urban centres it fell to *contrôleurs civils* to select Muslim intermediaries. In the countryside the same task fell to the military intelligence officers of the Service des affaires indigènes (native affairs service).[51] A similar network of French officials operated in Tunisia.[52] Lyautey also valued urban planners and medical professionals as vital elements of the colonial state. Not long before his death he addressed a French psychiatric congress in Rabat in 1933, telling his audience that physicians were 'the primary and most effective of our agents of penetration and pacification'.[53]

Morocco after the First World War still fell short of Lyautey's ideal. Certainly, until the French were drawn into the Rif war in 1924, their take-over in Morocco met less sustained resistance than the conquest of Algeria. But the 1912 protectorate treaty none the less split the Muslim elite, provoking a major rebellion led by Ahmed el-Hiba in the south of the country. Suppression of the southern revolt and dismissals of *makhzen* officials suspected of disloyalty to the Sultan or collusion with German and Ottoman agents reduced the number of permissible appointees for senior administrative posts. Corruption or, at best, the use of official titles to accrue personal wealth remained commonplace among those selected as *pashas*. So, too, did resentment at the French presence. There was recurrent factionalism among aristocratic families, rival tribal clans and merchant guilds, as well as between cities competing for commercial dominance and political influence. And a younger generation of French-educated bourgeois Moroccans were drawn to Arab nationalism and socialism. Ahmad Balafrej, the religious scholar Allal al-Fassi, Omar Ben Abdeljalil and Hassan al-Wazzani were all future nationalist leaders with similar backgrounds in the bourgeois milieux of Fez and Rabat.[54] They saw through the venality and fraudulence of associationist policy. They knew that French officials and security service officers intervened more or less surreptitiously to run affairs theoretically delegated to Moroccan personnel. Disdain for Arab appointees and a profound misunderstanding of Moroccan political culture lurked behind this residual French inclination to impose centralised control over local government. William Hoisington's studies of the high administrative turnover of *pashas* and *cadis* in Casablanca and Rabat are conclusive. Time after time the French administration refused to cede the necessary authority to local officials they despised: 'Almost everywhere in the Rabat that Lyautey remade and Frenchmen ruled, Moroccans lost prestige, influence and authority as well as land and money'. Indirect rule failed because Lyautey's staff never allowed it to work.[55]

What of the Indochina federation, another model of associationism? Albert Sarraut, twice governor, in 1911–13 and 1916–19, was but one in a sequence of committed associationists stretching back to Jean-Marie De Lanesson's pioneering governorship of 1891–94. In the post-war decade Sarraut's successors as governor-general – Maurice Montguillot, Maurice Long, Maurice Le Gallen, Martial Merlin, Alexandre Varenne and Pierre Pasquier – each carried the associationist torch. Of these, the socialist Alexandre Varenne – governor-general between June 1925 and October 1927 – was a particularly assiduous reformer, and spent little time in the governor's palace.[56] His governorship was divided into two distinct periods, the first between November 1925 and October 1926, the second between June and November 1927. During the first, he reorganised the consultative assemblies in Tonkin, Annam and Cambodia, renaming them Chambers of People's Representatives, and widening access to public office. Municipal government and port administrations were also opened up to additional local appointees. Varenne's social policy was equally reformist. He increased medical provision in rural areas, funding vaccination programmes and prophylactic treatment centres across the Vietnamese territories to combat the spread of epidemics. The new governor also pushed the Bank of Indochina to provide credit facilities to the agricultural sector, particularly through a farmers' co-operative bank (Crédit populaire agricole, CPA) established on 21 July 1927. The CPA provided loan capital, enabling peasant smallholders to invest in land, seed purchases and agricultural equipment. It undermined traditional usury, previously the sole source of borrowing for impoverished farmers. By 1933 twenty-four provincial banks owed their existence to Varenne's original support for rural credit facilities.[57]

During his second period in office, in late 1927, Varenne focused on widening access to basic education. He decentralised the educational service to encourage individual villages to invest in primary school construction. Provincial officials were empowered to select teaching staff regardless of race, provided they held basic qualifications.[58] Varenne stressed that his overriding objective was to retain the confidence of Indochina's indigenous elites, without which local government was impossible.[59] But, as in Morocco, by the end of the 1920s the effort to streamline colonial bureaucracy and facilitate economic modernisation in the Indochinese territories faltered. Associationism was supposed to be conducted in conformity with the demands of reliable local interest groups. In Indochina at least, these ideals soon went awry.[60] The inter-war period witnessed the introduction of sweeping fiscal reform, the codification of individual legal title to land and property, new civil and criminal codes, and the creation of new tiers of devolved authority at village, commune and provincial level. The underlying purpose of these measures was to create a modern commercial economy. The gradual replacement of customary law, communal land tenure, collective taxation and quasi-feudal obligation with French systems of civil and criminal law, property ownership, individual tax payment and hierarchical bureaucracy was intended to promote colonial exploitation of Indochina's resources. Fiscal reform yielded immediate results. According to Daniel Hémery, the extension of direct taxation obligations in Tonkin led to a 150 per cent rise in budgetary receipts from 2,544,000 piastres in 1920 to 4,100,000 in 1921.[61] But, far from respecting local tradition, such reforms struck at the foundations of civil society, village governance and customary farming practices.

Stung by criticism that they were tearing the fabric of society apart, associationists in Hanoi sketched out a tidy picture of colonial government that was little more than a cliché. In theory, the Indochina federation, already constituted as distinct kingdoms, protectorates and colonies, was, in the 1920s, rapidly subdivided into provinces and communes administered by French officials working in harmony with an indigenous administrative class – the mandarins – uniquely responsive to local custom. Here was an invented tradition that owed more to the way Vietnamese, Cambodian and Laotian society were represented by French ethnographers, settlers and officials than to official respect for indigenous methods of rule. In practice the colonial authorities still exercised stringent control over the membership and powers of scrutiny of the consultative assemblies and municipal councils restructured by Varenne in the mid-1920s. Again, Daniel Hémery is instructive. He suggests that before 1914 the imposition of commune administration in Cochin-China – supposedly modelled on existing Vietnamese village communities (*thon*) and their council of notables (*xa*) – actually undermined village autonomy and the power of the traditional elite. Similar efforts between the wars to superimpose French authority at village level in Tonkin and Annam by creating new structures of commune administration were strongly resisted, contributing to the outbreak of rebellion in 1930–31. Nor were the mandarins a homogeneous, monolithic class of one mind in matters of local politics.[62] Associationism compounded the rivalries between favoured mandarins, capitalist entrepreneurs and disaffected notables whose former authority was eroded.[63]

It was not supposed to be that way. In 1918–19 colonial officials and French academics with a professional interest in empire, notably social anthropologists and geographers, looked forward to a sustained period of peace. They drew parallels between the passing of the old European order and the end of the era of colonial conquest. Peace in Europe heralded a new age of colonial consolidation better attuned to local conditions. Colonial administration responsive to cultural *mores* meant in the first instance the recognition that subject peoples were more different from their French rulers than early assimilationists had assumed. In November 1921 the political affairs directorate of the Dakar government-general explained its thinking:

> The failure of the policy of assimilation became striking from the day that we noticed among the numerous *indigènes* turning up at our schools abruptly separated from their own *milieu* an attitude of mind [*orientation d'esprit*] different from our own, and a marked tendency to evade the discipline that a progressive society has the right to expect of its members.[64]

Associationist rhetoric put a moral gloss on administrative conservatism by portraying respect for colonial authority and tribal hierarchy as reassuring certainties to native populations rooted in tradition. The institutions of civil society in rural communities – tribal chiefs, village councils and extended family groups – were 'anchors' of social order. It was irresponsible to suggest that the mass of colonised peoples could become French without decades of political education and gradual economic advance. Denial of citizenship became ethically justifiable to prevent detribalisation and loss of cultural identity among the native masses.[65]

The Jonnart Law in Algeria

Algeria was the exception that proved the rule of ascendant associationism. France's most cherished colony was constitutionally, if not culturally, assimilated to France. Such was the theory at least. Algerian society was certainly transformed by French conquest and colonisation. But massive land expropriation, the economic marginalisation of the Muslim rural population, the growth of a large urban under-class and the dismantling of traditional rural hierarchies of power were hardly the basis for harmonious communal relations between the settler population and the Muslim majority.[66] Furthermore, French cultural signifiers, such as Catholic religious practice, taxation systems and intermarriage, were more prevalent in other territories, especially the *vieilles colonies* of the pre-Napoleonic age such as Martinique, Guadeloupe, Réunion and Saint-Louis in Senegal. By contrast, in France's Arab territories interracial marriage was 'statistically insignificant', and generally frowned upon by administrators and settlers. Before and after the First World War the stereotype of the unapproachable *femme arabe*, an object of exotic desire and of intense suspicion, abounded in French popular culture.[67] While inter-communal contact was closely regulated, economic exploitation, cultural subordination and racial discrimination were systematically pursued in Algeria owing to the scale of European settlement and its justification on grounds of complete assimilation. By 1914 the French dominated every facet of Algeria's economic and political life. France was building a nation in Algeria that was notionally a mirror image of the mother country, but in reality a servile adjunct of French society.

The oft-quoted language of colonialism in Algeria was distinctive. The country was alone in being referred to in both official rhetoric and popular vernacular as an extension of France. The cliché ran that, just as the Seine divided Paris, so the Mediterranean divided France and Algeria, two parts of the same whole. Moreover, as Kristin Ross points out, colonial rule in sub-Saharan Africa was articulated in terms of property ownership. France was *grand patron* of the lands of AOF and AEF. Algeria's situation was different. French domination of the country signified the imposition of all that was French on to a disparate, chaotic and pre-modern indigenous society. Algeria could 'mature' only as a subordinate part of the French nation.[68] Even Fernand Braudel, the founder of the *Annales* school, who taught at the Algiers Lycée Bugeaud between 1924 and 1932, admitted in hindsight that the colonial order of *Algérie française* seemed to him perfectly natural at the time.[69] By 1920 French settlers had already dispossessed the Algerian peasantry of an estimated 2,581,000 ha of prime cultivable land. This was not merely overlordship, it was land seizure on a scale unmatched anywhere else in the empire.[70]

Algiers was home to France's largest overseas administration. Algerians raised more regiments to fight the First World War than any other colony. And the power of the settler community increased as its numbers grew dramatically in the decade after 1918. It may seem surprising then that post-1919 policies in Algeria confirmed the French shift towards associationism. Surely these were propitious times for a renewed drive to

PLANNING AND ADMINISTRATIVE PRACTICE

assimilate the colony to France? In fact the further consolidation of settler influence ruled this out. The immigration of French, Spanish, Maltese and Italian settlers to Algeria gathered momentum in the early years of the Third Republic, driven in part by the emigration of French farmers seeking untarnished cheap land after the phylloxera outbreak of the late 1870s and 1880s had devastated French vineyards. The *colon* population grew from 245,000 in 1872 to 750,000 in 1914.[71] The number of Europeans in Algeria rose further to 900,000 in the 1920s. Higher levels of European colonisation registered in several ways: socially, in the development of a stronger settler identity as French Algerians; economically, in the further pauperisation of Muslim landowners and workers; politically, in the *colons'* determination to reserve the instruments of colonial power to themselves. Assimilationist policies were sure to encounter bitter settler opposition. Only less ambitious associationist reforms could survive *colon* obstructionism.

After four years of intermittent parliamentary debate, on 4 February 1919 the Jonnart Law enfranchised some 421,000 Muslim men. The scheme was named after the three times Algiers governor-general Charles Jonnart, who piloted the scheme through the Chamber of Deputies. The new electoral law actually marked a retreat from two more ambitious legislative projects formulated by two Socialist deputies, Henri Doizy and Marius Moutet. Before the war, Doizy sympathised with the demands of the Young Algerian movement for citizenship, equal voting rights and the retention of Muslim personal status. Led by Dr Belkacem Bentami, the Young Algerians were an elite group of educated junior administrators, mainly municipal councillors, whose opportunities for career advancement were limited by their second-class status within the colonial system. In June 1912 Young Algerian representatives took advantage of imminent French plans to extend military conscription to Algerian Muslims to secure an audience with President Raymond Poincaré. Bentami's supporters pressed for the abolition of the hated *indigénat* legal code, fairer taxation, equitable disbursement of public expenditure between Europeans and Muslims and the grant of citizenship to Muslim ex-servicemen. These proposals boiled down to one overarching demand: complete assimilation of a qualified Algerian Muslim elite. Doizy later refined the Young Algerians' programme into his own legislative project. His readiness to pursue an assimilationist policy guaranteed that the scheme would fail. Doizy's assimilationism was consistent with Socialist leader Jean Jaurès's insistence that colonialism was justifiable only in so far as French rights and benefits were extended to subject peoples. But no project that threatened the settlers' political dominance would get through Parliament, even in the changed atmosphere generated by the mass conscription of colonial subjects.[72]

Marius Moutet was a shrewder political operator than his party colleague Doizy. A renowned southern lawyer, Moutet sharpened his debating skills alongside future Radical Party leader Edouard Herriot. Together they founded the Lyons section of the League of the Rights of Man at the height of the Dreyfus affair in 1898. Like many of the liberal republican parliamentarians who first entered public life as committed Dreyfusards, during a political career spanning four decades from his entry to the Chamber on 7 August 1914 Moutet defended the rights of the individual against the needs of the state.[73] His wartime experience as a member of the parliamentary foreign and colonial affairs commission alerted him to the absence of basic human rights among colonial populations. It was as representative of this commission that Moutet first visited Algeria in 1916 to investigate the outbreak of disturbances in the Aurès mountains. He returned convinced that Muslim electors should be allowed to vote not only for representatives in Algeria but for the colony's parliamentary representatives in the French Chamber of Deputies and Senate as well. Moutet's willingness to dismantle the foundations of settler power after only twelve days spent in the colony earned him the lasting hatred of the *colon* press. His pacifism lent added venom to his critics in Algiers at a time when almost twenty per cent of the male settler population was in uniform.[74]

Moutet knew the strength of parliamentary and settler opposition he would encounter. He therefore watered down his original plans when he introduced an Algerian electoral Bill to the Chamber in March 1918. It was this revised scheme that formed the basis of the later Jonnart Law. Moutet believed that the case for an extended male Muslim electorate with the same legal rights and taxation obligations as the settler population was ethically self-evident. So he focused rather more on the means to reactivate genuine participatory democracy in Algerian local government. He regarded the traditional tribal council, or *djemâa*, as the key institution here. *Djemâas* still functioned in the army-administered Saharan territories of southern Algeria, exercising customary authority over financial, political and judicial affairs. But tribal councils had atrophied farther north for want of any real influence or monetary power. Like many liberal imperialists, Moutet respected the work of army Arab affairs specialists. The soldier-administrators of the native affairs service in Algeria's Saharan territories were the latest incarnation of the *bureaux arabes* – Arabic-speaking rural officials on whom the Algiers administration relied to extend the reach of the colonial state deep into the Algerian interior. The war's insatiable demand for troops provided a new measure of the army's administrative achievements. There was no formal conscription in the army-controlled territories, unlike the rest of Algeria where civil administration applied. Yet between 1 August 1914 and 31 December 1917 18,415 men of the southern territories volunteered for military service, and a further 10,753 for labour service in France. These figures represented 30.5 per cent of the adult male population aged between twenty and forty-nine, almost double the average recruitment in northern Algeria where conscription applied. Notwithstanding the obvious economic inducements to serve and the coercive power of military rule, the scale of voluntary enlistment in southern Algeria suggested that the army's associationist practices were particularly effective.[75] And *djemâas* were at the heart of the army system.

Moutet proposed to make *djemâas* elected bodies with the right to disburse tax revenue raised in communal budgets. In short, the indigenous population was to be trained in local democracy in preparation for fuller liberty in the remote future.[76] Moutet's *djemâa* scheme was overshadowed by the broader provisions of the Jonnart Law. It none the less marked a fundamental shift in the Socialist Party away from assimilationism toward a more pragmatic associationism. This bears emphasis, because historians have claimed that the SFIO remained wedded to assimilationism after 1918.[77] The fact that Moutet's overall project passed to Charles Jonnart was largely attributable to the political mood in Algiers at the close of the war. Prime Minister Clemenceau supported Moutet's plans in outline. But he was anxious to stem gathering opposition to them among the settlers. His close ally Jonnart, then serving as Minister of Blockade, commanded respect in Algiers. The obvious solution was to send Jonnart back there to defend a scheme more palatable to the settler community.

The central provisions of the 1919 law were calculated to deceive. Newly enfranchised male Muslim electors were automatically qualified to vote in municipal, communal and national elections that selected mayors, regional councils and the two nationally elected bodies: the financial delegations that scrutinised the colony's budget, and the Algerian supreme council originally established in 1898. But male Muslim electors were placed on a separate electoral roll from settler voters, unless they had qualified for French citizenship through educational qualification, a career in administration or military service. This electoral division was mirrored in the use of two electoral colleges to select all local and national assemblies. *Colon* voters selected the first, and more influential, electoral college. Settler predominance was also safeguarded by restrictions on the permissible number of Muslim representatives in regional and national assemblies. The maximum number of Muslim councillors in the regional councils was limited to twenty-five per cent of the total membership. Muslim representatives were elected to only one of the three financial delegations at national level. The other two were reserved to major property holders and French citizens. The final piece in the administrative jigsaw, the Algerian supreme council, was another closed shop. Twenty-eight of its fifty-nine members were nominees of the governor. The delegations and the regional councils elected the remaining thirty-one. A clever Muslim political tactician might make it all the way from a *djemâa* to the supreme council, but only by dancing to the French tune. And only in constituencies with few settler voters did a Muslim candidate stand any chance of election as one of the ten Deputies and three Senators elected to the French National Assembly.[78]

The Jonnart Law also limited the overall number of Arab and Berber bureaucrats at mayoral, communal and national level. In conformity with earlier Young Algerian demands, junior posts in Algeria's communal bureaucracy were opened up to Muslim candidates. Applicants aged between twenty-two and thirty (widened to thirty-five if they had completed five years' military service) could sit an annual civil service examination in Algiers, provided their local mayor entered them. The examination was divided into three parts. The first was a written paper focusing on mathematics and comprehension skills. The second was a typing test. Applicants then faced a final oral interview before a government selection panel. The complex selection process rooted out all but the most compliant 'Beni Oui Ouis' – the colloquial term of abuse for venal Muslim officials.[79]

A similar pattern was evident in plans to create additional opportunities for Muslim ex-servicemen in recognition of their war service. Soldiers who completed their tour of duty were already exempted from the *indigénat* legal code by a September 1912 decree. Wartime legislation in January 1916 and March 1917 confirmed this measure and reserved some public sector posts to former servicemen. These included clerical jobs in communal bureaucracy, low-grade employment in the railway industry and postal service, and admission to the rural police force. Jonnart introduced an annual quota of such posts, making 400 jobs available in 1919. These ranged from skilled professional employment, such as *khodjas* (public sector officials), Arabic interpreters for French judges and assistants (*commis*) to communal administrators, to unskilled labour as sanitation, railway and postal workers.[80] Overall numbers of returning veterans far outnumbered the posts made available to them. Yet in the scheme's first three years of operation between 1919 and 1922 scores of vacancies remained. The novelty of the scheme, the unattractiveness of some jobs, the inaccessibility of others, help explain this. Low self-esteem among former soldiers, high levels of illiteracy, and veterans' reluctance to work in isolated rural communities, added to the problem. But many ex-servicemen realised they were being fobbed off with unskilled work normally available anyway. In 1922 the Algiers government wound down the veterans' employment scheme. In 1926 it was abandoned altogether, by which time only fifty-one of 800 ex-servicemen candidates had secured a clerical post.[81] At much the same time, the Ministry of Colonies closed an administrative loophole whereby colonial subjects could secure citizenship status by volunteering for the Foreign Legion. Evidently, criminals could acquire French citizenship after service with the Legion but colonial subjects could not.[82]

The veterans' employment scheme was a microcosm of the wider failure of the 1919 reforms. There would be no democratic challenge to the settler oligarchy. The wartime precursors of the Jonnart Law had promised far more to Algerian male electors than the final legislation delivered. The slow trickle of Muslim applicants for 'naturalisation' as French citizens mirrored the derisory admission rates to departmental and communal administrations. Within the first five years of the law's operation only 359 Muslims applied for French citizenship. In the colonial empire as a whole only twenty-two naturalisations were approved in 1919.[83] The Algiers government insisted none the less that the Jonnart Law formed part of a longer-term scheme of political education constructed on associationist principles. The native affairs division envisaged a two-tier development of political consciousness among Algerian male electors. The existing educated urban elite was identified as the sole Muslim constituency that fully understood the Jonnart reforms. All Muslim electoral candidates were expected to emerge from this Europeanised community. As for the great majority of Muslim males, limited enfranchisement would acclimatise them to their subordinate role at the margins of the political community. In April 1919 the native affairs division explained its viewpoint:

> The masses that inhabit the vast territories of the *communes mixtes*, who live in slums or in tents, are still ignorant. They have not had time to become aware of their freedoms. Their minds are dormant, constrained by centuries of servitude to authority. The task we have embarked on is to open them up to fresh thinking. Village meetings have been convened by sub-prefects and administrators, all of whom are eager to carry out their new duty of political education.[84]

Convinced that the Jonnart reforms amounted to generous constitutional change, successive Algiers governments treated the colony's electoral arrangements as set in stone. The Jonnart Law remained in place for seventeen years until it was reviewed by Léon Blum's Popular Front ministry in 1936–37.

The Jonnart legislation had another important corollary: it influenced the administrative structures in place in the neighbouring Moroccan and Tunisian protectorates.[85] As in Algeria, so in Lyautey's Morocco, associationist administrators regarded tribal *djemâas* as the bedrock of rural authority. But at the regional level Morocco was divided into neither Algeria-style departments nor Ottoman-type *sanjaks*. Tribal loyalties were stronger, clan rivalries sharper and regional particularism more pronounced than in Algeria. The Rabat residency was therefore wary of vesting too much authority in locally respected *caïds* and *pachas* for fear of antagonising the central administration of the Sultanate (*mahkzen*), whose regional authority was, in some places, precarious. Native affairs policy in Morocco was also influenced by the stream of ethnographic, sociological and urban planning reports produced by French diplomats and academics specially commissioned to assist the consolidation of the protectorate before the First World War.[86] These specialists promoted co-operation with indigenous elites but, in the short term, the fast rising European population seemed a safer alternative. Morocco's settlers provided an untapped and assuredly conservative resource to assist Morocco's regional development. A renewed wave of settler immigration occurred between 1919 and 1921, bringing in 35,511 new arrivals. By 1926 there were 96,377 European settlers in French Morocco, and by 1937 over 150,000.[87] Historians have remarked on Lyautey's loathing for avaricious settlers, but he did little to slow their immigration.[88] The settler population was primarily identified with *petit commerce* and urban trades. Yet, by the time Lyautey left Morocco in late 1925, settlers owned nearly 500,000 ha of Moroccan land, half the area under European control on the eve of Moroccan independence in 1956.[89] Lyautey and his successors relied on settler representatives organised into consultative assemblies representing commercial, agricultural and industrial concerns, similar to the financial delegations in Algeria. The establishment of Morocco's government council in March 1919, a proto-parliament with limited powers of budgetary scrutiny, also echoed Algeria's system.[90]

The French administrative system was more entrenched in Tunisia. The protectorate was smaller and ethnically less diverse than its near neighbours. The country's Arab elite rarely contested the Tunisian Bey's royal authority. But, again, a three-tier administrative model applied.[91] The Tunis residency interfered least in local government, allowing councils of *caïds* to remain the focal point of district administration. From 1922 regional councils were selected in Tunisia's five administrative sectors: Tunis, Bizerta, Le Kef, Sousse and Sfax. Each could petition the residency direct for funding from the national budget, a process strictly controlled by the appointment of a residency nominee – a *contrôleur civil* – to chair all council sessions. A sixth council existed solely to represent the interests of the Jewish community in Tunis. Although obviously confined to a distinct religious group, this was the one truly democratic forum in Tunisian municipal government. Its twelve elected members served a four-year fixed term. The Tunisian national assembly, the grand council, was organised in March 1928 along similar lines to the Algiers supreme council. The selection system guaranteed a majority of French citizen representatives. They met in separate session from the *indigène* grand council members, thus minimising the chances of confrontation with the residency over budget expenditure. If, however, the two sections of the grand council remained at loggerheads, the Tunisian supreme council was called in to resolve matters. Membership of this final body was largely in the gift of the residency and the beylical authorities, thus ensuring an outcome to suit French interests.[92] Taken together, associationist government in the North African protectorates rested on a veneer of Muslim engagement sufficiently credible to conceal the commanding hand of colonial authority. The political history of inter-war Morocco and Tunisia is dominated by French efforts to protect that veneer against Arab efforts to replace it with genuine participatory government.

Associationism in black Africa

During the inter-war period the federal administration in AOF placed greater reliance on tribal elites previously derided as the embodiment of the obscurantism, backwardness and cruelty that French rule was supposed to eradicate. As Alice Conklin has shown, this spectacular policy reversal marked the adoption of a more conservative associationist style of republican imperialism in Africa.[93] Local alliances forged to promote economic exaction, military recruitment and the preservation of rural order reinforced the power of tribal chiefs willing to trade complicity in the colonial system for French recognition of their regional authority. Officials even argued that collaboration with the chiefs signified a democratisation of sorts. An African elite would learn the rules of responsible government, imparting their knowledge to the rural populations under their sway. *Evolués* would learn that their only means of advancement was to work within this system rather than to oppose it, a hope soon disappointed.[94]

During the 1920s favoured tribal elites in the rural interior of West African colonies assumed a more central role in judicial administration and the provision of labour. French district administrators (*commandants de cercle*) relied on African intermediaries to resolve local disputes in accordance with customary law. Chiefs, interpreters and village headmen were never passive agents of the colonial state. Many exploited their influence as colonial employees and community spokesmen to consolidate their power or to secure material gain, sometimes misleading those hapless French officials not conversant in local languages.[95] Yet both sides recognised that there was no viable alternative. Some 2,200 cantonal chiefs and around 48,000 village headmen kept the peace, and made tax collection, the provision of forced labour and army recruitment a viable proposition.[96] In the interior of the recently established Cameroon mandate, too, during the late 1920s the French high commission relied less on coercion to secure taxes and labour, attempting instead to distribute the burdens imposed more evenly among village populations.[97] The distribution of authority between individual colonial governments, regional administrators and their chiefly agents had shifted decisively.

In French Equatorial Africa government motives were rather different, although the outcome was much the same. In AEF greater devolution of authority to local chiefs was driven by one consideration above all: the chronic shortage of qualified French officials.[98] In 1923 the total registered European population of AEF – administrators, settlers, traders and their families – was still less than 2,000. As table 2.1 indicates, the European populations in the colonies of Oubangui-Chari and Chad were under 300.

Table 2.1 Registered European population in AEF, 1923

Colony	Men	Women	Children	Total
Moyen Congo	562	157	24	743
Gabon	505	80	20	605
Oubangui	190	44	0	234
Chad	271	25	0	296
Total	1,528	306	44	1,878

Source CAOM, Maurice Prouteaux papers, PA50/3/D11.

AEF's mission schools were too few in number to provide enough literate students to fill even junior clerical posts. The federal administration and local trading companies in Brazzaville imported African office staff from Gabon and West Africa.[99] With so few personnel to draw on, the Brazzaville authorities were attracted to the development of a distinct socio-legal category – *indigènes d'élite* – applicable to trusted chiefs and village headmen. These intermediaries would acquire preferential legal status but not full citizenship. Naturalisation as French citizens was a privilege conferred on only a handful of predominantly urban Africans in AEF each year – never enough to constitute a distinct administrative elite, and unlikely to accept postings in the rural interior.[100] The Brazzaville administration's hostility to wider access to citizenship was ultimately self-defeating. It was, however, consistent with Governor-general Raphaël Antonetti's refusal to modify the *indigénat* in the 1920s.[101] The punishments meted out by district officers under this legal code were unaltered since the original introduction of the *indigénat* to AEF in 1887. In one of its few acts of colonial reform, on 15 November 1924 the Cartel des gauches coalition passed decree legislation that reduced the punishments specified in the original *indigénat* decrees passed in the late nineteenth century. It was left to the Ministry of Colonies to oversee reforms colony by colony. Antonetti was not easily swayed. Over the next four years he insisted that the acute isolation of French officials in Equatorial Africa made draconian penalties essential. The capacity to dispense instant punishment was the best guarantee of order for rural administrators, often several hundred kilometres from the nearest police post or military garrison. Furthermore, Antonetti argued, a whip hand was essential to drag AEF's indigenous population, 'often close to barbarism', into the twentieth century.[102] On 1 May 1925 he wrote:

> Our entire native policy in Equatorial Africa boils down to the struggle against the individualism of subjects who profit from the general security we have established by evading their duties to society. [We are working] to reconstitute an indigenous society that, although once cohesive because any individual that dared to leave it faced slavery or death, has been disintegrating since these fears have disappeared. This society must be regenerated on a new basis of just social obligations, but these obligations are far from being voluntarily accepted because they are not yet understood.[103]

Antonetti's message was simple. It was out of the question to relax French punitive powers, just as it was impossible to concede citizenship rights to Africans unfamiliar with the basic tenets of capitalist organisation and French legal norms.[104] The governor was, however, happy for village headmen and councils of elders to dispense traditional justice. Continued application of customary law complemented the *indigénat*, kept administrative costs down, and avoided the troublesome requirement to explain the complexities of French legal process to isolated rural populations.[105] Over a decade later, on 28 December 1936, François-Joseph Reste, Antonetti's successor as governor-general, maintained that co-operation with African chiefs remained the first principle of colonial governance in AEF. By then the authority of the federal administration in Brazzaville over subordinate governors in matters of fiscal policy, budgetary spending and legal affairs had been further codified by decree legislation passed between 30 June 1934 and 1 January 1935.[106]

For all that, AEF remained a destination of last resort to members of the colonial service. A loyal hierarchy of local intermediaries remained essential to keep colonial government working.[107] Regional disorder was concentrated in areas where such hierarchies could not be established, a fact proved by the insurrection among the Gbaya-speaking peoples clustered in western Oubangui-Chari, north-east Cameroon and the Haute Sangha province of French Congo between 1928 and 1931 (discussed in chapter seven).[108] Other factors played their part in this more pragmatic associationism. During the 1920s the Brazzaville administration and the principal concessionary companies operating throughout the Congo basin strove hard to increase the profitability of commercial exploitation in AEF after the disruption to exports occasioned by the First World War. In 1924 Antonetti approved wider recourse to forced labour to ensure completion of the Congo–Océan railway and a road system linking the Cameroon mandate with Oubangui-Chari. More extensive plantations, vast lumber camps in Gabon and French Congo, and increased coffee cultivation all imposed new demands on tribal populations. The tax burden also increased markedly from 1925, just as improved communications enabled tax collectors to reach deeper into the interior.

There were thus important differences of emphasis between the associationist policies adopted for want of any alternative in AEF and the more ambitious policies pursued in AOF. In West Africa the pervasiveness of associationism after the First World War marked the triumph of those that the late François Manchuelle labelled the 'colonial humanists' in the federal government. Officials loyal to the reformist governor-general Joost Van Vollenhoven, whose brief term of office in 1917 had promised a re-vitalisation of methods of indirect rule, were generally unsympathetic to his successor, Gabriel Angoulvant, a long-standing proponent of centrali-sation and increased use of forced labour. Advocates of associationism warned of the adverse consequences for traditional agriculture, tribal hierarchy and local economies should the colonial authorities impose harsher direct control. Cantonal administrators were closely attuned to the cycles of regional arable production, labour migration and livestock rearing that were the bedrock of colonial economies in AOF's inland territories.[109] Most agreed with Maurice Delafosse, the influential anthropologist and colonial administrator, who condemned assimilationist policies, forced labour and military recruitment as inherently destructive of African societies.[110]

Many of the senior bureaucrats in Dakar were schooled in the directorate of political affairs first developed by Léon Faidherbe as governor of Senegal in the 1850s and 1860s. Faidherbe's determination to build an associationist central bureaucracy in Saint-Louis was matched by his reliance on co-operative tribal chiefs and his use of locally recruited military forces – the tirailleurs sénégalais – to consolidate French colonial power. The appoint-ment of Martial Merlin as AOF governor-general in succession to Angoulvant in 1919 marked the reassertion of these associationist princi-ples. Merlin was an old Africa hand. He had served as governor-general in AEF and Madagascar. It was in Senegal, however, that he learned his craft.[111] Merlin trained in the Dakar Political Affairs Bureau. As secretary-general to AOF governor Ernest Roume in the early 1900s, he refined the system of chieftaincy through which colonial authority in the rural interior was upheld. The new governor supervised a raft of administrative reforms initiated by his predecessor, Angoulvant. In 1918 the Dakar government defined the scope of its powers over individual colonial administrations in AOF's federal system. The role of the Dakar authorities was to co-ordinate the policies implemented colony by colony. Experience indicated that metro-politan supervision of colonial policy was impossible without a supranational authority intermediate between the French government and a remote colonial administration. More important, the process of colonial state building was far from complete. The federal authorities in AOF, like their counterparts in Equatorial Africa and the Indochina federation, tried to ensure common administrative standards and a consistent doctrine of government.[112] Dakar, Brazzaville and Hanoi were the hubs of associationist planning, initiating and regulating policy. In 1921 Merlin oversaw the replacement of the principal consultative assembly in AOF with a colonial council in which places were reserved to official nominees alongside elected members. The Dakar administration added collaborative chiefs as placemen within the council, strengthening conservative chiefly authority in the process.[113]

Earlier decree legislation passed on 4 December 1920 reorganised communal administration across AOF. Local consultative councils, *conseils des notables*, were instituted in administrative regions, or *cercles*, through which tribal leaders could relay the grievances of village elders to their French district officer, the *commandant de cercle*.[114] The creation of the advisory councils at cantonal and village level between 1928 and 1932 completed these reforms. Only Africans naturalised as French citizens secured any representation at national or federal level through two overlapping consultative bodies, the administrative council and the council of government. In Senegal tribal chiefs were also represented in a separate colonial council with limited deliberative powers over policy making in the colony.[115] Certain guiding principles underpinned these administrative reforms. The entire structure of consultative assemblies reinforced tribal hierarchy, revitalising the bonds between conservative tribal leaders and French administrators. These ties had been severely tested before 1914, and were further undermined by the economic and manpower demands of the war. Whereas tribal hierarchy was previously characterised as a barrier to colonial penetration, social progress and economic modernisation, in the changed circumstances of the 1920s chiefs became agents of a more co-operative and conservative colonialism that buttressed the foundations of African rural society.[116]

The AOF government also saw Muslim religious leaders as adjuncts of associationist policy. Official efforts to enlist Senegal's *grands marabouts* as agents of colonial power combined coercive pressure and close surveillance with limited concessions to favoured religious figures. Just as the French had permitted the growth of indigenous civil society in the four communes of Senegal, from the 1880s onward efforts were made to make Islamic institutions in the Senegalese interior accept French hegemony. These 'paths of accommodation' meshed with parallel attempts to co-opt tribal chiefs into the colonial hierarchy.[117] Yet *marabouts* rarely participated in colonial administration. Indeed, on occasion, Islamic leaders and local chiefs worked together to subvert the colonial system by persuading district administrators to implement policies directly beneficial to Sufi orders and tribal communities.[118] But the Islamic civil society that they represented was broadly tolerant of the French presence, and, in some cases, even allied with favoured governors. The support of Sufi leaders acquired more importance as the economic development of Senegal's peanut basin accelerated in the decade after 1918, spurred by the completion of the Thiès to Bamako railway. The goodwill of the Murid followers of Amadu Bamba Mbacke, the leading *marabout* in the peanut basin, became essential to increased labour recruitment. The co-option of Muslim leaders culminated in the emergence of Seydu Nuru Tal as *grand marabout* in the 1920s. The grandson of Umar Tal, Senegal's foremost Islamic resistance leader, Seydu Nuru Tal became a 'roving ambassador' for French colonialism in West Africa.[119]

A different path in Madagascar?

In Madagascar the issue of citizenship through naturalisation dominated the politics of colonial government in the 1920s. Two decrees promulgated in January 1926 and December 1930 established notables' councils in each administrative district. As in AOF, village headmen nominated cantonal delegates. They served for two years alongside French district administrators in the new assemblies. Council meetings, sometimes convened only once a year, discussed matters of local concern: cantonal administration, labour service (*prestation*), wage rates and tax levels.[120]

The new consultative system did not address the root causes of political opposition in Madagascar's urban centres. On the one hand, members of the indigenous Merina elite, junior officials, and Communist anti-colonialists shared a common interest in naturalisation. For the dispossessed Merina – the dominant group in pre-colonial Madagascar – citizenship promised re-entry to the political community. For Malagasy bureaucrats in Tananarive, Diego Suarez and Tamatave, citizen status was essential to career advancement. For ex-servicemen, citizenship was their due. And to marginalised opponents of the regime, restrictions on naturalisation proved the inequity of a colonial system based on Gallieni's *politique des races*.[121] Gallieni's strategy of divide and rule systematically excluded Merina leaders from positions of authority. A 1913 government-general circular warned provincial and district administrators that unwarranted reform might 'overturn the edifice of [tribal] society'. It conveniently ignored the shift in inter-communal power precipitated by the *politique des races*.[122] Ostracised by the colonial authorities, the Merina oligarchy therefore became a rallying point for popular opposition to French rule.[123]

The irony was that naturalisation in Madagascar was numerically insignificant. In 1922, for instance, eleven naturalisations were approved. Ten of these were doctors. Even this was too much. Between 1924 and 1929 Governor-general Marcel Olivier imposed more stringent qualification requirements. Regional administrators complained that naturalised Malagasy doctors headed for the capital, deserting rural practices where their skills were most needed, particularly as bubonic plague remained endemic. French traders and plantation owners also opposed naturalisation, fearing competition from an indigenous mercantile elite. Olivier agreed, and selected local intermediaries on the basis of their kinship ties with an influential Malagasy family of aristocratic lineage rather than past service to the colonial power. Ex-servicemen were excluded, except for a handful of exceptionally decorated veterans.[124]

The foundation in 1915 of the Merina-dominated Vy Vato Sakelika (VVS, literally, 'the network of iron and stone') was the root cause of governmental intransigence. The VVS rekindled memories among officials and settlers in Tananarive of earlier anti-colonial secret societies. Although the VVS sometimes claimed to be a Malagasy cultural association, its structure of local cell networks dominated by young, literate Merina convinced the authorities otherwise.[125] As a result, after 1915 the *sûreté* acquired greater influence over government policy. Governor Olivier's crackdown against Malagasy supporters of the League of the Rights of Man as well as VVS activists such as Jean Ralaimongo and Paul Dussac limited public expression of opposition to French naturalisation policy. In the immediate post-war years the island seemed politically calm. VVS members sentenced by tribunal in 1916 to long terms of forced labour even received a presidential pardon on 2 November 1922.[126]

The *sûreté* estimated that Malagasy with direct experience of life in France or in other colonies posed the greatest threat. Throughout the inter-war period, the security services in Madagascar monitored Ralaimongo and Dussac's activities obsessively.[127] Unlike his fellow autonomist leader Paul Dussac, a Frenchman born in the Crimea and raised in Réunion, Jean Ralaimongo represented an established community of educated Malagasy, principally of Merina descent, for whom the French arrival heralded a loss of social status and political power. Ralaimongo was born in 1885, the son of an *indigène* pastor attached to one of the island's many Protestant missions. After qualifying as a teacher, Ralaimongo made the first of many trips to France in 1910. Like so many of the first generation of anti-colonial nationalists in French Africa, he served in the First World War and then spent much of the early 1920s in Paris. At this stage, he was a committed assimilationist. An activist of the French League for native Malagasies' citizenship rights (Ligue française pour l'accession des indigènes de Madagascar aux droits de citoyen), Ralaimongo initially envisaged a more equitable distribution of power rather than an end to colonial government. But he became increasingly militant. Frustrated by French intransigence, he was attracted by the anti-colonialism of the Communist Third International. He was convicted of sedition on 10 July 1922. Faced with five years' forced residence on Mayotte Island, Ralaimongo fled to

Paris, where he founded a nationalist newspaper, *L'Opinion*, together with former VVS members, including Dr J. Ravoahangy. From the northern port of Diego Suarez, Ralaimongo also organised the distribution in Madagascar of *Le Paria* and *Les Continents*, two Communist periodicals targeted at a colonial audience.[128] The watchwords of this journalism were colonial citizenship, land redistribution, worker rights and autonomous majority rule in Madagascar.[129]

Ralaimongo, Ravoahangy and Dussac exposed the vacuum at the core of republican imperialist rhetoric. The introduction of local consultative assemblies after the war made little difference to the lives of ordinary Malagasy. Naturalisation for a select few offered nothing to impoverished colonial subjects. VVS supporters had turned the ideals of associationism against the colonial authorities, ensuring that public agitation for greater citizenship rights never died away. On 19 May 1929 around 3,000 Malagasy protesters marched through Tananarive after the police broke up a meeting addressed by Paul Dussac at the Excelsior cinema. Demonstrators converged on the governor's Cabinet Office 'brandishing sticks' and waving red flags – symbols of the 'Red Shawls' revolt of the 1890s as much as of Communist affiliation.[130] Their anger focused on an administration that closed off any prospect of political advancement for the vast majority of the population. Police repression made national heroes of the organisers of the 19 May demonstration. By the time Olivier's successor as governor-general, Léon Cayla, arrived in Madagascar in May 1930, support in the capital for mass citizenship was deeply entrenched.[131] Cayla increased the number of naturalisations, but only marginally. In 1931 ninety-three applications were approved; in 1935 only thirty-eight. By then Ralaimongo, Dussac and other early Malagasy nationalists had moved on. In the early 1930s their opposition to associationist colonial policy centred on the discriminatory *indigénat*, whose arbitrary punishments and fines invited administrative abuse.[132]

Conclusion

Theories of governance had a major impact on the direction of colonial policy after 1918. With the important exceptions of the *anciennes colonies*, the general resurgence of associationist ideas elsewhere in the 1920s empire stimulated fundamental changes in governmental practice and the development of indigenous civil society. More prosaic factors were also crucial. The associationists' supposed respect for pre-colonial societies, rural hierarchies and local custom masked their underlying need to limit popular dissent while keeping administrative costs down. Working with village headmen and tribal chiefs within the parameters of customary law bolstered the most conservative elements of rural society, facilitating colonial regulation of agriculture, labour supply and commerce. The rapid turnover of colonial governors and senior administrators was always a major barrier to administrative continuity. Differing levels of infrastructure development also precluded uniformity in policy. Isolated district officers in Niger, Chad or Oubangui-Chari faced a very different task from the burgeoning regional bureaucracy of the Indochina federation where much of the day-to-day work of public administration, tax collection and judicial arbitration was conducted on French behalf by the mandarin class. In the 1920s AOF averaged 500 French officials for a federation population of 15 million. Indochina averaged 5,000 for a population approaching 21.5 million.[133]

Official rhetoric throughout francophone colonial Africa insisted that administrative change was to be gradual, cautious and respectful of local tradition. In practice, it rested on a racialised conception of colonial society as too primitive to cope with the demands of mass political engagement. The federal government in Dakar claimed that the limitation of political rights to tribal leaders and naturalised citizens was consistent with efforts to prevent the 'deracialisation' of the African masses. It would be irresponsible to extend the wider citizenship rights and elective institutions enjoyed by the *originaires* (original inhabitants) of Senegal's four communes – the first outposts of French colonial penetration in West Africa – to the wider population of AOF.[134] After all, it was only through centuries of cultural contact, intermarriage, concubinage and Catholicism that the trading stations and island territories of the pre-Napoleonic French colonial empire, such as the 'model colonies' of Martinique and Guadeloupe, were assimilated to France. And here, too, clear racial hierarchies applied.[135] Hence the recurrent tendency in colonial policy statements to represent administrative reform as an educational process that affirmed French cultural superiority and infantilised the colonised population. The engagement of indigenous peoples in colonial government was determined by their 'political maturity' in coming to accept French rule.[136] Equipped with a seemingly infallible justification for colonial oligarchy, associationists dominated policy making in much of the French empire from the end of the First World War to the start of the Second.

Notes

1 Raymond Betts, *Assimilation and Association in French Colonial Theory, 1890–1914* (New York: Columbia University Press, 1961), is instructive.
2 John W. Cell, 'Colonial rule', in Judith Brown and Wm Roger Louis (eds), *The Oxford History of the British Empire. The Twentieth Century* (Oxford: Oxford University Press, 1999), 237–43.
3 The outstanding study of associationism in practice is Alice L. Conklin's *A Mission to Civilize*. See also Betts, *Assimilation and Association*, chapters 6–7.

4 Jean-Marc Bernardini, *Le Darwinisme social en France 1859–1918. Fascination et rejet d'une idéologie* (Paris: CNRS Editions, 1997), 185–95.
5 Alice L. Conklin, 'A force for civilization. Republican discourse and French administration in West Africa, 1895–1930', in Becker *et al.*, *AOF : réalités et héritages*, I, 283–302.
6 Kim Munholland, 'The French response to the Vietnamese nationalist movement, 1905–1914', *Journal of Modern History*, 47:4 (1975), 655–75.
7 Roshwald, 'Colonial dreams of the French right wing'. Roshwald identifies protagonists of indirect rule with the French right before 1914, but concedes that associationism drew wider support.
8 Charles Michelet, 'L'empire français et la constitution impériale', *Outre-Mer* 4:1 (1932), 30–48.
9 Introduction to Alec G. Hargreaves and Mark McKinney (eds), *Post-colonial Cultures in France* (London: Routledge, 1997), 21.
10 Elizabeth Ezra, *The Colonial Unconscious. Race and Culture in Interwar France* (Ithaca NY: Cornell University Press, 2000), 6.
11 Bernardini, *Le Darwinisme social*, 161–9; Charles Sowerine, *France since 1870. Culture, Politics and Society* (London: Palgrave, 2001), 58–9, 66, 70. In 1892 Drumont used the profits from *La France juive* to establish an antisemitic newspaper, *La Libre Parole* (*The Free Word*). In May 1898 he figured among four openly antisemitic candidates elected to parliament by *colon* voters in Algiers.
12 James D. Le Sueur, *Uncivil War. Intellectuals and Identity Politics during the Decolonization of Algeria* (Philadelphia: Pennsylvania University Press, 2001), 18–19.
13 Gary Wilder, 'Framing Greater France between the wars', *Journal of Historical Sociology*, 14:2 (2001), 198–225.
14 Conklin, 'Colonialism and human rights', 419–42.
15 Mahfoud Kaddache, *Histoire du nationalisme algérien* I. *Question nationale et politique algérienne 1919–1951* (2nd edn) (Algiers: Entreprise nationale du livre, 1993), 32.
16 Tony Smith, 'Muslim impoverishment in colonial Algeria', *Revue de l'Occident Musulman*, 156 (1974), 154–6. The *indigénat* was, for example, introduced to AEF by decree on 30 September 1887.
17 Bidwell, *Morocco*, 162–74; Philip S. Khoury, *Syria and the French Mandate. The Politics of Arab Nationalism, 1920–1945* (London: I. B. Tauris, 1987), 82–3.
18 Gilles Lafuente, *La Politique berbère de la France et le nationalisme marocain* (Paris: Editions l'Harmattan, 1999); William A. Hoisington Jr, 'Cities in revolt. The Berber Dahir (1930) and France's urban strategy in Morocco', *Journal of Contemporary History*, 13:4 (1978), 433–48.
19 MAE, série P: Tunisie 1917–40, vol. 387, Residency report, 'Conventions collectives de travail', 11 July 1936.
20 Jacques-W. Binoche-Guedra, 'La réprésentation parlementaire coloniale (1871–1940)', *Revue Historique*, 280:2 (1988), 522–33.
21 Martin Stuart-Fox, 'The French in Laos, 1887–1945', *Modern Asian Studies*, 29:1 (1995), 121, 137.
22 Tai, 'The politics of compromise', 371–91.
23 Fanny Colonna, *Instituteurs algériens 1883–1939* (Paris: Presses de la FNSP, 1975), 56–7.
24 Bernard Marcel Peyrouton, *Du Service public à la prison commune. Souvenirs: Tunis, Rabat, Buenos Aires, Vichy, Alger, Frèsnes* (Paris: Plon, 1950), 39. Peyrouton undertook this task between 1930 and 1933 on behalf of the Algiers governor.
25 Benjamin Stora, 'La gauche socialiste révolutionnaire, et la question du Maghreb au moment du Front populaire (1935–1938)', *Revue Française d'Histoire d'Outre-Mer*, 70: 258 (1983), 58–63.
26 ADA, Sarraut papers, 12J69, Interior Ministry, 'Note sur le Congrès Socialiste de Toulouse', n.d. 1934.
27 Semidei, 'Les Socialistes français', 1128–41.
28 Stora, 'La gauche socialiste', 58–9.
29 Wilder, 'Framing Greater France', 198–225 *passim*.
30 Eric T. Jennings, 'Monuments to Frenchness? The memory of the Great War and the politics of Guadeloupe's identity, 1914–1945', *French Historical Studies*, 21:4 (1998), 566–77. Jennings's work provides an interesting counterpoint to the local politics of

commemoration in 1920s France as discussed in Daniel J. Sherman, 'Bodies and names. The emergence of commemoration in interwar France', *American Historical Review*, 103:2 (1998), 443–66, and in Sherman, *The Construction of Memory in Interwar France* (Chicago: University of Chicago Press, 1999), chapter 2.

31 Gilbert Meynier, 'Volonté de propagande ou inconscient affiche? Images et imaginaire coloniaux français dans l'entre-deux-guerres', in Pascal Blanchard and Armelle Chatelier (eds), *Images et Colonies. Actes du colloque* (Paris: ACHAC, 1993), 41–2.

32 Peyrouton, *Du service public*, 27–9, 37. In 1922 Peyrouton had just completed a tour of duty in the Madagascar administration. A well connected Freemason, he used his personal contacts with the editors of the *Dépêche Coloniale* to secure a place as the paper's 'special correspondent', accompanying President Millerand on his official tour of the Maghreb.

33 Wilder, 'Framing Greater France', 205–8.

34 Alice L. Conklin, ' "Democracy" rediscovered. Civilization through association in French West Africa (1914–1930)', *Cahiers d'Etudes Africaines*, 145:37 (1997), 59–60.

35 Both quotes cited in Hargreaves, *The Colonial Experience in French Fiction*, 14–15.

36 An excellent biography is Marc Michel, *Gallieni* (Paris: Fayard, 1989); Patrice Morlat, *Les Affaires politiques de l'Indochine 1895–1923. Les grands commis du savoir au pouvoir* (Paris: Editions l'Harmattan, 1995), 251–4.

37 ADA, Sarraut Papers, 12J280, 'Discours d'Albert Sarraut sur la situation en Indochine devant la Chambre des Députés', n.d. 1919.

38 Conklin, *A Mission to Civilize*, 40–1.

39 There are striking similarities between Sarraut's ideas and those of Lord Lugard, Governor-general of Nigeria between 1912 and 1918. Like Sarraut, Lugard cemented his reputation as a theorist of colonial rule in the early 1920s with the publication of a book, *The Dual Mandate* (1922), which stressed the material benefits and ethical obligations of indirect rule. See Cell, 'Colonial rule', 240.

40 ADA, Sarraut papers, 12J162, Chambre des Députés, Douzième Législature, Session de 12 avril 1921, 'Projet de loi portant fixation d'un programme général de mise en valeur des colonies françaises', 16–35.

41 Wilder, 'Framing Greater France', 203–6; Agathe Larcher, 'La voie étroite des réformes coloniales et la "collaboration franco-annamite" (1917–1928)', *Revue Française d'Histoire d'Outre-Mer*, 82: 309 (1995), 387–420.

42 AN, Georges Bidault papers, 457/AP/115, 'Circulaire du Maréchal Lyautey: Politique du Protectorat', 18 November 1918.

43 William A. Hoisington, Jr, 'French rule and the Moroccan elite', *Maghreb Review*, 22:1 (1997), 138.

44 Daniel Rivet, *Lyautey et l'institution du protectorat français au Maroc*, 3 vols (Paris: Editions l'Harmattan, 1988); André Le Révérend, *Lyautey* (Paris: Fayard, 1983); William A. Hoisington, Jr, *Lyautey and the French Conquest of Morocco* (London: Macmillan, 1995). For Lyautey's pre-Moroccan career see Pascal Venier, *Lyautey avant Lyautey* (Paris: Editions l'Harmattan, 1997).

45 For a character sketch of Lyautey see Paul Rabinow, *French Modern. Norms and Forms of the Social Environment* (Chicago: University of Chicago Press, 1989), 105–25. Regarding Lyautey's sexuality see Robert Aldrich, *Colonialism and Homosexuality* (London: Routledge, 2003), 64–9, and his 'Homosexuality in the French colonies', in Jeffery Merrick and Michael Sibalis (eds), *Homosexuality in French History and Culture* (New York: Hawarth Press, 2001), 208–9.

46 On Lyautey's early Maghreb career see Munholland, 'Rival approaches', 328–43.

47 Hoisington, Jr, 'French rule', 138–9. Two volumes of Lyautey's *Lettres de Tonkin et du Madagascar 1894–1899* were published in Paris between 1920 and 1921.

48 Lyautey's article 'Du rôle colonial de l'armée', published in the *Revue des Deux Mondes* in January 1900, was the most authoritative explanation of pacification ever written by an army officer, see Venier, 'A campaign of colonial propaganda', 33–4.

49 Hoisington, Jr, 'French rule', 138.

50 Roger Gruner, *Du Maroc traditionnel au Maroc moderne. Le Contrôle civil au Maroc, 1912–1956* (Paris: Nouvelles Editions Latines, 1984), 73–4, 103–5, 205–9.

51 Rivet, *Lyautey et l'institution du protectorat* III, 195–212 *passim*.

52 Elisabeth Mouilleau, *Fonctionnaires de la République et artisans de l'empire. Le cas des contrôleurs civils en Tunisie (1881–1956)* (Paris: Editions l'Harmattan, 2000).

53 Richard Keller, 'Madness and colonization. Psychiatry in the British and French empires, 1800–1962', *Journal of Social History*, 35:2 (2001), 297, 313–17, quote at p. 297. In the early 1920s Lyautey supported the foundation of the Berrechid psychiatric hospital, the first such facility in Morocco. The Hôpital Psychiatrique de Blida in Algeria, training ground for Antoine Pirot's Algiers School of Psychiatry, was not established until 1938.

54 Hamid Irbouh, 'French colonial art education and the Moroccan feminine milieu. A case study from Fez, 1927–1930', *Maghreb Review*, 25:3–4 (2000), 286.

55 Hoisington, Jr, *Lyautey and the French Conquest*, chapters 6 and 7, quote at p. 134. Hoisington summarises his arguments in 'French rule and the Moroccan elite', 138–41. During Lyautey's term as Resident-general, six different pashas were appointed in Casablanca, and four of these appointees changed over a five-year period.

56 Francis Koerner, 'Un socialiste auvergnat Governeur-général d'Indochine. Le cas d'Alexandre Varenne (1925–1928)', *Revue Historique*, 285:1 (1991), 133–45.

57 CAOM, Marius Moutet Papers, PA28/4/Dossier Varenne, sous-dossier 59, 'Aperçu de l'oeuvre accompli en Indochine par Alexandre Varenne'.

58 *Ibid.*

59 ADA, Sarraut papers, 12J377, Varenne personal letter to Sarraut (then Minister of Interior), 8 August 1926.

60 Brocheux and Hémery, *Indochine. La colonisation ambiguë*, 101.

61 *Ibid.*, 102.

62 *Ibid.*, 102–5, 110–13.

63 ADA, Sarraut papers, 12J280, Directeur du Cabinet Pierre Pasquier (Hué) personal note to Sarraut, 2 April 1923.

64 CAOM, AOF, Fonds moderne, 17G40, Direction des affaires politiques (Dakar), 'Affaires politiques et indigènes', n.d., November 1921.

65 *Ibid.*

66 John Ruedy provides a penetrating examination of French colonial rule in Algeria before 1919 in his *Modern Algeria*, 80–113.

67 Peter Dunwoodie, *Writing French Algeria* (Oxford: Clarendon Press, 1998), 128–9; Julia Clancy-Smith and Frances Gouda (eds), *Domesticating the Empire. Race, Gender, and Family Life in French and Dutch Colonialism* (Charlottesville VA: University Press of Virginia, 1998), 5.

68 Kristin Ross, *Fast Cars, Clean Bodies. Decolonization and the Reordering of French Culture* (Cambridge MA: MIT Press, 1995), 123.

69 Fernand Braudel, 'Personal testimony', *Journal of Modern History*, 44:4 (1972), 451; also cited in Christelow, 'The mosque at the edge of the plaza', 289, 303 n. 2. One of Braudel's *lycée* colleagues was Louis Bertrand, a member of the Académie Française, whose racialist ideas became popular among the city's settler community.

70 John Ruedy, *Land Policy in Colonial Algeria* (Berkeley CA: University of California Press, 1967), 101; see also Mahfoud Bennoune, 'The introduction of nationalism into rural Algeria, 1919–1954', *Maghreb Review*, 2:3 (1977), 2.

71 Dunwoodie, *Writing French Algeria*, 15.

72 Vincent Confer, *France and Algeria. The Problem of Civil and Political Reform, 1870–1920* (Syracuse NY: Syracuse University Press, 1966), 62–74, 99–106 *passim*; Biondi, *Les Anticolonialistes*, 86–93 *passim*.

73 Moutet was the only French deputy elected during the First World War, but he achieved notoriety as defence lawyer for the Radical Party elder statesman, Joseph Caillaux, arrested at Clemenceau's instigation in 1917 for dealings with German contacts in pursuit of a negotiated peace.

74 It bears emphasis that not all settler ex-servicemen were hostile to pacifism. The Ligue internationale des combatants de la paix, the most influential of the militant pacifist organisations in inter-war France, established a strong presence in French North Africa in the early 1930s, see Norman Ingram, *The Politics of Dissent. Pacifism in France, 1919–1939* (Oxford: Clarendon Press, 1991), 134–43 *passim*.

75 CAOM, GGA, 11H/46, no. 908, Service des affaires indigènes, 'Note pour le Secrétaire Général du Gouvernement, Alger', 21 February 1918. In Algeria north of the Territoires du sud, under civil rule, 76,096 military conscripts and 60,359 labourers were recruited in the 1914–17 period. This represented 16.5 per cent of the adult male population aged twenty to forty-nine.
76 Confer, *France and Algeria*, 99–109.
77 See, for example, Semidei, 'Les Socialistes français', 1115–53; Stora, 'La gauche socialiste', 58.
78 AN, F⁶⁰202, Haut Comité Mediterranéen rapport no. 4, 'Les Assemblées élus en Afrique du Nord', March 1937 session.
79 CAOM, GGA, 9H32, no. 22148, Directeur des affaires indigènes, 'Note pour concours', 21 June 1928.
80 Cannon, 'Irreconciliability of reconciliation', 43–5.
81 *Ibid.*, 45–7; CAOM, affpol/21, Direction des services militaires (Colonies) to Direction de l'infanterie 2ème bureau (Guerre), 24 July 1926.
82 CAOM, GGA, 9H32, Service des affaires indigènes (Algiers), 'Note sur les emplois réservés aux anciens militaires indigènes', 5 July 1927.
83 Confer, *France and Algeria*, 113–21.
84 CAOM, GGA, 11H46, no. 3520, Direction des affaires indigènes, 'Rapport sur la situation politique et administrative des indigènes, mars 1919', 29 April 1919.
85 Lafuente, *La Politique berbère*, 80–4; Bidwell, *Morocco*, 285.
86 Edmund Burke III, 'Fez, the setting sun of Islam. A study of the politics of colonial ethnography', *Maghreb Review*, 2:4 (1977), 1–5.
87 Rivet, *Lyautey et l'institution du protectorat* III, 8.
88 C. R. Pennell, *Morocco since 1830. A History* (London: Hurst, 2000), 199; Robin Bidwell cites Lyautey's private correspondence criticising *colons* for their 'pure Boche' racism and lack of intelligence, see *Morocco under Colonial Rule*, 202.
89 Rivet, *Lyautey et l'institution du protectorat* III, 18–22; Pennell, *Morocco*, 199.
90 AN, F⁶⁰202, Haut Comité Méditerranéen rapport no. 4, 'Les Assemblées élus en Afrique du Nord', March 1937 session. In addition to the Government Council there were two other economic advisory councils in Morocco: the Comité permanent de défense économique and the Conseil supérieur du travail.
91 AN, F⁶⁰202, Haut Comité Méditerranéen rapport no. 4.
92 *Ibid.*
93 Conklin, *A Mission to Civilize*, 7–8, chapters 6 and 7.
94 Conklin, ' "Democracy" rediscovered', 68–74; Genova, *Colonial Ambivalence*, 78–80.
95 Osborn, ' "Circle of iron" ', 29–50.
96 Tony Chafer, *The End of Empire in French West Africa, 1936–1960. France's Successful Decolonization?* (Oxford: Berg, 2002), chapter 1; Conklin, *A Mission to Civilize*, 203–7.
97 Peter Geschiere, 'European planters, African peasants, and the colonial state. Alternatives in the *mise en valeur* of Makaland, south-east Cameroon, during the interbellum', *African Economic History*, 12 (1983), 88.
98 As an example: CAOM, GGAEF, 1D1, no. 220 bis, Governor-general Antonetti to Inspection générale du service de santé (Colonies), 4 March 1926. The chief medical inspectors for Moyen Congo, Gabon, Oubangui-Chari and Chad were all due to leave AEF, leaving no qualified healthcare staff to direct its medical services.
99 Phyllis M. Martin, 'Contesting clothes in colonial Brazzaville', *Journal of African History*, 35:3 (1994), 406.
100 CAOM, GGAEF, 1D4, no. 369, Antonetti to Direction des affaires politiques 4e bureau (Colonies), 20 April 1929. The idea of the *indigènes d'élite* category originated with the Supreme Colonial Council's legislative section.
101 CAOM, affpol/663/D1, no. 1050/C, Antonetti to Direction des affaires politiques 2ème bureau, 'Application de l'Indigénat', 15 December 1928.
102 *Ibid.*, no. 368, Antonetti to Direction des affaires politiques, 1 May 1925.
103 *Ibid.*
104 CAOM, GGAEF, 1D1, Antonetti to Direction des affaires politiques, 21 July 1926.
105 *Ibid.*, no. 330/L, Antonetti to Minister of Colonies Léon Perrier, 27 December 1926.

Antonetti warned that African subjects would misconstrue the adversarial nature of trial by jury as indicative of French indecisiveness.

106 SHA, 6H124/D1, Ministère de la France d'Outre-Mer, 'Notes documentaries: Oubangui-Chari', 8 May 1948: details the legal changes in inter-war AEF.
107 Elikia M'Bokolo, 'Forces sociales et idéologies dans la décolonisation de l'AEF', *Journal of African History*, 22 (1981), 394.
108 Thomas O'Toole, 'The 1928–1931 Gbaya insurrection in Ubangui-Shari. Messianic movement or village self-defense?' *Canadian Journal of African Studies*, 18:2 (1984), 330–3. For details of the affected regions see SHA, 6H124/D1.
109 Manchuelle, *Willing Migrants*, 149.
110 Marc Michel, 'Un programme réformiste en 1919. Maurice Delafosse et la politique indigène en AOF', *Cahiers d'Etudes Africaines*, 5:58 (1975), 313–27. On Delafosse's approach to ethnography see Filippo M. Zerilli, 'Maurice Delafosse, entre science et action', in Amselle and Sibeud, *Maurice Delafosse*, 144–65.
111 Conklin, *A Mission to Civilize*, 187–8.
112 CAOM, 17G40, 'Note du Gouvernement Général', n.d., 1918.
113 Robinson, *Paths of Accommodation*, 61–2, 73–4.
114 CAOM, 17G40, Direction des affaires politiques (Dakar), 'Affaires politiques et indigènes', n.d., November 1921.
115 Olatunji Oloruntimehin, 'The economy of French West Africa between the two World Wars', *Journal of African Studies*, 4:1 (1977), 54. The author suggests that, in Senegal at least, these measures were a retrograde step, as they supplanted the colony's *conseil général*, a more genuinely representative body.
116 Conklin, *A Mission to Civilize*, 142–9, 191–7 passim.
117 Ibid., 42–3.
118 John Glover, ' "The mosque is one thing, the administration is another." Murid *marabouts* and Wolof aristocrats in colonial Senegal', *International Journal of African Historical Studies*, 33:2 (2001), 351–65.
119 Robinson, *Paths of Accommodation*, 229–40.
120 CAOM, GGM, 4D44, Comité permanent d'études scientifiques et économiques et de la statistique, 'Madagascar. L'évolution politique et sociale de 1926 à 1937'.
121 Randrianja, *Société et luttes anticoloniales à Madagascar*, 168–74.
122 CAOM, GGM, 4D44, Comité permanent d'études scientifiques et économiques et de la statistique, 'Madagascar. L'évolution politique et sociale de 1926 à 1937'.
123 Stephen Ellis, 'The political elite of Imerina and the revolt of the Menalamba. The creation of a colonial myth in Madagascar, 1895–1898', *Journal of African History*, 21 (1980), 221–33.
124 Francis Koerner, *Madagascar. Colonisation française et nationalisme malgache XXe siècle* (Paris: Editions l'Harmattan, 1994), 189–92.
125 Randrianja, *Société et luttes anticoloniales à Madagascar*, 153–9.
126 CAOM, GGM, 4D44, 'Madagascar. L'évolution politique et sociale'.
127 See, for example, CAOM, GGM, 6(2)D39, 'Exposés annuels sur l'activité du service de la sûreté générale, 1933–38'.
128 CAOM GGM, 6(2)D/55, Propagande révolutionnaire 1925–41, sûreté générale (Tananarive), 'Organisation du Communisme à Madagascar', 8 January 1925.
129 CAOM, GGM, 4D44, 'Madagascar. L'évolution politique et sociale'.
130 CAOM, GGM, 6(2)D/55, 'Rapport du chef de la sûreté génerale', 29 May 1929.
131 Randrianja, *Société et luttes anticoloniales à Madagascar*, 185–7.
132 Koerner, *Madagascar*, 193–4, 277–9.
133 Andrew and Kanya-Forstner, *France Overseas*, 244. There were roughly equal numbers of European officials in French Indochina and British India in the 1920s.
134 Regarding citizenship status in the four communes, see Coquery-Vidrovitch, 'Nationalité et citoyenneté en Afrique occidentale française'. Municipal councils and a *conseil général* were established in Senegal between 1872 and 1879, see H. O. Idowu, 'The establishment of elective institutions in Senegal, 1869–1880', *Journal of African History*, 9:2 (1968), 261–77. On 1 October 1916 adult male *originaires* (original inhabitants) of the four communes were granted French citizenship without any revocation of their customary rights as practising Muslims.

135 J. D. Hargreaves, 'Assimilation in eighteenth-century Senegal', *Journal of African History*, 6:2 (1965), 177–84; D. H. Jones, 'The Catholic mission and some aspects of assimilation in Senegal, 1817–1852', *Journal of African History*, 21 (1980), 323–40.
136 CAOM, 17G90, no. 2811, Direction générale des affaires politiques, 'Rapport sur l'activité de la Direction politique, 1936–1937', 22 November 1937.

PART II

An empire for the masses? Economy, colonial society and popular imperialism

CHAPTER THREE

The empire and the French economy: complementarity or divorce?

The role of colonial subjects as economic producers and consumers varied markedly between territories. The affluence of most colonies depended on rising international demand for a limited range of primary commodities. As a result, colonial economies were acutely sensitive to market fluctuations in international raw material prices. Some territories would always remain *colonies d'exploitation*, so called because of their unsuitability for European settlement as *colonies du peuplement*. The economy of French Equatorial Africa, for example, was dominated by low-cost extraction of hardwood timber and rubber. Island territories, such as Martinique, Guadeloupe and New Caledonia, with longer histories of French colonisation, were by the 1920s reliant on exports of an even narrower range of commodities: sugar and rum in the Antilles, nickel in New Caledonia, phosphates and spices from French Oceania.[1] But in key territories – Indochina, Madagascar, Senegal and French North Africa – industrial diversification wrought dramatic changes on demographic distribution, class formation and inter-communal relations. Long a major rice producer, during the mid-1920s Indochina became a major rubber exporter and the largest coal-mining centre in South East Asia. Senegal's groundnut harvest remained pivotal to local prosperity, but the colony's role as the economic hub of AOF transformed local patterns of trade, internal migration and urban growth, changes symbolised by the ascendancy of Dakar. The colonial administration in Madagascar favoured investment in mineral production and promising new export crops such as vanilla and coffee. Officials were also eager to develop the island's role as an entrepôt for merchant vessels plying the Cape route. And in North Africa, the staple agricultural exports of wine, wheat and citrus fruits employed proportionately less labour as urban industries, mining and artisan trades expanded in the decade after the First World War.[2]

An imperial economy?

The idea of a unified French imperial economy in the inter-war years is misleading. Admittedly, certain factors made for economic unity. A common system of trade protectionism applied. French exporters were guaranteed preferential access to colonial markets, first through the 1892 Méline tariff, and then through the more liberal Kircher tariffs of 1928 that reduced the duties imposed on colonial goods imported to France. As Minister of Agriculture in 1883–85, then president of the Chamber of Deputies' committee on tariffs, and, finally, as prime minister between 1896–98, Jules Méline further ensured that French peasant farmers were protected from adverse competition from their colonial counterparts.[3] The colonies were also tied into the French monetary system. After 1919 the National Bloc coalition and French Finance Ministry officials favoured the restoration of a gold standard that set the parity of the franc against a determined measure of gold. In fact, at the Genoa economic conference in 1922 Raymond Poincaré's government signed up to a gold exchange standard. It was rather different, allowing states to hold convertible currencies as a substitute for gold reserves. The move ultimately drew widespread criticism in France, firstly because it was dangerously inflationary and, secondly, because it fuelled the American-led credit boom of the 1920s that collapsed so disastrously in October 1929.[4] For much of the inter-war period, the French financial community remained deeply dissatisfied with government monetary management.

In May 1928 the National Assembly ratified the drastic currency stabilisation enacted by Poincaré's administration in December 1926. This pegged the currency at 124 francs to the pound – effectively a four-fifths devaluation as against the franc's pre-war parity. The 'franc Poincaré' lasted until the next French devaluation enacted by the left-wing Popular Front government in September 1936. In the intervening eight years, successive governments struggled to defend the franc Poincaré against further depreciation. Orthodox financial policies were pursued in the depression years: deflationary spending cuts, a diminished money supply, defence of the currency. But as other industrial nations took bolder steps, and devalued their own currencies, the franc became severely overvalued, making French exports less price-competitive.[5] As we shall see, colonial economies were severely affected by the vicissitudes of French monetary policy – the inflationary consequences of the gold exchange standard, the upheaval of the 1928 devaluation, state attachment to deflationary economics in defence of the franc Poincaré, and the shock of three further franc devaluations between 1936 and 1938.

Preoccupied by currency instability, inter-war governments took it for granted that colonies should strive for self-sufficiency, and not become a burden on the French taxpayer. This returns us to my opening point. Since the empire was tied to France's monetary system, and most colonies were reliant on the French market, does it make sense to think in terms of a French imperial economy? In my view, the short answer is no. Comparison between colonies invites vague generalisation. In some territories a cash economy was barely established. In others, exporters suffered as the franc Poincaré became overvalued, while importers and consumers acquired greater purchasing power. In several colonies the hostility of metropolitan producers to competition from colonial products posed a more fundamental problem than monetary exchange rates. Algeria's wine producers – the backbone of the colony's economy – faced unremitting opposition from their French counterparts. The Lorraine metallurgical industry monitored the progress of strip mining for iron ore in Morocco and Tunisia with ill-disguised suspicion. The Colonial Union slogan, 'Buying colonial goods is buying French goods!' had a hollow ring for French farmers contemptuous of unfamiliar foodstuff imports such as Indochinese rice or for French school-children repelled by African tapioca.[6] Yet French industrialists were neither uniformly attracted to colonial trade nor unanimously hostile to colonial industrialisation. And a minority of wealthy French farmers had agricultural interests on both sides of the Mediterranean. Here again we encounter the problem of comparability. To take an obvious example, industrial diversification in the Indochina federation in the inter-war years, albeit limited, bears little correlation to the stifling of industrial growth in sub-Saharan French Africa by metropolitan imports of manufactured goods.[7]

Colonial federations, individual colonies and even regions within these colonies were highly disparate in terms of climate, topography, ecology, economic development, the local labour market and the growth of a wage economy. A snapshot of French Indochina on the eve of the depression is instructive. The North Vietnam territory of Tonkin (Bac Bo) was charac-terised by a high population density of over 1,000 people per square kilo-metre in the Tonkin delta, an equatorial climate suited to intensive crop cultivation, and an established irrigation network. Peasant smallholders typically farmed less than two hectares of land. Sixty-two per cent owned less than one-third of a hectare. Subsistence farming, sharecropping and the limited sale of any rice or maize surplus were the norm. Annam (Trung Bo), a larger expanse of coastal territory spanning central Vietnam, was more diverse, but population density was lower, soils were generally less fertile and agricultural output was less. In the South Vietnam colony of Cochin-China (Nam Bo), even in the fertile Mekong delta, population density was lower still: less than 200 per square kilometre. There were distinct dry and wet seasons, little soil irrigation, larger landholdings, more settlers, and a fast developing network of rubber plantations. Tenant farming largely based on fixed rent payments in kind was more common than in the other Vietnamese territories. Cochin-China also produced over sixty per cent of Indochina's rice exports in the 1920s. Linked via the Mekong delta, Cambodia was climatically and agriculturally similar to Cochin-China. Laos was the most thinly populated and least developed of Indochina's territories. Most Laotian peasants were subsistence farmers.[8] Although they were taxed heavily and required to perform *corvée* labour on public works, state revenue never covered the costs of colonial administration in Laos. The development of the colonial cash economy varied markedly from territory to territory, and between town and countryside. Rural wages and land rents were often paid in rice.[9]

Table 3.1 French Indochina population figures *c.* 1930 (000)

Territories	Population	Area under cultivation (000 ha)
Tonkin	8,096	1,200
Annam	5,122	800
Cochin-china	4,484	2,300
Cambodia	2,806	800
Laos	944	400
Total	21,452	5,200

Sources Figures derived from Hanoi government-general, annual statistical returns, 1930–31. Table adapted from Irene Nørlund, 'Rice and the colonial lobby. The economic crisis in French Indochina in the 1920s and 1930s', in Peter Boomgaard and Ian Brown (eds), *Weathering the Storm. The Economies of South East Asia in the 1930s Depression* (Singapore: ISEAS, 2000), 202, table 10.1.

The two sub-Saharan federations were also markedly different in economic terms. The communications infrastructure, internal markets and skilled work force available in AOF outstripped those of AEF, although French Equatorial Africa was geographically the more extensive and resource-rich.[10] The relative affluence of lower Senegal drew economic migrants from French Sudan, whose economy remained underdeveloped and desperately poor throughout the inter-war years. Yet French Sudan was also the centre of France's ambitious cotton production policy, intended to meet metropolitan demand for cotton.[11] Conversely, throughout the inter-war period the Senegalese population was taxed more heavily than the populations of poorer AOF colonies. The larger tax burden on the wealthier colonies of Senegal, Guinea, Ivory Coast and Dahomey helped the Dakar authorities to compensate for the limited revenues of Sudan, Niger and Mauritania, and so balance the federal budget.[12] Across French West Africa temporary labour migration and more permanent internal population movements represented a complex interaction of economic pressures, agricultural cycles, and social cleavages between differing ethno-religious groups and between former slaves and freeborn persons. Population movements, critical to the development of a more politicised African labour force, cannot therefore be wholly reduced to the impact of French colonialism.[13]

With a combined population of approximately 11.5 million after the First World War, AOF was thinly populated. But AEF had only a little over 5.5 million registered inhabitants in 1924.[14] Ironically, manpower shortages were no less severe in AOF because commercial activity, most of it highly labour-intensive, was far greater. Between 1914 and 1926 the number of French firms operating in AOF rose from sixty-nine to seventy-seven. In addition, seventeen other European companies worked in the federation. Thirty-nine of these businesses exported agricultural or forestry products. Most commercial houses were based in French West Africa's major export centres such as Bamako, Conakry, Abidjan, Porto Novo, Lomé and, above all, Dakar. Two in particular towered over the rest in the inter-war years: the Société commerciale de l'Ouest Africain (SCOA) and the Compagnie française de l'Afrique Occidentale (CFAO). Both these trading companies emerged from the First World War with an expanded capital base, having supplied a range of strategic raw materials for the war effort.[15] SCOA was the largest French trading company in West Africa, and offered investors huge returns before the depression years of the early 1930s.[16] Olatunji Oloruntimehin characterises the SCOA and the CFAO thus: 'These oligopolies, between them, dwarfed the other companies by the resources at their disposal, the multiplicity of their interests, the scale of their organisations, and the important links which they had with commercial and industrial groups in France'.[17]

In AEF, too, French trading companies were overwhelmingly concentrated in the coastal regions of Gabon and French Congo. The commercial dominance of these concessionary companies at the end of the First World War reflected the paucity of public funding in AEF before the conflict began. Government hopes prior to 1914 that private trading companies would stimulate the development of France's poorest African territories were misplaced.[18] Instead, the ability of the large concessionary companies to monopolise the local market in primary exports overshadowed ineffectual state activity and marginalised African traders unable to compete with their European rivals.[19] Between 1900 and 1913 state investment in the federation averaged less than one million francs per annum. Even the total capital reserves of AEF's trading companies amounted to only 70 million, most of it spent in the coastal colonies. Before the 1930s the inland territories of Oubangui-Chari and Chad scarcely possessed a cash economy at all. Inland railway projects were abandoned, river transport was slow and inefficient, anterior roads were impassable for much of the year. In 1927 there were only 384 registered motor vehicles in the entire federation.[20] Farther north, in the Maghreb, the Algerian and Tunisian road and rail networks were still largely unconnected in 1920.[21]

Of course, if anything unified the colonial empire, it was economic subordination to France. Metropolitan trade with the colonies was, in turn, conditioned by factors outside the control of colonial governments. French producers typically looked to colonial markets when domestic or continental demand declined. The dumping of high-priced metropolitan manufactured goods in the colonies relied on the closure of the empire to cheaper alternative sources of supply. Even after the 1928 Kirsher reforms, the imperial tariff system remained weighted in favour of metropolitan purchasers and producers. This was not about to change. Government financial experts such as Louis Loucheur, the much respected former Minister of Armaments, later to become Minister of Commerce in the National Bloc coalition, warned that French industry was especially vulnerable to pressure from American and Asian competitors. By 1927 Loucheur predicted that structural unemployment in France would probably stabilise at around ten per cent. And the consequences of the franc Poincaré devaluation were still unknown. In this economic environment, generous commercial concessions to colonial producers were unlikely.[22]

Such were the conditions in which the inter-war consolidation of French empire trade took place. As French industry struggled to compete with new rivals outside Europe, the colonies became a more important refuge for otherwise uncompetitive metropolitan manufactured goods. By 1939 the empire accounted for over forty per cent of total French exports, and thirty-seven per cent of imports to France.[23] Intra-colonial commerce was also conducted to benefit the French exchequer above all. West Indian sugar, African timber and Vietnamese rubber were re-exported to other colonies, but France determined the volumes traded and the tariffs set. Conversely, colonial exporters depended on foreign shipping to carry much of their produce, the French merchant fleet being too small to handle the bulk of colonial exports. Those French industries such as textiles, metallurgical manufacturing and food refining that used colonial raw materials made concerted efforts to keep commodity prices down. Their ability to purchase these raw materials from other sources gave them additional leverage.[24]

The dreams of policy makers

After 1919 the dominant preoccupation in colonial government was to make empire pay better, whatever the background noise of high-minded imperialist sentiment and administrative debate. Colonial tutelage to France was *ipso facto* intended to serve the material interests of those that directed the process. The economic relationship between France and its colonies was constantly adjusted in an effort to reconcile the demands of the state apparatus, imperial trading companies, private sector investors and settler producers. Raising the quality of life for local populations was desirable primarily because it was economically beneficial to France. Heightened colonial efficiency, understood in terms of improved life expectancy, additional labour and increased consumer spending, was essential to sustained economic growth, creating additional opportunities for exploitation of colonial markets and resources.

In 1919 the majority of colonies remained essentially agricultural economies characterised by customary forms of land tenure based on communal, family, or lineage-based land holding. Over the next twenty years a central objective of French colonialism was to transform patterns of land ownership from communal land holding to individual tenure. Whether by choice or coercion, individual landowners were more likely to farm for profit, specifically by growing export crops, the sale of which was fundamental to the profitability of the colonial system. With few exceptions, economic calculations such as these counted for more than abstract and *passé* concepts of civilising mission.[25] Colonial administrations adopted the rhetoric of economic determinism to resolve the tension between the economic exploitation of colonial populations and the imperial obligation to 'improve the natives'. Economic modernisation would benefit all levels of colonial society as general prosperity increased over time. Put simply, this was trickle-down economics. The harsh reality of the depression years brought such platitudes crashing down, revealing instead the extent of chronic poverty and coercive labour practices in colonial economies. And as the limited sources of private finance dried up, colonial dependence on state funding increased.[26] Nowhere was this more apparent than in French Sudan, a huge landlocked territory at the northern perimeter of AOF.[27]

French Sudan was singled out for dramatic economic modernisation in the inter-war period owing to its abundance of cultivable land, its history of textile production, and its location at the heart of the Niger River system. Long-running experiments with cotton production along the middle reaches of the Niger River provoked bitter disputes between colonial officials, regional administrators, agronomists and entrepreneurs. Arguments over how best to develop French Sudan's economic potential revealed competing racial assumptions about African labour and the capacity of peasant society to assimilate modern agricultural practices. The debate over cotton production mirrored disagreements over whether the subject population should be acknowledged as rational economic actors.[28]

After 1918 the quarrel over cotton policy in French Sudan became identifiable with two distinct groups of interested parties in France and AOF. One favoured market adjustment, incentives to peasant cultivators, the systematic introduction of new cotton varieties and other state inducements to persuade local growers to switch to cotton production for export. Others, led by Emile Bélime, an official in the colonial public works department, were more successful in convincing politicians and imperial lobbyists that a massive state-backed irrigation scheme held the key to unlock the cotton-growing potential of French Sudan's savannah. Albert Sarraut incorporated Bélime's ideas within his April 1921 colonial development scheme.[29]

Funding for the Sarraut plan in general, and the Niger irrigation scheme in particular, was not immediately forthcoming. Arguments dragged on among ministers, colonial bureaucrats, industrialists and speculators over the optimum means to transform French Sudan into a cotton-rich area comparable to America's deep south. Similar efforts to turn the northern Ivory Coast into part of an AOF cotton belt became increasingly coercive. Punitive tax hikes compelled savannah farmers to increase their output of cotton, which they then had to sell at official market places.[30] On 15 March 1924 AOF governor-general Jules Carde produced a decisive policy statement endorsing long-term investment in a Niger irrigation scheme. He focused on two underlying problems that bedevilled all previous attempts to increase West African cotton production: the supply of labour for European-run cotton plantations and irrigation projects, and the projected role of African farmers as export producers. Carde had the technical expertise of a private sector consortium, the Compagnie générale des colonies, at his disposal, but acknowledged his reliance on forced labour to provide the overwhelming majority of labourers needed to bring the project to fruition. Village chiefs in surrounding regions were required to provide manual labourers to dig ditches, canal systems and dams. But Carde also recognised the countervailing arguments for greater state support of small-scale peasant enterprise. Agronomic advice to farmers, increased provision of fertilisers and higher-yield cotton crops, plus an improved communications network, were just as essential as a massive irrigation project in promoting cotton production in French Sudan.[31]

Almost eight years later, in January 1932, as AOF faced mounting economic distress, the National Assembly finally approved the establishment of a quasi-public agency, the Office du Niger. It was to oversee a massive public works scheme that would finally bring Niger irrigation to fruition.[32] Emile Bélime was appointed its director-general.[33] Loosely administered by the AOF government-general and a supervisory council in Paris, the Office du Niger is remembered more for the maltreatment and high mortality rates among its African workers than for the far-reaching colonial production drive that inspired its creation. At the time, Bélime portrayed the scheme as an ethical project dedicated to the advancement of African living standards rather than as a harsh expedient to increase cotton output.[34] In the 1920s the AOF authorities faced a severe labour shortage. The Office du Niger project was the latest in a line of economic projects whose work force was largely supplied by coercive means.[35] In addition to forced labour, the colonial authorities implemented a compulsory resettlement scheme to provide the field labourers necessary to cotton production in irrigated areas.[36] By 1936 mounting public controversy surrounding recruitment to, and conditions in, Office du Niger labour camps prompted the Popular Front to exert tighter state control over the use of African labourers.[37] With Socialists and other Popular Front supporters at the rue Oudinot and in the senior echelons of the colonial bureaucracy, Bélime and the Office du Niger board of directors were increasingly isolated, vilified for their policies and ridiculed for their failure to produce a major cotton yield in West Africa.[38]

The Office du Niger scheme indicates that pressure to increase production was not confined to the colonial periphery. After its inaugural meeting in 1925, commercial considerations dominated proceedings in the supreme colonial council. But the council's large membership made for unproductive sessions. In July 1926 it was reorganised into a number of standing committees (sections permanentes) to dispense policy advice.[39] The most influential of these sections was the economic committee, a think-tank that reported to the rue Oudinot political affairs division on the empire's immediate economic priorities. Increasingly powerful, the economic committee's conclusions were sometimes forwarded verbatim to individual colonial governments as policy proposals. The committee had recurrent preoccupations: manpower provision, intensification of agricultural production, and closer integration of metropolitan–empire trade. Such was the volume of work delegated to it by the rue Oudinot that in 1927 the economic committee was divided into five permanent sub-committees offering specialist advice on agriculture and forestry, industry and commerce, public works, mining, and tourism development.[40]

The supreme colonial council was the one official forum in which Sarraut's development schemes lived on. Council members shared Sarraut's dream of a close-knit imperial trading system founded on long-term colonial development projects and the harmonisation of colonial export production with French demands. There was, however, a marked disparity between the weight of reports produced by the council's sub-committees and their translation into tangible economic change. By the time the depression eased in 1936, the council had produced hundreds of economic modernisation plans ranging from manpower allocation and communications to electricity distribution and merchant shipping. Few were wholly implemented.[41]

One explanation for the council's failure is that it was simply wrong to assume a match between France's import requirements and the empire's supply capacity. In 1984 historian Jacques Marseille fundamentally re-evaluated the economic relationship between France and its overseas empire. He overturned existing certainties about the economic complementarity between the two. Using a wealth of statistical data, he redefined the patterns of French overseas investment, as well as of commercial and industrial trade with the colonies. In what remains the foremost study of French empire economics, Marseille concluded that the inter-war period witnessed intense competition between metropolitan raw material producers and their colonial counterparts, as well as an abiding reluctance among France's newer industries to expand into colonial markets. By contrast, uncompetitive, traditional industries increasingly relied on a captive colonial market to fill the gap created by loss of European trade. Trading companies were less dominant than is often assumed. Marseille found that the majority of colonial businesses established after 1849 engaged in mining (twenty-six per cent), plantation agriculture (twenty-four per cent) and industry (sixteen per cent).[42] The depression wrought further changes. During 1930–32 the colonies acquired unprecedented importance as sources of imports and outlets for metropolitan exports. Greater interdependence was not mutually beneficial. In the 1930s especially the increase in the colonies' share of French exports reflected the unhealthy relationship between failing metropolitan industries and the colonial market. At the same time, falling commodity prices in the depression years diminished colonial purchasing power for now sorely over-priced French goods.[43]

Table 3.2 French commerce and the colonies, 1928–32 (million francs)

Year	Grand total	Imports from/Exports to the colonies	% of overall imports
French imports			
1928	53,443,900	6,855,800	12.7
1929	58,220,600	7,008,900	11.8
1930	52,510,800	6,530,600	12.4
1931	42,205,800	6,171,700	14.6
1932	29,825,800	6,220,000	20.8
French exports			
1928	52,103,600	9,025,400	17.3
1929	50,139,100	9,448,700	18.8
1930	42,835,200	8,851,300	20.6
1931	30,835,200	7,162,000	23.5
1932	19,693,200	6,202,400	31.5

Note All figures include trade with all French overseas territories.
Source ADA, Sarraut papers, 12J174, Ministry of Colonies, Direction Economique, 3e bureau, 'Projet de loi portant organisation de l'économie coloniale et intégration de cette économie dans l'économie métropolitaine', draft, n.d. 1933.

During the 1920s French private investors looked to the empire to provide healthy returns for venture capital after the calamitous loss of the Russian market in 1917 and the more widespread disruption of European investment patterns in the First World War. More joint stock companies were established in the colonies between 1915 and 1929 than in any other period of colonial rule.[44] But investors interested in imperial investment targeted the main chance. Spectacular short-term gains could be made in colonial investments during boom years such as 1924–28, but in times of recession investment capital melted away. Commodity price falls hit commercial investors and trading companies especially hard. After the mid-1920s boom in AOF, for example, the two dominant trading companies, SCOA and CFAO, suffered dramatic losses of revenue between 1930 and 1935, and did not restore their pre-1929 capital reserves until after 1945.[45]

The West African commercial situation was mirrored elsewhere. Between 1924 and 1930 foreign investment in Indochina spiralled to 2,870 million francs, driven in part by the appreciation of the Indochinese piastre against the French gold franc.[46] Almost 700 million francs were ploughed into hugely remunerative rubber plantations, principally in Cochin-China. The resultant rubber boom caused a chronic labour shortage in Cochin-China, offset by increased use of non-contract coolie labour. Additional manpower helped *per capita* national product in southern Vietnam to surge ahead, outstripping economic growth in Tonkin.[47] After 1930 Cochin-China's speculative boom was neither sustained nor repeated.[48] Between 1926 and 1929 78,600 ha of land was devoted to rubber plantation. Between 1930 and 1935 the figure declined to 13,500 ha. This remarkable contraction was temporary. By 1936 plantation production had recovered to 126,000 ha.[49] In this instance, government support rather than venture capital underpinned the recovery of plantation agriculture, a reflection of high settler involvement in the rubber industry. Planters received 139 million francs in government subsidies and loans in 1931–32 despite a calamitous ninety-two per cent net fall in rubber prices over the preceding seven years.[50] In many ways unusual, the case of Indochina's rubber industry is still revealing. The net growth in private investment in the colonies, from under twenty per cent of total capital invested overseas in 1914 to over forty per cent by 1939, masks the sharp fluctuations between good years and bad. It also conceals the gulf between private investment in high-profit export industries such as mining and hardwood timber and the dearth of private sector interest in colonial development.[51] Only the state could fill the gap. But successive governments were unwilling or unable to meet the colonies' desperate need for capital investment, particularly during periods of recession or currency instability. Colonial public spending in the depression years targeted settler interests. The colonies were always poor, remote cousins of the metropolitan economy rather than cherished members of a grand imperial family.[52]

Marseille's findings remain persuasive. His conclusion that the overseas empire was poorly integrated into French economic planning is at one with the image of an essentially Eurocentric France, where popular imperialism remained marginal to most people's daily lives. Paradoxically, the greater importance attached to the colonial market as a vital 'reservoir' for French exporters and investors in the 1930s obscured the dominance of state investment in the empire after 1930 and the higher material costs of colonial control.[53] A constant theme running through Jacques Marseille's work is that the economic performance of colonial economies rarely matched government and Parti colonial expectations. The explanation remained the shortage of investment – both public and private. But what did this actually mean in the inter-war period? The next section addresses this question.

Economic development and investment

In 1913 the French overseas empire accounted for thirteen per cent of French exports and 9.4 per cent of French imports. In that year, colonial trade was officially valued at 1,692 million francs, putting the empire a distant third behind commerce with Britain (2,569 million) and Germany (1,936 million). The bulk of French colonial trading before the First World War was concentrated in established colonies: Algeria, Senegal, Cochin-China and the French Antilles, which together accounted for over seventy per cent of the total. One explanation for this imbalance was a January 1892 customs law that distinguished between formally assimilated colonies (Algeria, Cochin-China, the Antilles, Guiana, Réunion, Mayotte, New Caledonia and, after 1897, Madagascar) and other non-assimilated territories. The former grouping acquired preferential trading rights with France, but was obliged to impose French tariff rates on all foreign imports. Jacques Marseille concludes that contemporary perceptions of the empire as a vital reserved market had more enduring impact in metropolitan politics than the dismal reality of limited economic compatibility between France and its colonies. Misperceptions also stemmed from the fact that in the early 1900s France exported more goods to the empire than were imported from it. Capital investment in colonial production was vital to correct this trade imbalance. The Ministry of Colonies set about the task in the 1900s, but a decade of state investment peaked in 1909. By that point the rate of growth in French colonial trade exceeded that of the British empire, although overall trade volume was far smaller.[54]

The pre-1914 trend toward greater public investment and tighter government regulation of capital movements within the empire prefigured the dominance of state funding agencies in colonial trade between the wars.

Without public sector spending to mask the fact, the reality of diminishing French industrial reliance on empire trade would have been more apparent in the inter-war years. In 1920–21, for instance, metropolitan demand for colonial raw materials collapsed. During the First World War French requirements for strategic raw materials and colonial foodstuffs had expanded. In 1919 colonial exporters still anticipated high profits from the wartime disruption of international markets and the brief post-war boom in France. They were soon disappointed. The resultant crisis of overproduction led to catastrophic falls in commodity prices. The metric tonne value of West African groundnuts, palm oil and cane sugar declined by anything from fifty to eighty per cent between April 1920 and May 1921. Although this downturn was short-lived, it lent weight to Albert Sarraut's arguments for long-term public sector investment to underpin colonial development.[55]

It was one thing to secure theoretical Cabinet support for infrastructure development and the diversification of colonial economies. It was quite another to win parliamentary backing for the expenditure involved. Sarraut kept *mise en valeur* in the public eye during his 1920–24 term at the rue Oudinot, but he did not fundamentally alter the mechanisms of imperial trade. By 1929 the empire's 12.5 per cent share of French import trade was only 2.5 per cent greater than in 1913. Over the same period French exports to the colonies climbed from fourteen to nineteen per cent, hardly the dramatic rise that Sarraut anticipated.[56] These small increases in the volume of exports to the colonies were easily accounted for. Colonial markets had become a safety net for declining French industries faced with unfilled domestic and European order books. Prominent examples included sugar refining, cotton weaving, soap making and the metallurgical industry. Jacques Marseille singles out one formerly large-scale employer, the French copper smelting industry, and one traditional artisan producer, the Marseilles candle-making industry, as examples of very different concerns that relied on colonial markets for their post-war survival.[57]

The impact of the depression between 1931 and 1935 led France's larger industrial producers to look on colonial territory as a solution to their loss of export markets elsewhere. The decline of international trade after the Wall Street Crash of October 1929 did not affect metropolitan France as rapidly as its principal industrial neighbours, Germany and Britain. France avoided forced devaluation in the early depression years, remaining the bastion of the 'gold bloc' states whose currencies remained tied to a gold standard. Between 1928 and 1932 Paris was a favoured destination for capital investors attracted by France's attachment to gold.[58]

Ultimately, the comparative strength of the franc was a poisoned chalice, especially for colonial economies dependent on overseas trade in primary products to assure their solvency. As one state after another devalued to cope with protracted recession in the early 1930s, so the gold-linked franc became increasingly overvalued, making colonial export products artificially expensive to former purchasers.[59] Key trade partners such as the United States, Britain and Japan either sharply reduced their commodity purchases in response to falling domestic industrial and consumer demand or sought cheaper sources of supply. The fate of colonial silk production illustrates the point. Producers of raw silk in Lebanon and Cambodia were devastated by the depression. Tied to the fortunes of the Lyons silk industry and the city's influential chamber of commerce, colonial silk makers were left high and dry when the Lyons Compagnie générale des soies cut back production.[60] Foreign demand for luxury products plummeted as the economic crisis deepened in North America, Western Europe and Turkey. Expansion of nylon production during the 1930s added to the problem. And once economic conditions improved from 1933 silk producers in Japan undercut their competitors in Beirut, Mount Lebanon and Phnom Penh because the Lebanese pound and the Indochinese piastre were tied to an overvalued franc.[61]

Wealthier Lebanese landowners could afford to replace mulberry trees with citrus or olive groves, but the wives of poor farmers, many of whom raised silkworms for essential supplementary income, lacked the means to diversify. Before the First World War over 12,000 women worked in silk mills in the towns of Mount Lebanon. By 1930 the figure was already down to approximately 3,000.[62] The Cambodian silk industry fared little better. Silk manufacturing in Phnom Penh was subordinated not only to metropolitan requirements but to the internal Indochina market as well. Cambodian manufacturers were obliged to buy silk cocoons farmed in Tonkin. By 1927 these cocoons cost an average twenty per cent more than their Chinese equivalents. Doubly disadvantaged, the Cambodian silk industry struggled to compete.[63] Once the depression struck Cambodia, the colonial government chose to invest in expanded maize production rather than attempt to revive the fortunes of the protectorate's beleaguered silk industry.[64] Meanwhile, the Lyons Chamber of Commerce increasingly viewed Indochina as a market for consumption rather than a producer of raw silk. Alarmed by rising Japanese competition, by 1934 the Lyonnais silk industry was pressing for greater protectionist measures to reserve the Indochina market to Lyons's refined silk products.[65] Ironically, colonial producers' inability to sell on international markets owing to the overvalued franc resulted in greater colonial trade dependence on France.[66] In 1929 France accounted for thirty-five per cent of the external trade of the Indochina federation. After the disastrous revaluation of the piastre in 1930 this proportion grew rapidly. Vital international markets were lost and strong protectionist tariffs remained in place, deterring Japanese inward investment in particular.[67] By 1935 France accounted for fifty per cent of all goods exports from Indochina. This increase did not signify complementarity between France and Indochina, but rather the inability of Indochina's exporters to break into other international markets.[68] Indochina faced an additional problem, the strength of the piastre against the Chinese currency, until the piastre was eventually devalued on 6 October 1936.[69] Here again, the suspension of piastre convertibility against gold in 1936 was designed to reduce the cost to France of essential Indochinese imports rather than to help Indochina's exporters recover market share in China.[70]

Declining global trade made commodity markets more price-competitive. Export producers fought harder to secure contracts, and accepted reduced profit margins or even short-term losses to sustain trading relationships. Colonial exporters therefore reduced their production costs wherever possible. In West Africa's plantations, Equatorial Africa's lumber camps, and Tonkin's anthracite mines, cutting labour costs proved the easiest means to economise. Reduced wages, deteriorating employment conditions and greater use of cheaper non-contract labour became the norm. By 1930 colonial administrations in French West Africa, Madagascar, the Antilles, and the Indochina federation no longer enjoyed the large budgetary surpluses built up between 1924–29 by high export volumes and limited public spending. As global demand for primary products diminished, smaller colonies with proportionately larger budgetary reserves, such as the French Indian enclaves, were better able to withstand the collapse in exports.[71] It was a different story in the colonial federations. There was widespread famine across AOF in 1931, and chronic food shortages elsewhere.[72] French industry also opposed any increase in colonial import tariffs, denying colonial governments a vital alternative source of short-term funding.[73] A snapshot of the AOF federal budget in the years leading up to and including the depression (Table 3.3) illustrates the fall in Treasury reserves and the cuts in federal expenditure that followed, particularly in 1933.

Table 3.3 Federal budget of Afrique Occidentale Française, 1928–33 (francs)

Budget year	Revenue	Expenditure	Recorded surplus	Recorded deficit
1928	297,107,380	210,568,494	86,538,886	
1929	282,243,077	235,288,320	46,954,757	
1930	313,188,785	282,496,387	30,692,398	
1931	252,384,588	311,185,052		58,800,464
1932	291,071,602	285,275,203	5,796,399	
1933	213,718,000	204,718,000	9,000,000	

Source CAOM, affpol/73, no. 473, Sénat Commission des Colonies, 'Rapport par Senateur Adolphe Messimy, séance du 26 juin 1934'.

In AEF the situation was rather different. The volume of trade conducted in AEF averaged only twenty per cent that of AOF. And trade volume in Equatorial Africa did not recover to the 1913 level until 1928. The imbalance between AEF's export trade and its tiny internal market for imported goods impeded economic growth. And the French government was not well placed to regulate AEF export prices. The bulk of the federation's rubber exports was traded in Antwerp, alongside the far larger quantities of rubber imported from the Belgian Congo. Similarly, most AEF hardwoods were shipped direct to the Hamburg timber market.[74] French Equatorial Africa did not so much descend into economic crisis after 1931 as merely return to the adverse economic conditions of the preceding decade. When the recession came to an end in 1936 *per capita* social spending on the AEF population was the lowest in colonial Africa, with the sole exception of the Togoland and Cameroon mandates.[75] But this sorry statistic was nothing new.

The overwhelming priority attached to export production, the reliance on a numerically small settler population to sustain a local monetary economy, and the poverty of colonial spending on the indigenous population that characterised the AEF economy in the 1920s was equally applicable to the French Pacific territories. A dynamic new governor, Georges Guyon, arrived in New Caledonia in early 1925. He invested heavily in public works at Nouméa and improved the road system on the Grand Terre. With a population of only 49,000 in 1930, New Caledonia's tiny fiscal base precluded major social spending. Between 1925 and 1929 Guyon relied on a combination of Bank of Indochina loans and stringent cuts in administrative costs to sustain his development programme.[76] The smaller islands of French Oceania, including the New Hebrides and Tahiti, were yet more vulnerable to the collapse of global commodity prices. The New Hebrides was dependent on capital investment from New Caledonia. And falling prices for Tahitian staples such as copra, coffee and vanilla were compounded by the island's nugatory commercial links with France.[77] Even in the archetypal colonial paradise the depression years were a disaster.

Between 1930 and 1935 successive centre-right governments in France followed a deflationary path out of depression. The one exception to this – Edouard Herriot's second short-lived Cartel des gauches Cabinet – held office for only six months between June and December 1932. Herriot also accepted the need for expenditure cuts, but encountered objections from his own supporters. The Cartel's attempt to cut budgetary expenditure by 5 billion francs over the two fiscal years 1932–33 fell foul of Radical and Socialist Party opposition in the National Assembly. After this body blow the coalition was decidedly unadventurous in economic policy.[78] More generally, between 1930 and 1935 government ministers, Ministry of Colonies planners and the influential parliamentary finance commissions expected overseas administrations to implement large expenditure cuts to keep colonial deficits in check. This was hardly unexpected. More remarkable was the extent to which colonial governors resisted demands for cutbacks in administrative spending. Personnel costs consumed between thirty and forty-five per cent of individual colonial budgets. In France, with a population of approximately 39.5 million, the cost of public administration absorbed closer to ten per cent of state revenue in 1931. In Tunisia, a small territory with 2.4 million inhabitants, the 1931 figure was forty-one per cent.[79]

In AEF administrative costs were proportionately larger still. The entire federation budget was not much larger than that of Senegal or Martinique. Yet AEF subjects supported five individual colonial governments in addition to the federal bureaucracy in Brazzaville. On 30 June 1934 Pierre Laval, then Minister of Colonies in Gaston Doumergue's government of national unity, proposed a fundamental reorganisation. AEF's colonial governors were to be reduced in status – and salary – to 'administrators-in-chief'. The federal government in Brazzaville was to become a unitary authority – effectively the solitary colonial government for AEF. Staff reductions were recommended throughout. Typically, although Laval's cost-cutting plan was passed into law, his plans were frustrated by bureaucratic obstructionism at the rue Oudinot and in Brazzaville.[80]

Colonial governors defended high expenditure on administrative services as the by-product of economic modernisation. Public works projects, educational provision, efficient policing and improved tax collection all added to the personnel payroll. In short, good government was expensive.[81] The flaws in this self-serving argument were easily discerned: it cut across the associationist ideal of indigenous involvement in colonial administration, it ignored the injustice of colonial officials paid on French wage scales but supported by native taxpayers, and it elided the fact that bureaucratic costs precluded substantial investment in colonial development.

As we have seen, the economic buoyancy of most colonial economies rested on maintaining high levels of export trade in a limited range of primary products. Understanding the depression in individual colonies requires a grasp of price fluctuations in key commodities. In 1928 rice accounted for sixty-nine per cent of Indochina's total export produce. By 1930 Indochina produced a quarter of the rice sold on the global market, and was China's principal rice supplier.[82] So the developing economic crisis in the federation was, above all, a rice crisis.[83] In AEF, Gabon colony went into deficit in 1932 as global demand for hardwood timber declined. Senegal also recorded budget deficits in 1932 and 1933 after groundnut prices crashed and the colony's main depots and ports fell idle.[84] Even more commercially diverse colonies still relied on exports of a solitary product. Algerian wine, Moroccan ores, Lebanese silk: all were mainstays of economies that were, by the standard of other French colonies, diversified. Madagascar initially escaped the worst of the depression because it exported a wide range of foodstuffs, spices and minerals. Demand for Madagascan graphite, maize and coffee held up in 1932–34. But by 1935 the general index of Madagascan trade revealed a steep fall in exports.[85]

In 1932 the Senate finance commission warned the Ministry of Colonies that during the preceding decade colonial governments had drawn too heavily on their limited budgetary reserves to fund public works. Colonial treasuries were empty, and the National Assembly would not vote short-term loan issues sufficient to fund public spending at previous rates. In February the previous year the National Assembly approved colonial loans totalling 3.9 billion francs. It would not do so again in a time of recession. The solution was to export more aggressively and raise taxes on colonial populations. Increased direct taxation of settler traders and landowners was identified as an immediate priority, since colonial labourers already faced a crushing tax burden. Yet colonial employers often recouped extra monies paid in tax by cutting wages.[86]

In these straitened times, the old island colonies attracted proportionately greater state support than the large colonial federations. In May 1931 the French Senate voted a 359 million franc loan to underwrite public works projects in Martinique, Guadeloupe, Guiana and Réunion started before the depression took hold. Two factors explain the continuation of state loan funding here. One was that the *vieilles colonies* were administered much like French departments, a distinct advantage when long-term infrastructure spending was contemplated. In Guadeloupe, for example, the authorities stuck to a twelve-year development plan funded from ordinary budget revenue, state loans and a disaster relief fund established after the island suffered a devastating hurricane on 12 September 1928. These monies covered road construction, water purification plants, the expansion of Pointe-à-Pitre port, and new government buildings, but left only 36.5 million francs for public health and education in a budgetary programme totalling 343.6 million francs.[87]

The revenue base of the island colonies was so small that they faced chronic deficits once demand for their staple exports collapsed. This was the second factor that helped assure them longer-term state support. Guadeloupe sugar was one such export commodity. The availability of cheaper sugar exports from Cuba and British West Indian colonies, the damage to refineries during the 1928 hurricane, and the recovery of French sugar beet production interrupted by the Great War, all contributed to greater state indulgence to the island's loan requirements.[88] The Indian Ocean island of Réunion also received a 63 million franc emergency loan in May 1931 to cover an otherwise unsustainable deficit. By contrast, New Caledonia avoided severe deficit problems because of buoyant demand for its two principal exports, nickel and chrome.[89] New Caledonia's nickel production broadly matched French and Belgian needs in the early 1930s. And the island's chrome was traded on the London commodities market, where demand increased once Britain and the United States emerged from the trough of depression in 1933.[90]

The economic exceptionalism of the old island colonies reminds us that none of the French governments in office during the depression years implemented an empire-wide economic recovery plan comparable to Britain's adoption of imperial preference under the Ottawa Agreement. In one sense, they had no need to do so. Imperial tariffs and colonial protectionism were always integral to French management of empire trade. But at no stage were such measures systematically revised to create a more coherent imperial trading bloc. Gaston Doumergue's government considered this option briefly in 1934, but abandoned an imperial preference scheme in the face of concerted opposition from the agricultural sector. France's wheat farmers, wine growers and fruit cultivators railed against cheaper colonial produce flooding the domestic market.[91] With minimal state intervention to prevent it, the empire sank further into depression between 1933 and 1935. In April 1934 Brazzaville governor-general Antonetti advised Pierre Laval to cancel plans to establish a colonisation service for AEF linked to the existing overseas settlement bureau, the Association nationale des colons français. Antonetti insisted that it was irresponsible to encourage French families to settle in Equatorial Africa in such dire times. Planned expenditure on the colonisation service was reallocated to two government agricultural specialists working in Brazzaville and Pointe-Noire to help strug-gling planters find new markets for their produce.[92]

One alternative to increasing the demands placed on colonial workers was to improve the infrastructure within colonial territory. Better commu-nications reduced transport costs, facilitated the export of perishable com-modities and promoted inter-colonial trade between neighbouring territories. Such a holistic, Keynesian approach to the economic slowdown was never seriously entertained. Instead, declining investment in communications networks was mirrored in colonial transport services. Most intra-colonial transport systems from the Damascus tram network to the rail systems of the colonial federations were privately owned corporations answerable to large-scale investors in France. Executive directors, conscious of investor pressure for retrenchment, tried to safeguard their companies without making demands for extra money on nervous shareholders back home. The temptation in periods of economic difficulty was to cut back rather than to risk new investment. One such case was the Dakar–Niger–Thiès railway. After four years of rising profits, in 1929 the railway company recorded a deficit. In 1930 the railway registered its worst losses of 10,418,168 francs after reducing business tariffs in a bid to maintain the volume of railway traffic transported through Senegal. The deficit triggered investor alarm, and capital investment in AOF's main rail company declined over the next four years.[93]

Only in exceptional cases did the colonial authorities fill the gap left by private corporations in recession. State involvement in the Office du Niger project increased in the early depression years. Similarly, the Brazzaville government bailed out the Compagnie générale des transports en Afrique (CGTA) in 1935, paying compensation for export products the CGTA transported at a loss. In this case, state support both ensured the solvency of the business and saved its main clients: settler rubber planters and timber exporters facing ruin.[94] None the less, such intervention was highly unusual. Colonial public works projects, for instance, were financed by a combination of state loan provision, construction and engineering company investment, and colonial taxation revenue. The French population might choose to invest in such schemes, but they could not be obligated to finance them through metropolitan taxes. The basic principle that colonies should pay their own way was inviolate. Hence the reliance on public loan issues raised on the Paris Bourse. However, state loan capital was less forthcoming in the 1930s. Loan issues were fundamental to early development schemes in Indochina before 1914, but declined as a proportion of public spending after the First World War. State loans accounted for 14.9 per cent of budgetary spending in Hanoi between 1915 and 1929, but for only 8.2 per cent between 1936 and 1940.[95] In Morocco, too, loan capital dried up after 1932. This compared with five major loan issues between 1916 and 1932 of between 242 million and 1,535 million francs, which funded vital public works including extensions to the port of Casablanca and a Moroccan telephone network.[96]

Elsewhere, state funding for public works resumed once the clouds of depression began to lift. In French West Africa Jules Brévié's federal administration injected funds into major infrastructure projects in late 1934. Extensive dredging of the Senegal River facilitated communications within Senegal, and between Senegal and Guinea. A long-term dock construction programme promised to increase the commercial capacity of key AOF ports. Building of an inter-colonial road network linking Senegal, Guinea and Ivory Coast continued apace. But in 1934–35 the AOF administration invested more heavily in railway development than road construction. 1,680 km of new track were laid between 1924–34 to create a more integrated rail system. Sixty-one additional locomotives and 370 freight wagons were brought into service in AOF between 1924 and 1930.[97] Additional rolling stock was imported to Guinea, enabling the colony's banana producers to export their crop through Abidjan within twenty-four hours of cutting. Railway development in Dahomey narrowed the economic gap separating the more prosperous coastal region between Porto Novo and Cotonou from the poverty of Dahomey's northern reaches.[98]

In the inter-war period as a whole, French corporate and private investors favoured projects offering high short-term gain, concentrating on primary products that could be gathered cheaply and that involved no secondary production costs. For instance, the export value of the rubber harvested in Cochin-China's plantations climbed by almost 300 per cent in the boom years of 1921–25. The resultant profits were largely repatriated to France. Even the major holding companies with longer-term commercial stakes in Indochina's plantation sector, such as the Société indochinoise de commerce, d'agriculture et de finances (set up in 1919) and the Franco-Belgian Société financière des caoutchoucs (founded in 1909), distributed most of their profits as shareholder dividends. Reinvestment in the rubber industry came a poor second. The wholesale withdrawal of French industry and capital that gathered pace in the Indochina war between 1946 and 1954 did not originate in the inter-war period. But Indochina's trading relationship with metropolitan France was always asymmetric. Money earned by foreign investors in Indochina rarely stayed there.[99]

Currency, banking and capital

The colonies' economic subordination to France, so apparent in the depression years, was facilitated by imposition of common monetary systems. Some territories, Algeria among them, were linked with France by customs unions dating from the nineteenth century. These colonies were especially reliant on the French import market. By late 1930 only the *anciennes colonies* of Martinique, Guadeloupe, French Guiana and Réunion were not tied to the gold standard, or its near equivalent, the gold exchange standard. In 1884 Algeria's economic subsidiarity to France was confirmed by the extension of customs union arrangements that reserved the conduct of bilateral trade to French merchant vessels. By 1920 Algeria was France's foremost colonial trade partner.[100] By 1938 France absorbed eighty-four per cent of Algeria's exports.[101]

In the 1920s common currencies – or at least commonly transferable currencies – were in general use throughout the empire. In some territories the introduction of the franc – or a franc-convertible equivalent – was very recent indeed. In 1920 the Moroccan state bank, controlled by shareholders of the Banque de Paris et des Pays-Bas, issued notes denominated in francs to replace the former currency, the hassani. Two years later the Moroccan franc was set at parity with its French equivalent.[102] By mid-decade the franc was in circulation in all dependent territories, with three exceptions – the Syrian–Lebanese pound, the Indochinese piastre and the roupee in France's Indian enclaves. In January 1924 the Beirut high commission linked the value of the Syrian–Lebanese pound to the franc in agreement with the newly founded Bank of Syria and Lebanon. After the regional economic dislocation occasioned by the First World War, the uprooting of Faisal's regime in Damascus, and the rupture of trade links with Turkey, it was only in 1923 that Syria's export economy began to recover. Exports increased threefold in the twelve months from May 1923. In the longer term, however, confidence in the Syrian–Lebanese pound deteriorated as the value of the franc plummeted between 1924 and 1926.[103] Resentment at the diminishing purchasing power of Syria's currency hardened opposition to France among the Sunni elite during the Great Revolt in 1925.[104] The Syrian–Lebanese pound lost sixty-four per cent of its exchange value against the US dollar over the twenty years from the establishment of the mandate in 1920.[105]

Events followed a similar course in Indochina. After 1926 the piastre was linked to the value of the devalued franc Poincaré. On 31 May 1930 the piastre was also tied to the gold standard, instigating a fall in its real value.[106] The currency was previously tied to the silver standard prevalent in East Asia, thanks to which the rate of exchange between piastres and francs increased by 633 per cent between 1915 and 1921 alone.[107] On 9 September 1934 the piastre was devalued again. A 'new piastre' came into circulation, its gold value reduced by twenty-five per cent against its pre-September equivalent. Following another piastre devaluation in 1936, the council of governors in Indochina lobbied for a reduction in import tariffs to compensate for the currency's diminished purchasing power. In 1937 they secured a reduction to thirteen per cent in the tariffs applied to Indochina's imports. Clearly, the piastre's loss of value was driven by the three successive franc devaluations between 1936 and 1938 rather than by changes in local economic conditions.[108] Only in French India was the local currency outside French control, hostage instead to the economic fortunes of the Raj. France regulated the use of the franc in all other colonies. The picture was completed during 1928 and 1929 when the Moroccan and Tunisian protectorates came into line with these currency regulations.[109]

Colonial banks, mutual societies and agricultural lending agencies also developed along broadly similar lines throughout the empire, serving French shareholders, trading companies and settler agriculturalists before diversifying – usually in response to state pressure – to provide limited capital facilities to indigenous traders and farmers. The first modern French colonial banks were established in Martinique, Guadeloupe and Réunion in July 1851. A month later the Bank of Algeria began operations. National colonial banks were subsequently created in French Guiana (1854), Senegal (1854), Indochina (1875), Morocco (1906), Syria (1924) and Madagascar (1925). All were closely tied to the French state, with the sole exception of the internationally regulated Bank of Morocco. The French Treasury guaranteed the liquidity of the national colonial banks, and the Finance

Ministry kept a tight rein on empire banking. Colonial bank presidents and senior directors were appointed by decree, and the Ministries of Finance and of Colonies vetted the nomination of branch managers. These two ministries also controlled the state regulatory authority for colonial banking, the Commission de surveillance des banques coloniales. Few colonial banks confined their operations to their colony of origin. By the early 1900s the Bank of Algeria had a strong presence in Tunisia. The Bank of Indochina set up branches in French India, French Somaliland, New Caledonia and French Oceania, in addition to its eleven branches in the Indochina federation in 1940. Traders in Equatorial Africa relied on French West African commercial banks to conduct much of their business. The tiny islands of Saint-Pierre et Miquelon off the Newfoundland coast were the sole colony without a local bank to issue currency.[110]

Governmental willingness to allow commercial banks the right to issue currency afforded these institutions enormous leverage within the colonial economy. The pattern was similar in those territories with a functioning stock market. A Beirut stock exchange began trading in 1920. Over the next decade, stock transactions were confined to seven investment houses, of which five were under French management, and two were Lebanese. During the 1930s the number of investment houses in Lebanon grew to twelve. Trading on the Beirut exchange was tied to the operations of the Paris Bourse, but was otherwise largely unregulated.[111] Indeed, the absence of financial controls and large short-term dividends were precisely what drew foreign capital investors. But the colonial banks were more central to individual colonial economies than stock market activity. With large capital reserves and a dual role as a retail bank and a bank of issue, the colonial banks influenced the availability of credit, the scale of commercial transactions, and the local money supply. This may be seen from table 3.4, which highlights the pivotal role of the Bank of Syria and Lebanon as a holder of capital in inter-war Lebanon.

Table 3.4 Principal holders of French capital in Lebanon during the mandate

Banks and utilities	Capital holdings (FF million)
Banque de Syrie et du Liban	300
Compagnie algérienne	267.30
Crédit Foncier d'Algérie et de Tunisie	125
Electricité de Beyrouth	75
Compagnie du port, des quais, et entrepôts de Beyrouth	16
Compagnie française du chemin de fer DHP	15

Source Adapted from Mohamed Amine el Hafez, La Structure et la politique économique en Syrie et au Liban (Beirut, 1953), 48.

Proponents of this closely integrated currency and banking system insisted that it facilitated intra-colonial commerce, as virtually the entire empire constituted a single monetary market. To these observers a common currency, much like a shared language, was fundamental to the development of a francophone imperial culture.[112] The major colonial banks were also important adjuncts of the state. Their directors discussed financial conditions, market prospects and capital issues with government officials.[113] When Indochina's major stock holding company, the Société française financière et coloniale, faced insolvency in 1930, André Tardieu's government persuaded the Banque de l'Indochine to save it.[114] Local opposition to the colonial monetary system was generally muted. Most colonies were essentially cash economies in which bank accounts, cheques and large-scale forward lending were the sole preserve of settlers and the indigenous commercial elite. Indochina was the major exception. The federation suffered acutely because the piastre–franc linkage put the currency out of step with other, similar economies in South East Asia that abandoned the gold or silver standard in the early 1930s. Indochina measured up better against the African colonial federations in the diversity of its savings institutions. Between 1925 and 1927 Alexandre Varenne, the first Socialist governor-general in Hanoi, pioneered small-scale savings schemes for peasant labourers, miners and factory workers, as well as insurance payments for industrial injury funded by employers' contributions. A former journalist, Varenne made his political reputation as a proponent of the income tax legislation introduced in France just before the First World War. He applied his understanding of fiscal reform to map out the framework of a social security system in Indochina. In the spirit of these earlier reforms, in July 1931 the Hanoi government introduced central regulation of seven insurance schemes, pension funds, public housing trusts and a rudimentary farmers' co-operative bank.[115]

Differential access to credit was a glaring source of discrimination in colonial economies. Borrowing money to fund the purchase of additional land, livestock or equipment presented insuperable problems for peasant cultivators from Tonkin to Morocco.[116] Usury rates were prohibitively high. And French agricultural lending agencies, such as the Crédit agricole, lent almost exclusively to settler farmers. In Algeria, European landowners enjoyed preferential access to the Caisse algérienne de Crédit agricole mutuelle, an agricultural co-operative bank modelled on its French equivalent. Moreover, settler cultivators had first call on the limited state funds set aside to assist farmers in poor harvest years. Such was the case in Constantine in 1920 after the failure of the wheat and barley crops. European farmers quickly restocked with seed for the coming year thanks to support from the Caisse régionale de Constantine. Algerian farmers were excluded. Numerous Muslim smallholders lost their livelihood while, for the most part, their European neighbours did not.[117]

A comparable process occurred in Tunisia and Morocco. The combination of falling market prices, recurrent harvest failure and limited borrowing facilities for Muslim farmers other than traditional usury left *indigène* cultivators facing ruin in the early 1930s. Creditors called in agricultural loans. Peasant smallholders were unable to pay land rents and tax demands. Those that continued farming were too poor to invest in the equipment, fertilisers or irrigation systems necessary to improve their yields. Prices for soft wheat, a Maghreb export staple, fell by fifty-five per cent between 1930 and 1933.[118] This was emblematic of policy failure: the North African administrations had invested heavily in wheat cultivation during the 1920s, aiming to turn the region into France's 'breadbasket'.[119] Once again settlers came first. When Tunisian wheat prices tumbled further in 1934 the Tunis government set a minimum wheat price to safeguard settler producers. Nothing was done to maintain olive oil prices, which had fallen by thirty-nine per cent over eight years, even though at least a third of Tunisia's Muslim population was supported by olive cultivation.[120] Contraction of the French North African agricultural sector reverberated through the region's economies. Opportunities for alternative employment in the mining and construction sectors fell away as these industries went into recession. The French authorities encouraged commercial managers to hire unemployed Europeans over local Muslims.[121] Proposals to establish farmers' co-operatives and agricultural banks backed by guaranteed state funding fell foul of the government's deflationary priorities.[122] Rural poverty in Tunisia was especially severe, and mirrored the decline of the country's phosphate mining industry. In 1929 Tunisia accounted for twenty-three per cent of global phosphate production. In 1937 the figure fell to seventeen per cent. Muslim smallholders, peasant sharecroppers, and miners were left destitute.[123]

The demands of European producers in French North Africa's agricultural market economy drowned out the more urgent needs of the Muslim peasant majority.[124] The emergence of *grand colon* estate owners exacerbated this trend. By 1930 almost seventy-five per cent of the total agricultural land in European hands had been consolidated into large farm estates. With better land, more capital and a cheap labour supply, settler farmers achieved far higher agricultural output per hectare. Having produced far more than their Muslim counterparts, they were less sensitive to price pressures when crops were sold.[125] The radicalisation of the North African countryside in the depression years was rooted in these economic pressures. The duality of the agricultural economy in colonial Algeria, wherein European farmers increasingly determined the economic activity of the Muslim peasantry, was replicated in the coastal cities. In Algeria's urban centres the settler population controlled industry, banking and export commerce. David Prochaska makes this abundantly clear in his pioneering study of Bône (now Annaba). Bône was very much a colonial city. Europeans outnumbered Muslims by at least two to one throughout the years 1848–1926. And the racial divide shaped the city's entire economic life:

> The chief distinguishing characteristic of the colonial Annaba economy was economic dualism. Taking the economy as a whole, commerce predominated over industry, the service sector overshadowed manufacturing. The main economic fault line ran, however, along ethnic lines, splitting Europeans from Algerians. Both had their industrial as well as commercial sectors, but the main point is that the European economy can be likened by and large to a company-centred, capitalist economy, while the Algerian economy can be compared to a bazaar-oriented, pre-capitalist economy.[126]

Conclusion

Increased trade dependence between France and the colonies in the decade after 1927 was driven by loss of export markets elsewhere rather than by significant net growth in colonial economies. In 1928 the colonial empire became France's most important trading partner. Once the depression hit the French economy in 1930–31 the empire served as a *réservoir colonial*, providing raw material resources and a captive market to metropolitan industries confronted with empty order books. The profits generated by colonial export trade became more vital to the French economy. And the ability to sell French products on French terms to French colonial subjects was critical to manufacturers unable to sell high-priced French goods elsewhere. In the longer term, however, this did neither France nor the colonies much good. Uncompetitive home industries limped on, thanks to the colonial market. And diversification in colonial economies was stunted by reliance on imported French manufactures. By 1930 the 'divorce' that Jacques Marseille identified between the long-term economic interests of France and the preservation of a closed colonial market system had begun.[127]

A number of colonies registered large increases in export volume after 1935. Budgetary income expanded markedly as economic recovery generated additional indirect tax revenue. The surge in colonial production in the immediate pre-war years confirmed how low previous output figures had been rather than indicating significant new productive capacity within colonial economies. Take Madagascar. Its external trade climbed from 588,774,000 francs in 1935 to 733,447,000 in 1936, a rise of twenty per cent. In the first six months of 1937 a further seventeen per cent increase was achieved. Deposits in the colony's banks showed similar improvements. None the less the preceding economic crisis had left its mark in business failures, lost markets and the worsened poverty of Madagascar's wage labourers.[128] Moreover, colonial industrialisation was in its infancy. In 1938 foodstuffs accounted for sixty-five per cent of colonial exports. And the fortunes of colonial markets were tied to the strength of the French economy through tariffs, customs agreements and currency use.[129]

It was left to the Third Republic's successors to pick up the pieces. In April 1944 the Free French Commissioner for Colonies, René Pleven, reminded the AEF government that a key objective of the Brazzaville conference four months earlier was to reverse the previous twenty-five years of governmental neglect and under-investment in sub-Saharan Africa especially.[130] The problems were just as daunting in those colonies where economic growth was more pronounced. Between the wars, greater urbanisation and industrial employment, declining infant mortality rates and increased life expectancy fed popular demand for education, better jobs, improved working conditions and tangible freedoms. As we shall see in the next chapter, French economic policies generated social change that proved impossible to contain.

Notes

1 Bouche, *Histoire de la colonisation française* II, chapter 4. In island territories a handful of large corporations typically cornered the local commodity export market. For example, phosphate mining in French Oceania was largely controlled by the Compagnie française des phosphates de l'Océanie.

2 Thobie *et al.*, *Histoire de la France coloniale*, 148–54.

3 Thomas F. Power, *Jules Ferry and the Renaissance of French Imperialism* (New York: Octagon Books, 1977), 29; Persell, *The French Colonial Lobby*, 129–31.

4 Kenneth Mouré, *Managing the Franc Poincaré. Economic Understanding and Political Constraint in French Monetary Policy, 1928–1936* (Cambridge: Cambridge University Press, 1991), 32–6.

5 Kenneth Mouré's introduction to the problems of the depression and French currency adjustment is invaluable: see *Managing the Franc Poincaré*, 1–45.

6 Ageron, *France coloniale ou parti colonial?* (Paris: Presses Universitaires de France, 1978), 255.

7 Irene Nørlund, 'The French Empire, the colonial state in Vietnam and economic policy, 1885–1940', *Australian Economic History Review*, 31:1 (1991), 72–89.

8 Irene Nørlund, 'Rice and the colonial lobby. The economic crisis in French Indochina in the 1920s and 1930s', in Peter Boomgaard and Ian Brown (eds), *Weathering the Storm. The Economies of South East Asia in the 1930s Depression* (Singapore: ISEAS, 2000), 201–11.

9 Pierre Brocheux, 'The state and the 1930s depression in French Indochina', in Boomgaard and Brown, *Weathering the Storm*, 252.

10 Catherine Coquery-Vidrovitch, *Le Congo au temps des grands compagnies concessionaires 1898–1930* (Paris: Mouton, 1972), 522–5.

11 The origins and eventual failure of *la politique cotonnière* are examined in Richard L. Roberts, *Two Worlds of Cotton. Colonialism and the Regional Economy in the French Sudan, 1800–1946* (Stanford CA: Stanford University Press, 1996).

12 CAOM, affpol/73, no. 473, Sénat Commission des Colonies, 'Rapport par Senateur Adolphe Messimy, séance du 26 juin 1934'.

13 The literature on labour migration in French West Africa is extensive. Indispensable introductions are Klein, *Slavery*; Manchuelle, *Willing Migrants*; A. I. Asiwaju, 'Migrations as revolt. The example of the Ivory Coast and the Upper Volta before 1945', *Journal of African History*, 17:4 (1976), 577–94; Myron Echenberg, 'Les migrations militaires en Afrique Occidentale Française 1900–1945', *Canadian Journal of African Studies*, 14:3

(1980), 429–50; Cordell and Gregory, 'Labour reservoirs', 205–24; Andrew F. Clark, 'Slavery and its demise in the Upper Senegal valley, West Africa, 1890–1920', *Slavery and Abolition*, 15:1 (1994), 51–71, and his 'Internal migrations and population movements in the Upper Senegal valley', 399–420.

14 Colonial population figures were rarely accurate. The collection of census data was unpopular, as it was closely identified with tax collection and labour supply. It is therefore probable that official population statistics significantly underestimated actual populations as local people evaded the census. Population statistics are further distorted by internal and external migration. For a general discussion of these pitfalls see Dennis D. Cordell and Joel W. Gregory, 'Historical demography and demographic history', *Canadian Journal of African Studies*, 14:3 (1980), 389–416. In 1924 War Ministry recruiters worked on the basis that the AOF population totalled 11,258,920, including approximately 500,000 in the Togoland mandate. The AEF population was then reckoned at 5,602,416, plus an additional 2,540,000 in the neighbouring Cameroon mandate, see SHA, 5H6/D1, Commission interministerielle des troupes indigènes, 2e sous-commission rapport, 'Recrutement', n.d. 1924, p. 22.

15 Catherine Coquery-Vidrovitch, 'L'impact des intérêts coloniaux. SCOA et CFAO dans l'ouest africain 1910–1965', *Journal of African History*, 16:4 (1975), 599. SCOA's capital reserves climbed from 3 million to 18 million between 1914 and 1919, CFAO from 9 million to 25 million.

16 ADA, Sarraut papers, 12J254, SCOA, 'Extrait du rapport présenté à l'Assemblée générale des actionnaires du 13 Octobre 1933'. A 500 franc investment with the SCOA in 1910 would have generated 4,075 francs by 1930. But the company went into crisis in September 1930 when it emerged that the Banque française d'Afrique was near collapse and could not cover 30 million francs held by SCOA on deposit.

17 Oloruntimehin, 'The economy of French West Africa', 54–6, quote at p. 60. Twenty-five of the French firms were based in Paris, thirty-five in Bordeaux and ten in Marseilles. Britain's United Africa Company provides a good comparison with the SCOA and the SFAO. See D. K. Fieldhouse, *Merchant Capital and Economic Decolonization. The United Africa Company* (Oxford: Clarendon Press, 1994).

18 Elisabeth Rabut, 'Le mythe parisien de la mise en valeur des colonies africaines à l'aube du XXe siècle. La commission des concessions coloniales 1898–1912', *Journal of African History*, 20:2 (1979), 271–87.

19 Christopher Gray, 'Lambaréné, Okoumé and the transformation of labor along the Middle Ogooué (Gabon), 1870–1945', *Journal of African History*, 40:1 (1999), 92–7.

20 Coquery-Vidrovitch, *Le Congo*, 519, 527. Apart from extra credits voted in 1901 and 1911, state spending in AEF averaged from 500,000 to 700,000 francs per annum.

21 Andrew and Kanya-Forstner, *France Overseas*, 19.

22 Hoover Institution, Louis Loucheur papers, box 3/folder 4, 'Discours prononcé par M. Loucheur devant la Conférence économique internationale, le 7 mai 1927'.

23 Jacques Marseille, *Empire colonial et capitalisme français. Histoire d'un divorce* (Paris: Albin Michel, 1984), 44–8, also cited in Nørlund, 'The French Empire, the colonial state in Vietnam', 76.

24 Andrew and Kanya-Forstner, *France Overseas*, 15.

25 Catherine Coquery-Vidrovitch, 'L'impérialisme français en Afrique noire : idéologie impériale et politique d'équipement 1924–1935', *Relations Internationales*, 7 (1976), 261–82. As an example of changing patterns of land tenure and the introduction of export crops see Robert M. Hecht, 'Immigration, land transfer and tenure changes in Divo, Ivory Coast, 1940–1980', *Africa*, 55:3 (1985), 319–21.

26 Catherine Coquery-Vidrovitch, 'L'Afrique coloniale française et la crise de 1930 : crise structurelle et genèse du sous-développement', *Revue Française d'Histoire d'Outre-Mer*, 63: 232 (1976), 386–424.

27 Laurence C. Becker, 'An experiment in the reorganisation of agricultural production in the French Sudan (Mali), 1920–1940', *Africa*, 64:3 (1994), 373–90.

28 Roberts *Two Worlds*, 286–90; Becker, 'An experiment', 374–5. Governor Carde made Bélime head of the Service générale des textiles et de l'hydraulique agricole.

29 Roberts *Two Worlds*, Part II, especially chapter 6, 118–44. Two years after the launch of

the Sarraut plan, Bélime summarised his own ideas in a short published study, *Les Irrigations du Niger. Discussions et controverses*.

30 Thomas Bassett, 'The development of cotton in northern Ivory Coast, 1910–1965', *Journal of African History*, 19:2 (1978), 276.

31 Roberts *Two Worlds*, 145–9; Becker, 'An experiment', 376–7.

32 'Mélanges et documents : l'Office du Niger', *Outre-Mer* 4:2–3 (1932), 221–2; ADA, Sarraut papers, 12J254, 'Rapport sur la situation économique de la Guinée Française, du Sudan, du Sénégal. La mise en valeur de l'AOF', par Jean Daramy d'Oxoby, Ancien Conseilleur Général et Colonial du Sénégal', November 1933, p. 58. Carde argued that the Office du Niger project had a social policy dimension, as it improved living standards in areas provided with a sure irrigated water supply.

33 Roberts *Two Worlds*, 223–38. Bélime remained director-general of the Office du Niger until 1943. Sarraut showed his continued support for the irrigation scheme by sitting on the Office's supervisory council.

34 Ernest Bélime, 'Fondements naturels, politiques et moraux des travaux nigériens', *Outre-Mer*, 6:2 (1934), 177–87.

35 Roberts *Two Worlds*, chapter 11; Bouboucar Fall, *Le Travail forcé en Afrique occidentale française 1900–1946* (Paris: Editions Karthala, 1993); Myron Echenberg and Jean Filipovich, 'African military labour and the building of the Office du Niger installations, 1925–1950', *Journal of African History*, 27 (1986), 533–51; Jean Filipovich, 'Destined to fail. Forced settlement at the Office du Niger, 1926–1945', *Journal of African History*, 42:2 (2001), 239–60.

36 Becker, 'An experiment', 378–80.

37 Roberts *Two Worlds*, 238–9; Nicole Bernard-Duquenot, 'Le Front populaire et le problème des prestations en AOF', *Cahiers d'Etudes Africaines*, 61 (1976), 159–72.

38 Filipovich, 'Destined to fail', 251–4.

39 CAOM, affpol/852, Note pour le Ministre, n.d. December 1927.

40 See, for example, CAOM, affpol/852, 'Questions examinées par le conseil économique pendant la session du Conseil supérieur des colonies 1927–28'.

41 CAOM, affpol/852, CSC session summaries, 1926–36.

42 Marseille, *Empire colonial et capitalisme français*, 105–10; also cited in Nørlund, 'The French Empire, the colonial state in Vietnam', 77.

43 *Ibid.*, 218–31.

44 Nørlund, 'The French Empire, the colonial state in Vietnam', 86–7; on the Russian market see: Martin Horn, *Britain, France, and the Financing of the First World War* (Montreal: McGill, 2002), 18–19, 183.

45 Coquery-Vidrovitch, 'L'impact des intérêts coloniaux', 604–5.

46 Andrew Hardy, 'The economics of French rule in Indochina. A biography of Paul Bernard (1892–1960)', *Modern Asian Studies*, 32:4 (1998), 808.

47 Anne Booth, 'Four colonies and a kingdom. A comparison of fiscal, trade, and exchange rate policies in South East Asia in the 1930s', *Modern Asian Studies*, 37:2 (2003), 432.

48 Marr, *Vietnamese Tradition on Trial*, 6; Nørlund, 'The French Empire, the colonial state in Vietnam', 85.

49 Nørlund, 'Rice and the colonial lobby', 208.

50 Brocheux, 'The state and the 1930s depression', 251–4; Nørlund, 'Rice', 208.

51 Marseille, *Empire colonial et capitalisme français*, 95–119; D. K. Fieldhouse, 'Review article. The economics of French empire', *Journal of African History*, 27 (1986), 169–72.

52 Marseille, *Empire colonial et capitalisme français*, 115–17.

53 *Ibid.*, 368–71.

54 Jacques Marseille, 'Les relations commerciales entre la France et son empire colonial de 1880 à 1913', *Revue d'Histoire Moderne et Contemporaine* 31:2 (1984), 286–97.

55 Sarraut defined his arguments in *La Mise en valeur des colonies françaises* (Paris: Payot, 1923), and refined them in his second, more analytical work, *Grandeur et servitude coloniales*.

56 Andrew and Kanya-Forstner, *France Overseas*, 226–8.

57 Marseille, 'Les relations commerciales', 303–7.

58 Kenneth Mouré, *The Gold Standard Illusion. France, the Bank of France, and the International Gold Standard, 1914–1939* (Oxford: Oxford University Press, 2002).

59 Mouré, *Managing the Franc Poincaré*, especially chapters 4 and 5.
60 Crédit Lyonnais played a key role as intermediary between Lyons silk merchants and the Beirut silk industry. See Khoury, *Syria*, 31.
61 John F. Laffey, 'Municipal imperialism in decline. The Lyon Chamber of Commerce, 1925–1938', *French Historical Studies*, 9:3–4 (1975), 345–8.
62 Thompson, *Colonial Citizens*, 33–5.
63 Brocheux and Hémery, *Indochine, la colonisation ambiguë*, 119.
64 PRO, FO 371/21590, Saigon Consulate, 'Report on conditions and events in French Indochina, July 1938'.
65 John F. Laffey, 'Lyonnais imperialism in the Far East, 1900–1938', *Modern Asian Studies*, 10:2 (1976), 243–7.
66 Marseille, *Empire colonial et capitalisme français*, 44–5.
67 Booth, 'Four colonies', 447–51.
68 CAOM, affpol/73, 1er Bureau, 'Project de rapport sur les monnaies et le change aux colonies', n.d. 1935.
69 Brocheux, 'The state and the 1930s depression', 268.
70 P-B. de la Brosse, 'La dévaluation du franc et la piastre indochinoise', *L'Asie Française*, 37:354 (November 1937), 275.
71 SHA, 9H1, Indes françaises, 'Exposé des motifs du projet de budget pour l'exercice 1930'. The authorities in Pondicherry managed to balance their 1930 budget at 2,811,825 rupees, and increased expenditure by 18,425 rupees over the previous year.
72 Cordell and Gregory, 'Labour reservoirs', 212; Bassett, 'The development of cotton', 278–9. Thomas Bassett points out that in Ivory Coast, where export revenue had risen markedly between 1924 and 1928, customs receipts declined by three-fifths between 1928 and 1932.
73 Brocheux and Hémery, *Indochine, la colonisation ambiguë*, 106.
74 Coquery-Vidrovitch, *Le Congo*, 522–6.
75 *Ibid.*, 528.
76 Gouverneur Guyon, 'La situation de la Nouvelle-Calédonie. Quatre années de gouvernement', *L'Océanie Française*, 25:109 (1929), 81–5; Mouren, 'La situation économique de la Nouvelle-Calédonie', *L'Océanie Française*, 27:118 (1931), 6–9.
77 Aldrich, *The French Presence*, 285–9.
78 Julian Jackson, *The Politics of Depression in France, 1932–1936* (Cambridge: Cambridge University Press, 1985), 58–9; Mouré, *Managing the Franc Poincaré*, 162.
79 MAE, série P: Tunisie 1930–40, vol. 377, Directeur-général des finances (Tunis), 'Comparaison entre les budgets tunisien et marocain', 18 January 1933. Administrative costs accounted for 38.6 per cent of the Moroccan ordinary budget when averaged out between 1931 and 1933.
80 CAOM, affpol/73, 2ème bureau (Colonies) report, 30 June 1934.
81 These arguments were all rehearsed by the Tunis residency in an effort to avert staff cuts, see MAE série P: Tunisie 1930–40, vol. 377, no. 1529, Residency report to Aristide Briand, 21 November 1931.
82 Brocheux and Hémery, *Indochine, la colonisation ambiguë*, 123.
83 Hardy, 'The economics of French rule', 815. This was the view of Paul Bernard, a leading economist and financier in Indochina.
84 See CAOM, affpol/73, lieutenant-governor, Gabon, 'Note sur l'évaluation des taxes au Gabon en harmonie avec la situation budgetaire', n.d. 1935; Sénat Commission des Colonies, 'Rapport par Senateur Adolphe Messimy, 26 juin 1934'.
85 SHA, 8H79, GGM, Monthly economic bulletins, December 1933–35; 'Bulletin économique', 4e trimestre 1935, 'Situation commerciale de Madagascar en 1935'.
86 CAOM, affpol/21, Léon Perrier, Sénat Commission des Finances, 1932 budget report; affpol/73, Dossier: 'Emprunts, loi du 22 février 1931'.
87 CAOM, affpol/73, no. 480, 'Rapport par M. Yves Le Trocquer, Sénat, annexe au procès-verbal de la séance du 28 mai 1931'.
88 CAOM, affpol/73, Dosser: Guadeloupe, questions diverses, Direction des affaires politiques memo, 'Exposé succincte des causes de la crise qui subit l'industrie sucrière et rhumière à la Guadeloupe', 26 June 1934.

89   'Le marché de nickel', *L'Océanie Française*, 33:150 (1937), 10–11.
90   CAOM, affpol/73, Dossier: Nouvelle-Caledonie, no. 5350, Louis Rollin letter to Ernest Lafont, Rapporteur du budget des colonies, 6 May 1935. New Caledonia's chrome mining industry was French-registered but controlled by British shareholders.
91   Frances M. B. Lynch, *France and the International Economy. From Vichy to the Treaty of Rome* (London: Routledge, 1997), 186.
92   CAOM, GGAEF: 1934, 1D9, no. 1158, Antonetti to Pierre Laval, 4 April 1934.
93   CAOM, AOF Fonds moderne, 17G329, Affaires Politiques rapport du projet, 'Un grand chemin de fer colonial', 21 November 1934.
94   *Ibid*.
95   Brocheux and Hémery, *Indochine, la colonisation ambiguë*, 150–3.
96   Jean-Claude Allain, 'Les emprunts d'état marocains avant 1939', in Charles-Robert Ageron (ed.), *Les Chemins de la decolonisation de l'empire française 1936–1956* (Paris: Editions CNRS, 1986), 131–41.
97   CAOM, 17G329, Affpol, 'Un grand chemin de fer colonial', 21 November 1934.
98   CAOM, 17G329, 'Tournée du gouverneur-général (décembre 1934–janvier 1935), Compte-rendu: éléments concernant les travaux publics'.
99   Brocheux and Hémery, *Indochine, la colonisation ambiguë*, 159–75.
100 Jacques Marseille, 'L'investissement public en Algérie après la deuxième guerre mondiale : vecteur de l'impérialisme ou avatar de la domination directe?' *Revue Française d'Histoire d'Outre-Mer*, 70:260 (1983), 180.
101 AN, F^{60}187, Dossier A2, Cabinet du Gouverneur Général de l'Algérie rapport, 'Situation économique et commerciale de l'Algérie en 1938'. The exception was iron ore. The three main Algerian iron ore mining companies, the Société d'Ouenza in Bône, the Société des mines de Zaccar near Algiers and the Société des mines de Timezrit near Bougie all faced stiff competition from Lorraine iron producers and relied on sales to Britain, Germany and Holland.
102 Pennell, *Morocco*, 197–8.
103 CADN, Fonds Beyrouth, Cabinet Politique, vol. 951/D7, no. 64/G. S. G. Direction du contrôle note, 8 March 1924; Cabinet secretariat note, n.d. May 1924. By March 1924 Damascus gold traders refused to accept the Syrian-Lebanese pound in commercial transactions. By 1927 the Bank of Syria's capital reserves of 25.5 million francs were dangerously low, see SHA, 2N70/D1, CSDN, 'Bulletin de la Banque de Syrie et du Grand Liban', 15 October 1927.
104 Khoury, *Syria*, 86–7, 93.
105 Gates, 'The historical role of political economy', 29.
106 'Stabilisation de la piastre indochinoise', *L'Asie Française*, 30:281 (1930), 216–22.
107 Brocheux and Hémery, *Indochine, la colonisation ambiguë*, 136.
108 Nørlund, 'Rice', 218.
109 CAOM, affpol/73, 1er Bureau, 'Project de rapport sur les monnaies et le change aux colonies', n.d. 1935.
110 *Ibid*.
111 *La Bourse de Beyrouth 1920–1970. Brochure editée par la Bourse de Beyrouth à l'occasion de son cinquantenaire*.
112 For a comparative assessment of common currency use as an aid to colonial penetration of African societies see D. K. Fieldhouse, 'The economic exploitation of Africa. Some British and French comparisons', in Prosser Gifford and Wm Roger Louis (eds), *France and Britain in Africa* (New Haven CT: Yale University Press, 1971), 593–662.
113 Brocheux and Hémery, *Indochine, la colonisation ambiguë*, 138–42. In 1940 the Bank of Indochina still controlled half of all currency transactions in the Indochina federation, having fought any reforms liable to undermine its primacy next to the other seven banking houses (two of them British) operating in Indochina after 1918.
114 Brocheux, 'The state and the 1930s depression', 253; Hardy, 'The economics of French rule', 810–11. The Société française financière et coloniale controlled nineteen companies in Indochina. Pierre Brocheux points out that the index of Indochina securities collapsed from 300 to 34 in the years 1927–31.

115 CAOM, affpol/76, Dossier 3, no. 907, Direction des affaires politiques, 'Note au sujet de la caisse des institutions sociales d'Indochine', 30 July 1931.
116 Pierre Rouveroux and Francis Murat, 'L'évolution du crédit agricole mutuel en Afrique du Nord', *L'Afrique Française*, 36:11 (November 1936), 609–12.
117 CAOM, GGA, 11H46, no. 6722, Commune mixte de Belezma, 'Rapport sur la situation agricole', 3 November 1920.
118 Pennell, *Morocco*, 219.
119 State support for wheat cultivation went furthest in Morocco, see Will D. Swearingen, 'In pursuit of the granary of Rome. France's wheat policy in Morocco, 1915–1931', *International Journal of Middle East Studies*, 17 (1985), 350–1.
120 Lisa Anderson, *The State and Social Transformation in Tunisia and Libya, 1830–1980* (Princeton NJ: Princeton University Press, 1986), 168.
121 Pennell, *Morocco*, 219–25.
122 MAE, série P: Tunisie 1930–40, vol. 377, Commission de l'Algérie et de Tunisie rapport par Michel Parès (Deputy for Oran), 'La crise tunisienne', 6 August 1933.
123 Abdelmajid Guelmami, *La Politique sociale en Tunisie de 1881 à nos jours* (Paris: Editions l'Harmattan, 1996), 82–3.
124 Charles-André Julien, *L'Afrique du Nord en marche. Algérie–Tunisie–Maroc 1880–1952* (Paris: Julliard, 1952. Rpt Paris: Omnibus, 2002), 55–7.
125 Dorothea M. Gallup, 'The French image of Algeria. Its origin, its place in colonial ideology, its effect on Algerian acculturation', University of California, Los Angeles, PhD, 1973, 435.
126 David Prochaska, 'Approaches to the economy of colonial Annaba, 1870–1920', *Africa*, 60:4 (1990), 508; also in Prochaska, *Making Algeria French. Colonialism in Bône, 1870–1920* (Cambridge: Cambridge University Press, 1990), 123–4.
127 Marseille, *Empire colonial et capitalisme français*, 370.
128 CAOM, GGM, sous-série 4D: rapports d'ensemble, 4D44, 'Rapport sur l'évolution politique et sociale à Madagascar de 1926 à 1937'.
129 Lynch, *France and the International Economy*, 187.
130 AN, René Pleven papers, 560AP/27, Pleven memo, 21 April 1944.

CHAPTER FOUR

Colonial economic demands and urban development in North Africa

A brief survey of the impact of inter-war economic change and urban planning in colonial territories must be selective. This chapter takes a 'top down' approach, drawing on the records of colonial government. The danger is that colonial subjects appear as mere economic instruments rather than actors in their own right. In an effort to overcome this, the chapter highlights three generic socio-economic issues that affected all strata of colonial society: taxation, labour supply, and urban development. The last subject is analysed in regard to French North Africa, the one colonial arena where Europeans in tens of thousands interacted directly with colonial populations.

Taxation

The French colonial state taxed subject populations to generate sufficient budgetary revenue to support its bureaucracy, military costs and limited social provision. As we saw in the previous chapter, colonial development, often the biggest single item of budgetary expenditure, was supported by a combination of fiscal revenue, state loans and private sector investment. The majority of colonial subjects liable to taxation were peasant small-holders and landless agricultural labourers. Most paid a simple poll tax, or *capitation*, for which heads of household were responsible. The requirement to pay taxes in cash had profound social consequences in colonies that lacked a developed monetary economy. Agricultural labour was increasingly performed to meet obligations to the colonial state, whereas previously it was more often determined by family and clan ties. Taxation thus hastened the emergence of colonial wage economies and a migratory labour force. In the Cameroon mandate, for instance, increases in direct taxation to balance the budget led more farm labourers from inland regions to migrate to the coast for paid employment on European and African-owned cocoa plantations.[1]

Across the French empire owners of land and livestock were taxed according to the amount of land farmed and the numbers of domestic animals
kept. Indirect taxes were also imposed on goods purchased and sold.
Transport taxes, internal customs charges and payment for essential
bureaucratic services such as travel permits and passports generated further
revenue. Tax collection in rural areas was linked to the cycle of annual harvests and, in the case of nomadic populations especially, the migration of
livestock to seasonal pastures. Taxes were easier to collect in times of abundance than in years of poor harvest or drought. Resistance to taxation usually
reflected chronic hardship and inability to pay more than political opposition.

Collecting colonial taxes was a coercive business whatever the prevailing
economic conditions. Use of police auxiliaries and regular troops was
commonplace. Financial inducements to indigenous intermediaries, whether
chiefs, *caïds* or mandarins, to collect revenue on behalf of the French
authorities led some to set about the task with unseemly zeal.[2] Fiscal
regimes were sometimes so severe that even thinly populated colonies with
tiny internal markets could generate a net profit for the colonial exchequer.
In Chad – along with Upper Volta, the most barren and undeveloped colony
in French Africa – from 1900 to 1920 the military administration adhered
scrupulously to the principle that the territory should be entirely self-
financing. A combination of high monetary taxation, the replacement of the
local currency, the thaler, with an overvalued franc, and official reluctance
to fund development established Chad as 'the richest of our poor colonies'
by the end of the First World War.[3] In 1918–19 and again in 1920–21
government survey missions criticised the severity of the colony's military
administration. These damning reports heralded the end of army control
over fiscal policy in Chad. Yet matters did not change overnight. Chad
registered budgetary surpluses throughout the early 1920s in spite of its low
population density and high occupation costs. By 1925 the Fort Lamy
authorities had amassed a budgetary reserve of almost 1.5 million francs.[4]

Albeit an extreme case, the Chad example demonstrates that there was
no clear equation between taxes paid and services provided. Nor was there
any systematic correlation between colonial taxation rates and subjects'
ability to pay. The Popular Front administration of 1936–37 was the sole
inter-war government that addressed this. Minister of Colonies Marius
Moutet made taxation a central element of a colonial governors' conference
convened in November 1936 to formulate structural economic reforms.
Taxation, he insisted, should be an instrument of positive social change,
not colonial oppression:

In a colonial country – where the monetary economy only came into existence under [French] authority – taxes are the sole means to draw the indigenous population out of a barter system and to direct them towards growing

export crops, the products of which serve to finance public works and administration. But the extent [of taxation] must be carefully monitored. If the *indigène* has the impression that he is made to work simply to pay taxes, and if each step in colonial development is accompanied by additional fiscal burdens, he will soon be discouraged and will only work to the limit of his fiscal obligations. That is a stumbling block [*écueil*] we must avoid.[5]

On 20 October 1936 Gaston Joseph, Moutet's chief political adviser, went further still, dwelling on the inequity of colonial taxes in Indochina. Vietnamese coolies earned on average nine piastres per month and paid five and a half in direct tax. A departmental head in the Hanoi government earned at least 1,000 piastres per month, fifty-five of which went in tax contributions. In other words, the coolie paid ten times as much in direct taxation as a proportion of his overall wage.[6] Well meaning it may have been, but the Popular Front was too short-lived to overhaul colonial taxation. Old habits died hard. In times of recession, colonial taxes cushioned the impact of declining export income, and, even in buoyant trading conditions, social spending was disproportionately allocated to settlers and town dwellers. In Tunisia, a relatively affluent society by colonial standards, until 1910 state welfare spending was channelled exclusively to the settler population. The protectorate authorities claimed that Muslim charity bequests provided a welfare net for the indigenous population. Demographic statistics suggested otherwise. Before 1914 the mortality rate among the Muslim population was, on average, three times higher than that of Tunisia's settler community. During the First World War the Tunis residency released additional funds for public health programmes, worker housing and primary school education. In the 1920s, however, the protectorate reverted to its pre-war practice of prioritising social spending of direct benefit to the settler population. Between 1918 and 1930 welfare funding never exceeded five per cent of Tunisia's general budget. The residency adopted a functionalist approach to improved public health, sanitation and the eradication of epidemics. Social spending was justified in terms of its knock-on effect on national efficiency and export output. A healthy colonial population was a vital economic resource, not an overriding policy objective.[7]

Europeans were similarly privileged in black Africa. Colonial government was more responsive to trading companies and plantation owners' pleas for financial concessions and tax breaks to avoid bankruptcy than to district officers' warnings about the untenable tax burden on *indigènes*.[8] As Catherine Coquery-Vidrovitch points out, West African taxpayers were doubly penalised in the depression years as real wages and employment fell and tax demands rose.[9] In AEF, too, in March 1931 Governor-general Antonetti estimated that fiscal revenue could be sustained thanks to growth in the federation's internal market. He rejected any reduction in the existing head tax of fifteen francs.[10] After a decade of constant tax increases, in

June 1935, mid-way through the last year of severe contraction in the AEF economy, acting Governor-general Marchessou finally acknowledged that the burden of personal taxation was unsustainable. Regional tax inspections revealed a population collapsing under fiscal charges.[11] AEF was the most extreme example of harsh state exaction, but it was far from unique. Indirect taxes on commercial transactions could be equally devastating, and hit indigenous traders disproportionately hard, as most lacked the capital resources of their European counterparts. Dahomey was one such case. Increased commercial charges after 1926 gradually excluded African traders in Porto Novo from the commodity market in palm oil, the colony's principal export.[12]

Colonial resistance to taxation, typically expressed by evading the tax collector, sometimes took a different turn. Popular resentment tended to be most acute in regions bordering non-French territory, where near neighbours across a colonial frontier, often of the same ethnic group, might be considered better off. These sentiments help explain the persistent movement of people from the AOF colonies of Guinea, Sudan, Niger and Dahomey to British-ruled Gold Coast and Nigeria. To some this was far more than economic migration, it was permanent flight – an act of political defiance as well as a sign of economic desperation.[13] Nomadic Bedouin in the Syrian Desert were equally astute. Year after year they traversed the frontiers of Transjordan and Iraq to elude tax collectors and find better grazing for their livestock, only returning to Syria once the revenue agents were gone.[14]

Variations in tax rates between colonies also sharpened popular anger. In the African and Indochina federations, cross-subsidisation between individual territories became well established after the First World War. And in smaller colonial territories, the tax burden generally reflected a number of local economic factors. These included the availability of alternate sources of state revenue, the cost of long-term public works, the proportion of comparatively wealthy settlers or Creoles in the overall population, the presence of expensive military or penal establishments, and the average wage of colonial workers. In the French Antilles all these factors shaped fiscal policy, albeit to varying degrees. The *bagne* penal colony played a prominent economic role in French Guiana, whereas the larger, more diverse populations of Martinique and Guadeloupe gave the local authorities more room to make fiscal adjustments. Natural disasters also played their part. Reconstruction after the 1928 hurricane in Guadeloupe distorted the island's economy for years afterwards. Much the same could be said of Réunion, the New Hebrides and New Caledonia, all of which suffered severe hurricane damage between 1928 and 1932.[15]

Tax receipts for 1938 from the three Caribbean colonies of Martinique, Guadeloupe and French Guiana reveal sharp variations in taxation, from an average payment of 247 francs per year in Guadeloupe to 627 francs in Guiana. It was a more straightforward task to spread the tax burden among Guadeloupe's 304,000 inhabitants than among Guiana's population of only 23,700. But the huge disparity was also explained by the absence of commercial revenue in Guiana, whose principal 'industry' remained the fearful *bagne*, the unfortunate inmates of which paid no taxes. As for Martinique, average *per capita* taxes in 1938 were 358 francs. Although Martinique's registered population of 246,700 was close to that of Guadeloupe, Martinique's infrastructure, administrative and education spending were far higher. In November 1938 the governors of the three Antilles colonies met to discuss common economic problems. They agreed that the high costs of Popular Front social reforms necessitated further tax increases of between four per cent (French Guiana) and nine per cent (Martinique).[16] At the end of the inter-war period, as at the beginning, recourse to increased taxation flowed naturally from the overriding need to balance budgets.

Labour supply

Colonial governments generally regulated workers' employment terms and labour conditions through decree legislation before the Popular Front took power in 1936. Unionisation, collective bargaining and freely negotiated labour contracts were extremely rare, and in much of francophone Africa non-existent. In some territories *indigène* wage labourers were admitted as rank-and-file members to unions set up for, and run by, European workers or naturalised colonial citizens. On occasion, colonial authorities blocked this by invoking legislation that limited membership of any union regulated by French law to French citizens.[17] The exceptions to the rule were the Middle East mandates, where worker rights were more entrenched, the Ottoman labour market having been liberalised after the 1908 Young Turk revolution.[18] Hostile to trade unions, it fell to colonial governments themselves to protect native workers from abuses by their employers. Worker protection was articulated in patriarchal terms. Officials determined the best interests of the labour force much like parents deciding on appropriate schooling for their child. Such at least was the theory. In practice, governors sought to balance three primordial needs.

The first was the social stability of their colony. It was politically imperative that labour exploitation did not provoke mass opposition to French control. Most administrators in the inter-war period regarded urbanisation and unionisation as preconditions to really threatening worker unrest. Stoppages and even violent protests in isolated plantations, labour camps and workshops were neither unexpected nor especially disquieting so long as they had little potential to spread elsewhere. The second fundamental requirement was to raise production levels. Even when faced with price falls caused by overproduction of a key export commodity, colonial governments sometimes encouraged greater output, thus compounding problems of over-supply and the difficulty of selling produce priced in overvalued francs.[19]

Furthermore, the colonial state made its own demands on labour that clashed with those of capitalist producers dependent on a cheap labour supply to ensure profitability. The need to balance state requirements against the rising manpower demands of the private sector informed the introduction of an AOF labour code in 1925. In return for state assistance in the provision of labour, private employers were required to provide basic facilities to their work force. These included food and housing, transport and health care.[20] But the Dakar authorities were poorly placed to act as an impartial arbiter in the West African labour market. Take Upper Volta, seen throughout the inter-war period as the largest 'reservoir' of labour in AOF. Here the colonial administration competed directly for manpower with large Ivory Coast forestry companies such as Holscherer de Côte d'Ivôire. The commercial pull of the Ivory Coast intensified in the 1920s. Timber production in the colony expanded from an export tonnage of 63,693 in 1922 to 137,520 tons in 1928. Between 1929 and 1934 exports of Ivory Coast timber declined as abruptly as they had risen, hitting an inter-war low of 28,193 tons in 1934. But the recession in the timber industry was offset by greater plantation production of rubber, palm oil, and cocoa. Ivory Coast was the fastest growing export economy within AOF over the inter-war period.[21] What did this mean for Upper Volta? The insatiable demand for Upper Volta manpower to work in Ivory Coast added to the state's heavy labour exactions. Regional administrators struggled to meet the annual quota for military recruits in addition to finding sufficient able-bodied men among the indigenous Mossi population to work on the construction gangs of the Dakar–Niger railway. Moreover, local chiefs and district officials together enforced the annual *prestations*, or day-labour requirements, through which the colonial state maintained the network of roads and telegraphs.[22] The affected populations sometimes refused mounting state and corporate demands for labour. Resistance to this colonial penetration took many forms. As we have seen, families moved between districts, or to British territory, to avoid liability for labour and head tax. And, whether by accident or design, peasant farmers often resisted incorporation into the monetary economy through their dogged attachment to subsistence agriculture contrary to official pressure to grow export crops.[23]

Whatever the short-term competition between them, there remained an underlying community of interest between colonial government and French trading companies, settler industrialists and landowners to ensure a continued supply of cheap local labour. In the light of this, the protection of workers, the third aspect of colonial economic policy, often fell short. Take perhaps the most extreme example – labour conditions in Equatorial Africa. On 4 May 1922 the Brazzaville government introduced a labour charter for AEF. The legislation authorised the authorities in Gabon, French Congo, Oubangui-Chari and Chad to determine the age limits, gender restrictions and permissible types of employment for the colonial work force. Albert Sarraut, once again Minister of Colonies, this time in Raymond Poincaré's second government, insisted that all workers in AEF taken on for over three months by a single employer should be offered labour contracts stipulating basic rights to lodgings, food and regular wages.[24] The federal government acted as guarantor of any locally negotiated labour contracts in which the colonial state had a direct interest, an edict that applied to labourers engaged in public works programmes. In practice, the Brazzaville authorities were preoccupied by the provision of labour rather than the protection of worker rights. Indeed, former Brazzaville governor Victor Augagneur was then under investigation for colluding with settler friends to divert the Pointe Noire railway, the largest public works project of the day, across their land.[25]

As there was a chronic labour shortage in the vast territory of Equatorial Africa, each year the AEF administrative council determined the maximum number of workers to be recruited in the federation's four component colonies. But this figure only included workers formally engaged as contract labourers. Those doing piecework were usually hired on a day-to-day basis with no contract – and consequently no formal employment protection. Hence, while contract employment on settler plantations and in the forestry industry was legally restricted to 'adult males', the use of women and children as day labourers remained unregulated.[26] Judged in terms of mortality rates, forced labour conditions in AEF were without parallel. Labourers on major public works schemes, in lumber camps and in plantations were treated as expendable commodities. Labour conditions were more severe in AEF in the ten years before the Wall Street crash than in the decade after it. And in the 1930s hostile media attention shifted to AOF's Office du Niger project.[27] Labour exactions in some AOF colonies such as Ivory Coast and Upper Volta by then approached the extreme cruelties of Equatorial Africa. In the Kong district of Ivory Coast administrators 'raided' villages in their search for labourers, taking off between seven and ten per cent of the total population in the years 1928 to 1930 alone.[28]

Officials in the French Pacific territories turned to imported contract labour to alleviate shortages. In the early decades of the twentieth century Asian workers from Java, Japan and, above all, Tonkin became essential to the New Caledonia and New Hebrides economies. From 1920 concerted efforts were made to secure skilled North Vietnamese labourers. But once these workers arrived it was left to individual employers to set their employment terms. In December 1920 a contributor to the journal *L'Océanie Française* advised readers of the characteristics of Vietnamese workers. They were praised as hardworking, commercially adept and skilled arable farmers. Many had experience of construction and mining, trades much in demand. Contract labourers could be housed in purpose-built villages where they would also receive basic French-language instruction.[29] Some employers were clearly tempted. By 1927 4,607 Indochinese labourers were working in the New Hebrides. Two years later the Asian population of 15,420 outnumbered the Europeans living in New Caledonia. The Hanoi government assisted the Nouméa authorities in their recruitment of North Vietnamese workers as part of the wider policy of 'inter-colonial support'. Intended to integrate the economies of the Pacific territories more closely with the Indochina federation, this policy took shape after the First World War as the flow of Indochinese workers was matched by the Bank of Indochina's deepening involvement in the New Caledonian economy.[30]

Labour migration into and out of Indochina in the 1920s was more extensive than in any other colonial federation. French officials had long regarded inward Vietnamese labour migration as one of three prerequisites – along with railway construction and capital investment – to the *mise en valeur* of Laos. By 1939 there were some 39,000 Vietnamese resident there, a fraction of the threefold population increase originally thought necessary to develop the Laotian economy.[31] From 1920 the federal government also recruited labourers in densely populated areas of Annam to work on the expanding rubber plantations of Cochin-China. Some were offered three-year work contracts, including free travel, accommodation, rudimentary medical care and a 700-gram daily rice ration. Others were employed on an informal basis in anticipation of a high attrition rate among existing plantation workers. Between 1922 and 1938 the number of contract labourers taken on in this way fluctuated between approximately 11,000 and 31,000. These workers, for the most part illiterate male peasant share-croppers, faced terrible working conditions that did not significantly im-prove over the inter-war period. Labourers were physically confined in plantation barracks whose poor location and cramped conditions left them vulnerable to malaria and tuberculosis. Contracts were summarily altered, wages cut and food rations ignored. And during the depression years it became abundantly clear that the corporate survival of the plantations counted for more with the Saigon administration than workers' rights.[32]

Official attachment to forced labour in some places, imported contract labour in others, is easily explained in economic terms, but no less shocking in its human costs. Yet settler producers consistently obstructed state labour reforms. At the height of Cochin-China's rubber boom between 1925 and 1927 Governor-general Varenne encountered stiff commercial opposition to his attempt to establish a Federal Labour Inspectorate. Transmigration of labourers from Yunnan, Siam, Burma, Laos and the Vietnamese territories was completely unregulated before Varenne's arrival, and only slowly improved after his departure. His network of government labour inspectors (contrôleurs du travail) ultimately became a model for later labour reforms in other colonial territories. But, in the short term, Varenne's introduction of work contracts to Tonkin's coal mining industry and Cochin-China's plantations in October 1927 provoked a month of vigorous settler protests that culminated in his dismissal.[33]

In the 1920s Varenne's labour reforms stood out. Elsewhere the focus of colonial economic planning was to stimulate additional commerce, not to regulate it. In AEF government backing for infrastructure spending and commercial enterprise slowly increased after the First World War. Government equipment loans totalled 393 million francs between 1914 and 1930. A further 1,513 million was voted between 1931 and 1939. In real terms, these sums represented more than a tenfold increase in state investment relative to pre-1914 figures.[34] Official efforts to stimulate economic growth in AEF were dogged by two perennial problems: budgetary deficits and the shortage of manpower. As forestry and mining (particularly diamond mining in Oubangui-Chari) took off in the late 1920s in response to rising global demand, so recourse to forced labour, prestations, and other forms of statutory labour increased. Traditional agriculture was severely disrupted in those regions most affected by commercial labour demands. Established patterns of family and village farming disintegrated. Women and children took on a greater share of arduous field work. Famines were common, and returning workers transmitted epidemic illnesses to isolated rural communities. During the 1920s the expansion of the timber industry along the Ogooué River system in Gabon drew in thousands of migrant labourers to work in temporary lumber camps. Paid in French francs, these forestry workers were tied to the colonial state by taxation demands and new restrictions on so-called 'free cutting' whereby men had previously supplemented their income by felling trees in unexploited forest areas. But lumber camps were transient phenomena. Their sole purpose was to extract timber at maximum profit before relocation to a new site. As a result, the timber industry brought few lasting benefits to a region. Participation in the cash economy did not mean better housing or diet. The greater commercialisation of the AEF economy in the 1920s produced a net decline in local living standards. Between 1920 and 1933 population levels actually fell in those regions where trading company activity was most intense, such as the Middle Congo and Oubangui-Chari.[35]

Buoyant demand for African hardwoods in the 1920s exacerbated AEF's labour shortage. Between 1924 and 1928 the market for okoumé mahogany from Gabon took off, quadrupling the colony's forestry revenue. Hardwood exports generated fifty-nine per cent of Gabon's budgetary revenue at their peak in 1928.[36] The federal authorities were anxious to tie African labourers into working for a particular timber company and sought to deter casual labourers from moving between lumber camps in search of more remunerative, temporary work. The answer was to grant major logging companies, such as the Société agricole forestière et industrielle africaine, long-term timber cutting concessions of ten to twenty years. These encouraged more systematic employment practices, including greater use of contract labour. The Brazzaville government saw a panacea: additional timber concessions would increase AEF's export output, labour migration would be more tightly confined, and more widespread use of labour contracts would reduce the problems associated with casual workers. In fact, labour shortages persisted until international demand for Gabonese hardwoods fell away between 1931 and 1935.[37] The forestry industry still relied on non-contract labour to supplement its permanent work force.[38]

After the First World War the international community was quicker to challenge this state of affairs than the French governmental establishment, which still turned a blind eye to labour abuses in Equatorial Africa. The International Labour Organisation (ILO) led the way. Established by the labour provisions of the Treaty of Versailles, the ILO brought together national representatives from government, industry and labour to formulate and monitor international labour legislation. Ironically, the ILO's first director was Albert Thomas, France's outstanding wartime Minister of Munitions. Between 1922 and 1926 Thomas campaigned for the legal enforcement of an eight-hour working day.[39] He focused on the major industrial powers, not the colonies. But his and subsequent ILO campaigns did expose the injustice of an unregulated colonial labour market.

Raphaël Antonetti's Brazzaville government opposed plans launched by the Cartel des gauches in 1924 to introduce statutory regulation of colonial working hours.[40] He also took a dim view of Cartel plans to reform the native legal code. The *indigénat* allowed district administrators to mete out fines and short jail terms for minor criminal offences without any formal trial procedure. In AEF the original *indigénat* provisions of 1887 remained in force. Edouard Herriot's government initiated a consultation process between the federal colonial administrations and individual colonial governors to test support for more widespread application of French criminal law and right to trial by jury. Antonetti justified the continuation of a summary punishment system with economic arguments. AEF's poor communications precluded a criminal code requiring law courts, travel to urban centres and the delays inherent in formal legal procedure. The accused would never grasp the concept of a contested trial, in which white Europeans openly argued about the alleged offence and the appropriate punishment. Above all, the *indigénat* gave district officers the means to compel the local population to work on French terms. There was no room for dialogue about economic modernisation. It had to be imposed. In this sense, administrative efforts to curb sleeping sickness and to increase agricultural production were two sides of the same coin. Each was incontrovertibly beneficial, each aroused local suspicions, and therefore each was enforced by recourse to the *indigénat*. In Antonetti's assessment, the racial inferiority of the indigenous population left the French authorities no alternative but to coerce them toward progress. On 1 May 1925 the governor-general confided his views to Minister of Colonies André-Hesse:

> The remedy is not discussion: we have to tell the *indigène* how to cultivate the soil that he scarcely knows how to scratch, teach him how to use the most basic hoes that he still ignores, force him to start more varied and seasonal [crop] cultivation on a sufficiently large scale to meet the dangers of bad weather and the depredations of wild boar. I choose the word 'force' because such is his apathy that without compulsion he would not even work hard enough to meet his one primordial need: to eat.[41]

Antonetti convinced the rue Oudinot to leave colonial working practices unchanged, but he was swimming against a rising tide of international opinion. In the mid-1920s the ILO turned its attention to colonial workers after several highly publicised scandals exposed high mortality rates among forced labourers, including those working in the AEF lumber trade and railway construction projects in the French Congo. In 1926 the League of Nations Slavery Convention accused the colonial powers of permitting working practices analogous to slave labour. The resultant three-year ILO investigation of colonial working conditions culminated in the passage of a Forced Labour Convention in 1930 signed by a majority of League states. The convention aimed to suppress 'forced or compulsory labour in all its forms within the shortest possible period'. Forced labour on essential public works was still permitted for a maximum of sixty days per year, but only in exceptional circumstances and at going rates of pay. Even so, France, Belgium and Portugal abstained, effectively opting out of the convention provisions. Each insisted that the ILO scheme ignored specific colonial economic conditions, and the French asserted their right to assign military conscripts to public works projects.[42]

Forced labour continued in French Africa until the end of the Second World War. The economic bureaucracy in AOF and AEF estimated that an adequate labour supply for infrastructure projects, military recruitment and settler-owned private enterprise could be secured only by coercive means. Manpower was unevenly spread across the two federations. Voluntary labour migration was also regionally confined, often seasonal, well established among some tribes, rare among others. Frederick Cooper sums up the position in reference to the cocoa plantations of Ivory Coast: 'Whereas the classic pattern of capitalist development in Europe entailed the assertion of the bourgeoisie's control over workers' time, the pattern of labor force recruitment in inter-war Africa came to depend more on the colonial states' control over space'.[43] The challenge was to get African labour where industry, settlers and administration wanted it without paying higher wages for the privilege. In 1927, for example, the Dakar authorities seized upon a measure devised by Marcel Olivier's administration in Madagascar a year earlier. Olivier's introduction of 'Labour Service for Public Interest Projects' enabled the colonial government to assign conscripts to work on railway construction for up to three years. African recruits could thus be redirected to work anywhere under the jurisdiction of their colonial government.[44]

Yet ILO scrutiny eventually made its mark. Even Antonetti's government introduced measures in January 1935 stipulating minimum age requirements, working hours, and meal breaks for nursing mothers working as casual labourers.[45] In the following year Blum's government at last ratified the 1930 ILO convention. The Popular Front's insistence on basic worker rights came as a rude shock to officials and settler producers throughout francophone black Africa. Yet even the Popular Front rejected the immediate abolition of forced labour, *prestations*, or forcible army recruitment. The worst abuses were tackled, but coercive practices survived. The Blum government certainly promoted voluntary African wage labour as a preferable alternative. And ministers accepted that forced labour, however economically expedient in the short term, was morally indefensible in the longer term. Yet the transition to a free labour system was to be gradual: officially sponsored, but not implemented legislatively overnight.[46]

Liberal colonial reformers also faced an uphill struggle against an obstructive colonial bureaucracy and the sheer scale of social deprivation in the empire. In 1936 the Ministry of Colonies turned to the Supreme Colonial Council (CSC) to determine urgent reform priorities. Under the Popular Front the CSC, reinvented in December 1935 as the Supreme Council for Overseas France (CSFOM), became a key advisory committee on social policy. The CSFOM president, Lucien Hubert, had served briefly as Minister of Justice in André Tardieu's Cabinet over the winter of 1929–30. Born in 1868, the avuncular Hubert was better known as a veteran colonial official, a committed pacifist and Radical Party elder. With Hubert in the chair, the CSFOM discussed employment reforms, the creation of more elected municipal councils, and the extension of colonial assembly powers over local budgets.[47] After Blum's government fell from office in June 1937 the CSFOM focused once more on economic problems to the exclusion of social policy. But by 1939 the committee had returned to its perennial concerns: efficient labour allocation between colonies, export production, transport policy and the imbalance of France–empire trade.[48] This was part of a broader shift. In its preparations for war, Edouard Daladier's government eroded the Popular Front's limited labour reforms still further.[49]

Urban development: contact between communities in French North Africa

French colonialism in the Maghreb was distinguished by the higher level of European settlement in the only overseas territories closely proximate to France. Algeria was the most favoured destination. Even after the surge in European immigration to Morocco after 1919, the settler population in 1926 was still less than 100,000.[50] Across North West Africa contacts between settlers and *indigènes* were increasingly urban. Colonial urbanism was therefore an important marker of the enduring French presence and the interplay between metropolitan design culture and colonial society. The growth and redesign of colonial cities was an important source of French imperial pride. But the movement of peoples between France and North Africa was never exclusively one-way. Having taken root during the First World War, Maghrebi immigration to France became more entrenched between the wars. Just as the French made their mark in North Africa through ambitious urban planning schemes, so Maghrebi immigrant communities altered the demographic structure of French cities, although less so than popular imagery of 'africanised' *quartiers* in France's inner cities might suggest. The development of colonial urbanism and official and public responses to colonial immigration indicate that the colonial state constructed relations between urban communities, and between metropolitan and immigrant populations, in racial terms that privileged white dominance. These racial stereotypes were reinforced by the French judicial discrimination against 'rootless' immigrant workers. Maghrebi immigrants especially were overwhelmingly single males living communally, often surviving on seasonal employment or casual labour, all factors which compounded their 'foreign' aspect.[51] Ironically, the growing French presence in colonial cities also generated sharper racial distinctions. The more that colonial cities acquired a Gallic veneer, and the greater the contact between the French and their colonial subjects, the more the racial hierarchies of empire became embedded.

The quickening pace of urbanisation after 1919 brought the European and Muslim communities of French North Africa into closer daily contact. Townsfolk, village communities and urban workers interacted across the racial divide, *colons* participating in the evening festivities of Ramadan, Muslims and settlers developing a distinct Franco-Arabic slang to describe the metropolitan French.[52] But urban overcrowding also accentuated inequality. The Maghreb was not alone in this respect. In Damascus the city's traditional organisational centres – mosques, Koranic schools, markets and bustling residential quarters – became focal points of opposition to French rule and emblems of the growing social divisions between rich and poor, educated and uneducated, French and Arabic-speakers.[53]

The spread of wage labour and internal economic migration fostered the growth of a larger urban colonial under-class in other French territories. The recorded population of Dakar almost doubled in size between 1930 and 1936, from 57,000 to 93,000.[54] Municipal authorities struggled to cope. Dakar's skeletal public health infrastructure had been in crisis for a generation by the time this population influx began. Rubbish collection services, improvements in sewage disposal and the expansion of fresh water supplies were disrupted by the advent of war and a bubonic plague epidemic in 1914.[55] Overcrowding, closer human proximity to rat-infested docks, rubbish tips and grain stores, as well as the inadequate diet of poor Senegalese, contributed to the recurrence of plague in Dakar in June 1919.[56]

Inter-communal friction in North Africa intensified as overcrowding worsened and demolition of Muslim housing areas increased.[57] Algerian Muslims were driven to political opposition, religious particularism and a reassertion of their Islamic identity by their iniquitous treatment at the hands of a colonial regime that upheld settler interests. Why was the majority of the *colon* population so reactionary? After 1918 the majority of settlers lived and worked in the coastal towns.[58] Yet *Algérie française* defined itself by reference to arcane ideals of peasant endeavour and small-town life. The docksides of Algeria's coastal ports evoked Marseilles and Toulon. But isolated Algerian market towns also mimicked their French equivalents from their flag-bedecked mayor's office to their ripe-smelling *pissotière*.[59] By the mid-1920s the central planks of settler identity – and of settlers' contempt for Paris authority – were in place. Right-wing commentators held up settler society as the bastion of a nationalist trinity: patriotism, Catholicism and tradition – all that was best in 'true France'.[60] The idealisation of the settler farmer as the embodiment of virile, patriotic dynamism echoed the ultra-rightism of French leagues such as the Croix de Feu. But French Algerians had matched words with deeds, forging a society anchored in hard graft, patriarchal hierarchy and large families. Inter-war France was decadent by comparison. Affluent city dwellers succumbed to modern vices. Workers were infected with revolutionary ideas. Bourgeois women rejected marriage, domesticity and reproduction as their natural heritage.[61]

Two distinctive literary movements to emerge from Algeria's settler community before 1940 tell us much about the underlying social environment of the colony. Between 1900 and 1919 the distinct 'Algerianism' that emerged in the literary production of settler writers reflected broader *colon* opposition to any traces of metropolitan liberalism in the Algiers administration. Algerianism's central claim was that colonial society had evolved a unique identity, distinctly French and yet different from, and in no way subordinate to, the dictates of Paris. The only true 'Algerians' were European settlers. The Muslim masses were an undifferentiated 'Other', objectified and unworthy of consideration as autonomous political and cultural actors. Their designation as Muslim and Arab confirmed their alien origins in an oriental theocratic community rooted in a territory more remote from Algeria than France.[62]

The Algerianists' denigration of Muslim culture, their insistence that settlers fashioned a modern polity from barbaric anarchy and their resentment toward metropolitan interference will be familiar to any student of colonial Algeria. They systematically erased the Arab contribution to the social evolution of Algeria and stereotyped the Muslim community as ignorant, predatory and cruel. As Peter Dunwoodie illustrates, Algerianist novelists of the early twentieth century were cultural militants. Writers such as René Garnier, founder of the *Revue nord africaine illustrée*, and Robert Randau (born Robert Arnaud), an Ecole coloniale graduate, former administrator, and co-founder in 1921 of the Association of Algerian Writers, were as intolerant of Muslim claims to greater rights and freedoms as they were of the patronising metropolitan clichés of the colonial exotic and the cultural naivety of settler society.[63] Instead, the Algerianists articulated the cultural triumphalism of settler domination. As the first editorial of the literary review *Afrique latine* phrased it in December 1921, Algeria had rediscovered its true Roman heritage after centuries of neglect 'in the voluptuous lethargy of oriental civilisation'.[64]

Whatever its claims to a separate cultural sphere and greater political autonomy, settler Algerianism derived much of its inspiration from the earlier writings of French antisemites and racial theorists such as de Gobineau and Drumont. The Algerianists' cultural arrogance borrowed from Charles Maurras and the ultra-nationalism of Action Française.[65] The most famous *colon* character of popular fiction in the early twentieth century was Cagayous, a working-class hero from the Algiers district of Bab-el-Oued. His adventures were regular fixtures in the settler press from the mid-1890s to 1920. Augustin Robinet, the creator of Cagayous, portrayed him as a lovable rogue, an anti-establishment figure of simple virtue and forthright opinions, including a lusty hatred of Jews, Muslims and metropolitan do-gooders.[66] In so far as Robinet and the subsequent wave of Algerianist writers favoured assimilationism, it was as a means to guarantee European institutional dominance of an Algeria integrated with France on settlers' terms. More tolerant, the two prominent women novelists in inter-war Algeria, Elissa Rhaïs and Lucienne Favre, placed Muslim women at the centre of their work but did not challenge the racial order.[67]

During the 1930s a younger, less triumphalist generation of settler writers emerged in Algiers. Dubbed the 'Ecole d'Alger school', writers including Gabriel Audisio, René-Jean Clot and, most famously, the young Albert Camus spurned the conscious racism of the Algerianists. Audisio, a Marseilles-born former civil servant of the Algiers government, broke through with his award-winning 1925 novel, *Trois hommes et un minaret*, a parody of the growing Maghrebi presence in Paris. Camus was better known in the Algiers of the late 1930s as a left-wing essayist and theatre impresario than as a novelist. The two men shared a more idealistic vision of Algerian society, not as an exclusively white preserve, but rather as part of a generic Mediterranean culture shaped by its ties with the sea. What Peter Dunwoodie terms 'Mediterraneity' stressed the bonds of coast and climate that linked the populations of the western Mediterranean region rather than the racial politics that divided them.[68] To their critics, the Ecole d'Alger school ignored the acute divisions in colonial Algeria and presumed a shared Franco-Muslim identity where none existed.[69]

Whatever their limitations, Audisio and Camus gave voice to a new hopefulness and liberality congruent with the emergence of the Popular Front in France. Assimilation in their eyes promised harmonious communal coexistence, albeit no equivalence of political rights. It is easy to pick holes in this idealistic, counterfactual outlook. To take Philip Dine's telling example, Camus liked to recall his inter-war experiences as an outstanding goalkeeper with the Racing Universitaire Algérois football team as evidence of inter-ethnic partnership. In Camus's idealistic recollections the cultural signifiers and social inequities between French and Muslim Algerians disappeared on the sportsfield.[70] But another promising young player of the day, Ahmed Ben Bella, the future FLN leader and president of independent Algeria, remembered his school football matches in Tlemcen rather differently. Muslim students relished the chance to compete with Europeans on genuinely equal terms in sport. But youth and professional teams in inter-war Algeria were usually racially segregated, and, in Ben Bella's recollection, settler players were physically larger because they were better nourished. The professional football teams that proliferated in urban Algeria during the 1920s were rigidly structured along ethnic lines, and drew their support accordingly. It was racial violence at inter-war football matches that compelled the Algiers government to introduce regulations in the 1930s specifying that all 'Muslim' teams should include at least three European players.[71]

The settler cult was a myth. The ideal of the imperial pioneer as a straight-talking son of the soil was, of course, not unique to French imperialism or to colonial Algeria. None the less, it was a gross distortion of recent history to suggest that the twin pillars of French Algeria were single-minded military conquest and the blood and sweat of the white farmer.[72] The military conquest was retarded by recurrent Muslim revolts. The army's suppression of this dissent, particularly in the late 1840s and in the early 1870s, was almost genocidal. Settler traditionalism conveniently ignored Europeans' drift from the land to urban *banlieus*, a pattern of internal migration that was well established by 1900. *Colon* leaders controlled Algerian municipal government during the Second and Third Republics. The authorities' demolition of Arab quarters, *souks* and even mosques was so severe that overall urban population levels diminished. In General Bugeaud's Algeria, mosques and *medinas* were destroyed or even recycled to make way for army barracks, administrative buildings, settler housing and Catholic churches. The resultant transformation, sometimes compared to the 'Hausmannisation' of Paris in the Second Empire, facilitated colonial control in densely populated urban areas.[73] But the demolition process ran roughshod over central tenets of the Muslim city: the schematic demarcation between male public space and female domestic space, the avoidance of public gaze into family homes, and the veneration of religious sites.[74]

Ironically, the nineteenth century waves of urban clearances were accompanied by the incorporation of Moorish and Islamic architectural styling – or *arabisances* – into the public buildings that supplanted Muslim housing areas in Algeria and, later, in Tunisia and Morocco as well.[75] The population of Algiers recovered to its 1830 level in 1860. But Tlemcen did not do so until 1891, Mascara until 1901, Constantine until 1911.[76] An unprecedented construction boom in the twenty years before 1914 transformed Algiers still further. Sixty-six new roads ploughed through Arab housing, and the new suburbs of Mustafa, Hamma and Belcourt sprang up to the west of the city. This largely *ad hoc* growth was fed by the doubling of the population of Greater Algiers from 120,000 in 1896 to 212,000 thirty years later. By 1926 Algiers had become a city utterly dominated by the requirements of its burgeoning settler population.[77] David Prochaska's study of Bône (Annaba) brings these dislocations to life. Between 1870 and 1920 the French *ville nouvelle* and sprawling districts of working-class housing engulfed the existing Arab city. By 1914 the city's main boulevard, the Cours Bertagna, was almost entirely French in aspect, construction and population. Muslims were concentrated in the poorest, outer *banlieues*. In Bône, as in other colonial cities, racial segregation existed in fact, if not in name.[78] Janet Abu-Lughod's study of Rabat, capital of the Moroccan protectorate, and Zeynep Çelik's investigation of the changing urban structure of Algiers make it plain that communal segregation characterised colonial urbanism throughout the Maghreb and French Africa more generally.[79] Colonial urban centres became archetypal 'dual cities' with distinct economic, cultural and architectural boundaries separating Europeans from the Muslim majority.[80]

The selective importation of French urban design deepened the gulf between rulers and ruled. It is a truism to state that French town planning emphasised the supposed permanence of the colonial presence. The public buildings, separate administrative districts, and settler new towns constructed in the inter-war years from Casablanca to Saigon monumentalised

French political power and racial dominance. A commentator at a 1927 colonial urban planning conference in Paris conceded, '[Colonial] urbanism is eugenics applied to towns'.[81] The superficial modernity of urban development in colonial cities masked the chronic poverty of the indigenous majority at their margins. The familiar tranquillity of French-designed settlements in the Algerian interior concealed the wholesale dispossession of the Muslim peasantry. The pattern of urban development in Tunisia was not dissimilar, although there was less outright dispossession of Muslim landowners. Two decrees passed a decade apart in December 1919 and July 1929 initiated affordable housing projects for the expanding industrial work force in Tunis and elsewhere. Municipal authorities in Tunis stressed that these projects would improve public health by demolishing the most overcrowded sections of the old city. It was no coincidence that these clearances also made urban policing and surveillance of the working class population much easier. Furthermore, Muslim inhabitants of Tunis's old quarters faced eviction as European workers took the lion's share of the new accommodation blocks, the so-called 'HBMs' (habitations à bon marché), built on the sites of old Arab dwellings.[82]

Aside from preferential treatment by municipal housing departments, European workers also had greater access to long-term credit. Of the twenty-eight mutual societies in inter-war Tunisia, only four catered to Muslims. During the depression the three capitals of French North Africa – Rabat, Algiers and Tunis – became more economically and racially segregated as unemployed peasant farmers flocked to the cities in search of work and existing urban workers struggled to find affordable accommodation within city limits. The *bidonvilles* at the fringes of these and other major cities in the Maghreb became home to Muslim economic migrants and local residents priced out of the housing market.[83]

Lyautey was always hostile to the corrosive effects of settler mercantilism on indigenous cultures. His protectorate administration was determined that French town planning in Morocco should avoid the destruction of Muslim civil society so evident in Algeria.[84] The Moroccan cities that Lyautey's urban planning directorate set out to create from 1913 onward were deliberately juxtaposed to Algiers, Constantine and Orléansville where successive waves of European settlement usurped Muslim property and public space.[85] But neither Lyautey, and still less his successors Théodore Steeg, Lucien Saint and Henri Ponsot, ever reversed the preferential allocation of land, social spending and public housing to the settler population. Morocco's *colons* were offered tax breaks, cheap land and property, and took a disproportionate share of municipal spending on utilities, education and health. The urban planning boom in Lyautey's Morocco that saw Rabat emerge as the national capital and Casablanca develop as the protectorate's commercial powerhouse was predicated on settler dominance of the Moroccan economy.[86] During the 1930s the urban poor of Rabat–Salé, the residency heartland, scratched out an existence among tents and lean-tos, a painful reminder of the limits of urban planning.[87]

Clearly, the new architectural aesthetic in Morocco had its limits, but it was certainly ambitious in concept. Gwendolyn Wright and Shirine Hamadeh draw out the parallels between urban planning under Lyautey and associationist theories of government. Hamadeh criticises the tendency among historians to view French colonial urbanism in orientalist terms as an imposed dichotomy between the colonial authorities' preservation of 'traditional' Muslim cities and their concurrent investment in the construction of 'modern' European cities. Yet she concedes that colonial urban planning in North Africa objectified Muslim settlements as areas to be preserved but not much invested in, while the flow of capital investment went instead to commercial centres and residential areas dominated by Europeans.[88] From Tunis to Rabat, these newer urban developments – or *villes nouvelles* – typically surrounded and thereby contained the pre-colonial towns. It was associationism applied to buildings and urban spaces.[89] In Lyautey's Morocco the Muslim city was to be preserved alongside – but separate from – its more dynamic French equivalent. In Janet Abu Lughod's words, this was 'urban apartheid'.[90] The walled city of Fez and Marrakech's Arab quarters were 'fossilised', preserved as living ethnographic exhibits, but starved of public funds. Matters were very different in Morocco's more northerly cities that attracted larger European populations. Casablanca and Rabat especially became laboratories for architectural modernism and unrestricted social engineering.[91] By the 1920s Rabat and Oudja on the Morocco–Algeria border were bustling commercial centres. The older imperial cities of Fez, Marrakech and Meknès that remained strongly Muslim in composition never enjoyed comparable levels of state support or economic growth.[92]

The development of Casablanca from the minor port of Dar El Beida was more dramatic still. In this instance, an entire city was constructed to a European model. Its commercial success and population growth were emblematic of French imperialism. A city built up from virtually nothing, Casablanca was, in William Hoisington's words, 'the French beachhead' in Morocco.[93] Moreover, in Casablanca roles were reversed: indigenous Moroccans were essential to build and administer an essentially European city, not vice versa. In Morocco's more established towns, urban development tested co-operation between residency planners and *makhzen* officials.[94] In Casablanca, however, a new façade of Muslim administration had to be created. The Muslim *pashas*, *cadis* (Shari'a court magistrates), and other indigenous municipal functionaries selected to run Casablanca's native affairs administration were brought in from elsewhere. But even here Lyautey favoured the appointment of officials chosen from the few aristocratic and merchant families local to the area. His appointees proved troublesome. A series of corruption scandals, a chronic shortage of willing Muslim intermediaries, the French obsession with surveillance of the Muslim population, and the economic stratification of Casablanca limited the opportunities for anything like a Franco-Muslim partnership in municipal government.[95]

Lyautey's urban planners were not so easily daunted. Led by his appointee Henri Prost, these developers were free of the planning constraints and popular pressure that prevented the wholesale redesign of French cities. Prost and his deputy, Albert Laprade, took advantage of their freedom of manoeuvre to plan urban development in Casablanca and Rabat that reconciled French commercial interests, the strategic requirements of colonial urban policing and Lyautey's insistence on a zonal framework for both business and residential districts that privileged the needs of the European and Moroccan elite.[96] Between 1913 and the completion of the Rabat development plan in 1930 the protectorate administration applied its sweeping arbitrary powers to undertake massive projects of urban renewal. The first town planning regulations enacted in Morocco in April 1914 were thus in advance of any comparable legislation in France. The modernisation of Rabat was quite unprecedented in the history of French state urbanism. More generally, the zonal segregation of the settlers' new towns from the established native quarters of the major cities; rigid standards for road construction, hygiene and water services; and the codification of strict building regulations to apply modern architectural aesthetics and uniformity in construction methods were all practices later adopted in other colonial cities from Hanoi and Dalat to Dakar and Tunis.[97]

In the Moroccan protectorate, title to property, urban planning codes and public funds were all skewed in favour of settlers. Everything, from the compulsory purchase of Muslim land situated on sites of planned new towns to the installation of water and sewerage systems, benefited the European urban population to the exclusion of the older Muslim medinas. On 12 August 1913 a *dahir* (Sharifian decree) established a new system of title to land modelled on the Torrens Act in Australia. Lyautey instructed officers of the army geographical service to undertake topographical surveys around Rabat, Casablanca and Oudja that parcelled land into available plots. Freehold land, collectively farmed pastures and even *habous* land administered by Muslim religious establishments could now be purchased by settlers or the state provided that the purchaser could indicate that expropriation served a public purpose, such as productive agriculture or urban development. Contested land claims were settled under French property law, and required written title to determine ownership, a caveat that favoured the European purchaser. The growth of urban Morocco in the 1920s, the quintessential model of colonial urbanism, rested on massive expropriation of Muslim land, often without compensation.[98]

It is not difficult to establish the veracity of Frantz Fanon's identification of the duality inherent in colonial cities in which European populations enjoyed the benefits of paved roads, clean water supplies and ample space while their indigenous subjects were crowded into the poorest housing with minimal public services. After attending the 1930 centennial celebrations of French rule in Algeria, even Le Corbusier, France's most renowned architect of the early twentieth century, produced an ambitious scheme for the urban redevelopment of Algiers, the Plan Obus, that assigned the Muslim population a subordinate role in a colonial metropolis designed as the hub of a modern industrial economy serving the needs of France.[99]

French North Africa was not the only colonial region affected by such dualistic urban development. By the 1920s numerous cities of the French empire had become concrete proof of the racial segregation and social exclusion of subject peoples within the colonial system.[100] Even the adoption of European clothing styles could reinforce ethnic boundaries rather than breaking them down. The African townspeople of colonial Brazzaville, for example, imitated European dress codes and social etiquettes. By 1920 the Compagnie française du Bas-Congo employed three tailors to run up clothes for African purchasers styled on French department store catalogues, including the Galeries Lafayette. But the clothing that most Africans could afford, including rubber sandals rather than pricey leather shoes, was far removed from the standard 'kit' of uniforms, heavy-weather gear and leisure wear recommended to colonial officials and their wives.[101] Meanwhile, from Brazzaville to Hanoi the physical separation of French residents from the indigenous inhabitants of colonial cities suggested a fear of contamination at variance with the declared official objective of colonial advancement through exposure to French culture.

Conclusion

The evidence offered here suggests that popular disaffection with French rule was likely to increase whether colonies got richer or poorer. Grinding poverty had an obvious political dynamic of its own. People with nothing to lose were inherently difficult to govern. But increased affluence generated another force for dissent that was just as dangerous to French authority: the power of rising expectations. If anything, limited economic modernisation heightened the injustice of colonial authoritarianism because its economic benefits were narrowly channelled to investors, trading companies and settlers. As Gray Wilder puts it, 'The challenge of Greater France was to include the colonies as integral elements of the French nation while locating colonial subjects outside the homogeneous juridical field that in practice defined the republican nation state.'[102] Here the colonial authorities fell down.

The degree to which colonial populations should be included in the republican imperial project was at the heart of inter-war debates over empire. Colonial urbanism in the Maghreb suggested that the French authorities favoured a stricter demarcation between rulers and ruled. Urban planning in North Africa marked a clear physical manifestation of associationist ideas. The Moroccan example is perhaps the clearest. Under Lyautey's guiding hand from 1913 onward urban development set out to entrench French rule while leaving existing Muslim settlement substantially intact.[103] The spatial segregation of 'traditional' Muslim cities from dynamic European *villes nouvelles* would mirror the social hierarchy of colonial domination. The gradual shift toward the preservation of Muslim cities, religious sites and cultural centres rather than the wholesale destruction of Arab housing and architecture that characterised the first decades of French rule in Algeria signified the adoption of the 'dual cities' approach to urban planning. European new towns surrounding – and generally supplanting – Muslim old towns represented the two communities, one of citizens, the other of subjects, typical of colonial society.

The growth of colonial cash economies hastened urbanisation and class formation, irrespective of developers' schemes. The spread of wage labour produced small, but increasingly organised, indigenous industrial work forces, albeit largely confined to colonial cities, ports and commercial centres. Official fear of systematic worker protest informed administrative hostility to the urbanisation and industrialisation of colonial societies. Anxious talk of 'detribalisation' in francophone Africa or of the decline of peasant tradition in Indochina were coded expressions of administrative worries that economic modernisation would unleash social pressures that would undermine colonial hierarchy. Alarmed by the impact of the depression, in the early 1930s an emerging generation of colonial technocrats, many of them educated at the Ecole polytechnique, pressed for an end to administrative hostility to colonial industrialisation. Men such as Paul Bernard of the Société financière française et coloniale (SFFC, French colonial and finance company) in Indochina, and the former SFFC chairman and later Inspector of Finances, Edmond Giscard d'Estaing, who compiled an influential report on the economic prospects of French Africa in 1932, insisted that a diverse industrial base and a growing wage labour force with increased purchasing power were fundamental to the long-term profitability of the colonial enterprise.[104] But their message was unpopular in government circles. The tight restrictions imposed on African labour forces in sub-Saharan Africa, the vigorous suppression of early African trade unionism and the abrupt reversal of Popular Front liberalisation in Africa,

Indochina and elsewhere revealed that modern industrial practices and worker rights were simply incompatible with colonial domination.[105] By the 1930s the colonial state faced the prospect of urban dissent and industrial unrest of a type common in Europe. These protests were but one facet of colonial experience with a clear gender dimension, the subject of the next chapter.

Notes

1 Jane Guyer, 'Head tax, social structure and rural incomes in Cameroon, 1922–1937', *Cahiers d'Etudes Africaines*, 20 (1980), 305–22, also cited in Andreas Eckert, 'African rural entrepreneurs and labor in the Cameroon littoral', *Journal of African History*, 40:1 (1999), 117–18. Douala landowners of the Cameroon littoral dominated cocoa cultivation until the 1930s depression. Douala entrepreneurship then declined owing to the collapse in export prices and the spread of labour-intensive plantation agriculture in the Cameroon interior following the development of new road systems.
2 Pennell, *Morocco*, 198. In Morocco, *caïds* (makhzen officials) received six per cent of the taxes collected.
3 Raymond Gervais, 'La plus riche des colonies pauvres : la politique monétaire et fiscale de la France au Tchad 1900–1920', *Canadian Journal of African Studies*, 16:1 (1982), 93–112.
4 *Ibid.*, 105–11. The 1925 budgetary surplus was recorded as 1,488,676 francs.
5 CAOM, Marius Moutet papers, PA28/1/D1, no. 1009, Moutet letter to Antonetti, 'Conférence des gouverneurs-généraux', 12 August 1936.
6 Jacques Marseille, 'La conférence des gouverneurs-généraux des colonies (novembre 1936)', *Le Mouvement social*, 101 (1977), 65–6.
7 Guelmami, *La Politique sociale en Tunisie*, 60–5, especially table I, p. 63.
8 Patrick Braibant, 'L'administration coloniale et le profit commercial en Côte d'Ivoire pendant la crise de 1929', *Revue Française d'Histoire d'Outre-Mer*, 63:3–4 (1976), 555–7.
9 Catherine Coquery-Vidrovitch, 'Mutation de l'impérialisme colonial français dans les années 1930', *African Economic History* 4 (1977), 129; Patrick Manning *Francophone Sub-Saharan Africa, 1880–1985* (Cambridge: Cambridge University Press, 1988), 51; also cited in Ghislaine Lydon, 'The unravelling of a neglected source. A report on women in francophone Africa in the 1930s', *Cahiers d'Etudes Africaines*, 147 (1997), 557.
10 CAOM, GGAEF, 1D6, no. 326, Antonetti to Colonies, 19 March 1931.
11 CAOM, GGAEF, 1D10, Marchessou to Affaires politiques, n.d. July 1935.
12 Bellarmin C. Codo and Sylvian C. Anignikin, 'Pouvoir colonial et tentatives d'intégration africaines dans le système capitaliste : le cas du Dahomey entre les deux guerres', *Canadian Journal of African Studies*, 16:2 (1982), 331–42.
13 The Dakar administration played down the significance of this migration to British territory. See, for example, CAOM, affpol/542, Dossier 10, 'Rapport politique du gouvernement-général de l'AOF, année 1935'. Regarding migration as political defiance, see Asiwaju, 'Migrations as revolt'. Male migration to avoid military recruiters was also endemic in early twentieth-century AOF, see Echenberg, 'Les migrations militaires', 429–50.
14 Martin Thomas, 'Bedouin tribes and the imperial intelligence services in Syria, Iraq and Trans-Jordan in the 1920s', *Journal of Contemporary History*, 38:4 (2003), 539–62.
15 CAOM, Marius Moutet papers, PA28/1/D9, no. 2857, Chambre des Députés, session de 1937, 16e Législature, Commission des finances, Report by Paul Reynaud, 'Budget général de l'exercice 1938: Colonies', 19 October 1937.
16 CAOM, affpol/757, 'Conférence des gouverneurs des Antilles et de la Guyane', 24 November 1938. Martinique had a chronic unemployment problem in the late 1930s.
17 See, for example, the case of *indigène* farm workers in French Oceania, whose membership of the two *syndicates agricoles* in the Windward Islands was restricted in this way: CAOM, affpol/76, Dossier 4, no. 2189, Direction des affaires économiques, 'Note pour la Direction politique', 6 June 1925.

18 For an interesting comparison of British colonial responses to Arab trade unionism see Zachary Lockman, 'British policy towards Egyptian labour activism, 1882–1936', *International Journal of Middle East Studies*, 20 (1988), 265–85, and his *Comrades and Enemies. Arab and Jewish Workers in Palestine, 1906–1948* (Berkeley CA: University of California Press, 1996), especially chapters 2, 5 and 6.

19 CAOM, affpol/73, Dossier: Madagascar et dépendances, Direction des affaires économiques, 1er bureau, to Ernest Lafont, 29 January 1935.

20 Conklin, 'Colonialism and human rights', 439.

21 Oloruntimehin, 'The economy of French West Africa', 57–9, 68. The fall in Ivory Coast timber exports in the 1930s also reflected the impact of deforestation.

22 Cordell and Gregory, 'Labour reservoirs and population', 207–15.

23 Dennis Cordell and Joel Gregory estimate that between 1923 and 1946 an annual average of sixteen per cent of young men in the Koudougou *cercle* in Upper Volta evaded labour service, see their 'Labour reservoirs and population', 220; see also Bassett, 'The development of cotton', 272–6.

24 CAOM, affpol/76, Dossier 2, *Journal Officiel*, 9 May 1925.

25 CAOM, affpol/119, Dossier 1, no. 1401, Victor Augagneur letter to Sarraut, 24 July 1923. The resale to the state of private land on the designated railway route offered huge profits to settler landowners. Augagneur was accused of corruption by the head of a family business that lost out in these dealings. Augagneur denied the charge.

26 CAOM, GGAEF, 1D10, no. 147, Secrétaire-général Marchessou to Direction des affaires politiques, 1er bureau, 24 January 1935.

27 Roberts, *Two Worlds*, 234–42.

28 Oloruntimehin, 'The economy of French West Africa', 74.

29 V. Tillinac, 'La main-d'oeuvre tonkinois', *L'Océanie Française*, 16:54 (November–December 1920), 118–121.

30 Aldrich, *The French Presence*, 163–4, 267.

31 Stuart-Fox, 'The French in Laos', 123–35.

32 Pierre Brocheux, 'Le prolétariat des plantations d'hévéas au Vietnam méridional : aspects sociaux et politiques (1927–1937)', *Le Mouvement Social*, 90:1 (1975), 55–87.

33 CAOM, Marius Moutet papers, PA28/4/Dossier Varenne, sous-dossier 59, 'Aperçu de l'oeuvre accompli en Indochine par Alexandre Varenne'.

34 Coquery-Vidrovitch, *Le Congo*, 519–20.

35 *Ibid.*, 516–21.

36 CAOM, affpol/73, 'Note sur l'évaluation des taxes au Gabon en harmonie avec la situation budgetaire', n.d. 1935.

37 Gray, 'Lambaréné, Okoumé and the transformation of labor', 99–105.

38 CAOM, GGAEF, 1D1, no. 413, Antonetti letter to Directeur Générale de l'Union Coloniale Française, 10 August 1926.

39 Martin Fine, 'Albert Thomas. A reformer's vision of modernization, 1914–32', *Journal of Contemporary History*, 12:3 (1977), 552–6.

40 CAOM, GGAEF, 1D1, Antonetti to Affaires économiques (Colonies), 6 June 1926.

41 CAOM, affpol/663/D1, Antonetti letter to Ministry of Colonies, 1 May 1925.

42 Frederick Cooper, *Decolonization and African Society. The Labor question in French and British Africa* (Cambridge: Cambridge University Press, 1996), 29–30. Aside from scandals over AEF colonies, labour abuses were reported in the Belgian Congo, Kenya and Angola.

43 Frederick Cooper, 'Conditions analogous to slavery. Imperialism and free labor in Africa', in Frederick Cooper, Thomas C. Holt and Rebecca J. Scott (eds), *Beyond Slavery. Explorations of Race, Labor and Citizenship in Postemancipation Societies* (Chapel Hill NC: University of North Carolina Press, 2000), 132.

44 Roberts *Two Worlds*, 227.

45 CAOM, AEFGG, 1D10, no. 147, Secrétaire-général Marchessou to Direction des affaires politiques, 1er bureau, 24 January 1935.

46 Cooper, 'Conditions analogous to slavery', 134–6.

47 CAOM, affpol/852, no. 1902/CS, Lucien Hubert, Président du bureau du CSFOM to Minister of Colonies, 10 December 1937.

48 CAOM, affpol/852, no. 7917, Direction des affaires économiques to Président du bureau du CSFOM, 10 October 1938.

49 Cooper 'Conditions analogous to slavery', 135–6.

50 Abu-Lughod, *Rabat. Urban Apartheid in Morocco*, 155 n. 3. By the end of the Moroccan protectorate in 1956 the European population had climbed to 350,000.

51 Mary Dewhurst Lewis, 'The strangeness of foreigners. Policing migration and nation in inter-war Marseille', *French Politics, Culture and Society*, 20:3 (2002), 72–7.

52 Ali Yedes, 'Social dynamics in colonial Algeria. The question of *pieds-noirs'* identity', in Stovall and Van Den Abbeele, *French Civilization*, 235–40.

53 Philip S. Khoury, 'Syrian urban politics in transition. The quarters of Damascus during the French Mandate', *International Journal of Middle East Studies*, 16:4 (1984), 507–9.

54 Yves Person, 'Le Front populaire au Sénégal (mai 1936–octobre 1938)', *Le Mouvement Social*, 107:2 (1979), 83.

55 Echenberg, *Black Death, White Medicine*, 30–1.

56 *Ibid.*, 190–7.

57 Christelow, 'The mosque at the edge of the plaza', 292–4.

58 Jeannine Verdès-Leroux, *Les Français d'Algérie de 1830 à aujourd-hui* (Paris: Fayard, 2001), 177–82.

59 These comparisons are drawn out in Verdès-Leroux, *Les Français d'Algérie*.

60 Herman Lebovics, *True France. The Wars over Cultural Identity, 1900–1945* (Ithaca NY: Cornell University Press, 1992).

61 Neil MacMaster, 'Writing French Algeria', *French Cultural Studies*, 11:1 (2000), 148–55.

62 Dunwoodie, *Writing French Algeria*, 4, citing Rabah Belamri, *L'Oeuvre de Louis Bertrand. Miroir de l'idéologie colonialiste* (Algiers: Presses Universitaires, 1980), 30–1, 200–1.

63 Dunwoodie, *Writing French Algeria*, 122–74.

64 *Ibid.*, 124.

65 René Garnier's 1905 demand of 'L'Algérie aux Algériens' evoked the notorious slogan 'La France aux Français' of Edouard Drumont's racist newspaper *La Libre Parole*, see Dunwoodie, *Writing French Algeria*, 126–7.

66 *Ibid.*, 89; David Prochaska, 'History as literature, literature as history. Cagayous of Algiers', *American Historical Review*, 101:3 (1996), 671–711.

67 Dunwoodie, *Writing French Algeria*, 148–9; Patricia M. E. Lorcin, 'Sex, gender, and race in the colonial novels of Elissa Rhaïs and Lucienne Favre', in Peabody and Stovall, *The Color of Liberty*, 124–5.

68 *Ibid.*, 175–217 *passim*.

69 David Carroll, 'Camus's Algeria. Birthrights, colonial injustice, the fiction of a French-Algerian people', *Modern Language Notes*, 112 (1997), 529–31.

70 Philip Dine, 'Un héroïsme problématique : le sport, la littérature et la guerre d'Algérie', *Europe* 806 (June/July 1996), 177–85.

71 Philip Dine, 'France, Algeria and sport. From colonisation to globalisation', *Modern and Contemporary France*, 10:4 (2002), 498.

72 The argument is discussed at length in Jean-François Guillaume, *Les Mythes fondateurs de l'Algérie française* (Paris: Editions l'Harmattan, 1992).

73 Michele Lamprakos, 'Le Corbusier and Algiers. The Plan Obus as colonial urbanism', and Shirine Hamadeh, 'Creating the traditional city. A French project', both in Nezar Al Sayyad (ed.), *Forms of Dominance. On the Architecture and Urbanism of the Colonial Enterprise* (Aldershot: Ashgate, 1992), 187 and 244.

74 These features are discussed in Janet Abu-Lughod, 'The Islamic city. Historic myth, Islamic essence, and contemporary relevance', *International Journal of Middle East Studies*, 19:2 (1987), 155–76.

75 Lamprakos, 'Le Corbusier', 189–91; Hamadeh, 'Creating the traditional city', 249.

76 Djilali Sari, 'The role of the medinas in the reconstruction of Algerian culture and identity', in Susan Slyomovics (ed.), *The Walled Arab City in Literature, Architecture and History. The Living Medina in the Maghrib* (London: Frank Cass, 2001), 70.

77 Zeynep Çelik, *Urban Forms and Colonial Confrontations. Algiers under French Rule* (Berkeley CA: University of California Press, 1997), 28–38, 67–70.

78 Prochaska, *Making Algeria French*, 153–65.

79 Abu-Lughod, *Rabat. Urban Apartheid in Morocco*; Çelik, *Urban Forms*. For similar segregationist policies south of the Sahara see Lynn Schler, 'Ambiguous spaces. The struggle over African identities and urban communities in colonial Douala, 1914–45', *Journal of African History*, 44:1 (2003), 51–72.

80 Janet Abu-Lughod, 'Tale of two cities. The origins of modern Cairo', *Comparative Studies in Society and History*, 7:4 (1965), 429; also cited in Anthony D. King, 'Writing colonial space. A review article', *Comparative Studies in Society and History*, 37:4 (1995), 541.

81 'L'urbanisme dans nos colonies : une exposition d'urbanisme colonial', *Le Monde Colonial illustré*, 146 (June 1927), 130.

82 Abdelmajid Guelmami, *La Politique sociale en Tunisie*, 65–6. Guelmami cites a figure of 924 cheap housing blocks built for Tunisian city workers between 1897 and 1928.

83 *Ibid.*

84 Paul Rabinow, 'Colonialism, modernity. The French in Morocco', in Al Sayyad, *Forms of Dominance*, 170–82.

85 Rabinow, *French Modern*, chapter 4.

86 Abu-Lughod, *Rabat. Urban Apartheid in Morocco*, 150–73.

87 Pennell, *Morocco*, 199, 223.

88 Hamadeh, 'Creating the traditional city', 241–3, 250. The fullest treatment of colonial urban design in French Morocco is Gwendolyn Wright, *The Politics of Design in French Colonial Urbanism* (Chicago: University of Chicago Press, 1991).

89 Rabinow, 'Colonialism, modernity', 172.

90 Abu-Lughod, *Rabat. Urban Apartheid in Morocco*.

91 Irbouh, 'French colonial art education', 275.

92 Abu-Lughod, *Rabat. Urban Apartheid in Morocco*, 153–5. By 1921 the registered population of Casablanca was only forty-six per cent Muslim. In Rabat the figure was fifty-nine per cent, and in Oudja fifty-one per cent. By contrast, in the same year, Europeans made up only one per cent of the registered population in Marrakech, three per cent in Fez and eleven per cent in Meknès.

93 William A. Hoisington, Jr, 'In search of a native elite. Casablanca and French urban policy, 1914–1924', *Maghreb Revew*, 12:5–6 (1987), 160.

94 Abu-Lughod, *Rabat. Urban Apartheid in Morocco*, 174–5.

95 Hoisington, Jr, 'In search of a native elite', 160–5.

96 Rabinow, 'Colonialism, modernity', 173–8.

97 Rabinow, *French Modern*, 288–92; Raymond F. Betts, 'Imperial designs. French colonial architecture and urban planning in sub-Saharan Africa', in Wesley Johnson, *Double Impact*, 194–205.

98 Abu-Lughod, *Rabat. Urban Apartheid in Morocco*, 159–69.

99 Lamprakos, 'Le Corbusier', 193–203. Never implemented, the centrepiece of the Plan Obus was a 100 m high curved viaduct linking the city's business district with settler residential areas.

100 Frantz Fanon, *The Wretched of the Earth* (English translation, New York, 1968), 38–9, also cited in Çelik, *Urban Forms*, 3–4.

101 Martin, 'Contesting clothes in colonial Brazzaville', 407–17. Martin points out that Japanese clothing suppliers dominated the supply of cheap clothes and especially canvas and rubber shoes to Africans in inter-war AEF.

102 Wilder, 'Framing Greater France', 210.

103 Rabinow, *French Modern*, 288–94; Wright, *The Politics of Design*.

104 Hardy, 'The economics of French rule', 812–14.

105 Frederick Cooper, 'The dialectics of decolonisation. Nationalism and labor movements in postwar French Africa', in Frederick Cooper and Ann Laura Stoler (eds), *Tensions of Empire. Colonial Cultures in a Bourgeois World* (Berkeley CA: University of California Press, 1997), 409–11.

CHAPTER FIVE

Women and colonialism and colonial education

This chapter explores some of the ways in which the clash of metropolitan and colonial cultures affected an oft-times ignored colonial majority – women and children in the empire. The fact that French imperialism was a predominantly masculine enterprise makes the study of gender all the more important. Conquest, colonisation and governance were primarily the result of men's decisions and men's actions. There was a pronounced gender imbalance within the European population of the empire. Government officials, company representatives, landowners and planters, policemen and army officers inhabited a very masculine world.[1] And the entire colonial project is sometimes interpreted in gendered terms of white male dominance: 'virile' Nordic imperialists controlling feminised, colonised societies.[2] Furthermore, the hierarchy of colonial rule created unequal power relationships between races and sexes. The colonies presented vast opportunities for social and sexual exploitation of women and transgression of metropolitan codes of behaviour. By the early twentieth century unregulated contact between communities was increasingly frowned upon, less out of respect for indigenous cultures than out of suspicion of them. But contacts were difficult to control. The prevalence of domestic service led Europeans to develop close relationships – professional, personal or sexual – with servants. Concubinage and prostitution remained commonplace, particularly in Indochina, where *encongayement* – taking a Vietnamese concubine, or *con gaï* – stimulated government efforts after 1919 to increase the proportion of French women among the white population. As Michael Vann puts it, 'With more white women about, it became less common and less acceptable to be openly *encongaïé'*.[3]

Mounting official hostility to interracial mixing after the First World War was one reason why more and more French women joined their partners in colonial postings or travelled independently in the empire. Even so, men dominated French colonial communities politically, numerically and culturally.[4] Colonialism affected not only relations between the sexes but same-sex relationships as well. As Robert Aldrich reminds us, 'Hierarchical relations – master to slave, entrepreneur to employee, officer to subaltern, colonist to houseboy – facilitated sexual expectations and demands'.[5] Hardly surprising, then, that the intensely masculine milieux of colonial garrisons, administrations and corporations were also sites of what Aldrich terms 'situational' homosexuality.[6] Gender politics then were a central feature of colonial rule. And gender was as important as colour and creed in determining the educational opportunities open to children in the empire.

Women in the empire

The social history of indigenous women in the colonies is a vast subject of such diversity that only a few tentative conclusions may be advanced here. One is that contemporary political debate about women living under colonial rule refracted metropolitan controversies about the role of women. Although it would be crass to reduce women's history in inter-war France to the matter of voting rights, it does bear emphasis that, while numerous Bills introducing universal suffrage in France were tabled in the Chamber of Deputies between 1919 and 1933, none survived the opposition or procrastination of the Senate and the abiding doubts of Radical Party anticlericals about the voting intentions of devout French women. As early as May 1919 the Chamber voted for equal political rights for both sexes, only to be blocked by the Senate three years later. Republican universalism excluded women from the centres of power just as systematically as it excluded colonial subjects.[7] Women's rights in inter-war France were much discussed, if rarely conceded. What about the colonies? Here, too, official interest in the status of women gradually increased. After 1918 the creation of the League of Nations and a raft of interventionist non-governmental organisations spearheaded international scrutiny of labour exploitation, human trafficking, family law and women's living conditions in colonial societies. In the 1920s colonial governments and international agencies were still relatively inexperienced in their methods of data collection, and their local knowledge about women's lives was often limited. This was reflected in their tendency to treat women of very different origins and in very different colonial environments as a homogeneous group.

Contemporary debate about the role of indigenous women was also informed by their social and cultural relationship with white women.[8] While indigenous women were, in most cases, doubly subordinated to men and to the colonial state, European women in the French empire lived in a male-dominated world as 'the inferior sex within the superior race'.[9] White women were often caught between their own second-class status and anxiety to uphold the 'correct' racial, sexual and gender boundaries between Europeans and subject peoples prescribed by the colonial authorities.

French women were there to domesticate their menfolk, maintain a proper distance from the indigenous population, and personify the values of respectable gentility that befitted imperial administration. The pressure to conform was intense.[10] The problems encountered by European women in colonial societies have tended to dominate the women's history of twentieth-century empires. Sometimes cast as villains in the downfall of the male-dominated imperial project, sometimes as heroes in challenging male authority and the adversity of colonial life, European women in the colonies are at last being analysed in their own right as active members of diverse communities, often split along lines of class as well as race.[11]

Another general observation concerns colonial women's importance as economic actors and active members of a political community. These subjects are now being more intensively studied in Muslim, Vietnamese and African colonial societies.[12] Margaret Meriwether and Judith Tucker provide a useful typology of the study of women in the Ottoman and colonial Middle East that is broadly applicable to women's experience of colonialism more generally. They discern several strands of historical writing on Middle Eastern women. Some historians have focused on high-ranking women of influence – members of urban or tribal notable families. Their biographies provide a window into the wider world of colonial society and Islamic hierarchy. Others have concentrated on the early political history of pioneering women's groups, whether charitable foundations, cultural circles or overtly political movements. Work on these groups has highlighted women's contribution to nationalist struggles commonly regarded as dominated by men. Most recently, scholars have increasingly approached women's history in colonial states in terms of gender discourse, linking male predominance in colonial society and culture with a gendered view of power distribution between the sexes.[13] But perhaps the most illuminating studies are those that reveal the social history of women as artisans and workers, family and community members.[14] In short, studies that recognise women as politically and economically proactive, rather than passive objects of state policy and social change. A final point regarding women's social organisation in colonial states concerns its feminist dimension. The connections between the economic behaviour and political engagement of women as colonial subjects and an overtly feminist struggle for women's rights are sometimes difficult to make. But, whether explicitly feminist or not, women's efforts to secure an enhanced economic role, a greater political voice or just a decent living challenged the colonial order.

The birth rate and women's rights

The post-war campaign to augment the French birth rate, or pro-natalism as it was more generically known, drew supporters from across the political spectrum. Catholic clerics keen to reassert patriarchal authority, female domesticity and religious observance found common cause with secular republicans anxious about the declining national efficiency of an ageing population.[15] But tax breaks, additional allowances for large families and the introduction in 1920 of legal bans on abortion and contraception did little to stimulate French population growth in the immediate aftermath of the First World War. Government statistics for 1924 indicated that the metropolitan population had remained static at 39.2 million since 1919, a drop of over 2 million from the 1913 figure. The pro-natalist lobby was more anxious about two emergent long-term trends. First was the dramatic fall in registered marriages after a brief post-war surge in 1919–20. Second was the steady decline in the annual birth rate from a post-war high of 834,411 in 1920 to 752,101 in 1924.[16] The psychological scars of the Great War, and the pervasive cultural identification of the conflict with death and loss rather than victory and achievement, may also have affected the population debate.[17] In 1930, twelve years after the armistice, war veterans still constituted forty-five per cent of adult French males aged over twenty. A powerful voice in domestic politics, veterans were also pivotal to the politics of *natalité*.[18]

Other less obvious factors were instrumental in shaping men's attitudes to French women's rights. Mary Louise Roberts has examined the media scandal that followed the 1922 publication of Victor Margueritte's million-selling novel *La Garçonne* – the story of a promiscuous young woman who defies social convention by living a single life in Paris. Roberts uses the furore over *La Garçonne* to show how growing anxiety among the political elite, Catholic religious leaders, war veterans, and right-wing intellectuals about the social and political changes unleashed by the First World War meshed with hostility to the growing assertiveness of a minority of French women in bourgeois society.[19] In this environment, pro-natalism drew increasing support as a means to keep women in their place.

During the 1920s France's leading pro-natalist pressure group, the Alliance nationale pour l'accroissement de la population française, and its official backers in the Ministry of Public Health's advisory council on the birth rate, saw in foreign immigration a temporary solution to France's worsening shortage of workers and reproductive families. Between 1920 and 1930 more than 100,000 French women married foreign men. Women who contracted a marriage to a foreigner automatically surrendered their French nationality. Legislation passed on 10 August 1927 to correct this was meant to ensure a net increase in France's population, not to confer legal equality on women. Until 1938 married French women remained legally incapacitated. They had no right to plead in court, administer property, or enter commercial employment without their husband's formal consent.[20]

The pro-natalist debate spilled over into the colonies even though colonial subjects were typically considered more fertile, or at least more reconciled to rearing large families, than their French counterparts. Colonial authorities privileged women's obligation to reproduce over their rights as individuals. In December 1931 Dr S. Abbatucci, head of the colonial army's office of social hygiene, wrote an article in *Outre-Mer*, the in-house journal of the Ecole coloniale, proposing various measures to increase the colonial birth rate in black Africa. Abbatucci identified several empirical and cultural factors detrimental to women's role as childbearers. These ranged from genital mutilation in adolescence (clitoridectomy) and polygamy in adulthood to the high incidence of epidemics, venereal disease and tuberculosis among indigenous women. Abbatucci's solution was to harness improved medical provision to French requirements for an increased colonial population. Women's primary duty in francophone Africa was to 'fabriquer du noir'.[21] Abbatucci's arguments resonated with those of the pro-natalist lobby in France, which became more strident in placing reproductive duty above individual women's freedom to choose as war approached in 1938–39.[22]

French efforts to increase the metropolitan birth rate were constructed on grounds of race as well as gender. Most advocates of foreign immigration and inter-marriage between overseas workers and French women excluded colonial immigrants from the process. The cultural gulf between the two parties was simply too great. Even feminist writers such as Alice Berthet accepted this premise. Marriage to a colonial subject supposedly debased the white woman. It exposed her to unacceptable cultural norms, from veiling to polygamy.[23] Pro-natalists may have precluded racial mixing, but national debate about the social conditions of colonial women was more wide-ranging. In the inter-war period humanitarian organisations, welfare groups and social policy think-tanks proliferated in France, as in Britain. Women played an influential role in these networks, some of which linked concern about the social improvement of working-class conditions and women's rights in industrial societies to interest in women's living standards in the colonies.[24]

The reordering of the international system after the First World War, and the wider public interest in humanitarian projects generated by the horrors of the conflict, nourished the growth of official, quasi-official and non-governmental agencies dedicated to the codification and monitoring of human rights. The very term 'human rights' entered the vernacular of international diplomacy as never before. International pressure groups such as the Women's Suffrage Alliance and the International Council of Women pressed the League of Nations to recognise women's right to independent nationality, an issue with wide ramifications in a colonial context.[25] The ILO was the most successful of the reformist agencies operating in

Geneva. High-profile ILO campaigns against forced labour caused profound embarrassment – if not immediate policy changes – in French government (*travail forcé* was given the milder appellation *travail obligatoire* in official policy statements).[26] For all its flaws as a forum for conflict resolution between states, the League of Nations and its affiliated agencies incontestably counted in matters of ethics. Their power to humiliate the imperial powers through condemnatory reportage was a real constraint on their *modus operandi* in colonial policy. Much the same could be said of high-profile international aid organisations such as the International Committee of the Red Cross.

During the 1920s the League of Nations established an annual cycle of reports from individual colonies on the treatment of women and children in the workplace, by the courts, and even under indigenous customary law. These reports were little more than questionnaires that gathered basic statistics about employment, working conditions, criminal convictions, child labour, human trafficking and prostitution in dependent territories. But even dry columns of tables and figures provided a qualitative measurement of stock justifications for colonial rule such as improved living standards and declining infant mortality rates, as well as the more nebulous concept of 'moral improvement'.[27] Yet colonial governments were sometimes reluctant to respond to League pressure to curb manifest abuses of basic rights. In AEF, for instance, the Brazzaville administration maintained that women and even children working in the colonial wage economy had greater economic freedom than their counterparts engaged in traditional subsistence agriculture.[28]

Recalcitrant imperial governments could not ignore League scrutiny entirely. At the very least, regular reportage to the League compelled colonial authorities to keep better records about their subjects. From 1926, for instance, the Brazzaville administration began collecting data on women's economic migration and employment patterns, in addition to gathering information on prostitution and imprisonment.[29] International scrutiny also affected policing priorities. In Syria, which, as a mandate, was subject to closer League of Nations monitoring, the *sûreté* paid greater attention to prostitution, trafficking in female sex workers and the regulation of local brothels than, for example, in Indochina, where prostitution, human trafficking and drug use were more widespread. The *sûreté* presence in Indochina was stronger, but, unlike Syria, the hostile gaze of international opinion was not an issue.[30]

Living conditions

In February 1939 the most popular of the imperialist periodicals, the monthly *Le Monde Colonial illustré*, began one of its special feature, tabloid-style 'Inquiries' into the living conditions of black African women. Bursting with righteous indignation, the periodical demanded an end to polygamy and closer regulation of African women's working lives. Reducing gender inequality in the colonies was *le devoir des blancs*, 'the whites' duty'. The periodical took up the same theme in a 'debate' between colonial experts four months later.[31] Rue Oudinot officials were by this time engaged in much the same sort of investigation. Two months after the outbreak of war in September 1939 a Ministry of Colonies survey of the status of indigenous women in colonial societies acknowledged that most faced a life of subordination to male authority. The survey conclusions for Indochina were fairly typical:

> It is not an undue claim to make that the Annamite woman lived in an almost completely self-effacing manner [état d'effacement].
>   From an early age, a girl was introduced to arduous work in the fields. She looked after the buffalo, did the chores, went to market, planted and harvested the rice. All children, girls and boys, were under the absolute authority of their father, who held extensive power over them. Annamite society admits of only two conditions: an individual may be head of a family or a family member. One holds all the power, the other has all the duties. A girl remains responsible to her father until she achieves emancipation on her wedding day. But we must be clear that in this case the term 'emancipation' merely signifies a transfer of authority from the father to the husband.[32]

Inter-war reforms such as the stipulation of minimum marital ages, legal restrictions on a husband's right to repudiate his wife, inheritance rights for divorced wives with dependent children, the prohibition of night labour by women, and legislative regulation of prostitution (but no outright ban) did not affect the basic gender hierarchy. Nor were they intended to do so.[33] Colonial reform trod a thin line between Western modernisation and the associationist requirement to preserve traditional culture. The colonial state placed women's social status and political rights within the boundaries of a hierarchical society it sought to maintain, thereby spurring women's deepening engagement in oppositional politics. Take Indochina. By the early 1920s Vietnamese women were active in several anti-colonial groups, including the Vietnamese Youth League and the VNQDD. In Tonkin, where censorship was less rigorous than in Annam and Cochin-China, Vietnamese journalistic debate about women's emancipation, education and socio-economic roles stimulated further political activism among women who linked rejection of Confucian deference and financial subordination to men with their hostility to the French colonial presence.[34] Between its inception in May 1929 and its closure in December 1934 an ostensibly apolitical periodical, *Phu Nu Tan Van* (*Women's News*), criticised social provision indirectly by profiling women's daily lives, including the hardships and injustices they encountered. Even in Hué, the royal capital, a Women's Labour Study Association challenged the French authorities and mandarin officials by inviting Phan Boi Chau, Vietnam's foremost liberal nationalist and a condemned criminal, to address the Association's opening ceremony on 28 June 1926.[35]

The second-class status of women in colonial societies was not, of course, simply a by-product of colonialism itself. For subject populations the social construction of relations between the sexes was determined by customs, religious practices and divisions of labour that were only slowly modified by the colonial presence.[36] Extraneous factors also intervened. Myron Echenberg demonstrates how devastating bubonic plague epidemics in north-west Senegal reordered the gender roles of Sereer women who played a leading part in funeral rites and public obituaries for plague victims. But while the collective grieving process added to their visibility and influence, Sereer women paid dearly as they also assumed primary responsibility for the care of patients in lazarettos and isolation huts, a duty that exposed them to greater risk of infection than their partners.[37]

In January 1935 the secretary-general of the AEF government defined women's status in Equatorial Africa entirely in relation to male family members: 'The native woman is essentially an instrument of production. A man's standing and prestige within the village are directly linked with the number of wives he has. A heavy burden of expectation weighs upon the woman until childbirth, and resumes soon afterward'.[38] Secretary-general Marchessou's comments made no allowance for the complexities of social organisation in tribal society. But he correctly recognised that women's reproductive role was valued above all else. And the labour under-taken by women in peasant communities was tied to the continuation of traditional forms of agriculture and trade. Childbearing and the types of rural work performed were, however, transformed by colonialism. Women entered colonial wage economies later and in fewer numbers than men. Those that did so were generally paid less than male counterparts. Fewer women were unionised, and many remained in small-scale artisan enterprises without employment protection. Meanwhile the spread of colonial plantations, waged employment and increased male labour migration added to women's domestic responsibilities. In most colonies male heads of household controlled the acquisition and distribution of family cash income.[39] The tiny colony of Gabon in Equatorial Africa was one such. During the 1920s Gabonese men departed for seasonal employment or paid work in the colony's burgeoning lumber camps, leaving women to shoulder a heavier burden in maintaining family smallholdings. This pattern of direct male participation in the wage economy and greater female involvement in field labour was commonplace.[40] In nearby Cameroon, Duala women also took on a greater share of agricultural work when male family members sought paid employment in the colonial wage economy.[41] Women performed increasingly arduous tasks as the customary division of male–female agricultural labour collapsed.

The struggle to make ends meet dominated women's lives in much of the colonial empire. Hardly surprising then that women played a prominent part in urban political dissent that originated in protests against food shortages, price rises or the burden of taxation. Hardship stimulated political engagement. In January 1933 women traders in Togoland demanded the release of two native leaders arrested for organising opposition to tax increases and state spending cuts.[42] Such outbreaks were typically non-violent, short-lived and spontaneous. None the less, in January 1928 the Brazzaville government cited the predominance of women traders in urban market centres, and their capacity to cause 'public disturbances', to justify the retention of arbitrary punishments for local women under the *indigénat* legal code.[43]

Women in Arab territories

European settlement in French North Africa disrupted traditional forms of land tenure, inheritance rights, and marital arrangements. Introduction of French legal codes also confronted women with unprecedented challenges. The application of French property law in Algeria undermined systems of communal and tribal land holding in which access to designated cultivatable plots was an inalienable right. Economic expedients such as sharecropping, economic migration and the break-up of extended family networks increased, with detrimental results for women. Husbands and close blood relatives were forced to travel greater distances in search of work. Links with tribe, village and community became correspondingly weaker. Daughters were expected to work from an earlier age, and the onus on bridal dowry wealth increased as Muslim land ownership declined. The persistence of polygamy in rural communities reflected the diminished economic assets that a bride's family could pledge at marriage.[44]

Furthermore, whereas rural women in early colonial Algeria played a highly visible role in the economic life of their village, often working in the service sector as market traders, midwives, laundresses or entertainers, by the 1900s these jobs did not confer comparable influence or social visibility in urban Algeria.[45] Muslim women at work in the Algerian city blended into the background of a political community dominated by settlers and a male Muslim elite. Meanwhile, by the 1920s the remaining female artisans in rural and small-town Algeria, such as the textile weavers of Tlemcen or the potters and mat makers of Kabylia, were disadvantaged by fundamental changes in the Algerian economy, including increased competition from urban textile manufacturers and the growth of a female wage labour force in the major cities. Skilled rural workers typically combined production for the household with larger-scale production for the local market and itinerant traders. But as more such women migrated to the coastal cities, and urban mass manufacture of comparable goods increased, the less cohesive these long-established artisan networks became.[46]

French codification of marriage law in North Africa did little to advance women's interests, despite official insistence that such regulation freed Muslim (and especially Kabyle Berber) women from iniquitous Islamic marital rites. From the 1880s until the late 1950s French legislators in Algeria tried to curb polygamy, forced marriage, child betrothal and male divorcees' avoidance of economic responsibility for their former wives. But legal regulation enforced French control over the Muslim population rather than affording women greater individual freedom.[47] The few attempts before the Second World War to give repudiated Muslim women greater legal protection against the loss of inheritance rights and compensation demands from former husbands did not succeed. Nor were these women treated as legally equal to men. They did not have equivalent rights to hold property in perpetuity or to be guardians of children. Algerian women were not regarded as legally competent or capable of independent judgement in court cases. Husbands, fathers or brothers usually spoke on their behalf. The fact that Algerian women remained objects of legislative change rather than agents of it allowed ingrained stereotypes to persist.[48] In the 1930s psychiatrists of the Algiers Faculty of Medicine argued, for example, that Maghrebi women generally succumbed to mental illness less frequently than their menfolk precisely because they were sheltered from 'the psychological burdens of civilisation' conferred by education and a more public role.[49]

In Islamic societies, and in urban centres especially, Muslim community leaders, *ulamas* and *marabouts* generally upheld the segregation of women in public. And administrators oscillated between viewing Muslim women as victims of male tyranny and as an unpredictable constituency, at once alluringly sensuous and dangerously unknown.[50] Conflict between colonial authorities and indigenous community leaders over the status and rights of women did, however, arise. For one side, unveiling and the acceptance of French civil law signified women's recognition of the benefits of European social norms. For the other, women's domestic roles in Muslim families were a last line of defence against the seepage of European culture into the Arab world. In Algeria Abd al-Hamid Ben Badis's Association of Reformist *Ulamas* insisted that veiling protected women from 'depersonalisation'. The *ulamas* also defended differential rights to divorce and to inheritance as key planks of Islamic teaching.[51] In Tunisia, too, the clerics of the Zitouna Grand Mosque and the executive of the Old Destour Party insisted that veiling was at once an affirmation of Tunisian women's Muslim identity and a rejection of Western assimilation. The veil was not just a sign of modesty, it was a politicised rejection of French values. Women who adhered to their customary domestic role remained true to their Muslim cultural identity. Men determined women's best interests in each case.[52]

Some women challenged these value judgements. In March 1928 Nazira Zayn al-Din caused a storm of male protest with the publication of her book *Unveiling and Veiling* (*al-Sufur wa al'hijab*), a closely argued 420 page study which insisted that equality between the sexes was at the essence of Islam. Elizabeth Thompson describes how Zayn al-Din questioned the scope of Shar'ia law, *ulamas' claim* to enforce it, and Muslim codes of behaviour that condemned women to second-class status. The issue of veiling was the *Leitmotif* of her thesis that the corruption of Islam in the Levant denied women genuine freedom of choice. Only twenty years old in 1928, Zayn al-Din was a Beirut Druze, the daughter of a court judge. Like most other city-dwelling Druze women, she wore a headscarf in public, but not a veil. Lebanon's Muslim establishment, personified by Sheikh Mustafa Ghalayini of the Beirut Islamic College, condemned her presumption in attacking *ulama* authority. But Zayn al-Din addressed her appeal for women's rights squarely at High Commissioner Henri Ponsot, to whom she sent ten copies of her book. Was France serious in its commitment to liberal modernisation of Lebanon and Syria? If so, it was duty-bound to promote women's rights. Her attempt to make a legal case for unveiling was ultimately self-defeating. Religious patriarchs reaffirmed that veiling fell within the parameters of Shar'ia law and was therefore obligatory. Ponsot's administration shied away from a controversy liable to impair relations with trusted Muslim community leaders.[53]

Muslim women were clearly important political actors. Between 1918 and 1920 women in Faisal's Syria participated in anti-government demonstrations, food riots and the mobilisation of popular committees. Some even joined local Arab militias and military nursing teams. Conversely, those women who chose to wear European dress were liable to attack by lower-class youths supportive of the popular committees' anti-Westernism.[54] And while the urban notables, or so-called 'men of culture' (*mutanawwirūn*), in Syria's major towns often supported women's suffrage and wider educational opportunity, they remained divided over whether women should enter politics or whether Muslim girls should receive a scientific education.[55]

The picture was remarkably similar in the Maghreb. Even the Muslim schoolmasters educated at the Bouzaréah teacher training college in Algiers (discussed below), seen as apostles of Western values, sometimes dismissed their spouses as intellectually juvenile. In their journal *La Voix des humbles* (*The Poor People's Voice*), first published in May 1922, these liberals promoted women's rights, but on their own terms.[56] To the east, in Tunis, two conferences, the first in 1924, the second in 1929, were held to protest against public veiling, high illiteracy rates among women and forced marriage. These meetings heralded the emergence of a Muslim women's movement in Tunisia.[57] Their organisers faced an uphill task. In 1930 the feminist author Tahar Haddad published *Notre femme, la législation islamique et la société* (*Tunisian Women, Islamic Law and Society*), a work that challenged prevailing male assumptions about Islamic teaching on women, polygamy and sexual discrimination. Like Nazira Zayn al-Din in Beirut two years before, Haddad concluded that women's emancipation was consistent with Islam. A leading Koranic scholar, Haddad's suggestion that a whole raft of women's rights conformed to Islamic law aroused bitter opposition, orchestrated by his former mentors at the Zitouna Grand Mosque.[58] In this instance, Tunisian women were victims of a longer-running dispute between the modernist and tradition-alist factions of the Grand Mosque, the beylical administration and the French residency. A founder of the Tunisian trade union confederation, Haddad was widely regarded as a moderniser, if not overtly secularist then close to it in his support for women's rights and a Western, scientific curriculum in girls' schools.[59] But it was the conservatives who won out. They persuaded the Tunis grand council that Haddad's views were inspired by Kemalist republicanism, anathema to the Tunisian monarchy.[60] Haddad's writings were duly banned.

In Algeria, Western-educated followers of Ferhat Abbas advocated fewer restrictions on women's dress and public behaviour, but none the less defended women's subordinate role within the patriarchal structure of the Muslim family. In 1938–39 Messali Hadj's Parti du Peuple Algérien encouraged women to participate in nationalist protest. None the less, tension remained. Messalists insisted that Arabic education, respect for Islam and, therefore, the maintenance of women's domestic role were central aspects of integral Algerian nationalism. Yet Messali Hadj admitted the contradiction between Algerian women's increasing prominence as nationalist militants and their traditional role as guardians of Muslim family values.[61] As Monique Gadant puts it, 'Women found themselves trapped by a conservative vision of their role in society justified by anti-colonialism'.[62]

By contrast, in Syria and Lebanon, where women's journalism emerged strongly from the 1890s onward, writers viewed matters in a very different light. Arab women journalists increasingly connected their preservation of Arab identity with the defence of their nation state. Acceptance of their role as wives and mothers did not signify the rejection of political engage-ment. Quite the reverse. Between 1923 and 1927 the Beirut monthly women's review *Minerva* encouraged its readers to improve their education and seek professional employment, while at the same time preserving their identity as Arab family women opposed to Westernisation.[63] As the case of Nazira Zayn al-Din discussed above indicates, cultural practices, and particular styles of dress, were always contested ground between Arab nationalists and the French authorities, as well as between Muslim men and women. Yet the mandate authorities dodged these issues, preferring to promote Western fashion indirectly and incrementally. In the month war broke out in Europe a contributor to *Le Monde Colonial illustré* was quick to exploit the more general adoption of Western dress by educated Syrian and Lebanese women as proof that the Muslim elite accepted Western values, longing to become 'très parisienne'.[64]

Women and reform

French feminist engagement with the underlying economic injustice of colonial rule was rare indeed. Denise Moran Savineau's official survey of the social condition of women in French West Africa, conducted on behalf of Governor-general Marcel de Coppet in 1937–38, was highly unusual. Moran was a colonial education specialist who made her name with a devastating critique of colonial government in Chad, where she spent several years working with her husband. When de Coppet appointed her in October 1937 Moran was a senior educational adviser to the Dakar government. After nine months travelling AOF in 1937–38 Moran produced thirty-five reports and a 232 page final study. Her investigation of women's role in the colonial economy revealed a catalogue of administrative neglect, oppressive work practices and chronic poverty during the depression years.[65]

Moran's 1938 survey remains the fullest contemporary analysis of women's lives available to historians of francophone Africa. Ghislaine Lydon's examination of Moran's findings highlights the paucity of women's rights in economic, legal and educational matters. Moran shared the abiding preoccupation of French missionary societies with social processes liable to disrupt African women's domestic role as wives, mothers and daughters.[66] But Moran was no Catholic evangelist. Her conclusions were impeccably republican – empirical and secular.

Viewed in hindsight, Moran's arguments seem depressingly familiar. African women faced entrenched discrimination. Their subordinate roles in tribal society and in marital relations left women little choice in the domestic work and agricultural labour they were assigned. They were paid less than their male counterparts, often for longer working hours. Industries that retained large numbers of women workers such as textile dyeing, pottery making and market trading were highly labour-intensive. When the gathering, refinement, production, transportation and final sale of a dyed cloth, household pottery or oil-based foodstuffs were reckoned together, the hourly wage rates were ludicrously low. In other respects, women's contribution to the colonial economy was not formally recognised at all. Numerous African women were effectively indentured labourers, whether transporting goods and water or working as unpaid adjuncts to their husbands.[67] Women's status as wives was influenced by their husband's calculation of their economic utility as childbearers, labourers and, on rare occasions, as a tradable resource. In this connection, Moran observed instances in the Ivory Coast, Guinea and the town of Ougadougou of women and children pawned by their husbands or fathers as security for a debt repayment. African women appeared most often in French colonial courts to petition for divorce or to answer criminal charges, the most frequent being minor theft. Those sent to prison had little protection against abuse by staff and male inmates.[68]

The Popular Front's willingness to dispatch investigative missions to the colonies to study living conditions, the treatment of women, and healthcare provision turned a spotlight on long neglected aspects of social policy that had previously elicited little comment in government. Thrown on to the defensive, colonial authorities discovered a sudden interest in social reform. It was no coincidence that on 25 June 1936 Jules Brévié, predecessor to de Coppet as AOF governor-general, revived proposals to provide legislative protection for African wives and children against forced marriage, polygamy and loss of inheritance. These plans had lain dormant since September 1932 and the Dakar administration had earlier shown little enthusiasm for interference in such sensitive matters of customary law. But in June 1936 Brévié faced imminent demotion. Whatever his motives, the governor-general couched reform of family law in associationist terms: respect for indigenous tradition was balanced against altruistic concern for freedom of the individual. But the core element in the scheme – statements of free consent to marriage by both spouses – threatened to undermine arranged marriage, negotiated bride price and parental power over their children.[69] Brévié's revived scheme culminated in a 7 May 1937 circular issued by the Dakar political affairs directorate stipulating new regulations for civil marriage among African subjects and the status of juveniles under customary law. A minimum age for legal marriage (sixteen for boys, fourteen for girls) was established, and both intending spouses were required to indicate their free consent. Wives acquired the legal right to divorce if a husband's polygamy could be proved.[70]

It took two years before these provisions were written into law. The delay resulted less from the intervening collapse of the Popular Front than from the abiding bureaucratic reluctance to interfere in customary family law. None the less, decree legislation passed on 15 June 1939 applied the regulations throughout AOF and AEF, and a further decree passed on 27 August 1939 extended the reforms to Cameroon. The Ministry of Colonies considered it unnecessary to extend the scheme to the other colonial federations. In Indochina minimum ages for marriage (again sixteen and fourteen, except in Tonkin, where the required ages were eighteen for boys, seventeen for girls), parental agreement, the free consent of spouses and restrictions on polygamy and remarriage had been in place since March 1931. In Madagascar male and female spouses were considered to hold equal rights under law, although male partners retained preferential rights to two-thirds of marital property.[71]

In May 1937 the Ministry of Colonies set about improving medical provision in AOF. The rue Oudinot focused on three targets: prophylactic treatments to combat epidemics, greater funding for rural nursing and midwifery, and the establishment of *postes médicales indigènes* to provide basic medical services to rural communities. Ministry officials modelled their proposals on a pilot project in Dahomey, initiated in 1929, which provided regular medical checks to a study group of 625 children. Results indicated a dramatic fall in infant mortality from a colony average of forty-five per cent for infants aged less than one year, to only 6.2 per cent among those in the study group.[72] Ironically, Popular Front Minister of Colonies Marius Moutet struggled to secure the necessary funds. It fell to his successor, Georges Mandel, appointed to Edouard Daladier's April 1938 Cabinet, to revitalise the scheme.

Mandel proved a worthy champion of colonial health care reformers. He endorsed an increase in AOF's public health budget from 100 million to 146 million francs in 1939. In line with Moutet's original plans, the increased funding was channelled into rural health care, much of it specifically aimed at women, both as nursing staff and rural health care providers, and as key recipients of preventive treatments. Each of the AOF colonies was to have a network of maternity units, midwifery training centres and mobile medical dispensaries providing prophylactic treatments for West Africa's three main epidemics: malaria, trypanosomiasis and syphilis. Daladier's government also acted on recommendations by the colonial health inspectorate to equip additional African district nurses, dispensary workers and midwives at a Dakar training centre completed three years earlier in 1935. In short, Mandel kept in place Popular Front plans to establish a total of 208 medical centres, 125 maternity units, 107 dispensaries, 74 nursing centres and 622 rural treatment centres.[73] The *évolué* midwives trained in AOF's *service de la santé* were among the most highly educated African women in inter-war West Africa. Many later joined nationalist movements, surely influenced by their experiences of the patriarchal and military style of the colonial health service.[74]

Official interest in training African women as health care providers reflected an underlying assumption prevalent among colonial governments. In French and British African territories indigenous women were seen as key agents of welfare and development policy. Colonial officials and metropolitan welfare groups generally agreed that only by educating African women could the domestic lives of colonial subjects be transformed. It was axiomatic in French West Africa, for example, that African mothers held a pivotal role in transmitting French cultural values to their daughters.[75] Educational provision facilitated the regulation of this process. In Muslim societies and African tribal villages, the domestic sphere and public spaces reserved for women such as single-sex bathhouses and workshops were simply off-limits to colonial officials. Education broke down these barriers to colonial domination, and was readily justified in terms of improved health and living standards. Some commentators even endorsed wider educational access for women on the grounds that educated African men would reject uneducated wives.[76] As Hamid Irbouh puts it with regard to the craft schools established for Muslim girls in Fez, the French assigned girls' education a ' "social mission", not a truly pedagogic one'.[77] From 1927 Renée Ravès, director of the Dar 'Adiyel craft school in the Fez medina, provided classes in French, embroidery, domestic science and Koranic scripture to well-to-do daughters of the Muslim bourgeoisie. This peculiar curriculum was designed to meet parents' demands that their daughters' education should increase their standing with prospective husbands. Ravès's French colleague, Louise Soulé, set up a very different girls' school in the working-class district of Fez Jdid. Soulé's establishment catered for poorer girls, principally of Berber origin. The Fez Jdid school curriculum devoted most time to child care and vocational handicrafts. The choice of crafts studied mirrored the artisan industries in Fez's working-class quarters. Girls' education in Fez replicated the racial and class boundaries of the colonial city.[78] Not everyone saw matters that way. Abd al-Hamid Ben Badis, leader of Algeria's Association of Reformist *Ulamas*, emerged in the 1930s as a strong proponent of increased access to basic education for Muslim women. But, as we have seen, he regarded Arabic Koranic education as an underpinning of girls' traditional household and reproductive roles within Muslim society. This was traditional education mobilised in opposition to the values that French educators hoped to transmit.[79]

Miscegenation

No discussion of gender issues in the French empire can overlook the so-called '*métis* problem' of miscegenation. Colonial society rested on unequal power relations between whites and *indigènes*, and between men and women. And, since the mid-nineteenth century era of General Louis Faidherbe, *métissage* was physical proof of it.[80] As Owen White has shown, there is much to be learned regarding contradictory French attitudes to colonial women in the long-running administrative debate in France and francophone Africa over the social integration of mixed-race children. Born following relationships between white men and black women, these *métis* and *métisses* presented intractable dilemmas to officials and missionary groups, not to mention to their African mothers and the French fathers, who, in most cases, refused to acknowledge them either personally or legally. Official reportage often described the plight of mixed-race children in lurid terms of 'abandonment', a concept more applicable to the absent fathers than to the mothers left to cope alone, their difficulties sometimes compounded by the occasional reluctance of maternal African relatives to acknowledge *métis(se)* offspring.[81] Without legal affirmation of parentage it was impossible to claim financial support from the absent father. In 1912 French legislators modified the Napoleonic Civil Code to facilitate paternity suits. At the instigation of Maurice Viollette, this legislation was partially extended to the empire, but was confined to cases where at least one of the parties involved was a French citizen. Even Viollette conceded that colonial governors should retain discretionary powers to limit paternity claims to cases where both father and mother held French citizenship.[82] The 1912 reform made little impact. It was not applied throughout the colonies, and was not extended to AOF until 1949.[83]

It remained utterly taboo to contemplate colonial men producing children with French women, but marriages of French men and colonial *métisses* drew qualified official support. During the 1937 Paris International Exhibition, for example, a 'Miss Overseas France' beauty contest was held in which nine of the ten finalists were young women of mixed race. The message was clear: colonial women might serve as suitable reproductive partners for French men. The resulting progeny would be good patriots, capable of integration with French racial stock. For the state, the challenge was to legitimise a practice that was as old as empire itself, but which colonial officials, some of them practitioners of double standards in their own sexual liaisons, still frowned upon. Government agencies were thus drawn to the pseudo-scientific theories of contemporary eugenicist commentators such as the physicians René Martial and Georges Schreiber. Somehow the exclusionary theories of the eugenicist movement had to be reconciled with the urgent requirement for more French babies, even mixed-race ones. The answer was to blur the definitions of what constituted 'Frenchness' by concocting a sliding scale of colonial races to discern those ethnic groups with which interbreeding was permissible, even positively desirable. It was no coincidence that a Miss Casalan of Guadeloupe, the eventual winner of the 1937 beauty contest, was praised for the whiteness of her skin.[84]

In other respects, attitudes to miscegenation were slower to change. The mere hint that a white woman might give birth to a black colonial subject's child (actually very rare indeed) could provoke official hysteria. Fear of interracial contact influenced government discouragement of spouses joining their husbands in the more inhospitable postings of black Africa and South East Asia. Conversely, in the 1920s spouses were increasingly encouraged to join their bureaucrat husbands, both to prevent them from straying and to reinforce the racial separation between white administrators and the colonial population.[85] In the French empire, as in the British, racist double standards were starkest of all when it came to sex.[86]

Missionaries and educational provision

Educational provision in colonial states is immensely revealing of metropolitan priorities, racial hierarchies and official assumptions about indigenous societies.[87] Education and religious conversion were perhaps the foremost means by which metropolitan culture could be replicated in dependent territories. The two were inextricably linked.[88] Missionaries, religious orders and other church-affiliated institutions retained considerable influence over educational provision in the colonies. In Pondicherry, first settled by the French in 1674, missionary educational establishments helped consolidate a francophone elite after the eighteenth century upheavals of Franco-British rivalry in India.[89] In Senegal two religious orders, the Soeurs de Saint-Joseph de Cluny and the Frères de l'instruction Chrétienne de Ploërmel, dominated the education of European and mixed-race children in the latter nineteenth century. The Ploërmel brothers built on their earlier experience of educational provision in the Antilles, assigned to their control under an 1837 convention.[90] By 1885 there were eight Catholic primary schools in Senegal, four for girls and four for boys.[91] Senegal's first *lycée*, established with government support at Saint-Louis in 1910, was modelled on the secondary courses previously provided by the Frères de Ploërmel.[92] Catholic missionary schools held less of a monopoly in the inter-war period. The French separation of church and state in 1905 reverberated through the empire, although it was not rigidly applied in the colonies. And the prevalence of Islamic observance in West Africa led colonial officials to question the suitability of missionary schooling. Even so, Catholic missionaries remained a force as colonial educators.[93] Republican anticlerical politicians rarely took issue with the blurring of the church–state divide in the colonies. Nor was there strong pressure for a secular curriculum from the minority of families that secured school places for their children. In 1914 the mayor of Brazzaville sought to establish why the town's mission school remained more popular with African parents than the local state school. The answer had less to do with Catholicism than with the missionaries' provision of a free school uniform and a daily meal.[94]

In Tunisia the African missionary brothers (Frères missionnaires d'Afrique) took charge of French-language schooling. The Frères missionnaires' order was created by the pioneer of missionary education in Africa, Cardinal Charles Martial Lavigerie, who dominated the Catholic educational establishment in the Maghreb. A statue of Lavigerie sited at the entrance to the Tunis medina in 1931 depicted the cardinal, cross in hand, challenging the inhabitants of the Arab old town.[95] Under his direction the Collège Saint Charles was founded in Tunis in 1882 both to offer a Catholic education and to eclipse the Collège Sadiki, the one Muslim secondary school for children of the capital's elite. Missionary institutions were also prominent in girls' education in Tunisia. The Sisters of St Joseph established Tunisia's first girls' school in 1843. It was a further sixty years before the first school reserved for Muslim girls opened in Tunis in 1901. Flying the tricolour in colonial education usually came with a pronounced Catholic message.[96]

In smaller colonies, particularly isolated island territories, missionaries had an even greater impact. Missionary influence in French Oceania was particularly apparent. During the nineteenth century Catholic and Protestant missions competed for dominance in New Caledonia and the New Hebrides, both among themselves and against foreign rivals. The islands of Wallis and Futuna – declared French protectorates in 1886 – were effectively run by Marist priests, in conjunction with the francophile monarchs of the islands. Papeete witnessed bitter in-fighting between opposing churches until an 1860 decree recognised Protestantism as Tahiti's official religion – a unique event in the French empire.[97] Little wonder that French Oceania and the *vieilles colonies* of the empire such as the French Antilles were exempted from France's 1905 anticlerical legislation. The notorious Third Republic maxim, variously attributed to two leading imperialists, Léon Gambetta and Paul Bert, that anticlericalism was not for export, certainly held sway in colonial education policy.

Missionary schools were also at the vanguard of French cultural imperialism in the Levant. French mission activity and educational investment in the Ottoman empire took off in the aftermath of the Crimean War. The Quai d'Orsay backed French educational projects to buttress France's claim to preferential influence in the Ottoman Sultanate. The resultant financial commitments swallowed around five per cent of the Foreign Ministry budget by 1914. Funding in support of French cultural penetration in the Levant resumed in 1920. A cultural affairs and schools office was created to oversee the promotion of French cultural projects.[98]

From the 1860s two monastic orders, the Capuchins and the Lazarists, received state funding for their Middle East missions, a practice that continued after 1905. The 3,000 or so Catholic missionaries working in Ottoman territory were state educational agents. When war broke out there were over 500 French-controlled schools with over 100,000 students across the Ottoman Middle East. In addition to the two main Catholic mission agencies, Propagation de la Foi (Propagation of the Faith) and L'Oeuvre des écoles de l'Orient (Eastern Schools Project), a Jewish educational organisation, the Alliance israélite universelle (AIU), pioneered by Adolphe Crémieux and Narcisse Leven between 1860 and 1880, taught 48,000 Jewish pupils in the Middle East by 1914. The AIU promoted French cultural values but cannot be compared with the Catholic missions, as Jewish educators confined their teaching to their own faith community. By contrast, the nearest equivalent lay organisation, the Mission laïque française, initially concentrated its activities in existing French colonies, although five of its schools were also established in Ottoman territory by 1914 thanks to Foreign Ministry grants. The Mission laïque subscribed to a more functional imperialism that valued French schooling as a means to increase the economic utility of the indigenous population.[99]

Schooling in Indochina and French Africa

A more fundamental question than whether colonial subjects should be raised as practising Catholics was whether they should be educated at all. Governors Paul Beau and Albert Sarraut nurtured the colonial education service established in the three Vietnamese territories in 1906. A 1918 code of public instruction delineated entry requirements for primary schools, lycées and the federation's four teacher training colleges. But colonial officials disputed the merits of wider educational access for young Vietnamese for years afterward.[100] Indochina's education bureaucracy was stunted by recurrent arguments over Vietnamese versus French-language schooling, and the wisdom of teaching France's revolutionary history or Vietnam's national past. These disagreements refracted official fears about the spread of nationalist ideas among Vietnam's scholar gentry.[101] After the First World War educational provision was limited to the privileged few. The Tonkin resident-general even claimed in his annual report for 1922 that Vietnamese mandarins objected to broader public access to elementary schooling. Literate children were less deferential. So educating the Vietnamese peasantry might endanger the hierarchical structure of Vietnamese society.[102] Doubts about the wisdom of advanced education were not confined to the empire. Argument continued in France over girls' right to sit the baccalauréat, the high school examination that was a prerequisite of higher education. Only a small minority attended secondary schools or lycées, each of which remained fee-paying.[103]

By 1929 32,646 children were enrolled in French-language primary schools in Vietnam, around double that figure by 1939. Far fewer progressed any further. David Marr estimates that in the entire inter-war period only some 20,000 Vietnamese studied in more advanced upper primary school (école primaire supérieure).[104] Complex bureaucratic structures were one thing, mass education quite another. The indigenous village school that taught children in local languages outside French control remained the principal 'formal' education for Indochina's subject races.[105]

In 1927, his final year as governor-general in Hanoi, Alexandre Varenne challenged received wisdom about the dangers of mass education, arguing in associationist terms that higher literacy rates and improved access to secondary education created an efficient work force and a collaborative elite. Varenne initiated a programme of primary school construction in 1927. He made compulsory primary schooling a priority in the colony of Cochin-China. Varenne also instructed the colonial school inspectorate to produce textbooks written in Vietnamese, Cambodian, Laotian and other local languages, breaking with official preference for instruction in *quoc-ngu*, the version of Vietnamese in Latinised script.[106] And the introduction in May 1927 of a three-year training course for secondary school teachers targeted young bourgeois outside the established mandarin elite.[107] Indigenous Vietnamese village schools continued to dominate ten years after the Varenne reforms. In 1938 416,057 pupils were registered in elementary and primary schools across Vietnam. Fewer than 400 were in the elite secondary schools. Fewer than one in ten school-age children attended classes for three years or more.[108]

In French Africa the educational debate in French Africa was less about the behaviour of a literate indigenous elite than about the creation of any such group. The AOF government established a federal educational service on 24 November 1903. Successive governors before and after the First World War linked the provision of basic schooling with the economic and administrative requirements of the federation.[109] Georges Hardy, the future director of the Ecole coloniale, cut his teeth as an educationalist directing the education service in Senegal between 1913 and 1921.[110] During these years all the colonies of AOF, barring Mauritania and Niger, established their own *écoles primaires supérieures* (EPS) to train clerks, primary school teachers and commercial agents. Schooling for an elite minority of Africans was thus intended to provide junior officials and specialist technicians: in short, reliable intermediaries. The spread of these 'EPS' schools met Hardy's objective – to spread French values to a select few Africans through the medium of a French-language curriculum.[111] The plurality of local languages in West Africa made common use of French essential if uniform standards were to be achieved, but ran the risk of alienating the children educated from their indigenous cultural environment. Cultural distance could become physical. The brightest children were encouraged to attend the William Ponty teacher training college, established near Dakar in 1903. By 1920 this establishment also offered rudimentary medical and clerical training tailored to the requirements of the federal government. Expansion of the William Ponty college after the First World War was stimulated by official embarrassment that educational provision in French Africa lagged behind its German equivalent in the two black African mandates – Cameroon and Togoland – largely transferred to French control in

1919–20. In 1913 German-administered Togo and Cameroon boasted pupil numbers of 14,000 and 41,000: a combined total that exceeded AOF's overall school population in 1920.[112]

In 1921 Sarraut explained the connections between education and colonial development in associationist terms:

> The principal effect of education should be to increase the value of colonial production substantially while heightening the quality and range of skills of the masses of indigenous workers. It should also separate out from the working masses a collaborative elite who, as technical staff, foremen, supervisors or managerial assistants, will make up for the shortages of Europeans and meet the increasing demands of agricultural, industrial and commercial enterprises. A more methodical education policy should also train a body of local administrators that impose less of a burden on colonial budgets that are stretched by the costs of European personnel . . . Finally, at a time when the generous and far-sighted application of associationist policy has widened access for indigenous representatives to consultative assemblies where they discuss matters of collective interest, education must develop their skills and capacity for useful and reasonable collaboration with us.[113]

His was a common administrative view. Education for male colonial subjects was designed to produce better workers, cheap clerical staff and a loyal colonial elite. Education for colonial girls, although conceived in similarly utilitarian terms, sought to reinforce domesticity. Colonial authorities saw several advantages in confining girls' education to practical skills, domestic sciences and moral instruction. With its vocational orientation, colonial education privileged French-language instruction: in AOF and AEF largely delivered as oral rote learning; in Indochina and the old island colonies more book-based. The AOF school inspectorate did produce a textbook series for the study of history, geography, folklore and hygiene, but focused on an invented African tradition that stressed the stability and practicality of daily life in West Africa. The study of history was carefully sanitised. In AOF schools, pre-colonial African history featured only in juxtaposition to the benefits of the colonial presence. In Indochina's curriculum the decadence of pre-colonial Vietnam and Cambodia was contrasted with the efficiency and ethical standards of French governance. In both federations, teachers made little reference to the revolutionary origins of French republicanism.[114] A narrowly confined curriculum promised immediate results. It was widely assumed that questions of hygiene, diet and household management, once taught, were quickly applied and never forgotten. Vocational teaching was also cheaper than academic studies because larger numbers of trained local intermediaries could be employed as educators. And practical education was less politically explosive than a curriculum that privileged literacy and the humanities. Why arm the natives with the tools to think critically and evaluate their political environment by comparison with other societies? Such risks were worthwhile only for a select elite whose political energies could be safely diverted into junior administrative service and eventual assimilation into the apparatus of colonial society.[115] It was no coincidence that the Association amicale des instituteurs du Sénégal – one of AOF's first trade unions – was founded in 1930 by Senegalese teachers, mainly graduates of the William Ponty college in Dakar.[116] By its very nature, education had unpredictable consequences.

In the early 1930s Jules Brévié, who had written extensively about schooling as a facet of colonisation, breathed new life into AOF education policy as governor-general. Brévié judged increased educational provision essential in the absence of a large settler population to propel economic modernisation. His utilitarian approach to schooling precluded access to a classic French educational curriculum to all but a privileged urban elite. At the same time, Brévié's administration saw colonial education in more ambitious terms. Schooling was an instrument of pacification, a tool of social engineering, and an ethical imperative, which would ensure that an African civil society respectful of French values gradually discarded the primitivism of tribal society.[117] Such was the theory. Dakar education service officials were well aware of the disjuncture between academic schooling for an elite minority and the vocational curriculum devised for the rural masses. Some warned of the divisive social effects inherent in targeting resources at the training of junior native auxiliaries. Efforts were therefore made to extend vocational education to the African peasantry through a network of *écoles normales rurales*.[118] In November 1937 the Dakar authorities reaffirmed that education for the wider masses should promote practical and linguistic skills, without, in the process, 'detribalising' or 'deracialising' infants destined to remain subjects, not citizens.[119]

It was largely a paper exercise. In 1938 under three per cent of school-age children in French West Africa were in full-time education, according to Gail P. Kelly, a total of 56,135. As there was no secondary education to speak of, the best that this minority of primary school pupils could hope for was rudimentary 'semi-schooling'.[120] Peggy Sabatier produces a higher estimate of 68,416 children in primary schools and 717 in EPS schools in 1938, still derisory figures.[121] And in the 1937–38 academic year, girls comprised only 5,892 of the recorded school population.[122] The opening of a federal teacher training college for young women, the Ecole normale de jeunes filles, in Rufisque in 1938 joined the Dakar School of Medicine and Midwifery established twenty years earlier as the only avenue of advancement for West African girls in post-primary education.[123]

In French Equatorial Africa, poorest and least developed of the colonial federations, secondary schooling remained entirely unavailable to *indigènes* in the mid-1930s. The last complete government statistics for pre-war school attendance in AEF indicated that 9,038 African children attended primary schools in 1938. The first black African trainee teachers in AEF were due to graduate from AEF's one teacher training establishment, the Ecole Edouard Renard, in February 1939.[124] The tiny minority of Africans educated in the federation's seventy-eight primary schools were strictly separated from settler children. In February 1934 Brazzaville Governor Antonetti justified this segregation, claiming that black children held back their white counterparts owing to their 'primitive mentality'. He even rejected Ministry of Colonies proposals to promote metropolitan–colonial contact through a 'pen friend' scheme, arguing that impressionable black schoolchildren would never comprehend a French pen pal's lifestyle.[125] Even the writer André Gide, the most eloquent inter-war critic of colonialism in Equatorial Africa, depicted the indigenous population stereotypically: spiritually pure, physically attractive but intellectually inferior.[126]

Much as the 'métis problem' affected colonial attitudes to interracial mixing, miscegenation also influenced colonial education policy. On the one hand, mixed-race children were living examples of the possibilities of assimilation. Some colonial officials considered them ideally suited to careers as fonctionnaires. Their French blood would facilitate their acculturation; their African upbringing offered unique access to indigenous society. Strongly influenced by Sarraut's ideas of increased colonial productivity, this treatment of mixed-race children as a valuable economic resource – what Owen White has dubbed la mise en valeur des métis – did not get very far.[127] The reality was very different. In inter-war AOF, for example, most métis(ses) faced uncertain futures. Boys and girls were educated separately. But for the majority, and for mixed-race girls in particular, education meant a strict regime in mission schools and designated orphanages (orphélinats de métis) such as those at Kayes in Senegal and Bamako in French Guinea. Far from being systematically trained to supply future administrative cadres, métis(ses) in AOF and AEF were taught in a closed Catholic environment where the shame of their origin was made to weigh especially heavy. Some boys were trained with a specific career in mind, such as medical auxiliaries in the Assistance médicale indigène, the principal public health organisation responsible for vaccination programmes across AOF. The majority of mixed-race girls, however, were prepared for their anticipated role as wives and mothers. The state authorities valued these girls' capacity to spread French language usage in their family circle over any wider contribution to the colonial economy.[128]

In the AEF mission schools in Brazzaville, Libreville, Pointe-Noire and Bangui métis schooling also focused on moral instruction and vocational training rather than a broader French curriculum necessary to gain admission to the colonial bureaucracy. The official objective was to afford métis greater social opportunities than their African mothers while still differentiating them from the white population. In practice the limited education offered was an unhappy compromise that achieved neither desired result. By 1939 French Africa's burgeoning mixed-race population was a threat to the colonial order rather than a pillar of it.[129]

Education in French North Africa

If the *métis* problem exposed the contradictions of educational provision in sub-Saharan Africa, in the Maghreb, where miscegenation was far less common, officials none the less rehearsed arguments over schooling familiar elsewhere. Some regarded schooling for Muslim children in purely instrumental terms as a means to increase national efficiency. Others stressed the moral benefits of making French cultural values accessible to a collaborative elite. But what sort of cultural attributes could be safely transmitted to subject populations? Jacobin republicanism? Scientific modernism? Belief in democracy and meritocracy? Obviously not. Lyautey supported the establishment of Moroccan schools ordered on lines of ethnicity and class, but opposed instruction in modern sciences and humanities. Teaching Moroccans to reason in French terms would be 'a fatal mistake'.[130]

The restrictions imposed on access to secondary education in North Africa echoed those in Indochina. In both cases, the status of the indigenous elite was the primary concern. In Algeria, decree legislation passed in April 1886 created secondary school bursaries for the sons of *caïds* and junior Muslim *fonctionnaires* in the colonial bureaucracy. During the First World War Governor-general Lutard reaffirmed that Muslim access to *lycées* should be reserved for sons of trusted notables, a policy strictly adhered to after the war. Some 386 Muslims attended *lycées* in 1914; 776 in 1930 (or 7.7 per cent of total *lycée* students in Algeria at that date). Access to the University of Algiers was similarly controlled, with ninety-three Muslim students enrolled in 1930, ninety-four in 1938 and eighty-nine in 1940.[131] In the 1920–21 academic year only 509 Muslim children received any kind of secondary education, whether in public or private schools or in advanced *écoles normales*. Muslim children thus comprised under six per cent of Algeria's secondary school population. Admittedly, overall numbers in colonial primary schools were far higher. Some 42,904 Algerian Muslim children were registered in the colony's primary schools in 1920–21. But this figure is less impressive when placed in the context of Algeria's ethnic composition. Although Europeans numbered less than twenty per cent of the Algerian population, 112,223 European children attended primary school in the same year.[132]

The educational statistics for the mass of the population reveal the marginality of the colonial school system. By the time the Popular Front government took office in 1936 only 2.1 per cent of Algerian men could read French. When the Popular Front finally collapsed in April 1938 less than ten per cent of school-age children received any formal education in the colony. There were also pronounced regional variations in literacy rates: in the Algérois the figure was 3.5 per cent; in the department of Constantine, only 1.1 per cent.[133] Equivalent educational provision for the Maghreb's European and Muslim communities was out of the question.

Fanny Colonna's research into the first cohorts of Algerian Muslim students to graduate from the colony's one teacher training college open to *évolués*, the École normale de Bouzaréah, reveals that their French instructors valued candidates' personal values above their academic performance. Most Bouzaréah attendees came from urban or suburban families in which at least one parent was a French-language speaker. As adjuncts of the colonial state, Algeria's primary school teachers were expected to transmit core values of loyalty, service and obedience. Their purpose was to uphold the existing social order, not to disrupt it. The Popular Front supported an increased intake of Arab and Berber candidates to Bouzaréah. But it never questioned the institution's guiding principle that academic content held less significance than inculcation of subservience to the colonial system. The class of 1936 comprised thirty-two Arabs and twenty-eight Berbers in addition to eighty-six European and Jewish teacher trainees. The curriculum was integrationist, stressing republican universalist values, Algeria's junior status in the French polity, and the cultural and material benefits of assimilation. Despite its republicanism, Bouzaréah was far from egalitarian. The best rooms, seats, even crockery, were reserved for *colon* students. Muslim teacher trainees were expected not only to assimilate French values but, just as important, to know their place as subordinates to their European masters.[134]

Such were the economic pressures on Muslim households that few families that sent children to primary schooling could afford to keep them there until they sat the primary school certificate (CEP) essential to win a place in secondary school. In 1924, for example, only thirteen per cent of the 7,000 children to finish primary school in Algeria took the CEP; less than half of these progressed to secondary education.[135] In 1939 11.4 per cent of Algeria's school-age children received a formal education, a total of around 110,000 pupils, and an increase of over fifty per cent on the numbers attending school in the 1920s. When population growth is taken into account, however, it becomes clear that greater educational provision failed to keep pace with Algeria's burgeoning child population.[136]

Expansion of the apparatus of protectorate government in Tunisia between 1881 and 1914 stimulated stronger demand for educated staff to fill the lower ranks of the French and beylical bureaucracy. Here, too, wider access to schooling created its own problems. The French requirement of a broad curriculum to produce versatile students proficient in French clashed with the beylical defence of Koranic education and classes conducted exclusively in Arabic. In defiance of beylical preferences, the residency education budget supported French-language schools geared to the needs of the settler population. As French demands won out, so a greater proportion of the young Arab elite attended *médersas* whose Koranic teachers opposed French acculturation. In February 1936 students at the Zitouna Grand Mosque protested against residency plans to increase the French and Arabic language requirements for admission to state bureaucracy. The students had no quarrel with harder entrance examinations, but insisted that the new regulations were another insidious attack on Islamic culture, an argument that resonated throughout Tunisian Arab society.[137]

In 1920 Sheikh Abdelaziz Taalbi, founding father of the Destour Party, raised the more fundamental problem. National independence would be unachievable until all Tunisians secured some rudimentary schooling. Destour and Néo-Destour propaganda accused the French authorities of denying formal education to Tunisians to stifle nationalist support. Ironically, the protectorate's schools were more numerous and better funded than in any other French African territory. Even so, although Muslims always constituted over ninety per cent of Tunisia's population, before 1930 Muslim children never made up more than forty-six per cent of school enrolment. Gender bias was still more pronounced. In 1930 only 11.4 per cent of school-age Muslim girls received a formal education.[138] By 1937 approximately thirty per cent of Muslim children completed primary schooling, but less than nine per cent of Muslims went on to secondary education. For the majority, Tunisia's 500 traditional Koranic schools (*kouttabs*) were the only education on offer.[139]

Conclusion

It is difficult to generalise about women's experience of French colonialism, easier to discern similarities in colonial education. And any historian's tentative conclusions should acknowledge the debt to scholars in other disciplines – area studies, social anthropology and sociology – that have studied women and children in colonial societies as discrete groups. Since the 1980s our knowledge of the daily lives of African women in particular has been enriched by research into their experience as economic producers and as victims of the colonial system – what Margaret Jean Hay termed the shift in scholarship from queens to prostitutes and peasants.[140] Most women in French colonial societies did not have free access to the labour market. Economic roles traditionally performed by women, such as the transportation of village produce and the sale of goods in local markets, were disrupted by mechanised transport systems, the growth of shops, and state regulation of market trading.[141] In Muslim territories rules dictating the public separation of the sexes (infiçal) placed women in a unique position in the eyes of both the colonial state and Islamic clerics determined to revitalise Muslim cultural values eroded by colonialism. But, as we have seen, Muslim women were usually treated as the objects of male policy making rather than originators of legislative change.

After the First World War French women faced official pressure to conform to a traditional gender role in which their prime civic duty was to marry and produce children for a depleted France. The linkage here with the colonies as a source of military power and of demographic replenishment for metropolitan France reminds us of the connections between the eugenics movement, Catholic and nationalist promoters of natalité, and state efforts to increase the French population. During the 1930s the demographic gap between France and Germany widened further. In these circumstances, imperialists, eugenicists and even Catholic supporters of strict marital values questioned the undesirability of mixed race marriages between French men and women from colonial territories. Colonial social policy, it seemed, was as much affected by changes in French national preoccupations as by local colonial conditions.

Formal education of subject populations was always conducted with racial assumptions and the requirements of administrative control much in mind. Universal primary education was never contemplated. It was too expensive and impossible to resource. Mass literacy would give rise to unwelcome political demands as economic expectations and awareness of wealth disparities increased. Colonial officials and anti-colonial nationalists agreed that schooling was a potent weapon – a double-edged sword that assisted the colonial power by providing a more skilled work force, but that could easily be turned against colonial authority as soon as an educated, literate public sought greater rights and privileges. Controlled access to schooling was therefore part of the fabric of social control. Admission restrictions were matched by careful regulation of curriculum content. The variations in subjects taught reveal a good deal regarding French attitudes about racial hierarchy. Hence Vietnamese children were deemed more intellectually capable than black Africans. It followed that the school curriculum in Indochina required tighter regulation. The Hanoi authorities attached greater importance to the systematic denigration of pre-colonial Vietnam than the Dakar government did to discussion of the pre-colonial kingdoms of West Africa.[142]

But, in one sense, all the colonial federations were more or less comparable. Educational opportunity was the preserve of a select minority. Even on the eve of the Algerian revolution in 1954, only 16.5 per cent of Muslim children attended primary schools, and less than one per cent attended secondary school on a full-time basis.[143] These dismal figures put the achievement of primary school teachers across Algeria in implanting francophone culture and republican values among the educated Muslim minority into context. For every Ferhat Abbas and Mouloud Feraoun educated to believe in the ideal of Franco-Muslim integration, there were eight or nine of their contemporaries for whom formal schooling remained a dream.[144]

Notes

1 Ann Laura Stoler, *Carnal Knowledge and Imperial Power. Race and the Intimate in Colonial Rule* (Berkeley CA: University of California Press, 2002), 1–4.
2 For recent discussions see Cooper, *France in Indochina*, 134–8; Yaël Simpson Fletcher, ' "Irresistible seductions". Gendered representations of colonial Algeria around 1930', in Clancy-Smith and Gouda, *Domesticating the Empire*, 193–210.
3 Cooper, *France in Indochina*, chapter 2, 154–9; Michael G. Vann, 'The good, the bad, and the ugly. Variation and difference in French racism in colonial Indochina', in Peabody and Stovall, *The Color of Liberty*, 191.
4 Stoler, *Carnal Knowledge*, 53–61.
5 Aldrich, *Colonialism and Homosexuality*, 4.
6 *Ibid.*, 2–3, quote at p. 3.
7 Reynolds, *France between the Wars*, chapter 9. For universal suffrage proposals see Paul Smith, *Feminism and the Third Republic. Women's Political and Civil Rights in France, 1918–1945* (Oxford: Oxford University Press, 1996).
8 See, for example, Clotilde Chivas-Baron, *La Femme française aux colonies* (Paris: Larose Editeurs, 1929).
9 Margaret Strobel, *European Women and the Second British Empire* (Bloomington IN: Indiana University Press, 1991), also cited in Frances Gouda, 'Nyonyas on the colonial divide. White women in the Dutch East Indies, 1900–1942', *Gender and History*, 5:3 (1993), 319.
10 Gouda, 'Nyonyas', 318–23; Ann Laura Stoler, 'Making empire respectable. The politics of race and sexual morality in twentieth-century colonial cultures', *American Ethnologist*, 16:4 (1989), 634–60, also cited in Stovall, 'Love, labor, and race', 301.
11 Malia B. Formes, 'Beyond complicity versus resistance. Recent work on gender and European imperialism', *Journal of Social History*, 23:3 (1995), 629–41. Ann Laura Stoler's work on European women in the Dutch colonial empire provides wider insights into white women's lives in colonial society. See her 'Making empire respectable. The politics of race and sexual morality in twentieth-century colonial cultures', *American Ethnologist*, 16:4 (1989), 634–60; 'Rethinking colonial categories. European communities and the boundaries of rule', *Comparative Studies in Society and History*, 31:1 (1989), 134–61; and 'Sexual affronts and racial frontiers. European identities and the cultural politics of exclusion in colonial South East Asia', *Comparative Studies in Society and History*, 34:3 (1992), 514–51. Several of her articles are collected in Stoler, *Carnal Knowledge*.
12 See, for example, James Gelvin, 'Demonstrating communities in post-Ottoman Syria', *Journal of Interdisciplinary History*, 25:1 (1994), 23–44; Beth Baron, *The Women's Awakening in Egypt. Culture, Society, and the Press* (New Haven CT: Yale University Press, 1994) and her 'The politics of female notables in postwar Egypt', in Billie Melman (ed.), *Borderlines. Gender and Identities in War and Peace, 1870–1930* (London: Routledge, 1998), 329–50; Ellen L. Fleischmann, 'The emergence of the Palestinian women's movement, 1929–39', *Journal of Palestine Studies*, 29:3 (2000), 16–32; Hue-Tam Ho Tai, *Radicalism and the Origins of the Vietnamese Revolution* (Cambridge MA: Harvard University Press, 1992), especially chapters 3 and 7; Jean Allman, Susan Geiger and Nakanike Musisi (eds), *Women in African Colonial Histories* (Bloomington IN: Indiana University Press, 2002).
13 Margaret L. Meriwether and Judith E. Tucker (eds), 'Introduction' to *Women and Gender in the Modern Middle East* (Boulder CO: Westview Press, 1999), 3–8.

14 An excellent recent study of this kind is Allman *et al.*, *Women in African Colonial Histories*. See also Nancy Rose Hunt, 'Placing African women's history and locating gender', *Social History*, 14:3 (1989), 359–79.

15 Reynolds, *France between the Wars*, 18–27 passim; Marie-Monique Huss, 'Pronatalism in inter-war France', *Journal of Contemporary History*, 25:1 (1990), 39–68.

16 PRO, FO 371/11052, W2625/2625/17, Lord Crewe (Paris) to FO, 24 March 1924. *Journal Officiel*: 'Statistique annuelle du mouvement de la population de la France'. The precise population figures were as follows: 1913: 41,476,272; 1924: 39,209,518. Not surprisingly, immediately after the war, registered marriages increased sharply to 623,869 in 1920. The 1924 figure was 355,923.

17 Prost, *Republican Identities*, 98–9. Antoine Prost notes that after 1918 war was usually represented in terms of casualties and death, not heroism and victory.

18 *Ibid.*, 97, 277–305 passim.

19 Mary Louise Roberts, ' "This civilization no longer has sexes". *La Garçonne* and cultural crisis in France after World War I', *Gender and History*, 4:1 (1992), 49–69. *La Garçonne* was published the same day that the Senate rejected votes for women, see Sowerine, *France since 1870*, 127.

20 Elisa Camiscioli, 'Intermarriage, independent nationality, and the individual rights of French women. The law of 10 August 1927', *French Politics, Culture and Society*, 17:3–4 (1999), 53–7.

21 S. Abbatucci, 'La maternité en Afrique Noire', *Outre-Mer* 3:4 (1931), 434–5.

22 Cheryl Koos, 'Gender, anti-individualism, and nationalism. The Alliance nationale and the pronatalist backlash against the *femme moderne*, 1933–1940', *French Historical Studies*, 19:4 (1996), 699–723.

23 Camiscioli, 'Intermarriage', 63–4.

24 In the British context see Joanna Lewis, *Empire State-building. War and Welfare in Kenya, 1925–52* (Oxford: James Currey, 2000), 26–8, 52–4.

25 Carol Miller, 'Lobbying the League. Women's international organizations and the League of Nations', Oxford University DPhil, 1992; cited in Pat Thane, 'The British imperial state and the construction of national identities', in Melman, *Borderlines*, 38.

26 Cooper, *Decolonization and African Society*, 29–30.

27 See, for example, the full set of annual reports submitted by the Brazzaville administration in CAOM, GGAEF: 1D1–10.

28 CAOM, GGAEF, 1D8, no. 400, Acting governor-general Alfassa to Direction des affaires politiques 1er bureau, 11 April 1933.

29 CAOM, GGAEF, 1D1, no. 294, Antonetti to Direction des affaires politiques 1er bureau, 3 April 1926.

30 CADN, Fonds Beyrouth, Cabinet politique, vol. 843/D1, no. 551/CP, Comte de Martel to Foreign Ministry, 3 August 1934; vol. 843/D2, 'Rapport annuel de la sûreté générale, 1934', 7 March 1935. In 1934 the Levant high commission expelled sixteen individuals from Syria for prostitution and pimping offences, and closed thirty so-called *maisons de rendez-vous* in Syria and Lebanon.

31 'Notre Enquête. La femme noire en Afrique Française. Le Devoir des Blancs', *Le Monde Colonial illustré*, 188 (February 1939), 30, and 192 (June 1939), 143.

32 CAOM, affpol/541/D1, Direction des affaires politiques 2ème bureau, 'L'évolution et la condition juridique de la femme indigène en Indochine', 29 November 1939.

33 *Ibid.*

34 Tai, *Radicalism*, 88–104, 220–1.

35 Marr, *Vietnamese Tradition*, 214–15, 220–1.

36 Soeur Marie-André du Sacré-Coeur, 'Vers l'évolution de la femme indigène en AOF', *Le Monde Colonial illustré*, 178 (April 1938), 68–9.

37 Echenberg, *Black Death, White Medicine*, 179, 202.

38 CAOM, GGAEF, 1D10, no. 147, Secrétaire-général Marchessou to Direction des affaires politiques, 1er bureau, 24 January 1935.

39 Phyllis Martin notes that Brazzaville townswomen bought fewer clothes than their menfolk, and at weddings bridegrooms often wore shoes while brides remained barefoot. See her 'Contesting clothes in colonial Brazzaville', 414.

40 Gray, 'Lambaréné, Okoumé and the transformation of labor', 87.
41 Eckert, 'African rural entrepreneurs', 111.
42 André Osterhaus and Claude Sissau, 'Les révoltes de femmes en Afrique durant la période coloniale', in Groupe Afrique noire, *L'Histoire des femmes en Afrique*, Cahier 11 (Paris: Editions l'Harmattan, 1987), 39–41; LaRay Denzer, 'Towards a study of the history of West African women's participation in nationalist politics. The early phase, 1935–1960', *Africana Research Bulletin*, 6:4 (1976), 65–85.
43 CAOM, affpol/663/D1, no. 1050/C, Antonetti to Affaires politiques 2ème bureau, 'Application de l'indigénat', 15 December 1928.
44 Marnia Lazreg, *The Eloquence of Silence. Algerian Women in Question* (London: Routledge, 1994), 98–105.
45 Julia Clancy-Smith, 'A woman without her distaff. Gender, work, and handicraft production in colonial North Africa', in Meriwether and Tucker, *Women and Gender*, 25–62.
46 *Ibid.*, 36–43.
47 Lazreg, *The Eloquence of Silence*, 88–9.
48 *Ibid.*, 89–91.
49 Keller, 'Madness and colonization', 314.
50 Gallup, 'The French image of Algeria', 106–17.
51 Lazreg, *The Eloquence of Silence*, 86.
52 Monique Gadant, *Le Nationalisme algérien et les femmes* (Paris: Editions l'Harmattan, 1995), 118–21. There are interesting comparisons with unveiling in Egypt, see Beth Baron, 'Unveiling in early twentieth-century Egypt. Practical and symbolic considerations', *Middle Eastern Studies*, 25:3 (1989), 370–86.
53 Thompson, *Colonial Citizens*, 127–35.
54 Gelvin, *Divided Loyalties*, 148–9, 213–14.
55 *Ibid.*, 191–2.
56 Gadant, *Le Nationalisme algérien et les femmes*, 122–4.
57 Ilhem Marzouki, *Le Mouvement des femmes en Tunisie au XXème siècle. Feminisme et politique* (Tunis: Cérès productions, 1993), 35.
58 Gadant, *Le Nationalisme algérien et les femmes*, 128; Lazreg, *The Eloquence of Silence*, 86.
59 Noureddine Sraieb, 'Islam, réformisme et condition feminine en Tunisie : Tahar Haddad (1898–1935)', *Clio. Histoire, Femmes et Sociétés*, 9 (1999), 77–85.
60 CAOM, affpol/907, no. 1559, Manceron (Tunis) to Foreign Ministry, Direction Afrique-Levant, 20 November 1930.
61 See *Les Mémoires de Messali Hadj* (Paris: J. C. Lattès, 1982), 152; also cited in Gadant, *Le Nationalisme algérien et les femmes*, 130. Messali stated that he considered his French wife his 'surest collaborator'.
62 Gadant, *Le Nationalisme algérien et les femmes*, 122.
63 Souad Slim and Anne-Laure Dupont, 'La vie intellectuelle des femmes à Beyrouth dans les années 1920 à travers la revue *Minerva*', *Revue des Mondes Musulmans et de la Méditerranée*, 95–98 (2002), 381–406.
64 Marthe Oulié, 'Femmes du Liban et de Syrie', *Le Monde Colonial illustré*, 195 (September 1939), 210–11.
65 Lydon, 'The unravelling of a neglected source'.
66 *Ibid.*, 555–84; Bernard Salvaing, 'La femme dahoméenne vue par les missionaires : arrogance culturelle ou antiféminisme clerical?' *Cahiers d'Etudes Africaines*, 84 (1981), 507–22.
67 Lydon, 'The unravelling of a neglected source', 565–72.
68 *Ibid.*, 555–84. See also Ghislaine Lydon, 'Women, children and the Popular Front's missions of inquiry in French West Africa', in Tony Chafer and Amanda Sackur (eds), *French Colonial Empire and Popular Front. Hope and Disillusion* (London: Macmillan, 1999), 170–87. Moran made a point of visiting prison establishments in AOF. She found that some women prisoners were assigned to prepare all inmates' food. Others were held in isolation to prevent sexual abuse by male prisoners.
69 CAOM, affpol/541, no. 349/AP/2, Brévié to lieutenant-governors (AOF), 25 June 1936.
70 CAOM, affpol/541, Direction des affaires politiques, 'Note annexe à la circulaire no. 290/AP/2 du 7 mai 1937 au sujet du marriage indigène'.

71 CAOM, affpol/541/D1, Direction des affaires politiques, 2ème bureau, 'Le statut juridique de la femme dans les colonies françaises', 29 November 1939.

72 CAOM, Marius Moutet papers, PA28/1/D4, no. 3278, Inspection générale du service de santé des colonies, 'Rapport au Ministre', 11 May 1937.

73 CAOM, affpol/541, no. 8457, Inspection générale du service de santé des colonies letter to Georges Mandel, 30 November 1938. At this point there were still only 141 trained midwives and eighty-three district nurses registered in AOF.

74 Jane Turrittin, 'Colonial midwives and modernizing childbirth in French West Africa', in Allman et al., Women in African Colonial Histories, 72–6. The AOF colonial health service was transferred to civilian control in 1918, but was still run along military lines in the inter-war years.

75 I am very grateful to Dr Ruth Ginio for her advice on this subject.

76 Mathéa Gaudry, 'L'instruction de la femme indigène en Algérie', L'Afrique Française, 46:1 (January 1936), 28–9.

77 Irbouh, 'French colonial art education', 277.

78 Ibid., 277–81.

79 Lazreg, The Eloquence of Silence, 86–8.

80 Owen White, Children of the French Empire. Miscegenation and Colonial Society in French West Africa, 1895–1960 (Oxford: Oxford University Press, 1999), 10–12; Stoler, 'Rethinking colonial categories', 134–61.

81 White, Children, 57–9.

82 Jean Elizabeth Pederson, ' "Special Customs". Paternity suits and citizenship in France and the colonies, 1870–1912', in Clancy-Smith and Gouda, Domesticating the Empire, 55–7.

83 White, Children, 37.

84 Elizabeth Ezra, 'Colonialism Exposed. Miss France d'Outre-mer, 1937', in Steven Ungar and Tom Conley (eds), Identity Papers. Contested Nationhood in Twentieth Century France (Minneapolis MN: University of Minnesota Press, 1996), 50–9.

85 For AOF see White, Children, 24–7; and Conklin, A Mission to Civilize, 169–71. For colonial Asia see Ann Laura Stoler, 'Carnal knowledge and imperial power. Gender, race and morality in colonial Asia', in Micaela di Leonardo (ed.), Gender at the Crossroads of Knowledge. Feminist Anthropology in the Postmodern Era (Berkeley CA: University of California Press, 1991), 64–8. For the Dutch East Indies comparison see Gouda, 'Nyonyas', 327–36.

86 Regarding the British Empire see Ronald Hyam, Empire and Sexuality. The British Experience (Manchester: Manchester University Press, 1990); and his 'Concubinage and the colonial service. The Crewe circular (1909)', Journal of Imperial and Common-wealth History, 14 (1986), 170–86. Compare also the attempt by British East African governors to regulate the practice of clitoridectomy in 1920s Kenya, see Susan Pederson, 'National bodies, unspeakable acts. The sexual politics of colonial policy-making', Journal of Modern History, 63:4 (1991), 647–80.

87 The most comprehensive study of education policy in francophone Africa in the preceding colonial period is Denise Bouche, L'Enseignement dans les territoires français de l'Afrique occidentale de 1817 à 1920. Mission civilisatrice ou formation d'une élite? 2 vols (Paris: Honoré Champion, 1975).

88 Olatunji Oluruntimehin, 'Education for colonial dominance in French West Africa from 1900 to the Second World War', Journal of the Historical Society of Nigeria, 7:2 (1974), 347–55.

89 Preeti Chopra, 'Pondicherry. A French enclave in India', in Al Sayyad, Forms of Dominance, 110–17.

90 Jones, 'The Catholic mission', 329–32; Bouche, Histoire de la colonisation française, 104.

91 H. O. Idowu, 'The establishment of elective institutions in Senegal, 1869–1880', Journal of African History, 9:2 (1968), 264.

92 Peggy R. Sabatier, ' "Elite" education in French West Africa. The era of limits, 1903–1945', International Journal of African Historical Studies, 11:2 (1978), 250.

93 Bouche, L'Enseignement; White, Children, 41–49, 54–5.

94 Martin, 'Contesting clothes in colonial Brazzaville', 410.
95 Annie Rey-Goldzeiguer, 'Réflexions sur l'image et la perception du maghreb et des maghrebins dans la France du XIXe et XXe siècles', in Blanchard and Chatelier, *Images et Colonies*, 37.
96 MAE, série P: Tunisie 1917–40, vol. 388, SE (Tunis) renseignement, 'L'enseignement des indigènes en Tunisie', 3 February 1937.
97 Aldrich, *The French Presence*, 26–7, 36–68.
98 Matthew Burrows, *'Mission civilisatrice'*. French cultural policy in the Middle East, 1860–1914', *Historical Journal*, 29:1 (1986), 130–2.
99 *Ibid.*, 109–35; John Spagnolo, 'The definition of a style of internal politics of the French educational investment in Ottoman Beirut', *French Historical Studies*, 8:4 (1974), 563–84; Jacques Thobie, 'La France a-t-elle une politique culturelle dans l'empire ottoman à la veille de la première guerre mondiale?' *Relations Internationales*, 25:1 (1981), 21–40.
100 P-B. de la Brosse, 'L'organisation de l'enseignement populaire en Indochine', *L'Asie Française*, 35:333 (October 1935), 264–5.
101 Munholland, 'The French response to the Vietnamese nationalist movement', 657–61; Tai, *Radicalism*, 93–6.
102 CAOM, GGI, 64191, Tonkin residency, 'Rapport sur la situation du Tonkin à la fin de l'année 1922', 3 February 1923. The Hanoi government-general disagreed with the Resident's reading of mandarin attitudes.
103 Karen Offen, 'The second sex and the *baccalauréat* in republican France, 1880–1924', *French Historical Studies*, 13:2 (1983), 252–86; Reynolds, *France between the Wars*, 144–5; Sowerine, *France since 1870*, 126. In early 1924 Minister of Education Léon Bérard, a noted opponent of women's suffrage, established a *baccalauréat* stream for girls' schools.
104 Marr, *Vietnamese Tradition*, 37–9.
105 Gail P. Kelly, 'The presentation of indigenous society in the schools of French West Africa and Indochina, 1918 to 1938', *Comparative Studies in Society and History*, 26:3 (1984), 524.
106 Brosse, 'L'organisation de l'enseignement populaire en Indochine', 265.
107 CAOM, Marius Moutet papers, PA28/4/Dossier Varenne, sous-dossier 59, 'Aperçu de l'oeuvre accompli en Indochine par Alexandre Varenne'. From 15 July 1927 intending secondary school teachers were required to sit a final examination, the *Brevet de capacité de l'enseignement secondaire franco-indigène* (Certificate of Competence in Franco-indigène Secondary School teaching) that focused on teachers' ability to deliver a French-language curriculum to Vietnamese children.
108 Kelly, 'The presentation of indigenous society', 526. The registered school population for the 1937–38 academic year was slightly higher: 62,464.
109 Sabatier, ' "Elite" education in French West Africa', 247; Oluruntimehin, 'Education for colonial dominance', 352–4.
110 Sabatier, ' "Elite" education in French West Africa', 249–51.
111 Person, 'Le Front populaire au Sénégal', 81.
112 Oluruntimehin, 'Education for colonial dominance', 350.
113 ADA, Sarraut papers, 12J163, Chambre des Députés, Douzième Législature, Session de 1921, procès-verbal, séance du 12 avril 1921, 'Projet de loi portant fixation d'un programme général de mise en valeur des colonies françaises', 37–8.
114 Gail P. Kelly, 'Interwar schools and the development of African history in French West Africa', *History in Africa*, 10 (1983), 162–9; Kelly, 'The presentation of indigenous culture', 528–38.
115 For a British comparison see Joanna Lewis's discussion of the feminisation of colonial education policy in inter-war Kenya in *Empire State-building*, 52–67.
116 Person, 'Le Front populaire au Sénégal', 81.
117 Albert Charton (AOF Inspector-general of Education), 'Rôle social de l'enseignement en Afrique Occidentale Française', *Outre-Mer*, 6:2 (1934), 188–99. Brévié refined these ideas in his book, *Islamisme contre naturisme*.
118 A. Rémondet, 'La création des Écoles Normales rurales en AOF', *Outre-Mer* 7:2–3 (1935), 201–3.

119 CAOM, AOF Fonds moderne, 17G90, no. 2811, 'Rapport sur l'activité de la Direction politique 1936–37', 22 November 1937.
120 Kelly, 'The presentation of indigenous society', 526–7.
121 Sabatier, ' "Elite" education in French West Africa', 256, table 1.
122 Rokhaya Fall, 'Le système d'enseignement en AOF', and Papa Momar Diop 'L'enseignement de la fille indigène en AOF 1903–1958', both in Becker et al., AOF : réalités et heritages II, 1071–80 and 1081–96. There were 18,395 registered pupils in AOF schools in 1919–20, of whom 400 were girls. Figures from Diop, 'L'enseignement', table 1, p. 1096.
123 Sabatier, ' "Elite" education in French West Africa', 252–3.
124 SHA, 2N70/D4, CSDN Secretariat, 'La Situation de l'AEF en 1938'.
125 CAOM, GGAEF, 1934, 1D4, no. 178, Antonetti to Conseil de l'instruction publique (Colonies), 5 February 1934.
126 Aldrich, Colonialism and Homosexuality, 331–44. Robert Aldrich demonstrates convincingly that Gide's view of Algerian culture, Maghrebi society and, to a lesser extent, the peoples of AEF was shaped by his romantic attachments to young indigène men and the less inhibited attitude to homosexuality in the colonies.
127 White, Children, 68.
128 Ibid., 63–80.
129 CAOM, GGAEF, 1D10, Secrétaire-général Marchessou (Brazzaville) to Direction des affaires politiques, 24 January 1935.
130 Irbouh, 'French colonial art education', 275–6.
131 Charles-Robert Ageron, Histoire de l'Algérie contemporaine (Paris: Presses Universitaires de France, 1964), 605, 850; Colonna, Instituteurs algériens, 92–3.
132 Figures taken from Kaddache, Histoire du nationalisme algérien, I, 39.
133 Colonna, Instituteurs algériens, 56.
134 Dunwoodie, Writing French Algeria, 22–4.
135 Colonna, Instituteurs algériens, 58.
136 Julien, L'Afrique du Nord en marche, 40–1.
137 MAE, série P: Tunisie 1917–40, vol. 387, no. 466, Direction des affaires politiques memo, 'Grève des étudiants de la Grande Mosquée', 6 March 1936.
138 Guelmami, La Politique sociale en Tunisie, 68–9. A snapshot of educational statistics for the 1920s does reveal an increasing proportion of Muslim children attending primary schools: 25.56 per cent in 1918; 40.65 per cent in 1925; and 46.42 per cent in 1930. See Guelmami, La Politique, p. 69, table 3.
139 MAE, série P: Tunisie 1917–40, vol. 388, SE (Tunis), 'L'enseignement des indigènes en Tunisie', 3 February 1937.
140 Historiographical trends in the study of African women, are reviewed by Margaret Jean Hay, 'Queens, prostitutes and peasants. Historical perspectives on African women, 1971–1986', Canadian Journal of African Studies, 22:3 (1988), 431–47; and Dorothy L. Hodgson and Sheryl McCurdy, 'Wayward wives, misfit mothers, and disobedient daughters. "Wicked" women and the reconfiguration of gender in Africa', Canadian Journal of African Studies, 30:1 (1996), 1–9.
141 Osterhaus and Sissau, 'Les révoltes de femmes en Afrique', 36–7.
142 Kelly, 'The presentation of indigenous society', 529–31. See also Kelly, 'Colonial schools in Vietnam. Policy and practice', in Phillip G. Altbach and Gail P. Kelly (eds), Education and Colonialism (London: Longman, 1978), 96–121.
143 Smith, 'Colonial impoverishment', 148.
144 James D. Le Sueur (ed.), Mouloud Feraoun, Journal 1955–1962. Reflections on the French–Algerian War (Lincoln NE: University of Nebraska Press, 2000). Mouloud Feraoun was a leading Algerian writer and educator from Kabylia. He was assassinated by the right-wing Organisation de l'Armée Secrète in March 1962.

CHAPTER SIX

'Thinking imperially'?
Popular imperialism in France

Until recently, historians of the colonial empire treated the concept of French 'popular imperialism' as an oxymoron.[1] The French, it is assumed, were wrapped up in domestic politics, too fond of home-grown pleasures, too contemptuous of the wider world to take fervent pride in their colonies. For those at the heart of power in Paris, the hubbub of Third Republic politics and metropolitan culture drowned out the call to empire. Those that raised their gaze beyond the horizon of French society were either consumed by European threats, or part of an eclectic minority of genuine 'imperialists', regarded with a mixture of indulgence and disdain by the majority of the political community. In deepest rural France the colonies were dimly understood as an agglomeration of largely unconnected territories and an unwelcome source of competition for the agricultural produce of French farmers and winegrowers. Imperialism at the provincial level was confined to those ports and cities with valued commercial connections to colonial territories. Public attitudes to empire were far more sophisticated and complex than this picture admits.

Yet evaluating popular imperialism in inter-war France is none the less problematic. The most interesting and frequently used evidence is representational. It ranges from analyses of colonial exhibitions, museums and the proliferation of colonial or colonial-inspired art and literature to the proliferation of colonial themes in popular cinema and French advertising.[2] The beginnings of opinion polling in the late 1930s have also been examined in an attempt to pin down public attitudes to empire. As John MacKenzie has shown in the British context, government propaganda often took second place to a plethora of non-state agencies dedicated to the imperial cause. Much as in Britain, imperialist geographical societies, missionary groups, ex-servicemen's associations and scouting movements, corporate advertisers and popular entertainers all promoted France's colonial connection. Cinema films, the Pathé and Gaumont newsreel companies, entertainers and songsters, the popular press, illustrated magazines and children's comics brought popular imperialism into the mass media age.[3] Radio Paris, for instance, allocated a fortnightly slot to discussion of colonial issues in 1930, increased to a weekly programme a year later.[4]

Colonial reportage also became a more regular feature in the Paris press. *Le Temps* published a weekly colonial supplement. From 1929 *L'Echo de Paris* produced a brace of 'empire' special editions each year. And tabloid-style newspapers such as *Le Petit Parisien* that popularised colonial conquest in the late nineteenth century still captivated their readers with sensationalist colonial reportage in the inter-war years. Not all such coverage was positive. In 1928 the writer Albert Londres chose *Le Petit Parisien* to recount in graphic detail the dreadful working conditions on AEF's Congo–Océan railway. His claim that over 17,000 labourers died during the construction of a 140 km section of track caused a media storm.[5] Far less critical were the metropolitan newspapers specifically dedicated to colonial news coverage, including the *Dépêche Coloniale et Maritime* (established in 1892). These overtly imperialist newssheets registered increased sales in the 1920s, but still catered to a specialist readership, many with personal, bureaucratic or commercial ties to the empire. More marginal still were the monthly publications of the various Parti colonial regional committees. All these were established between 1890 and 1911, but none achieved a mass circulation. *L'Afrique Française*, produced by the French Africa and Morocco committee, was by far the largest. Targeted at settlers, officials and imperial traders, the range and depth of articles in the Parti colonial press were offset by the fact that, year after year, individual journals relied on a handful of contributors to provide most of their copy. Senator de la Brosse in *L'Asie Française*, Eugène Pelleray in *L'Océanie Française* and Henri Labouret and Robert Delavignette in *L'Afrique Française* were old colonial hands whose editorial line rarely varied, and who simply preached to the converted.[6] Finally, a clutch of anti-colonial newspapers edited by colonial immigrants and university students began publication in Paris soon after the First World War. The best known of these – and the most frequently banned by the Interior Ministry – were *Les Continents* and *Le Paria Tribune des populations des colonies*, both vociferous critics of colonial oppression.[7] By 1929 this anti-colonialist press had working links with the PCF and was synonymous in the eyes of police censors with Comintern propaganda.

But were the French public paying much attention? There was an obvious disjuncture between profuse imperial coverage and an immutable public apathy toward colonial problems.[8] As Minister of Colonies in 1920 Albert Sarraut articulated the challenge facing the imperialist lobby:

> It is absolutely indispensable that a methodical, responsible, and constant [imperial] propaganda be brought to bear in our country on adults and

children through imagery, newspapers, conferences, films and exhibitions . . . In our primary schools, colleges and *lycées* we must improve and enlarge the cursory education that pupils receive about our history and our colonial possessions. It is vital that this education should be livelier, more expressive and more practical; that visual imagery and film are used to educate and entertain French youth out of ignorance about our colonies.[9]

Sarraut's call to arms elicited a mixed response. French enthusiasm for empire remained fitful, clichéd, sometimes superficial. As Jean-Pierre Biondi puts it, ' "La France profonde" was probably not colonialist, [but] it was not anti-colonialist . . . The masses that broadly approved of empire faced a minority that was passionate about it'.[10] If anything, in France, as in Britain, imperial propaganda encouraged the domestic 'under-classes' to behave as imperial 'over-classes'.[11] Herman Lebovics has highlighted a marked shift toward cultural conformity in France and its empire in the early twentieth century. Political, juridical, cultural and anthropological definitions of authentically 'French' qualities became a battleground between left and right. Racial stereotypes became more prevalent in consequence. So, too, did governmental hostility to interracial 'mixing', whether in France or in the colonies, something abundantly clear in official attitudes to *métissage* and colonial concubines. A clearer linkage was established between Frenchness and political rights that left little room for any significant emancipation of subject peoples.[12] Cultural historians have found support for Lebovics's thesis in French celebrations of empire after 1919.[13] This chapter revisits these issues, broadly surveying inter-war popular imperialism.

Empire and popular culture in France

The high and low points of French imperialism in the early Third Republic registered less on the Richter scale of domestic public opinion than their British equivalents, and their long-term aftershocks were correspondingly weaker too.[14] The towns of Annam, western Sudan, Madagascar and Morocco – all brought under the French yoke between 1880 and 1914 – did not have the ring of Mafeking or Ladysmith, principally because French settlers were of marginal importance in each case. In terms of popular imperialism the national stereotypes of Anglo-Saxon reserve and high Gallic emotion were reversed. Few in France paid close attention to colonial events. Fewer still influenced colonial policy. Morocco was a case in point. Consolidation of the recently established protectorate was broadly popular, but the fragility of French control over Sultan Moulay Youssef ben Hassan's administration was poorly appreciated at home. Before 1914 the Third Republic never saw an outpouring of popular jingoism comparable to the British public reaction to the South African War at the turn of the century. Celebration of noted triumphs, as in early twentieth-century Morocco, was, by British standards, restrained. Embarrassing defeats brought down ministries less out of wounded imperial pride than because of harm to French standing in Europe. Parisian crowds bayed for Prime Minister Jules Ferry's blood in 1885 after French defeat at Langson in Tonkin. British 'jingoism' found no echo in provincial France. The one exception – the return home of the leader of the Fashoda expedition, Major Jean-Baptiste Marchand, in 1898 – prompted an outpouring of anglophobic nationalism rather than an affirmation of popular imperialism. Yet even Ferry's most vociferous Radical Party opponents, Georges Clemenceau among them, would not renounce possession of colonial territory, once it was acquired.

The contradiction between underlying imperialist resolve and widespread public apathy persisted after 1919. The historian searching for evidence of empire in the day-to-day life of inter-war France has little difficulty finding it. Colonial conquest was everywhere memorialised in street names, city squares, Parisian metro stations, war memorials and municipal museums. Imperial explorers, noted governors and, above all, the nineteenth-century *conquistadors* of Africa, South East Asia and the Pacific were immortalised in Parisian street signs, especially in and around Vincennes and the administrative district of the *septième*.[15] Provincial towns such as Bordeaux, Lyons and Marseilles also advertised their long-standing colonial heritage in boulevards and back alleys given imperial epithets.

Colonial postcards, some scenic, some depicting heroic achievement, others pornographic, circulated in vast numbers before and after the First World War. Sunny vistas of colonial capitals, tableaux of Coloniale engagements against tribal hordes, and studio 'studies' of disrobed colonial women were commonplace. By 1914 there were at least fifty-four publishers of colonial postcards in sub-Saharan French Africa.[16] Between 1900 and 1925 a single photographer's studio in Dakar produced over 6,000 images for the local postcard trade.[17] Before 1914 Lyautey's Rabat residency, generously funded by the Parti colonial's Moroccan committee, employed war correspondents to photograph notable campaign victories later replicated in official postcard sets.[18] The producers of the principal genre of Algerian colonial postcard – the so-called 'scenes and types' – upheld rigid distinctions of race and class in the urban landscapes, public buildings and 'typical' scenes of workaday life they recorded. Algerian Muslims, even blue-collar settlers, might, for instance, be depicted at work, but white-collar Europeans were not.[19]

Writers, artists, film makers, musicians, museum curators and club owners were also drawn to colonial imagery of various kinds. After 1919 the French *avant-garde* drew inspiration and entertainment from colonial cultures as never before. Jazz – often referred to as *une musique nègre* –

was in vogue. So was so-called *négrophile* writing and colonial cinema. Colonial exoticism was a recurrent theme in French advertising and high fashion.[20] The overall impact of these aesthetic shifts is hard to gauge. Some were short-lived, and most traded in crude racial stereotypes. Writers had a more lasting impact. Several of André Gide's novels and his auto-biography, *Si le grain ne meurt*, helped mould the popular image of the colonies, French North Africa especially, as eroticised paradises.[21] Elizabeth Ezra is surely right to conclude that artistic engagement with empire themes generated a 'colonial unconscious' in inter-war French – and especially Parisian – culture.[22]

In 1925 the French secondary school curriculum was redesigned to incorporate more explicit reference to the colonies. A compulsory colonial question was added to the geography *baccalauréat* examination. In 1926 an advisory committee of colonial officials and academics working under the aegis of the Supreme Colonial Council began investigating further curriculum changes intended to ensure that schoolchildren grasped the empire's importance to France. Heroes of imperial exploration and conquest featured more heavily in the national history taught in secondary schools and *lycées*. Lyautey held pride of place among these figures following the 1931 publication of André Malraux's effusive, best-selling biography of the Moroccan marshal. Primary schools came into line with the altera-tions made to the secondary school curriculum. Classroom maps were republished with overseas possessions more prominently displayed.[23] Even so, empire was hardly omnipresent in the classroom. After the 1925 cur-riculum reforms, *lycées* and colleges were obliged to incorporate 'France and its colonies' into a one-hour weekly geography class. 'The history of French colonisation' became one of the nineteen compulsory elements in the two hours assigned per week to first-year French history classes. Similarly, the post-1848 administrative structure of the empire figured among the twenty-two elements of the *lycée* philosophy curriculum.[24] In rare instances com-mitted imperialists went further. The Lyons Chamber of Commerce patronised an *école de préparation coloniale* whose students took classes in colonial geography, history and four oriental languages in a curriculum that trained them for colonial commercial careers. But enrolment fell away in the depression years, as did the Lyons businessmen's funding.[25]

Study of the empire was more entrenched at university level. The colo-nial legal system was integrated into the law curriculum in July 1889. Colonial geography was taught at the Sorbonne's *faculté des lettres* from 1893, and the Universities of Bordeaux and Marseilles followed suit in 1897 and 1899 respectively.[26] Thanks to the efforts of Indochina governor-general Paul Doumer and the spate of advances in microbiology and epide-miology, a Paris institute of colonial medicine was established in 1902, a metropolitan counterpart to the Pasteur medical research laboratories set up across the empire in the late nineteenth century. French medical dispensaries established in southern China illustrated the links between Western medicine, improvements in public health and cultural imperialism. In addition to providing advance warning to Indochina of likely epidemics introduced from China, these dispensaries proved that investment in colonial medicine strengthened the imperial cause.[27] The imperialist lobby wanted more. Eager to capitalise on the public interest fired by the 1931 Vincennes colonial exhibition, in September that year the Colonies and Sciences Association, a loose grouping of colonial lobbyists, Ecole coloniale staff and Education Ministry bureaucrats, proposed the further incorporation of colonial subjects into the school curriculum and specialist university degrees.[28] The association pressed for the creation of university professorships dedicated to the natural sciences, whose recipients would conduct research into the geology, botany and zoology of colonial territories. Invited speakers proposed the establishment of additional specialist laboratories for research into parasitology, tropical medicine and agronomy.[29]

In April 1933 Minister of National Education Anatole de Monzie responded positively to an offer by the managerial board of the magazine *Le Monde Colonial illustré* to distribute the publication free of charge to all *écoles normales primaires* in France. De Monzie was bound to be accommodating. The board in question included Sarraut, former governors Théodore Steeg and Martial Merlin, as well as two Marshals of France, Lyautey and Louis Franchet d'Esperey, hero of the Marne, plus the presidents of the two parliamentary Chambers.[30] But comic books and children's magazines were probably more influential on young minds than the arid reading of *Le Monde Colonial illustré*. Ever the virtuous Belgian boy scout, Hergé's Tintin, roamed over Africa; the 'Amazing adventures of Dache' transported young readers to zouave encampments; and mass-circulation Catholic magazines for girls, such as *La semaine de Suzette* and *Bécassine*, ran page after page praising missionary work.[31]

French commercial life also revealed the imperial connection, whether in the businesses dependent on exporting to colonial markets, in the Marseilles dockyards crammed with colonial goods, in the colonial foodstuffs that enriched the French diet, or in the produce advertised with empire motifs. The most famous of these was surely Banania cocoa powder. Redesigned in 1917, its wrapper depicted a smiling *tirailleur* pronouncing in pidgin French, 'Ya bon', 'It's good'. Using Anne McLintock's terminology, Anne Donadey characterises Banania's imagery as 'commodity racism', stressing that advertisers' depictions of colonial subjects played on the greater visibility of colonial peoples to the French population during and after the First World War.[32] Just as Banania's motif hit the food shelves, West African troops serving on the western front also featured prominently in overtly racist postcards and dirty jokes as the embodiment of male sexuality. This was typical: the juxtaposition of a crude racial stereotype – guileless, stupid, savage, sexually promiscuous – with an idealisation of the colonies themselves as an unspoilt paradise. After the war, commercial trademark images of colonial subjects remained racially stratified, North Africans frequently represented as a martial race, black Africans as child-like and Vietnamese as cultured artisans or figures of exotic beauty.[33]

Colonial exoticism was an established leitmotif by 1918. Muslim terri-tories were stereotypically personified in tourism advertising as an erotic, veiled dancer that symbolised a land of promise to settlers and tourists alike. Railway station hoardings tempted commuters to imagine the pleasures of an imperial cruise. In the late 1920s the Art Deco styling of shipping line posters advertising trips to North Africa, Indochina, Lebanon and the Antilles became instantly recognisable. A hierarchy of *chic* tourist havens emerged as more exclusive and remote colonial destinations became accessible to the richest travellers. Shipping company plans in 1913 to offer cruises from Le Havre to New York, then overland via Niagara Falls to San Francisco, and thence aboard a Union Steam Ship to Tahiti, were interrupted by the war.[34] But in 1921 a newly created Oceania tourism committee revived these schemes, in conjunction with tourist information bureaux and the French Touring Club's colonial arm – the Touring Club colonial. The new committee boasted an impressive mem-bership that included the vice-president of the French Touring Club, two shipping line presidents (of the Compagnie générale transatlantique and the Compagnie des messageries maritimes), and Paul Froment-Guieysse, director of the French Oceania committee. Confident that tourism would flourish in Polynesia, Tahiti especially, their task was simply to encourage the 'right sort' of tourist.[35]

While those taking Oceanic cruises in the 1920s tended, at the very least, to be *haut bourgeois*, three shipping lines – the Compagnie générale trans-atlantique, the Messageries maritimes and the Chargeurs réunis – strove to develop more affordable colonial tourism, providing hotel accommo-dation, excursions and inland transport as part of imperial 'package tours'. Prodded by the North African governors, commercial airlines eventually followed suit once France's trans-African air route linking Algiers to Tananarive came into operation in 1938.[36] Year after year the Supreme Colonial Council reminded ministers that the development of empire tourism should be integrated into colonial policy. Indochina led the way. With official encouragement, its rich cultural heritage and oriental exoticism became staples in tourist industry advertising. In 1926 Governor-general Varenne appointed an assistant to liaise with French film makers and advertisers on behalf of the Hanoi authorities. A subsidised Indochina tourism association was soon established. By 1927 the association had opened branches in Saigon, Pnom-Penh, Hué, Tourane and Haiphong, offering brochures, postcards, posters and local timetables to prospective clients.[37] Over the next three years similar marketing drives began in AOF, AEF and Madagascar, the intention being to incorporate francophone African territories in 'grand tour' packages sold to wealthy tourist clients.[38] As the depression bit harder colonial governments revaluated tourism as a precious source of revenue and a means to bring colonial needs to public attention. In 1933, for example, the Brazzaville government organised an extensive itinerary for the Ligue maritime et coloniale director Rondet-Saint, and publicised the achievements of Maryse Hiltz, the first woman aviator to traverse Africa by air. Their message was clear: 'darkest Africa' was no longer impenetrable.[39]

The Popular Front's institution of annual paid holiday leave in 1936 presented the possibility of colonial travel to workers who saved diligently for the holiday of a lifetime. But for most French working families the advent of the much-loved *congés payés* meant short breaks to the seaside and the country rather than trips overseas. The Popular Front's promotion of leisure, sport and other recreational activity had a strongly metropolitan focus. The provinces rather than the colonies were overrun with city folk enjoying time off – or so more affluent country dwellers complained.[40] Aside from those with family connections in the empire, colonial tourism remained an overwhelmingly bourgeois affair. By the mid-1930s ferry services to the Maghreb were widely available, offering a cheap way to reach imperial territory within twenty-four hours of departure. Direct telephone connections and commercial air flights from France to North Africa were also established in the ten years before 1940.[41] A full-page advertisement in the November 1937 issue of the Paris monthly review *Corréspondance d'Orient* played on this accessibility. Against a sketched backdrop of a walled medina surrounded by date palms, the advert coaxed readers to visit Morocco by evoking the pursuits typical of the bourgeois tourist:

> Morocco offers you all the joys of camping in the mountains, winter sports in exquisite locations among the eternal snows of the Atlas Mountains with their hidden Alpine refuges at over 3,000 metres above sea level. And in the towns, the most demanding tourist will find sumptuous palaces and comfortable hotels at reasonable prices.[42]

The French Touring Club, France's largest private tourist association, with up to 300,000 members in the 1930s, was particularly receptive to such enticement. It capitalised on growing public interest in colonial tourism by producing elaborate publicity brochures and tour guides depicting colonial vacations as at once exotic, educational and a patriotic duty. Travellers could sample 'authentic' indigenous cultures while revelling in France's imperial achievement. Cheap prophylactic treatments available over the pharmacy counter, including Prémaline and Quinacrine, kept mosquitoes and malaria at bay.[43] What imperial pioneers had conquered with the rifle the intrepid tourist could capture with the camera. But contact with local populations was strictly limited. Tour guides selected daily outings appropriate for their clients, shielding them from insalubrious sights, sounds and smells. A quick visit to the *souk* or the street-side market for the obligatory souvenirs was enough local colour for most paying customers. Besides, for many this was highbrow tourism, a chance to sample ancient cultures, not the reality of modern colonialism. The new French tourist elite was, in Ellen Furlough's words invited 'to view clichés' from African tribalism and Vietnamese exoticism to the vestiges of lost civilisations allegedly salvaged by French intervention such as Cambodia's Angkor Wat temple complex or the Tunisian ruins of ancient Carthage.[44]

Members of the Touring Club often took to the road with the relevant copy of a Michelin Guide to hand. In the inter-war period France's leading tyre maker was at the forefront of tourism marketing. The makers of the Michelin Guide also widened their purview from the diversity of provincial France to the richness of the colonies, publishing a new guide to the Maghreb territories to coincide with the 1930 centenary of the French landings in Algeria. Michelin's new North African guidebook made telling assumptions about what French tourists should do. The local water was to be avoided. But so, too, was ethnic cuisine, other than in exceptional cases, such as Fez, where the city's main attraction was immersion in the labyrinthine streets and casbahs of the old town. Here the venturesome traveller might risk some *gâteaux arabes*. More generally, Michelin anticipated that its tourist clients would prefer sightseeing and comfortable European hotels to the humdrum existence of North Africa's cities. Tourists were thus set apart in deliberate mimicry of colonial officialdom.[45]

It was also taken for granted that the discerning tourist would travel separately from the colonial populations being observed. In August 1938 the French Touring Club seized on completion of the *transindochinois* road network linking all the territories of the Indochina federation as an opportunity for its clientele to begin Michelin Guide-style tourism in the Far East. Car travellers could at last explore Indochina without straying from the safety of its arterial road system.[46] Africa was not far behind. On 31 May 1939 AEF governor-general Alfassa told an invited Touring Club audience that colonial tourism could integrate France and the empire more fully. The colonies were the obvious venue for the true tourist patriot.[47]

Cosseted though they were, tourists were an important constituency in challenging received wisdom about specific colonies. The popular representation of Indochina as morally degenerative and physically unhealthy tells us much about the construction of the federation in the French official mind. Exotic, even glamorous, it may have been, but *l'Indochine française* was also inherently threatening. The climate, the impenetrable jungles, the Asiatic culture, even the people were potentially corruptive influences best kept at arm's length by those designated to run the territory. By the 1920s the stereotypical image of the colonial *fonctionnaire* in Indochina was of a restless individual, a misfit served by his concubine or *con gaï*. As his years of colonial service rolled by, the ravages of a decadent lifestyle and an unhealthy climate exacted a heavy toll. In 1907 the Hanoi government banned opium smoking by government personnel. In later years it cracked down on mixed-race relationships with local women. Both were facets of *indigénisation*, or 'going native', a transgression of the normative boundaries between rulers and ruled.[48]

If tourism offered fresher perspectives, it also promised thrills. Hunting was a favoured niche recreation for the rich tourist pioneer. By the early 1930s trophy hunters had decimated much of the big game of Equatorial Africa. Such was the scale of the slaughter that in February 1934 the AEF authorities set up country parks in each of the Equatorial African states. Gabon was the sole exception, deemed too inhospitable and malaria-ridden for any sportsman. Elsewhere, the Brazzaville government's hunting inspectorate drew up the park boundaries with an eye to a sustainable big game market. Shooting permits for the most prized species, first codified in 1929, were increased in price to deter the casual amateur. African villagers living inside the new parks were forcibly relocated, officially to safeguard their crops from wildlife destruction, actually to curb traditional hunting, thereby reserving choice animals for the remunerative safari market.[49]

At a more mundane level, day-to-day contacts between France and colonies also increased over time. Those for whom overseas vacations remained an unaffordable luxury could sample imperial adventure, if only vicariously, by purchasing a cinema ticket. In the 1920s French documentary makers still drew inspiration from the colonies, the first ethnographic films of colonial life having been made as far back as 1897.[50] But cinemagoers favoured escapism. Such was the French film industry's production of empire-related films that they became an identifiable genre: *cinéma colonial*.[51] Exotic settings, plotlines of doomed interracial love and romantic heroes devoted to imperial self-sacrifice also figured large in popular fiction. Even Marcel Pagnol, best remembered for his affectionate evocations of Provençale life, introduced colonial aspects to his work. In his screenplays for the films *Marius* (1931) and *Manon des sources* (1953) it emerges that the eponymous Marius is drawn to a more exciting lifestyle in the African empire, and that Manon's mother had sung in Dakar and Saigon.[52] Empire, it seemed, intruded everywhere. Visitors flocked to the three major colonial exhibitions of the inter-war period: the Marseilles colonial exhibition of 1922, the 1930 celebrations of the centenary of French rule in Algeria, and the massive 1931 colonial exhibition in the Vincennes parkland on the eastern fringes of Paris.

Reminders of empire abounded in French popular culture. Why then is the idea of popular imperialism in inter-war France so elusive? The difficulty here is the chasm between received imagery and lived experience, between the empire of the popular imagination and the reality of colonialism. The French public readily embraced the former, but only a small minority ever confronted the latter. It is doubtful, for example, that the reading public in France were as affected by the opposing literary styles of Algerianist and Ecole d'Alger writers described more fully in chapter four as by the escapism of Pierre Loti's best known pulp novels, *Le Mariage de Loti* (1880) and *Le Roman d'un spahi* (1881). In 1930, seven years after his death, the standard catalogue guide to French books in print devoted twenty-seven pages to Loti's work. A prolific author, Loti's colonial fiction fitted the mould of classic orientalist exoticism: as untaxing on the reader as it was crudely racist.[53] Metropolitan consumerism was equally dominated by idealised visions of empire – whether as an exotic utopia, a land of illicit pleasures, a bottomless pit of economic resource or a reservoir of military strength. These clichés bore little resemblance to the daily realities of colonial rule. Understandably, the French public preferred a simplified and romanticised view of empire that provided fresh sources of diversion and comfort during long years of economic crisis and worsening international threats.

The superficiality characteristic of popular perceptions of colonised peoples was also apparent in the *négrophile* literature of the period. The novelists Paul Morand and Céline (Louis-Ferdinand Destouches), later to emerge as prominent Vichyites, wrote fiction featuring stereotypical colonial characters, African-Americans, and other 'primitives'. Bardamu, hero of Céline's first novel, *Voyage au bout de la nuit* (*Journey to the End of the Night*, published in 1932), ventures through colonial Africa and, subsequently, the heart of industrial America. The dehumanising effects of colonial oppression and Fordist industrial practices reinforce Céline's faith in the superiority of French culture.[54] More overtly racist, Paul Morand's writing etches a thin line separating black peoples from savagery. His 1928 collection of short stories *Magie noire* (*Black Magic*) includes African and African-American characters typecast as racially inferior, barbaric and predatory. Their underlying primitivism endures beneath the trappings of Western codes of behaviour.[55]

Popular literature increased the public's appetite for colonial escapism, but did not stimulate national debate about the costs and benefits of empire. This remained the preserve of the colonial lobbyists. The loudest cries of ardent imperialism in inter-war France emanated from the corridors of 8 rue de la Boëtie in Paris, home of the French Maritime and Colonial League (Ligue maritime et coloniale française), inter-war successor of the Parti colonial. It claimed 600,000 supporters at its peak in 1925, and insisted that membership rolls would eventually top a million. The figures were a gross exaggeration: the League had only 20,145 paid-up individual members in 1927–28.[56] It did, however, secure official endorsement. Backed by the prestigious Académie française, the League took shape in June 1920 with the merger of two imperialist pressure groups, the Ligue maritime française and the Ligue coloniale française. The new organisation set three objectives: increased colonial trade and development; sponsorship of advanced study of colonial societies; and promotion of empire interests. The League's bulletin, media articles, books, documentaries and a cycle of academic conferences stressed the empire's centrality to French prosperity and power. The League also funded academic prizes in *lycées* and *grandes écoles*, encouraging promising students to join the colonial service. Much like its Parti colonial forebear, the League was both an agglomeration of pressure groups and a quasi-official mouthpiece of government. Its executive committee included former ministers and governors, many of them founders of the French Africa committee, the French Asia committee and the French Oceania committee.[57]

The membership of these committees was a roll call of leading lights in parliamentary politics, academia and the business world. In January 1930 the French Asia committee included President of the Republic Paul Doumer, president of the Senate and Republican Federation leader Louis Marin, current premier André Tardieu, former premier Raymond Poincaré, Quai d'Orsay secretary-general Philip Berthelot, Naval Minister Georges Leygues, Professor Louis Massignon of the Collège de France and the armaments magnate Eugène Schneider.[58] Most were enthusiastic backers of the French Maritime and Colonial League, ensuring that from 1921 it received generous funding paid directly by colonial governments in annual subventions.[59] In 1927 the League director Rondet-Saint persuaded the Poincaré government to institute an annual 'Empire Week'. Free cinema screenings of colonial documentaries, radio talks, pamphlet distributions and local conferences took place throughout France each year until 1939.[60] Organisers were disheartened by the results. Even the 1931 Vincennes colonial exhibition was more colonial 'theme park' than empire education forum. The exhibition's board of management admitted as much: 'What the colonies suffer from most are the indifference and ignorance of [French] public opinion . . . Overall, there still exists a "metropolitan" mentality in which the "colony" remains a remote image, an exotic curiosity, an object of luxury'.[61]

The colonies exhibited

Staging colonial exhibitions in inter-war France combined big business, government propaganda, popular racism and high farce. In February 1922 the Dakar political affairs directorate requested West African governors to nominate chiefs and Muslim notables to attend the colonial exhibition scheduled to open in April in Marseilles. Similar instructions went out to other colonies. Blaise Diagne, Senegal's first black deputy to the National Assembly, fired off a string of angry letters to Albert Sarraut at the rue Oudinot, indignant that no elected colonial representatives received invitations. African politicians that voted AOF's 1922 budget were now systematically excluded from an event supposed to illustrate the federation's economic potential. Visitors to Marseilles were sold a version of empire in which Frenchmen alone controlled the colonies' economic destiny.[62] The 1922 exhibition was primarily designed to impress French industrialists, traders and the wider public with the empire's untapped potential. It served the same purpose for trusted colonial intermediaries. The organising committee saw no place for Western-dressed colonial politicians with ideas of their own. The more compliant chiefs and tribal elders selected spent four weeks at the Marseilles exhibition. On their return home they were then expected to advise clients and dependants of French imperial might.[63]

The elite colonial visitors to the Marseilles exhibition and its successor, the far larger Vincennes colonial exhibition of 1931, were also objectified as tourist attractions. Closely monitored during their time in France, colonial dignitaries were required to 'play the part' of the colonised: exotic, colourful and deferential.[64] In full royal garb the Vietnamese puppet king Khai Dinh drew most interest among the visiting public, and most adverse comment among Vietnam's intelligentsia.[65]

Objectification of colonial populations was also apparent in the centennial celebration of the French conquest of Algeria. During the spring and summer of 1930 official ceremonies, museum exhibitions, military processions, sporting events, firework displays, banquets and public speeches honoured French achievements in Algeria.[66] The French press agency, Agence Havas, distributed 532 articles on the subject. The Algiers government produced over 14,000 press releases and printed 1.2 million brochures – *Cahiers du centenaire* – for libraries and schools. Some 6.6 per cent of Algeria's 1930 budget went to centennial propaganda. Some 80,000 French visitors descended on the colony during the year. These figures included a remarkable 306 members of the National Assembly, most of them formally received by Algiers mayor Brunel. Algeria's governor, Pierre Bordes, proved less indefatigable. Nervous exhaustion forced him to retire from public life before the year was out.[67]

The unifying theme of these commemorations was clearly expressed by two monuments unveiled in a welter of publicity in 1930. The more imposing was at Boufarik, 35 km south of Algiers. It was a huge white sculpted mural, 15 m high and 40 m wide. Bearing the inscription 'To the glory of French colonisation', the entire edifice celebrated settlers' pioneer spirit in a series of bas-reliefs. The *colons*' conquest of adversity also signified their triumph over the indigenous population. An editorial in *La Revue Indigène* conceded this, but hoped that Muslim Algerians would participate in the celebrations none the less because subordination to France conferred tangible economic benefits and an interdenominational electoral system. The other major Algerian centennial monument was erected at Sidi Ferruch, site of the original French landings west of Algiers in June 1830. Here, the conquest itself was celebrated in a frieze commemorating the military achievements of the Armée d'Afrique. French leadership harnessed Maghrebi soldiers' martial prowess to a greater imperial purpose.[68]

As if these monumental messages were not plain enough, the submission of Algeria's Muslim population was symbolically re-enacted at the Caroubier hippodrome in Algiers. French President Gaston Doumergue was presented with an Arab stallion, 'symbol of submission and obedience'.[69] The centennial organising committee led by the CSC member Ernest Mercier had other, more permanent testaments to the conquest of Algeria in mind. Mercier's committee spent most of its 82 million franc budget on three new museums in Constantine, Oran and the magnificent setting of the Algiers Villa du Bardo. Each was to house a combination of European paintings and sculpture, 'the best artistic work' from Algeria, specimens of Islamic art and a collection of Roman artefacts intended to illustrate the 'true lineage' of French Algeria. In addition, municipal authorities and *maisons d'agriculture* received subventions to finance exhibits representing the achievements of 'ordinary' settler farmers.[70] This was museum staging as pure imperialist propaganda.

As celebrations of colonial rule, it was sadly inevitable that the centennial ceremonies contrasted French order with the preceding anarchy of Ottoman North Africa. On 10 May 1930 Doumergue addressed a banquet of dignitaries in Algiers. He evoked the beauty of the port, a city framed by the sea from which 'misery, fear and violence' had been eradicated by French governance.[71] Government posters depicted France variously personified as Marianne, a redoubtable *petit colon* or a pragmatic, shirt-sleeved official, surrounded by the fruits of a century of altruistic enterprise: tilled fields, abundant produce, healthy children, a gleaming modern city in the distance.[72] The French Communist Party and various anti-colonial groups pilloried the hypocrisy of the centennial, subverting the official representation of Franco-Muslim partnership. Far from sharing the spoils of colonial modernisation, ordinary Algerians were impoverished by it.

The Communists produced the more striking imagery, but they could never match the profusion of state propaganda. The raft of official celebrations confirmed the resurgence of a more self-confident republican imperialism. France had much to be proud of in Algeria. Its ports were expanding fast, its economy was closely tied to France, its population proved their loyalty in the trenches. Over a 100 year period the army, settlers and bureaucrats had constructed a uniquely Gallic society in the Maghreb. The official line was entirely predictable, and certainly not new. More note-worthy was that few beyond the extreme left in France questioned such a trite characterisation of Algerian society. The centenary fabricated a con-venient historical reality that absolved France of difficult choices. The depression notwithstanding, Algeria was doing just fine. And the 1930 celebrations were merely a prelude.

The 1931 colonial exhibition

A lot has been written about the Vincennes colonial exhibition of 1931. Historians have used it to reconstruct imperialist perceptions of what the empire could and should be. Others have analysed the exhibition from the perspective of relations between colonisers and colonised, and through the medium of postmodernism to deconstruct the cultural meaning behind the colonies exhibited. The exhibition's enormous commercial success revealed not only how little the French public really understood what went on in 'their' empire, but also how little they wanted to know. As Prime Minister André Tardieu conceded in a famous article in L'Illustration, 'the concept of empire has yet to be created'.[73]

The essential paradox of any 'celebration' of colonial domination was manifest in the colonial pavilions laid out in the Vincennes parkland. Each was designed to legitimise the imperialist vision of the exhibition or-ganisers, and transmit that vision to the French public at large. Originally scheduled for 1929, the exhibition finally opened on 6 May 1931. Some 33.5 million tickets were sold over its five-month duration.[74] President Doumergue, fresh from his extensive tour of Algeria the previous year, led the opening ceremony at Vincennes. Marshal Lyautey, the exhibition patron, joined him on the podium, as did Albert Sarraut, the exhibition's chief advocate in the National Assembly. Paul Reynaud, then Minister of Colonies in Pierre Laval's first government, also took part. Bao Daï, the young Emperor of Annam, added a dash of colonial colour. His presence as newly restored head of state served as a reminder of France's recent sup-pression of the 1930 Nghê-Tinh rebellion in colonial Vietnam.

Four years in the making, the Vincennes exhibition was far larger than originally planned. Its displays provided paying customers with sanitised points of contact with idealised colonial societies. Pavilion imagery appealed to French stereotypes of primitivism, exotic fantasy and subject populations brought from savagery to civilisation by altruistic colonial intervention. Exhibition symbolism was rarely subtle. Visitors struggling to get their bearings could home in on the exhibition's central fountain: a statue of Marianne, the embodiment of the republic, apron in hand, gathering a tribute of gold coins from four colonial subjects.[75] From here, visitors toured pavilions representing each of France's overseas territories. These pavilions were arranged around the exhibition centrepiece, a massive reconstruction of the Khmer temple of Angkor Wat. Collectively, the exhibits suggested a clear racial hierarchy, from the advanced cultures of South East Asia rediscovered by French exploration after centuries of neglect, through the Islamic traditionalism of the Maghreb conserved by judicious French urban planning and sensitivity to Muslim culture, to the tribalism of black African peoples respected by associationist colonial policy. The positive forces of economic modernisation, *francophonie* and social enlightenment unified these very different cultures. Significantly, Algeria, the colony forged in France's image, was not dignified with an architectural monument of uniquely Algerian origin.[76]

As Elizabeth Ezra reminds us, the Vincennes exhibition promoted 'cultural contact in order, paradoxically, to reinforce the divisions among groups'.[77] Small troupes acting out 'typical' scenes of indigenous life represented subject populations in the individual colonial pavilions. These performers became objects of tourist consumption, mimicking the imagined lifestyle of the tribal festival, the artisan workshop and the generic 'African village'.[78] Their choreographed performances underscored France's cultural sophistication, and whetted visitors' appetites for colonial produce without need for explanation of how goods and services were actually obtained. The cumulative experience of an exhibition visit simulated an imperial grand tour without the discomfort of real travel or physical contact with different races.[79] Although impossible to verify, it seems that repeat visitors eager to view more of the pavilions accounted for the 10,032,630 entrance fees paid at the gate, most first-time visitors having bought their tickets in advance. Each colonial government, as well as the protectorate and mandate administrations of North Africa and the Levant, helped fund the construction of their respective pavilion displays. Chambers of commerce with regional colonial interests chipped in. The Lyons silk industry provided over half a million francs; the city's chamber of commerce helped fund the Catholic missionary pavilion and installed its own information bureau near by.[80] The total cost of these installations eventually rose to 44 million francs, the largest single item in the overall exhibition budget of 220.5 million. The Hanoi government made by far the largest single colonial contribution of 29 million francs, needed to fund the replica of Angkor Wat.[81]

The Vincennes exhibition was a mass of contradictions. Between the vigorous promotion of French global power and the reality of a fragmented, bit-part empire. Between the organisers' lofty ambitions to depict France's imperial achievements and their willingness to titillate visitors with gaudy shows of the exotic.[82] Nicola Cooper captures this disjuncture with reference to the Vietnamese and Cambodian exhibits:

Indochina figured in the exhibition as a site of ambivalence. Lauded as an advanced society and a worthy recipient of French colonial action, the goal of continued French rule was only possible if this image was tempered with a simultaneous view of Indochina as chaotic and weak, a needy inferior clamouring for French intervention and aid.[83]

The displays sought to prove that in science, culture, government, education and medicine French colonialism represented the best of modernity rather than the worst of capitalist exploitation. In this the exhibit failed. Visitors retained memories of dancing girls, unfamiliar food and ludicrous shows of tribal primitivism rather than a deeper appreciation of the *mission civilisatrice*. Plans for a permanent colonial institute, funded by exhibition receipts, to commemorate colonial endeavour and sustain public interest in the empire atrophied in the depression years.[84] A lesser cousin, the Paris colonial museum on avenue Daumesnil, designed between 1931 and 1933 by architect Albert Laprade to house exhibition materials, became more widely renowned for its Art Deco styling and intricate ironwork than for its exhibits.[85]

Almost unnoticed in 1931, Vietnamese and African students studying in Paris joined forces with the Comintern-funded Anti-imperialist League and leading lights of the Paris surrealist movement in staging a counter-exhibition of their own. Their 'anti-exhibition' highlighted colonial oppression, and was assembled on a shoestring budget. It was small-scale, amateurish and seen by only a handful of Parisians.[86] Yet its theme was the more prophetic. France would encounter violent opposition to the imperial mission laid out in Vincennes. Over the summer of 1931 the PCF colonial section reiterated this message in *L'Humanité* reports on colonial living conditions.[87]

The indulgent portrayal of traditional colonial societies at Vincennes could be compared with the regionalist themes of the French entries in the two World Fairs staged in Paris during the inter-war period. At the Arts décoratifs exhibition in 1925 and the International Exhibition of 1937 numerous pavilions depicted local customs, folklore and village life.[88] These displays of French culture evoked rural communities free of the decadence of modern industrial society. This fitted a longer-term pattern, the popularisation of ethnography in late nineteenth-century France having reflected widespread interest in local folklore as regional dialects and traditions receded in the face of economic modernisation. The parallel between this glorification of regionalism and the focus on colonial traditionalism seems clear. In French national and municipal museums the ethnographic representation of non-European cultures and the folklorists' celebration of rural tradition cast peasant society, village hierarchy and strict gender roles as pillars of social order.[89] There was no place for colonial nationalism in colonial exhibition pavilions, and no place for class warfare in the peasant idyll of French regionalism portrayed at the World Fairs. The fact that a leftist Popular Front administration endorsed the celebration of regionalism in 1937 suggests that nostalgia for the comforting certainties of peasant life spanned the political spectrum in the post-depression years.[90] As international tensions mounted, faith in France's redoubtable peasant stock was matched by a rediscovery of the solid virtues of loyal colonial populations soon to be called upon to defend French soil.

Cinéma colonial

Carrie Tarr has noted the reluctance of French cinema to address its colonial heritage. She takes her criticism a step further: 'As a medium for constructing subjectivities and identities, Western cinema normally works to (re-)produce ethnic hierarchies founded on the assumed supremacy of white metropolitan culture and identity, largely through the absence or marginalizing of the voices and perspectives of the troubling ethnic Others'.[91] Framed in the context of postcolonial French culture, her comments resonate with the inter-war period. Colonial censors, usually attached to the local *sûreté*, were intolerant of cinematic images that questioned French institutions or the supremacy of the French race. In 1934, for instance, the Beirut *sûreté* censorship bureau viewed a total of 433 films for distribution in Syria and Lebanon. Sixteen were cut and eleven were banned outright.[92] Three of the banned films stood out. *Le Juif errant* (*The Wandering Jew*), an English-language film, was disbarred for presenting Jews 'in a grotesque light' liable to incite racial hatred. Conversely, two French films, *Mam'zelle Spahi* and *Les gaietés d'escadron* (*The Delights of the Platoon*) were proscribed for unflattering depictions of the army inimical to imperial prestige.[93]

There was no comparable censorship in French cinemas to prevent racist typecasting of colonial subjects. During the 1920s and 1930s films with strong colonial themes enjoyed enormous popularity. Jacques Feyder's *L'Atlantide* (1921) set the trend for *cinéma colonial*, and remained the highest-grossing French film of the decade. A big-budget film, shot on location in North Africa, *L'Atlantide* tells the story of a French officer ravaged by drugs, the hardships of desert life among the Tuareg and a mysterious temptress, who eventually murders his superior officer.[94] In their taste for depictions of imperial adventure, military conquests and eastern exoticism French cinemagoers resembled their British counterparts.[95]

L'Atlantide reveals a good deal about popular imperialism immediately after the First World War. Originally released as silent films, several of the early colonial cinema productions including *L'Atlantide* and its lurid cousin, *L'Esclave blanche* (1927), enjoyed renewed commercial success when remade in the 1930s as 'talkies'.[96] The spread of soundtrack technology in the 1930s reinvigorated the public appetite for colonial escapism. Tales of martial valour, forlorn love and epic tragedy, films such as *L'Occident* (1928), *Le Grand Jeu* (1934) and *La Bandera* (1935) were among the blockbusters of their day.[97] Their dramatic content and box office success were remarkably similar to the patriotic fare of the Korda brothers at London Films, including *Sanders of the River* (1935), *The Drum* (1938) and *The Four Feathers* (1939).[98] Lovers of *cinéma colonial* were rewarded with a spate of films set in Morocco. In 1934 directors Jean Benoît-Levy and Marie Epstein produced *Itto*. The film was a remarkably sensitive treatment of Berber resistance to Lyautey's consolidation of the protectorate. The plot explored divisions in a leading Berber clan, whose family members were played by local actors. *Itto* was unusual. Colonial cinema typically dealt in racial stereotypes. In the most popular genre of its type – the Foreign Legion movie – the action in films such as Jacques Sévérac's *Les Réprouvés* (*The Outcasts*) culminated in an outnumbered garrison repulsing undifferentiated Arab hordes.[99] In David Slavin's words, *cinéma colonial* 'came to inhabit the settler's moral universe' of white supremacy and xenophobic nationalism.[100]

The artistic and Bacchanalian communities in Jazz Age Paris were also never far from empire associations, whether in the popularity of African-influenced music and fashion, the proliferation of ethnic restaurants catering for colonial immigrants or the *risqué* world of mixed-race jazz dance clubs. The most famous of these, the Bal colonial on rue Blomet in the fifteenth *arrondissement*, originated in 1924 as a dance club for the 10,000-strong Antillais community in Paris. By 1928 it drew a more diverse crowd, including Montparnasse artists and writers such as André Gide and Ernest Hemingway. But its main fee payers were bourgeois Parisians drawn to live Afro-Caribbean music and the normally taboo practice of erotic mixed-race dancing.[101]

The Parisian career of the African-American star Josephine Baker exemplified these cultural connections. A symbol of Jazz-Age Paris, where she starred in the Revue nègre, Baker was also a star of *cinéma colonial* and an omnipresent figure in consumer advertising. A truly iconic figure, she endorsed products with implicit colonial links such as bananas and skin-tanning cream. Elizabeth Ezra has shown how the transformations of Baker's media image from the bawdy star of the Folies Bergères in 1926–27 to the heroine in two films, *Zouzou* (1934) and *Princess Tam Tam* (1935), capitalised on her racial difference to entice French audiences toward an exoticised vision of the colonial world. Significantly, in each of her hit films Baker played a character compelled to assume a different identity but ultimately trapped by her racial origins. As a music hall artiste from Martinique in *Zouzou* and as a Tunisian shepherdess undergoing a Pygmalion-type transformation in *Princess Tam Tam*, Baker ultimately fails to integrate into modern French society. As *Princess Tam Tam* Baker's shepherdess character assumes an unsustainable position in Parisian high society that ultimately proves her undoing. Her original identity becomes corrupted. Her adoption of French ways seems at once hopeless and ridiculous. Baker's role as seductress in both films was typical of the colonial cinema genre in portraying colonial women as primitive *femmes fatales*. And the political allegory in *Princess Tam Tam* is stark: assimilationism is doomed to fail; the boundaries and hierarchies between races should not be breached.[102]

On the eve of war the vogue for colonial film was harnessed to the upsurge in public interest in empire as a vital source of national strength. Romance and exoticism gave way to equally stylised plotlines of army heroism and victory over adversity. Four film releases of 1938–39 typified this shift. Each set in the Saharan Maghreb, *SOS Sahara*, *La Piste du Sud*, *Légions d'honneur* and *Trois de Saint-Cyr* (another Jacques Feyder film) offered reassuring portrayals of indomitable French military spirit. Much as *L'Atlantide* had set the trend for cinematic representation of empire after the First World War, so *Trois de Saint-Cyr* touched a nerve with a nation girding for war. French troops drive off wave after wave of Arab attacks on a remote Saharan outpost. The relief column of cavalry eventually arrives to save the day, but not before the valiant outpost commander, shrouded in a tricolour, gasps his last breath. Government approval of the film's message of unity and sacrifice was underscored by Premier Daladier's presence at the Paris première in 1939.[103] Yet these films marked the end of a cinema era depicting empire as a source of national salvation. Two films produced in 1948 that evoked the imperial heroism of an earlier age, *Le Paradis des pilots perdus* and *L'Escadron blanc*, failed to grip the public imagination.[104]

Conclusion

The imperialist press, the more frequent allusions to empire in school curricula, the greater accessibility of the colonies as tourist destinations, the cycle of colonial exhibitions, and the changing physiognomy of *cinéma colonial*, were all facets of a new cultural imperialism after 1919. Yet their cumulative power to change public opinion in France proved limited. As war loomed, most colonial lobbyists conceded that they had not transformed France into an imperial nation. In March 1937 a contributor to the Ecole coloniale journal *Outre-Mer* captured the mood, ' "France, a nation of 104 million inhabitants"? That's a joke, because France has no imperial mentality.'[105] Much as in 1914–18, it took an external threat to the mainland to galvanise public interest in the colonies. The recrudescence of interest in colonial resources and manpower in 1938–39 was, however, superficial, born of a desperate search for comfort rather than any more lasting access of imperial pride. The problems of empire were not, then, a regular feature of political life, cultural intercourse or national debate in inter-war France. It is worth bearing this in mind as we now turn to the rebellions that convulsed the French empire between the wars.

Notes

1 Chafer and Sackur, *Promoting the Colonial Idea*, challenge this viewpoint.
2 See, for instance, Paul S. Landau and Deborah D. Kaspin (eds), *Images and Empires. Visuality in Colonial and Postcolonial Africa* (Berkeley CA: University of California Press, 2002).
3 These issues are discussed in John M. MacKenzie, *Propaganda and Empire* (Manchester: Manchester University Press, 1984), and in his *Imperialism and Popular Culture* (Manchester: Manchester University Press, 1986), 1–14. For France, see Alain Ruscio, *Que le temps était belle au temps des colonies* (Paris: Larose, 2000).
4 Meynier, 'Volonté de propagande ou inconscient affiche?', 42; Thobie *et al.*, *Histoire de la France coloniale*, 134.
5 Ageron, 'Les colonies devant l'opinion publique', 47.
6 Stanford University's Hoover Institution collection of Parti colonial journals contains the inter-war runs of *L'Afrique Française*, *L'Asie Française* and *L'Océanie Française*. *L'Afrique Française* began publication in 1890, *L'Asie Française* in 1900 and *L'Océanie Française* in 1911.
7 See, for example, ADA, Sarraut papers, 12J172, *Le Paria Tribune des populations des colonies*, issue 4, 1 July 1922.
8 Ageron, *France coloniale ou Parti colonial*, 250–67 passim.
9 Cited in Jacques Marseille, 'Les images de l'Afrique en France (des années 1880 aux années 1930)', *Canadian Journal of African Studies*, 22:1 (1988), 121.
10 Biondi, *Les Anticolonialistes*, 16.
11 MacKenzie, *Propaganda and Empire*, 254.
12 Lebovics, *True France*, xii–xiv.
13 See, for example, Norindr, *Phantasmagoric Indochina*; Ezra, *The Colonial Unconscious*.
14 Thomas F. Power, *Jules Ferry and the Renaissance of French Imperialism* (New York: Octagon Books, 1977). Regarding the South African War and British popular culture see Andrew Thompson, 'Publicity, philanthropy and commemoration. British society and the war', in David Omissi and Andrew Thompson (eds), *The Impact of the South African War* (London: Palgrave, 2002), 9–123. On the longer-term impact of the South African War see Donal Lowry, ' "The Boers were the beginning of the end"? The wider impact of the South African War', in Donal Lowry (ed.), *The South African War Reappraised* (Manchester: Manchester University Press, 2000), 203–46.
15 Aldrich, 'Putting the colonies on the map', 214–18. Robert Aldrich notes that from 1929 to 1936 – years bisected by the 1931 Colonial Exhibition – twenty-six Parisian streets acquired empire-related names.
16 Marseille, 'Les images de l'Afrique en France', 122.
17 Quinn, *The French Overseas Empire*, 201.
18 Rey-Goldzeiguer, 'Réflexions sur l'image et la perception du maghreb', 34.
19 Prochaska, 'Approaches to the economy of colonial Annaba', 515–18.
20 Jeffrey H. Jackson, 'Making jazz French. The reception of jazz music in Paris, 1927–1934', *French Historical Studies*, 25:1 (2002), 154–5; David Henry Slavin, *Colonial Cinema and Imperial France, 1919–1939. White Blind Spots, Male Fantasies, Settler Myths* (Baltimore MD: Johns Hopkins University Press, 2001). The huge popularity of African-American entertainer Josephine Baker, whose seasons at the Folies Bergères in the mid-1920s played on colonial exoticism, was among the most visible signs of the changing aesthetic mood, see Ezra, *The Colonial Unconscious*, 109–12.
21 Aldrich, *Colonialism and Homosexuality*, 338–9.
22 See Elizabeth Ezra's illuminating discussion of inter-war colonial culture in Paris in *The Colonial Unconscious*, 1–20.

23 CAOM, affpol/852, Conseil supérieur des colonies, session 1926–27.
24 Raymond Ronze, 'L'enseignement colonial dans les lycées et collèges français', *Outre-Mer* 3:3 (1931), 222–3.
25 Laffey, 'Municipal imperialism in decline', 340–1.
26 Augustin Bernard, 'L'enseignement colonial dans les facultés des lettres', *Outre-Mer* 3:3 (1931), 227; A. Girault, 'L'enseignement colonial dans les facultés de droit', *Outre-Mer* 3:3 (1931), 239.
27 Louis Tanon, 'L'Institut de médecine coloniale de Paris', *Outre-Mer* 3:3 (1931), 244; Florence Bretelle-Establet, 'Resistance and reciprocity. French colonial medicine in south-west China, 1898–1930', *Modern China*, 25:2 (1999), 171–203.
28 'Compte rendus du Congrès de l'enseignement colonial en France (28–29 septembre 1931)', *Outre-Mer* 3:3 (1931).
29 Charles Jacob, 'L'enseignement supérieur scientifique et les colonies françaises', *Outre-Mer* 3:3 (1931), 233–8; H. Bonnin, 'L'enseignement de la médicine coloniale', *Outre-Mer* 3:3 (1931), 258.
30 ADA, Sarraut papers, 12J172, Anatole de Monzie to administrateur délegué, 'Le Monde Colonial illustré', 30 April 1933.
31 Thobie *et al.*, *Histoire de la France coloniale*, 135; Marseille, 'Les images de l'Afrique en France', 122.
32 Anne Donadey, ' "Y'a bon Banania". Ethics and cultural criticism in the colonial context', *French Cultural Studies*, 11:1 (2000), 11–14. Anne McClintock coined the idea of 'commodity racism' regarding British imperial advertising: *Imperial Leather. Race, Gender, and Sexuality in a Colonial Context* (London: Routledge, 1995), chapter 5.
33 Melzer, 'Spectacles and sexualities', 216–23; Dana S. Hale, 'French images of race on product trade marks during the Third Republic', in Peabody and Stovall, *The Color of Liberty*, 131–46.
34 Report on tourism survey in *L'Océanie Française*, 10:31 (January 1914), 17.
35 G.H., 'Le tourisme en Océanie', *L'Océanie Française*, 17:55 (January–February 1921), 12–13.
36 The sixth North African governors' conference in July 1930 urged Air Minister André Laurent-Eynac to subsidise the introduction of multi-engine aircraft on the commercial air routes to the Maghreb, see SHA, 2N65/D3, CSDN, VI conférence nord-africaine, deuxième séance, 3 July 1930.
37 CAOM, Moutet papers, PA28/4/Dossier Varenne, sous-dossier 59, 'Aperçu de l'oeuvre accompli en Indochine par Alexandre Varenne'.
38 CAOM, affpol/852, Conseil supérieur des colonies, Section du tourism, session 1926–27, 'Questions examinées par le conseil économique pendant la session du conseil supérieur des colonies, 1927–1928'.
39 CAOM, GGAEF, 1D8, no. 1323, Alfassa to Minister of Colonies, 10 December 1933.
40 Julian Jackson, *The Popular Front in France. Defending Democracy, 1934–1938* (Cambridge: Cambridge University Press, 1988), 131–6.
41 Dunwoodie, *Writing French Algeria*, 29, 149.
42 ADA, Sarraut papers, 12J118, *Corréspondance d'Orient*, no. 479, November 1937 issue. The review began publication in 1887.
43 Both products were advertised in the Parti colonial press as the best treatments against malaria, see, for example, *L'Asie Française*, 38:357 (February 1938).
44 Ellen Furlough, '*Une leçon des choses*. Tourism, empire, and the nation in interwar France', *French Historical Studies*, 25:3 (2002), 449–52, 457–8.
45 Stephen L. Harp, *Marketing Michelin. Advertising and Cultural Identity in Twentieth Century France* (Baltimore MD: Johns Hopkins University Press, 2001), 252.
46 'Au group colonial du Touring-Club de France, Le tourisme en Indochine', *Le Monde Colonial illustré*, 182 (August 1938), 150–1.
47 Touring-Club de France, 'L'heure de l'Afrique', *Le Monde Colonial illustré*, 193 (July 1939), 163.
48 Cooper, *France in Indochina*, 154–63.
49 CAOM, GGAEF, 1D9, nos. 284 and 291, Antonetti to Ministry of Colonies, Direction des affaires économiques, 28 February and 3 March 1934.

50 Alison Murray, 'Teaching colonial history through film', *French Historical Studies*, 25:1 (2002), 42–3; Slavin, *Colonial Cinema*, 59–62.
51 Slavin, *Colonial Cinema*.
52 Lynn A. Higgins, 'Pagnol and the paradoxes of Frenchness', in Ungar and Conley, *Identity Papers*, 91, 107.
53 Sharif Gemie, 'Loti, orientalism and the French colonial experience', *Journal of European Area Studies*, 8:2 (2000), 149–65. 'Pierre Loti' was the pseudonym for Louis-Marie-Julien Viaud.
54 Jackson, *France. The Dark Years*, 39–42.
55 Ezra, *The Colonial Unconscious*, 129–44 *passim*.
56 Ageron, *France coloniale ou Parti colonial*; also cited in Thobie *et al.*, *Histoire de la France coloniale*, 135–6.
57 CAOM, affpol/21, Dossier: 'Ligue Maritime et Coloniale Française', no. 390, Touzet circular to colonial governors, 1 June 1921.
58 *L'Asie Française. Bulletin mensuel du comité de l'Asie française:* committee membership details, vol. 30 (1930).
59 CAOM, affpol/21, Dossier: 'Ligue Maritime et Coloniale Française', no. 390, André Touzet, circular to colonial governors, 1 June 1921.
60 Ageron, 'Les colonies devant l'opinion publique', 46.
61 ADA, Albert Sarraut papers, 12J172, 'Quelques aspects de la propagande réalisée par "Le Monde Colonial illustré" ', 15 April 1933.
62 See, for example, CAOM, affpol/542, Dossier 8, Blaise Diagne letters to Albert Sarraut, 9 June and 8 July 1922.
63 CAOM, AOF Fonds moderne, 17G41, Direction des affaires politiques (Dakar), circular to AOF lieutenant-governors, 9 February 1922.
64 Pham Quynh, a Vietnamese journalist invited to attend the Vincennes Exposition, complained that colonial delegates were assigned a 'walk-on part' in the staging of the exhibition. See Furlough, '*Une leçon des choses*', 449.
65 Marr, *Vietnamese Tradition*, 6 n. 2.
66 Rey-Goldzeiguer, 'Réflexions sur l'image et la perception du maghreb', 37. Eighteen separate exhibitions and fifty-nine conferences celebrated the centenary.
67 Peyrouton, *Du service public*, 37, 39.
68 *La Revue Indigène*, 25: 258–9 (1930): special issue: 'Le centenaire de l'Algérie', 124.
69 Kaddache, *Histoire du nationalisme algérien* I, 237–40, quote at 238.
70 ADA, Sarraut papers, 12J259, Commissariat général du centenaire de l'Algérie, 'L'oeuvre du centenaire de l'Algérie', n.d. 1930.
71 Verdès-Leroux, *Les Français d'Algérie*, 177–85, Doumergue quote at 179.
72 Rey-Goldzeiguer, 'Réflexions sur l'image et la perception du maghreb', 34–5.
73 Ageron, *France coloniale ou Parti colonial*, 254.
74 Bouche, *Histoire de la colonisation française*, 304–5. The figure of 33.5 million exhibition visitors compares with 27.1 million for the British Empire Exhibition held at Wembley over a longer period in 1924–25, see John MacKenzie, 'The popular culture of empire in Britain', in Brown and Louis, *The Oxford History of the British Empire. The Twentieth Century*, 214.
75 Sowerine, *France since 1870*, 255.
76 Lebovics, *True France*, chapter 2.
77 Ezra, *The Colonial Unconscious*, 47.
78 Furlough, '*Une leçon des choses*', 442–6, quote at 442. West African and Chinese representatives were used in a similar fashion at Britain's Wembley Empire Exhibition in 1924–25, see MacKenzie, *Propaganda and Empire*, 108–9.
79 Pavilions representing life, art and European material improvement in individual colonies were familiar, having been adopted at the 1922 Marseilles Colonial Exhibition and the Wembley Empire Exhibition in 1924. See Yaël Simpson Fletcher, ' "Capital of the colonies". Real and imagined boundaries between metropole and empire in 1920s Marseilles', in Felix Driver and David Gilbert (eds), *Imperial Cities. Landscape, Display and Identity* (Manchester: Manchester University Press, 1999), 136–54; MacKenzie, *Propaganda and Empire*, 107–11.

80 Laffey, 'Municipal imperialism in decline', 338.
81 CAOM, affpol/21, Léon Perrier, Sénat commission des finances: 1932 colonial budget report.
82 The style of the exhibition and the popular response to it recall Jules Ferry's exasperation with the crowds at the 1889 Paris exhibition: 'All that interests the French public about the Empire is the belly dance'. Quoted in Andrew and Kanya-Forstner, *France Overseas*, 17.
83 Cooper, *France in Indochina*, 86.
84 CAOM, affpol/21, Léon Perrier, Senate commission des finances, 1932 colonial budget report.
85 Marie-France Boyer, *Trading Spaces* (London, 2002).
86 Lebovics, *True France*, 56, 105–10.
87 AN, F⁷13412/D4, CGSPA, 'L'action révolutionnaire aux colonies', 4 June 1931.
88 See Shanny Peer, *France on Display. Peasants, Provincials and Folklore in the 1937 Paris World's Fair* (Albany NY: State University of New York Press, 1998); also cited in Julian Jackson, *France. The Dark Years* (Oxford: Oxford University Press, 2001), 30.
89 Martine Segalen, 'Here but invisible. The presentation of women in French ethnography museums', *Gender and History*, 6:3 (1994), 335–8; Daniel J. Sherman, ' "People's Ethnographic": Objects, Museums, and the Colonial Inheritance of French Ethnography,' *French Historical Studies*, 27:3 (2004), 674–86.
90 Shanny Peer, 'Peasants in Paris. Representations of rural France in the 1937 International Exposition', in Ungar and Conley, *Identity Papers*, 21–3.
91 Carrie Tarr, 'French cinema and post-colonial minorities', in Hargreaves and McKinney, *Post-colonial Cultures*, 59.
92 CADN, Fonds Beyrouth, vol. 843/D2, no. 1894/SG, 'Rapport annuel de la sûreté générale, 1934', 7 March 1935. British colonial officials were also animated by the tension between the corruptive potential and educational impact of film, see Rosaleen Smyth, 'The development of British colonial film policy, 1927–1939, with special reference to East and Central Africa', *Journal of African History*, 20:3 (1979), 437–50.
93 CADN, Fonds Beyrouth, vol. 843/D1, no. 551/CP, High Commissioner de Martel to Foreign Ministry, 3 August 1934.
94 Slavin, *Colonial Cinema*, 33–4; Ezra, *The Colonial Unconscious*, 3.
95 MacKenzie, *Propaganda and Empire*, 81–4.
96 David H. Slavin, 'Heart of darkness, heart of light. The civilizing mission in *L'Atlantide*', in Ungar and Conley, *Identity Papers*, 113–35; see also Slavin, *Colonial Cinema*, 35–57.
97 Pierre Sorlin, 'The fanciful empire. French feature films and the colonies in the 1930s', *French Cultural Studies*, 2 (1991), 135–51.
98 For a succinct treatment of pre-war British colonial cinema see Jeffrey Richards, 'Boy's Own Empire. Feature films and imperialism in the 1930s', in MacKenzie, *Imperialism and Popular Culture*, 140–64, quote at 162.
99 David H. Slavin, 'French colonial cinema before and after *Itto*. From Berber myth to race war', *French Historical Studies*, 21:1 (1998), 132–3, 154–5; and *Colonial Cinema*, 114–37.
100 Slavin, *Colonial Cinema*, 16.
101 Brett A. Berliner, 'Dancing dangerously. Colonizing the exotic at the Bal Nègre in the inter-war years', *French Cultural Studies*, 12:1 (2001), 59–75. The Bal colonial was held in a studio previously owned by the artists Joan Miró and André Masson. Brett Berliner suggests that its heyday lasted from 1928 to 1932.
102 Ezra, *The Colonial Unconscious*, 97–128 passim.
103 Jackson, *France. The Dark Years*, 101–2.
104 Rémy Pithon, 'Opinions publiques et représentations culturelles face aux problèmes de la puissance : le témoignage du cinema français (1938–1939)', *Relations Internationales*, 33 (1983), 91–102; Pascal Ory, 'Introduction to an Era of Doubt. Cultural reflections of 'French power' around the year 1948', in Josef Becker and Franz Knipping (eds), *Power in Europe? Great Britain, France, Italy and Germany in a Postwar World, 1945–1950* (Berlin: Walter de Gruyter, 1986), 398.
105 J. Fayet, 'Un programme de propagande impériale', *Outre-Mer*, 9:1 (1937), 21.

PART III

An empire in trouble: opposition, revolt and war

CHAPTER SEVEN

An empire in revolt? The Rif war, the Syrian rebellion, Yen Bay and the Kongo Wara

Four distinct rebellions shook the French empire between the wars. The Rif war in northern Morocco and the Syrian revolt originating in the autonomous state of the Jabal Druze were major uprisings that had some claim to be national rebellions. They were suppressed only by the deployment of overwhelming French military firepower. The Yen Bay mutiny in Indochina triggered wider unrest that convulsed northern Annam and four provinces of Tonkin during 1930–31. The Kongo Wara (literally, 'the war of the hoe handle') in the Haute Sangha region of AEF is the smallest and least well known of these inter-war anti-colonial revolts. Obscure in origin and remote from any urban centres, the Kongo Wara none the less took three years to eradicate. Few in France ever knew of the violence in the Haute Sangha, and the French political community was only dimly aware that socio-political disturbances lasted for years after order was supposedly restored in each of the affected territories described here.

These inter-war revolts will be related to wider imperial problems. Belief in French aptitude as a ruler of Muslim societies was a cornerstone of republican imperialism. Uprisings in Muslim territories exposed the bankruptcy of imperialist claims that France was Europe's one true 'Muslim power'. By contrast, the Yen Bay mutiny was widely regarded as a Communist-directed uprising, concentrated among the garrison forces of North Annam, Soviet-style factory committees and the emerging proletariat of Indochina's plantation economy. Whereas few politicians, media commentators or colonial officials remarked on the Kongo Wara rebellion, the Rif war, the Syrian revolt and the Yen Bay mutiny reverberated through French politics more than any other colonial issues during the inter-war period. Hence the discussion of these events also considers the impact of colonial rebellion on French party politics, the mobilisation of French Communist opposition to empire, and the development of strategies of colonial warfare and imperial policing.

The Rif war

In a book confined to the French empire it is doubly important to contextualise the French campaign against Mohammed Abd el-Krim el Khattabi's Rif republic in the highlands straddling the French and Spanish Moroccan protectorates as the by-product of a much longer struggle between Rif Berber tribes and the Spanish authorities.[1] The largest of these tribes, the Beni Uriaghel, dominated the eastern Rif and resisted the encroachment of Spanish colonialism after the establishment of the dual protectorate in Morocco in 1912.[2] French forces sustained heavy losses in their initial attempts to 'pacify' Berber regions in 1913–14. Under Lyautey's guiding hand, native affairs officers increasingly sought to conciliate tribal leaders, notably through a series of legislative decrees (*dahirs*) that privileged Berber customary law.[3] These measures drove a wedge between Berber areas and those regions of the Sultanate administered by Shari'a law as part of the *makhzen*. Once the First World War was over, Lyautey's government quickened the pace of pacification, focusing on the subjugation of *Le Maroc utile*, literally 'useful Morocco', where mineral, agricultural, demographic and water resources made economic development viable.[4]

This new phase of French pacification meshed with the continuing Spanish war against the Rif Berbers. On 22 July 1921 Rif guerrillas defeated the Spanish colonial army at the battle of Anual, a signal event that broadened the Rif coalition, produced a vicious transformation in Spanish strategy and set alarm bells ringing in French-controlled Morocco to the south. After further Spanish reverses in 1924, on 12 April 1925 the Rif army mounted an offensive into the French zone, seizing the opportunity to expel French forces before Lyautey's commanders could consolidate their defences.[5] The attack was devastating. Over forty border posts were overrun. French casualties exceeded 1,000 killed, 3,700 wounded and a further thousand missing – representing losses of over twenty per cent of the forces deployed in the Rif.[6] Severely overstretched, Lyautey's remaining garrison forces could not guarantee the security of the northern towns of Taza and Fez.[7] In May the French sought urgent conversations with Primo de Rivera's Spanish regime to plan joint operations against the expanding Rif republic. On 8 September Spanish amphibious assaults began at Al Hoceima (Alhucemas Bay) that opened a final decisive phase of the conflict. Rif forces were pushed inland, and by late October faced mounting Spanish and French pressure on all fronts. Winter weather stepped in to halt the carnage but Rif resistance was decisively crushed between February and May 1926.[8]

The colonial state eventually deployed the full military resources of a first-class European military power to crush tribal resistance. Lyautey's complex formulas for indirect control gave way to Marshal Pétain's ruthless prosecution of a general offensive backed by artillery and air power.[9] The origins of this change of strategy were as much political as military, and confirmed a breakdown in relations between the French government and the Rabat residency brought on by the stresses of the war. Lyautey was exasperated with Edouard Herriot's Cartel des gauches Cabinet formed on 31 May 1924. His requests for more troops went unheeded; his efforts to conciliate tribal leaders were unappreciated. Long-planned operations were scaled back.[10] On 23 July he confided to his old friend Wladimir d'Ormesson that he felt frozen out by the new government. Several ministers wanted him replaced; none was receptive to his argument that the protectorate faced imminent attack.[11] In consequence, Lyautey was denied essential resources made available to his successor three months later.[12]

Lyautey was further convinced that Primo de Rivera's Spanish regime planned to cut a deal with Abd el-Krim that would leave French Morocco alone to confront a consolidated Rif republic supported by Britain and Germany.[13] He was right about his declining standing in Paris, but wrong about Spanish intentions. It was difficult to interpret Primo de Rivera's strategy, which seems to have rested on a more stringent Rif blockade and a sustained campaign of aerial bombardment.[14] Lyautey, however, was not apprised of this. And in France his stock of political capital was almost exhausted. Herriot's coalition wanted him out. But it was Paul Painlevé's more conservative Cabinet formed on 17 April 1925 that finally pushed Lyautey from office.[15] The turning point came in early August following Pétain's tour of inspection along the French northern front in Morocco. Pétain submitted a decisive report to Painlevé's government that heralded a fundamental change in strategy, the deployment of overwhelming force and the end of Lyautey's career.[16] On 24 September the marshal submitted his resignation to Foreign Minister Aristide Briand. In October a more compliant civilian appointee took over as resident. Théodore Steeg, a bookish Radical Party stalwart from the Gironde, seemed a safe pair of hands. His past experience as Governor of Algeria stood him in good stead to conciliate Morocco's settlers, unnerved by Lyautey's failure to stem the Rif rebellion.

In early 1925 Lyautey had accurately predicted a Rif attack, citing intelligence gathered by native affairs officers along the northern frontier.[17] The same information helped convince him that the protectorate would eventually collapse, not simply as a result of operations in the Rif but because Berber and Arab Moroccans alike would ultimately reject French hegemony.[18] Part of Lyautey's genius lay in his capacity to anticipate the long-term consequences of France's colonial presence. By 1925 he was a profoundly pessimistic man. His reading of the Rif war antagonised his political superiors in Paris because he saw beyond the steps needed to achieve short-term victory. French ministers wanted quick fixes in 1924–25.

Consumed by a mounting financial crisis at home, the Herriot and Painlevé governments were ill at ease with colonial problems that threatened to split the Cartel coalition.[19] Lyautey told them an unpalatable truth. Behind the mountain skirmishes, garrison sieges and punitive aerial bombardments of tribal settlements that characterised the Rif war, the conflict was essentially a battle for hearts and minds that required massive long-term state investment. Much the same could be said of the Syrian revolt, then still in its early stages.[20] The more punitive the French operational strategy, the harder it would be to win the respect of tribal leaders and urban elites. Submission to French control could be achieved, but it was not a sound basis for Franco-Moroccan coexistence.[21]

By March 1925 Rif resistance was far more than tribal rebellion. The Rif administration governed a mini-state, with a functioning central bureaucracy, a complex Muslim legal code, a prison system and an international supply network. Abd el-Krim's nascent republic upheld Islamic observance and Shari'a principles of individual responsibility, but in other ways it was closer in spirit to Kemalist Turkey than a Muslim sultanate. The Rif leader was impatient with hierarchic tribal society, and customary laws that upheld order through collective oaths, compensation payments and inter-clan feuds.[22] Shifting tribal allegiances, the difficulties of governing an isolated state blockaded by powerful neighbours and the overriding need to consolidate Abd el-Krim's executive authority make it impossible to classify the Rif republic as either a new-style Islamic state or a nationalist republic-in-the-making. Nor is it wise to compartmentalise the Rif war as either a primary resistance movement or a nationalist revolt.[23] The Riffian state was a unique enterprise.

In 1927 a by then exiled Abd el-Krim gave an interview in an Egyptian journal indicating that his aim had been to create an Islamic state. This had aroused the suspicions of tribal sheikhs fearful of a loss of influence in a theocratic regime. But the composition of the Rif republic administration, which included sheikhs, Muslim *caïds* and *cadis*, suggests that the need to establish functioning bureaucratic and judicial structures determined the type of civil society created.[24] The rebellion, too, was less a holy war against Western encroachment than a reasoned attempt to limit the socio-economic impact of the protectorate system.[25] Conscription for men and women applied among the region's main Berber tribes, and military duties were demarcated between the sexes. Rif women conveyed munitions and supplies to front-line fighters, served as medical orderlies and worked as spies in Spanish and French-held territory.[26] Zemmour and Romara tribeswomen exacted high standards from their menfolk, failure to fight the French being considered legitimate grounds for divorce.[27] Abd el-Krim's forces were a genuine 'people's army' in terms of composition, if not ideology. They undertook complex manoeuvres across a broad front.

Their offensive capacity was enhanced by their mobility and the advantage of surprise. Rebel forces were equipped with repeat-firing rifles, principally Mausers captured from Spanish army units. Between 13 and 18 April 1925 several thousand Rif tribesmen organised into three *harkas* traversed the northern perimeter of the French protectorate, advancing towards Ouezzan and Amjot in the west and down the Ouergha river valley towards Taza in the east. By 26 April they had attained their immediate objective. The two main tribal federations in the region, the Beni Zeroual and Abd el-Krim's own Beni Uriaghel, joined the rebellion. By early May up to 20,000 additional tribesmen and women had joined the Rif cause. Many came armed with guns previously supplied by the French army in recognition of earlier submission to protectorate authority.[28]

In these first months, before the French deployed artillery and aircraft in any number, the conflict was of low intensity. Individual engagements were, however, bitterly contested. Casualties among Foreign Legion units ran into the hundreds, West African troops suffered appallingly from inadequate winter clothing, and Rif forces pounded isolated French positions with artillery captured in past encounters with Spanish units.[29] In a contest as much about prestige as about pitched battles the symbolic importance of seizures of territory and the rout of French garrisons should not be underestimated. Above all, the war along this northern front was a struggle for the allegiance of the indigenous Berber tribes.[30] Initially at least, the Beni Zeroual and the Beni Uriaghel fought within the confines of their tribal territory for more autonomous control over their land. The issue was whether the Rif republic or the French protectorate promised them a more stable future.[31] Each side exploited military success to impose its authority on wavering tribal leaders. But tribal pacification was tenuous. Women hostages were often taken to force the hand of recalcitrant clans.[32]

True to his convictions, Lyautey planned to cut off Abd el-Krim's local sources of support by exploiting intelligence about tribal allegiance, and distributing funds, favours and military support accordingly. His preference for politically targeted pacification against rebellious tribes did not promise the swift victory that Painlevé's ministers expected. On 2 May 1925 Lyautey wrote once more to his confidant, Wladimir d'Ormesson:

> I have just spent the hardest and most anxious week I have known since Fez in 1912. Without any prior indication, during the twenty-four hours of 25 April, there was a mass break-out of Abd el-Krim's forces across our entire northern front, precipitating the defection of four frontier tribes and unsettling others as far south as Fez. The town is under threat, eight border posts have been taken, all telegraph wires have been cut, the insurgents have cut the Fez-Taza road and all other northern routes. Our detachments have been routed [*bousculés*]; and over four days French losses alone were thirty-six killed, including four officers, and forty-three injured, five of whom were officers.[33]

In fact, Abd el-Krim's initial breakthroughs did not presage a collapse of the French position. The situation on the northern front quickly stabilised. The Rif leader opted to consolidate his authority among newly dissident tribes before marching on Fez, always his major goal. Yet Lyautey could hardly claim any success. Although he had correctly predicted the timing and direction of the Rif attack, his preparations for it were sorely inadequate. Numerous military outposts and pillboxes in the Ouergha river region were overrun, encircled or cut off. Early relief efforts directed by his appointee, General Aldebert de Chambrun, were abandoned on 27 May.[34]

These problems notwithstanding, General Serrigny, sent by Painlevé to conduct a tour of inspection in Morocco on behalf of the Supreme Defence Council, commended Lyautey's strategic vision in a preliminary report submitted on 4 June. The residency's division of the northern front into three military sectors made sense. Lyautey was now willing to countenance a much broader offensive to recapture lost territory. Mobile operations would resume once reinforcements were deployed. The marshal even impressed Serrigny with more wistful discussion of combined Franco-Spanish assaults to force the surrender of Ajdir, the Rif republic's capital just south of Alhucemas Bay.[35] In the short term, the army air force units of the 37e régiment d'aviation were preparing a relentless bombardment of rebel positions.[36] For all that, Lyautey simply did not convince as a proponent of firepower tactics. Serrigny was more critical in a final report submitted on 11 June in which he derided Lyautey's extensive delegation of military responsibility to subordinates. Painlevé, then serving as both Premier and War Minister, used this as the pretext to divide Lyautey's civil and military functions. The resident was stripped of his role as military commander, and a government appointee, General Stanislas Naulin, a Rhineland occupation army commander, arrived in Rabat to direct the reconquest of the Rif.[37]

The French political community reacted to the Rif war with a mixture of indignation and shock. The conflict divided the Cartel des gauches in the National Assembly, although the rank and file of Herriot's governing Radical Party swung behind the war effort. Socialist criticism of the war focused on the government's failure to keep Parliament and public well informed about the course of operations. But Socialist complaints were half-hearted at best. Between 29 May and 23 June 1925 Painlevé's new Cabinet survived three votes of confidence over its conduct of the war, in large part because only a minority of SFIO Deputies joined the Communists in opposing the government.[38] In general terms, both the Radicals in power and their Socialist supporters in the National Assembly were more animated by mounting financial problems – a depreciating franc, Bank of France hostility to exchange policy, and the flight of investor capital from France – than by colonial conflict.[39]

In late 1924 the Cartel des gauches coalition began to split. The Rif war became a political football as old rivalries between the Radicals, the Socialists and the Communist Party re-emerged. Léon Blum's SFIO calculated that support for the war was essential to prevent any haemorrhage of bourgeois voter support to the Radicals.[40] The one voice of dissent was Jacques Doriot, then the PCF's leading spokesman on colonial affairs. Acting on Comintern advice, between May 1925 and March 1926 Doriot orchestrated parliamentary debates, trade union protests, anti-war committees, Young Communist action groups and mass meetings in opposition to the war. Nine such meetings took place in Paris. In the largest, Doriot addressed a crowd variously estimated at between 3,500 and 15,000 amid the fairground attractions of Paris Luna Park on 26 May 1925. Here Doriot exploited Jean Jaurès's principled opposition to the original annexation of Morocco to fuel his condemnation of the Socialists for voting military credits for a war of oppression that claimed increasing numbers of working-class casualties on both sides. In addition, Communist activists staged seventy-three anti-war meetings in the provinces, drawing crowds often several hundred strong. In Périgueux, Rivesaltes, Bourges, Strasbourg, and Douai, attendances of over 2,000 were registered.[41] Doriot's biting invective was memorable: the Rif war and the Druze uprising illustrated the bankruptcy of strategies of indirect rule in France's Muslim territories. But he did not speak for the French Communist Party, still less for the French left as a whole. Norman Ingram's assessment of the PCF's equivocal attitude to pacifism could be applied in equal measure to anti-colonialism: 'French Communism in the inter-war period was intermittently and opportunistically antimilitarist and internationalist, but hardly pacifist'.[42]

In 1925 only the Communist youth section lent Doriot wholehearted support. The party's executive committee, its provincial federations and its trade union affiliates refused to condemn France's presence in Morocco outright. French involvement in the Rif escalated soon after the bruising experience of the Ruhr occupation, another issue over which the PCF faced right-wing accusations of damaging national interests by opposing state policy. The PCF leadership was therefore sensitive to similar accusations of treasonous anti-militarism regarding the Rif campaign. So docile was the Communist leadership that the Comintern rebuked PCF leader Maurice Thorez for his party's lukewarm opposition to the war. Ultimately the PCF adopted an anti-militarist message to mobilise rank-and-file support for protests and strike action against army operations. Doriot's unrestrained anti-colonialism was far less popular. He did co-ordinate CGTU plans for work stoppages in protest at operations in the Rif, as well as attempts to persuade armament workers, transport staff and Marseilles dock workers to disrupt the resupply of French forces in Morocco. It proved harder to replicate the Ruhr campaign for soldier fraternisation with the local population, largely because there was no functioning Communist Party in Morocco to spread propaganda among the French garrison.[43]

French forces had established superiority along the decisive northern front by October 1925. Large areas remained under rebel control, but the key strategic centres of Fez and Taza were made secure.[44] Ironically, once Pétain's application of overwhelming firepower had driven Riffian forces into retreat the general adopted a strategy more akin to Lyautey's methods. With the approval of Morocco's civilian resident-general, Théodore Steeg, in late 1925 heavily defended *centres de résistance* were established along the margins of the northern front to bar southerly penetration by Abd el-Krim's forces. Pétain's defensive screen enabled army tribal affairs specialists to redouble their efforts to rally local clan groups one by one.[45] Between December 1925 and February 1926 an estimated 17,000 Berber clan families formally submitted to Muslim affairs officers. In June 1926 Abd el-Krim's most ardent supporters in the Beni Zeroual clan followed suit, as did two other Berber clan groupings, the Ghezaoua and the Beni Mestara. Active resistance was by then largely confined to the eastern reaches of the Ouezzan region. Skirmishing also continued on routes between Taza, Fez and Oujda. In July the army command concluded that pacification of *Maroc utile* was more or less complete.[46] In fact, the annual cycle of military campaigns in the Rif, the Atlas and the southern desert continued for a further eight years until Morocco was misleadingly declared fully 'pacified' in 1934.[47]

The Syrian revolt and constitutional impasse in the Levant, 1925–30

Historical interest in the Syrian revolt of the mid-1920s has focused on one question above all. How did a local tribal uprising of southern Syria's Druze clans in the summer of 1925 so quickly escalate into a national rebellion against French imperial authority? Behind this enquiry lie several others. How far did the Syrian revolt mark the incorporation of Syria's predominantly rural, peasant population into a national polity previously identifiable with a Damascene elite? In other words, did the revolt reactivate the mass opposition to foreign rule evident in the Faisal period? The famine and economic disorder of First World War Syria exacerbated the gulf separating rich and poor. This wide economic gap was pivotal to the intensification of the 1925 revolt and the changing modes of political organisation that followed it.[48] Agricultural production did not recover to pre-1914 levels until 1928. Urbanisation meanwhile gathered momentum as peasant cultivators sought industrial employment. The population of Damascus more than doubled from 184,000 immediately after the First World War to 286,000 by the start of the Second. Population growth in Aleppo was faster still, from 127,000 in 1914 to 320,000 in 1943.[49]

In the 1930s the focus of political opposition to the French presence shifted back to the towns, but was articulated in the more recognisably modern forms of disciplined political parties, mass youth movements, trade unions and women's groups. This raises a further question about the Syrian revolt. How far did it signify the transition from predominantly tribal and elite forms of political opposition to a more inclusive Syrian nationalism? By the time the Popular Front took office in May 1936 Syrian workers, political parties and women's organisations demanded social reforms and citizens' rights commensurate with those of metropolitan France, and used the weapon of the general strike to achieve them. In Syrian urban politics at least, issues of class and gender had assumed equivalent importance to the older social cleavages of communal identity, religious affiliation and family origins.[50] That is not to say that communal sectarianism declined in importance in either Syria or Lebanon. Nor is it to challenge the dominant historiographical tendency to represent French policy in both states as, at root, an attempt to divide and rule by exploiting and amplifying inter-communal tensions.[51] Rather, it is to acknowledge the diversity of civil opposition to French authority and the underlying economic injustice that propelled it.

From 1920 the practices of indirect rule refined by Lyautey's Moroccan administration were broadly applied to Syria and Lebanon. French officials exploited the distinctive ethno-religious composition of each country to lessen the probability of unified opposition to mandate government.[52] In the months preceding the French seizure of power in Damascus, General Gouraud staffed a skeletal 'Levant administrative service' with native affairs specialists selected by preference from French North Africa. Experienced army personnel were designated as military governors to administer former Ottoman *wilayets* in Syria and Lebanon, and officers were also selected as deputy governors for each district or *caza*.[53] Throughout the term of the Levant mandates provincial and rural government retained this strongly military aspect, although more civilian advisers were introduced in Lebanon.[54] Once established in Beirut, the Levant high commission pursued a divisive strategy, setting countryside against city, Christian against Muslim, and according various minority groups privileged status at the expense of the Sunni Muslim majority. These actions were a crude adaptation of Lyautey's more sophisticated approach to Moroccan local government and inter-communal relations.[55]

The French decision in September 1920 to incorporate four predominantly Muslim *cazas* previously attached to Syria within Greater Lebanon had serious ramifications. The 1920 boundary settlement worsened inter-communal tensions in Lebanon, and antagonised Syria's Sunni community.[56] Between 1922 and 1924 High Commissioner Maxime Weygand, the second high-ranking general appointed to head Levant government, instituted a federal system of Syrian 'states', each with its own autonomous administration. By the end of 1924 functioning Alawite and Druze states were in place, respectively based on their 'compact minority' populations of predominantly Shi'ite Alawites and Druze clans. The Alawite region centred on Latakia in the north-west, the Jabal Druze to the far south, the *sanjak* of Alexandretta on the margins of Turkish Anatolia and the remote Jazirah region in the north-east were thus bureaucratically isolated from a Syrian state based on the Damascus hinterland and the Aleppo region to the north. After the humiliation of Syrian–Lebanese partition in 1920, the Sunni Arab elite in Damascus now confronted another disaster: the apparent triumph of the policy championed since 1918 by Robert de Caix and the French Asia committee that treated the Levant as an agglomeration of religious groups rather than the epicentre of the Arab 'nation'.[57] The 'minorities policy' that entrenched Maronite Christian dominance in Greater Lebanon in 1920 was now extended to Syria, the consolidation of distinct communal regions clearly designed to preclude unitary nationalist government from Damascus.[58]

It was thus inevitable that the 1924 administrative reorganisation would alienate Syria's Arab population as the prospect of a unitary state directed by a strong central government receded.[59] Weygand's experiment with federalism in Syria soon backfired. Distinct local administrations were prohibitively expensive. Their divisive effects undermined co-operation with a conservative, pro-Western Arab elite, something that the British seemed to be achieving in neighbouring Iraq. In Syria, by contrast, matters went from bad to worse. On 16 January 1924 Damascene notables underlined their hostility to the new constitutional structure when the Syrian Federal Council voted itself out of existence by supporting a proposal for a unitary state.[60]

The demarcation of the Syrian–Lebanese administrative structure also destroyed the febrile communal balance between Christian and Muslim populations in the new Lebanon. Leaders of the Maronite community rejected the choice inherent in the 1920 settlement between the stabilisation of the enlarged Lebanese state through conciliation of the country's Muslims or acceptance of an eventual return to the narrower geographical confines of Mount Lebanon to reinforce the country's Christian identity. Instead, the French high commission colluded with Maronite leaders to prevent Muslim majority rule. Additional qualifications for Lebanese citizenship favoured the Christian community. And these regulations were further codified in the bureaucratic arrangements for the 1932 Lebanese census, subsequently used as the basis of voter registration.[61]

Divide-and-rule tactics in Syria were not merely a corruption of Lyautey's associationism. They also reflected the political outlook of the security services in the Levant territories. Mandate government rested on a network of regional military intelligence offices, native affairs bureaux and police agencies that together provided the central administration with information on public opinion, crime, disorder and sedition.[62] These threat assessments were instrumental in forming senior officials' mental map of the Middle East. Throughout the early 1920s high-commission policy rested on geo-strategic assumptions drawn from this incoming intelligence reportage. French Syria was represented as a state under siege. The principal external enemies were Turkish irredentism in the north, British imperial aggrandisement from the south and east, and Comintern sponsorship of Arab unrest. Factionalised Muslim elites, pan-Islamism, tribal dissent and simmering inter-communal antagonisms threatened to undermine the Syrian polity from within.[63] Whatever the veracity of these threat perceptions, high-commission policy gave them tangible form. Convinced that internal security hung by a thread, successive high commissioners ceded limited authority to venal collaborators and religious minorities while withholding power from the Syrian parliament. As a result, popular mistrust of the mandate authorities ran deep. In 1924, for example, it was widely rumoured that the high commission deliberately spread the smallpox virus in the Hama region to quell local disorder.[64]

A year later, after Sultan al'Atrash's uprising in the Jabal Druze had spread to Damascus and Hama, High Commissioner General Maurice Sarrail and his Radical Party and Republican-Socialist sponsors in Paris still refused to concede that French authority was generally despised.[65] From September 1925 onward the political engine of the Syrian rebellion was the alliance between the Druze rebel chiefs and Dr 'Abd al-Rahman Shahbandar's Syrian People's Party. Established earlier in the spring, the People's Party (Hizb-al-Sha'b) was the first overtly nationalist grouping legally established under the mandate.[66] In September 1925 Shahbandar and his Druze allies created a provisional national government in the Jabal Druze capital, Soueida. Unfortunately for the rebels, the Syrian–Palestine Congress, principal external backer and paymaster of the revolt, was by this point divided into two competing factions, one led by Emir Shakib Arslan, the other by Michel Lutfallah, leading member of a wealthy Lebanese *émigré* family in Cairo. Arslan's supporters, many of whom were members of the Istiqlal Party (the descendant of the Syrian Arab Independence Party), were generally pan-Arabist, anti-Hashemite and committed to the Arab struggle in Palestine. But Shahbandar was tied to Lutfallah's rival faction. Both men were Western-educated members of the Arab elite. They typified the first generation of People's Party leaders in championing Western-style secular nationalism. At first, these competing visions of Syrian nationalism were disputed among the leaders themselves, but did not affect the groundswell of popular support for rebellion.[67]

Public contempt for French rule turned to profound alienation among native Damascenes in mid-October 1925. On 18 October the Levant army commander, General Maurice Gamelin, authorised a bombardment of the central and southern quarters of Damascus that were occasionally infiltrated by Druze forces. The rebels' most recent incursion had been spectacular. Druze fighters penetrated the south and east of the capital and even set fire to the French administrative headquarters in the 'Azm Palace.[68] Gamelin was bound to react. That said, the shelling of civilian housing was militarily futile. Druze militiamen were not urban guerrillas, nor were they fervently supported by ordinary townspeople, for whom their predations and mere presence presented a grave risk. Moreover, the Druze militias fled the city before Gamelin's artillery bombardment began. The results were devastating. Civilian casualties, hotly disputed by French commanders at the time, ran to almost a thousand dead.[69] The October bombardment was not the last of its kind. The city was shelled again in April 1926. These actions represented imperial policing at its very worst. Gamelin's decision to permit artillery firing with splinter shells revealed a callous disdain for civilian life redolent of General Dwyer's actions in the more famous Amritsar massacre six years earlier.[70]

Sarrail's right-wing opponents in France were gunning for his dismissal before news of Gamelin's October 1925 bombardment reached Paris. Indeed, the carnage in Damascus had little bearing on Sarrail's downfall. Like Joseph Gallieni before him, Sarrail was a rare breed: an ardently republican, left-leaning general. Unlike Gallieni, Sarrail evoked bilious hatred among the parliamentary right and ultra-nationalist leagues such as Action Française unmatched since the height of the Dreyfus crisis in the 1890s. Sensing their opportunity to oust the high commissioner and embarrass the Cartel des gauches, anti-Cartel Deputies ignored the long-term causes of Druze and Arab rebellion. The extensive parliamentary inquest into the Syrian revolt focused solely on Sarrail's term in Beirut from January 1925. The anti-Cartel press followed suit, concentrating on the two initial military disasters in the summer of 1925 that encouraged wider rebellion in October.[71]

Sarrail's replacement was Henry de Jouvenel, who disembarked at Beirut in early December 1925. The new high commissioner arrived after a brief detour to Cairo where he tried without success to negotiate an end to the revolt with representatives of the Syrian–Palestine Congress, acknowledged as the controlling agency of radical Arab nationalism.[72] De Jouvenel was a liberal senator for the Corrèze, and former editor of the Paris daily Le Matin. He was much respected by Foreign Minister Briand, who had engineered his appointment to Beirut. More important in the Syrian context was his strong attachment to the League of Nations where he served on the French delegation.[73] His appointment rekindled hopes among moderate Damascus politicians of a more sympathetic French approach to the rebellion. But the divisions in the Syrian–Palestine

Congress were once more projected on to the Syrian revolt. Arguments over tactics and the distribution of charitable donations to support the rebellion grew more intense. And Shakib Arslan's decision in November 1925 to parley with de Jouvenel prior to his departure from Paris provoked disarray among rebel leaders in Syria just as Gamelin's forces turned to the offensive. Arslan and de Jouvenel discussed a compromise settlement based on French recognition of Syria's national independence and plebiscites on reunification in the four *cazas* of Greater Syria attached to Lebanon in 1920. The Syrian state would concede exclusive strategic, cultural and economic privileges to France, including the use of bases, French training of a Syrian army, and the right to raise loan issues in Damascus.[74]

By the time these proposals were tabled in Paris the outlines of a more aggressive French military strategy were already in place. In the short term, the War Ministry and the Levant army command effectively quashed the emerging Quai d'Orsay scheme for a Syrian constitutional settlement based on French withdrawal in return for long-term privileges in post-independence Syria. The liberal high commissioner and his secretary and confidant, Jean-Louis Aujol, were stymied before they began.[75] Gamelin planned additional sweep operations into the Jabal Druze and the Aleppo region. Levant army regiments and mobile units of Circassian irregulars and Syrian *gendarmerie* pursued rebel bands deeper into the countryside.[76] Meanwhile, the French municipal administrations in Aleppo and Homs, and military intelligence officers in the interior, provided weapons, bribes and other inducements to local leaders willing to assist the containment of unrest.[77] These divisive tactics built on the distinct regional and commercial interests of Syria's main provincial towns. In Aleppo in particular, long-standing economic ties with Turkey, a history of resistance to central government control, and a heterogeneous population of Arabs, Turks, Alawites and Armenian refugees made fertile ground for French intervention. But playing different communities and rival leaders off against each other was explosive, and in January 1926 ignited further disorder. In late December 1925 de Jouvenel announced that elections would be held on 8 and 12 January 1926 in the Alawite territory and in those parts of the Syrian state where martial law did not apply. He further insisted that elected representatives from each administrative district should convene separately to discuss the proposed constitutional changes. This smacked of divide and rule. Nationalist leaders in Aleppo led by Ibrahim Hananu organised an election boycott. Their colleagues in Homs and Hama did the same, prompting the mandate authorities to arrest those notables held responsible.[78]

Demonstrations in support of the Aleppo detainees triggered renewed violence. In the worst incident, the town garrison fired on a crowd of nationalist demonstrators, leaving eight dead. The extent of public anger at French repression became apparent when only twenty-two per cent of the Aleppo electorate voted in the January 1926 elections.[79] Meanwhile, in Damascus, de Jouvenel's new deputy, high-commission delegate De Reffye, sought out influential politicians willing to join the French in marginalising the Syrian People's Party, by then regarded as the key political ally of the rebel Druze chiefs.[80] Hence de Jouvenel's first act of any significance was to dismiss Subhi Barakat as Syrian president and install a more 'reliable' government in the capital.[81]

In the new year four main centres of unrest remained. First among these was Soueida, always the top military priority as the symbolic heart of the rebellion. Second was the Ghouta oasis, a semi-rural district east of the capital from which an estimated 600 Druze fighters raided French targets in and around Damascus. Third was a more diffuse rebel group operating around Mount Hermon on the Syrian–Lebanese border. Finally, a smaller cluster of rebel groups remained active around En Nebk, midway between Damascus and Homs.[82] By July 1926 the revolt was largely contained. On paper, General Andréa's recapture of Soueida in April was the decisive strategic turning point.[83] In practice, by the time Andréa's forces marched into the Druze capital, fewer Syrian town dwellers, peasant farmers and Bedouin tribesmen were willing to risk the consequences of dissent. French officials were particularly relieved by the collapse of Bedouin tribal resistance. Rebel enlistment of Bedouin support in early 1926 briefly threatened to rekindle more widespread rural disorder.[84]

Bedouin reticence reflected the severity of the summary punishment meted out by the irregular forces at the cutting edge of mobile operations rather than any new-found respect for French rule. Regional officials and tribal affairs specialists of the Contrôle bédouin were hard-pressed to rebuild contacts with community leaders appalled by French conduct and outraged by the widespread imposition of collective fines on villages, tribes and city districts.[85] Their first priority was to convince tribal sheikhs, village headmen (mukhtars) and smallholders of the probity of rural administration. The revolt destroyed the progress made by district and tribal authorities in this regard since 1920. A couple of examples illustrate the point. Since November 1922 Colonel Georges Catroux, head of the Levant military intelligence service, had pressed for the introduction of common fiscal obligations throughout the country rather than differing rates of taxation in the Syrian states. In similar vein, in July 1923 the Levant army command introduced more stringent regulations governing aerial bombardments of civilian populations. Suppression of the rebellion flouted these guidelines. Tax collection became more coercive and uneven. Collective fines and destruction of villages and Bedouin encampments made a mockery of French claims of equitable rural governance.[86]

Following the Syrian revolt, the country's nationalist leaders saw no middle ground between French colonialism and a treaty of independence.[87]

Their reluctance to compromise explained the failure of a package of constitutional revisions that Henri Ponsot, successor to de Jouvenel as high commissioner, and his secretary-general Maugras released to journalists in Beirut on 26 July 1927. Characteristically, the taciturn high commissioner left it to Colonel Catroux to explain the measures that included promises to devise a new constitutional settlement reintegrating the minority states into a Syrian national polity.[88] The July 1927 proposals fell short of the constitution promulgated in Lebanon on 23 May 1926. Loosely modelled on the institutions of the Third Republic, the Lebanese constitution actually consolidated the system of 'political sectarianism' that privileged the Maronite community in Beirut and Mount Lebanon and, to a lesser extent, the Sunni notables and absentee landlords of Beirut, Tripoli and Tyre. Together, these groups formed a powerful conservative elite that dominated Lebanese national politics until 1932. Ponsot's further revision of Lebanon's constitution in October 1927, which fused the two Chambers of the Beirut parliament, did not significantly alter the role of the dominant political elite. Throughout the late 1920s Lebanon's new governmental establishment stifled the growth of Muslim civil society and representative political parties.[89]

Meanwhile, Ponsot's experiments with parliamentary government in Syria dissolved into acrimony. Following a six-day conference in Beirut, on 25 October 1927 senior nationalist figures from Syria's four main towns of Damascus, Aleppo, Hama and Homs repudiated the high-commission reforms proposed in July. The conference delegates had more ambitious demands: an end to martial law, the release of all political prisoners, restoration of individual and press freedoms, and negotiation of an independence treaty.[90] This Beirut conference also sired the most influential nationalist movement in the Syrian mandate: the National Bloc (al-Kutla al-wataniyya). It was another five years before the National Bloc formally defined its programme and structure at a Homs congress in November 1932. None the less, the Bloc was a functioning political organisation by the end of 1927. It enjoyed the dual advantage of widespread urban support combined with a remarkably homogeneous leadership drawn from the educated elite of urban professionals, ex-Ottoman officials and full-time Arab politicians. Most were born in the 1880s and came from eminent Sunni families. Several were absentee landowners, but a larger number were lawyers, doctors or former civil servants.[91] In short, the National Bloc offered the best hope of French dialogue with a moderate nationalist movement.

Ponsot's government tried to create a more convivial political climate in Syria in the months prior to parliamentary elections scheduled for April 1928. But this was shrewd politics rather than far-sighted concession. By late 1927 the last embers of the Great Revolt were almost out. The high commission was convinced that final suppression of the revolt presented a window of opportunity to rally a collaborative elite akin to its Lebanese equivalent. To that end, Ponsot issued an amnesty for sixty-four leading nationalist politicians a month before the elections. The release list was selective. The Damascus military intelligence bureau warned that the Syrian People's Party was committed to independence, and therefore deaf to compromise.[92] The political amnesty was therefore designed to intensify nascent splits between National Bloc and People's Party supporters liable to be as destructive as the earlier factionalism in the Syrian–Palestine Congress.[93] But if Ponsot's military advisers were satisfied, the Foreign Ministry was not. The Quai d'Orsay Levant division was exasperated at Ponsot's refusal to clarify his plans. This, in turn, reflected deeper anger that Ponsot's timid reformism did not measure up to that of de Jouvenel, who was every bit the Foreign Ministry's man. It seemed reasonably clear that Ponsot felt obliged to follow the British precedent in Iraq and at least prepare for negotiation of a treaty of independence. But with whom did he plan to negotiate? And on what basis? These questions went unanswered.[94] Meanwhile the high commissioner sailed blithely on, comforted by the National Bloc's decision to contest the elections.

Military intelligence officers were also wary of Ponsot's true intentions, but worked hard to ensure the election of pro-government candidates in rural areas. It was a different story in the towns. Nationalist candidates predominated in Damascus, Aleppo, Homs and Hama. Bitter rivals they may have been, but National Bloc and Syrian People's Party candidates were not easily cajoled. The new Constituent Assembly was determined to vote through a Syrian constitution establishing a parliamentary republic immune to French manipulation. The Assembly's commitment to restore a Greater Syria incorporating Lebanon and a good deal of British mandated territory added fuel to the fire. Faced with mounting right-wing criticism in Paris, Quai d'Orsay complaints, and the ill-disguised contempt of his all-important military intelligence staff, Ponsot turned from conciliator to autocrat. On 11 August 1928 he adjourned the Constituent Assembly, ostensibly for three months. In fact this signalled the end of Syria's brief experiment with Lebanese-style collaborative parliamentary government.[95] In November 1928 Ponsot extended the adjournment. In February 1929 the Damascus parliament was prorogued indefinitely. In May 1930 it was formally dissolved pending nationalist acceptance of the high commission's preferred constitutional settlement. For the next six years a cycle of acrimonious elections, short-lived Damascus governments and failed treaty proposals dominated national politics in Syria until a major escalation of political violence beginning with a general strike in January 1936 unblocked the path to treaty talks.[96]

Rebellion in Indochina: the Yen Bay mutiny and its aftermath

On 10 February 1930 Vietnamese infantrymen of the Yen Bay garrison on the Red River north-west of Hanoi mutinied, killing two French officers, four NCOs and two of their fellow *tirailleurs*. Another garrison at Hung Hoa in Phu-Thô province and administrative headquarters across Tonkin were also attacked by former soldiers, peasant labourers and workers, some armed with knives and staves. In Hanoi an army brigadier was wounded.[97] The Vietnamese Nationalist Party (Viet Nam Quoc Dan Dang, VNQDD) co-ordinated the attacks.[98] The party was founded in December 1927, weeks after the departure of Indochina's last genuinely reformist governor, Alexandre Varenne. In its short, turbulent existence the VNQDD was led by a group of young Vietnamese journalists, schoolteachers and clerks, several of them linked with the Hanoi Nam Dong publishing house. It was fiercely patriotic and determinedly anti-colonial. VNQDD cadres imitated Communist organisational methods but drew inspiration from a utopian Confucianism rather than Marxist ideology. Indeed, its main Vietnamese rival, the Comintern-affiliated Revolutionary Youth League, tried, but failed, to develop links with the VNQDD in conformity with the Comintern's 'united front' strategy in 1927–28.[99] In the more repressive atmosphere created after Varenne's departure, a *sûreté* clampdown on the VNQDD's senior ranks in 1929 provoked the insurrection of February 1930 as party activists made a final bid to overthrow the colonial order.[100]

As in Morocco and Syria in 1925, when violence erupted in Tonkin in February 1930, officials in Indochina pondered whether local unrest bore the seeds of a national revolt. But there was also a key difference. Few in René Robin's Tonkin residency, in Governor-general Pierre Pasquier's federal government or in François Piétri's Ministry of Colonies harboured any illusions that northern Vietnam was fully pacified before, during or after the 1930 disturbances. The attempted assassination of Governor-general Merlin by the Vietnamese revolutionary Pham Hong Thai in 1924, and the arrest of Vietnam's foremost anti-colonial leader, Phan Boi Chau, in the following year signalled the eclipse of the secret societies that spearheaded opposition to colonial control in the first two decades of the twentieth century. Stronger, more ideologically driven groups soon took their place. The most important of these was the Vietnam Revolutionary Youth League, precursor of the first Communist movement in Vietnam, established in Canton by Nguyen Ai Quoc (Ho Chi Minh) during 1925. By the time the Yen Bay mutiny began, Ho Chi Minh had returned to Indochina to supervise the unification of rival Communist groups in Tonkin and Annam.[101] Once news of the violence reached Paris, Albert Sarraut advised his fellow senators that army mutinies, prison violence and local rebellions were endemic in the

Vietnamese territories.[102] Reaction in the Chamber of Deputies was more mixed. Jacques Doriot ascribed the violence to the inherent flaws of the colonial prison system. But the champagne magnate Pierre Taittinger, leader of the ultra-rightist Patriot Youth league (Jeunesses Patriotes), called on the government to protect settlers against Communism.[103]

Violent, well organised resistance to French rule in Indochina certainly had longer antecedents than in France's Muslim territories.[104] Before the First World War nationalist secret societies proliferated in Annam and Tonkin. Directed by Vietnamese exiles of the scholar gentry, first in Japan and, after the 1911 Chinese revolution, in southern China, these anti-colonial groups were audacious in their methods and consistent in their objectives.[105] An attempt by sympathetic army cooks and soldiers to poison the Hanoi garrison in June 1908, and a spate of anarchist-style bombings, including an assassination attempt on Governor Sarraut in 1913, led the colonial authorities to rely more heavily on *sûreté* surveillance, informer networks and harsh legal penalties to contain Vietnamese dissent. Some regional officials acknowledged that rural sympathy for Vietnamese nationalism was rooted in punitive direct taxes, minimal public services and the privileges enjoyed by settlers and mandarins. Armed with heightened police powers, however, the federal government did little to address these underlying causes of popular antagonism to French authority.[106]

Governor-general Pasquier shared the conviction that political violence was a fact of life in Indochina, something to be suppressed rather than assuaged. In a report remarkable for its complacency, he advised the Ministry of Colonies in June 1930 that the VNQDD, the Vietnamese Communist leadership and their rank-and-file supporters lacked ideological coherence. Anti-colonial groups borrowed from diverse intellectual sources. VNQDD tracts were sprinkled with references to Rousseau, Sun Yat-sen and Confucius. Communist propaganda slavishly followed Comintern instruction.[107] Pasquier's comments reflected an article of faith among Hanoi officials: the Vietnamese peasantry was incapable of sustained political engagement. In 1925–27 provincial administrators used these arguments to undermine Varenne's case for rural reform. Farmers and landless labourers had neither the time nor the inclination to look beyond the horizon of the village. The cycles of crop cultivation and the vicissitudes of the weather counted for more than political change in Hanoi, Saigon or Hué. Talk of a Vietnamese national community was nonsense. The administration was better advised to reinforce the traditional hierarchy of the mandarins and landlords than to meddle in social reforms that might foster national consciousness by imposing uniform standards across the federation.[108]

The severity of French repression in 1930–31 stemmed from the shocking realisation that arrogant assumptions about uneducated Vietnamese had been proved so wrong. Yet the first wave of violence in February 1930 was quickly contained. The Yen Bay mutiny lasted barely twenty-four hours. VNQDD cells, decimated by the earlier *sûreté* crackdown, were utterly shattered by the end of February. Activists that escaped the security forces eventually regrouped in the southern Chinese provinces of Yunnan and Canton, but could not compete with the mounting influence of the Indochinese Communist Party (ICP)[109] inside Vietnam.[110] Meanwhile, over the spring of 1930, villages suspected of pro-rebel activity faced aerial bombardment or ruthless clean-ups by army foot patrols.[111] Fast-track criminal tribunals hastily set up in Tonkin tried 1,086 individuals for sedition to the acclaim of the settler press. Thirteen VNQDD leaders were marched to the centre of Yen Bay on 17 June and guillotined.[112]

The Hanoi government had no time to reflect on the success of this first wave of repression. During April and May 1930 more widespread disturbances broke out in northern Annam. Railway tracks were sabotaged near Da Nang and police fired on May Day protesters at Ben Thuy in Vinh province, killing five. On 5 May police swept through the worst affected villages in the Nghê-Tinh region, leaving sixteen dead. The federal authorities were more unnerved by the first outbreaks of major unrest in Cochin-China. There, too, security forces fired on May Day demonstrators. The pattern of 'revolutionary demonstrations', police shootings and round-ups of protesters in and around Saigon continued until November 1930. Farther north, political violence in Annam became more sporadic after the initial clampdown in May. But by September the provinces of Nghê-An and Ha Tinh had become ungovernable. Both were densely populated. The affected areas of the Vinh region contained some 400,000 inhabitants grouped into 934 villages. Attacks on property were rife; huge crowds sacked army guard installations. On 8 September army intelligence reported that an insurrectionary force of 8,000 attacked a *garde indigène* post at Do-Luong, 40 km west of Vinh.[113]

The colonial authorities in Annam's imperial capital, Hué, went on the offensive in response. A string of military posts was set up across central Vietnam. A special mobile police column was created to track down Communist agitators in the worst affected provinces.[114] During September army aircraft bombarded Nghê-Tinh villages and strafed any rebel columns they could find. Units of Vietnamese colonial forces were gradually replaced with more trusted detachments of foreign colonial troops. A Foreign Legion battalion that shipped into Haiphong on 29 August, plus two companies of colonial infantry and a squadron of non-Vietnamese Tho tribesmen, fanned out from Vinh in early October. Days later this 'repression column' engaged the largest armed rebel bands at Thanh-Qua and Vo-Liet in the bloodiest confrontations of the year. Lightly armed peasants were mown down by machine gun fire and Legionnaires swept through rebel villages over successive nights, leaving a trail of devastation.[115]

Official casualty figures for the period 10 February to 10 October recorded 345 rebels killed, 124 wounded and 429 arrested. (The comparatively low number of wounded lends weight to Vietnamese accusations that French troops were ordered to take no prisoners.) There were no French casualties after the initial killings at Yen Bay, an indication both of the rebels' lack of modern weapons and the security forces' shoot-on-sight policy.[116]

What made the 1930 rebellion different was the incontrovertible evidence of Communist co-ordination of otherwise disparate unrest. More alarming still was the speed and skill with which the Vietnamese Communist movement established a network of control in rural Annam, creating 'Red Villages' (*lang do*) in which Soviet-style reforms were immediately applied. There was ample evidence that the ICP directed the rural revolution in northern Annam and the worker-driven protests in Cochin-China. In the Nghê-Tinh region, the ICP organised rural soviets, land redistribution, peasant strikes, tax and market boycotts, and the coercion of recalcitrants.[117] A heady, utopian revolutionary atmosphere briefly took hold. Peasants acquired land, Communist schools sprang up, and Vietnamese women helped run factory soviets and city protests in which demonstrators marched behind red flags emblazoned with Soviet emblems.[118] *Sûreté* officers concluded that a cell of twenty-seven Vietnamese Communist *émigrés* controlled the entire rebellion in fulfilment of a precise Comintern scheme to overthrow the colonial state.[119]

Communist tactics became bolder still after scores of ICP organisers were locked up. In August preparations were in hand for a general strike.[120] By September villagers in Nghê-Tinh faced reprisals if they refused to participate in demonstrations. Symbols of colonialism from government offices to prisons, schools and nurseries were besieged, some even destroyed. Agitators spread rumours of renewed mutinies and imminent Chinese army landings, and promised an end to taxation under Communist rule.[121] *Sûreté* headquarters in Hanoi compared the 1930 rebellion with the much larger 1926 Communist uprising against the Dutch colonial authorities in Java. And on 28 June 1930 the French Chamber of Deputies declared over-whelming support for Piétri and Pasquier's efforts to contain 'the Communist challenge', setting the stage for the more savage repression of the autumn.[122] By early October prisoner 'interrogations' and the seizure of ICP central committee documents revealed Communist plans to prepare local insur-rections in support of the Nghê-Tinh revolt.[123] Confessions later extracted from VNQDD suspects during 1931–32 enabled the *sûreté* to build up a similar picture of secret meetings, *émigré* influence, agent contacts and propagandist cells in Tonkin.[124]

Pasquier's government was also alarmed by Communist success in politicising the migrant labour force employed on Cochin-China's largest rubber plantations. Work stoppages, demands for improved conditions and intermittent violence against French labour recruiters and plantation managers were attributed to Comintern agitation rather than ascribed to the squalor and brutality of life as a plantation worker.[125] In the year of the Yen Bay uprising 30,637 contract labourers and 24,666 non-contract casual workers were recruited to Cochin-China's plantations. Their living conditions and food rations were abysmal, their contracts frequently ignored by unscrupulous employers. Malaria depleted the work-force, many of whom fled at the first opportunity. This propensity to flight helps explain the casual brutality of plantation overseers, which, in turn, made a largely illiterate plantation labour force receptive to Communist propaganda.[126]

On 9 February, eve of the Yen Bay mutiny, VNQDD members assassinated the director of the Indochinese manpower office, an organisation that pressed coolies into service in Cochin-China and New Caledonia.[127] News of the killing spread fast. During the Tet festival from 4 to 11 February 1930 over 6,000 workers went on strike at the Michelin company's vast plantation at Phu-Rieng, north of Saigon. The strikers' demands were unremarkable: wage increases, sick pay, compensation for industrial injury, an eight-hour working day and an end to corporal punishments. But their insistence that Tran Van Cung, an allegedly Communist labour organiser, be released from detention led Michelin representatives and the Saigon authorities to conclude that the stoppage was long planned and Communist-inspired. When labourers disarmed a *garde indigène* unit sent to quell the dissent, the authorities ruled out any compromise, and sent in the army. The strike leaders were sentenced to five years' penal servitude. The 1930 repression set the pattern for official responses to later strikes on Cochin-China's plantations in 1932 and 1936–37. What often began as spontaneous work stoppages provoked by arbitrary wage cuts or incidents of overseer violence against labourers were savagely put down on the grounds that Communist subversion lay behind all such industrial unrest.[128]

The Yen Bay mutiny, the foundation of the ICP and disturbances in the plantation sector almost coincided with the depression in Indochina's economy and the devaluation of the piastre.[129] But, as Pierre Brocheux has argued, it is misleading to assume a simple causal link between political unrest and the economic slowdown in 1930–31. For one thing, the effects of collapsing commodity prices were felt most acutely in Cochin-China, where rice production for export and the rubber boom of the mid-1920s made the colony more vulnerable to declining international demand. Peasant producers in northern Annam, the epicentre of rebellion, were less integrated into the monetary economy. Landless labourers stood to benefit from cheaper rice, their staple food. Furthermore, between 1930–39 a key long-term trend in Indochina's economy was rising dependence on French capital and metropolitan consumption of Vietnamese goods as traditional markets in China and South East Asia contracted. Moreover,

Indochina's export decline in the early 1930s was less catastrophic than in other colonies. The socio-political consequences of the depression registered in more indirect ways. Wage earners hit by the piastre devaluation faced proportionately higher taxes. Managers faced with collapsing prices pushed plantation labourers to harvest greater volumes of rubber and rice. Widespread lay-offs and breaches of labour contracts ensued. In short, the depression helped precipitate rebellion and a more formal organisation of Vietnamese Communism, whose origins lay elsewhere.[130]

In 1931 rebellion in colonial Vietnam became more chaotic. By the summer most of the ICP leadership were killed, imprisoned or driven back into exile. And the party was split over tactics and ideology. The familiar Stalinist accusation of 'right deviationism' took a heavy toll of senior rank-and-filers purged by former comrades determined to keep fighting. The ICP central committee and the bulk of its regional apparatus collapsed. The Red Villages were restored to French control, and urban disaffection with the limited gains achieved discredited the ICP, particularly among educated Vietnamese.[131] Ostensibly the uprisings had achieved little. But Vietnamese politics were never the same again. City and countryside, worker and peasant, were united in hatred of French colonialism as never before. Although decimated in the early 1930s, the ICP confirmed its status as the sole force capable of marshalling nationwide resistance to French rule. The long road to the Indochina war had begun.

The Kongo Wara

The Nghê-Tinh rebellion was the most ideologically driven anti-colonial uprising the French confronted before 1940. At first glance it bears little comparison with the least known of the inter-war anti-colonial revolts – the Kongo Wara rebellion in Equatorial Africa's Haute Sangha region. What unites them is the speed with which the instruments of colonial authority collapsed, albeit temporarily, in the face of determined opposition and relatively low-level violence by poorly armed peasants.

In his devastating 1927 critique of administrative abuse in Equatorial Africa, André Gide warned that the combination of corrupt officials, thuggish auxiliaries and unrestricted capitalist exploitation by monopolistic trading companies was bound to generate resistance if left unchecked. Two years later the unlikely figure of André Maginot acknowledged that Gide was right. Maginot was an imposing politician, immensely tall and prodigiously clever. Inevitably, his name will always be associated with French defence strategy rather than colonial policy. Yet Maginot served three terms at the rue Oudinot, and began his career in public service at the Algiers government before the First World War.[132] As Minister of Colonies in April 1929 Maginot intervened in the case of an official in the N'Gotto sub-district in AEF. On 9 December 1926 the local correctional tribunal passed a curious verdict on the man, a Monsieur Pacha, finding him guilty of 'acts of homicide by imprudence'. A separate criminal trial also convicted Pacha for other acts of violence against the local population. He was fined 500 francs for the former crime, and sentenced to a year's imprisonment for the latter. Soon afterward, Maginot was pressed by the League for the Rights of Man to institute a formal commission of inquiry into separate allegations of state brutality in AEF made by Gide and his fellow writer Albert Londres. Maginot's rue Oudinot advisers scented danger. The campaign might generate adverse publicity comparable to the exposure of Belgian abuses in turn-of-the-century Congo by E. D. Morel's Congo Reform Association. The Brazzaville authorities were less contrite, sweeping Pacha's case under the carpet.[133] It seems irrefutable that a minority of junior officials in Equatorial Africa held African life very cheap indeed. Against this background, reports of disorder in the Gbaya tribal districts of Oubangui-Chari's Haute Sangha region filtered through to the federal capital.

Thomas O'Toole points to the excesses of traders, planters and police auxiliaries in provoking violence in Gbaya villages in 1928.[134] Elsewhere, the Gbaya insurrection, or Kongo Wara ('War of the Hoe Handle') has been portrayed as a millenarian revolt led by a charismatic leader, 'Karnu' (rendered in French as Karinou; literally, 'the roller up of the earth').[135] That was certainly how the colonial authorities in Bangui and the AEF army command represented it at the time. Karnu was dubbed a *fétisheur*: a fanatical prophet whose followers wore magic charms to fend off bullets. The soldiers who eventually killed him made much of the fact that his hut contained an improvised altar and throne.[136] Since independence, nationalist writers have seen Kongo Wara as Oubangui's first popular resistance movement against colonial oppression. Thomas O'Toole and Elikia M'Bokolo suggest that Karnu's role as leader of the Kongo Wara became part of an Oubangui-Chari 'resistance myth' later exploited by Barthélemy Boganda, the 'father' of independence in the Central African Republic. These characterisations have some validity. But the rebellion's diffuseness suggests that it arose from a combination of French exactions, inter-tribal rivalries and the absence of effective policing.[137]

The Kongo Wara revolt began in June 1928 in Karnu's adopted village of Nahim in the Bouar-Baboua administrative district of the Haute Sangha. Villagers attacked the sub-district officer, allegedly encouraged to do so by Karnu's millenarian predictions of a decisive conflict with French colonisers. Attacks on European travellers were subsequently reported throughout the Haute Sangha. Bangui governor Lamblin and the AEF army commander General Thiry agreed to make an example of Karnu's supporters. Within weeks Karnu was dead. He and his brother were shot on 11 December 1928 when a company of 132 Senegalese riflemen entered Nahim village.

Their bodies were put on public display to confirm that neither held magical powers. Low-intensity pacification operations continued for a further two years. Tribesmen armed with poisoned arrows and traditional spears were shot on sight.[138]

Initially, however, the scorched earth tactics employed by the French relief column to stamp out opposition provoked wider disorder. In a major escalation of the revolt, in January 1929 seven local police auxiliaries were murdered at Deng Deng across the Oubangui frontier in Cameroon. With no prospect of dialogue with advancing French forces, some village leaders appear to have concluded that their sole options were resistance or flight.[139] The resultant penalties were severe. On 13 June 1930 the Brazzaville government council sentenced twelve alleged tribal ringleaders in Haute Sangha to ten years' internment. A further eleven *indigène* notables received lesser sentences of five years.[140] Yet the Kongo Wara underscored the fact that colonial stability rested on a dependable rural elite. In the Bouar-Baboua district – heartland of the rebellion – it fell to the army lieutenant who led the original attack on Nahim to restore tribal co-operation.[141] Ostensibly, this marked a return to associationist policies interrupted by the disorder of the previous three years. Protracted army operations and the larger police presence none the less indicated the fragility of colonial control, and the absence of checks upon it, in the African interior. After the flurry of government and media interest in AEF social conditions following Gide's high-profile visit, one wonders how far the casual state violence that preceded the Kongo Wara revolt went unremarked in the years that followed it.

Conclusion: order after revolt?

National rebellion did not break out again in Morocco or Syria after 1927. Yet public order, tribal unrest and ethnic separatism remained perennial problems in both countries until the French departed. A snapshot of army pacification in Morocco in 1933 gives some idea of the scale of the task. Between May and September six battalions of Algerian and West African infantry scoured the mountains of the High Atlas, clashing with Berber tribal forces. By October some 2,500 families of the Ait Isha, Ait Haddidou and Ait Sokhman tribes had submitted to French authority at a cost of over 100 soldiers killed.[142] These engagements received hardly a mention, even in the Parti colonial press. The hill country of the Rif, the mountainous tribal domains of the Middle and High Atlas and the pre-Saharan reaches of south-east Morocco were the focal point of military pacification in the years 1927–34.[143] Levant army operations in the Jabal Druze, the southern Hauran and, above all, in Upper Jazirah on the frontiers of Turkish and Iraqi Kurdistan were remarkably similar. The hallmarks of these unseen dirty colonial wars were skirmishes between tribesmen and French irregular forces such as Moroccan *goums* and Circassian cavalry, punitive aerial bombardment or army dynamiting of dissentient villages, land and live-stock confiscations, and the consequent dislocation of tribal communities.

During the 1930s, however, only urban protest in Morocco and Syria elicited Cabinet interest in Paris. Persistent French attempts to exploit inter-communal divisions transformed food riots, inter-ethnic clashes and industrial unrest into well organised Arab nationalist opposition. In Morocco, the introduction of the so-called Berber *dahir* in May 1930 provoked an unprecedented wave of marches, public meetings and riotous confrontations with security forces in Casablanca, Rabat, Salé, Fez and Marrakech that lasted throughout the summer.[144] The ferocity of this popular opposition stemmed from the conviction that the *dahir* privileged the Berber community in order to divide the Muslim population as a whole. The residency insisted that the *dahir* was merely a legal instrument to bring the administration of customary justice and property law in Berber terri-tory into line with French judicial practice. There was a grain of truth to this. But the fact remained that the *dahir* superseded Shari'a law, thus undermining the Sultanate's jurisdiction in Berber lands. To many Moroccans it confirmed their long-held suspicion that the French con-sidered the Berbers a community capable of assimilation to France, unlike their more oriental Arab cousins. Resident-general Lucien Saint and his head of native affairs, General Charles Noguès, knew that the *dahir* would arouse Arab resentment, but underestimated its scale.[145] Similar decrees in 1914–15 that affirmed the separate status of customary law in Berber lands had passed off more or less without incident.[146]

At least three fundamental changes had occurred in the intervening years. First was the development of organised political opposition to French imposition of juridical and cultural boundaries between Berbers and Arabs, transparently intended to divide and weaken the Muslim population. Second was the *ad hoc* alliance between Muslim clerics and a new genera-tion of bourgeois students, many of whom returned from university educa-tion in Paris as fully fledged nationalists inspired by the arguments and organisational methods of Messali Hadj's Etoile Nord-Africaine. Third was the radicalisation of a fast-growing urban under-class: under-employed, poorly housed and faced with worsening conditions as the depression hit Morocco's export-driven economy.[147] Over the summer of 1930 city demonstrations against the hated *dahir* formed a bridge between the ear-lier era of cultural opposition to French erosion of Muslim civil society and the emergence of populist nationalism that articulated demands for Moroccan self-rule.[148] Mohammed Hassan al-Ouezzani personified this shift. Ouezzani returned from his studies at the Paris Ecole des sciences politiques an accomplished Maghrebi student leader, a nationalist organiser and a disciple of Shakib Arslan. In June and July 1930 he led protests against the *dahir* in Fez, imploring mosque congregations to fight against a menace to Islam and the Moroccan national community. Residency officials, anxious that the Sultan's representatives should be seen to back the forces of order, were delighted that the *pasha* of Fez had Ouezzani arrested after Friday prayers on 18 July and then publicly flogged.[149]

Over subsequent months, city *pashas* took the lead in containing disorder, armed with security service intelligence regarding known agitators.[150] On the one hand, the furore over the Berber *dahir* suggested that ordinary Moroccans were wise to the duplicity at the heart of supposed 'indirect rule'. Urbain Blanc, Foreign Ministry delegate in Rabat and second-in-command at the residency, admitted as much. On the other hand, Blanc's fellow officials took comfort in the vigour with which their Moroccan appointees suppressed the *dahir* riots. The *pasha* of Fez, Mohammed el-Baghdadi, and his counterpart in Rabat, Abderrahman Bargach, proved their undying loyalty to France. But the cost was more profound popular hostility to French administration and venal *makhzen* officials.[151]

No matter how well *gendarmes* and Moroccan troops cowed protesters into submission, Muslim antagonism to French rule had entered a new phase. The adverse impact of the depression crystallised these resentments into mass support for Morocco's first genuinely nationalist political party, the Comité d'Action Marocaine (literally Moroccan Action Committee, more usually designated the National Action Bloc). In 1934 the National Action Bloc published a detailed list of constitutional reforms, hoping that the emergence of the Rassemblement Populaire in France signalled a new indulgence toward colonial reform among the liberal left.[152] The Popular Front electoral victory in May 1936 represented the culmination of the Rassemblement Populaire, the looser coalition of republican parties, trade unions, pressure groups and intellectual organisations committed to oppose the ultra-rightist leagues in France. In Morocco, as in other colonial territories, political expectations reached unprecedented heights. The Popular Front's colonial reforms are discussed in detail in chapter nine. What concerns us here is the speed with which Muslim optimism in the early summer of 1936 turned to bitter disappointment in the autumn. Between 14 and 17 November 1936 mass meetings convened in Casablanca, Salé and Fez in support of the National Action Bloc's 1934 demands. The police broke up these demonstrations, arresting over 150 alleged ringleaders. It seemed that the events of 1930 were repeating themselves – but with one important difference. In November 1936 the young Sultan Mohammed Ben Youssef came out decisively in opposition to National Action Bloc protests. He summoned René Thierry, Urbain Blanc's successor as Foreign Ministry delegate, to demand immediate suppression of the demonstrations and punishment of those arrested. Resident-general Charles Noguès confessed that the Sultan's iron resolve surprised him – pleasantly so. Noguès was a Popular Front appointee and a loyal disciple of Lyautey. Armed with the Sultan's personal instructions, he could clamp down on nationalist dissent without acting contrary to the Popular Front's more liberal inclinations.[153]

The political situation in Syria also deteriorated markedly in the depression years. The relatively successful implementation of the Anglo-Iraqi treaty of independence between 1930–32 sharpened popular disaffection in Syria at declining living standards and the attachment of the Syrian pound to an over-valued franc.[154] Hostility to French rule peaked in a thirty-six-day general strike called by the National Bloc, but organised by student radicals in Damascus on 27 January 1936. The suspension of parliamentary institutions, the manipulation of successive governments and French efforts to marginalise nationalist groups nourished urban support for street protests and a more radical nationalist alternative. The more widespread popular political engagement characteristic of Feisal's regime resumed with a vengeance. The Syrian People's Party made the transition from a cliquish group of urban notables to a modern secular party with a mass membership. Students' organisations, women's groups and paramilitary scouting groups proliferated. Ironically, it was the National Bloc, cornered into supporting the general strike, that profited most – using mounting public anger to coax the Sarraut and Blum governments into conceding negotiations over a treaty of independence.[155]

At street level, the spectacular growth of radical youth movements revealed the heightened militancy among nationalist protesters. In Syria, Lebanon and Morocco Muslim Scouting associations were as potent a force for youthful patriotism as their equivalents in Europe. In the Levant states especially, teenage Scouts often graduated to more overtly paramilitary organisations. Most of these were established in the freer atmosphere of the Popular Front period in 1936–37 as protests intensified in anticipation of the long delayed conclusion of Syrian and Lebanese independence treaties. Uniformed groups such as the Damascus Steel Shirts, the 'National Guards' in Aleppo, the 'Young Arabs' in Homs, and the pan-Arabist Najjada in Lebanon were noisy and intimidating. By July 1936 even small Syrian towns like Azaz, Idlib and Ercha boasted their own National Guard formations.[156] In Christian East Beirut, two Maronite-dominated organisations, the Lebanese Phalanges and the White Shirts, became caught up in the city's sectarian rivalries, adding to the inter-communal friction stirred by Syrian demands for reunification.[157] The youth groups' mimicry of European fascist rallies and insignia added to their menace. Staff of the high commission civil cabinet warned the Foreign Ministry that youth groups, manipulated by senior nationalist politicians, might be the 'shock troops' of a *coup d'état*.[158] French diplomatic staff in Damascus further advised that if the National Bloc failed to secure a treaty, a new generation of more militant leaders such as Nizhat Memlouk, Nassib

Bakri and Fakhri Baroudi, schooled in these youth movements, might eventually take over.[159] On 20 June 1936 the Popular Front stepped in to end Foreign Ministry procrastination, and conceded full treaty negotiations with a Syrian government delegation. By then the Syrian mandate was almost ungovernable, brought to a standstill by urban protests, work stoppages and street violence.[160]

Colonial Indochina, too, was racked by political violence and social upheaval during the depression years and the subsequent period of Popular Front reform. Governor Varenne's efforts to liberalise admission to the Indochinese bureaucracy between 1925 and 1927 did not survive his departure.[161] Murderous state repression of the Yen Bay and Nghê Tinh uprisings in 1930–31 was accompanied by renewed reliance on Vietnam's conservative elite. This constituency was too small and unpopular – perhaps four per cent of the total indigenous population – to provide the basis for stability. Meanwhile, such was the scale of French repression that the Tan Viet and the VNQDD were liquidated as political groups. It was a costly loss. These organisations might conceivably have developed as moderate, non-Communist nationalist parties with which the French authorities could ultimately negotiate. As it was, only the ICP survived as a viable – and more radical – opposition movement.[162] The destabilisation of the agricultural market in the depression years of 1931–35 cemented the bonds between an impoverished Vietnamese peasantry and a radicalised urban work force, a phenomenon examined in chapter nine.

Turning to the Haute Sangha region in AEF, the last of the regions examined here, the reversion to associationist policies after three years of sporadic disorder enabled the Brazzaville government to claim that the Kongo Wara was an anomalous incident rather than an indication of the limits of colonial authority in the Equatorial African interior. The Kongo Wara, and the rural dissent that followed the killing of Karnu in December 1928, much like the other revolts described above, remind us that the French colonial state faced endemic opposition throughout the inter-war years. The differing scale and organisational sophistication of these rebellions makes direct comparison between them difficult. In each case, however, control was restored only after overwhelming force had been deployed. This was a protracted process that emphasised the fragility of colonial order. And in all cases, once order was restored, the crying need for fundamental reform was either muffled or ignored.

Notes

1 The best English-language treatment of the war remains C. R. Pennell, *A Country with a Government and a Flag. The Rif War in Morocco* (Wisbech: Middle East and North African Studies Press, 1986). David S. Woolman, *Rebels in the Rif. Abd-el-Krim and the Rif Rebellion* (Stanford CA: Stanford University Press, 1968) is also useful. An outstanding

examination of Spain's involvement is Sebastian Balfour, *Deadly Embrace. Morocco and the Road to the Spanish Civil War* (Oxford: Oxford University Press, 2002). A more lurid account is José E. Àlvarez, *The Betrothed of Death. The Spanish Foreign Legion during the Rif Rebellion, 1920–1927* (Westport CT: Greenwood Press, 2001). French military strategy is analysed by Gershovich, *French Military Rule*, chapter 5. On the background to French involvement see Rivet, *Lyautey et l'institution du protectorat français au Maroc*, and Georges Oved, *La Gauche française et le nationalisme marocain 1905–1954* I (Paris: Editions l'Harmattan, 1984).

2 C. R. Pennell, 'Ideology and practical politics. A case study of the Rif War in Morocco, 1921–1926', *International Journal of Middle East Studies*, 14 (1982), 20.

3 Charles-Robert Ageron, 'La politique berbère du protectorat marocain de 1913 à 1934', *Revue d'Histoire Moderne et Contemporaine*, 18:1 (1971), 62–74.

4 AN, Paul Painlevé papers, 313AP/244/D4, no. 522/Cabinet militaire (Rabat) to War Ministry/EMA, summary report, 22 March 1924; Pennell, *Morocco*, 186–7.

5 SHA, 3H107, War Ministry, 'Projet de conférence des opérations au Maroc: Note au sujet des origines de l'agression rifiane', n.d. 1926.

6 Pennell, *A Country with a Government*, 186–91.

7 SHA, 3H101, tel. 101, Rabat residency, 'Bulletin périodique du 29 avril 1925'.

8 Balfour, *Deadly Embrace*, 98–117; Hoisington, Jr, *Lyautey and the French Conquest*, 196–204.

9 Gershovich, *French Military Rule*, 137–40; Meynier, 'Volonté de propagande ou inconscient affiche?', 47. The final phase of the Spanish offensive was bloodier still, involving the use of TNT shells, mustard gas and free-fire tactics: see Balfour, *Deadly Embrace*, chapters 4–5.

10 AN, Lyautey papers, 475AP/86, no. 227 Lyautey report, 'Bulletin périodique de renseignements: Situation sur le front de l'Ouergha', 4 July 1924; tels. 315, 498 and 500, Lyautey to EMA-2, 14 August, 1 October, 19 October 1924.

11 André Le Révérend (ed.), *Un Lyautey inconnu. Corréspondance et journal inédits* (Paris: Perrin, 1980), Lyautey letter to d'Ormesson, 23 July 1924, 310–12.

12 AN, Painlevé papers, 313AP/246/D1, EMA Section d'études, 'Note sur les envois de renforts au Maroc en 1925'. The first phase of army reinforcement from January to April 1925 was insufficient to permit offensive operations.

13 Le Révérend, *Un Lyautey inconnu*, Lyautey letter to d'Ormesson, 23 July 1924, 310–12. Regarding Primo de Rivera's policy, see Shannon E. Fleming and Ann K. Fleming, 'Primo de Rivera and Spain's Moroccan problem, 1923–27', *Journal of Contemporary History*, 12 (1977), 88–9.

14 Balfour, *Deadly Embrace*, 95–6.

15 Painlevé formed another government on 29 October 1925 after a Cabinet reshuffle.

16 SHA, 3H602, Pétain report to War Ministry/Premier's Office, 4 August 1925.

17 MAE, série M, vol. 89, Direction des affaires indigènes/SR, 'Rapport mensuel sur la situation politique et militaire au Maroc, mars 1925'. The report identified heightened Riffian military movements along the northern front.

18 Rabinow, *French Modern*, 318.

19 Jean-Noël Jeanneney, *Leçon d'histoire pour une gauche au pouvoir. La faillite du Cartel 1924–1926* (Paris: Editions du Seuil, 1977), chapters 6–7.

20 AN, Painlevé papers, 313AP/248, Captain Carbillet report to Painlevé, 'La situation actuelle en Syrie', n.d. 1925.

21 Bidwell, *Morocco*, 25–6.

22 David M. Hart, *Tribe and Society in Rural Morocco* (London: Frank Cass, 2000), 15, 52.

23 Pennell, 'Ideology and practical politics', 19–20.

24 *Ibid.*, 22–31.

25 Ageron, 'La presse parisienne', 7.

26 C. R. Pennell, 'Women and resistance to colonialism in Morocco. The Rif, 1916–1926', *Journal of African History*, 28 (1987), 110–17.

27 Assia Benadada, 'Les femmes dans le mouvement nationaliste marocain', *Clio. Histoire, Femmes et Sociétés*, 9 (1999), 68.

28 SHA, 2N243/D2, General Serrigny report on Moroccan tour of inspection, 4 June 1925; Gershovich, *French Military Rule*, 130–2.
29 SHA, 9N269/D7: 'Troupes coloniales au Maroc, 1921–1927'.
30 MAE, série Maroc, vol. 89, Direction des affaires indigènes/SR, 'Rapport mensuel d'ensemble du protectorat, avril 1925'.
31 SHA, 2N243/D2, Serrigny report on Moroccan tour of inspection, 4 June 1925.
32 Bidwell, *Morocco*, 101.
33 Le Révérend, *Un Lyautey inconnu*, Lyautey letter to d'Ormesson, 2 May 1925, 312–13.
34 Gershovich, *French Military Rule*, 131.
35 SHA, 2N243/D2, Serrigny report on Moroccan tour of inspection, 4 June 1925.
36 SHAA, 2C35D1, Commandement Général du Front Nord, 3ème Bureau, 'Projet de programme de bombardements aériens des arrières ennemis', 1 June 1925.
37 AN, Painlevé papers, 313AP/244/D2, Painlevé letter to Lyautey, 26 June 1925; Gershovich, *French Military Rule*, 134; Hoisington Jr, *Lyautey and the French Conquest*, 200.
38 Oved, *La Gauche française* I, 198–213.
39 Jeanneney, *Leçon d'histoire pour une gauche au pouvoir*.
40 On Doriot's role and left-wing responses to the Rif War more generally see David H. Slavin, 'The French left and the Rif War, 1924–25. Racism and the limits of internationalism', *Journal of Contemporary History*, 26 (1991), 5–32.
41 Oved, *La Gauche française* I, 231–7, See Oved's tables on pp. 236–7 detailing the public meetings held to oppose the war. The crowd figure was officially recorded as. 3,500, but the Communist daily *L'Humanité* published the higher figure of 15,000. ADA, 12J 43, 'Meeting organisé par le Comité d'Action de la Région Parisienne du Parti Communiste, Luna Park', 16 May 1925.
42 Ingram, *The Politics of Dissent*, 5.
43 Jean-Jacques Becker and Serge Berstein, *Histoire de l'Anti-communisme* (Paris: Olivier Orban, 1987), 172–7; Nicole Le Guenac, 'Le PCF et la guerre du Rif', *Le Mouvement Social*, 78:1 (1972), 50–6.
44 CADN, Fonds Protectorat du Maroc, sous-série: Direction des affaires chérifiennes 1912–1956, vol. 163/Dossier: Les Fronts, décembre 1927, Army command memo, 'Stabilisation du Front Nord. Nos avances vers le Sud'.
45 CADN, Fonds Protectorat du Maroc, sous-série: Direction des affaires chérifiennes 1912–1956, vol. 163, no. 2281, Steeg to Foreign Ministry, 1 December 1925.
46 CADN, Fonds Protectorat du Maroc, sous-série: Direction des affaires chérifiennes 1912–1956, vol. 163/Dossier: Les Fronts, Décembre 1927, Army command memo, 'Stabilisation du Front Nord. Nos avances vers le Sud'.
47 AN Lyautey Papers, 475AP/189, 'Les dernières étapes de la pacification de l'Atlas central', 13 October 1933; 'La pacification de l'Anti-Atlas', 4e trimestre 1933; Gershovich, *French Military Rule*, 146–61 *passim*.
48 Khoury, 'The Syrian independence movement and the growth of economic nationalism in Damascus'.
49 Thompson, *Colonial Citizens*, 29–31.
50 *Ibid.*, 11–12, 155–70 *passim*.
51 Khoury, *Syria and the French Mandate*; Lenka Bokova, *La Confrontation franco-syrienne à l'époque du Mandat 1925–1927* (Paris: Editions l'Harmattan, 1990); N. E. Bou-Nacklie, 'Les Troupes Spéciales. Religious and ethnic recruitment, 1916–46', *International Journal of Middle East Studies*, 25:4 (1993), 645–60.
52 Edmund Burke III, 'A comparative view of French native policy in Morocco and Syria, 1912–1925', *Middle Eastern Studies*, 9 (1973), 175–86; Khoury, *Syria and the French Mandate*, 55–6; and Khoury 'Factionalism among Syrian nationalists during the French mandate', 453.
53 CADN, Fonds Beyrouth, Cabinet politique, vol. 840/D1, 'Service de Renseignements organisation et directives', n.d. 1930.
54 CADN, Fonds Beyrouth, Cabinet politique, vol. 840/D2, SR Service Central note, 'A/S action politique des commandants de colonnes', 6 January 1926.
55 Khoury, *Syria and the French Mandate*, 156.
56 Tauber, *The Formation of Modern Syria and Iraq*, 66–7.

57 Itamar Rabinovitch, 'The compact minorities and the Syrian state, 1918–45', *Journal of Contemporary History*, 14:4 (1979), 693–7.

58 Yossi Olmert, 'A false dilemma? Syria and Lebanon's independence during the mandatory period', *Middle Eastern Studies*, 32:3 (1996), 42.

59 CAOM, 19G21: Propagande musulmane, 1914–29, Services des affaires musulmanes 'Renseignements sur les questions musulmanes au 4 septembre 1923'.

60 Khoury, *Syria and the French Mandate*, 54, 136–8. Philip Khoury points out that, on the eve of his departure from Beirut, Weygand recognised the error of his policies, especially the missed opportunity to conciliate moderate Arab nationalists.

61 Rania Maktabi, 'The Lebanese census of 1932 revisited. Who are the Lebanese?' *British Journal of Middle Eastern Studies*, 26:2 (1999), 219–41.

62 As examples, see CADN, Fonds Beyrouth: sous-série Sûreté générale, Syrie 1926–41 vol. 842, and vol. 895: Armée, Gendarmerie, Police.

63 As an early example: SHA, 20N1089/D4, no. 773, Haut commissariat service de renseignements, 'Syrie et Liban, rapport mensuel d'ensemble, mois de juin 1921'.

64 N. E. Bou-Nacklie, 'Tumult in Syria's Hama in 1925. The failure of a revolt', *Journal of Contemporary History*, 33:2 (1998), 279.

65 MAE, série E: Levant, vol. 193, tel. 233/Cabinet civil, Sarrail to Foreign Ministry, 4 September 1925.

66 Khoury, *Syria and the French Mandate*, 141–7. The People's Party took shape in January 1925 and by June claimed 1,000 members in Damascus, most of them educated Arab professionals.

67 Khoury 'Factionalism among Syrian nationalists', 447–56.

68 MAE, série E: Levant, vol. 194, tel. 600/KD, Sarrail to Foreign Ministry, 25 October 1925.

69 PRO, FO 371/10852, E7250/357/89, consul W. A. Smart (Damascus) to Austen Chamberlain, 10 November 1925. The Levant army command admitted to 150 deaths.

70 Sir Charles W. Gwynn, *Imperial Policing* (London: Macmillan, 1936), chapters 3 and 9.

71 Jan Karl Tanenbaum, *General Maurice Sarrail 1856–1929. The French Army and Left-wing Politics* (Chapel Hill NC: University of North Carolina Press, 1974), 208–21.

72 Safiuddin Joarder, 'The Syrian nationalist uprising (1925–1927) and Henri de Jouvenel', *Muslim World*, 68 (July 1977), 194.

73 Christine Manigand, 'Henry de Jouvenel, Haut-commissaire de la République française en Syrie et au Liban (1925–1926)', *Guerres Mondiales et Conflits Contemporains*, 192 (1998), 102–5.

74 Khoury 'Factionalism among Syrian nationalists', 456–64.

75 Manigand, 'Henry de Jouvenel', 104–8.

76 CADN, Fonds Beyrouth, Cabinet politique, vol. 840/D1, 'Service de Renseignements organisation et directives', n.d. 1930. There were thirty such mobile units operating in Syria by December 1925. They were later reorganised into nineteen *escadrons légers*, permanently on hand to contain communal unrest.

77 CADN, Fonds Beyrouth, Cabinet politique, vol. 894, no. 611/ES, Pierre Alype memo, 'Situation dans le vilayet d'Alep', 26 January 1926; no. 32/HS/3, Captain Miatrot (SR bureau chief, Homs) to Levant SR, 28 January 1926.

78 Joarder, 'The Syrian nationalist uprising', 198–9.

79 Peter Sluglett, 'Urban dissidence in mandatory Syria. Aleppo, 1918–1936', in Kenneth Brown, Bernard Hourcade, Michèle Jolé, Claude Liauzu, Peter Sluglett and Sami Zubaida (eds), *Etat, ville et mouvements sociaux au Maghreb et en Moyen Orient* (Paris: Editions l'Harmattan, 1989), 305–8.

80 MAE, Henry de Jouvenel papers, vol. 4, no. 403, De Reffye (Beirut) to Foreign Ministry, 15 June 1926.

81 Khoury, *Syria and the French Mandate*, 182–4.

82 CADN, Fonds Beyrouth, Cabinet politique, vol. 840/D2, no. 428/2, EMA-2, 'Recherche de renseignements', 25 February 1926.

83 That was certainly how Andréa represented it in his memoir of the conflict: Général C. J. E. Andréa, *La Révolte druze et l'insurrection de Damas* (Paris: Payot, 1937).

84 CADN, Fonds Beyrouth, Cabinet politique, vol. 986/D24, no. 9520/ES/2, Captain Mortier (Jabal Druze SR) to SR Levant, 23 November 1926.

85 CADN, Fonds Beyrouth, Cabinet politique, vol. 840/D2, no. 4537/K3, Direction du SR du Levant, 'Directives sur l'action du SR pendant la phase de consolidation politique', 14 September 1926.
86 CADN, Fonds Beyrouth, Cabinet politique, vol. 486/Dossier: Affaires bédouines, no. 1894/SP, Catroux to Gouraud, 7 November 1922; SR Service central note, 18 February 1924. Regarding air operations and targeting in the Druze revolt see SHAA, 1C8/D4: 'Répression de la révolte Druze (1925–1927)'.
87 CADN, Fonds Beyrouth, Cabinet politique, vol. 466, tel. 250, Ponsot to Foreign Ministry, 14 January 1928.
88 Khoury, *Syria and the French Mandate*, 246.
89 Zamir, *Lebanon's Quest*, 31–55 *passim*.
90 Khoury, *Syria and the French Mandate*, 247–8.
91 *Ibid.*, 249–66.
92 CADN, no. 763/DV, SR Damas ville, 'Renseignement au sujet de l'activité des extrémistes de Damas', 20 March 1928.
93 Khoury, *Syria and the French Mandate*, 249.
94 CADN, Fonds Beyrouth, Cabinet politique, vol. 466/D1, tel. 284, Diplomatie (Paris) to Ponsot (Beirut), 16 January 1928.
95 Khoury, *Syria and the French Mandate*, 327–48 *passim*; Peter Shambrook, *French Imperialism in Syria 1927–1936* (Reading MA: Ithaca Press, 1998), 27–35.
96 Sluglett, 'Urban dissidence', 303; Khoury, *Syria and the French Mandate*, 20–1; on parliamentary politics in 1930s Syria see Shambrook, *French Imperialism*, chapters 2–4.
97 ADA, Sarraut papers, 12J301, 'Etat des incidents survenus en Indochine depuis le 10 février 1930'.
98 Yves Gras, 'L'Indochine française et le nationalisme vietnamien (de la conquête à 1939)', *Revue Historique des Armées*, 4 (1984), 40; Brocheux and Hémery, *Indochine. La colonisation ambiguë*, 300–6.
99 Tai, *Radicalism*, 217–23; Khánh, *Vietnamese Communism*, 91–3; William J. Duiker, 'The Revolutionary Youth League: cradle of Communism in Vietnam', *China Quarterly*, 51 (July–September 1972), 484–6.
100 Marr, *Vietnamese Tradition*, 336, 377–8; Khánh, *Vietnamese Communism*, 95.
101 ADA, Sarraut papers, 12J307/Dossier: Evénements de Yen Bay, Pierre Pasquier preliminary report on the Yen Bay uprising, 6 June 1930. Piétri took over at the rue Oudinot on 2 March 1930. His predecessor, Lucien Lamoureux, was briefly Minister of Colonies when the original outbreak began in February 1930. Duiker, 'The Revolutionary Youth League', 479–80, 492–4.
102 'Les événements d'Indochine : l'opinion de M. Albert Sarraut', *Journal des Débats*, 14 February 1930.
103 SHA, 6N53/D3, no. 6612, War Ministry secretariat, 'Note pour la direction des troupes coloniales', 18 February 1930.
104 The fullest treatment in English remains David G. Marr, *Vietnamese Anticolonialism, 1885–1925* (Berkeley CA: University of California Press, 1971).
105 ADA, Sarraut papers, 12J301/*sûreté* dossier, 'L'agitation anti-française dans les pays Annamites de 1905 à 1918'.
106 Munholland, 'French response to the Vietnamese nationalist movement', 655–75.
107 ADA, Sarraut papers, 12J307/Dossier: Evénements de Yen Bay, Pierre Pasquier preliminary report on the Yen Bay uprising, 6 June 1930.
108 CAOM, GGI, série F, affpol/64193, no. 41/SCR, Tonkin residency report, 'Situation politique du Tonkin', 11 April 1926.
109 After previously divided Communist factions adopted the name Vietnamese Communist Party in February 1930, the Party's Central Committee followed Comintern instructions to change the party name to Indochinese Communist Party (ICP) in October, as an inclusive, internationalist gesture towards potential supporters in Laos and Cambodia. The ICP none the less remained overwhelmingly Vietnamese in composition.
110 CAOM, GGI, affpol/65444, *sûreté* report, 'Le Viet Nam Quôc Dan Dang ou Parti National Annamite des Emigrés en Chine (1933–1937)'.

111 ADA, Sarraut papers, 12J301/Dossier: 'Agitation Communiste en Indochine, 1930'.
112 Marr, *Vietnamese Tradition*, 377; Khánh, *Vietnamese Communism*, 95–6.
113 SHA, 6N503/D3, no. 1497, EMA Section d'études, 'Note pour le secrétariat général', 20 June 1931.
114 ADA, Sarraut papers, 12J301, no. 5648/SCR *sûreté générale* (Hanoi) to Direction des affaires politiques, 8 October 1930; Khánh, *Vietnamese Communism*, 156–7.
115 SHA, 6N503/D3, no. 1497, EMA Section d'études, 'Note pour le secrétariat général', 20 June 1931.
116 ADA, Sarraut papers, 12J301, 'Etat des incidents survenus en Indochine depuis le 10 février 1930'. Firearms licensing helped ensure that the rebels had access only to small arms, mutineers' weapons and guns stolen from army and police posts.
117 Khánh, *Vietnamese Communism*, 150–5; Pierre Brocheux, 'L'implantation du mouvement communiste en Indochine française : le cas du Nghe-Tinh (1930–1931)', *Revue d'Histoire Moderne et Contemporaine*, 24:1 (1977), 49–74.
118 Marr, *Vietnamese Tradition*, 244–5.
119 ADA, Sarraut papers, 12J301, Unsigned *sûreté* intelligence report, 'Localisation de l'agitation', 21 November 1930.
120 ADA, Sarraut papers, 12J301, no. 466-C, French Resident (Vinh) Guilleminet, to Hué residency, 9 September 1930.
121 ADA, Sarraut papers, 12J301, no. 267/RS, Annam Resident Le Fol to Governor-general Pasquier, 'A/S des incidents de Vinh et Ha-Tinh, septembre 1930'.
122 'Le Débat sur l'Indochine', *Le Temps*, 29 June 1930.
123 ADA, Sarraut papers, 12J301, no. 5648/SCR *sûreté générale* (Hanoi) to Colonies, Direction des affaires politiques, 8 October 1930.
124 CAOM, GGI, affpol/65444: *sûreté générale* VNQDD interrogation reports, 1930–37. The army command in Indochina was less informed about rebel objectives, see SHA, 6N503/D3, EMA Section d'études, 'Evénements d'Indochine', 16 June 1931.
125 'Le mouvement révolutionnaire en Indochine', *Le Temps*, 13 May 1930.
126 Brocheux, 'Le prolétariat des plantations', 62–7.
127 Khánh *Vietnamese Communism*, 94.
128 Brocheux, 'Le proletariat des plantations', 80–6.
129 For details see Smith, 'The foundation of the Indochinese Communist Party'.
130 Pierre Brocheux, 'Crise économique et société en Indochine française', *Revue Française d'Histoire d'Outre-Mer*, 63:232 (1976), 655–67.
131 Khánh, *Vietnamese Communism*, 158–61.
132 André Maginot maximised the colonial war effort during his first term as Minister of Colonies in Alexandre Ribot's government between March and September 1917. He supported the National Bloc and backed French occupation of the Rhineland, see Marc Sorlot, 'Les entourages militaires d'André Maginot dans les années 1920', in Olivier Forcade, Eric Duhamel and Philippe Vial (eds) *Militaires en République 1870–1962. Les officiers, le pouvoir et la vie publique en France* (Paris: Publications de la Sorbonne, 1999), 143–51. Maginot returned to the rue Oudinot in 1928–29, serving successively in Raymond Poincaré's fifth Cabinet and in Aristide Briand's eleventh.
133 CAOM, affpol/119/D2, Maginot letter to Raphaël Antonetti (Brazzaville), 16 April 1929; André Gide, *Voyage au Congo. Carnets de route* (Paris: Gallimard, 1927).
134 O'Toole, 'The 1928–1931 Gbaya insurrection', 333–6.
135 Karnu's family name was Barka Ngainoumey.
136 SHA, 6H124/D1, sous-dossier 5: 'Cahier de renseignements sur Bouar-Baboua', n.d. 1932; sous-dossier 4: 'La pacification du Pays Baya en 1928–1931', par le Lieutenant-colonel Prugnat, 19 October 1951.
137 O'Toole, 'The 1928–1931 Gbaya insurrection', 341; Elikia M'Bokolo, 'Forces sociales et ideologies dans la décolonisation de l'AEF', *Journal of African History*, 22 (1981), 393; Coquery-Vidrovitch, *Le Congo*, 201–11.
138 SHA, 6H124/D1, sous-dossier 4: 'La pacification du Pays Baya en 1928–1931', par le Lieutenant-colonel Prugnat, 19 October 1951, 2–14.
139 O'Toole, 'The 1928–1931 Gbaya insurrection', 336–42. On the killings in Cameroon

see SHA, 6H124/D1, sous-dossier 5: 'Cahier de renseignements sur Bouar-Baboua', n.d. 1932.

140 CAOM, affpol/663/D1, no. 1010, affpol (Brazzaville), arrête, 13 June 1930: records decisions of the Commission permanente de conseil de gouvernement.

141 SHA, 6H124/D1, sous-dossier 4: 'La pacification du Pays Baya en 1928–1931', par le Lieutenant-Colonel Prugnat, 19 October 1951, 14.

142 AN, Lyautey papers, 475AP/189, 'Rapport d'ensemble sur les opérations de Groupe mobile du Tadla en 1933', 20 October 1933.

143 Summary reports in MAE, série M, vol. 89, Direction des affaires indigènes/SR, 'Rapports Mensuels d'Ensemble du Protectorat', and 7N4093, EMA, Section d'Outre-Mer, 'Bulletins de renseignements mensuels des questions musulmanes, 1937–1940'.

144 William A. Hoisington, Jr, *The Casablanca Connection. French Colonial Policy, 1936–1943* (Chapel Hill NC: University of North Carolina Press, 1984), 29–32. The most detailed account is now Lafuente, *La politique berbère*, 190–241 *passim*.

145 Hoisington Jr, 'Cities in revolt', 433–5.

146 Ageron, 'La politique berbère', 62–5; Irbouh, 'French colonial art education', 284.

147 Ageron, 'La politique berbère', 78–83; Pennell, *Morocco*, 219.

148 Hoisington, Jr, 'Cities in revolt', 436–41.

149 Pennell, *Morocco*, 227–32; Ageron, 'La politique berbère', 79.

150 Hoisington, Jr, 'Cities in revolt', 436, 441–4.

151 Hoisington, Jr, 'French rule and the Moroccan elite', 141–2.

152 In autumn 1933 Ouezzani established a French-language newspaper, *L'Action du Peuple*, in an effort to win over liberal settlers and sympathetic French observers. The paper was banned on 11 May 1934.

153 Hoisington, Jr, *The Casablanca Connection*, 40–51.

154 CADN, Fonds Beyrouth, Cabinet politique, vol. 477/D1, Cabinet politique memo, 'Comparaison entre les divers traits intervenus dans le Proche Orient', n.d. 1936.

155 Khoury, *Syria and the French Mandate*, 458–67.

156 CADN, Fonds Beyrouth, vol. 481/D2, nos 701 and 721, Meyrier (Beirut), reports to Direction Afrique-Levant, 10 and 18 July 1936.

157 Zamir, *Lebanon's Quest*, 233–5.

158 CADN, Fonds Beyrouth, Cabinet politique, vol. 481/D2, no. 70, Meyrier to Foreign Ministry, 10 July 1936. The three Syrian groups mentioned all belonged to an umbrella organisation, the 'Jeunesse Nationale' (National Youth), and stemmed from student organisations in individual towns. In early July 1936 two Jeunesse Nationale members were accused of an apparently motiveless killing in Homs.

159 CADN, Fonds Beyrouth, Cabinet politique, vol. 481/D2, no. 1039/CP, Damascus delegate to Meyrier (Beirut), 17 July 1936.

160 Shambrook, *French Imperialism*, 213–15.

161 Francis Koerner, 'Un Socialiste auvergnat Gouverneur Général d'Indochine. Le cas d'Alexandre Varenne (1925–1928)', *Revue Historique*, 285:1 (1991), 133–45.

162 Tony Smith, 'A comparative study of French and British decolonization', *Comparative Studies in Society and History*, 20:1 (1978), 94.

CHAPTER EIGHT

Anti-colonial nationalism:
The examples of Algeria and Tunisia

This chapter discusses forms of public opposition to empire in two North African territories that typified the differing strands of republican imperialism in the inter-war period. Official commitment to assimilationism in Algeria stood in marked contrast to indirect, associationist rule in the Tunisian protectorate. Yet in both locations, integral nationalist groups were deeply entrenched by 1939. Distinct constituencies of support drove the organisation of early nationalist groups in French North Africa. These included opponents of empire among the colonial immigrant population in French cities, educated bourgeois elites excluded from high office or professional advancement in their home towns, in addition to the rank-and-file cadres of nationalist supporters. The minority of French men and women opposed to colonial rule also helped cultivate a metropolitan environment in which immigrant workers and university students from the colonies could exchange ideas and organise. Differences in the socio-economic background and generational profile of inter-war nationalist leaders were refracted in the wide spectrum of nationalist attitudes to the French colonial presence. Some were unequivocally anti-colonial. Most were not. But all argued for greater rights, freedoms and privileges. They did so by identifying Muslim national communities that pre-existed colonial rule and that were disadvantaged by it. This common thread makes the generic appellation 'nationalist' appropriate to otherwise disparate organisations.

Before 1939 Algeria and Tunisia were not sites of inter-war rebellion comparable to Morocco, Syria or Indochina. As we have seen, armed conflict and nationalist consolidation in these latter territories were intertwined. The emergence of popular nationalist groups in Algeria and Tunisia followed a different path. Immigrant workers in France and Maghrebi university students in French cities coalesced in forming nationalist attitudes and disciplined party organisations. Contacts with French Communists and anti-colonialists – also significant in the emergence of leftist anti-colonial movements in Vietnam and Madagascar – were similarly critical in the North African case. But unlike Madagascar, where, as we shall see in chapter nine, Communist sympathisers among the educated Merina elite and the settler population helped construct an autonomist movement in the 1930s, in Algeria and Tunisia oppositional party politics developed soon after the First World War. The patterns in sub-Saharan French Africa were different again. Mass political parties were largely absent during the inter-war period, and African trade unionism, Sufi brotherhoods and tribal affiliations were more important foci of opposition to French rule. In several assimilated *anciennes colonies*, including Senegal's Four Communes, the French Antilles and New Caledonia, local representatives of French political parties dominated the electoral process to the exclusion of uniquely indigenous political groupings. Algeria stood out as the one large colony where metropolitan political parties competed side by side with local organisations representing both the enfranchised Muslim elite and the much larger disenfranchised Muslim majority. Opposition to French authority in Tunisia was also unusual, primarily because here, more than in any other territory, the major nationalist grouping, the Néo-Destour, worked hand-in-glove with a well established militant trade union movement, the General Confederation of Tunisian Workers (Confédération générale des travailleurs tunisiens). A less distinctive, but crucial, feature in both the Algerian and Tunisian cases is that the dominant nationalist parties to emerge by 1939 remained at the forefront of the continuing struggle for national independence after 1945.

Early opposition to French rule in Algeria

In late nineteenth-century Algeria the Islamic revivalist movement Nahda sought to protect Muslim culture against the corrosive effects of French colonisation. And in the decade before the First World War French-educated members of the Young Algerian movement distinguished between the liberal republican values of 'true France' and the exclusionary colonial policies practised in the empire.[1] These groups privileged cultural opposition, pleading for greater respect of Arab learning and Islamic tradition.[2] Following the 1916 Arab revolt and the disappointments of the Middle East partition between 1918 and 1921, nationalist sentiment and cultural assertiveness among Muslim populations in the Maghreb and the Middle East became more pronounced. The growth of populist supranationalism – based on a sense of belonging to a distinct Muslim community at odds with Western imperialism – throughout the Arab territories of North Africa, the Fertile Crescent and the Arabian peninsula was tied to several factors. Urbanisation, increased literacy rates, the growth of an anti-colonial Arabic press, Islamic revivalism, the impact of the global depression and the mounting international instability of the 1930s all played a part.[3]

Pan-Arab nationalists' identification of a shared Arab heritage reinforced the linguistic and religious ties that defined a greater Arab nation unjustly divided by European partition. By contrast, for those that, in the Egyptian context, Israel Gershoni and James Jankowski term 'territorial nationalists' nationalist thought mirrored the racial distinctiveness of particular Arab nation states.[4] Egypt was a model of both Arab supranationalism and territorial nationalist ideas. It was no coincidence that Abd al-Hamid Ben Badis, Algeria's foremost *ulama* leader, modelled his programme on the actions of Egyptian Muslim scholars led by Mohammad Abduh and Rashid Rida.[5] All variants of oppositional Arab nationalism shared a common trait: each identified foreign rule as the principal obstacle to overcome. The intensification of the Arab–Zionist conflict in the Palestine mandate united Muslims more than any other issue. The Palestine Revolt of 1936–39 catalysed inter-Arab co-operation and hardened popular antagonism to European imperialism in general.[6]

As we saw in chapter two, the institutionalisation of Algeria's second college electoral system through the 1919 Jonnart Law entrenched the second-class status of the Muslim electorate and their Arab and Berber representatives in local and national assemblies. The three financial delegations, the one forum with genuine financial muscle, remained under European control throughout the inter-war period. Democratisation was, of course, never envisaged in a colonial society that reserved political and economic power to the settler population. Yet the *colon* community was sufficiently unnerved by the enfranchisement of 421,000 Muslims to set itself against any constitutional reform for the next generation. Far from breaking the mould of Muslim–settler confrontation in Algerian politics, the 1919 reforms reinforced it. The Jonnart system made co-operative Muslim appointees lackeys of the colonial state. Irrevocably tarred with the colonial brush, these 'Beni Oui Ouis' lost credibility as legitimate representatives of Muslim majority opinion. They left a political void soon to be filled by the secular nationalism of the Etoile Nord-Africaine and the Islamic exclusivity of the Association of Reformist *Ulamas*.[7]

Settler opposition to any blurring of the boundaries between rulers and natives was a constant feature of the political landscape in inter-war Algeria. The first Algiers municipal elections held after the passage of the Jonnart Law were indicative. Emir Khaled, grandson of Abd el-Kadir, and a power-ful symbol of national resistance in the eyes of Algiers Muslims, scored a resounding victory, defeating a string of pro-administration candidates in the November 1919 municipal poll. Khaled's demands for greater Muslim representation in Parliament, the award of citizenship with retention of Muslim status, and the use of Arabic in the Algerian educational system, confirmed that newly enfranchised Muslim male voters were unimpressed by the concessions granted hitherto. The Algiers native affairs division thought otherwise, insisting that the municipal and *djemâa* elections in Algiers, Oran and Tlemcen were dominated by local concerns to the exclusion of anything resembling Algerian 'nationalist' politics. The profusion of Muslim candidates, much encouraged by French officials in order to split potential opposition, was held as affirmation that personal followings and clan rivalries predominated over coherent political programmes. Muslim male voters in rural communes cared about the harvest and the state of the agricultural market, not nationalist abstraction. The Constantine prefecture was alone in acknowledging the strength of anti-French feeling.[8]

The Algiers government annulled the municipal vote after raucous settler protests at the outcome. But Khaled did not go away. His subsequent election to the Algiers general council and the Muslim financial delegation kept him at the forefront of Arab opposition to an intransigent colonial administration. Khaled personified the hopes of the Young Algerian movement. Sometimes compared to the Arab clubs dominated by disenchanted Arab officials and army officers in the Ottoman Middle East before the First World War, the Young Algerian movement emerged somewhat earlier, in the 1880s. However, it achieved national prominence only with the publication of its definitive list of political demands in 1912. Khaled injected new life into the movement after the war. He was an inspiring figurehead and a shrewd political operator. French officials compared him to Egypt's Saad Zaghloul, populist leader of the 1919 revolt against British imperial authority in Cairo. In 1920 the prefect of Algiers even warned the Interior Ministry that Khaled was too powerful a national symbol to risk taking decisive action against. The Algiers government secretariat tried to buy him off instead, promising an undisclosed payout and a generous pension if the Emir would abandon politics.[9]

Khaled was immune to bribery, but he was no nationalist firebrand.[10] His cosmopolitan upbringing in Algeria, Syria and France culminated in graduation from the Lazarist Brothers' College in Damascus and the Saint-Cyr military academy. He was also a decorated French army officer. Khaled represented a cultured urban elite ousted from national, provincial and municipal authority by French colonisation. Their central demand was to share power in a more plural colonial system. The Young Algerians thus campaigned for wider citizenship rights without the prior requirement for renunciation of their personal status as Muslims (the process dubbed 'naturalisation'). Khaled turned assimilationist rhetoric against the colonial system it was supposed to justify, demanding equal rights for Muslims who clearly fulfilled assimilationist criteria for citizenship, whether through education, personal wealth or public service.[11] He also reminded the authorities of Algerian Muslims' contribution to the French war effort. And he exposed government hypocrisy in refusing to implement the Jonnart reforms. These guileless demands for fair treatment made the colonial authorities squirm.[12] Yet Khaled restricted his campaign to elite Muslim participation in Algerian politics. In August 1922 he proposed that Muslims should select two-fifths of the membership of all Algerian Assemblies, a formula devised to leave French hegemony intact while opening access to political and bureaucratic posts to the educated Muslim elite.[13] Colonial autocracy could have survived even had his demands been met. Khaled's speeches and writings, notably in *L'Ikdam*, the Arabic newspaper devoted to his cause, were attuned to the cycle of Algerian national and municipal elections. The Emir made little attempt to rally mass support against the colonial system as a whole.[14] His profound conservatism exposed the Young Algerians' Achilles' heel. By self-definition, they were elitists. The Young Algerian movement overlooked the hardships of most Algerian subjects. In their determination to break into Algeria's administrative system the Young Algerians became an adjunct to the colonial state in the eyes of Islamic leaders and the urban poor.[15]

Khaled recognised that the Young Algerians risked being labelled 'Beni Oui Ouis' desperate to secure an entrée to privileged colonial society. In the early 1920s he began to show more interest in the plight of Algeria's Muslim under-class, using the pages of *L'Ikdam* to denounce educated Muslims who took no interest in their poorer brethren.[16] He was genuinely appalled by the wholesale dispossession of the peasantry, and was painfully aware of the socio-economic gulf separating the wealthy few from the mass of rural poor. In a searing critique of French native policy published in August 1922 he noted that to travel beyond the coastal cities, the model settlements and the fertile flood plain south of Algiers was to step back in time. The destruction of the conquest was everywhere apparent. The supposed benefits of colonisation – roads, schools, hospitals and the rest – were nowhere to be seen.[17]

The gradual emergence of this more radical, populist Khaled sealed his political fate. In 1923 the Algiers authorities moved against him, first sending him into exile, then allowing him to settle in Syria in 1926. 'Khaledism' did not long survive the Emir's departure. Between 1919 and 1923 neither the Young Algerians in general nor Emir Khaled in particular made the transition from elite lobbyists to party politicians. That said, the Emir's ideas did permeate the later activities of the Federation of Elected Muslims (Fédération des élus musulmans), a non-violent, elite grouping that was the natural inheritor of Young Algerianist thinking. So, too, the Emir's assertion of Algeria's Muslim and Arab identity struck a chord with the country's *ulamas* (Koranic instructors) such as Sheikh Tayyib al-'Uqbi, the foremost *ulama* in Algiers, that were otherwise disdainful of Khaled's cosmopolitanism.[18]

After the furore over the 1919 reforms and the rise of Khaledism, the settler community rejected even the narrowest of political concessions to the Muslim majority.[19] In November 1927 Pierre Bordes succeeded the Socialist Maurice Viollette as Algiers governor-general.[20] The outgoing governor was hounded from office by a loose coalition of wealthy settlers. During the 1926 and 1928 budgetary rounds, European members of the Algiers financial delegations blocked Viollette's spending plans, first on social reform, and second on the construction of a local munitions industry.[21] Petitions demanding the governor's dismissal were sent to Premier Poincaré and Sarraut, then responsible for Algeria as Interior Minister. Viollette's crime? To have proposed more equitable tax rises and land reforms to raise peasant living standards. He diverted state funds to irrigation projects, clean water supplies and other public health services of general benefit. He established an Algerian Crédit agricole to provide loan facilities to poor settlers and Muslim smallholders.[22] And Viollette tolerated religious dissent. In 1925 he refused to punish Ahmed Tawfiq al-Madani, a renowned cleric expelled from Tunisia for incitement, for his inflammatory denunciation of assimilationism as a political fraud that sapped Muslim cultural identity. Viollette opted instead to conciliate Islamic leaders in Algiers, founding the 'Progress Club' in the Place du Gouvernement, the capital's administrative centre, as a forum for dialogue between clerics, bourgeois Arab leaders and French officials.[23] Viollette's unbiased approach to inter-communal relations provoked settler fury. In September 1927 Viollette's cabinet staff warned Sarraut of 'a real risk of worse [settler] violence' unless the governor left Algiers soon.[24]

Viollette's resignation on 31 October 1927 revealed the settlers' influence at the heart of government in Paris. And it radicalised previously moderate Muslim politicians in Algeria. The Federation of Elected Muslims, the League for the Rights of Man, Socialist Party representatives, workers' groups and the local civil service association petitioned Viollette to stay.[25] But European members of the financial delegations proved more powerful. They co-ordinated the campaign against the governor, mobilised the Algiers press against him and marginalised Muslim representatives that spoke in his defence. For moderates such as Ferhat Abbas this was a watershed.[26] The bruising experience of Viollette's eviction in 1927 changed the course of Muslim politics in Algeria, but, as Gilbert Meynier has noted, throughout the inter-war period Algeria's Muslim elite were at once fascinated and repelled by the constitutional model of French republican democracy.[27] Again and again, settler politicians and their press allies pilloried the few Algerian Muslims in the upper reaches of local government as subversive nationalists when most were unabashedly francophile and attached to assimilationist ideals.

Until the rise of Islamist movements in North Africa in the 1980s few political analysts privileged the religious component in early Maghrebi nationalism.[28] Empirical evidence suggests that only slowly was the incompatibility between Muslim cultural identity and French colonial rule clearly discerned. For much of the inter-war period even Abd al-Hamid Ben Badis, leader of the Association of Reformist *Ulamas*, concluded that the interests of Islam in Algeria were best served by co-operation with France.[29] The Association was formally established on 5 May 1931 under the presidency of Ben Badis and his deputy, Muhammad al-Bashir al-Ibrahimi.[30] From July 1925 both men worked with like-minded Islamic reformists in producing two periodicals, *al-Muntaquid* and *al-Shihab*, which, much like the Wahabi in Saudi Arabia, advocated a return to the puritanical essence of Islamic observance.[31] There was no talk of evicting the French outright. Ben Badis rejected French suzerainty only when the Algiers authorities clamped down on the Association from 1933 onward. In February that year the Algiers government banned Association *ulama* from preaching in government-controlled mosques. The Algiers Cultural Association, established by Jonnart in 1905 to allow Muslim clerics greater autonomy in mosque administration, was also dissolved. Jean Mirante, director of the Algiers native affairs division, justified this attack on an Islamic institution by claiming that *ulama* teaching fostered Muslim rejection of both colonial authority and the 'correct' Islamic doctrine of officially sanctioned *marabouts* (leaders of popular Sufi orders) in the Algerian interior. The *ulamas* threatened colonial authority precisely because they called upon Muslims to reassert their separate identity as Algerians. Indeed, it was Tayyib al-'Uqbi's teaching at the new mosque on the edge of the Place du Gouvernement that triggered the initial ban. Al-'Uqbi's uncompromising style, equally critical of the assimilated Muslim elite as of French officialdom, suggested that Viollette's vision of inter-communal partnership was a mirage.[32]

It was far easier to deal with Westernised Muslims demanding citizenship rights than to cope with a religious movement that implored its followers to turn away *en masse* from French regulation as both a sacred obligation and a national duty. Yet the *ulamas* did not demand Algerian independence. Al-'Uqbi called for mass naturalisation of the Muslim majority, a viewpoint endorsed by Albert Camus and France's pre-eminent scholar of Islam, Louis Massignon.[33] And Ben Badis used Koranic teachings to impress on Muslim men that subordination to France conflicted with their primary duties under Shari'a law. The *ulamas* warned that development of the French-controlled wage economy threatened the Muslim family by undermining customary gender roles and the inviolability of domestic space. The adulteration of Islamic values by colonialism was blamed for the ills of modern society, from prostitution to illiteracy. After 1933 Ben Badis did not compete for influence within the colonial order; he simply rejected it.[34]

State repression of the reformist *ulamas* climaxed in 1936 when Al-'Uqbi, by then the Association secretary-general, was imprisoned for allegedly killing Bendali Mahmoud, the Maliki Mufti of Algiers. The Mufti questioned the right of the Association of Reformist *Ulamas* to petition the newly elected Popular Front government on behalf of all Muslims. His killing gave the authorities the opportunity to stem the *ulamas'* growing influence, while consolidating ties with the government's traditional Muslim allies, the Sufi *marabouts*.[35] Settler leaders welcomed the resultant crackdown as long overdue. Yet state repression misfired. The *ulamas* adopted a more integral Algerian nationalism, which attracted still greater Muslim support. In al-Bashir al-Ibrahimi's regional power base of Tlemcen, for example, 171 Muslim sponsors supported the foundation in 1936 of an *ulama*-backed 'free school' dedicated to Koranic teaching and a wholly Arabic curriculum. These sponsors included prominent Tlemcen families, but also naturalised French Algerian citizens, serving Muslim army officers, a lawyer and a banker – in other words, a diffuse constituency committed to the preservation of Algeria's cultural integrity.[36]

Economic factors

Mortality rates declined sharply in inter-war Algeria. The registered Muslim population increased from 4,923,186 in 1921 to 6,201,144 in 1936, an increase of 29.5 per cent. Throughout this period, Muslims constituted at least eighty-six per cent of the total population. Most were still tied to the land. In 1919 the government classified nine out of ten Muslim families as peasants.[37] Over the next two decades two economic processes, both equally detrimental to the Muslim majority, converged. The first was the worsening marginalisation of Muslim smallholders within Algeria's agricultural economy. The second, linked with the first, was the sharp growth in internal migration to the colony's principal cities. Decades of French pressure on peasant land radicalised the rural poor. Peasant smallholders became a vital reservoir of nationalist support and helped set the agenda of nationalist demands.[38]

The colonial legal system undermined established patterns of Muslim land ownership and traditional farming practices.[39] Land laws favoured the settler community, denying Muslim rights to common grazing and cultivable land unless written title could be produced. French colonisation displaced Muslim cultivators from ancestral holdings, creating what Mohamed Khenouf describes as an 'ecological disequilibrium'.[40] In 1917 settlers possessed 2.31 million hectares of farmland. By 1940 the figure stood at 2.7 million.[41] Displacement was particularly marked in the fertile, heavily populated plains of the Tell.[42] In densely cultivated areas of eastern Algeria, where Muslim farmers typically worked communal plots of less than 10 hectares, few could prevent settler 'purchase' of their land. Traditional grazing grounds became inaccessible as more land fell under European control, leading to the collapse of Arab livestock holding and the further impoverishment of nomadic Bedouin. Landless Arab peasants forced to sell off animals faced an uncertain future in a settler-dominated pastoral economy as farm workers or sharecroppers (*khammès*) who sold their labour in return for one-fifth of the eventual harvest. These peasant labourers were doubly disadvantaged. They were at the bottom of the colonial cash economy, and their remaining arable plots were insufficient to ensure basic family subsistence. Thus to Khenouf's ecological disequilibrium we should add an economic one, evident in increased peasant migration to the coastal cities and overseas to join the immigrant work force in France.[43]

In their analyses of these changes Charles-Robert Ageron, André Nouschi and Tony Smith reach similar conclusions. Only rarely were Muslim farmers compelled to abandon agriculture entirely. It suited wealthy European estate owners and poorer settler farmers employing only a handful of seasonal workers to maintain the peasant labour supply. Muslim farm workers cost less to employ than their French or Spanish equivalents and were easier to dismiss in times of shortage. Rather than destroying peasant society outright, the injustice of colonialism lay in the impoverishment of Muslim agriculture within the colonial economy.[44] Muslim smallholders lost access to prime arable land and traditional grazing sites, pushing them to cultivate more arid plots that demanded greater labour for less reward. As a result, peasant agricultural output declined steadily over the inter-war period. Grain production *per capita* never recovered to pre-1914 levels before 1939. The national sheep herd fell by 2.5 million between 1919 and 1939. Livestock numbers had declined since the 1860s, but what these statistics do not reveal is that Europeans owned most remaining herds.[45]

Not all Muslim farmers suffered in this way. Algeria's foodstuff exports to France – wheat, citrus fruits, olives and, of course, wine – increased during the 1920s, buoyed by protectionist tariffs and the franc's artificially high value. Abolition of the discriminatory Arab taxes – the *impôts arabes* – in 1919 helped generate *per capita* increases in wheat and maize consumption. The 1920s were not, however, a decade of uninterrupted growth. Bad harvests, localised famines, land expropriation, fluctuating metropolitan demand for wheat and wine, plus government refusal to open Algeria's commodity market to other nations, all limited the scope for Muslim farmers to achieve good returns.[46] None the less, some did thrive. Ahmed Henni has even argued that the expanding French market for agricultural produce precipitated the emergence of a kulak-type middle class of Muslim landowners that farmed for profit by growing crops solely for export. This group often purchased additional land to establish farms of between 10 and 50 hectares with a waged labour force. A tiny minority, these more affluent Muslim landowners formed the backbone of rural support for the moderate, integrationist politicians of the Federation of Elected Muslims.[47]

Henni further contends that the proliferation of modern farming methods, the growth of a cash economy in rural communes, and the few instances of Muslims repurchasing land from European settlers give the lie to Frantz Fanon's characterisation of a monolithic, downtrodden peasantry denied any outlet for wealth creation within colonial society. The number of registered Muslim wine growers in Algeria tripled from 3,280 in 1913 to 9,100 in 1931, although these figures say nothing about the size of farms involved. And the number of *khammès* sharecroppers actually diminished in the 1920s as traditional forms of peasant subsistence declined in the new wage economy.[48] These examples overlook a vital point: namely that by 1914 settlers had already expropriated most prime agricultural land.

Conditions in the 1930s were also very different from the isolated instances of greater rural affluence that Henni describes in the decade after 1919. André Nouschi and Daniel Lefeuvre emphasise the severity of Algeria's socio-economic crisis between 1930 and 1935. The economy stagnated as staple producers lost markets and the industrial sector went into recession.[49] Declining real wages compelled peasant families to fall back on unproductive plots and inadequate livestock. The burden of land and mortgage debts increased.[50] Prior to the franc devaluation of September 1936 Algeria's key exports – wine, wheat, soft fruits and metal ores – were not internationally price-competitive, resulting in greater dependence on the French market. But French demand contracted in the depression, and was further curbed by rival domestically produced goods. Muslim wheat producers, mine workers and peasant day labourers were hard hit by this trade crisis, as were the unemployed Algerian immigrants returning in greater numbers from France. The colony's registered population had risen from 5,231,800 in 1906 to 6,553,400 in 1931. In 1936 it reached 7,234,700. These figures become more striking when we consider the disparity between Muslim and European population growth. Between 1887 and 1926 the registered population of French citizens in Algeria grew from 219,000 to 828,000.[51] But between 1926 and 1936 the settler population increased by some 110,900, the Muslim population by 954,400. The settler community was increasingly outnumbered, its status as a privileged minority harder to conceal.[52]

Additional government measures to restrict Muslims' freedom of movement and curb economic migration to France were introduced from 1924 onward. Tighter regulation on the indigenous work force served several objectives. For one, it met Cartel des gauches anxiety about uncontrolled Algerian immigration, a concern stimulated by abundant signs of French blue-collar racism and union antagonism to employers' use of casual immigrant labour.[53] After the double murder in 1923 of two Parisian women on the rue Fondary by a Kabyle immigrant, Interior Minister Camille Chautemps toughened up immigration checks.[54] Colonial immigrants faced arbitrary repatriation unless they could produce identity cards with photographs, medical certificates and evidence of cash reserves. Once he took over at the Interior Ministry in Poincaré's July 1926 Cabinet, Albert Sarraut increased police surveillance of colonial immigrants, targeting Maghrebi nationalist groups above all.[55] The Algerian prefectures also policed internal travel between communes to control Muslim economic migration and monitor criminal behaviour. Stricter regulation played well with settler representatives demanding that the Muslim majority be kept out of European areas – residential and commercial – other than for work purposes.[56]

European penetration of the Berber uplands of Kabylia was significantly weaker than in the Arab flatlands south of the coastal fringes. Kabylia was difficult to farm, and the Berber population was less tied to the cycle of agricultural production. Artisan production such as tanning, and the small-scale manufacture of specialist goods, from jewellery and pottery to gunpowder, was increasingly prevalent. Kabylia was also the principal centre of rural Algerian emigration to the coastal cities and, more notably, to France. The colonial authorities viewed Berbers favourably next to their Arab compatriots. Mountainous Kabylia was even likened to the Auvergne: a peasant heartland of 'true France'.[57] And Kabyle Berbers were stereotyped as a race apart: a redoubtable community of ancient Latinate stock resistant to Arab Islamisation. The Berber majority in Morocco was similarly typecast in the colonial imagination, largely to undercut the power of the Arab Sultanate.[58] Yet the myth that North Africa's Berbers were less Islamic and therefore more open to Western influence than the Arab population intensified French suspicion of Kabyle immigrants, considered naturally susceptible to leftist ideology.[59] This became increasingly problematic. Kabylia's Berber-dominated Tizi–Ouzou region produced more inter-war colonial immigrants than any other area of comparable size in the empire. Temporary economic migration was embedded in Kabyle culture by the 1920s. Young men in Berber villages were expected to seek industrial employment in Algiers or France, and relied on their older kinfolk and fellow villagers to find them jobs in the mines of northern France, the factories of Paris and Marseilles, or the artisan workshops of Algiers. Industrial employers sought out new workers with similar backgrounds and expectations to those already employed. Existing employees helped relatives and neighbours to join them. Between 1914 and 1929, for instance, French mine owners in Epinac-les-Mines employed a Kabyle agent to recruit annual quotas of workers.[60]

Population pressure in the Algerian countryside fuelled urbanisation, leading to greater overcrowding in the cities. Settlers benefited most from new housing programmes, rents being prohibitively expensive to the indigenous economic migrants crammed into city *casbahs* and makeshift suburban settlements.[61] In the early 1930s Algiers witnessed the emergence of its first shanty towns, or *bidonvilles*, named after the gas bottles (*bidons*) frequently cannibalised to build corrugated iron shelters on the fringes of established suburbs.[62] But it was in the acute overcrowding of the inner city *casbahs*, encircled by European-controlled commercial districts and suburbs, that nationalism fomented. The oppositional community of the Algiers *casbah* that came to prominence in the war of independence in the 1950s originated in the miserable housing conditions and economic hardship of the 1930s when many of the future leadership of the National Liberation Front grew to adulthood.

Overseas contacts

The centralised structure of the imperial system, and its hegemonic assertion of French cultural supremacy, encouraged indigenous elites from Vietnam to Morocco to send their sons to study in colonial *lycées* or in metropolitan universities. Articulate, francophone colonial students supplied the cadres and journalistic voices of what Mahfoud Kaddache terms the *avant-garde révolutionnaire* of anti-colonial nationalism.[63] There are close parallels between the Vietnamese and Chinese students drawn to Communist internationalism in 1920s Paris and the *negritude* movement of the 1930s which brought together francophone African, Caribbean and Madagascan students such as Léopold Sédar Senghor, Tiemorho Garan Kouyaté, Aimé Césaire, Gaston Monnerville and Jean Ralaimongo with leading Afro-American campaigners.[64] In the 1920s West African students in Paris drew on pan-Africanism, both to express their criticisms of French colonialism and to distinguish them from African proponents of assimilationism such as Blaise Diagne. Indeed, hostility to Diagne's avowed commitment to assimilationism became a focal point for younger pan-Africanists determined to assert their distinct cultural identity. As one might expect, there was a powerful undercurrent of intergenerational conflict in colonial student politics. The Ligue universelle pour la défense de la race noire and its successor groups, the Comité de la défense de la race nègre and the Ligue de la défense de la race nègre, were forcing grounds for a rising generation of young French African nationalists that rose to greater prominence in the 1930s and 1940s. Many of these overseas students in inter-war Paris also worked side by side in an umbrella organisation, the Committee of Inter-colonial Union.[65]

Jean Ralaimongo, for one, a wartime member of Madagascar's first proto-nationalist group, the VVS, sharpened his journalistic skills and organisational abilities through work with Communist-affiliated groups in Paris such as the Anti-imperialist League and International Red Aid, as well as the PCF.[66] So, too, did Tiemorho Garan Kouyaté, a native of French Sudan, who was among the first generation of African students to link colonial emancipation with Communist internationalism, initially as organiser of the League for the Defence of the Negro Race and then, from 1933, as founder of the League for the Independence of the Peoples of Senegal and French Sudan, an overtly pro-Communist group.[67] More famously, Nguyen Ai Quoc, better known as Ho Chi Minh, followed a similar path to Ralaimongo in early 1920s Paris. Ho was the principal contributor on Vietnamese matters to the first anti-colonial newspaper run by colonial students in Paris, *Le Paria Tribune des populations des colonies*. Founded in 1922, *Le Paria* (*The Outcast*) combined the exposure of colonial oppression with Marxist ideological content.[68] A vibrant anti-colonial press developed in the 1920s. The limited circulation of papers such as *Le Paria*, *La Nation Annamite*, *El Ouma* (*The Islamic Community*), and *Le cri des nègres* was no guide to their importance. Ho's early journalistic experience and his contacts with French Socialists and Communists in Paris deepened his commitment to anti-colonialism, Vietnamese nationalism and Communism well before he left for southern China in 1924 to work with Comintern representatives in Canton in building a Vietnamese Communist movement. Future Moroccan nationalist leader Allal el-Fassi, Néo-Destour founder Habib Bourguiba, and Senegalese leader Léopold Sedar Senghor also sharpened their rhetorical skills as young journalists in Paris.[69]

Much like the anti-colonial press, the statements of colonial student organisations in inter-war France are less well remembered than the individuals who took part. Tunisian nationalist leaders – including Habib Thameur, Slimane ben Slimane and Mongi Slim – cut their teeth in the largest, most prominent such group, the Association des étudiants musulmans nord-africains (North African Muslim Students' Association, AEMNA), founded by a fellow Tunisian student, Chadly ben Mustafa Khaïrallah in December 1927. Most North African, Syrian and Lebanese students in France were caught between support for secular socialism, pan-Arabism and the unity of the Muslim community.[70] Student associations ensured unity in diversity among Muslims studying in French universities and colleges, their organisational platform facilitating links with political parties and trade unions.[71] Dominated by Tunisian and Moroccan students – more numerous and better funded than their colleagues from Algeria – the AEMNA had close ties with Tunisia's Destour Party, the Moroccan free school movement, the Etoile Nord-Africaine, and Shakib Arslan's Syrian–Palestinian Congress.[72] If anything, the experience of political liberties in France sharpened their awareness of colonial injustice. And their freedom of expression should not be overstated. The Paris prefecture of police took a close interest in AEMNA meetings. Hundreds of colonial students, exiles and intellectuals, Khaïrallah among them, were expelled for seditious activity.

Student activism was a forcing ground for nationalist ideas, but it was among Algerian immigrant workers in France that integral nationalism, leftist idealism and political militancy first coalesced in the inter-war period. Marginalised and sometimes vilified by employers and co-workers alike, the colonial immigrant communities in French cities were particularly receptive to an emerging nationalist rhetoric that praised their cultural resilience.[73] The tendency to infantilise colonial immigrants as irresponsible, insalubrious and incapable of autonomous organisation was by no means confined to the French right. Racial stereotyping of this kind was fundamental to the PCF's official designation of Algeria as 'a nation in formation'. The phrase distanced the Communists from untrammelled colonial domination, yet it justified continued French rule on the grounds that Algerians lacked the political maturity necessary for self-government. Party leader Maurice Thorez, the main proponent of this formulation, was loath to admit that French Communists favoured Gallic colonialism over Muslim nationalism, but such was the case. In Thorez's assessment colonial industrialisation was essential if Communists were to win support among an emergent colonial proletariat. PCF leaders were dismissive of the integral nationalism of Algeria's one mass-based leftist party, Messali Hadj's Etoile Nord-Africaine (North African Star, ENA). 'Messalism' represented a new strain of Algerian nationalism: modernist, secular, and committed to national independence rather than limited concessions to favoured social groups among Algeria's Muslims.[74] The ENA came of age at the inaugural Brussels congress of the League against Imperialism and Colonial Oppression in 1927.[75] The League was sponsored by the Comintern, but was a broader coalition than that implies. It united colonial nationalists, immigrant leaders, European pacifists and intellectuals, as well as Communist fellow travellers. Albert Einstein, Labour MP Fenner Brockway, Jawaharlal Nehru and Victor Basch, a key figure in the League for the Rights of Man, ranked among its more famous supporters. The ENA figured among the best organised of its colonial groups alongside the South African National Congress.[76] It took the stand to become the first nationalist party to call openly for Algerian independence.

The construction of Algerian nationalism

The Brussels congress signified a fundamental shift in Algerian nationalism. The ENA leadership was the first to frame its demands in terms of a distinct nation state. Algerians began the process, but others soon followed. The Comité d'Action Marocaine (Moroccan Action Committee) and the Néo-Destour (New Constitution Party) made national independence their ultimate goal.

Yet in the late 1920s most opposition to French rule in the Maghreb was still articulated as cultural self-defence. In Algeria the Federation of Elected Muslims and the *ulamas* championed Islamic institutions, education and learning. In Tunisia the Destour movement attacked French infringements of beylical authority. And in Morocco the Salafiyyist free school movement defended Koranic teaching and Morocco's Islamic cultural heritage as part of a wider resistance to the cultural assimilation of alien Western values.[77] Five free schools – denoting the absence of state regulation – were set up in Fez by graduates of the city's Qaraouiyne University. Three more followed in Rabat and one in Casablanca. Some school staff later made the transition to proto-nationalist secret societies such as the *zawiya* set up in Fez in 1930.[78] The government's introduction of the hated Berber *dahir* in May that year boosted popular support for Moroccan nationalism precisely because it challenged a key pillar of Islamic authority: Shari'a law implemented through the Sultanate. The *dahir* therefore struck at the legitimacy of a Muslim Moroccan 'nation' composed of Arabs and Berbers alike. This perceived attack on Moroccan national unity catalysed the shift from cultural preservation to an overtly political nationalism that privileged individual rights and constitutional freedoms. Former student journalists were central to this transition, con- tributing to the journals *Maghreb* and *L'Action du Peuple*, which laid down the core demands of the Moroccan Action Committee during 1932–33. The country's first nationalist political party, the Moroccan Action Committee listed these demands in a fifteen-chapter Reform Plan submitted to the Rabat residency and Foreign Minister Pierre Laval on 1 December 1934. The Reform Plan set the agenda for nationalist opposition in Morocco until the detention of Moroccan Action Committee leaders in late 1937 restored a semblance of calm to the protectorate.[79]

Algerian integral nationalism posed a greater threat. The Parti du Peuple Algérien (PPA, Algerian People's Party), established, like its ENA forebear, under the direction of Messali Hadj, utterly rejected Algeria's assimilation to France.[80] Returning to Algeria from France on 2 August 1936 Messali Hadj electrified the crowd that greeted him at Algiers' main football stadium. 'I bent down and I picked up a handful of [Algerian] soil and I said to myself that this earth cannot be sold. The entire people are its heirs. You don't sell your country! You don't assimilate your country!'[81] Eight months later on 11 March 1937 the PPA political bureau held its inaugural meeting before 300 immigrant workers at Nanterre in the Paris suburbs. The new party set itself against the sectarian interests of the Muslim elite from which most indigenous political leaders sprang. PPA leaders eschewed the Islamic revivalism of the *ulama* and the elite interests of the Federation of Elected Muslims, claiming instead to represent all oppressed Algerians, regardless of race, class or religion, under the slogan 'Neither assimilation nor separation, but emancipation'.[82]

The core constituency of the ENA and later PPA remained immigrant Algerian workers embittered by endemic French racism that restricted their economic opportunities, curtailed their freedom of movement and denigrated their cultural inheritance. Messalists appealed to Algerians to connect their distinct ethnicity with the needs of the Algerian nation. The discrimination they suffered as individuals mirrored the oppression of the Algerian national community as a whole. ENA supporters also evoked the rhetoric of 1789, challenging the French authorities to live up to republican universalist ideals of democracy, equality and common citizenship.[83] Interviewed by the radical journal *La Justice* on 17 August 1937, Messali Hadj depicted Algerian nationalism as heir to the French Revolution. PPA members were true Jacobins: supporters of democratic choice and the right of the poor to overthrow a feudal colonial order. Yet even this secular nationalism was, by default, pro-Islamic for the simple reason that Algeria's right to majority rule was bound to result in the reassertion of its distinct Muslim culture.[84]

French governments, Algiers officials and the settler lobby still maintained that Algeria was a French construction built on virgin soil from the administrative chaos of the Ottoman era. The concept of the Algerian nation as either Muslim, oriental and pre-colonial or French, Latinate and Westernised was fiercely contested. Was Abd el-Kadir the leader of a national community facing foreign oppression? Or was he just a tribal emir whose resistance to French expansion between 1835 and 1847 represented the last gasp of a dying feudal order? Did the vast expropriation of Muslim agricultural land in the late nineteenth century signify the destruction of traditional Algerian society or the construction of an entirely new agrarian state by settler pioneers? Did the introduction of the *indigénat* in 1874 institutionalise racial oppression of the indigenous majority to whom separate, harsher legal penalties applied or confirm that the French alone brought judicial coherence to Algeria?[85] The most contentious issue in pre-war Algerian politics was bound up with these questions. If, as the French authorities insisted, Algeria was a product of French initiative, what did the Muslim majority have to do to earn admission to this new society? If the answer was to assimilate into French culture, then how could France justify withholding the economic and educational opportunities as well as the basic political freedoms essential for any Muslims to emulate their French masters?

Until 1936 Muslim political engagement in the politics of Algerian constitutional reform was essentially restricted to an indigenous elite committed to extend the rights and privileges of Muslims within the colonial order. The ENA may have been founded a decade earlier, but it was based in France. In the early 1930s the Association of Reformist *Ulamas* did more to transform nationalist discourse in Algeria's cities by spurning reform proposals whose underlying purpose was to tie political freedoms to the adoption of French cultural values, something that Muslims of conscience could not do. But the political impact of these arguments was diminished because *ulama* supporters never developed the sophisticated party structure of leading religious groups in other Arab states, such as the Muslim Brotherhood or the Young Men's Muslim Association in Egypt.[86] And too few Muslims served in Algeria's colonial bureaucracy to constitute something akin to the bourgeois *effendiyya* class of Muslim junior officials so critical in the nationalist politics of Egypt and Iraq.[87] Those Muslims that had acquired positions in commune, prefecture or even central government were generally of two types: Europeanised and French-educated or deeply conservative and reconciled to the colonial order. The restrictions on Muslim political activity, the absence of basic rights of association, plus the illiteracy and grinding poverty of the urban poor and the rural peasantry, further impeded organised nationalist protest. It was no coincidence that integral nationalism developed outside Algeria, among the immigrant community in France. The under-class of Algerian immigrants in inter-war French cities had the social cohesion necessary to a unified movement. Their shared experience of low-paid jobs, poor housing and racial discrimination fed their militancy.

It would be wrong, however, to view the Muslim poor in Algeria as peripheral to the growth of anti-colonial nationalism. Popular support for the ENA/PPA spread quickly from France to Algeria, assisted by the constant cycle of economic trans-migration across the Mediterranean. The nationalist presence certainly varied between town and countryside, fertile plains and Saharan interior. Yet it would also be misleading to assume that urban Algerian workers were drawn to the leftist secularism of the ENA/PPA, while peasant villagers favoured the *ulamas'* Islamic revivalism. Returning Algerian immigrants unlocked the simmering resentment felt by their compatriots left behind in rural communes. Peasants, encouraged by the French authorities to channel their political energies into local *djemâa* councils, subverted the system by selecting candidates affiliated to the ENA and, later, the PPA as their *djemâa* representatives. Nationalist party politics penetrated to the very base of local government organisation in rural Algeria before 1939.[88]

Local economic conditions affected support for nationalist parties. Between 1937 and 1939 the PPA made its greatest inroads in areas where settler land ownership and control of agricultural markets were most pronounced. Labour conditions were highly significant. Industries that adopted modern production methods were susceptible to nationalist agitation among shopfloor workers performing repetitive tasks in a constrained working environment. Canning factories, bottling plants, textile manufacturers and, especially, mineworks became focal points of political activity. In the entire southern territories the mining centres of Touggourt and Ghardaïa were the sole areas to witness nationalist unrest in the years of Popular

Front government.[89] Personality politics also played a part. The eastern Algerian origins of Messali Hadj and Ferhat Abbas were pivotal to their powerful support networks in Constantine towns such as Sétif, Guelma, Bougie, Kherrata and Philippeville. Another *Constantinois*, Dr Mohamed Bendjelloul, leader of the Federation of Elected Muslims, drew audiences of 1,200 to 8,000 in these towns during an August 1937 lecture tour after the collapse of Popular Front reforms.[90] In the urban centres of Constantine, as in Kabylia, higher levels of Muslim emigration and literacy nourished contested popular politics. More often than not, however, Algerians backed several organisations at once. Allegiance to the PPA did not preclude support for reformist *ulamas*, and a respected local councillor might attract the votes of Muslims nominally attached to rival political groups. In the late 1930s Algerian prefectures predicted that the survival of this clientage system would impede the growth of disciplined mass parties capable of mobilising voter support in local and national elections.[91]

Algerian politicians were sometimes exasperated by the fluidity of their rank-and-file support. Over the summer of 1937 PPA activists infuriated at Bendjelloul's reluctance to speak out against French detention of Messali Hadj felt compelled to attend Federation of Elected Muslims meetings in the knowledge that many in the audience supported both groups. The Association of Reformist *Ulamas* campaigned alongside the atheistic Algerian Communist Party for a boycott of cantonal elections in September 1937. Algerians accepted these contradictions knowing that each organisation opposed the existing order.[92] But the fact remains that factionalism, party splits and bitter rivalries retarded the development of a unified nationalist movement. In 1938 the Federation of Elected Muslims, still the leading moderate Muslim voice, split into regional groups. Bendjelloul's Constantine federation, the movement's founding section, detached itself and became the moving force of a new coalition, the Rassemblement Franco-Musulman Algérien (RFMA), launched on 31 July 1938. This new grouping aligned Bendjelloul's followers with the Association of Reformist *Ulamas*. Six weeks earlier, on 9 June 1938, Bendjelloul and Ben Badis attended the opening of the Sidi Lakhdar*medersa* in Constantine. The ceremony capped a developing partnership between them. Bendjelloul supported *ulama* calls for Muslim unity and greater Islamic observance; Ben Badis backed Bendjelloul's efforts to win political influence in Algiers.[93] There was less unity between them over core demands. Bendjelloul's primary interest in additional voting rights, constitutional reforms and wider access to French citizenship was hard to reconcile with Ben Badis's rejection of the Europeanisation of Algerian society and his call for the institutionalisation of a Muslim educational system. Few were surprised when conflict re-emerged between the two. In 1939 the *ulamas* struck a more militant tone, criticising Bendjelloul's lavish personal expenditure and calling for a genuinely representative Muslim national assembly in Algeria.[94]

The split within the Federation of Elected Muslims over the summer of 1938 provoked another decisive realignment. On 28 July 1938 Ferhat Abbas announced the formation of a new party, the Union Populaire Algérienne (UPA). In the words of his biographers Benjamin Stora and Zakya Daoud, the foundation of the UPA 'consummated the rupture' between Ferhat Abbas and Mohamed Bendjelloul. Where Bendjelloul chose the tried and trusted tactic of an electoral coalition of like-minded notables, Abbas embraced the Messalist concept of a mass 'party of the people for the people'. The UPA, he declared, would canvass support in *souks*, cafés and city slums. The UPA programme included a minimum wage and basic primary education for all alongside more familiar demands for racial equality, wider voting and citizenship rights.[95] It also broke with the RFMA in its emphasis on Algeria's distinct national identity and its rejection of the 'eastern' obscurantism of the *ulamas*.[96] Ferhat Abbas may have respected Messali's organisational tactics, but he was far less radical. He did not call for independence, but envisaged a Franco-Algerian relationship built on partnership rather than colonial dependence. These grand words had limited impact. The UPA made few inroads into PPA support beyond Abbas's stronghold of Constantine, and the party leadership remained divided over its reform proposals.

Within the Association of Reformist *Ulamas* the long-standing differences between Ben Badis and Sheikh al-'Uqbi receded in 1938. Al-'Uqbi signalled his partial retirement from public life, having been released following police investigation of the 1936 killing of Bendali Mahmoud. But *ulama* clerics were always held together by their sense that colonialism threatened the very fabric of Muslim culture and Islamic teaching. Speakers lined up to reiterate *ulama* demands for Arabic schooling and the 're-Islamisation' of Algeria at the Association's annual assembly in Algiers in late September 1938.[97] Whereas the *ulamas* consolidated their local influence in the late 1930s, the PPA faced more formidable obstacles between 1937 and 1939. Messali and a clutch of senior PPA leaders were by then under house arrest, in prison or in exile. Police informants infiltrated PPA meetings and reported activists' movements. The *sûreté* broke up PPA gatherings. In June 1939 the Algiers prefecture simply annulled council elections once it became clear that a PPA candidate would win.[98]

True to its origins among the Maghrebi immigrant community in France, in the late 1930s the Messalist leadership was closer to the principal nationalist groups in Morocco and Tunisia than to the UPA or other elite groups in Algeria. The Moroccan Action Committee and Néo-Destour were more conducive partners to the PPA than rival Algerian parties committed to retain constitutional ties with France. The *ulamas* remained suspicious of the PPA's leftist rhetoric but shared the party's pan-Maghrebi outlook. Much as Messalists cultivated links with like-minded nationalists in the neighbouring protectorates, so by 1937 Ben Badis was committed to establish an *ulama* association spanning the three French North African territories.[99]

The Algerian Communist Party (Parti Communiste Algérien, PCA) suffered comparable state repression to the ENA/PPA after 1925, when PCA membership and the party newspaper, *La Lutte sociale*, were first proscribed by governor-general Viollette following settler outrage at the party's anti-militarist campaign against the Rif war. Equal victimisation was no basis for co-operation between them. More promising was their initial enthusiasm for Popular Frontism in 1935–36.[100] Throughout the 1930s, however, underlying antagonism between the PCA and the ENA/PPA endured. Messalists accused French Communists of conspiring in the government ban imposed on the ENA in January 1937.[101] Disappointed by the failure of Popular Front reforms, and faced with a renewed wave of state repression, in February 1938 the PPA rejected co-operation with Léon Blum's second government.[102] Messali's followers also resented the PCA's efforts to 'Algerianise' its membership cadres and 'Arabise' its image, a policy the settler-dominated Algerian Communist movement had pursued since the Comintern issued general instructions to colonial Communist movements to seek mass indigenous support in July 1924. PCA efforts to indigenise were a failure.[103] In 1936 the PCA was still rooted among settler workers and intellectuals in Algiers and Oran. There was something phoney to the PCA central committee's enthusiasm for the mandatory teaching of Arabic in schools, something Machiavellian in its approaches to the Algerian Muslim Congress, the reformist *ulamas* and a lesser known creation of the Popular Front years, the Bloc des organisations musulmanes d'Oranie. These manoeuvres were not completely fruitless. By 1938 increasing numbers of PPA supporters in Constantine department, the heartland of Messalist nationalism, joined the PCA as well. The process cut both ways. In November 1938 Ahmed Boumendjel, long-serving lawyer for the ENA/PPA, won a seat on Algiers municipal council thanks to cross-party backing from PPA and PCA.[104]

As preparations for war intensified in 1939 some Algerian political groups fell into line with French policy. Prefects, mayors, *sûreté* officials and army intelligence officers took full advantage of the Daladier government's willingness to allow them a free hand in the repression of Muslim political activity. A fortnight after the outbreak of war in September the Algiers *sûreté* concluded that 'the activities of the various political parties [in Algeria] have virtually ceased'.[105] Most pleasing was the attitude of the forty-year-old Ferhat Abbas. Too old for the first call-up, Abbas still rejoined his former regiment, telling supporters in his home town of Sétif that he felt duty-bound to suspend all political activity and fight for France.[106] The Association of Reformist *Ulamas* also deferred to French wishes, cancelling its annual September Congress in Algiers. Faithful to their assimilationist ideals, senior leaders of the Federation of Elected Muslims endorsed the French war effort.[107]

More militant organisations were laid low. PPA leader Messali Hadj was under constant police surveillance at his brother-in-law Mohamed Mamchaoui's home in Tlemcen. The Algerian Communist Party, along with its French counterpart, was soon banned outright.[108] Far from disappearing, the underlying economic and social causes of Muslim alienation would soon loom larger than ever. There was no reversal of the decades of land seizures, no end to the institutionalised discrimination against Muslim workers and peasants. Health and educational provision remained pitiful, the welfare net still little more than that provided by Islamic charitable bequests. Imperial patriotism did not run deep among the Muslim poor.

Tunisia

Nationalist protest in Tunisia provides a useful comparison with events in Algeria. Despite their proximity, the two territories were, in theory at least, ruled very differently. Tunisian nationalism in the early 1920s was an elitist, exclusive affair dominated by the country's Arab bourgeoisie. But national politics was transformed by a major dock strike in August 1924. There were by then over 100,000 urban industrial workers in Tunisia, including over 45,000 Europeans organised into local branches of French trade unions.[109] Muslim dockers in the ports of Tunis and Bizerta broke ranks with their European co-workers and instead aligned with young Tunisian nationalists in the Destour movement who had launched a workers' co-operative two months earlier in June 1924. This new generation of nationalist leaders led the two most important nationalist groups to emerge in inter-war Tunisia: the Néo-Destour party and the Confédération générale des travailleurs tunisiens (CGTT), a national trade union confederation dedicated to Muslim workers' rights and Tunisian self-reliance.[110] Both organisations rejected French suzerainty and the reformist gradualism of the established Destour party.

In November 1924 M'hamed Ali and Tahar Haddad drew up the UGTT statutes, having successfully mobilised mass support for the striking dockers in Tunis and Bizerta. State reaction was swift. CGTT leaders were imprisoned in 1925, and the movement was bitterly opposed by its CGT rival. The foundation of the CGTT was none the less a quantum leap forward, not least as the grass-roots strength of the Tunisian labour movement became a counterfoil to the factionalism of the nationalist parties.[111] CGTT organisers were unequivocally anti-colonial, seeing Tunisian capitalism and French colonialism as two sides of the same coin. Indigenous workers suffered racial and class discrimination, and were systematically excluded from any share in the wealth generated by their labour.[112]

After the 1924 dock strikes Tunisian opinion divided along two fault lines. The first was the division between modernisers and traditionalists, often expressed as a conflict between those that embraced Western forms of social organisation and those that regarded such change as inimical to Tunisia's Muslim identity. The second split was between the proponents of mass politics and elitist notables that exerted influence through older systems of clientage. In 1933–34 the dominant voice in Tunisian nationalism – the Destour movement – split irrevocably. Radicals formed the Parti Libéral Constitutionaliste Tunisien, better known as Néo-Destour. Its leadership was Europeanised in educational background and intellectual formation. Several had French university degrees and trained as lawyers, doctors or pharmacists.[113] None the less, the two branches of the Destour movement stemmed from common social roots and similar economic background. French-speaking bourgeois urban Arabs dominated both. Néos was reluctant to concede this, attacking the established Destour movement as *trop embourgeoisé* because it remained aloof from the Tunisian masses. But the singular difference between them was a matter not of class but of generation. As their name implied, Néo-Destour's founders were younger, more Westernised and less connected with the apparatus of the beylical state.[114]

Destour drew most of its support in Tunis, while Néo-Destour garnered wider backing in provincial towns and the outlying Sahel. But the two factions were less divided on local issues than over questions of organisation and tactics. Both wings of the Destourian movement sought national independence, and only a small minority within Néo-Destour advocated social revolution. The distinguishing principle of Néo-Destour was its avowed modernism. It copied the PCF model of a central political bureau, disciplined regional federations and a network of local party cells as the first point of contact with grass-roots party members. Its programme of secular nationalism facilitated co-operation with the Tunisian socialist movement and the CGTT.[115]

The Old Destour movement and the academics and *ulamas* trained in the university of the Zitouna Grand Mosque in Tunis typified the traditionalist elite. By the time of the 1934 schism Old Destour notables seemed increasingly self-serving and irrelevant to a population on the brink of starvation. The senior echelons of the Zitouna Grand Mosque, dominated by aristocratic families of the northern cities, faced mounting criticism for their failure to connect with the suffering of the people. A power struggle developed between 1930 and 1933 within the mosque establishment as disaffected students led by Tahar Ben Achour insisted that Zitouna should defend the interests of the entire Muslim population. This contest paralleled that between the two branches of the Destour movement.[116] From 1934 onward Tunisia's younger generation of nationalist leaders drew their following from a Muslim under-class driven into chronic poverty in the depression years. Mass urban protest, popular committees, trade union organisations and women's groups all coalesced as poverty, unemployment and famine conditions gripped Tunisia between 1931 and 1935.[117]

Néo-Destour also won important support among Tunisian women. In the early 1930s women's organisations in Tunisia were largely confined to the bureaucratic elite and prominent Muslim clerical families in Tunis. On 29 February 1932 the wife of Resident-general Manceron and two Tunisian princesses announced the creation of the Société des Dames Musulmanes, effectively a high-class dining society that raised money for disaster victims. This was far removed from the feminist women's association that Tunisian journalist Hédi Laabidi had tried to establish in support of Tahar Haddad's emancipationist programme discussed in chapter five.

Modelled on the more militant women's movement then coalescing in Egypt, Laabidi tried but failed to establish an equivalent Tunisian association.[118] Instead, a more socially conservative group, the Tunisian Muslim Women's Union (Union musulmane des femmes de Tunisie, UMFT), came to prominence in Tunis during the Popular Front interlude. The UMFT drew up its statutes in 1936. These stressed civic duty, moral instruction, and wider access to education above the more contentious issues raised by Haddad and Laabidi six years earlier.[119] Significantly, the UMFT retained close links with the Zitouna Grand Mosque, and avoided police sanctions by stressing its religious credentials. UMFT president, Bchira Ben Mrad, was married to a Zitouna cleric, and was the daughter of Tunisia's 'Sheikh al Islam', Mohammed Salah Ben Mrad, the former antagonist of Tahar Haddad. Under Bchira Ben Mrad's leadership the UMFT organised charity fund-raisers for male Tunisian university students studying in France. It confined its support for women's education to a campaign for universal primary education for girls. The UMFT never challenged the Muslim gender hierarchy, but it did lend support to Néo-Destour. In their first overtly political action, the twelve women of the UMFT executive bureau led calls for the release of nationalist detainees rounded up two years earlier on 3 September 1934. The UMFT's greater clarity over nationalist politics than women's emancipation mirrored that of the nationalist leadership. Progressive nationalist leaders in the Maghreb remained ambivalent about Muslim women's public role. In the 1920s Habib Bourguiba rejected enfranchisement for women. But after he broke with Old Destour to lead its Néo-Destour rival, he endorsed women's participation in nationalist protest. Wassila Ben Ammar, his future wife, worked with Bchira Ben Mrad in the UMFT. And in 1938–39 Bourguiba's nieces, Saïda and Chadlia

Bouzgarrou, led demonstrations against the detention of Néo-Destour organisers. Both were jailed for a month for disrupting Premier Edouard Daladier's state visit to Tunis on 3 January 1939.[120]

Radicalism among Tunisian men and women was exacerbated by the severe deflationary policies and harsher police repression that characterised Marcel Peyrouton's three-year term as Tunis resident-general between 1933 and 1936.[121] Peyrouton's appointment in 1933 signified the first Daladier government's determination to crack down on dissent in the North African territories.[122] Peyrouton was instructed to make the cuts necessary to restore a balanced budget, and told not to let nationalist protest stand in his way.[123]

The French authorities thus responded quickly to Néo-Destour militancy.[124] In May 1933 the residency secured wider decree powers to intern individuals suspected of subversion for up to two years without trial. Néo-Destour was officially banned by decree on 31 May 1933. Three pro-nationalist newspapers, L'Action Tunisienne, La Voix du Tunisie and the Voix du Peuple, were also proscribed. Public reaction was muted. Néo-Destour activists pressed reluctant shopkeepers and market vendors in Tunis to cease trading for three days in protest at the ban. The capital's tram service was boycotted, as were conspicuous French products such as tobacco.[125] Tunisia's beylical administration caused the residency greater concern, leading Peyrouton to justify repression as a defence of Tunisia's monarchy.[126] After a wave of violent protests in the summer of 1934, in September Peyrouton dispatched eight senior Néo-Destour leaders to internal exile, invoking article 3 of the 1881 Treaty of Bardo by which France pledged to protect the Tunisian dynasty against any threat.[127] These sentences brought the total number of nationalist organisers in internal exile to twenty-two. With senior leaders in detention, in February 1935 the day-to-day running of Néo-Destour fell to a more moderate figure, Chadly Khaïrallah, a former official of the beylical administration and the son of the Bey's ex-chief of protocol. Residency tactics soon became clear – to sow dissension in Néo-Destour ranks. Peyrouton planned to exploit Khaïrallah's loyalty to the Bey as the lever to split the Néo-Destour. Khaïrallah was expected to favour dialogue with the beylical administration and the residency over the detainees' known preference for continued protest. Peyrouton approved further sanctions against unlicensed meetings and a stricter regime for the detainees to help tip the balance.[128] By late 1935 the residency's hard line seemed to be working. Fearful of further arrests, in September 1935 Néo-Destour rejected Communist proposals for a united front.[129]

The election of the Popular Front in May 1936 – discussed at greater length in the next chapter – led to feverish anticipation among educated Muslims of major constitutional and economic reforms in North Africa.

Rising public expectations triggered Néo-Destour's breakthrough as a mass movement. Party leaders were released as part of the Blum government's general colonial amnesty for political prisoners. Press restrictions were lifted and greater freedom of assembly was restored. The introduction of labour reforms modelled on the June 1936 Matignon industrial accords in France encouraged Néo-Destour to cement ties with a CGTT leadership eager to make use of newly granted rights to strike action and collective bargaining. And there was a more conciliatory face at the residency. On 21 March Armand Guillon replaced Peyrouton as resident-general. The new appointee backed Popular Front reforms, and had direct experience of industrial disputes and urban poverty as a Nord prefect and Paris public health official.[130] But the hopes engendered by the Popular Front left Guillon floundering. He knew that concessions intended to stimulate multi-party pluralism in Tunisia would merely confirm Néo-Destour's dominance, antagonising the settler population and the Bey's conservative advisers.[131]

Over the winter of 1936–37 district officers reported settler disquiet. Sure of its primacy in Tunis, Bizerta and Sfax, Néo-Destour was by then campaigning more vigorously in rural areas for wage increases and the unionisation of agricultural labourers. Settler farmers complained that their workers were less deferential, emboldened by the relaxation of ordinances prohibiting any criticism of the authorities. European landowners isolated among an overwhelmingly Muslim rural population read the worst from any changes in Arab peasant attitudes, seeing the slightest questioning of authority as heralding a revolutionary sea change.[132] On 23 January M. R. Vénèque, president of the Tunis Chamber of Agriculture, lambasted these 'declining standards' in an open letter to Guillon published in the settlers' newspaper, *Le Colon Français*. Vénèque articulated the apocalyptic paranoia and hectoring indignation of a community confronted for the first time with a loss of privilege. The residency was ignorant of the 'real' state of things; Tunisia was on the brink of a bloody pan-Islamic revolution, and the Popular Front was to blame.[133]

Inter-communal tensions became caught up in the ideological polarisation characteristic of the Popular Front era. The annual Bastille Day military parade in July 1937 was intended to remind people who was really in charge. But no sooner had it ended than several hundred Communists and assorted Popular Front supporters organised a counter-demonstration. They were soon in undisputed control of the capital's main thoroughfares, with no police in sight. The demonstrators marched close by a group of immaculately dressed women, mainly officers' wives, who had watched the earlier review from a café terrace. The women were not easily intimidated, and replied to the clenched fists and shouts of 'L'Internationale' and 'Les soviets partout' with fascist salutes and cries of 'A bas les Juifs', 'Vive la France' and, in a few cases, 'Vive le roi'. The café was later vandalised.[134]

By this point, the combination of unrelenting settler criticism and warnings from *contrôleurs civils* that the security forces were severely overstretched had already provoked a reversal of residency policy.[135] Repressive policing and a crackdown on nationalist activity resumed in March 1937. Violent confrontations between police and shipyard workers at Métline near Bizerta left six dead.[136] There was worse carnage in the iron ore and phosphate mines of southern Tunisia, where many of the workmen were either from Tripolitania or Algeria. Those most affected were at Djerissa, Metlaoui, Redeyef, Moulares and M'dillah. At Metlaoui strikers occupied the company offices and blockaded a building containing 300 rifles and ammunition for civil defence purposes, as well as a stock of dynamite. Senegalese troops tried and failed to secure the compound, so reinforcements of *gendarmes* and troops were brought in to surround the depot. A *gendarmerie* officer was assaulted while trying to clear the area, and shots were exchanged. Sixteen strikers were killed. It was a sorry end to Guillon's hopes of phased reform. These incidents occurred on the very day that the resident-general left for Paris to attend the government's Mediterranean High Committee (Haut Comité Méditerranéen). He held emergency talks with ministers and the director of the Gafsa Phosphates Company. These were inconclusive. Guillon's misfortunes continued – journeying south, his train collided with a car at a level crossing.[137]

The frustration of reform in 1937 produced a rift among the Néo-Destour leadership. At the party's 1937 congress in Tunis from 30 October to 1 November 1937 divisions emerged between Bourguiba's supporters, who advocated further protests and a general strike, and more moderate leaders grouped around party president Dr Mahmoud Materi, who rejected violent confrontation with the French authorities. Three weeks later Habib Bourguiba issued a call for mass protest in *El Amal*, a newspaper under his personal control. The residency considered his statement sufficiently inflammatory to initiate judicial proceedings against him.[138] Bourguiba was not so easily cowed. On 31 December Materi resigned his position in protest at pressure from fellow executive members for a campaign of street action. Bourguiba assumed the party presidency and orchestrated a series of protests and work stoppages. On 8 April the Néo-Destour political bureau called for a general strike. The next day Tunis descended into anarchy. Barred from marching on the Palais de Justice, demonstrators rioted in the capital's Muslim *quartiers*. An unidentified assailant slit a *gendarme's* throat. Police sprayed machine-gun fire among the crowds. The residency admitted a death toll of twenty-two. Protesters claimed it was closer to 200. Whatever, it was a watershed event. The new Daladier government declared a state of siege in Tunisia and renewed the ban on Néo-Destour.[139] A wave of arrests of party activists followed that far exceeded anything attempted by Peyrouton. Martial law restrictions were relaxed on

17 August 1938, but there was no let-up in the crackdown on nationalist opposition. Announcing the lifting of the state of siege, the commander of French troops in Tunisia, General Hanote, told a press conference that the security forces had arrested 908 individuals for sedition, 380 of whom remained in prison. But the French Foreign Ministry conceded retrospectively that by 1939 over 2,000 Néo-Destour members were detained. Between 2,000 and 3,000 party activists were locked up. Bourguiba and senior party aides were interned at Fort Saint-Nicholas in the Bouches-du-Rhône, and remained in captivity until freed at German and Italian behest in 1942.[140]

Epilogue

Between its appointment in April 1938 and the French declaration of war on 3 September 1939 the Daladier government authorised the most severe repression of nationalist dissent in the empire since the punitive operations in Indochina following the Yen Bay mutiny in 1930–31. State-of-siege regulations comparable to those in Tunisia were imposed throughout colonial territories during the summer and autumn of 1939. French preparation for war provides a partial explanation for this repression. But renewed official determination to silence anti-colonial nationalists was also part of a wider right-wing backlash against the liberalism of the Popular Front, discussed in the next chapter. As France mobilised in September 1939 conditions were ripe for an explosion of violent mass opposition to colonial rule. Restrictions on freedom of movement and association were harsher than at any point since 1918. Nationalist leaders were either imprisoned, in exile, or under close police surveillance. Colonial trade unions were dissolved or denied the opportunity to act on behalf of their members. Settler interests dominated the local assemblies that remained in place. And the war compounded the social and economic pressures in colonial societies as recruitment, requisitioning, rationing, foodstuff shortages, price inflation and greater use of coerced colonial labour disrupted the empire's economic recovery after the worst depression years.

Notes

1 'Le "Manifest Jeune Algérien" (juin 1912)', in Claude Collot and Jean-Robert Henry (eds), *Le Mouvement national algérien. Textes 1912–1954* (Paris: Editions l'Harmattan, 1978), 23–4.
2 Charles-Robert Ageron, *Les Musulmans algériens et la France 1871–1919* II, (Paris: Presses Universitaires de France, 1968), chapter 37; also cited in Gadant, *Le Nationalisme algérien et les femmes*, 118–19.
3 The wide-ranging literature on constructions of early Arab nationalism in the Middle East has outstripped discussion of its anti-colonial dimension. See, for example, Rashid Khalidi, Lisa Anderson, Muhammad Muslih and Reeva S. Simon (eds), *The Origins of Arab Nationalism* (New York: Columbia University Press, 1991); Israel Gershoni, 'Rethinking the formation of Arab nationalism in the Middle East, 1920–1945. Old and

new narratives', in James Jankowski and Israel Gershoni (eds), *Rethinking Nationalism in the Arab Middle East* (New York: Columbia University Press, 1997), 3–25; C. Ernest Dawn, 'The Formation of pan-Arab ideology in the inter-war years', *International Journal of Middle East Studies*, 20 (1988), 67–91; Mahmoud Haddad, 'The origins of Arab nationalism reconsidered', *International Journal of Middle East Studies*, 26 (1994), 201–22. The French response to Arab nationalism is discussed in A. Mahafzah, 'La France et le mouvement nationaliste arabe de 1914 à 1950', *Relations Internationales*, 19 (1979), 295–312. Common aspects of colonial nationalism are discussed in B. Arcidiacono, 'Aux racines du nationalisme en terrain colonisé : quelques cas de l'entre-deux-guerres (Maghreb, Indochine, Indonesie, Inde et Nigeria)', *Relations Internationales*, 18 (1979), 149–88.

4 Israel Gershoni and James P. Jankowski, *Redefining the Egyptian Nation, 1930–1945* (Cambridge: Cambridge University Press, 1995), Part I.

5 Lazreg, *The Eloquence of Silence*, 81.

6 James Jankowski, 'Egyptian responses to the Palestine problem in the inter-war period', *International Journal of Middle East Studies* 12:1 (1980), 1–38; Philip S. Khoury, 'Divided loyalties? Syria and the question of Palestine, 1919–1939', *Middle Eastern Studies*, 21:3 (1985), 324–48; Basheer M. Nafi, *Arabism, Nationalism and the Palestine Question, 1908–1941* (Reading MA: Ithaca Press, 1998), chapter 6.

7 See Vincent Confer's arguments in *France and Algeria*, 113–21.

8 CAOM, GGA, 11H46, Direction des affaires indigènes, 'Rapport mensuel sur la situation politique des indigènes pendant le mois de novembre 1919'.

9 Ahmed Koulakssis and Gilbert Meynier, *L'Emir Khaled premier za'im? Identité algérienne et colonialisme français* (Paris: Editions l'Harmattan, 1987), 263–4.

10 Charles-Robert Ageron, 'Enquête sur les origines du nationalisme algérien : l'emir Khâled, petit-fils d'Abd El-Kader, fut-il le premier nationaliste algérien?' *Revue de l'Occident Musulman*, 2 (1967), 9–49.

11 Koulakssis and Meynier *L'Emir Khaled premier za'im?* 198–206.

12 Mahfoud Kaddache, *L'Emir Khaled. Documents et témoignages pour servir à l'étude du nationalisme algérien* (Algiers: Office des Publications universitaires, 1987), 112–15: 'La représentation des musulmans algériens', 22 December 1922.

13 Khaled, 'Les plus immédiats de nos desiderata', *L'Ikdam*, 4 August 1922, in Collot and Henry (eds), *Le Mouvement national algérien*, 31.

14 Koulakssis and Meynier *L'Emir Khaled premier za'im?* 265–86 *passim*.

15 Christelow, 'The mosque at the edge of the plaza', 295.

16 Kaddache, *Histoire du nationalisme algérien* I, 97–118 *passim*.

17 Kaddache, *L'Emir Khaled. Documents*, 109–12: 'Le problème indigène', 11 August 1922.

18 Koulakssis and Meynier *L'Emir Khaled premier za'im?* 303–4.

19 Daniel Rivet, *Le Maghreb à l'epreuve de la colonisation* (Paris: Hachette, 2002), chapter 9.

20 ADA, Sarraut papers, 12J259. Bordes was identifiable with the 1919 reforms, having served as Jonnart's secretary-general in Algiers, see ADA, Sarraut papers, 12J259, Jonnart to Minister of Interior, Jules Pams, 29 June 1919.

21 Jacques Cantier, 'Les gouverneurs Viollette et Bordes et la politique algérienne de la France à la fin des années 1920', *Revue Française d'Histoire d'Outre-Mer*, 84:314 (1997), 30–5; Benjamin Stora, *Nationalistes algériens et révolutionnaires français au temps du Front populaire* (Paris: Editions l'Harmattan, 1987), 28.

22 ADA, Sarraut papers, 12J259, Viollette letter to Sarraut, 6 October 1927.

23 Christelow, 'The mosque at the edge of the plaza', 298–9.

24 ADA, Sarraut papers, 12J259, 'Visite Morinaud: Algérie', 16 September 1927.

25 ADA, Sarraut papers, 12J259, tel. 2951, Viollette (Algiers) to Ministry of Interior/Cabinet, 31 October 1927.

26 Cantier, 'Les gouverneurs Viollette et Bordes', 25–49.

27 Gilbert Meynier, *Histoire Intérieure du FLN 1954–1962* (Paris: Fayard, 2002), 46.

28 Since the 1992 annulment of the FIS election victory in Algeria, analysis of early North African nationalism more generally has shifted. For a recent example see Pierre Vermeren, *La Formation des élites marocaines et tunisiennes. Des nationalistes aux islamistes 1920–2000* (Paris: Editions La Découverte, 2002), 17–98 *passim*.

29 Benjamin Stora and Zakya Daoud, *Ferhat Abbas une utopie algérienne* (Paris: Editions Denoël, 1995), 57.

30 Allen Christelow, 'Ritual, culture and the politics of Islamic reformism in Algeria', *Middle Eastern Studies*, 23:3 (1987), 256–63.

31 Stora and Daoud, *Ferhat Abbas*, 16–17.

32 Christelow, 'The mosque at the edge of the plaza', 299–300. Tayyib al-'Uqbi's key patron was Muhammad Bin Siam, head of the Algiers cultural association and the principal administrator of the newest Algiers mosque.

33 *Ibid.*, 300–1.

34 Gadant, *Le Nationalisme algérien et les femmes*, 120–1; Lazreg, *The Eloquence of Silence*, 81–2. Ben Badis also campaigned against the 'un-Islamic' practices of popular Sufism, such as veneration of saints and leaders of Sufi orders.

35 Ruedy, *Modern Algeria*, 135.

36 Sari, 'The role of the medinas in the reconstruction of Algerian culture and identity', 75–6.

37 André Nouschi, *L'Algérie amère 1914–1994*, (Paris: Editions de la Maison des Sciences de l'Homme, 1995), 63–4.

38 Mahfoud Bennoune, 'The introduction of nationalism into rural Algeria 1919–1954', *Maghreb Review*, 2:3 (1977), 1–3.

39 Mahfoud Bennoune, 'Socio-economic changes in rural Algeria, 1830–1954', *Peasant Studies Newsletter*, 11:2 (1973), 12–13.

40 Mohamed Khenouf, review of Johan H. Mueleman, *Le Constantinois entre les deux guerres*, *Journal of African History*, 19:2 (1978), 558.

41 Bennoune, 'Socio-economic changes', 16. Bennoune illustrates the displacement of traditional Muslim agriculture by settler farms geared to export production by reference to declining livestock ownership, and falling cereal and olive cultivation, between 1867 and 1940.

42 Neil MacMaster, 'Patterns of emigration, 1905–1954. "Kabyles" and "Arabs" ', in Alec Hargreaves and Michael J. Heffernan (eds), *French and Algerian Identities from Colonial Times to the Present. A Century of Interaction* (Lewiston NY: Edwin Mellen Press, 1993), 22–4.

43 Nouschi, *L'Algérie amère*, 66–70.

44 Ageron, *Les Musulmans algériens et la France*, chapter 29; Nouschi, *L'Algérie amère*, 66–70; Tony Smith, 'Muslim impoverishment in colonial Algeria', *Revue de l'Occident Musulman et de la Méditerranée*, 156 (1974), 140–1, 150–1.

45 Bennoune, 'The introduction of nationalism into rural Algeria', 2. In 1911 livestock figures for every 1,000 persons in Algeria were as follows: 200 cattle, 1,553 sheep and 694 goats. On the eve of the Algerian war of independence, in 1953, the corresponding figures were 91 cattle, 631 sheep and 339 goats.

46 Dunwoodie, *Writing French Algeria*, 26.

47 Ahmed Henni, 'La naissance d'une classe moyenne paysanne musulmane après la première guerre mondiale', *Revue Française d'Histoire d'Outre-Mer* 83:311 (1996), 47–64.

48 *Ibid.*, 56–61.

49 Nouschi, *Algérie amère*, 53–62; Daniel Lefeuvre, *Chère Algérie. Comptes et mécomptes de la tutelle coloniale 1930–1962* (Paris: Société française d'histoire d'outre-mer, 1977), 35–51.

50 Dunwoodie, *Writing French Algeria*, 18.

51 Gallup, 'The French image of Algeria', 433.

52 Lefeuvre, *Chère Algérie*, 57–9. French census figures almost certainly miscounted the total Muslim population, underestimating the population of internal economic migrants living at the margins of the coastal cities.

53 ADA, Sarraut papers, 12J172, 'Note pour Monsieur le chef du Service du contrôle et de l'assistance des indigènes en France', 8 September 1924.

54 Neil MacMaster, 'The Rue Fondary murders of 1923 and the origins of anti-Arab racism', in Jan Windebank and Renate Gunther (eds), *Violence and Conflict in the Politics and Society of Modern France* (Lampeter: Edwin Mellen Press, 1995), 149–60.

55 See, for example, APP, série BA: Carton BA2170: Etoile Nord-Africaine. For a subtle

[273]

examination of Sarraut's ideas on race and immigration see Clifford Rosenberg, 'Albert Sarraut and republican racial thought', *French Politics, Culture and Society* 20:3 (2002), 97–114.

56 MacMaster, 'Patterns of emigration', 36.
57 Ageron, 'La politique berbère', 50–3.
58 Patricia M. E. Lorcin, *Imperial Identities. Stereotyping, Prejudice and Race in Colonial Algeria* (London: I. B. Tauris, 1999); Lafuente, *La Politique berbère*, 84–93.
59 CAOM, GGA, 11H46, Direction de la securité générale (Algiers), 'Etat numérique des ouvriers indigènes embarqués pour la métropole ou débarqués pendant le mois de juin 1918'. Regarding the Kabyle myth, see Lorcin, *Imperial Identities*.
60 MacMaster, 'Patterns of emigration', 21–31.
61 Nouschi, *Algérie amère*, 73. Muslim overcrowding was particularly acute in Algiers. André Nouschi cites the example of the Algiers *casbah*, where population density increased from 2,028 inhabitants per hectare in 1921 to 2,819 in 1931.
62 Çelik, *Urban Forms*, 79.
63 Kaddache, *Histoire du nationalisme algérien* I, 182; Daniel Hémery, 'Du patriotisme au marxisme : l'immigration vietnamienne en France de 1926 à 1930', *Le Mouvement Social*, 90:1 (1975), 3–54.
64 Koerner, *Madagascar*, 189.
65 J. Ayo Langley, 'Pan-Africanism in Paris, 1924–36', *Journal of Modern African Studies*, 7:1 (1969), 69–94; CAOM GGM, 6(2)D/55, 'Note sur la propagande révolutionnaire interessant les pays d'outre-mer', 15 January 1925.
66 CAOM GGM, 6(2)D/55, *sûreté générale* (Tananarive), 'Organisation du Communisme à Madagascar', 8 January 1925.
67 Person, 'Le Front populaire au Sénégal', 86–7. Kouyaté was shot during the wartime occupation of France.
68 ADA, Sarraut papers, 12J172, *Le Paria*, issues 1–4, 1922.
69 Duiker, 'The Revolutionary Youth League', 475–7; Driss El Yazami, 'France's ethnic minority press', in Hargreaves and McKinney, *Post-colonial Cultures*, 116–17.
70 For nationalist politics among North African students in inter-war France see Guy Pervillé, *Les Étudiants algériens de l'université française 1880–1962* (Paris: CNRS, 1984), and his 'Le sentiment national des étudiants algériens de culture français de 1912 à 1942', *Relations Internationales*, 2 (1974), 233–59; Charles-Robert Ageron, 'L'association des étudiants musulmans nord-africains en France durant l'entre-deux-guerres. Contribution à l'étude des nationalismes maghrébins', *Revue Française d'Histoire d'Outre-Mer* 70:258 (1983), 25–56.
71 AN, F⁷13411, Contrôle général des services de police administrative, 'Association de la jeunesse syrienne', 21 June 1922; APP, BA2183: Police dossier, 'Affaires diverses concernant le Liban : colonie libanaise de Paris', 7 June 1929.
72 Ageron, 'L'association des étudiants', 26–30; John P. Halstead, 'The changing character of Moroccan reformism, 1921–1934', *Journal of African History*, 5:3 (1964), 441. Contrary to Ageron, Halstead suggests that Moroccan students dominated the AEMNA.
73 Benjamin Stora, 'La construction d'un imaginaire politique dans l'espace migratoire : les Algériens en France 1920–1954', *Maghreb Review*, 16:3 (1991), 198.
74 Kaddache, *Histoire du nationalisme algérien* I, 202.
75 ' "Revendications algériennes" présentées par Messali au Congrès de Bruxelles (10–14 février 1927', in Collot and Henry, *Le Mouvement national algérien*, 39.
76 Biondi, *Les Anticolonialistes*, 158–9.
77 John P. Halstead, *Rebirth of a Nation. The Origins and Rise of Moroccan Nationalism, 1912–1944* (Cambridge MA: Harvard University Press, 1967), 61–2.
78 Halstead, 'The changing character of Moroccan reformism', 438–43; Pennell, *Morocco*, 227.
79 E. G. H. Joffé, 'The Moroccan nationalist movement. Istiqlal, the Sultan and the country', *Journal of African History*, 26 (1985), 290–4; Halstead, 'The changing character of Moroccan reformism', 445–6.
80 'Constitution du PPA', in Collot and Henry, *Le Mouvement national algérien*, 91–3.
81 Stora, *Nationalistes Algériens*, 40.

82 Mahfoud Kaddache, *Le Parti du Peuple Algérien 1937–1939. Documents et témoignages pour servir à l'étude du nationalisme algérien* (Algiers: Office des publications universitaires, 1985), 'Déclaration du bureau politique du PPA', 22–3.

83 Rabah Aissaoui, ' "Nous voulons déchirer le baillon et briser nos chaînes": Racism, colonialism and universalism in the discourse of Algerian nationalists in France between the wars', *French History*, 17:2 (2003), 186–209.

84 Kaddache, *Le Parti du Peuple Algérien*, 27–31.

85 Algeria's colonial history is surveyed in Dunwoodie, *Writing French Algeria*, 1–35.

86 Gershoni and Jankowski, *Redefining the Egyptian Nation*, 15–16, 168–85 *passim*.

87 Michael Eppel, 'The elite, the *effendiyya*, and the growth of nationalism and pan-Arabism in Hashemite Iraq, 1921–1958', *International Journal of Middle East Studies*, 30:2 (1998), 227–50; Gershoni and Jankowski, *Redefining the Egyptian Nation*, 7–11.

88 Bennoune, 'The introduction of nationalism into rural Algeria', 2–5.

89 AN, F⁶⁰187, Dossier A2, Cabinet (Algiers), 'Situation politique et économique des territoires du sud en 1938'.

90 CAOM, 9H32, Direction de la sécurité générale (Algiers) 'Rapport sur les faits importants intéressant l'ordre et la sécurité. Mois d'août 1937'.

91 CAOM, GGA, 9H29/D1, sous-prefecture de Sétif, 'Rapport de quinzaine sur l'état d'esprit des indigènes, période du 5 au 20 janvier 1937'; 'Rapport de l'administrateur de la commune mixte d'Ain M'Lila', 10 September 1937.

92 CAOM, GGA, 9H32, Direction de la sécurité générale (Algiers) 'Rapport sur les faits importants intéressant l'ordre et la sécurité. Mois d'août 1937'.

93 CAOM, GGA, 9H18, Surveillance des indigènes, Direction des affaires indigènes note, 'Autour du mouvement d'union des musulmans algériens', 9 June 1938.

94 AN, F⁶⁰187, Dossier A2, Cabinet (Algiers), 'Situation politique indigène de l'Algérie', 15 February 1939.

95 Stora and Daoud, *Ferhat Abbas*, 91–2.

96 AN, F⁶⁰187/Dossier A2, Ferhat Abbas pamphlet, *Pourquoi nous créons l'Union populaire algérienne*, n.d.

97 Stora and Daoud, *Ferhat Abbas*, 94.

98 CAOM, GGA, 9H18, Surveillance des indigènes, no. 307, Cabinet (Algiers) note, 'Le PPA et l'annulation de l'élection du conseilleur général Douar', 15 June 1939.

99 CAOM, GGA, 9H32, Direction de la sécurité générale (Algiers) 'Rapport sur les faits importants intéressant l'ordre et la sécurité. Mois d'août 1937'.

100 Emmanuel Sivan, *Communisme et nationalisme en Algérie 1920–1962* (Paris: FNSP, 1976), 37–8; François Alexandre, 'Le PCA de 1919 à 1939 – données en vue d'eclaircir son action et son rôle', *Revue Algérienne des Sciences Juridiques, Economiques et Politiques*, 11:4 (1974), 175–214. ENA reactions to Communist tactics are described in Stora, *Nationalistes Algériens*, 32–45.

101 Stora, 'La gauche socialiste', 69.

102 Mohammed Touari, 'Pourquoi le PPA est contre le projet Viollette', in Kaddache, *Le Parti du Peuple Algérien*, 57–9.

103 Allison Drew, 'Bolshevizing Communist Parties. The Algerian and South African experiences', *International Review of Social History*, 48 (2003), 167–87.

104 AN, F⁶⁰187, Dossier A2, Cabinet (Algiers), 'Situation politique indigène de l'Algérie', 15 February 1939.

105 CAOM, GGA, 9H32, no. 17,269, Direction de la sécurité générale (Algiers), 'Rapport hebdomadaire', 16 September 1939.

106 Stora and Daoud, *Ferhat Abbas*, 98.

107 CAOM, GGA, 9H32, no. 17,675, Direction de la sécurité générale (Algiers), 'Rapport hebdomadaire', 23 September 1939.

108 *Ibid.*, Direction de la Sécurité Générale (Algiers), 'Rapport hebdomadaire', 30 September 1939.

109 Juliette Bessis provides a figure of 110,000 industrial workers in Tunisia by 1926, see 'Le mouvement ouvrier tunisien : de ses origines à l'indépendance', *Le Mouvement Social*, (1974), 91.

110 Eqbal Ahmad and Stuart Schaar, 'M'hamed Ali, Tunisian labor organizer', in Edmund

Burke III (ed.), *Struggle and Survival in the Modern Middle East* (London: I. B. Tauris, 1993), 199.
111 *Ibid.*, 199–203.
112 Guelmami, *La Politique sociale en Tunisie*, 85.
113 Those with professional training included Habib Bourguiba, Tahar Zaouche, his brother Nourredine Zaouche, Salah Ben Youssef and Tahar Sfar.
114 MAE, série P: Tunisie 1917–1940, vol. 388, Rapport du Capitaine Macquart, 'Le mouvement Destourien', 22 June 1937.
115 MAE, série Tunisie, 1944–55, vol. 335, Direction Afrique–Levant, 'Etude sur le Parti du Néo-Destour', n.d.
116 Marzouki, *Le Mouvement des femmes en Tunisie*, 27–34.
117 For background see Guelmami, *La Politique sociale en Tunisie*.
118 Souad Bakalti, *La femme tunisienne au temps de la colonisation 1881–1956* (Paris: Editions l'Harmattan, 1996), 74–5; Beth Baron, *The Women's Awakening in Egypt. Culture, Society, and the Press* (New Haven CT: Yale University Press, 1994).
119 Marzouki, *Le Mouvement des femmes en Tunisie*, 46–7.
120 Bakalti, *La Femme tunisienne au temps de la colonisation*, 76–84.
121 For instance, MAE, série P: Tunisie 1917–40, vol. 386, residency security reports: 'A/S agitation Destourienne', 8 January, 10 March and 13 April 1935.
122 Daladier's interest in North Africa should not be taken too far. His second Ministry – brought down by the 6 February 1934 riots in Paris and, with an eleven-day life span, the shortest of the Third Republic – was less resolute. After the rioting, Daladier infamously offered the Moroccan residency to Paris Prefect of Police Jean Chiappe in a bid to get rid of the troublesome police official at a time of acute political tension in the capital.
123 Peyrouton, *Du service public à la prison commune*, 46–9.
124 Juliette Bessis, 'Sur Moncef Bey et le Moncefisme : la Tunisie de 1942 à 1948', *Revue Française d'Histoire d'Outre-Mer*, 70:260 (1983), 98–9.
125 MAE, série P: Tunisie 1930–40, vol. 377, no. 791, Tunis residency to Joseph Paul Boncour, 12 June 1933.
126 MAE, série P: Tunisie 1917–40, vol. 386, RG1, Peyrouton to Foreign Ministry, 8 January 1935. On 2 January 1935 the detainees were sent to the southern desert territories ruled by the French military.
127 Peyrouton, *Du service public*, 48.
128 *Ibid.*, no. 544, Direction des affaires politiques et commerciales (Tunis) report to Foreign Ministry, 13 April 1935.
129 *Ibid.*, no. 1373, Peyrouton letter to Pierre Laval, 24 September 1935.
130 Julien, *L'Afrique du Nord en marche*, 77–8.
131 MAE, série P: Tunisie 1917–40, vol. 387, Tunis residency, 'Rapport – conventions collectives de travail', 11 July 1936; SG1663, Direction des affaires politiques rapport, 'Législation sur les libertés publiques', 18 July 1936.
132 See, for example, MAE, série P: Tunisie 1917–40, vol. 387, no. 91, Guillon to Yvon Delbos, 25 January 1937.
133 *Ibid.*, vol. 387, *Le Colon français*, 23 January 1937: 'Lettre du Président de la Chambre d'Agriculture à M. le Résident Général'.
134 PRO, FO 371/20695, C5254/238/17, consul Knight (Tunis) to FO, 16 July 1937.
135 MAE, série P: Tunisie 1917–40, vol. 388, 'Note sur les principaux incidents survenus en Tunisie depuis le mois de mars 1937'.
136 Julien, *L'Afrique du Nord en marche*, 81.
137 PRO, FO 371/20695, C2224/238/17, consul Satow (Tunis) to FO, 8 March 1937.
138 'L'exposé de M. Albert Sarraut sur l'Afrique du Nord', *Le Temps*, 28 November 1937.
139 Julien, *L'Afrique du Nord en marche*, 83–4.
140 MAE, série Tunisie, 1944–55, vol. 300, Section Afrique-Levant memo, 'Habib Bourguiba', n.d., 1951.

CHAPTER NINE

Reform frustrated: the Popular
Front experiment and the French empire

Until the 1980s few historians dissented from the view that the Socialist-led Popular Front government experimented with colonial reform but failed to bring about fundamental change in the social and political life of the colonies.[1] The metropolitan authorities lacked the political will and the monetary means to effect significant improvements in living conditions or individual freedoms. The new coalition held office for too short a time and faced too many entrenched opponents, from the French Senate to colonial officials and settler interests, to achieve much in practice.[2] In sum, the Popular Front prepared reformist legislation only a fraction of which was implemented piecemeal within various overseas territories. Few of these laws remained on the statute book for long. Some were quickly revoked in 1937–38. Others were locally undermined, or blocked by parliamentary opposition. Most were simply inadequate to make any difference to the mass of colonial subjects. Paved with good intentions, the road to Popular Front colonial reform was a cul-de-sac.

Historical interpretations change. The publication of a groundbreaking edited collection in 1998 has encouraged a more subtle reading of the Popular Front's imperial endeavours.[3] Where analysts of Popular Front policies in individual colonies once highlighted the lack of radical legislative change and the absence of long-term state investment in social projects, most now stress the importance of contextualisation. At a time when outright rejection of colonialism was confined to the intellectual margins, the government's attempt to construct a 'colonialist humanism' based on gradual reform and a paternalist sense of responsibility for colonised peoples should be judged on its own terms. Even so, the contradictions of *la colonisation altruiste* proved impossible to conceal. Popular Front reformers never challenged a racially ordered colonial system, believing that the white man's burden derived from the innate superiority of republican cultural values.[4]

Communists, immigrants and colonialism

The Popular Front ministry elected in May 1936 was the only government in inter-war France led by the Socialist Party. In another first, SFIO leader Léon Blum headed the only inter-war Cabinet to receive the parliamentary backing of the French Communist Party. Three women, Cécile Brunschvicg, Irène Joliot-Curie and Suzanne Lacore, were among the thirty-five ministers and under-secretaries of state in Blum's government, a striking, if long overdue, departure for French women still denied the vote.[5] Reformist in intent, and bold in composition, the first Blum government seemed to herald a new political dawn. It was also the sole inter-war government to include commitments to colonial reform in its election programme, although these were vague and non-specific. The Rassemblement populaire programme called for the appointment of a parliamentary committee of inquiry into political, economic and social conditions in the colonies, singling out French North Africa and the Indochina federation for special attention. And the SFIO annual congress, which opened in Paris on 30 May with the scent of electoral victory still sweet, provided a forum for Socialist Party members from French Africa to air their grievances over forced labour, limited welfare provision and the incarceration of political prisoners. Significantly, however, delegates failed to pass a single resolution committing the SFIO to any precise colonial reforms.[6] None of the Popular Front's component parties was wholeheartedly anti-colonialist. Even the PCF saw in empire a means to reinforce Popular Frontism against the fascist challenge.

The Communists were never at ease in matters of colonialism. The party did not adopt an unequivocally anti-colonialist position before 1939. Its criticisms of colonial rule were elliptical, subsumed in more generic criticism of 'militarism' as in the Rif conflict, or of 'imperialist aggression' as in its support for the Amsterdam Congress against Imperialist War convened in August 1932 by France's pre-eminent pacifists, Romain Rolland and Henri Barbusse.[7] Communist parties in the colonies posed a more direct threat to imperial control than their French counterpart.[8] During the Popular Front interlude the PCF broadly adhered to the instructions of the seventh Comintern Congress in May 1935 to subordinate class warfare to the overarching objective of an anti-fascist front in France. These tactics won few friends among anti-colonial nationalists with a natural affiliation to the hard left. As we have seen, anger at PCF toadying to bourgeois non-Communist groups in France explained the ENA/PPA's revulsion at the hypocrisy of the Algerian Communist Party.

During 1937 leading integral nationalist groups in North Africa – ENA/PPA, the Moroccan Action Committee and the CGTT – distanced themselves from the governing coalition as the Popular Front reform programme ran out of steam. In hindsight, this is unsurprising. The greater ideological polarisation in French party politics evident after clashes between Communists and the ultra-rightist leagues sparked rioting in Paris on 6 February 1934 rippled outwards to North Africa. Maghrebi nationalists established stronger ties with the only anti-colonialist voices remaining on the French extreme left: Marceau Pivert's Gauche révolutionnaire faction in the SFIO, and Trotskyite and anarchist groups that became a more visible presence once the flow of Spanish Republican exiles to North Africa increased after the outbreak of civil war in Spain in July 1936.[9] Meanwhile, the dynamics of Popular Frontism constrained the PCF's anti-colonialism still further as the Communists worked alongside openly imperialist coalition partners. The PCF central committee was, broadly speaking, more willing to contemplate limited self-rule for certain territories than rank-and-file members. But Jacques Doriot, former Young Communist leader and the PCF's most eloquent and forceful critic of colonial oppression in the 1920s, was, by 1936, the party's bitterest critic. After his expulsion from the PCF in June 1934, Doriot performed a remarkable feat of ideological gymnastics. In July 1936 he completed his personal reinvention, emerging as the tub-thumping pro-Nazi leader of the Parti Populaire Français (PPF), the most incendiary of the ultra-rightist parties.[10] To the PPF, colonies were the rightful inheritance of the French race.

Doriot's transformation was less unusual than it first appeared. Even the PCF applied concepts of racial hierarchy to gauge the 'societal evolution', and hence the revolutionary potential, of individual colonies. Abd el-Krim merited Communist support in 1924–25, but five years later the 'uncivilised' leaders of tribal revolt in the Kongo-Wara did not.[11] Racism remained common among left-voting blue-collar workers, particularly after the sharp increase in immigration during the years 1922–24 and 1925–31. In 1931 the foreign component of the French labour force reached 1,599,000 immigrant workers, an inter-war peak. Colonial immigrants comprised a significant part of this figure, although the fastest-growing immigrant communities over the preceding decade were of Italians, Poles and Spaniards.[12] Between 1931 and 1939 immigrant numbers stabilised at around 7.5 per cent of the working population. Figures compiled by the Mediterranean High Committee in March 1937 illustrated the distribution of the largest colonial immigrant group – Maghrebi labourers. North African and other colonial immigrants were kept at the bottom of the employment pile. And immigrant workers in general were officially designated a supplementary work force, codified as *travailleurs immigrés* (immigrant workers) or *main d'oeuvre étrangère* (foreign manpower), the expectation being that the flow of immigrant labour could be turned on or off as economic circumstance dictated. Colonial immigrants in particular were not encouraged to put down deep roots in France, and were monitored by dedicated police bureaux and the Ministry of Colonies' Service du contrôle et de l'assistance des indigènes coloniaux en France.[13]

Table 9.1 Distribution of North African immigrants in France, March 1937

Department	Algerians	Moroccans	Tunisians	Total
Ardennes	No precise figures			931
Bouches du Rhône	14,666	166	168	15,000
Gard	No precise figures			1,580
Haute Garonne		15	20	170
Loire	No precise figures			3,000
Meurthe et Moselle	No precise figures			1,350
Moselle	No precise figures			1,350
Nord	1,927	172	6	2,150
Pas de Calais	Omitted	58	4	62
Puy de Dôme	277	21	1	299
Rhône	2,840	140	20	3,000
Seine	27,000	5,000	100	32,100
Seine Inférieure	394	279	102	775
Seine et Oise	Omitted	337	24	361
Grand Total				62,083

Source CAOM, GGA, 8H61, Haut Comité Méditerranéen, Dossier 1, HCM rapport no. 3 'Les Nords-Africains en France', March 1937 session, annex II. Although some prefects submitted inaccurate or incomplete information, the regional distribution of North African immigrant workers, and the predominance of Algerians among them, are clear enough.

French co-workers sometimes vilified colonial immigrants as non-unionised strike-breakers and unskilled day labourers whose desperation for employment caused downward pressure on wages. The PCF's inconsistency over colonialism and its hostility to non-unionised labour allowed this bigotry to persist. It was all a far cry from Doriot's early campaigning against colonial injustice. In 1924 the party established a colonial commission, and organised a congress of Maghreb workers in Paris in December. Communist sympathisers were sought out in the Maghrebi and Vietnamese immigrant communities. Newspapers and tracts in French, Arabic and Vietnamese were published in an effort to woo immigrant workers. As we saw in chapter eight, several leading anti-colonial nationalists made their entry to politics through pro-Communist student journalism in the 1920s. But these initiatives soon lost momentum. Neither the central committee nor PCF rank-and-filers showed much fellow feeling toward colonial comrades.[14] It was all too easy to juxtapose downtrodden colonial workers with the colonial troops sent in to put down André Marty's

Communist mutineers in the French Black Sea fleet in April 1919. In 1920, the year of the definitive breach between French Communists and Socialists, the Communist International stated that it was incumbent on the proletariat in imperial nations to shepherd workers in their dependent territories toward socialism. Careful guidance would enable colonial states to avoid the transitional stages of industrial capitalism on the road to socialist transformation. These instructions were used to justify the PCF's patronising approach to colonial populations for years afterward.[15]

At a more prosaic level, after the December 1920 Socialist–Communist split at the Tours congress, the PCF was unwilling to jeopardise its bid for mass support by adopting a stridently anti-colonialist line. Declining PCF membership rolls and the recovery of SFIO support in the late 1920s added to Communist caution. The irony was that delegates at Tours implored the French left to tackle the oppression of workers in all its forms.[16] It failed to do so. The PCF leadership went through the motions of opposing colonialism at the party's annual congress in Arles in December 1937. Party leader Maurice Thorez referred to *indigène* populations as 'slaves' (as distinct from proletarian 'wage slaves' in France). Gabriel Péri, Doriot's successor as the PCF's principal spokesman on empire affairs, decried colonial living conditions. And Kaddour Ben Kaim and Khaled Bagdache, secretaries of the Algerian and Syrian Communist Parties, took the floor to denounce colonial oppression.[17] No one in power was listening. The Popular Front was nearing final collapse, and the reformist mood of the previous year had given way to a return to colonial authoritarianism.

The PCF spoke out much too late. With no pressure from its left wing for a more radical alternative, it was little wonder that the Popular Front coalition tried instead to find new legitimacy for France's imperial presence. It was reform, not retreat. Most Popular Front ministers were unsure of their feet in colonial affairs. At the outset of the Popular Front experiment colonial reform refracted previously enacted domestic policies. Only after several months in power did Blum's government contemplate local reforms attuned to individual colonial requirements.

During late 1936 industrial legislation, increased trade union rights, worker education schemes and additional welfare benefits were selectively transposed to imperial territories, albeit in much diluted form.[18] This reflected a longer-term trend. Wider bureaucratic engagement in social policy and welfare planning after the end of the First World War rubbed off on Colonial Ministry officials and colonial governments. During December 1934 and January 1935 Louis Rollin, Minister of Colonies in Pierre-Etienne Flandin's centre-right government, hosted a French imperial economic conference in Paris, whose proceedings were dominated by five study commissions. Their membership represented a broad range of old Parti colonial interests – provincial commerce, employers' groups, the army and the

Paris Bourse. The commissions proposed measures to increase colonial production, provide greater welfare provision, equip colonial industries with modern machinery, and improve the financial management of colonial bureaucracy. Each commission then put forward its suggestions to the plenary economic conference. Paul Bernard, principal economic adviser to the Hanoi government, took advantage of the conference to put the case for state-backed industrialisation in Indochina, an idea he developed more fully in a book, Le Problème économique indochinois, published earlier in 1934. Bernard pointed out that the established *pacte colonial* whereby the colonies furnished primary products to France in return for manufactured goods was deeply prejudicial to colonial economic growth.[19] Minister of Colonies Rollin was enthused.[20] His fellow ministers, then in the throes of major spending cuts, were not. The imperial economic conference was stillborn. Its only outcome was a committee for colonisation and peasant affairs in the Ministry of Colonies, intended to co-ordinate overseas settlement with the government's colonial development priorities.[21]

Eighteen months later the prospects of substantial increases in colonial expenditure were brighter. And the Popular Front was the first French government to correlate metropolitan social reform and colonial welfare. Robert Delavignette, the outstanding intellect of the French colonial service, celebrated the new era in gushing prose: 'If there is one ministerial department to which apply the three famous catchwords – "Peace", "Bread", and "Liberty" – that rallied the Popular Front, it is certainly the Ministry of Colonies'.[22] The elaboration of government reforms, the expectations they generated and their ultimate rejection by settlers, some colonial officials and the French National Assembly are discussed below.

Marius Moutet and his opponents: the colonial governors' conference and the Guernut commission

Four members of the Blum government held primary responsibility for the articulation of colonial reform. Blum appointed the Senator and former Governor-general of Algeria, Maurice Viollette, a minister of state without portfolio. In 1936 Viollette was vice-president of a small, but influential, parliamentary grouping, the Union Socialiste et Républicaine, led by his fellow Senator, Joseph Paul-Boncour. Viollette's delicate mission was to pilot a package of Algerian constitutional reform through the choppy waters of parliamentary opposition. Pierre Viénot took on an analogous job for the North African protectorates and the Middle East mandates as under-secretary of state at the Quai d'Orsay. Viénot made his name as an expert on Muslim territories in the early 1920s when he served in Lyautey's personal cabinet in Rabat. He was soon immersed in negotiation of the long-overdue treaties of independence with Syria and Lebanon. The third individual selected to steer through reforms in Arab states was Charles-André Julien, a liberal academic and an outstanding Arabist. Julien did not serve in the government, but became secretary-general of the Mediterranean High Committee. His brief was to make the committee a vehicle for reformist policy formulation in North Africa and the Levant.[23]

Finally, there was the Socialist Minister of Colonies, Marius Moutet. As we saw in chapter two, Moutet's commitment to colonial reform had been evident since the First World War. His task was to mould the governing coalition's diffuse, and often contradictory, schemes for colonial renovation into legislative measures that could survive hostile parliamentary scrutiny in France and bitter settler opposition in the colonies.[24] Two months after taking office, Moutet wrote the preface to a book on colonial policy by Louis Mérat, a renowned economist attached to the rue Oudinot staff. Mérat advocated the creation of an empire-wide managed economy. The idea appealed to Moutet as marking a definitive transition from one-sided commercial exploitation to a new age of economic integration between France and the colonies. Moutet hoped to align the interests of French and colonised peoples, arguing that better colonial living standards were essential to imperial economic development.[25]

Moutet's path was eased by a sweeping clear-out of colonial governors known to be most resistant to reforms. Eighteen of the thirty colonial governors and residents were transferred, pushed into retirement or otherwise replaced.[26] Among the most significant victims of this purge was Marcel Peyrouton, evicted from the Rabat residency after less than six months *in situ*. Indochina's governor-general René Robin also lost his job. Others clung on, aware they were out of favour in Paris, but either unable or unwilling to tone down their hatred of Blum's government. Léon Cayla, the *pied noir* governor-general of Madagascar, was one such. And, like Peyrouton, Cayla later achieved notoriety in the Vichy regime.[27] The best remembered of those to benefit from the redistribution of governorships was Félix Éboué, a long-serving black Guyanese official and Colo graduate, appointed Governor of Guadeloupe.[28]

Moutet also gathered a reformist team around him in Paris. He brought in close associates to run the colonial inspectorate at the rue Oudinot, the ministry's economic division and its all-important personnel department. René Barthes proved a capable director of Moutet's ministerial office. Gaston Joseph, director of political affairs, was a long-standing proponent of reform. And Robert Delavignette became a pivotal figure in policy formulation from his position as director of the *Ecole nationale et la France d'Outre-Mer* (since 1934 the more liberal appellation of the Ecole colonial).[29] Opponents of the Popular Front among the existing colonial bureaucracy always presented a more formidable obstacle to constructive reform than the anti-colonialism of the extreme left. Moutet's purge was therefore vital. It had most impact in Africa, where eleven out of sixteen African governorships changed hands.[30] Even so, Moutet faced stubborn opposition from officials like Léon Cayla in Tananarive: men ideologically at odds with the Popular Front and sceptical that limited colonial demo-cratisation could work. In the weeks before the May 1936 elections, contributors to *La Quinzaine coloniale* (*Fortnightly Colonial News*), a mouthpiece for colonial service personnel, voiced their dread of a Popular Front election victory. As if to confirm their fears, on 24 June 1936, three weeks after taking over at the rue Oudinot, Moutet wrote to colonial governors deploring the bureaucracy's blindness to the imperative need for reform.[31]

Moutet was in no mood to waste time. His first ministerial pronounce-ments stressed his overriding concern to ameliorate living conditions for colonial subjects rather than export conditions for capital investors and trading companies. On 29 June 1936 the rue Oudinot announced plans to extend recently passed metropolitan social legislation to the colonies. The crux of these measures was a fixed working week, paid holidays, sickness and insurance benefits for workers, and the right to free collective bargain-ing.[32] Moutet also took immediate steps to implement colonial social legislation approved by previous governments, but never before enforced. Decree legislation dating from January 1933 that outlawed child labour and night work by women in Indochina was imposed for the first time in August 1936. A further decree of 9 September 1934 recognising employers' liability for industrial injuries was also brought into effect in the African federations.[33]

It proved difficult to sustain this early reformist impetus. Extension to the empire of the Matignon Accords – the series of industrial and trade union reforms promulgated in France on 7 June 1936 – was never entirely accomplished. On 14 December the National Assembly approved three decrees extending the forty-hour working week, paid holidays and collec-tive bargaining contracts to workers in the five *anciennes colonies* of Martinique, Guadeloupe, French Guiana, Réunion and New Caledonia.[34] But in other larger colonies, social legislation was more bitterly contested. In broad terms, colonial governments raised more objections to proposed electoral reforms and wider trade union rights than to social welfare meas-ures that posed less of a challenge to European dominance. That said, colonial governors, chambers of commerce in the empire and at home, and other settler lobby groups frustrated even marginal social reforms, insisting that the costs involved were prohibitively high and would be borne by European taxpayers in the colonies.[35]

Moutet's Ministry of Colonies requested colonial governments to im-plement welfare changes colony by colony in spite of the clear indications that hostile officials would undermine the process. Probably unavoidable, this was none the less a fatal mistake. The colonial federations were to convene investigative commissions composed of senior bureaucrats, chamber of commerce representatives, industrial and agricultural leaders, and a handful of selected notables. Individual colonial governments were also given a say. These commissions became a barrier to reform every bit as obstructive as the French Senate.[36] The investigative commission in Brazzaville whittled down social reforms covering taxation, *prestation*, commune administration and the regulation of internal economic migration put before the federal government council in late December 1936.[37] The consultation process in Madagascar was equally flawed. The island's financial and economic delegations discussed reform proposals put forward by the labour inspectorate in response to local concerns. Paid holidays were approved in theory. So, too, was the introduction of a forty-hour week to factories and businesses. Planters were advised to make their own arrangements with their workforce representatives to apply a forty-hour week where possible. But the fine detail of these labour reforms revealed how far they were watered down. Malagasy workers were not expected to take holiday allowances in full. Indigenous workers had to satisfy their employers that they had *worked* a full forty hours, rather than merely being on site for that time, a discriminatory requirement not applied to European employees on the grounds that only white workers respected 'the discipline of the workplace'. Collective bargaining rights in the agricultural sector were still regulated by the pre-existing system of 'verbal contracts' between plantation owners and migrant workers. Seasonal industries and agricultural employers were allowed to apply an eight-hour working day, rather than a forty-hour week, in recognition of their reliance on casual workers. Madagascar's labour code in its final form bore no comparison with its French equivalent.[38]

Moutet, meanwhile, tried another tack. On 12 August 1936 he announced that a governor-generals' conference would convene in early November to discuss reform priorities. The conference agenda focused on easing the colonial tax burden to stimulate purchasing power, fiscal incentives to local producers, funding for additional public works schemes, and the reduction of bureaucracy. These were plans bound to antagonise colonial officials.[39] It is tempting to say they were calculated to do so. There was certainly a discernible bullishness in rue Oudinot preparations for the November meetings. To take but one example, Moutet chided federation governors for their failure to avert widespread famine from northern Annam to Niger and Oubangui-Chari. The new minister made his views plain: '*I believe that a colonial system is not viable unless it is animated by the needs of the indigenous population who should benefit from it*'.[40]

The governors' conference was the decisive showdown between the reformist central government and the forces of reaction in the colonial state. But there were always limits to this confrontation for the simple reason that both parties were mutually reliant. On 5 November 1936 Moutet opened the first conference session at the Prime Minister's official Paris residence, the Hôtel Matignon. He reiterated on three occasions that whatever the residual conservatism among colonial governments, reform would be the product of specialist advice and dialogue between centre and periphery rather than a centrally imposed programme. Indeed, Moutet and his key ally Gaston Joseph relied on experienced officials to formulate specific plans for tax reform, increased social provision and public works spending. The reformist measures considered by the colonial governors' conference reflected a longer tradition of technocratic planning in colonial policy that continued into the Vichy years.[41]

Social spending was severely constrained by the September devaluation of the franc. The measure, initially resisted by Blum's Cabinet, established a free-floating *franc élastique*.[42] The currency was effectively devalued by between twenty-five and thirty-five per cent. Nor was this the last pre-war depreciation of the franc. French investment capital continued to flow overseas throughout the lifetime of the first Popular Front. Two further devaluations took place in 1937 and 1938. Necessarily responsive to specialist advice, Moutet was now further hemmed in by the government's declining financial position. Two fundamental beliefs continued to guide him. First, he sought to revitalise Socialist identification with a reformist republican imperialism whose cardinal tenet was that the transmission of material benefits and cultural enlightenment to dependent populations could justify colonial control. Second, he believed in assimilationism, selectively and gradually applied. Success would be calibrated statistically through indices of life expectancy, improved infant survival rates, better diet, greater political engagement and educational provision. After six years of severe recession in which the Ministry of Colonies had become obsessed with export output and budgetary deficits, it was time to elevate colonial government to a higher purpose than mere accounting and capitalist profit.[43] Moutet's rejection of mercantilism was all very well, but it still fell to the colonies to finance their own social transformation. Franc devaluation, the high costs of labour reform and the crippling burden of the Popular Front's ambitious four-year rearmament programme left no scope for major welfare spending on colonial peoples.

It was never likely that colonial governors would carry the torch of reforms that cut their staff and curbed their personal authority. The purge of colonial governorships had made little fundamental difference. If Moutet's team were to keep the reform process alive, they would have to look elsewhere. The answer seemed to lie in the tried and trusted combination of parliamentarians with a keen interest in colonial problems, academic specialists, colonial service experts and high-profile government supporters capable of pricking the nation's conscience. In other words, the Popular Front worked with its own adaptation of the old Parti colonial, seeking out a constituency of liberal imperialists committed to structural reform of the colonial system. The embodiment of this coalition was the Guernut commission.

Blum's government approved the creation of a commission of inquiry to investigate 'the needs and legitimate aspirations' of colonial populations on 11 August 1936. It was another six months before the Senate finally approved the establishment of the commission on 30 January 1937. Those familiar with the crucial part played by obstructive conservative Senators in the downfall of Blum's government in June 1937 will find their hostility to colonial reform unremarkable. Ultimately, Senate opposition made a mockery of the Popular Front's colonial commission of inquiry. Led by Henri Guernut, a leading member of the League for the Rights of Man, Radical deputy for Aisne, and Minister of Education in the preceding Sarraut Cabinet, his eponymous commission was subdivided into three geographical sections.[44] The forty-two parliamentarians, colonial officials, professors and noted reformists assigned to these constituted an impressive, if heterogeneous, outfit. They included five Senators and eleven Deputies. Among these were Théodore Steeg, the former resident-minister in Morocco and governor in Algiers, who chaired the Senate's standing committee on colonial affairs. His opposite number in the Chamber of Deputies, the Socialist Jean-Baptiste Nouelle, also took part. Professor Paul Rivet of the Museum of Natural History and Professor Marcheux of the Academy of Medicine represented the academic world. More household names included novelist André Gide, still acclaimed for his damning critique of colonialism in the Congo,[45] and Victor Basch, president of the League for the Rights of Man. Outstanding colonial specialists included Robert Delavignette, Charles-André Julien and Hubert Deschamps. The Socialist Party's colonial section was strongly represented by, among others, André Philip, Maurice Paz and Daniel Guérin, the most outspoken anti-colonialist then in the Socialist ranks.[46] The commission's impressive membership lent gravitas to the government's avowed intention to correct manifest abuses of colonial rule. Its three regional sub-committees duly investigated the local needs of the North African protectorates – black Africa, the Antilles and Indian Ocean islands – and France's Asian and Pacific territories.[47]

Much of the disappointment surrounding Popular Front colonial reform stems from the fact that the Guernut commission amassed its evidence too late for the Blum ministry to act on it. Blum's government resigned on 22 June, the Senate having withheld emergency powers to cope with deepening financial crisis. The commissioners set to work in July. Two of the three regional sub-committees held only three sessions. The third, the sub-committee for the Asian and Pacific territories, met more frequently, thanks to the energetic chairmanship of Victor Basch. All three sub-committees invited reform schemes from interested groups in the colonies. Local Socialist Party federations and colonial Masonic lodges proved especially keen respondents. Nationalist groups submitted analogous demands – democratisation, freedom of association and equal rights for colonial subjects.[48]

Armed with this information, the Guernut commission began its more arduous task: on-the-spot inspection missions. Here, too, a combination of two factors – Senate opposition and the passage of time – ensured its failure. Conservative Senators led by the Radical elder statesman Joseph Caillaux blocked plans for potentially embarrassing fact-finding missions.[49] And the reformist impulse had passed by the time the Guernut commission finalised its plans. Camille Chautemps's ministry, in power from June 1937 to March 1938, and Edouard Daladier's third government that took office on 10 April ignored the commission's findings. Guernut disbanded the entire investigative apparatus in July 1938 with its work still incomplete. Historians have stressed the Guernut commission's significance as a barometer – and precursor – of colonial reform.[50] None the less, the historian seeking evidence of changes enacted in 1936–37 must look elsewhere.

Constitutional and penal reforms

The Popular Front's resumption of assimilationist policies was too short-lived to bring about significant increases in the overall numbers of colonial citizens. Madagascar was not untypical. The colonial authorities passed decree legislation in October 1936 that conferred citizenship on those Malagasy that could meet predetermined educational, linguistic and economic criteria. The numbers naturalised under this and later legislation passed in April 1938 ran to some 2,000. The figure represented a major advance over the handful of naturalisations enacted by Léon Cayla's government in the early 1930s. Still, the measure affected only a narrow educated elite. The Popular Front's decision to ease the burden of forced labour had a greater bearing on the lives of most Malagasy. Here, too, disappointment followed high hopes. Celebration in 1936 at the abolition of the hated public works manpower service that administered the provision of forced labourers proved premature. Two years later the forced labour system was resurrected to assist French preparations for war.[51]

In similar vein, releases of political prisoners were soon aborted. Amnesties for political detainees followed by their re-arrest when the political temperature increased was nothing new; prisoner releases were always bargaining chips in colonial politics. In Syria, for instance, a general amnesty for leaders of the Great Revolt in March 1928 was applied selectively in an effort to split the newly formed Syrian National Bloc. Eight years later, on 26 February 1936 157 detainees imprisoned for public order offences during the two-month Syrian general strike were freed to bolster public support for a venal government in Damascus.[52] The Popular Front release programme was so important because it reversed the clampdown on colonial dissent that began in 1929 and lasted until 1935. Indochina, French North Africa and Madagascar were the territories most affected. The number of detainees in Madagascar was exceptionally high, Léon Cayla proving an especially repressive governor in his crackdown on Communist and autonomist groups between 1932–35. With Comintern encouragement, from early 1933 International Red Aid, the Anti-imperialist League and the PCF daily *L'Humanité* campaigned on behalf of over 400 Malagasy workers imprisoned by the Tananarive authorities, initiating legal proceedings to secure their release.[53]

On 16 June 1936 Moutet intervened. Cayla, recalled to Paris a month earlier, was forced to look on from Paris as his interim replacement, Governor Jore, implemented Popular Front reforms in his absence.[54] Scores of political prisoners were freed, including the autonomist leader Jean Ralaimongo, Paul Dussac and Emmanuel Razafindrakoto: the troika of leading Communist organisers on the island.[55] Cayla's conservative supporters on the island now regarded the Popular Front's electoral victory, the menace of Communism and the breakdown of colonial control as inseparable. Their nightmares soon took concrete form. Within days of the first political prisoner releases, a series of nationalist protests began. The high public profile of the recently freed activists, pent-up antagonism against Cayla's government and high expectations of fundamental reform precipitated a festive, quasi-revolutionary atmosphere. During late June, July and August 1936 mass meetings in Tananarive, Tamatave, Majunga, Antanimena and Diego Suarez, often several thousand strong, became more threatening. On 12 August 1936 180 Communist supporters attended the inaugural meeting of the Parti communiste de la région de Madagasacar (PCRM) at the Hôtel Glacier in downtown Tananarive. Paul Dussac, secretary-general of this Madagascan section of the PCF, led calls for the mass conferment of citizenship, a thinly veiled demand for autonomy, if not outright independence. Settlers and traders set up a rival organisation, the Union franco-malgache, to contest Dussac's autonomist demands. Clashes between the opposing groups offered a pretext for the authorities in Tananarive to backtrack on reform. During the autumn of 1936 the authorities outlawed all political meetings as a threat to public security. The focal point of urban opposition then shifted to a series of wildcat strikes by workers in the island's major colonial trading companies, beginning with stoppages on 18 October 1936 at the Société industrielle et commerciale de l'emyrne in Tananarive.[56] This first strike wave was soon followed by more protracted industrial action that began in February 1937 with a ferrymen's strike in Diego Suarez. The PCRM co-ordinated these stoppages, as the government suspected. But it was the disintegration of Popular Front reform that gave the Communists an ideological platform in Madagascar's factories.[57]

Events in Madagascar were instructive. The Popular Front's more liberal approach to naturalisation did not touch the great majority of colonial subjects. Nor did the release of political detainees and the growing urban militancy that followed. For every agitator detained in the early 1930s, tens of thousands of Malagasy peasants faced arbitrary arrest under the *indigénat*. In 1933 43,466 *indigénat* infractions were punished. In 1934 the figure rose sharply to 64,537: a forty-eight per cent increase that represented the cutting edge of Cayla's authoritarianism. Individual prison terms were generally short, the fines imposed were not crippling, but they affected a broader cross-section of the subject population than direct involvement in nationalist dissent.[58] In the Madagascan countryside peasant communities driven close to famine by the depression manifested their frustration very differently from the urban population. During 1936–37 entire villages registered their hostility to officialdom in all its forms by boycotting state vaccination programmes, particularly the long-running campaign against bubonic plague. Vaccination rates across the island fell by an estimated fifty per cent in 1936 alone, some 715,000 vaccinations having been administered in the previous year throughout Madagascar's high plateaux. Public health officers, convinced of the underlying political motives involved, complained of a vicious circle: the inevitable resurgence of plague infection was, in turn, attributed to the French. For all the governmental angst about Communist sedition, intense rural suspicion of colonial interventionism presented the more intractable dilemma. By June 1937 the re-arrest of leading nationalists, Paul Dussac's repatriation to France and severe press restrictions contained nationalist dissent. But large swathes of the countryside remained implacably hostile to district administration.[59]

The growth of popular militancy in Madagascar catalysed by the reversal of early reforms was repeated across the empire. The previous chapter described the radicalisation of Algerian and Tunisian nationalism in the Popular Front years. Widespread expectation of reform, popular frustration with government inaction in 1936–37, and draconian repression in 1937–39 were much the same in both places. In Indochina these transitions were equally abrupt. The Popular Front's first priority here had been to end lingering repression in the Vietnamese territories consequent upon the rebellions of 1930–31. Moutet campaigned from the back benches for clemency toward those convicted of involvement in Yen Bay and the Nghê-Tinh soviets in 1930, highlighting a notorious instance when the Saigon criminal commission handed down thirty-four death sentences and eighty-three terms of forced labour in a single day. Six years later Moutet's ministerial aides advised that clemency towards Vietnamese detainees was a prerequisite to political progress in Hanoi, Hué and Saigon. Not everyone agreed. Governor Robin's implacable opposition to prisoner amnesties in June 1936 may have triggered his dismissal.[60] The Vietnam releases had a snowball effect, the government announcing further amnesties in the Antilles, Réunion and French Guiana on 11 August 1936, and in all other colonial territories on 27 August. Some 2,028 jail inmates were freed in the Vietnamese territories alone, of whom 1,352 were officially designated political prisoners. The 499 political prisoners freed by the Tonkin government were the largest single cohort of detainees released by a colonial government during 1936–37.[61]

Moutet did not intend to stop there. He reserved the right to scrutinise all police dossiers of convicted political prisoners, enabling him to override locally imposed sentences that appeared unduly harsh. The rue Oudinot also made Indochina the principal focus of its penal reforms. ICP members imprisoned during the uprisings of 1930–31 had little difficulty indoctrinating a new generation of Communist recruits, many of them juvenile offenders, amidst the insanitary conditions, chronic overcrowding and appalling brutality of Vietnamese jails.[62] On 20 July 1936 Moutet demanded improvements. Decent rations, regular family visits, daily exercise, library facilities and better medical treatment, including the isolation of the many colonial prisoners infected with tuberculosis, were all pioneered in Vietnam before being introduced in other colonies. The colonial magistrature was overhauled, and mixed juries of European and *indigène* representatives tried cases involving settler violence against the local population.[63] Penal reforms in Indochina attracted less media attention in France than attempts to restructure the notorious *bagne* penal colony in French Guiana, popularly regarded as the harshest of all colonial prisons. But Vietnam's political environment changed fundamentally. ICP cadres in Tonkin and Cochin-China exploited Popular Frontism to the full, forging partnerships with Trotskyite groups, the more bourgeois Constitutionalist Party in Saigon and even local branches of the SFIO. Under the cover of plans for a multi-party Indochinese Congress, ICP activists organised an entire committee network across the south.[64]

The federal government in Dakar shared many of the conservative preoccupations of their colleagues in Hanoi, and felt vindicated in their cautious approach to social and electoral reform, having shepherded French West Africa through the depression without encountering major unrest. The Dakar political affairs directorate defended associationist policies, such as the consolidation of tribal hierarchy and the creation of local consultative assemblies (*conseils des notables indigènes*) in May 1919, which, it claimed, were guided 'by long experience of primitive societies, and based on a liberalism precisely adjusted to the aspirations and aptitudes of individuals and native communities'.[65] Occasionally chinks appeared in the façade of governmental complacency. Dissent in AOF was actually widespread immediately before the Popular Front took office. But disturbances, for the most part, remained sporadic and local. Between 1933 and 1936, for example, *évolués* in Benin protested at their lack of economic opportunities, animists in Côte d'Ivoire resisted Christian proselytising and tribesmen in the western Sahara blocked European settlement.[66] In the eastern reaches of AOF, popular opposition appeared especially threatening. During 1933–34 protests against colonial restrictions spread through the major commercial centres in the Gulf of Guinea, prompting heightened police surveillance in the Togo mandate, Dahomey and Cameroon.[67]

The Dakar government opposed Popular Front reforms, but did so more subtly than its counterparts in Hanoi and Tananarive, arguing that rapid socio-political change was irresponsible. The social diversity and physical extent of West African territories made them ill suited to a reform programme that extended political rights wholesale and threatened to disrupt the all-important labour market. The most obvious distinction was between Senegal and other federation territories. With its four *originaire* communes, in 1936 Senegal counted 21,000 citizens with full electoral rights among a population of approximately 1.6 million. There were only 2,400 French African citizens among the wider AOF population. Government in Senegal was similarly unusual, divided between the lieutenant-governor's office, the federal authorities and influential municipal councils. The growth of Senegalese party politics also set the colony apart. After Blaise Diagne's death in 1934, Galandieu Diouf and Lamine Guèye – well educated *évolués* that rose to prominence as Diagne supporters in the Jeune Sénégal youth movement – dominated black politics in the colony. Each followed Diagne in constructing a local party machine. Where Diagne made the local section of the Radical Socialist Party his own fiefdom, during 1934–35 Diouf and Guèye established political parties – respectively, the Parti Républicain Nationaliste and the Parti Socialiste Sénégalais – imprinted with their own vision for Senegal.[68] Diouf and Guèye could rely on a network of experienced *originaire* politicians in the municipalities of the four communes, as well as supportive local newspapers, to spread their message of equal rights for *évolués*, and improved pay and conditions for African workers.[69] With a functioning party system, an outspoken press, and a politically astute elite, by 1936 Senegalese politics set the agenda for political change in the rest of French West Africa. Tony Chafer puts it nicely, 'The key significance of the Popular Front was thus that it marked the point at which the discourse and values of French republicanism were first used beyond the confines of the Four Communes to mobilise a campaign against the colonial regime in French West Africa'.[70]

With a deeply conservative, and self-confident, federal government in Dakar and a nascent nationalist party politics in Senegal, political confrontation in AOF seemed inevitable once the Popular Front's willingness to contemplate colonial reform became generally known. With this in mind, Moutet resolved on a change at the top. On 8 August 1936 the socialist Marcel de Coppet took up the post of governor-general in Dakar, transferring south from his previous posting in Mauritania. De Coppet was an Africa veteran with impeccable liberal credentials and powerful friends, including André Gide and Moutet himself.[71] He immediately addressed highly publicised labour abuses on the Office du Niger project, and conceded that AOF's cotton cultivation programme should rely less on coercion and more on market incentives to producers.[72] In a breakthrough measure, on 6 January 1937 Moutet approved de Coppet's decision to exempt women from the *indigénat*.[73]

The new governor-general also realised that African trade unions and other employee groups were integral to colonial civil society. On 11 March 1937 de Coppet legalised trade unions and professional associations. A week later he confirmed government support for collective bargaining. The Dakar authorities thereby recognised a host of union organisations that sprang up in late 1936. These included employee associations in commerce, banking, the insurance industry and the building trade, as well as more conventional labour unions of dockers and metallurgical industry workers. On 21 December 1936 Senegal's newly founded dockers' union was among the first to organise strike action in support of its demands.[74] The Dakar authorities also signed up to Geneva Convention provisions regulating forced labour. Insurance against industrial accidents, an eight-hour working day for industrial employees and restrictions on the employment of women and children followed.[75]

As for political reforms, reviewing its policies over the twelve months of Blum's government, the AOF political affairs directorate concluded that citizenship was accessible to those ready and willing to seek it: 'The doors of the city have been largely opened to the [indigenous] elite, but rare are those that show any wish to pass through'. In this reading of events, registration of only fifty or so citizenship requests in 1936 represented not a failure of policy but confirmation that *indigènes* were profoundly attached to their own culture. The majority of those seeking French citizenship were junior bureaucrats whose career experience prepared them for the social transformation inherent in naturalisation.[76]

By contrast, in Senegal's four original communes, where African citizenship rights had long applied, voters went to the polls three times in 1936. On 26 April Galandou Diouf narrowly defeated Lamine Guèye in elections to the French Chamber of Deputies. A month later Senegal's single electoral college selected members of the colony's colonial council.

And in October representatives of the Conseil supérieur de la France d'outre-mer were elected.[77] If male electors in Senegal could be trusted, then why not their counterparts in other densely populated West African colonies, such as Côte d'Ivoire, Guinea and Dahomey? And when would the African women entering the work force in increasing numbers by the late 1930s be judged to have attained 'political maturity'? As matters stood, the electoral process in Senegal tended to highlight the absence of constitutional progress elsewhere.

In 1936 François-Joseph Reste, the newly appointed governor in Brazzaville, cited the Dakar government as the model for administrative reforms in Equatorial Africa. Reorganisation of central government in AEF began within weeks of the Popular Front's election in May. A federal inves-tigative commission approved the establishment of a native council modelled on AOF's *conseils des notables indigènes*. The native council was the first consultative assembly of any kind in AEF in which African representation was assured. It was to meet annually to scrutinise tax rates, public works projects and the *prestation* system of compulsory day labour. Places were reserved for between eight to sixteen African delegates, subject to the governor's personal approval. Three leading notables – all of whom were naturalised French citizens – were, in addition, admitted to the gov-ernor's administrative council.[78] These measures were hardly substantial democratisation, but the beginnings of collaboration with a conservative native elite marked an important step forward. After the unholy trinity between Reste's predecessor, Governor-general Raphaël Antonetti, European trading companies, and plantation owners, any changes in the complexion of government in France's poorest colonial federation were welcome.

From industrial reform to colonial strike wave

Moutet's instruction to colonial governors on 29 June 1936 to study the application of French labour legislation within their territories seemed to augur a new era in which colonial industrial relations might come to resemble their metropolitan equivalent. But colonial expectations of col-lective bargaining rights, restricted working hours and improved factory conditions, modelled on the Matignon labour laws, encountered determined bureaucratic opposition. The Matignon agreements of early June followed weeks of strike action, factory occupations and mass protest in France – confrontational and political, certainly, but not especially violent. Many on the French right none the less viewed the June 1936 strike wave in cataclysmic terms: at best as the decline of working-class deference, at worst as the harbinger of revolution.[79]

These fears were amplified among colonial officials and settlers. As in France, colonial workers sometimes walked out without first elaborating their industrial demands, action seen as revolutionary and probably Communist-inspired. Most colonial strikers, however, demanded Matignon-style concessions – an eight-hour working day, minimum working conditions and the right to collective bargaining. They met a far harsher official response than did the French strikers. On 11 June European trade union organisers called a strike at the massive Cosuma sugar refinery in Casablanca, claiming that the management refused to negotiate with a workers' group that included Muslim members. Foreign Ministry advisers blocked Residency plans to exile the union leaders concerned and a negotiated settlement soon followed. A similar dispute among the predominantly Muslim work force at the Khouribga phosphate mine was handled very differently. Foreign Legion units coerced the men back to work. These strikes indicated that the imperial response to industrial action would be determined by considerations of race as well as class.[80] In the French Indian enclave of Pondicherry repression of strike action was firmer still. Local textile workers began sit-in strikes in July 1936 that evoked the earlier factory occupations in France. Strike leaders highlighted mill workers' insufferable conditions. Midday temperatures in Pondicherry's mills often exceeded 45°C. Shifts averaged between eleven and twelve hours, far longer than the norm in nearby British Indian textile factories.[81] Yet within hours of the first stoppage the authorities resolved to end the sit-ins by force. Police clearance of the affected mills left ten textile workers dead.[82]

The sequence of popular strike action broken by state violence was hardly unprecedented. Syria offered the most recent evidence of this. Between 20 January and 6 March 1936 Damascus was gripped by a general strike that exposed the fragility of imperial rule when confronted by well organised economic protest.[83] Work stoppages began among shopkeepers, merchants and university students enraged by the closure of a National Bloc office in Damascus and the arrest of Fakri al-Barudi, a leading Bloc spokesman in the capital, and Sayf al-Din al-Ma'mun, head of the nationalist youth movement.[84] Riots, the closure of bazaars, and nationalist demonstrations quickly spread to other Syrian towns, bringing the country to 'the verge of a complete shut-down'.[85] High Commissioner Comte Damien de Martel travelled inland from Beirut to take personal charge of the situation. Neither politicians nor public were in any mood to listen. The embarrassing spectacle of the high commissioner trading insults with Fa'iz al-Khury, an experienced barrister and organiser of the National Bloc's Damascus branch, exemplified the shifting balance of power between the mandatory state and the Syrian nationalist movement. De Martel resorted to carrot and stick. Troops repeatedly fired on demonstrators both to clear the streets and to break the strikers' resolve. But the high commissioner conceded to National Bloc delegates that negotiations for a treaty of independence should begin.[86] The Syrian general strike sent shock waves through the empire.

Colonial strikers had wrested concessions by direct action before the Popular Front took office.

Indochina was also in the grip of politicised industrial action by the time Blum's Cabinet first convened in May 1936. The vast Michelin rubber plantation at Dau Tiêng in Cochin-China was the scene of communal violence between South Vietnamese labourers and North Vietnamese coolies. These confrontations were soon eclipsed by a more general protest movement against starvation wages and squalid living conditions among workers housed in purpose-built plantation villages.[87] And strikes on rubber plantations were, in turn, overshadowed by industrial unrest in Vietnamese cities. During 1936–37 resentment against the Popular Front among Indochina's European population centred on this wave of factory strikes unleashed by the government's labour reforms.[88] Moutet was unmoved. On 5 February 1937 he told Governor-general Brévié in no uncertain terms who was to blame. Worker militancy stemmed first and foremost from employers' reluctance to negotiate fair labour contracts and their readiness to replace employees with non-contract labourers at the first sign of dissent. The minister then struck a more conciliatory tone, imploring the colonial government to begin mediation efforts through the labour inspectorate set up by Alexandre Varenne a decade earlier.[89] His plea fell on deaf ears.

Saigon, in particular, witnessed unprecedented industrial unrest. Having struck for improved pay in early November 1936, workers at the port's naval arsenal walked out again on 6 April 1937 in protest at a new split shift system introduced to speed up urgent repairs to the warship *Savorgnan de Brazza*. Within two days 945 of the arsenal's total work force of 1,280 downed tools.[90] The Saigon arsenal strike was politically explosive for two reasons. First, to the delight of local business leaders, the naval authorities rejected arbitration by the government labour inspectorate. Second, it was clear that ICP organisers directed the arsenal strike through factory committees redolent of the action committees created during the 1930–31 uprisings.[91] Acting on *sûreté* intelligence, Brévié concluded that Communist agitators were dragging out the dispute through worker intimidation, intensive propaganda and manipulation of the collective bargaining system established by Popular Front labour legislation.[92]

Protests in Cochin-China reached new heights in May 1937. Communist activists led noisy May Day celebrations in Saigon, encouraged by the election of two ICP Stalinists and one Trotskyite to the municipal council. Between 7 and 10 May peasant demonstrators in Cholon province demanded an end to the poll tax, the revocation of the tobacco tax and the settlement of the arsenal strike. Days later, an estimated 1,500 coolies from the Michelin rubber plantations at Dau-Tiêng, dissatisfied with a day rate increased from twenty-seven to thirty-two piastres, marched on Saigon to lay their grievances before the director of labour. Communist organisers, it seemed, were everywhere. The Saigon governor set out by car and intercepted the column en route, imploring the labourers to return to the plantation.[93] This intervention, at once desperate and conciliatory, exposed the weakness of the colonial authorities. In this charged environment the arsenal strike finally ended on 12 May after the Saigon naval commander relented, inviting in labour inspectors to settle matters. The Vietnamese Communist press hailed a landmark victory – proof of workers' organisational power, the need for state regulation of the labour market and ICP capacity to co-ordinate industrial action. The Saigon authorities drew much the same conclusions, but found no cause to celebrate. The arsenal dispute, and the mobilisation of rural support behind it, raised the spectre of a Communist-controlled general strike in Cochin-China, a fear that coloured official attitudes to all local industrial disputes thereafter.[94]

The federal government took little convincing of ICP involvement in a later strike wave among railway workers on the Saigon–Mytho and Saigon–Dalat lines, their colleagues in northern Annam, and locomotive workshop employees in Dian (near Saigon) and Vinh (Annam) in July 1937. Workers in several rail depots allegedly walked out without submitting any demands. Only later did strike organisers demand reinstatement of employees previously dismissed for sedition.[95] Meanwhile, the balance of forces tilted the authorities' way. The four-year alliance between Stalinists and Trotskyites in Cochin-China, co-ordinated by the publishers of the Saigon newspaper *La Lutte (The Struggle)*, disintegrated once the *sûreté* moved decisively against them in late 1937. Duong Bach-Mai, a Stalinist journalist on another Communist daily, *Le Peuple*, Ta-Thu-Thau, director of *La Lutte*, and his partner, Nguyen van-Tao, were disbarred from Cochin-China for ten years. In-fighting among South Vietnamese Communists resumed just as the new Chautemps government gave the Indochina government *carte blanche* to crack down.[96]

Attempting reform in Algeria: the Blum–Viollette project

To Algerian settlers, Popular Front reforms were identifiable with one man – Minister of State Maurice Viollette. 'Viollette-l'Arabe' as he was pejoratively known, had remained a hate figure since his Algiers governorship of 1925–27. The loathing was mutual. Just as ultra-rightists threatened the Third Republic in the 1930s, so Viollette identified reactionary settlers as the principal barrier to colonial progress. On his departure from Algiers in 1927 he issued a remarkable public warning to the colonists who had ousted him from office. The European population would eventually be overthrown if it continued to deny the indigenous population the most basic rights and freedoms.[97] In a Senate speech eight years later on 22 March 1935 Viollette turned his fire on France's political elite.

One government after another ascribed inter-communal friction to Muslim ingratitude. None faced up to the abject failure of reform. Little wonder that Muslims saw no hope in French politicians: 'when they protest against the abuses all around them, you become indignant; when they applaud [reform] you become suspicious, and when they keep quiet you fear them'.[98]

For all his outspoken prescience, Viollette was also a committed imperialist. He was convinced that the unique virtue of the French colonial mission was its transmission of republican political culture.[99] In May 1936 Viollette was deputy leader of the independent Socialist Party (Union Socialiste et Républicaine), an influential position from which to advance his scheme for the enfranchisement of some 25,000 Algerian Muslims. But he still faced intractable obstacles. Viollette had to work alongside Raoul Aubaud, under-secretary of state at the Interior Ministry, a conservative Radical with responsibility for Algerian internal administration. Aubaud formulated strict qualifications for Muslim voting rights.[100] Even these restrictions did not assuage Senate antagonism to the entire scheme. Under Viollette's proposals, as interpreted by Aubaud, only ex-servicemen, members of regional and local councils, recognised trade union officials and those with a university degree could anticipate enfranchisement. Hence, two aspects of the so-called Blum–Viollette project are immediately striking: first, the narrow limits to the reform, and, second, the bitterness of right-wing opposition to it.[101] In this sense, the project holds a mirror to the failed Jonnart legislation of 1919. The fact that Viollette's reforms also ran into the sand indicates how little the French political elite, the Algerian settler community and the colonial state had changed since the end of the First World War.

How may one account for such vitriol when the reform enfranchised less than two per cent of the Muslim adult male population? The answer lies in those clauses that, for the first time, granted Algerians the right to vote without renouncing their personal legal status as Muslims. It was this prospect that provoked nearly 200 *colon* mayors and their deputies, including those of Algiers, Oran and Constantine, to stage a mass resignation in protest at Viollette's Bill on 8 March 1938. Well aware that in over seventy years fewer than 5,000 Algerians had relinquished their Muslim personal status to acquire French citizenship, settlers and the French right would never admit that Muslim colonial citizens could vote alongside their European counterparts without a prior commitment to subordinate their indigenous culture to the aspiration to become French. In purely legal terms, a fully enfranchised citizen of Algeria could not be French and Muslim at the same time. Defeat of the Blum–Viollette project was catastrophic because it destroyed any prospect of the development of a loyalist Muslim elite attached to France but allowed to retain its distinct religious identity. The mayors' shared nightmare of a rural commune controlled by its

Muslim 'citizens' actually killed off any prospect of more harmonious inter-communal politics.[102]

The fate of the Etoile Nord–Africaine under the Popular Front under-lined the impossibility of extracting substantial political rights from even a liberal government. On 14 July 1935 ENA members in Paris joined the crowds marching in support of the Rassemblement Populaire. A year later Messalists were also quick to transmit their political demands to Blum's Cabinet. The ENA called for abolition of the *indigénat*, wider Muslim vot-ing rights in Algeria and France, and greater social spending on Algeria's Muslim majority. Messali Hadj moderated calls for Algerian independ-ence in the spirit of Popular Front unity, aware that ENA contacts with the SFIO's Gauche révolutionnaire faction afforded some leverage over Socialist policy.[103] But Messali struggled to direct ENA strategy. On 24 January 1935 he received a six-month jail sentence for inciting Muslim soldiers to desert. On 14 May he was handed down a further one-year sentence for the same crime. Faced with renewed incarceration, he fled to Geneva, working along-side the pan-Arabist Syrian–Palestine Congress.[104]

The Popular Front political prisoner amnesties allowed Messali to return to France and Algeria, whereupon he reiterated that *Algérie française* was a fiction masking a century's colonial oppression. The ENA's uncompromis-ing rejection of the Blum–Viollette project – centrepiece of the government's North African reforms – sealed its fate. Messali lambasted the scheme's restriction of citizenship to between 21,000 and 25,000 members of the Muslim elite. Far from democratising Algeria, the Blum–Viollette project perpetuated sectarian division, the dilution of Muslim culture and the sub-jugation of the Arab majority.[105] In late 1936 political unrest in Algeria increased as reforms disintegrated. It was too much for Blum's ministers to stomach. On 27 January 1937 Blum's Cabinet introduced legislation out-lawing ultra-rightist, anti-republican groups, or leagues. It used these pow-ers to impose a fresh ban on the ENA. Much as some of the outlawed French leagues reconstituted themselves in new guise as political parties, so, too, the ENA reinvented itself as the Parti du Peuple Algérien in March.

The Popular Front was positively hostile to the PPA, recognising it as a more formidable opponent of colonialism than the ENA. From late 1937 the ENA's core constituency of immigrant Algerian labourers was over-shadowed by the surge in support for the PPA inside Algeria. Messali returned to Algiers on the eve of the collapse of the Blum government in June 1937. Three weeks later he led a 14 July parade of some 3,000 PPA supporters, marching through the centre of Algiers behind the party's dis-tinctive green flag.[106] Messali's popularity increased still further after he and four other PPA leaders were re-arrested on 27 August 1937 for inciting sedition. On 15 October Messali, by then imprisoned, won forty-nine per cent of the vote in the Algiers cantonal elections, a repeat performance of

Emir Khaled's electoral success seventeen years earlier. Messali's position as figurehead of integral Algerian nationalism was assured. Muslim voters, it seemed, demanded to be heard even when their spokesmen were muzzled by the Algiers regime.[107] Yet, as in 1919, so in 1937 the Algiers prefecture simply annulled the vote.

The ban imposed on the ENA was replicated by official proscription of the Néo-Destour and the Moroccan Action Party, successor to the Moroccan Action Committee. Both parties were banned in March 1937. Contacts between the three Maghrebi groups, fostered by their joint membership of a permanent Muslim committee set up in 1935, grew in response to the severity of state repression against them. By the end of 1936 the three parties co-ordinated their political operations in France through a central agency in Paris. Maghreb unity also featured prominently in the North African Muslim student association programme. By 1937 the AEMNA was largely run by Tunisian university students in Paris. Like their political masters, they, too, faced more severe police restrictions in 1937–38.[108] So did Tunisia's CGTT, still the most cohesive trade union confederation in the empire. Maghrebi nationalist parties, trade union groups and the AEMNA saw the unification of the three Maghreb territories as politically expedient. But co-operation was more than a marriage of convenience. The collapse of reform gave vent to pan-Arab sentiments subsumed beneath the distinct national objectives of the separate organisations.

By March 1937 the North African authorities were more concerned about worker protests than about party political activity. Much as in Vietnam, West Africa and the French Antilles, increasing labour militancy erupted in strike waves that spread across Algeria and, above all, Tunisia during 1937–38. As in the Vietnamese territories, Maghrebi strikers appended overtly political demands to their industrial grievances. Striking labourers pressed for the release of nationalist leaders or union officials jailed for sedition. European workers in North Africa also pressed their demands for better wages and working conditions. But fraternisation between the two communities of strikers was rare. The disparity between the limited state violence employed against settler strikers and that meted out to *indigène* workers revealed the racism at the heart of the colonial project in North Africa, whatever the Popular Front's high-minded efforts to mitigate its effects. In August 1937 settler construction workers in Algiers and dock labourers in the port of Nemours downed tools. Both strikes were resolved without incident after stoppages of a fortnight and three weeks respectively. In the same month 2,200 striking Muslim miners in Tébessa and Bône were coerced back to work by the Garde mobile. A series of wildcat strikes among peasant grape pickers in Constantine followed a similar course. The Garde républicaine intervened after shots were exchanged between striking farm labourers and those willing to resume work.[109]

In late 1937 and the first four months of 1938 the French authorities pursued a systematic crackdown against Muslim political dissent and industrial unrest across North Africa. This was most effective in Morocco, where the recently founded Moroccan Action Party was targeted. The Rabat residency tolerated limited nationalist activity only in so far as it remained the preserve of the urban elite and lacked a popular organisational base. In 1937 these preconditions collapsed. Security service monitoring of nationalist meeting points and political intelligence from the rural interior indicated a worrying surge in tribal support for the Moroccan Action Party programme.[110] The prospect of urban protest reverberating through the Moroccan countryside and recently pacified tribal areas alarmed residency officials.[111] Poor harvests in 1935–37 and reports of starvation conditions among Morocco's peasantry added to residency fears. Export restrictions were introduced in 1937 to safeguard Morocco's foodstuff supply. And Noguès's administration approved successive increases in the minimum daily wage introduced in June 1936 in an effort to ensure that rural wages at least kept pace with rising food costs. But the primary focus of residency policy remained the nationalist threat. As mentioned above, the Moroccan Action Party was duly dissolved by decree on 18 March 1937. Resident-general Noguès and his deputy, Jean Morize, authorised more systematic repression once it became clear in July that the organisation had merely gone underground and canvassed wider support. Arrests were made, newspapers shut down, meetings broken up and rioters shot down. The worst violence occurred in early September 1937 in Meknès, hitherto one of the protectorate's quieter cities. Public outcry over the municipal authorities' diversion of precious water resources from the Boufekrane River to irrigate European farms culminated in rioting between protesters, police, infantry and *spahi* units. Thirteen demonstrators were killed and scores injured.[112] Clashes continued in other Moroccan cities during September and October 1937 until most senior nationalist leaders were either arrested or exiled. Ugly scenes of cavalry charging at rioters, soldiers firing on protesters and troops patrolling medinas suggested a brutal edge to the 'protectorate' concept.[113]

By this point the Blum–Viollette project was dead. The French Senate would never pass it, settlers would never accept it, and Algerian nationalists turned against it. In an article in the Néo-Destour newspaper *L'Action Tunisienne* published on 26 February 1938, Mohammed Touari, PPA organiser in the town of Blida, south of Algiers, pointed out that settler furore over such meagre reforms was fuelling mass support for the PPA and the Association of Reformist *Ulamas*.[114] Elitist groups such as the Young Algerians and the Federation of Elected Muslims had had their day. Muslims wanted a genuine nationalist alternative.[115]

Albert Camus's activities during 1936–37 echoed the hopes and disillusion of the period. In April 1937 Camus presided at the opening of the

Algiers Maison de la culture, an organisation that brought together settler writers and artists enthused by the advent of the Popular Front. He spoke of Algeria's *nouvelle culture méditerranéenne*: a unique Franco-Muslim heritage shaped by proximity to other Mediterranean societies. Idealistic and, as yet, poorly understood in France, Camus's rejection of untrammelled settler dominance formed part of a broader attack on the fascist ideology seeping across the western Mediterranean from Italy and Spain.[116] Yet Camus's inclusive vision of a new Algerian society had limits. Critical of settler conservatism, he stopped short of support for Algerian emancipation. Camus and other artists of the Ecole d'Alger drew upon the left republican tradition of humanist imperialism, blurring the distinctions between French and Arab, *colon* and *indigène*. But their vision of a harmonious, 'liberal' empire was out of step with settler interests and French parliamentary opinion.

Camus's experience points to the fact that the ideological polarisation of Popular Front France was replicated in those colonial territories with large settler populations. In Algeria, Cochin-China and Madagascar splits between liberal and right-wing settlers were superimposed on the struggle between colonial nationalists and their opponents. In Algeria, colonists' backing for the anti-parliamentary leagues signified rejection of secular republicanism, hatred of the Blum government and the assertion of white racial supremacy. Conversely, the European membership of the Algerian Communist Party combined vocal support for Republican Spain with sympathy toward Muslim demands for greater rights. The PCA remained a small minority interest. The leagues did not. Colonel de La Rocque's Croix de Feu, founded in 1928, was the most popular of the leagues in 1930s France. By 1934 La Rocque claimed 150,000 supporters. And the Croix de Feu and its more overtly fascistic rival, Jacques Doriot's Parti Populaire Français, were the sole French political organisations to mobilise mass settler followings in urban Algeria.[117] One of the three ultra-rightist leagues banned by the Blum government, La Rocque reinvented the Croix de Feu as the Parti Social Français. PSF cadres expanded rapidly, although the party's claim of up to 2 million supporters was a gross inflation of a membership that probably peaked at less than half that figure.[118] In this sense, Algeria simply followed the same pattern as France. The PSF and PPF held mass meetings, and intimidated left-wing opponents with paramilitary parades, street violence and vicious press polemic. And on 10 June 1936 the SFIO branch in Oudja, western Algeria, warned Blum that La Rocque's supporters had distributed 194 guns to 'reliable' Muslims in anticipation of a Communist uprising.[119] The PSF and PPF journals, *La Flamme* and *Le Pionnier*, were a familiar sight in settler *quartiers*. And Doriot planned to take a controlling stake in *Oran-Matin*, a popular daily in the city where PPF support was strongest.[120]

The difference between the metropolitan and Algerian settler versions of ultra-rightism emerged most clearly on questions of race. The racism implicit in PSF nationalism and explicit in PPF proto-fascism was painted in starker colours in the Algerian context. Signing up to the PSF in France could be a gesture of protest against Popular Front social and industrial reform. In Algeria it was an affirmation that the Muslim population should be kept in their place. Algeria's Jewish community was another target of ultra-rightist vitriol. These trends became apparent once the PSF made its electoral breakthrough in the February 1938 ballot for the financial delegations. In Oran and Constantine, cities with a proportionately larger, more visible Jewish community than Algiers, Bône or Bougie, antisemitism became a rallying cry to PPF supporters. But in the capital, where the PSF garnered more votes than the PPF, hostility to Muslim enfranchisement was paramount. Both La Rocque and Doriot toured Algeria's cities in 1938. La Rocque chose Constantine as the venue for the PSF annual congress in October 1938. And Doriot drew audiences of up to 5,000 during two national tours in May and November.[121] The end of the Popular Front era saw Algerian communal politics more sharply divided than ever.

Towards independence in the Levant mandates?

From June 1936 the Blum government pushed ahead with treaties of independence with Syria and Lebanon foreshadowed in the original terms of the Type A mandates, but repeatedly postponed in the decade after the Syrian revolt. A draft Franco-Syrian treaty was initialled in Paris in early September 1936 after five months of faltering talks between a Syrian delegation dominated by National Bloc leaders and a Quai d'Orsay negotiating team led first by outgoing foreign minister Pierre-Etienne Flandin and then by Pierre Viénot.[122] In theory, Syrian national independence was to be confirmed by French parliamentary ratification of the treaty after a three-year probationary period. The French retained exclusive military privileges, including two major bases and a garrison of unspecified size, as part of a twenty-five-year Franco-Syrian alliance.[123] Alawi councillors and Druze tribal leaders lobbied Blum's foreign minister, Yvon Delbos, to uphold their autonomy. Mindful of the infamous Iraqi army massacre of Assyrians in 1934, Viénot's negotiating team insisted on explicit safeguards for Syria's ethnic and religious minorities. Certain administrative structures of the autonomous Jabal Druze and the Alawite regions were retained under the treaty arrangements.[124] But the National Bloc government packed the Alawite and Druze provincial authorities with Syrian nationalists to weaken the autonomy of the compact minority states.[125] It seemed likely that an independent Syria would be a unitary state rather than a strongly federal one, as most minority leaders preferred.[126]

Once the treaty terms were published on 22 October, a carnival atmosphere developed in Damascus that culminated in the triumphant return home of the Syrian delegation three weeks later.[127] Co-ordinated by the National Bloc and its paramilitary youth wing, the Steel Shirts, these celebrations were premature. The Damascus parliament ratified the treaty on 27 December. But it became clear in the new year that a powerful alliance of Parti colonial veterans, right-wing politicians, high-commission insiders, military leaders and press magnates were determined to block French ratification. Popular Front assent to the three-year probationary period, understandable given the strength of parliamentary opposition to full Syrian independence, was none the less a grave mistake. 'The treaty that never was', as Philip Khoury terms it, was further stymied by the descent into war in 1939.[128]

Lebanese independence, too, was conditionally postponed in 1939. But the Franco-Lebanese treaty, closely modelled on the earlier Anglo-Iraqi treaty of 1930, was more swiftly negotiated and ratified in Beirut and Paris. Lessons were learnt from the earlier Syrian negotiations. Speed was of the essence because of deteriorating inter-communal relations in Lebanon's cities. After the conclusion of the Franco-Syrian talks in the second week of September 1936, Viénot and Levant high commissioner de Martel immediately focused on a Lebanese treaty. The stumbling blocks to agreement were much the same: the rights of minority groups, the demarcation of Syrian political influence in Lebanese internal affairs, French military and cultural privileges, and the terms on which constitutional arrangements devised for the mandate in the 1920s would be applied to Lebanon as a sovereign state. The one arrangement unique to the Lebanese treaty was the enormous freedom of action left to the French military to use Lebanon as a base of operations throughout the treaty term. In a complete reversal of roles, Lebanon's Sunni Muslims, whose co-religionists were the majority religious group in Syria, emerged as the most outspoken opponents of the Lebanese treaty. Minority opposition to the Syrian treaty centred on fears of a unitary Arab Islamic state liable to trample on the rights and cultures of the country's non-Sunni communities. By contrast, in Lebanon, the country's Sunni Muslims led by Riad al-Sulh rejected a constitutional system that cemented Maronites' political dominance. Two days after signature of the Franco-Lebanese treaty, the start of Ramadan on 15 November heralded an explosion of violence in Muslim West Beirut. Running street battles between Muslim demonstrators and security forces engulfed the city centre, threatening the security of the high commission. Disturbances spread to Tripoli on 20 November. Scores of casualties were reported in both places. It was a sad epitaph after years of expectation. If anything, the 1936 treaties intensified inter-communal tension and reignited Lebanese fears of Syrian irredentism.[129]

Conclusion

The virulence of popular reaction to colonial reform in 1936–38 should not blind us to the fact that empire was marginal to Popular Front legislators and most of their metropolitan supporters, from parties and trade unions to anti-fascist groups and intellectuals' organisations. Only a specialist few became animated by colonial questions. The French left had long years in the political wilderness in which to formulate plans for imperial renovation. Colonial reform was on the Blum government's agenda, but the experience of 1936–37 indicated how little preparation had been made. Well-meaning concern was no substitute for systematic planning. The Popular Front lacked clarity, unity and leadership when it came to imperial issues. The energy of individuals such as Moutet and Viollette was not enough. A stronger governmental lead was essential if vested commercial interests, outraged settler opinion and obstructionist colonial bureaucracy were to be overcome. By 1938 the most eloquent voices of colonial opposition were the very French-educated *évolués* that welcomed the Popular Front to power. The Popular Front was more concerned with widening access to benefits than with a complete overhaul of previous practice.[130] As the international situation deteriorated, Socialist and PCF leaders sacrificed their 'humanistic' imperialism on the altar of national defence. The fascist threat was not, however, the sole reason for the abrupt return to more oppressive colonial policies in 1938–39. Repression overseas mirrored the rolling back of the Popular Front's industrial and associational reforms in France as the Daladier government, enthusiastically supported by employers' groups, moved decisively rightward from November 1938 on.[131]

Ministers that championed social reforms, cultural freedom and human rights at home were noticeably silent about analogous issues in the colonies. Léon Blum never made colonial change a priority. More urgent domestic and European preoccupations from industrial strife and a depreciating franc to the civil war in Spain help explain this. But in 1936–37 the Socialist Party leadership was as timorous about empire reform as it was about women's suffrage, another issue that Blum's ministers sidelined. On both matters, Blum delegated difficult reform schemes to relatively junior ministers, and then declined to push through reformist legislation by decree in the teeth of parliamentary opposition.[132] Coalition dynamics played their part. The Radical Party, the group with the largest reservoir of imperial expertise among its senior ranks, was never credible as an agency of colonial renovation (and was united in opposition to votes for women). Radical leaders were solidly imperialist, broadly sympathetic to settler interests and the plight of European *petits commerçants* in the empire. The 'young Turks' loyal to Edouard Daladier wanted to maximise the material benefits of colonial markets and the pool of empire manpower. The PCF obeyed Comintern instructions to the letter in colonial matters. Communist leaders refused to jeopardise their commitment to Popular Frontism by rekindling the PCF's former anti-colonialism in direct opposition to the Radicals and the SFIO. Maurice Thorez and the Communist Party central committee showed remarkably little fellow feeling for Vietnamese, Algerians or Malagasys faced with arbitrary arrest and indefinite imprisonment, something on which French Communist leaders would have more time to reflect when the PCF was outlawed following the Nazi–Soviet Pact in 1939. Nor was there strong pressure from the Communist Party rank and file to adopt a more anti-colonialist position, or to protect the interests of colonial workers in France.[133] The Popular Front's colonial reformers, then, were set apart. They were never in the mainstream of government policy making. There was no rank-and-file pressure from Popular Front supporters in France to accelerate imperial reform. Without it, or wholehearted government backing, colonial renovation was doomed.

Notes

1 A classic expression of the traditional view is Georges Lefranc, *Histoire du Front populaire* (Paris: Payot, 1974), 301. Two participants in the Popular Front's colonial reforms, Charles-André Julien, and Daniel Guérin, a member of the SFIO's Colonial Commission, also lamented the failure of policy: Charles-André Julien, 'Léon Blum et les pays d'Outre-Mer', in Pierre Renouvin and René Rémond (eds), *Léon Blum. Chef de Gouvernement 1936–1937* (Paris: FNSP, 1967), 377–90; Daniel Guérin, *Front populaire, révolution manquée* (Paris: Maspero, 1970). An exception to this trend is Person, 'Le Front populaire au Sénégal'. Other work, innovative regarding the metropolitan facets of Popular Frontism, overlooks its colonial aspect, for example, Martin S. Alexander and Helen Graham (eds), *The French and Spanish Popular Fronts. Comparative Perspectives* (Cambridge: Cambridge University Press, 1989).

2 The life span of the Popular Front is contested. A coalition of republican parties, trade unions, civic organisations and intellectuals committed to defend French democracy came together as the Rassemblement Populaire in 1934 in reaction to the perceived threat of an anti-republican *coup* by ultra-rightist leagues such as the Croix de Feu. A group of left-liberal intellectuals, the Comité de vigilance des intellectuels antifascists, pushed the main political parties toward co-operation. Apologists consider Léon Blum's Ministry (May 1936–June 1937) the only genuine Popular Front government. Blum drew support from the Socialist, Communist and Radical parties as well as the CGT trade union confederation. Deputy Premier Camille Chautemps succeeded Blum as Prime Minister. His government (June 1937–March 1938) kept the appellation 'Popular Front' and completed the nationalisation of the French rail industry. But the Chautemps Cabinet was dominated by the Radicals and faced mounting criticism from the PCF. In a ministerial reshuffle on 18 January 1938 Chautemps dispensed with his remaining Socialist Ministers. This second Chautemps government collapsed prior to the March 1938 *Anschluss*. Blum then tried, but failed, to form a government of national unity embracing left and right. Instead, he briefly led a second government (March–April 1938) dominated by Socialists and left independents. The collapse of this Ministry, and its replacement on 10 April 1938 by Edouard

Daladier's Radical-led government, marked the definitive end of the Popular Front. The best history of these events is Jackson, *The Popular Front in France*.

3   Chafer and Sackur, *French Colonial Empire and Popular Front*. Prior to this work, the last major collection devoted to Popular Front colonial policies was a special issue of the journal *Le Mouvement Social*: 107 (avril–juin, 1979).

4   See Eric Jennings's thoughtful review of Tony Chafer and Amanda Sackur's work in *Journal of Modern History* (2001), 182–4.

5   Siân Reynolds, 'Women and the Popular Front. The case of the three women Ministers', *French History*, 8:2 (1994), 196–224; and her *France between the Wars*, 150–4. The women had ties with the three main parties of the Popular Front, and Brunschvicg was president of the French Women's Suffrage Union.

6   PRO, FO 371/19875, C4181/1211/17, Sir George Clerk (Paris) to Anthony Eden, 9 June 1936.

7   Ingram, *The Politics of Dissent*, 153–4. Both men wrote searing indictments of modern warfare. Rolland's *Au-dessus de la mêlée* (*Above the Fray*) was published in September 1914; Barbusse's novel *Le Feu* (*Under Fire*) in August 1916.

8   ADA, Sarraut papers, 12J172, 'Le Communisme et les colonies', n.d.

9   Stora, 'La gauche socialiste', 59–69; also in Stora, *Nationalistes algériens*, chapter 2.

10   Doriot's remarkable career has drawn several biographers, including Philippe Burrin, *La Dérive fasciste. Doriot, Déat, Bergery, 1933–1945* (Paris: Seuil, 1986); Brunet, *Jacques Doriot*.

11   Meynier, 'Volonté de propagande ou inconscient affiche?' 47.

12   Paul Lawrence, ' "Un flot d'agitateurs politiques, de fauteurs de désordre et de criminels". Adverse perceptions of immigrants in France between the wars', *French History*, 14:2 (2000), 204–5.

13   Maxim Silverman, *Deconstructing the Nation. Immigration, Racism and Citizenship in Modern France* (London: Routledge, 1992), 10–11; Clifford Rosenberg, 'The colonial politics of healthcare provision in interwar Paris', *French Historical Studies*, 27:3 (2004), 637–68.

14   Neil MacMaster, *Colonial Migrants and Racism. Algerians in France, 1900–62* (London: Macmillan, 1997), 125–6.

15   Sorum, *Intellectuals and Decolonization in France*, 44.

16   Semidei, 'Les Socialistes Français et le problème colonial', 1125.

17   CAOM GGM, 6(2)D/55, PCF Section colonial, 'La France du Front Populaire et les peuples coloniaux', pamphlet for the Arles Congress, 25–29 December 1937.

18   These reforms are surveyed in Chafer and Sackur, *French Colonial Empire and Popular Front*.

19   Jacques Marseille, 'L'industrialisation des colonies. Affaiblissement ou renforcement de la puissance française?' *Revue Française d'Histoire d'Outre-Mer*, 69:254 (1982), 23; for general discussion of Bernard's ideas see Andrew Hardy, 'The economics of French rule', 807–48.

20   SHA, 2N64, CSDN: 'Conférence économique de la France métropolitaine et d'outre-mer, 1934–1935'. The five study commissions were as follows: commission générale des productions; commission de la prévoyance sociale; commission de l'outillage colonial; commission des finances; commission de l'économie générale.

21   CAOM, Moutet papers, PA28/1/D5: Questions économiques, 'Comité d'action colonisatrice et de paysanne indigène', n.d. September 1935.

22   CAOM, Marius Moutet papers, PA28/1/D1, sous-dossier D: Delavignette note, 'Marius Moutet au Ministère des Colonies'.

23   William A. Hoisington, Jr, 'The Mediterranean Committee and French North Africa, 1935–1940', *Historian*, 53:2 (1991), 259–60.

24   Jackson, *The Popular Front*, 154–8.

25   Marius Moutet, preface to Louis Mérat, *L'Heure de l'économie dirigée d'intérêt général aux colonies* (Paris: Sirey, 1936), iii–iv.

26   William B. Cohen, 'The colonial policy of the Popular Front', *French Historical Studies*, 7:3 (1972), 368–93; Irwin M. Wall, 'Socialists and bureaucrats. The Blum government and the French administration, 1936–37', *International Review of Social History*, 19:3 (1974), 325–46.

27   Peyrouton, *Du service public*, 55; Eric T. Jennings, *Vichy in the Tropics. Pétain's National Revolution in Madagascar, Guadeloupe, and Indochina, 1940–1944* (Stanford CA: Stanford

University Press, 2001), 41. Peyrouton's memoirs suggest obliquely that his instructions to cut Moroccan public spending clashed with Popular Front social reforms. Governor Cayla made no secret of his loathing for the government and its Jewish Premier.

28 René Belanus, 'Félix Éboué, gouverneur nègre du Front Populaire à la Guadeloupe', in Lucien Abenon, Danielle Bégot and Jean-Pierre Sainton (eds), Construire l'histoire antillais (Paris: Editions du CTHS, 2002), 173–95. Éboué previously served in Martinique and French Sudan between 1922 and 1936.

29 Robert Delavignette, 'Le Front populaire devant l'Afrique noire', L'Afrique Française, 46:5 (May 1936), 252–5; Cohen, Rulers of Empire, 98–104.

30 Robert Delavignette, 'La politique de Marius Moutet au Ministère des Colonies', in Renouvin and Rémond, Léon Blum Chef de gouvernement 1936–1937, 391–4.

31 Marseille, 'La conférence des gouverneurs-généraux des colonies', 61–2.

32 CAOM, Moutet papers, PA28/1/D3, 2ème Bureau (Colonies) note, n.d. 1937.

33 Ibid., PA28/1/D1, Delavignette note, 'Marius Moutet au Ministère des Colonies', n.d. 1936.

34 Ibid., PA28/1/D3, 2ème Bureau (Colonies) note, n.d. 1937.

35 Laffey, 'Municipal imperialism in decline', 339–40.

36 CAOM, GGAEF, 1D11, no. 1477, Reste to Marius Moutet, 24 October 1936.

37 Ibid., no. 1817, Reste to Direction des affaires politiques, 31 December 1936.

38 CAOM, GGM, série B: Corréspondance, 3B92, no. 2422, Gouverneur par interim to Direction des affaires politiques 1er bureau, 10 November 1936.

39 CAOM, Moutet papers, PA28/1/D1, no. 1009, Moutet letter to Antonetti (Brazzaville), 'Conférence des gouverneurs-généraux', 12 August 1936.

40 Ibid., PA28/1/D11, Moutet circular, n.d. 1936. Underlined in the original text.

41 Marseille, 'La conférence des gouverneurs-généraux des colonies', 69–72.

42 Kenneth Mouré, ' "Une éventualité absolument exclue". French reluctance to devalue, 1933–1936', French Historical Studies, 15:3 (1988), 479–505; Mouré, Managing the Franc Poincaré, chapter 7.

43 CAOM, AOF Fonds moderne, 17G88, Conférence des gouverneurs-généraux: Discours prononcé par M. Marius Moutet', 5 November 1936.

44 Marc Lagana, 'L'échec de la commission d'enquête coloniale du Front populaire', Historical Reflections, 16:1 (1989), 79–97.

45 André Gide's Voyage au Congo. Carnets de route, published in 1927, became an unlikely bestseller. Gide also produced a documentary with Marc Allégret recording his experiences in AEF, see André Sauvage, 'Oghanda – scenes de la vie indigène en Afrique Equatoriale', Le Monde Colonial illustré, 42 (February 1927), 47.

46 Lagana, 'L'échec de la commission d'enquête coloniale', 82–3.

47 Ibid., 84; Les Archives Nationales, Etat Général des Fonds, Tome III, 515 ff.

48 Lagana, 'L'échec de la commission d'enquête coloniale', 87–90.

49 Ibid., 91–5.

50 Catherine Coquery-Vidrovitch, 'The Popular Front and the colonial question. French West Africa: an example of reformist colonialism', and Lydon, 'Women, children and the Popular Front's missions of inquiry in French West Africa', both in Chafer and Sackur, French Colonial Empire and Popular Front, 157–9 and 173–6; Lydon, 'The unravelling of a neglected source', 555–84.

51 Jennings, Vichy in the Tropics, 58, 70.

52 Michael G. Fry and Itamar Rabinovitch (eds), Despatches from Damascus. Gilbert MacKereth and British policy in the Levant, 1933–1939 (Tel Aviv: Dayan Centre, 1985), Doc. 24. Damascus quarterly report: January 1 to March 31, 1936.

53 CAOM, GGM, 4D44, Comité permanent d'études scientifiques et économiques et de la statistique, 'Madagascar : l'évolution politique et sociale de 1926 à 1937'.

54 Randrianja, Société et luttes anticoloniales à Madagascar, 285–6.

55 Ibid., 295–6.

56 CAOM, GGM, 4D44, Comité permanent d'études scientifiques et économiques et de la statistique, 'Madagascar : L'évolution politique et sociale de 1926 à 1937'.

57 Randrianja, Société et luttes anticoloniales à Madagascar, 368–73. Wildcat strikes continued in Madagascar until the outbreak of war in 1939.

58 Koerner, Madagascar, 310–11.

59 CAOM, GGM, 4D44, Comité permanent d'études scientifiques et économiques et de la statistique, 'Madagascar: L'évolution politique et sociale de 1926 à 1937'. Regarding later surveillance of Communist activity in Madagascar: CAOM, 6(2)D55, no. 1215/DISCF, Police régionale mobile, 2e brigade Tamatave rapport, 15 July 1938.

60 Zinoman, *The Colonial Bastille*, 267–78.

61 CAOM, Moutet papers, PA28/1/D1, sous-dossier C: 'Notes sur les réalisations d'ordre politique du ministère, 1936–1937'.

62 Zinoman, *The Colonial Bastille*, chapters 7 and 8.

63 CAOM, Moutet papers, PA28/1/D2, sous-dossier A: 'Textes et circulaires concernant les problèmes judiciaries coloniaux: Réforme de la Justice, 1936–1937'.

64 Khánh, *Vietnamese Communism*, 211–15; Marr, *Vietnamese Tradition*, 392–6.

65 CAOM, 17G90, no. 2811, Direction général des affaires politiques, 'Rapport sur l'activité de la Direction politique, 1936–1937', 22 November 1937.

66 *Ibid.*, Direction des affaires politiques, 'Note détaillée sur la situation politique de l'AOF en 1936', 5 November 1936.

67 CAOM, AOF Fonds moderne, 21G47, Governor-general Brévié to 2ème bureau (Colonies), 3 February 1934.

68 Person, 'Le Front populaire au Sénégal', 84–5.

69 *Ibid.*, 85. Diouf was backed by *Le Sénégal*, a paper run by his principal supporter, Alfred Goux, the mayor of Dakar. Guèye's PSS was supported by two more left-wing newspapers, *L'AOF* and *Le Périscope*.

70 Chafer, *The End of Empire in French West Africa*, 35.

71 Marcel de Coppet previously served in Casamance (Senegal), Chad, Dahomey, Somalia and Mauritania, see Chafer, *The End of Empire in West Africa*, 32.

72 Thomas Bassett, 'The development of cotton in northern Ivory Coast', 279.

73 Person, 'Le Front populaire au Sénégal', 94.

74 *Ibid.*, 91–2.

75 Ibrahima Thioub, 'Economie coloniale et rémunération de la force de travail : le salaire de manoeuvre à Dakar de 1930 à 1954', *Revue Française d'Histoire d'Outre-Mer*, 81:305 (1994), 437–8; see also N. Bernard-Duquenet, *Le Sénégal et le Front Populaire* (Paris: Editions l'Harmattan, 1985).

76 CAOM, AOF Fonds moderne, 17G90, no. 2811, 'Rapport sur l'activité de la Direction politique, 1936–1937', 22 November 1937.

77 *Ibid.*, 'Note sur la situation administrative de l'AOF en 1936', 5 November 1936.

78 CAOM, GGAEF, 1D11, 1936, no. 898, Brazzaville government to Ministry of Colonies/Cabinet, 13 June 1936.

79 Prost, *Republican Identities in War and Peace*, 311–32; and his earlier 'Les grèves de Juin 1936 : essai d'interprétation', in Renouvin and Rémond, *Léon Blum*, 67–87; Jackson, *The Popular Front*, 87–104.

80 Pennell. *Morocco*, 242.

81 It bears emphasis that the Delhi government offered troops to help put down the Pondicherry strikes, and that one of the enclave's three spinning mills was British-owned, see PRO, FO 371/19874, C7320/374/17, Victor Perowne (Paris) to FO, 14 October 1936; and C7432/374/17, Lloyd-Thomas (Paris) to FO, 20 October 1936.

82 Jacques Weber, *Pondichéry et les comptoirs de l'Inde française après Dupleix* (Paris: Editions Denoël, 1996), 332–4.

83 Fry and Rabinovitch, *Despatches from Damascus*, Doc. 24. Damascus quarterly report: 1 January to 31 March 1936.

84 MAE, série E: Levant, vol. 492, Comte de Martel report to Foreign Ministry, 3 January 1936; Subki Bey Barakat letter to de Martel, 22 January 1936.

85 Khoury, *Syria and the French Mandate*, 456–63, quote at 457.

86 Fry and Rabinovitch, *Despatches from Damascus*, Doc. 24. Damascus quarterly report: 1 January to 31 March 1936.

87 CAOM, Moutet papers, PA28/4/Dossier Varenne, 'Manifestation des ouvriers annamites employés sur les plantations de la Société Michelin'.

88 CAOM, Moutet papers, PA28/4/Dossier Varenne, sous-dossier 75, Moutet letter to Brévié (Hanoi), 5 February 1937.

89 *Ibid.*
90 CAOM, Moutet papers, PA28/4/Dossier Varenne, sous-dossier 71, no. 1756/SG, Brévié to Ministry of Colonies, 23 April 1937.
91 CAOM, Moutet papers, PA28/2/D16, no. 682/2/SRM, SR Troupes d'Indochine, bulletin de renseignements no. 33, 31 July 1937.
92 CAOM, Moutet papers, PA28/4/Dossier Varenne, sous-dossier 71, no. 1638, Brévié to Direction des affaires politiques/3e Bureau, 28 May 1937.
93 PRO, FO 371/20695, C4680/240/17, consul Hogg (Saigon) to FO, 27 May 1937.
94 CAOM, Moutet papers, PA28/4/Dossier Varenne, sous-dossier 71, no 649/C, Cochin-China Governor Pages to Brévié, 14 May 1937.
95 CAOM, Moutet papers, PA28/4/Dossier Varenne, sous-dossier 72, no. 334/S, Brévié to Moutet, 18 August 1937.
96 PRO, FO 371/22921, C4684/249/17, consul H. C. Walsh (Saigon), Report on conditions in Indochina during February 1939; Khánh, *Vietnamese Communism*, 224–6; Marr, *Vietnamese Tradition*, 388–9. The sentences on *La Lutte* group members were revoked in 1939.
97 Dunwoodie, *Writing French Algeria*, 29; for more details see F. Gaspard, *Maurice Viollette, homme politique et éditorialiste* (Paris: Editions Edijac, 1986).
98 Ferhat Abbas cited Viollette's remarks in a 1946 parliamentary debate on repression in Algeria. See *Journal Officiel*, 1er Séance, Assemblée Consultative, 23 August 1946.
99 Conklin, 'A force for civilization', 292.
100 Jackson, *The Popular Front*, 154.
101 SHA, Fonds de Moscou, C1109/D667, SEA (Algiers), 'A/S du projet de loi Viollette pour l'attribution des droits politiques aux indigènes', 5 February 1937.
102 PRO, FO 371/21601, Algiers consulate quarterly report no. 3, 31 March 1938.
103 Stora, *Nationalistes algériens*, 33–5.
104 ADA, Sarraut papers, 12J118, 'L'exposé de M. Albert Sarraut sur l'Afrique du Nord', *Le Temps*, 28 November 1937.
105 Stora, *Nationalistes algériens*, 30–1, 85–104 *passim*.
106 'L'exposé de M. Albert Sarraut sur l'Afrique du Nord', *Le Temps*, 28 November 1937.
107 Stora, *Nationalistes algériens*, 20–2; Dunwoodie, *Writing French Algeria*, 29–33.
108 Ageron, 'L'association des étudiants musulmans', 43–4.
109 CAOM, GGA, 9H32, Direction de la Sécurité Générale (Algiers), 'Rapport sur les faits importants intéressant l'ordre et la sécurité, mois d'août 1937'.
110 Hoisington Jr, *The Casablanca Connection*, 55–60.
111 Moroccan smallholders that bought cheap land in the Depression years were widely seen as a bedrock of rural conservatism, see Joffé, 'The Moroccan nationalist movement', 296–9.
112 MAE, série Maroc, vol. 92, no. 1977, Rabat residency report, 'Situation politique et économique (période du 28 août au 10 septembre 1937)', 11 October 1937.
113 Hoisington Jr, *The Casablanca Connection*, 61–73.
114 Kaddache, *Le Parti du peuple algérien 1937–1939*, 'Pourquoi le PPA est contre le projet Viollette', 57–9.
115 Kaddache, *Histoire du nationalisme algérien*, 459–62.
116 Dunwoodie, *Writing French Algeria*, 185.
117 In contrast to the Croix de Feu, Action Française, the longest established of the ultra-rightist groups, had little to say on colonial questions, see Heffernan, 'The French right and the overseas empire', 100–1.
118 Jackson, *The Popular Front*, 252–4. On PSF membership see Soucy, *French Fascism. The Second Wave*, 113–14; Passmore, *From Liberalism to Fascism*, 249.
119 AN, F^{60}201/Dossier Peyrouton, Michel Faurant (Section SFIO d'Oudja) letter to Blum, 10 June 1936.
120 AN, F^{60}187/Dossier A2, Cabinet (Algiers), 'Situation politique européenne de l'Algérie en 1938'.
121 *Ibid.* Doriot spoke at eight Algerian venues in May 1938: Algiers, Oran (twice), Bône, Sidi Bel-Abbès, Mostaganem, Constantine and Tiaret.
122 The treaty negotiations are extensively discussed in Khoury, *Syria and the French*

Mandate, 464–8, 485–93; and Peter Shambrook, *French Imperialism in Syria*, 198–228.

123 SHA, 7N4190/D1, EMA Section d'Outre-Mer, 'Traité Franco-Syrien : projet de convention militaire', n.d. September 1936; Fry and Rabinovitch, *Despatches from Damascus*, Doc. 27, Damascus quarterly report: 1 October to 21 December 1936.

124 MAE, série E: Levant, vol. 493, Ibrahim el Kinj letter to Yvn Delbos, 25 June 1936, tel. 655/Cabinet politique, Délégué Général Meyrier to Delbos, 27 June 1936.

125 Rabinovitch, 'The compact minorities and the Syrian state', 700–5.

126 CADN, Fonds Beyrouth, Cabinet politique, vol. 494, Cabinet politique note, 'Observations sur la protection des droits des minorités en Syrie', n.d. 1936. Leaders of the Alawite, Druze, Armenian and Circassian communities failed to secure places in the Syrian delegation to Paris, diminishing their ability to shape the treaty terms.

127 Fry and Rabinovitch, *Despatches from Damascus*, Doc. 27, Damascus quarterly report: 1 October to 21 December 1936.

128 Khoury, *Syria and the French Mandate*, 485–93. Regarding military responses to the treaty, see Maurice Albord, *L'armée française et les états du Levant 1936–1946* (Paris: CNRS, 2000).

129 Zamir, *Lebanon's Quest*, 194–214.

130 Jackson, *The Popular Front*, 126–8.

131 The question of whether business leaders exacted 'revenge' on the Popular Front in 1938–39 divides historians, see Ingo Kolboom, *La Revanche des patrons. Le patronat français face au Front populaire* (Paris: Flammarion, 1986), and, for a contrary view, Richard Vinen, *The Politics of French Business, 1936–1945* (Cambridge: Cambridge University Press, 1992).

132 Paul Smith, 'Political parties, parliament and women's suffrage in France, 1919–1939', *French History*, 11:3 (1997), 355.

133 See Yaël Simpson Fletcher, ' "A more perfect equality?" Colonial workers and French Communists in Marseilles, 1936–1938', *Proceedings of the Western Society for French History*, 24 (1997), 506–15.

CHAPTER TEN

Approaching war: the empire and international crisis in the 1930s

As international tension increased during the 1930s, the idea that the empire could compensate for French demographic, economic and military weakness next to the fascist powers gained favour in Paris. It was widely assumed in government and parliament that the colonial contribution to any future war in Europe would exceed that of 1914–18. And from 1924 onward the colonies were tied into the financing of French defence expenditure. Colonial governments contributed to service ministry budgets and the Finance Ministry placed increased onus on colonial taxpayers to meet the costs of local port improvements and other fixed defences. Algeria made the largest single contribution. Between 1924 and 1937 six per cent of the colony's budgetary income was allocated to metropolitan defence.[1] In 1937 Algerian taxpayers were landed with an additional 289 million franc bill for the modernisation of the Mers el-Kébir fleet base, and on 24 June 1939 Albert Sarraut, then Interior Minister, and his colleague Paul Reynaud at Finance, set Algeria's annual contribution to the French defence budget at 85 million francs for the next decade.[2]

Heightened imperial contributions did not, however, generate much confidence among politicians in France. After the trauma of the Czechoslovak crisis in 1938, French political parties remained sorely divided internally and between one another over French capacity for war against Germany, Italy and, probably, Japan. The Communist leadership, caught between its theoretical commitment to worker internationalism, residual support for Popular Frontism and the growing threat of proscription, took refuge in a concept of French power based on the abiding strength of populist republicanism.[3] The Socialists struggled to come to terms with the collapse of the European collective security system that Blum's first Popular Front government had tried to preserve.[4] The Christian Democrat groupings, Jeune République and the Popular Democratic Party, marginal in parliamentary terms, shared the Socialists' lament at the disintegration of an international system based on League of Nations principles.[5] The

Democratic Alliance, the largest right-wing parliamentary party, with eighty-four Deputies, had split in September 1938 when Paul Reynaud led a parliamentary group that left the Alliance in disgust at party leader Pierre-Etienne Flandin's outspoken defeatism.[6] And the internal divisions of the Radical-Socialists, still the quintessential party of government under Edouard Daladier, replicated the wider societal divisions between advocates of 'firmness' against Hitler and increasingly desperate appeasers.[7]

One feature common to the entire political spectrum in 1938–39 was nostalgia for French imperial grandeur, typified in the public mind by the colonies' contribution to victory in 1914–18.[8] Julian Jackson gets to the heart of the matter: 'The sudden popularity of the Empire in 1938 was clearly an emotional compensation for the dramatic loss of French influence in Europe which Munich seemed to presage'.[9] The climax of the Czechoslovak crisis left a deeper psychological scar in France than in Britain. Mobilisation began on 24 September; private savers rushed to withdraw their money from the banks; and, with the abandonment of its one faithful eastern ally, and Britain still reluctant to commit to a full-blooded alliance, France stood more alone than ever.[10] The shock to French society registered in a fundamental reversal of left–right splits over foreign policy. Elements of the nationalist right became more openly pessimistic, and in rare cases, defeatist. Much of the non-Communist left and liberal centre rose to the challenge of preparing France for war.[11] As we saw in chapter six, a host of imperialist films enjoyed box-office success in the twelve months following the September 1938 war scare. The spectacle of France's imperial legions triumphing against overwhelming odds made comforting viewing.[12] With war imminent, on 29 July 1939 the Daladier administration established a Department of Information (Commissariat général à l'information) to co-ordinate state propaganda. The new organisation added to public expectations of the colonial contribution to the war effort. During the early months of the Phony War ministers and high-ranking generals trod the red carpet at the cinema premières of *L'Homme du Niger* and *Brazza, l'épopée du Congo*, two films that identified France as a great African power. A similar film, *La France est un empire*, was selected for the Cannes film festival. Whatever happened, France could rely on its colonies.[13] Or so the official line went. In fact belief in this *salut par l'empire* ('salvation by empire') was superficial, founded on ignorance of colonial conditions rather than a careful calculation of the empire's contribution to France's economy and military strength.[14] With these points in mind, this chapter considers the viability of French imperial defence planning and the empire contribution to it.

Threat perceptions and imperial defence priorities

French imperial defence planning differed from that of Britain in at least three key respects. The first was the different onus placed on continental obligations. Recurrent disputes over strategic priorities and the allocation of precious military resources were common to both colonial powers. But, in France, few questioned the principle that defence of empire was subordinate to continental commitments in Europe. It could not be otherwise. It was self-evident to politicians and planners that the empire should contribute to French national survival. In a global conflict the net movement of men and resources would be from the colonies to France, not the other way round.[15] By 1937 the Ministry of Colonies defence budget was substantially devoted to measures to facilitate the transfer of colonial men and materials to France in time of war. Between 1935 and 1938 the Chamber of Deputies finance commission approved the allocation of a greater proportion of the overall Ministry of Colonies budget to military expenditure. In 1935 612 million francs was reserved for colonial defence spending. In 1936 the figure climbed to 668 million, and in 1938 to 677 million. These increases were justified as part of France's preparation for war rather than as a means to consolidate the defensive capacity of the colonies themselves.[16]

During the winter of 1922–23 the War Ministry imposed its authority over the organisation, recruitment and training of colonial regiments. The Ministry of Colonies military section retained responsibility for raising defence revenue within individual territories, and the assignment of security forces for internal policing. This shift in jurisdictional power represented a deeper attitudinal change among imperial defence planners. It marked the first major reassignment of inter-ministerial responsibility for colonial forces since the turn of the century. In July 1900 colonial regiments, until then collectively designated *troupes de la marine* (a reflection of the navy's key role in early conquests), came under the joint authority of the War Ministry and the Ministry of Colonies. In November 1922 the War Ministry went much further. French imperial forces were henceforth designated a supplementary reserve for European war. Justified at the time on the specious grounds that the era of colonial pacification was over, the measure fundamentally redefined the primary purpose of France's colonial armies.[17] By 1922 War Ministry planners already anticipated a standing colonial reserve of six fully equipped divisions, each of four combined infantry and artillery regiments trained to fight against a first-rank European power.[18]

These changes were consistent with the foremost imperial lesson of the First World War: the colonies helped France to win in Europe.[19] No surprises there. For France, 1914–18 was overwhelmingly a European conflict. The Middle Eastern war against Ottoman Turkey was peripheral, and primarily a British imperial affair. Seizures of German territory in Africa were more ephemeral still. There was no hostile East Asian power to worry about. Imperial lobbyists clamoured for the post-war spoils in the Levant and black Africa, but the wider French public knew that victory emerged from the mud of the trenches. Militarily, politically and, above all, emotionally the western front experience reinforced the Eurocentricity of French post-war strategy. In the French mind set, total war was not global war. Rather, the totality of metropolitan and imperial resources was required to defeat Germany. In the words of Deputy Chief of Staff General Alphonse Georges, 'the colonies would be defended on the Rhine'.[20] Britain's blue-water imperialism did not resonate in France, where imperial power denoted the capacity to bring colonial resources to bear in defence of the home country. Global commitment would fatally dissipate limited strategic assets. French strategic planning thus differed from British in its recognition that the survival of colonies was reliant on *a priori* defence of the motherland. As a result, French governments and general staffs were less troubled than their British counterparts by fine calculations of how best to defend far-flung dependencies.[21]

Herein lay a second key difference between French and British imperial strategy. Colonial defence was never allowed to impede metropolitan preparations for war in Europe. Put simply, the defence of France consumed the overwhelming majority of French resources and attention. Indochina was the major loser as a result of this. There was no French equivalent to the 'Singapore strategy' of Far Eastern imperial contingency planning. Given the disastrous consequences of that strategy for Britain, Singapore, colonial Malaya and Australasia, one is tempted to applaud the French for their greater pragmatism. Yet contradictions remained. The limited horizons of French imperial strategy did not correspond either with successive governments' declared commitment to maintain the empire intact or with Indochina's pivotal position as France's second most important captive economic market after North Africa. No French Far Eastern squadron was set to arrive in Camranh Bay – the federation's major fleet base, still incomplete in 1940. No major transfers of men or mechanised equipment to Indochina were envisaged to keep Japanese invaders at bay. After talks with Cochin-China governor Pages in January 1936, Vice-admiral Jean Esteva, naval forces commander in Indochina, warned that officials, settlers and Chinese traders were 'extraordinarily apprehensive' about Japan.[22] They had good reason. A December 1936 report on the federation's few remaining tank units revealed the state of things, 'those in Saigon are only wheeled out on the 14th July; those in Tonkin are beyond repair and are nothing more than scrap iron'.[23]

Strategic neglect of Indochina was nothing new. The alarm expressed by Daladier's ministers at the parlous state of France's Far Eastern defences in 1938–39 echoed the shocked outrage among politicians and public about the withdrawal of French forces from Langson in Tonkin that brought down Jules Ferry's government in April 1885. French empire defence planning always looked to Africa before Asia. Elsewhere, the French Antilles, Saint-Pierre et Miquelon, French Oceania and the French outposts in India were substantially protected by Anglo-American naval power. The inevitable priority attached to European defence against Germany left no alternative to the slow decline of French defensive capacity in South East Asia. Again, one should acknowledge the commonsense realism of Eurocentric strategic planners. No matter how many men, money or materials were poured into Indochina, they could not match the offensive capacity of Japanese forces. The significance of pre-war understanding of Indochina's indefensibility is more symbolic. It is sadly ironic in the light of the desperate French efforts to cling on to Indochina after 1945 that in 1939 the defence establishment tacitly accepted its loss.

The third factor differentiating French and British imperial defence lay in the culture that informed it. British empire defence planning drew on maritime tradition, the pivotal importance of the white Dominions to Britain's global standing as the centre of an English-speaking world and the huge resources of British India as a military reserve. French empire defence schemes drew on the martial traditions of its two distinct colonial armies: one, the Armée d'Afrique, the title assigned to the standing forces in French North Africa; the other, la Coloniale, the appellation of the colonial infantry regiments raised in black Africa, Indochina, Madagascar and the Antilles.

After full mobilisation in October 1939, these imperial land forces ran to hundreds of thousands. Their commanders and cadres shared the imperial preoccupations and extensive fighting experience of their British equivalents in the Indian Army. But their primary role in war was not to protect the colonial inheritance but to supplement the line in France. Algeria, France's main colony of white settlement, held pride of place in imperial strategy, but it was no Dominion. Constitutionally, of course, it was far more: Algeria was France. But the legal niceties and rhetorical claims of *Algérie française* disarmed Algiers governors that pressed the case for North African defence because, in purely constitutional terms, defence of France was *ipso facto* defence of Algeria. French imperial strategy made little allowance for dialogue between the metropolitan centre and imperial outposts. The imperial conferences, high commissions and Dominion Office bureaucracy that linked London, Ottawa, Cape Town, Canberra and Wellington made no sense in the French context. Their nearest equivalent – the regular cycle of North African governors' conferences – had no impact on strategic thinking in Paris. Pushed by Dominion governments, Britain's imperial strategists argued bitterly over building fighters or bombers, sending battleships to the South China Sea and preparing a small army to fight in Europe. French strategic planners paid lip service to the integrity of *la plus grande France*, but in practice the Cabinet and the senior generals scarcely raised their eyes beyond the continental horizon. France's imperial defence culture was confined to specialists at the margins of government. Its practitioners were long-serving overseas commanders, the colonial bureaucracy and a separate, and subordinate, military planning agency in Paris. Reduced to its essence, empire defence was an unaffordable luxury to a France struggling to meet the threat of German invasion.

Recruitment, colonial control and strategy

The proportion of colonial troops serving in the French armed forces as a whole declined after the first Popular Front government introduced a four-year rearmament programme costing an estimated 14 billion francs in September 1936. This did not represent any easing of colonial recruitment, but was the consequence of the expansion of the metropolitan land army. In 1930 colonial units comprised thirty-six per cent of overall army strength. This fell to twenty-eight per cent in 1934, and to twenty-four per cent in 1936. After mobilisation in September 1939 the 520,250 colonial soldiers represented eleven per cent of France's 'mobilised manpower'.[24]

Tirailleur sénégalais units in the First World War were employed as shock troops against German positions, but the experience of trench warfare left colonial regimental commands convinced that black African troops were ill suited to combat in harsh European winters.[25] Coloniale regiments were typically garrisoned in the Midi. Their transportation to and from Mediterranean ports was made easier; tuberculosis infection and other pulmonary illnesses associated with cold conditions were minimised.[26] The War Ministry colonial section regulated the use of these colonial troops in counter-insurgency operations such as the Syrian revolt of 1925–26 and pacification operations in Morocco. Disdain for the combat effectiveness of Indochinese, Malagasy and Equatorial African regiments persisted. In April 1922 Lyautey pleaded with the War Ministry to replace the Equatorial African troops deployed in northern Morocco with hardier West Africans capable of withstanding difficult terrain and the army diet of rice and meat.[27] But during the winter 1925 campaign against Abd el-Krim's forces in the Rif highlands hundreds of *tirailleur sénégalais* were invalided out of the line. During November and December 1925 alone army surgeons conducted almost 200 foot amputations on frostbite victims. These casualties suggested that any shortcomings of colonial troops resulted from inadequate equipment (in this case a lack of winter boots and woollen socks) and poor health care, not inherent racial characteristics.[28] Shortages of doctors, surgical equipment, prophylactic treatments and medical facilities dogged colonial regiments until the 1940 *débâcle*.[29]

If the cash-strapped army bureaucracy was less than assiduous about equipment, the same could not be said of its monitoring of colonial units for signs of political unrest.[30] The army's principal concern was always Communist infiltration. PCF anti-militarism and its incitement of desertion among soldiers sent to the Rif front in 1925 raised lasting fears of mutinous colonial troops. And the authorities' focus on leftist sedition seemed justified by the fact that two pro-Communist nationalist parties, the ENA and the ICP, tried to disrupt military recruitment in the 1930s. After the suppression of the Yen Bay mutiny, ICP success in enlisting support among detainees in Vietnam's prison system added to alarm about Communist influence among Vietnamese conscripts.[31] Individual colonial commands submitted regular reports on garrison 'morale', an innocuous term usually read as 'unrest'. Time after time the recipients of these memoranda circled, scored or otherwise highlighted any passages referring to Communist activity – appropriately enough, in red pencil.[32] Political surveillance of colonial troops in the 1930s indicated one trait above all. With the notable exception of Indochina, regiments stationed in the colonies were 'uninfected' by Communism. By contrast, those based in France were more prone to dissent and 'dangerous ideas'.[33] Imperial defence planning took this into consideration. Colonial regiments were assigned longer periods on policing and frontier protection duties overseas. Garrisons in France were increasingly fortress-like. Contact with the civilian population was discouraged. Mobilisation schemes envisaged the wholesale transfer of Armée d'Afrique formations and Coloniale infantry and artillery regiments within days of the outbreak of war, but not before it.[34]

After the First World War defence planning staffs were established in each of the French North African territories to link local civil administration with the general staff bureaucracy in Paris. Improved co-ordination between strategic planners and Maghreb officials ensured that Moroccan, Algerian and Tunisian defence requirements were subordinated to the primordial needs of metropolitan security.[35] The swingeing defence cuts of the depression years increased the burden placed on cheaply maintained Armée d'Afrique and Coloniale regiments. Meanwhile, army preoccupation with Germany enabled the Naval Ministry to recoup its influence over empire defence planning. In 1920 the general staff concluded that the protection of francophone Africa was best assured by French fleet supremacy in the western Mediterranean and a strong naval presence off the West African coast.[36] Provided the navy controlled these waters, communications links, troop and supply transfers, and the reinforcement of key naval bases from Bizerta to Dakar, presented few problems. Costly stockpiling and troop reinforcement would assume higher priority only if the navy could not prevent enemy landings.[37]

In October 1922 the general staff defined the Maghreb's strategic needs.

In the absence of any pressing European threat, the planners focused on increased coastal patrols, improved port defences, strategic raw material supplies, the development of an integrated rail system and the construction of additional military airbases.[38] In May 1923 the War Ministry approved plans to increase Tunisia's production of ferrous ores, extend the territory's transport network and develop a metallurgical industry around Tunis. The army staff planning section conceded that the measures were uneconomical, but judged it vital to achieve Maghreb self-sufficiency in strategic raw materials.[39] By this point, French naval strength in the western Mediterranean faced more severe challenge. The Washington Naval Conference of 1921–22 intensified Franco-Italian naval competition.[40] And the French navy's strategic commitment to empire protection was impossible to reconcile with the National Bloc's determination to keep defence spending in check during the military occupation of the Ruhr in 1923–24.[41]

The navy's importance as guarantor of African security was not about to disappear. Army squabbling made sure of that. Between 1920 and 1924 the War Ministry sought to establish the principle that Morocco's *corps d'occupation* – always the strongest and best equipped army command in French North Africa – should provide the first reserve for the defence of Algeria and Tunisia against external attack. Should general war arise, the three North African territories would become a single strategic whole. Moroccan regiments were expected to make up the shortfall as other North African units were sent to fight in France. The army staff planned to transfer Armée d'Afrique cadres in Algeria and Tunisia to France to form the core of four divisions (85e to 88e) operating alongside the metropolitan army. Lyautey demurred at this. The Rabat residency preferred to reduce the French elements in existing Armée d'Afrique formations, in particular among units of *zouaves* (infantry) and *chasseurs d'Afrique* (cavalry), in which French volunteers predominated. French servicemen could thus be reassigned to metropolitan regiments, allowing thorough 'Africanisation' of the Armée d'Afrique in terms of composition and strategic role. In short, Lyautey wanted a Maghreb army uniquely trained and preserved for North African defence.[42]

Arguments over the use of North African troops were soon subsumed by the more pressing crisis of the Rif war. War Ministry planners imposed their preferred alternatives thereafter. By that point Lyautey was gone. His civilian replacement, Théodore Steeg, was no match for his predecessor in matters of imperial defence. And, after all, Abd el-Krim was finally overwhelmed by Pétain's distinctly metropolitan methods of colonial warfare – artillery barrages, poison gas, aerial bombardment and frontal infantry assaults. In June 1926 the Supreme Council of National Defence (Conseil Supérieur de la Défense Nationale, CSDN), then France's foremost civil–military strategic planning committee, acknowledged that the empire's role as a net contributor to French defence made it impossible to determine the allocation of military resources to individual colonies. The complexion of any future Mediterranean or North African conflict was obscure. It was probable that war in Africa would be the by-product of a European conflagration. In a very real sense, the defence of France was the defence of its empire.[43]

Four years later, on 12 October 1930, André Tardieu's government created the post of commander-in-chief for French North Africa. The appointee was selected from the military membership of the supreme war council. But the functions of the commander-in-chief were reserved for periods of crisis such as internal rebellion and the consequent declaration of martial law, or the imminent threat of invasion by land or sea. In early September 1938 Daladier's government finally codified the duties involved, the post having been assigned to the Rabat resident-general Charles Noguès.[44] It was the prospect of war in Europe – not in Africa – that compelled the French authorities to clarify the chain of command in the empire, the reason being that Noguès was to supervise the transfer of African troops to France.

In July 1935 the CSDN considered a revised plan for the long-term division of Armée d'Afrique regiments between France and North Africa. Eleven battalions of North African troops were already deployed in France between October 1933 and December 1934. These troop transfers formed part of the CSDN scheme to integrate North African formations alongside metropolitan army units to compensate for the so-called *années creuses* – the years 1935–40 in which the annual contingent of French conscripts would fall because of the reduced birth rate during the First World War. These preparations aside, the most striking feature of the CSDN's strategic planning in 1935 was its preoccupation with internal disorder and potential disloyalty among Maghrebi troops. The scale of the violence unleashed during the Constantine riots in August 1934 shook the military establishment.[45] Plans to use professional Maghrebi soldiers interchangeably with their French counterparts were abandoned, except in specialist units, such as cavalry and artillery, facing acute manpower shortages. The prime minister's office assumed responsibility for the co-ordination of inter-ministerial intelligence on Muslim affairs. The danger of Arab revolt forced a rethink of manpower allocation.[46] Clearer distinctions were made between Armée d'Afrique units largely composed of Muslim troops and so-called 'sovereignty troops', such as Foreign Legion and *zouave* regiments, where Europeans were more numerous. The latter took on more internal policing duties in French North Africa. After the Constantine disturbances Gardes mobiles units, three armoured car squadrons and several cavalry formations were also earmarked to deal with urban unrest. Similar precautions were taken in France. Maghrebi servicemen stationed around Paris, in Lyons and in bases in and around Marseilles were segregated from French troops.[47]

Government, general staff, service and colonial ministries co-ordinated long-term imperial strategy only from 1936 onward. 'Empire defence plans' featured on the general staff agenda from time to time after the Rif war. But the issue never won much attention until the shake-up of the civil–military apparatus of general staff advisory committees in 1936–37. The rue Oudinot's senior strategic planning body, the Consultative Committee on Colonial Defence (Comité Consultatif de Défense des Colonies, CCDC), acquired unprecedented influence under the Popular Front as an advisory committee to the newly established Standing National Defence Committee (Comité Permanent de la Défense Nationale, CPDN), the highest-ranking civil–military committee in government between 1936–40. Both of France's last two peacetime Ministers of Colonies, Marius Moutet and Georges Mandel, supported the CCDC, which had an exceptional secretariat under General Eugène Mordant, later assigned the thankless task of army command in Indochina in 1939–40. Through the revitalised CCDC the Ministry of Colonies at last acquired a voice in strategic planning, submitting policy advice to the CPDN at seven meetings held between 1936 and 1939. It was not enough. On 12 May 1938 a distinct colonial general staff was created. Only then did colonial requirements make their mark at governmental level.[48]

Waking up to the problem of imperial defence was one thing, agreeing on how best to solve it quite another. The bureaucratic changes of 1936–38 were the outcome of a jurisdictional battle between the rue Oudinot's military affairs service and the War Ministry's colonial section. Impelled by the two inspectors-general of colonial troops of the 1936–40 period, Generals Gaston Billotte and Jules-Antoine Bührer, the Ministry of Colonies combated War Ministry and general staff reluctance to concede time or resources to imperial defence. The War Ministry's iron grip on North African defence planning, the navy's predominance in questions of Mediterranean strategy and the Air Ministry's unwillingness to send the precious modern aircraft just beginning to roll off the production lines in Toulouse and Paris to far-off colonial airbases left little room for manoeuvre. Defence forces in black Africa, Indochina, Madagascar, the Antilles and other island colonies were technically under rue Oudinot control. But in practice the service ministries expected colonial governments to pay for local regiments and fixed defences, and the metropolitan military establishment to control their eventual use. In crude terms, the colonial bureaucracy did the leg work of recruitment and financing, but the service bureaucracy took the strategic decisions. The facts of life in French strategy could not be altered: colonial defence was about the crumbs left at the table after the planners of war with Germany had gone. In March 1939 General Bührer, successor to Billotte and principal spokesman on imperial defence, toured colonial garrisons in the Midi. His visits to barracks in Fréjus,

Toulon and Marseilles left him unimpressed. Soldiers 'left a lot to be desired . . . greatcoats [*capotes*] too long or too short, untidy clothing, badges either dirty or in poor condition'.[49] Behind Bührer's complaints about the troops' slovenly appearance was something more revealing: the army command expected the same of colonial regiments as their French counterparts.

The Mediterranean territories: French North Africa and the Levant mandates

Italy, not Germany, was the greatest menace to colonial security in Africa and the Mediterranean. Italian designs on Tunisia, French Somaliland and the Dodecanese islands off the Turkish coast became clearer as Mussolini's imperial ambitions increased after the initial conquest of Abyssinia in 1936.[50] Italian military support for Franco's forces in Spain raised the prospect of Italian access to ports and airbases in the Balearic Islands – particularly Minorca – from which maritime communications between France and the Maghreb might be disrupted.[51] And Rome's *détente* with the Yugoslav government in early 1937 hammered another nail in the coffin of France's vestigial Eastern European alliance system.[52] By December 1936 Franco's imperial schemes were also clearer. The Algiers authorities monitored radio broadcasts from Seville inciting the Muslim populations of Morocco and Oranie to cast off French control.[53] On 18 December, five months after the outbreak of the Spanish civil war, General Georges, a former corps commander in Algeria, warned his general staff colleagues that greater resources were needed to forestall a rupture in communications between France and the Maghreb in a war with Italy and possibly Spain.[54] And the CSDN estimated that defence of the Maghreb's land borders and sea approaches precluded a naval assault on the Balearics, or a rapid overland march into Spanish Morocco, both options seen as a way to knock Franco's Spain out of a multilateral conflict.[55] Customarily net contributors to metropolitan defence, the North African territories might become a drain on strategic raw materials, naval units, anti-aircraft batteries and Armée d'Afrique regiments needed in France.[56]

In November 1936 Marius Moutet visited garrisons and port installations in AOF. On returning to France, he and General Billotte pressed the case for imperial defence requirements to be integrated into the Popular Front's rearmament scheme.[57] The CPDN acceded to this request on 15 February 1937. At its next meeting, on 15 April 1937, the CPDN further agreed at Daladier's insistence to devote greater resources to Maghreb defence and fleet protection of the vital western Mediterranean transit route.[58] Blum's government was deeply hostile to Fascist Italy, whose increasingly flagrant intervention in Spain remained a bitter source of division between left and right in France.[59] This ideological animus triggered right-wing accusations, shared by some general staff members, that Blum's ministers destroyed all prospect of Franco-Italian reconciliation. The concept of a partnership with Rome to check German ambitions in Central and Eastern Europe was an *idée fixée* in right-wing circles, and conversations between the French and Italian army and air staffs were held between March and June 1935.[60] Military co-operation between France and Italy was always easier to envisage in a Central European context than an African one. And the Abyssinian war and the Spanish conflict undermined the earlier foundations of collaboration between the two general staffs. By 1937 the notion of a lost opportunity to conciliate Mussolini's regime was little more than a stick used by opponents of the Popular Front to beat the government for allegedly sacrificing strategic interest to misguided idealism.

Italian aggrandisement was not the chief consideration in Mediterranean strategy anyway. Germany had to take precedence. Although Italy was the more likely aggressor in North Africa, the general staff necessarily focused on the more pressing German threat in Europe. If France could not withstand a German attack, then all was lost. In North Africa and Indochina the Daladier government approved accelerated mobilisation measures, raw material stockpiling and the construction of local workshops to repair aircraft and military equipment, rather than any significant reinforcement of garrisons.[61] Permanent defence councils were established in Morocco, Algeria and Tunisia to work in conjunction with the military cabinets of the North African resident-ministers and governors.[62] Noguès, still Moroccan resident, supervised a North African defence scheme as designated commander-in-chief of the Maghreb theatre.[63] From June 1938 the North African authorities held a regular cycle of meetings on military supply, mobilisation and civil defence.[64] The mechanisms of bureaucratic control and the sophistication of Maghreb strategic planning were unmatched anywhere else in the empire. But no government could reassign precious forces to any colony: the Nazi menace was paramount.

French defence planning in Syria and Lebanon was strongly influenced by the Maghreb example. There were two obvious reasons for this. The Levant territories were similarly exposed to possible Italian attack. And the grandly named Levant Army was a composite force of North African (mainly Algerian) regiments, supplemented by units of West African and Madagascan infantrymen. Arab Syrians were largely confined to *gendarmerie* and other paramilitary formations: the *forces supplétives* and *troupes spéciales*.[65] Before 1939 the politics of mandatory control precluded anything more. To raise national armies in the Levant mandates would be to create powerful symbols of Syrian and Lebanese sovereign independence.

Defence planning in the Levant territories rested on a number of strategic assumptions. First, and most fundamental, France was obliged to defend Syria against attack by any state. This general statement masked a specific duty: to contain Turkish irredentism in northern Syria. Syrian nationalists pointed out that the French record here was poor. French withdrawal from Cilicia in 1922 signalled the end of open hostilities with Ankara. Tentative co-operation developed as the fascist threat loomed larger, something Turkish President Kemal Atatürk seemed ready to confront.[66] This was not entirely good news for Syrian Arabs. Disputed sovereignty over the Alexandretta *sanjak*, the thorniest issue in relations between Paris, Ankara and Damascus, was resolved to Turkish benefit when, to Arab and Armenian dismay, the formerly Syrian territory was transferred to Ankara's control in July 1938.[67] France subordinated legitimate Syrian claims to the region to the requirement for Turkish goodwill in any future European conflict.[68] General staff anxiety over Soviet incursion into the Middle East complicated matters. Between 1934 and 1939 the likelihood of Soviet penetration was increasingly discounted, but the Nazi–Soviet Pact undermined all previous assessments. A stronger certainty was that French communications to the Levant would be disrupted in the initial stages of general European war.[69] The Levant high commission began stockpiling food, fuel and munitions in 1939. Syria had no substantial oil reserves of its own. The Syrian pipeline system terminating at the port of Tripoli was, however, integral to the export of Iraqi crude.[70] When Britain took possession of Mosul in 1919 it conceded France a 23.75 per cent stake in Iraqi oil exports. Paris governments relied on Iraq's oil to keep the wheels of French industry turning.[71] Once France allied with Britain in 1939, contingency plans readied additional supplies of petroleum products and foodstuffs for the Levant states from neighbouring British territories.[72] These preparations highlighted a final strategic expectation: British support in the Middle East. The Italian threat and the internationalisation of the Palestine revolt between 1936 and 1939 drove the imperial powers into joint strategic planning, their chequered history of regional competition notwithstanding.[73]

Between 10 and 17 October 1936 the Levant Army conducted its biggest manoeuvres since the Syrian revolt a decade earlier. Air force squadrons joined combined operations staged around Homs. The Levant manoeuvres sent a clear signal of French resolve to Rome.[74] But French anxiety about Italian intentions focused primarily on Tunisia. In the early 1930s two regiments of *tirailleurs sénégalais* formed the backbone of the protectorate garrison. War Ministry plans to reinforce Tunisia with units drawn from Morocco and Algeria to repel an attack from Italian Libya were shelved following defence cuts enacted between 1929 and 1933.[75] Meanwhile another Italian danger emerged. Franco-Italian imperial relations in East Africa never recovered after the Italian invasion of Abyssinia in 1935–36. Aerial incursions into French Somaliland and skirmishes along the Ethiopian–Somali border became a matter of routine in 1937. Mussolini's government pressed the Quai d'Orsay to negotiate over frontier delimitation, knowing that French consent to do so would amount to *de facto* recognition of Italy's Abyssinian conquest. French diplomats sidestepped Italian demands by proposing a neutral zone along the French Somaliland border. Rue Oudinot officials then objected that any such zone meant a loss of territory. Minister of Colonies Georges Mandel was determined to stop the rot. In April 1938 he appointed thirty-eight-year-old Hubert Deschamps, a rising star of the Ecole nationale et la France d'Outre-Mer, as governor in Djibouti. Deschamps set out to make French Somaliland something worth defending. He expanded the port, built a new hospital and rural dispensaries for the Somali population, and created a veterinary service to meet the demands of Somali herdsmen.[76]

While Deschamps breathed new life into the colony, a Ministry of Colonies cartographer arrived in Djibouti in May 1938 to map out the border. The Italians sent their own delimitation commission a week later. Over the next two months the rival cartographers drew very different maps. The result was a formal French request in late July 1938 for Italian evacuation of some 2,700 km^2 of Somali territory around Ali Sabiet. Italy's non-compliance is less remarkable than the fact that the formal boundaries of colonial rule in East Africa meant so little. Paper commitments counted for nothing against a revisionist imperialist power.[77]

Meanwhile, in September 1938 Deschamps and the regional army commander, Colonel Truffert, identified three main Italian threats to French colonial control in Somaliland: an overland attack by forces in Ethiopia; air attacks; and an uprising in Djibouti by the Italian commercial community. Deschamps had few resources to call upon. Truffert's garrison amounted to about a thousand West African and Somali *tirailleurs*. There were a few ageing Potez aircraft and one anti-aircraft battery in Djibouti port. Some 200 sundry irregulars and lightly armed policemen were available in the capital, as well as an estimated 400 settler 'partisans' allegedly willing to resist the Italians with anything from hunting rifles to their kitchen cutlery. Reinforcement from Madagascar would take too long; reinforcement from British Aden had yet to be agreed.[78] In January 1939 two battalions of *tirailleurs sénégalais* disembarked at Djibouti, and a squadron of modern Déwoitine fighters replaced the decrepit Potezes. The local population was suitably impressed: with irrepressible optimism Deschamps telegraphed that French prestige was restored.[79] More important, French intelligence gathering on Italian troop movements improved. The *opéra bouffe* aspect of the situation in Somaliland belies the fact that it represented in microcosm the general staff's inability to devise a long-term imperial defence strategy. Djibouti commanded a vital strategic position at the entrance to the Red Sea. So, too, did British Aden. The former remained a sleepy commercial port. The latter was set to become a key command centre.

Turkey still featured prominently in French imperial threat assessments in 1938–40. At first glance, this seems odd. Alexandretta was ceded. And during the spring and summer of 1939 French negotiators spearheaded efforts to cement the Western powers' 'Balkan front' through the conclusion of a tripartite Franco-British-Turkish military alliance. In October 1939 these negotiations bore fruit. Why then did French mistrust of the Ankara regime persist? Abiding suspicion stemmed from a combination of ingrained prejudice, undue expectations and the struggle for long-term regional influence. Old Syria hands in the Foreign and War Ministries, not to mention the Beirut high commission, believed that Turkey's new government under Ismet İnönü harboured designs on additional Syrian territory, from Aleppo in the west to the Haute Djezireh in the east.[80] French inability to contain Arab nationalism or regional separatism in Syria sharpened these anxieties. By 1937 the Levant Army's military intelligence division and the *sûreté générale* had amassed a wealth of material confirming Ankara's links with Turkic communities in northern Syria, other separatist groups and even Syrian nationalist politicians.[81]

French ambivalence toward Turkey indicated deeper uncertainty about whether the long-sought-after Balkan alliance could ever work. There were formidable problems to overcome even if – as was officially proposed – French, Turkish and British forces only undertook joint operations against Italy in the eastern Mediterranean. Would Italy enter the war at all? Would the Turkish general staff commit a large proportion of its front-line divisions to such operations after the Nazi–Soviet Pact resurrected the Soviet threat to eastern Anatolia? And would the three alliance partners ever provide adequate resources to assure a quick victory? By the winter of 1939–40 it was becoming clear that the answer to all three questions was no. An amicable Franco-Turkish relationship was unattainable; their Near Eastern interests simply did not coincide. Each saw virtue in the rapid overthrow of Italian fascism and the containment of the Soviet threat to the Middle East. And there is little doubt that the Ankara regime favoured an allied victory over an Axis-dominated Europe. But Turkey's historic dominance along the northern tier of the Arab world was incompatible with French aspirations to remain a Middle Eastern power.

By the end of 1938 the military authorities in North Africa and the Levant were positively ebullient in their anticipation of war with fascist Italy, whatever Turkey's position. The Naval Ministry and the naval staff under Admiral François Darlan, always influential in Mediterranean strategy, rose to the challenge of additional Italian capital ship construction and secured funding for two additional 35,000 tonne battleships on 2 May 1938.[82] The Rabat and Tunis residencies saw war with Mussolini's regime as a means to end persistent Italian demands for territorial concessions and special privileges for the large Italian immigrant communities in Tunis and Casablanca. Hostile Italian radio and press propaganda, much of it co-ordinated by the Radio Bari broadcasting station, intensified after Mussolini's reiteration of Italian claims to territory in Tunisia and Somaliland in November 1938.[83] During 1939 Radio Berlin's Arabic broadcasts also increased in violence.[84]

In 1939 the Daladier government at last fought fire with fire. On 3 January the premier arrived in the port of Bizerta aboard the cruiser *Foch* to begin a three-day tour of Tunisia. He stopped off in Corsica, another territory with strong historic ties to Italy. The prime minister's visit had a martial flavour, and steeled the Maghreb population for war.[85] Daladier led a military parade of *spahi* cavalry in Tunis, he inspected fortifications in Gabès and presented the regimental standard to colonial artillery in Sousse. Public meetings with the Tunisian Bey and Mohammed Chenik, Destourian vice-president of the Tunisian grand council, followed.[86] Symbolic handshakes were exchanged, the 45,000 Tunisians that fell in the Great War were recalled, and speeches were made affirming Tunisia's resolve to stand shoulder-to-shoulder with France. Italian colonial demands were clearly counterproductive. Elements of the Radical Party and the French right desperate to withdraw from Eastern Europe were not about to give up on the empire. Daladier, the contemplative former teacher and southern baker's son, returned home an imperial statesman, looking, it must be said, as sullen as ever. He refuted Italian claims that France had forfeited the respect of its Muslim subjects.[87] To drive the point home, in February 1939 Algerian officials of the Paris mosque affirmed Muslim loyalty to France in a French radio address recorded after a ceremony for fallen Muslim troops at the tomb of the unknown soldier.[88] The site was highly symbolic. At the height of ultra-rightist activity in 1934–36 veterans' groups often gathered at the tomb's eternal flame to protest at the Third Republic's betrayal of the war generation. The February 1939 commemoration reclaimed the tomb as a monument to republican imperialism.

On 20 February Algiers governor-general Georges Le Beau advised the Interior Ministry that the Muslim population was much impressed by French resolve to check Italy in North Africa.[89] Arab hostility to Mussolini's regime still ran high after brutal Italian repression of the Senussi in Libya in the early 1930s, so much so that General Henri Simon, a leading commentator on the Armée d'Afrique, thought any repeat of the First World War disorders in Algeria and Tunisia inconceivable.[90] If anything, Arab opinion was more sensitive to signs of French weakness. Spurred by Daladier's visit, in early 1939 Noguès won government support for reinforcement of the Fezzan, the swathe of territory in south-west Libya that formed a vital nexus between the Maghreb, AOF and Chad, the northernmost colony of AEF. Foreign Legion garrisons in a string of Fezzan oases, and regular sorties by *méhariste* columns through the Tibesti mountains along the Chad–Libya border, protected AEF and kept open trans-Saharan communications and east–west air routes from AOF to French Somaliland.[91] Daladier's Cabinet also approved supplements to the North African defence budget in 1939 and again in 1940. Increased port defences from Casablanca to Bizerta, new jetties at Agadir and Mers el-Kébir, additional rolling stock for troop transport, and improvements to road and telephone communications improved the defensive position in the Maghreb, the shortcomings of which were exposed by the Czech crisis mobilisation in September 1938.[92] But the spending was dictated as much by metropolitan as by imperial needs. After all, port and infrastructure modernisation facilitated the interchange of forces between North Africa and France.

The black African territories: AOF, AEF and Madagascar

During the inter-war years the War Ministry inspectorate of colonial troops judged AOF the securest region of the empire. In colonies such as French Sudan and Niger, isolated, makeshift garrisons were considered sufficient to keep order. The likelihood of external invasion was nugatory. Party political opposition, nationalist protest and worker unrest were sporadic, and generally soon contained. Army intelligence officers regarded Islamism as a more potent threat.[93] Between 29 January and 1 March 1925 Marshal Pétain visited thirteen West African districts in which the local population resisted military recruitment during the First World War. His summary report was dismissive. The causes of unrest were disparate. In some areas, otherwise loyal populations harboured a grievance against army impositions. In others, the belief that the British were less exacting proved decisive. But, in typically curt fashion, Pétain singled out 'Islamisme' and 'Fétichisme' as the principal contributory factors. Excessive recruitment was not the problem, insensitivity to local belief systems was.[94] Respect Islamic observance and get Muslim leaders – especially *grand marabout* Seydu Nuru, grandson of Senegal's venerated Islamic resistance leader, Umar Tal – to co-operate and all would be well.[95] Pétain's opinions were widely shared by civilian officials and military bureaucracy. There was certainly no let-up in conscription targets. West Africa was expected to supply the highest proportion of recruits for overseas service of any colonial federation. In 1923 the annual *contingent* of 11,000 new recruits to be sent overseas was calculated as in table 10.1.

Thirteen years later recruitment for *tirailleur* regiments was further increased after a four-week West African tour by General Billotte.[96] Like Pétain, Billotte saw little prospect of imminent external attack or internal disorder in the region. He recommended that the German commercial presence in the Canary Islands and the Spanish enclave of Rio de Oro should be carefully assessed, and that the port of Dakar should be better equipped with shore batteries and anti-aircraft weaponry. But he was generally sanguine about the future of French rule in West Africa. His priority was therefore to maximise the recruitment of *tirailleur* units for service in Europe. The annual *contingent* was increased to 15,000; the AOF garrison was reduced to 10,000; West African regiments serving in Indochina were redeployed straight to France. Billotte inherited the mantle of General Mangin, architect of the *force noire*, setting a target of 400,000 West African soldiers after full mobilisation.[97]

Table 10.1 Tirailleur Sénégalais recruitment for overseas service, 1923

Colony	Recruits	Embarkation
French Sudan	2,000	Dakar
Upper Volta	2,500	Conakry Dakar
Guinea	1,850	Dakar
Niger	400	Cotonou
Dahomey	950	Cotonou
Ivory Coast	1,500	Grand-Bassam
Senegal	1,700	Dakar
Mauritania	100	Dakar

Source SHA, 5H6/D1, War Ministry Direction des troupes coloniales, 'Renseignements concernant la formation du contingent sénégalais de relève pour 1923'.

Civil–military discussion of black African colonies always boiled down to manpower. Colonial recruits plugged gaps in metropolitan forces, but could be temporarily run down or maintained on a shoestring to reduce local budget deficits. During the devaluation crisis in November 1926 Poincaré's Minister of Colonies, Léon Perrier, signed off a new defence scheme for AEF that achieved all these objectives. Between 1933 and 1935 earlier colonial defence cuts were steadily reversed – this at a time when the metropolitan army still faced financial retrenchment. Cheaply maintained, versatile Coloniale regiments were a winning formula to Treasury accountants. By June 1935 a series of supplementary defence schemes for the black African federations were in place. Matters came full circle in the following year. On 24 September 1936 Billotte and Moutet proposed a definitive defence scheme for the sub-Saharan federations that attached top priority to war with Germany, thus ensuring a larger pool of *tirailleur* regiments for service in France.[98]

In Madagascar, too, strategic planning was tied to metropolitan defensive needs. In 1931 the rue Oudinot's military affairs division chose the Vincennes Colonial Exhibition to announce the establishment of an East

African Defence Group composed of two Malagasy infantry regiments and two specialist artillery groups. These forces were designated a strategic reserve to protect Madagascar and reinforce nearby Réunion and French Somaliland.[99] Thereafter, annual army manoeuvres in Madagascar posited the rapid deployment of these troops to the island's major ports and strategic locations. Sometimes little more than paper exercises, these manoeuvres made it plain that the army units in Madagascar were hopelessly overstretched.[100] In 1936 the Ministry of Colonies promised the East African Defence Group new weaponry, equipment and motorised transport. There was a catch. Malagasy regiments were placed on stand-by for deployment in France or in the Mediterranean theatre within weeks of the outbreak of war.[101]

The importance attached to African colonies as a military reservoir must be set against the recrudescence of colonial appeasement in the years 1936–38. The Blum government sent out conciliatory messages to Berlin about the possible cession of former German territories that flatly contradicted its commitments to colonial reform and more integrated imperial defence. Senior members of the Popular Front coalition, including the former Young Radicals Pierre Cot and Jacques Kayser and several pacifist Socialists, had endorsed colonial restitution to Weimar Germany. Between 1929 and 1933 Radical Party elder statesmen such as Albert Sarraut and Joseph Caillaux toyed with plans for a Franco-German customs union in black Africa during complementary bilateral talks over closer economic co-operation in Europe. Blum's government linked these two issues, tying retrocession of colonies to creation of a 'Eurafrican' trading zone.[102]

Two dark clouds hung over colonial appeasement. It was unlikely that France and Britain could agree a package of African territorial concessions and colonial economic sweeteners adequate to persuade Hitler's government to curb its expansionist ambitions in Eastern Europe. And it stretched credulity to believe the German Führer was animated by the restitution of former colonies.[103] In hindsight, it is abundantly clear that the whole idea was hopelessly unrealistic. Surrendering colonies as a solution to the worsening European crisis provoked by Nazi aggression was preposterous. Colonial appeasement is interesting primarily because of what it indicates about official attitudes to overseas possessions and the state's obligation to dependent peoples. The fact was that Popular Front ministers, Léon Blum included, did contemplate transferring the Cameroon and Togoland mandates to Nazi control. So much for 'colonial humanism'.

South East Asia and the Pacific

The Indochina federation remained a lucrative asset to France in the 1930s. The rubber boom of the preceding decade was never repeated, but successive governments pumped in funds to keep export producers afloat during the worst of the depression.[104] Indochina became a safe haven for investors unnerved by France's three successive franc devaluations between 1936 and 1938. It also produced key strategic raw materials – rubber, coal, zinc and tungsten. The federation registered a net balance of payments surplus throughout the inter-war period, except in three years of sharp recession: 1922, 1930 and 1931. More important, Indochina was a captive market for high-priced French goods and generated foreign exchange earnings by exporting rice and minerals to the China market. Between 1936 and 1939 Indochina's export volumes increased rapidly. In 1937 the port of Saigon handled 2,140,000 metric tonnes of commercial cargo, making it France's sixth busiest port.[105]

The resignation with which the French political community contemplated the loss of Indochina in a war with Japan suggested that economic considerations had little bearing on the long-term trajectory of imperial decline in Asia. Immediately after the First World War, ministers, strategic planners and lobbyists in the French Asia and French Oceania committees had few illusions about the decisive shift in the Pacific balance of power. Rising American and Japanese regional influence was intimately connected with the European powers' expenditure of blood and treasure on the western front. The French Oceania committee observed the outcome of the 1921–22 Washington Naval Conference with unease, sceptical that naval disarmament would work, and certain that French strategic capability in the Pacific was in eclipse.[106] Instability in mainland China, fuelled by the first clashes of the Chinese civil war in 1927–28, was another complication. Soviet support for Asian revolutionary movements heightened imperialists' fears of what Sarraut dubbed a 'monstrous coalition' in the Far East between the Soviet Union, China and Japan, in which anticolonial nationalists might serve as proxies to undermine the European colonial presence.[107] French eagerness to conclude a Franco-Chinese treaty with the Kuomintang government makes sense in this light. Signature of this bilateral accord on 16 May 1930 normalised relations between the Chinese government and the Indochina authorities but also created a hostage to fortune as Sino-Japanese relations descended into crisis. After the Manchurian Crisis of 1931–32 Japanese foreign and commercial policy became a constant preoccupation in the pages of the specialist colonial press. The French Asia committee journal monitored Japan's penetration of China, correctly predicting an eventual Japanese drive into South East Asia.[108]

General staff strategists harboured similar doubts about French capacity to resist Japanese expansionism, although few voiced their anxieties in public.[109] Their pessimism derived in large part from the advice of Admiral Raoul Castex, former commander of the North Atlantic fleet. Castex was the most influential strategist of French imperial defence. In his five-volume study, *Théories stratégiques*, published between 1930 and 1935, he insisted that France's naval resources should be devoted to the preservation of Atlantic, Mediterranean and African interests. The Pacific was beyond the reach of French naval power; the defence of Indochina *une chimère absolue*.[110] Castex's viewpoint mirrored thinking within the Germanocentric army staff. Admiral Darlan was also alert to Castex's views, and to the testing responsibilities of empire protection. As naval commander in Algeria in August 1930 Darlan oversaw the initial extension of the Mers el-Kébir fleet base. As adviser to Naval Minister François Piétri in March 1934 he refined naval strategy for war against Italy and Germany, leaving no scope for operations in the Far East. As chief of naval staff in April 1939 he rejected untenable commitments in Asia.[111]

Government and party political opinion about the Far Eastern situation split along left–right lines as the Japanese menace to Indochina grew. The mainstream parliamentary right advocated conciliation of Tokyo as the sole viable option, and regarded Japan as a vital buffer against Communism in East Asia. Commercial investors, including a consortium of four French banks that funded extensive railway construction in Indochina and the southern Chinese province of Yunnan, were understandably anxious to safeguard their investments.[112] By contrast, left-wing Radicals, Socialists and the PCF replayed their arguments in defence of Republican Spain with regard to the Chinese Republic. Marius Moutet and Henri Guernut were particularly outspoken in their condemnation of Japan at the outset of the Sino-Japanese war in July 1937.[113]

From June 1938 the Daladier government became more sharply critical of Japanese expansionism in China. But Foreign Minister Georges Bonnet held his ministerial colleagues' condemnatory rhetoric in check by initiating more active appeasement of Tokyo.[114] The general staff did not take issue with him. In October 1938 CSDN plans to resupply Indochina in wartime conceded that convoys were unlikely to get through uninterrupted. The War Ministry and the Ministry of Colonies vested greater hopes in the development of a local armament and munition sector capable of producing sufficient war *matériel* to maintain Indochina's garrison forces over a period of months if communications with France were severed.[115] But the military command in Hanoi and General Bührer's colonial general staff knew that Indochina was indefensible. In early 1939 a French military mission under air force General Berger provided technical support to Chiang Kai Chek's forces. However, the Kuomintang government contracted the services of the Berger mission privately, enabling the French authorities to deny its existence.[116] Berger's secret mission symbolised French policy. What the Foreign Ministry termed a policy of 'balance' was a hopeless mess: *ad hoc* concessions to Japan, abortive efforts to increase Indochina's defences, and occasional gestures of support for Chiang Kai Chek.[117]

Japanese pressure on Indochina intensified in spring 1939. Fighting in Yunnan brought Japanese forces to the Tonkin frontier. The China campaign revealed that the Japanese army was capable of complex amphibious operations to secure a beachhead in hostile territory.[118] So the Hanoi authorities were understandably dismayed by Japan's seizure of Hainan in February, and Tokyo's formal announcement on 31 March that the Spratley islands came under the jurisdiction of the Japanese colonial government in Taiwan.[119] Control of these islands afforded Japanese assault forces a commanding position at the entrance to the Gulf of Tonkin and the approaches to Saigon farther south. French military observers became convinced that Japan's southward drive to the South China Sea would accelerate once international circumstances permitted it.[120]

During 1939–40 French aid to Chinese Nationalist forces, whether through ageing *matériel*, transport facilities through Tonkin, preferential credit or sympathetic publicity, was nothing more than a pinprick to Japan's southward advance.[121] Daladier and Georges Mandel were reluctant to bow to Japanese pressure. But in Hanoi governors-general Jules Brévié and Georges Catroux assessed their situation with the brutal realism of the underdog.[122] Repeated postponements in the building of a submarine base at Camranh Bay underscored the fact that France could not divert substantial military resources from the impending conflict with Germany. Wistfully referred to as 'notre Singapore' by naval staff planners, Camranh Bay, like the trans-Saharan railway before it, remained a pipe dream of imperial strategists.[123] In June 1939 Naval Minister César Campinchi finally pledged funding to begin construction of the Camranh base and to enlarge the dockyard facilities at Saigon. Neither changed Indochina's immediate defensive prospects.[124] It was with this in view that representatives of the Indochina military command headed for staff talks in Singapore between 22 to 27 June 1939 with Admiral Sir Percy Noble, commander of Britain's China Station forces. The discussions brought together over fifty participants, including senior British staff officers from Hong Kong, India, Burma and Ceylon. Behind the warm words characteristic of the first months of the Anglo-French alliance, the Singapore conference promised little.[125] Compared with parallel discussions held in Aden in early June regarding joint action in defence of the Indian Ocean and the Red Sea approaches, the talks in Singapore were inconclusive.[126] The British rejected any commitment beyond the Malay barrier.[127]

The disparity between declared strategic intentions and limited defensive means was equally apparent in France's island territories of the Pacific and Indian Oceans. In the 1920s the commercial value and strategic importance of New Caledonia's mineral exports made the island a precious colonial resource. The territories of French Oceania – New Caledonia, New Hebrides and Tahiti especially – were hard hit by collapsing commodity prices in the depression. None the less, after 1934 New Caledonia's nickel-based economy soon recovered its importance to the French exchequer.[128] On 22 June 1933 the CCDC approved a New Caledonia defence scheme. After mobilisation, a single company of colonial infantry, three machine-gun units, one mortar group, a lone coastal battery protecting the entrance to Nouméa port, and a volunteer network of 'coast watchers' were all that protected the territory from invasion. The governor was given discretion to call up additional reservists if need be. The Naval Ministry pledged to replace the one ageing steamer on stand-by in Nouméa with an unspeci-fied vessel that would 'harass the attacker's supply lines'.[129]

The Heath Robinson aspect of defence planning in the French Pacific territories became more apparent as the decade wore on. British mining interests controlled the bulk of New Caledonia's nickel production, but Japanese commercial investment in the island expanded in the inter-war years, boosted by cheaper methods of iron ore extraction.[130] Once Japan's campaign in China resumed, New Caledonia's nickel resources became a more tempting prize, a fact proved by competitive tendering between French, British and US government purchasers.[131] The Nouméa authorities responded quickly. Manoeuvres were organised in August 1937 predicated on Japanese landings in the Voh-Koné region on the north-west coast. They descended into farce. Manoeuvres were first postponed after a viru-lent outbreak of measles among the reservists, and then further delayed because the vessel loaned by the island's main nickel company to trans-port troops from Nouméa to Koné had meanwhile resumed commercial operations.[132] Over the weekend of 16 September 1939, the final manoeuvres held in New Caledonia before the fall of France posited a staged retreat to Nouméa in the south after hostile landings along the northern coasts.[133] The spirit of self-sacrifice implicit in these plans con-firmed that no French naval support could be expected.[134] The security of New Caledonia, like that of the other French Oceanic territories of Tahiti, Wallis and Futuna, ultimately rested on American, British and Australian maritime control of the South Pacific.

The empire goes to war, 1939–40

In the 150th anniversary year of the French Revolution, the Paris Bastille Day celebrations on 14 July 1939 occasioned the greatest show of imperial power since the victory parades of 1918–19. The traditional march down the Champs Elysées was larger and more colourful than usual, featuring colonial regiments in full battledress. A column of *tirailleurs sénégalais* led the parade. Minister of National Education Jean Zay invited honorary colonial delegations to attend the celebrations, but excluded political representatives.[135] In line with the greater solemnity and military

ceremonial accorded to the twentieth anniversary Armistice Day commemorations on 11 November 1938, the Dakar government transformed
its 1939 Bastille Day parade into a symbolic call for colonial unity. The
crowds that applauded the march-past by the Dakar garrison were less
racially segregated than in previous years. Veterans of 1914–18, settlers
and *indigènes* paraded side by side in Rufisque.[136]

These 14 July commemorations gave expression to the stronger public
conviction in France that the empire was fundamental to national
survival. Ministerial statements stressed that colonial troops and labour,
strategic raw materials, foodstuffs and foreign exchange earnings closed
the demographic, economic and military gaps between France and the
fascist powers. At best, the *salut par l'empire* remained a vague concept. At
worst, it was an official deception. Yet the new imperial unity in 1939 was
not entirely bogus. As war loomed in August, fifty-three per cent of respondents in a French opinion poll stated that the loss of any colony would
be as painful as the surrender of metropolitan territory.[137] The empire was
harnessed to the French war effort in 1939–40, and the military contribution of colonial regiments in the battle for France was considerable. But
colonial men and materials were but one component in what remained
first and foremost a Franco-German war. Moreover the common imperial
purpose that underpinned the *salut par l'empire* idea was as much the product
of rigorous policing and state control as of genuinely francophile sentiment.

The so-called Phoney War lasted from Daladier's declaration of war
on 3 September 1939 until the German attack on France and the Low
Countries on 10 May 1940. Numerous settler organisations declared their
unflinching loyalty in this nine-month period. More interesting were the
range of *évolué* groups for whom willingness to serve marked a renaissance of assimilationist idealism and an opportunity to reassert claims to
equal rights as French citizens. A conflict that pitched republican values
against fascism was surely a struggle to end racial discrimination. Such
reactions were apparent in Algeria. Cherrid Missoum, secretary of the youth
wing of the Algerian Muslim Congress, and Muslim representatives of
Algeria's financial delegations recognised the war's unifying potential.[138]
Djemâa councils, the Muslim ex-servicemen's association and the leaders
of Algeria's principal sufi orders rushed to identify with the fight against
Nazism. Muslim community leaders reminded their constituents of
Hitler's racist attitude towards Arabs as well as Jews.[139]

In the Levant states the declarations of loyalty were more fervent still.[140]
In September 1939 a remarkable cross-section of political opinion backed
the French war effort. Supportive statements from Lebanese President Emile
Eddé, the Maronite patriarch Abdallah Khouri and the leaders of other
Lebanese Christian churches were to be expected. Affirmations of loyalty
from Druze and Alawite chiefs, representatives of Syria's main compact

minorities, were noteworthy. But similar declarations from National Bloc and People's Party leaders made more impact. Jamal Mardam's comment on 3 September 1939 was not untypical: 'To serve France is to serve the cause of humanity'.[141] Effusive perhaps, but nationalist politicians had ample reason to wear pro-French credentials on their sleeve at a time when the *sûreté* was arresting Syrian and Lebanese Communist Party activists.[142]

Any hopes that expressions of colonial loyalty would be rewarded with additional freedoms were disappointed. There was little indication before the French defeat that the Daladier or Reynaud governments contemplated greater civil rights for colonial subjects or servicemen, although professional troops could still claim citizenship rights on completion of their service term. War came to colonial streets in a different guise. State-of-siege regulations were widely imposed on the outbreak of hostilities. By October 1939 a massive round-up of nationalists, Communist sympathisers and sundry undesirables was under way from Saigon to Fort-de-France. In Algeria, for example, the PPA and the Association of Reformist *Ulamas* were 'decapitated' by the incarceration of their senior leaders.[143] Wartime regulation amounted to martial law, conferring arbitrary powers of arrest and detention on civil officials and colonial commands. Most – Noguès in Rabat, Georges Le Beau in Algiers, Léon Cayla in Tananarive, Gabriel Puaux in Beirut, Georges Catroux in Hanoi, naval commanders in the Antilles – targeted politicians, clerics, youth leaders and trade unionists that had been under police surveillance for months, even years. Daladier's Cabinet was equally security-conscious, having had to cope with the spread of colonial strikes and disorders when the Popular Front experiment collapsed.

Police repression in 1939–40, the assembly of colonial conscripts after mobilisation and the transition to a rudimentary war economy in the colonies were racially constructed. Racial differentiation was clearest in government rationing schemes. Foodstuff rationing went furthest in French North Africa. On 31 May 1938 the Ministry of Agriculture agreed to stockpile one million tonnes of wheat and flour in the Maghreb territories, to be managed by the National Wheat Office created by the Popular Front.[144] Plans drawn up over the summer of 1938 allocated very different rations of flour and other reserved foodstuffs to Europeans and Muslims. High-quality soft wheat was almost entirely assigned to settlers, each of whom was allotted 200 kg of wheat flour per year. Algerian Muslims were allowed only 32 kg. Rationing schemes for meat, vegetable products, tea and coffee, finalised in August 1938, were similarly discriminatory. The meat ration was calculated on the basis of average annual consumption over the years 1935–37. Europeans were estimated to consume 17 kg of beef, 5 kg of pork and 1.2 kg of horsemeat per year. Muslim meat consumption was reckoned at 3 kg of lamb per year, even less (1.7 kg) in the Saharan territories.

Religious, dietary and cultural differences aside, it was clear that the settler population were better fed in peacetime and better catered for in wartime than their Muslim subjects.[145]

On 4 October 1939 General Noguès, now commander-in-chief in North Africa, suspended commercial exports from the Maghreb. Henceforth, exporters required a government licence to sell any produce overseas. The French state assumed authority to commandeer vital export commodities, and the North African authorities permitted commercial exchanges between the Maghreb territories only after French supply needs were met.[146] Subordination of imperial economic requirements to those of France was inherent in the colonial relationship, and should not surprise. Since 1927 French North African contingency planning for war in Europe was designed to meet French industrial demand for strategic raw materials and the food-stuff requirements of the metropolitan population. North Africa's zinc, lead, tungsten and other metal ores, as well as its wheat, wine and wool, were earmarked for exclusive use in a French war economy. The demands of local industrial producers and the dietary needs of the Muslim popula-tion were secondary considerations.[147]

As in Indochina, so in French North Africa the general staff toyed with plans to establish the bare bones of a munitions industry, the objective being to make the Maghreb territories self-sufficient in cartridges, gun-powder and explosive.[148] Parliamentary proposals in 1927 for wider indus-trial diversification in French North Africa were stifled by primordial metropolitan demand for a wide range of Maghrebi goods – all of which were strategically important to the French economy in wartime.[149] Between 1928 and 1932 War Ministry attention shifted instead to an audit of North Africa's strategic raw material requirements and the expansion of local port capacity as a prelude to the stockpiling of war *matériel* and foodstuffs in the three Maghreb territories.[150] The foundations of French North Africa's war economy were laid down in the mobilisation decrees issued at the height of the Czech crisis between 23 August and 28 September 1938. The Maghreb railway system and commercial shipping came under mili-tary jurisdiction. Algerian prefectures regulated use of the colony's telephone network. Munitions workers were subject to military discipline. The state-of-siege regulations rubber-stamped by Morocco's Sultan Mohammed V and Tunisia's Ahmed Pacha Bey on 1 and 3 September 1939 were drawn up a year earlier.[151]

Indochina was the other principal colonial cash cow for the French war economy in 1939–40. Indochinese defence loans raised in each year of the First World War raised a total of 192 million francs for the French war effort. The Hanoi government expected to exceed these contributions in 1939–40. The French Treasury capitalised on Indochina's balance of pay-ments surplus to generate additional revenue from Vietnamese exports.

Duties on Tonkin coal were increased from 4.5 per cent to 7.5 per cent in 1936. A colonial defence loan raised in late 1938 produced 440 million francs for French rearmament. By 1939 Indochina was also France's third largest supplier of strategic raw materials.[152]

French expectation that Indochina's major contribution to the imperial war effort would be economic rather than military distinguished it from most other colonies that placed a stronger emphasis on manpower mobilisation. The Ministry of Colonies was reluctant to impose financial burdens on other colonial populations equivalent to those in Indochina. The experience of the depression years suggested that the existing tax burden in French Africa was unsustainable. Budgetary revenue for 1938–39 in AOF, AEF, Madagascar, the French Antilles, Réunion and French Oceania registered large increases over previous years. But the franc devaluations of 1936–38 nullified the additional sums raised. The CSDN estimated that the AOF general budget of 349 millions francs for 1939 was roughly equivalent to that of 1938, even though the 349 million figure represented a nominal twenty per cent increase in revenue.[153] A similar fifteen per cent revenue increase in Madagascar's budget for 1939 was also cancelled out by the earlier franc depreciation.[154] Réunion, Martinique, Guadeloupe, New Caledonia and French Polynesia all registered growth in foreign trade during 1938–39 as French, US and British demand for primary goods strengthened.[155] Réunion, for instance, recorded a net trade surplus of almost 40 million francs in 1938, its first after a decade of budget deficits. But Governor Court warned the island's general council on 10 July 1939 that the surpluses generated by Réunion's trade boom would be swallowed by public works schemes previously run at a loss.[156] Réunion was typical. Urgent port and communication improvements in the French island territories on the eve of war gobbled up the extra funds generated as overseas demand for raw materials picked up.

The long-anticipated imperial contribution to war faced its greatest test when German forces poured into France and the Low Countries in May 1940. Even before mobilisation in September 1939, the Armée d'Afrique counted 127,875 Muslim troops, seventy-three per cent of them volunteer enlistments.[157] These men formed the core of the Algerian, Moroccan and Tunisian regiments that spent the following spring dug in along France's north-eastern frontier. Coloniale units were generally called forward later, in conformity with the *hivernage* system of holding black African regiments in reserve in the warmer climes of a Midi winter. Ten colonial divisions, seven of them African, took part in the battle for France, nine per cent of the total forces deployed to protect France, and a higher proportion than in 1914.[158]

West Africans played a leading role in three distinct sectors on the western front in May and June 1940. *Tirailleurs sénégalais* of the 1st and

6th colonial infantry divisions engaged German forces around the Aisne and the Argonne forest from 16 May to 9 June. The War Ministry later praised these colonial units for mounting repeated counter-attacks against the German lines before completing a final orderly retreat to the Vosges on the day of the Franco-German armistice. Mixed *tirailleur* regiments incorporated into the 4th, 5th and 7th colonial infantry divisions fared worse. These regiments held a line on the Somme for a fortnight after initial engagements on 23 May, but several units were 'wiped out' (*anéantie*) during a renewed Wehrmacht offensive south west of Amiens on 5 June. Finally, West African regiments of the 2nd and 8th colonial light infantry divisions were progressively withdrawn from the Aisne and the Somme, finishing the campaign close to the Seine.[159] In February 1942 the Vichy Secretariat of War estimated 4,439 colonial troops killed during the 1940 campaign. An additional 11,504 were classified as missing presumed dead, while estimates of the numbers of colonial POWs ranged from 25,000 to 80,000.[160]

Conclusion

Heavy colonial losses in the battle for France showed that the empire made an important contribution to France's war effort in 1940. The colonies paid the blood tax, albeit over a much shorter period than in 1914–18. The fact that colonial troops once again died fighting for France was not proof of a united empire. For an imperial nation the challenge of total war was to weld its colonial system into a major strategic asset. Vital raw materials and foodstuffs, additional human capacity, colonial taxation revenue and strategic bases were the hard currency of imperial power in war. Just as important from the metropolitan perspective was the additional confidence and common purpose that a cohesive empire might confer on an embattled population. There was, of course, an entirely different construction of empire in a global conflict. Far-flung colonies and prized bases were strategically exposed and difficult to defend. Overseas possessions dissipated precious military assets. Some colonies became a drain on resources rather than a reservoir of manpower, money and supplies. Strategic policy makers inevitably prioritised their imperial defence obligations in an effort to match global commitments to limited military means. They had no other choice: the future of every colony rested on the defence of the Rhine. As a result, three gaps in French imperial defence had grown too wide to conceal by 1939. First, French Indochina was indefensible against Japanese attack by land and sea. Second, the programme of imperial port defences initiated in 1936 was far from complete. Key fleet bases lacked anti-aircraft defences, effective coastal batteries and adequate docking and repair facilities. Third, the overriding needs of metropolitan defence denuded colonies of the garrison strength necessary for local protection against external invasion or internal disorder – unsurprising, given the primordial German threat, but an affirmation that, as always, the colonies existed to serve France.[161]

Notes

1 SHA, 2N66/D3, Note pour le Président du Conseil, 'Contribution de l'Algérie aux dépenses militaires de la métropole', n.d. 1939.
2 'Algérie. Contribution à la défense nationale', *L'Afrique Française*, 49:1 (January 1939), 22; SHA, 2N66/D3, 'Emploi de la contribution militaire de l'Algérie'; 'Décret rélatif à la participation de l'Algérie aux dépenses de la défense nationale', 24 June 1939.
3 Jean-Jacques Becker, 'La perception de la puissance par le Parti Communiste', *Revue d'Histoire Moderne et Contemporaine*, 31:4 (1984), 636–42.
4 B. D. Graham, *Choice and Democratic Order, The French Socialist Party, 1937–1950* (Cambridge: Cambridge University Press, 1994), 224–42 *passim*.
5 Danièle Zeraffa, 'La perception de la puissance dans la formation Démocrate Chrétienne', *Revue d'Histoire Moderne et Contemporaine*, 31:4 (1984), 658–65.
6 Rosemonde Sanson, 'La perception de la puissance par l'Alliance Démocratique', *Revue d'Histoire Moderne et Contemporaine*, 31:4 (1984), 636–57.
7 Serge Berstein, 'La perception de la puissance par le Parti Radical-Socialiste', *Revue d'Histoire Moderne et Contemporaine*, 31:4 (1984), 619–35.
8 As an example: General Maxime Weygand, 'L'Armée coloniale 1914–1918', *Le Monde Colonial illustré*, 180 (June 1939), 112–15.
9 Jackson, *France. The Dark Years*, 94.
10 Martin Thomas, 'France and the Czechoslovak crisis', *Diplomacy and Statecraft*, 10:2–3 (1999), 139–45.
11 Ingram, *The Politics of Dissent*, 9; Georges Vidal, 'Le Parti communiste français et la défense nationale (septembre 1937–septembre 1939)', *Revue Historique*, 306:2 (2004), 333–69.
12 Pithon, 'Opinions publiques et représentations culturelles', 94–5.
13 Pithon, 'French film propaganda July 1939–June 1940', in K. R. M. Short (ed.), *Film and Radio Propaganda in World War II* (London: Croom Helm, 1983), 78–84.
14 Marc Michel terms this rediscovery of imperial pride a 'conscience impériale', see his 'La puissance par l'empire', 35; Charles-Robert Ageron, 'A propos d'une prétendue politique de "répli imperial" dans la France des années 1938–39', *Revue d'Histoire Maghrébine*, 12 (1978), 228–37.
15 For a more general discussion see Thomas, 'At the heart of things?', 325–61.
16 CAOM, Moutet papers, PA28/1/D9, no. 2857, Chambre des Députés, session de 1937, 16e Législature, Commission des finances, Report by Paul Reynaud, 'Budget général de l'exercice 1938: Colonies', 19 October 1937.
17 SHA, 9N268/Dossier: Organisation, War Ministry Direction des troupes coloniales, no. 3228/1/8, 'Note pour l'Etat-Major de l'Armée 1er bureau', 22 November 1922.
18 SHA, 9N268/Dossier: Organisation, no. 3731/1/8, Directeur des troupes coloniales memo, 'Organisation des troupes coloniales', 1 October 1921.
19 Dennis E. Showalter, 'Plans, weapons, doctrines. The strategic cultures of interwar Europe', in Roger Chickering and Stig Forster (eds), *The Shadows of Total War. Europe, East Asia, and the United States, 1919–1939* (Cambridge: Cambridge University Press, 2003), 76–8.
20 Henry Dutailly, 'Weaknesses in French military planning on the eve of the Second World War', in B. J. C. McKercher and Roch Legault (eds), *Military Planning and the Origins of the Second World War in Europe* (Westport CT: Greenwood Press, 2001), 95.
21 For British naval comparisons see the essays in Greg Kennedy and Keith Neilson (eds), *Far-flung Lines. Studies in Imperial Defence in Honour of Donald MacKenzie Schurman* (London: Frank Cass, 1996); Christopher M. Bell, 'The "Singapore strategy" and the deterrence of Japan. Winston Churchill, the Admiralty and the dispatch of Force Z', *English Historical Review*, 114:662 (2001), 609–14.

22 ADA, Sarraut papers, 12J280, Esteva letter to Charles Piétri, 31 January 1936.
23 CCDC meeting, 23 December 1936, quote cited in Michel, 'La puissance par l'empire', 41.
24 Dutailly, 'Weaknesses in French military planning', 93.
25 See the testimonies in Lunn, *Memoirs of the Maelstrom*.
26 Martin Thomas, 'The Vichy government and French colonial prisoners of war, 1940–1944', *French Historical Studies*, 25:4 (2002), 681–2.
27 SHA, 9N270, no. 135/SC2, Lyautey to War Ministry 8ème Direction, Section coloniale, 4 April 1922.
28 SHA, 9N269/D7, 'Rapport du Général Claudel, Inspecteur-général des troupes coloniales au sujet des troupes indigènes au Maroc (Taza)', 12 January 1926.
29 SHA, 2N9/D3, CSDN, 'Note concernant les besoins de nos colonies en *personnel médical* et les measures destinées à y satisfaire', n.d. March 1925.
30 French units were also monitored, see Becker and Berstein, *Histoire de l'Anti-communisme*, 197–202.
31 Recham, *Les Musulmans algériens dans l'armée française*, chapters 4–6; Zinoman, *The Colonial Bastille*, 200–39 *passim*.
32 As examples: SHA, Archives de Moscou, C623/D1419, no. 1880, EMA-2, Cabinet militaire, 'Troupes de groupe d'Indochine, Rapport annuel 1930'; C609/D374, SEL (Beirut), 'Activité Communiste en TSMF', 12 April 1940; Etat-Major des Colonies, 5ème Bureau, 'Activité soviétique en Extrême-Orient', 27 May 1940.
33 See, for instance, MAE, série P: Tunisie 1930–40, vol. 386, Cabinet militaire (Tunis), 'A/S propagande communiste dans les unités indigènes', 21 May 1935.
34 SHA, Archives de Moscou, C223/D122, no. 2906/G, SEA, 'Note sur les conditions psychologiques d'une mobilisation générale en Algérie (Mai 1935)', 22 May 1935.
35 SHA, 2N245/D1, Direction Afrique-Levant to Comte de Martel (Beirut), 5 February 1934.
36 SHA, 2N243/D2, CSDN memo, 'Défense de l'Afrique du Nord', n.d. 1920.
37 SHA, 7N3887/D1, EMA-3, War Ministry note, 'Défense de la Tunisie', 8 September 1922.
38 SHA, 7N3887/D3, EMA, Section d'Afrique et d'Orient, 'Etude sur la défense de l'Afrique du Nord, année 1922'.
39 SHA, 7N3887/D2, EMG, Section d'Afrique et d'Orient note, 28 May 1923.
40 Joel Blatt, 'The parity that meant superiority. French naval policy toward Italy at the Washington Naval Conference and inter-war French foreign policy', *French Historical Studies*, 12:2 (1981), 223–48; and Blatt, 'France and the Washington Conference', *Diplomacy and Statecraft*, 4:3 (1993), 192–219.
41 The financial pressures that drove France toward Ruhr occupation are discussed in Stephen Schuker, *The End of French Predominance in Europe. The Ruhr Occupation and the Dawes Plan, 1923–1924* (Chapel Hill NC: University of North Carolina Press, 1976), 20–6; John F. V. Keiger, 'Raymond Poincaré and the Ruhr crisis', in Robert Boyce (ed.), *French Foreign and Defence Policy, 1918–1940. The Decline and Fall of a Great Power* (London: Routledge, 1998), 49–70.
42 SHA, 7N3887/D4, EMA-3, 'Défense de l'Algérie et Tunisie', 29 April 1924; EMA-3, 'Défense de l'Afrique du Nord contre une attaque extérieure', 9 September 1924.
43 SHA, 2N243/D2, no. 494, Ministre de l'Intérieur, Direction des affaires algériennes note, 10 June 1926.
44 SHA, 2N243/D1, no. 688/DNS, CSDN, Secrétariat général, 'Instruction interministerielle pour l'application du décret du 12 Octobre 1930', 6 September 1938; Hoisington, Jr, *The Casablanca Connection*, 159–65 *passim*.
45 Intelligence gathering on public opinion in Algeria intensified after the Constantine riots, see SHA, Archives de Moscou, C223/D122, SEA 2ème Bureau (Algiers), 'A/S Etat d'esprit à Constantine', 18 September 1936.
46 SHA, 2N243/D2, Sous-commission de contrôle de la défense nationale, 'Rapport sur les questions intéressant la défense nationale en Afrique du Nord', 31 July 1935.
47 *Ibid*.
48 Michel, 'La puissance par l'empire', 35–42.
49 SHA, 9N270/D12, no. 83/IGC, General Bührer, 'Note pour le Général directeur des troupes coloniales', 23 March 1939.

50 Romain Rainero, 'La politique fasciste à l'égard de l'Afrique du Nord : l'épée de l'Islam et la revendication sur la Tunisie', *Revue Française d'Histoire d'Outre-Mer*, 64:237 (1977), 498–515.
51 PRO, FO 371/19913, C6903/4/18, Quai d'Orsay memo, 2 October 1936.
52 Reynolds M. Salerno, 'Britain, France and the emerging Italian threat, 1935–38', in Martin S. Alexander and William J. Philpott (eds), *Anglo-French Defence Relations between the Wars* (London: Palgrave, 2002), 76–80.
53 AN, F⁶⁰201, no. 436, Algiers government to Premier's Office, 10 December 1936.
54 SHA, 2N65/D3, CSDN, General Georges to Daladier note, 'Organisation de l'Afrique du Nord pour le temps de guerre', 18 December 1936. Regarding Georges's difficult relationship with his military master, Chief of General Staff General Maurice Gamelin, see Alexander, *The Republic in Danger*, 99–100.
55 SHA, 7N3908, CSDN note, 10 November 1936.
56 Christine Levisse-Touzé, 'La préparation économique, industrielle et militaire de l'Afrique du Nord à la veille de la guerre', *Revue d'Histoire de la Deuxième Guerre Mondiale*, 142 (1986), 2–17.
57 SHA, 2N22/D1 bis, Moutet letter to Daladier, 30 November 1936.
58 SHA, 2N22/D1, CSDN secretariat, 'CPDN séance du 5 février 1937', and 'CPDN séance du 15 avril 1937'.
59 William I. Shorrock, *From Ally to Enemy. The Enigma of Fascist Italy in French Diplomacy, 1920–1940* (Kent OH: Kent State University Press, 1988), 191–5.
60 MAE, Joseph Avenol papers, vol. 29, 'Le rapprochement franco-italien et le voyage de M. Laval', 22 November 1934; Robert J. Young, 'French military intelligence and the Franco-Italian alliance, 1933–1939', *Historical Journal*, 28:1 (1985), 143–68.
61 Levisse-Touzé, 'La préparation économique', 2–6; SHAA, Guy La Chambre papers, Z14403/D1, 'Note sur la fabrication d'avions en Indochine', 8 February 1939.
62 Thomas, 'At the heart of things?' 345.
63 Hoisington, Jr, *The Casablanca Connection*, 159–65 passim.
64 SHA, 2N65/D4, no. 524/DN/I, Secrétariat permanent de la défense nationale (Algiers), 'Liaison entre les SPDN en Afrique du Nord', 14 June 1938.
65 Bou-Nacklie, 'Les Troupes Spéciales', 645–60.
66 Aryeh Shmuelevitz, 'Atatürk's policy toward the Great Powers. Principles and guidelines', in Uriel Dann (ed.), *The Great Powers in the Middle East, 1919–1939* (New York: Holmes & Meier, 1988), 313; Brock Millman, 'Turkish foreign and strategic policy, 1934–42', *Middle Eastern Studies*, 31:3 (1995), 483–508.
67 The most detailed – and pro-Kemalist – treatment of the issue is now Yücel Güçlü, *The Question of the Sanjak of Alexandretta. A Study of French–Turkish–Syrian Relations* (Ankara: Turkish Historical Society, 2001).
68 Jacques Thobie, 'Le nouveau cours des relations franco-turques et l'affaire du sandjak d'Alexandrette 1921–1939', *Relations Internationales*, 19 (autumn 1979), 355–74; Martin Thomas, 'Imperial defence or diversionary attack? Anglo-French strategic planning in the Near East, 1936–1940', in Alexander and Philpott, *Anglo-French Defence Relations*, 168–72.
69 SHA, 2N245/D1, Direction Afrique-Levant to Comte de Martel, 5 February 1934; 7N4190/D1, Commission d'études de la défense des états du mandat, rapport, 28 December 1938.
70 SHA, 2N245/D5, EMA-4, 'Note pour le President du Conseil', 25 March 1928; PRO, WO 33/1507/COS 691, 'Mediterranean, Middle East and North Africa Strategic Appreciation', 21 February 1938.
71 Andrew and Kanya-Forstner, *France Overseas*, 188–92; Itamar Rabinovitch, 'Oil and local politics. The French–Iraqi negotiations of the early 1930s', in Dann, *The Great Powers in the Middle East*, 172–82.
72 See the Eastern Mediterranean and Balkan Front strategic planning reports in PRO, WO 193/955 and WO 106/2019.
73 Thomas, 'Imperial defence or diversionary attack?', 157–85; regarding the international ramifications of the Palestine Revolt see Nafi, *Arabism*, chapters 5 and 6.
74 CADN, Fonds Beyrouth, Cabinet politique, vol. 904/D4, EMA-3, General Huntziger 'Ordre général no. 269/A', 21 October 1936.

75 MAE, série P: Tunisie 1917–40, vol. 633, B/4,587, Resident-general Manceron to Foreign Ministry, 6 May 1933.
76 CAOM, Hubert Deschamps papers, PA 36/1/D1: Côte Française des Somalis, 1938–40.
77 AN, F⁶⁰201, Foreign Ministry Section Afrique-Levant note, 'Empiètements de l'Italie sur le territoire de notre colonie des Somalis', 9 February 1939.
78 CAOM, Deschamps papers, PA 36/1/D2, CFS Cabinet memo, 'Défense de la colonie', 18 September 1938.
79 CAOM, Deschamps papers, PA 36/1/D2, Deschamps to Mandel, 24 January 1939.
80 AN, F⁶⁰201, Dossier Turquie, Section Afrique-Levant, memo to Haut Comité Méditerranéen, 13 February 1939.
81 SHA, Archives de Moscou, C581/D371, SR note, 'Aspect politique de la question du Sandjak', 2 January 1937; C878/D998, SCR renseignement, 'Activité étrangère', n.d. July 1937.
82 Hervé Coutou-Bégarie and Claude Huan (eds), Lettres et notes de l'Amiral Darlan (Paris: Economica, 1992), 72; Peter Jackson, France and the Nazi Menace. Intelligence and Policy Making, 1933–1939 (Oxford: Oxford University Press, 2000), 266–7.
83 AN, F⁶⁰201, Foreign Ministry Section Afrique-Levant memo, 17 December 1938.
84 SHA, 2N243/D4, no. 295/CAB, Noguès to Gamelin, 26 October 1939, sends 'Procès-verbal de la conférence des services généraux d'information des trois gouvernements nord-africains'.
85 Alfred Silbert, 'Avec M. Daladier en Tunisie', Le Monde Colonial illustré, 188 (February 1939), 3; Jackson, France. The Dark Years, 101.
86 'Le Président Daladier en Tunisie', Revue Française d'Outre-Mer, 762 (January 1939), 6–7.
87 Alfred Silbert, 'Avec M. Daladier en Tunisie', 3. Talbot Imlay, Facing the Second World War. Strategy, Politics, and Economics in Britain and France, 1938–1940 (Oxford: Oxford University Press, 2003), 358.
88 'Un beau marriage France–Islam dans le grand armorial de l'empire', Le Monde Colonial illustré, 189 (March 1939).
89 SHA, 2N243/D5, Georges Le Beau letter to Interior Ministry, 20 February 1939.
90 General Henri Simon, 'La leçon d'une mobilisation en Afrique du Nord', Revue Française d'Outre-Mer, 762 (January 1939), 5.
91 SHA, 2N243/D5, Gamelin 'Note sur la défense des colonies', 1 February 1939; Foreign Ministry, 'Note au sujet des négociations franco-italiennes', n.d. 1939; Noguès letter to Gamelin, 'Action politique en Libye', 24 March 1939.
92 SHA, 2N243/D3, Daladier letter to Noguès, 1 November 1939; Le Beau letter to Daladier, 'Contribution militaire de l'Algérie pour 1940', 23 January 1940.
93 SHA, 5H6/D1, Commission interministerielle des troupes indigènes, 2e sous-commission rapport, 'Recrutement', n.d. 1924.
94 SHA, 5H6/D2, Pétain report, 'Troubles et soulèvements intérieurs en Afrique Occidentale Française pendant la guerre 1914–1918', 26 March 1925.
95 Robinson, Paths of Accommodation, 229–40.
96 SHA, 5H6/D3, General Billotte, mission d'inspection en AOF, 1936, 26 June 1936.
97 Ibid.
98 SHA, 7N414/D6, CCDC, 'Plan de mobilisation du groupe AEF-Cameroun', 20 November 1937.
99 SHA, 8H81/D2, no. 31/MOB, General du Buisson, Commandant, Groupe de l'Afrique Orientale Française, note to EMA service historique, 22 February 1935.
100 SHA, 8H81/D1, Etat-Major (Tananarive), 'Exercice sur la carte executé en Septembre 1936 à Tananarive', 28 September 1936; 8H81/D2, 'Madagascar : emplacement des troupes du groupe de l'Afrique Orientale Française', 1 March 1937.
101 SHA, 8H73/D5, no. 2065/1/1, Moutet to Tananarive governor, 5 September 1936.
102 Charles-Robert Ageron, 'L'idée d'Eurafrique et le débat colonial franco-allemand de l'entre-deux-guerres', Revue d'Histoire Moderne et Contemporaine, 22:3 (1975), 455–68.
103 For background see Chantal Metzger, L'Empire colonial français dans la stratégie du Troisième Reich 1936–1945 (Brussels: Peter Lang, 2002); and her 'L'empire colonial français dans la stratégie du Troisième Reich (1936–1945)', Relations Internationales,

101:1 (2000), 41–55; Andrew J. Crozier, *Appeasement and Germany's Last Bid for Colonies* (London: Macmillan, 1988); Ngando, *La France au Cameroun*; Léonard I. Sah, 'Activités allemandes et germanophilie au Cameroun (1936–1939)', *Revue Française d'Histoire d'Outre-Mer*, 69:255 (1982), 129–44; and, more controversially, K. A. N'Dumbre, *Hitler voulait l'Afrique. Le projet Troisième Reich sur le continent africain* (Paris: Editions l'Harmattan, 1980).

104   Nørlund, 'Rice and the colonial lobby', 204–6.
105   Brocheux and Hémery, *Indochine, la colonisation ambiguë*, 129, 169.
106   Several articles in the 1921, 1922 and 1923 issues of *L'Océanie Française* analysed the implications of the Washington naval conference for the French Pacific territories. See, for example, two articles by E. Pelleray, 'La conférence de Washington', *L'Océanie Française*, 17:58 (July–September 1921), 74–7; and 'Après Washington : la situation dans le Pacifique', *L'Océanie Française*, 19:70 (1923), 70–5.
107   Jacques Binoche, 'La politique extrême-orientale française et les relations franco-japonaises 1919–1939', *Revue Française d'Histoire d'Outre-Mer* 86 (1989), 531–3.
108   See, for example, editorial: 'La France et le conflit sino-japonais', *L'Asie Française*, 32:296 (January 1932), 7–9; G. Besnard, 'La politique extérieure du Japon', *L'Asie Française*, 33:313 (September–October 1933), 281–3; A.M., 'La politique d'expansion commerciale du Japon', *L'Asie Française*, 34:319 (1934), 112–14.
109   John F. Laffey, 'French Far Eastern policy in the 1930s', *Modern Asian Studies*, 23:1 (1989), 117 n. 1.
110   Duroselle, *La Décadence*, 266–7; O. Louis, 'De Bizerte à Mers el-Kébir : Les bases navales d'Afrique du Nord dans l'entre-deux-guerres', *Revue Historique des Armées*, 4 (1999), 36–7.
111   *Lettres et notes de l'Amiral Darlan*, 28–9, 49–53, 95–6.
112   Georges Taboulet, 'La France et l'Angleterre face au conflit sino-japonais (1937–1939)', *Revue d'Histoire Diplomatique* 88 (January 1974), 133.
113   Binoche, 'La politique extrême-orientale française', 533–6.
114   Laffey, 'French Far Eastern policy', 138–46.
115   SHA, 2N70/D2, CSDN Secretariat, 'Note sur l'organisation de la défense autonome de l'Union Indochinoise', 27 October 1938.
116   Taboulet, 'La France et l'Angleterre', 125.
117   *Ibid.*, 126–43.
118   Allan R. Millett, 'Assault from the sea. The development of amphibious warfare between the wars: the American, British and Japanese experiences', in Williamson Murray and Allan R. Millett (eds), *Military Innovation in the Interwar Period* (Cambridge: Cambridge University Press, 1998), 68–9.
119   Taboulet, 'La France et l'Angleterre', 128–30.
120   B.Q., 'Japon : le marche vers les mers du sud', *Revue Française d'Outre-Mer*, 766 (May 1939), 139–40.
121   SHM, 2BB7/T1, EMG-2, Tokyo naval attaché, 'L'annexation des îles Spratley par le Japon', 1 May 1939; John E. Dreifort, *Myopic Grandeur. The Ambivalence of French Foreign Policy toward the Far East, 1919–1945* (Kent OH: Kent State University Press, 1991), 149–53.
122   Bertrand Favreau, *Georges Mandel ou la passion de la République 1885–1944* (Paris: Fayard, 1996), 42, 334. Mandel appointed Catroux to succeed Brévié on 16 July 1939.
123   SHA, 7N2837/D2, SHA-2, 'Singapour – La conférence franco-britannique', n.d. June 1939.
124   PRO, CO 825/28/5, C10342/249/17, H. F. C. Walsh (Saigon) to FO, 12 July 1939.
125   *DDF*, 2nd series, vol. XVII, final report of Singapore talks, pp. 42–55.
126   SHM, TTD 821/Dossier FNEO, Station navale de l'Océan Indien 'Bougainville', 'Conférence anglo-française, Aden, 29 mai au 3 juin 1939'.
127   Dreifort, *Myopic Grandeur*, 164.
128   Robert Aldrich, *The French Presence*, 288–90, 318–20. Robert Aldrich notes that the CSDN acknowledged New Caledonia's commercial and strategic value in 1927.
129   SHA, 12H3, no. 1508, Colonies to Governor (Nouméa), 11 September 1933.
130   Aldrich, *The French Presence*, 290–4.

131 Louis Hubert, 'La production de nickel et la défense nationale', *L'Océanie Française*, 27:122 (1931), 103–4.
132 SHA, 12H3, no. 243/S, Commandant Supérieur des Troupes, Groupe du Pacifique, 'Compte-rendu sur les manoeuvres de 1937', 1 August 1937.
133 SHA, 12H3, Commandant Supérieur des Troupes, Groupe du Pacifique, 'Exercice du cadres du Samedi 16 Septembre 1939'.
134 Pelleray, 'La France en guerre', 61–2.
135 CAOM, GGA, 9H18, no. 1143, Centre d'informations et d'études (Constantine department) report, 'Echos dans les milieux indigènes de la célébration du 14 juillet à Paris', 19 July 1939. Members of the Association el Myad el Kheiri, a non-political organisation, were the sole Algerian delegates invited to attend the Paris celebrations.
136 Marc Michel, ' "Mémoire officielle", discours et pratique coloniale. Le 14 juillet et le 11 novembre au Sénégal entre les deux guerres', *Revue Française d'Histoire d'Outre-Mer*, 77:287 (1990), 150–3; regarding the ideologically polarised responses to Bastille Day celebrations in 1939, see Joan Tumblety, ' "Civil wars of the mind". The commemoration of the 1789 revolution in the Parisian press of the radical right, 1939', *Journal of Contemporary History*, 30:3 (2000), 389–429.
137 Sorum, *Intellectuals and Decolonization in France*, 25, citing Raoul Girardet, *L'Idée coloniale en France de 1871 à 1962* (Paris: Table Ronde, 1972), 134. Girardet stressed the other aspect of this opinion poll, namely that over forty per cent of respondents did not judge the loss of colonial territory to be especially grave.
138 AN, F60187/DA1, Algiers Chamber of Agriculture motion proposed by M. Vagnon, n.d. December 1939; Cherrid Missoum to Daladier, 10 December 1939; no. 51054, Le Beau (Algiers) to Ministry of Interior/Cabinet, 28 May 1940.
139 'L'Afrique du Nord et la guerre', *L'Afrique Française*, 49:8–9 (September 1939), 212–13.
140 'Levant : généralités', *L'Asie Française*, 39:367 (February 1939), 72.
141 'Les populations du Levant sous mandat français et la guerre', *L'Asie Française*, 39:373 (September–October 1939), 275–7.
142 SHA, Archives de Moscou, C623/D1419, SEL note, 'Conversation avec M. Puaux', n.d. August 1939.
143 Mahfoud Kaddache, 'L'opinion politique musulmane en Algérie et l'administration française (1939–1942)', *Revue d'Histoire de la Deuxième Guerre Mondiale*, 114 (1979), 103–6.
144 SHA, 2N66/D1, no. 5159–2, Daladier letter to Henri Queuille, 6 September 1938.
145 SHA, 2N66/D1, no. 4739, 'Note de renseignements pour l'évaluation des besoins de la population civile en denrées de première nécessité d'après la moyenne des consommations au cours des années 1935, 1936, 1937', Algiers, 23 August 1938.
146 SHA, 2N65/D3, no. 2161/DNAFN, Noguès to Daladier/CSDN, 4 October 1939.
147 SHA, 2N65/D3, CSDN, 'Le développement et l'équipement économique de l'Afrique du Nord', n.d. November 1927.
148 SHA, 2N66/D1, 'Extrait du rapport du Général Girod en date du 16 juin 1927'.
149 SHA, 2N65/D2, no. 4993, CSDN, 'Extrait du projet de proposition de résolution', 11 June 1927.
150 As examples for Algeria see SHA, 2N66/D1, Ministry of Interior report to CSDN: Direction du Contrôle, 'Recensement des ressources et des besoins en Algérie en temps de guerre', n.d. August 1931; 'Les ports de l'Algérie', 7 November 1932.
151 'L'Afrique du Nord et la guerre', 215–19.
152 'L'Indochine et la défense de l'empire', *L'Asie Française*, 39 (June 1939), 197–9.
153 SHA, 2N70/D3, CSDN Secretariat, 'Le Budget générale l'Afrique Occidentale Française pour l'exercice de 1939'.
154 SHA, 2N70/D5, CSDN Secretariat, 'Le Budget local de Madagascar pour 1939', 26 January 1939.
155 See the statistical returns in SHA, 2N70/D7–8, 'Commerce extérieure – premier semestre, 1939'.
156 SHA, 2N70/D5, CSDN Secretariat, 'La Réunion : la situation de la colonie'.
157 Recham, *Les Musulmans algériens dans l'armée française*, 66–7.
158 Echenberg, *Colonial Conscripts*, 88.

159 Regarding *Tirailleurs Sénégalais* in the battle for France, see SHA, 9N268: Troupes coloniales, Secrétariat d'état à la guerre (Vichy), 'Note sur la participation à la campagne 1939–40 des unités sénégalaises', 20 February 1941.
160 SHA, 15H142, 'Participation des troupes coloniales à la campagne 1939–1940', 1 February 1942; Thomas, 'The Vichy government', 663–76.
161 Michel, 'La puissance par l'empire', 38–41.

CONCLUSION

Prelude to decolonisation?
The inter-war empire revisited

By 1939 France was a declining European power in crisis, with an unmanageable colonial empire. But so it was in 1920. What, if anything, changed in the intervening twenty years? Is 'the inter-war empire' of any use as an analytical tool, or is it merely a historical construct and nothing more? The histories of the colonial system, and of its individual components between 1919 and 1939, are absorbing in themselves. But few would question the truism that the two World Wars wrought fundamental changes to the international system, to European colonialism and to French society. The French empire after 1919 was fundamentally different from that of 1914, just as the French Union of 1946 did not replicate the colonial system of the inter-war years.

In trying to unravel what sets the inter-war years apart as a discrete period of colonial change, this book has addressed several larger issues. One has been to trace the origins of decolonisation in the rise of colonial nationalism, anti-colonial movements, violent protest and rebellion against imperial authority after 1919. Another objective has been to connect theories of republican imperialism and colonial governance with the lived experience of colonial rule in a twenty-year period scarred by war and economic dislocation. Examination of inter-war reforms or, more precisely, of the frustration of reformist initiatives, suggests that the problems of empire in 1939 were the consequence of French reluctance to contemplate any fundamental redistribution of power within colonial states. Yet examination of popular imperialism, imperialist lobbying and colonial policy making indicates that decisions of lasting import to the empire were made with minimal ministerial, parliamentary or public discussion in France. The French population was neither mobilised in opposition to colonial reform, nor in support of it. Municipal imperialism, once a powerful influence on colonial economic policy and a stimulus to public support for empire, was weakened by the impact of the depression and changes in the international system that made remote colonies seem more a liability than

[347]

an asset. On the eve of war France took refuge in the idea that colonial resources might cancel out the nation's economic and demographic inferiority next to Nazi Germany. This did not indicate a broader popular imperialist horizon, but a narrower one. Everything imperial was secondary to defence of the Rhine frontier. For the empire to hold, France had to hold first. A final question thus confronts us: how far did the French empire matter to inter-war France?

An essential paradox of French imperialism was that France's governing elite remained overwhelmingly Eurocentric in outlook despite the global reach of colonial rule. French governments rarely placed empire at the forefront of decisions made in economic or foreign policy. This assertion may jar. After the Great War the sharp decline of the franc, the urgent need to increase export volume, the imminent redistribution of territory under the peace settlement and the powerful tide of nationalist sentiment enhanced parliamentary and public interest in the colonies. The wartime contribution of colonial troops attained almost folkloric status, enhanced by the prominence of imperial regiments in the Rhine occupation – and the bitter German complaints against them.[1] French gratification at the deployment of colonial regiments as occupiers in Germany was itself double-edged. Many were relieved to see them go, a sentiment captured in the phrase 'pas chez nous, chez eux' (colloquially, 'not in our backyard, but in theirs').[2]

The sky-blue Chamber of 1920–24 was fervently nationalistic. Even so, empire remained peripheral to National Bloc politics. Colonial modernisation and constitutional reform were rejected. Empire was there to serve, to be dwelt upon only when urgently required in the assistance of France. Colonial policy making was a specialist affair, a matter for those peculiarly drawn to the exotic attractions of the colonies or, as was commonly assumed, unable to win access to more esteemed branches of government. Between the wars the business of running the French empire was a political backwater. Important administrative changes occurred none the less. By the 1920s colonial policy formulation was centralised in Paris to a far greater extent than before 1914 when local colonial commanders frequently seized new territory in a chaotic process of frontier imperialism pursued in defiance of government instruction. In the inter-war period the growing bureaucratic complexity of strategic policy making made it harder for Parti colonial interests to wield decisive influence at Cabinet or departmental level.

On those occasions when significant parliamentary time was devoted to questions of empire, as, for example, during the extended debate over colonial development between 1921 and 1923, or in response to the rebellions in Morocco and Syria during 1925–26, most Deputies used discussion of colonial policy as a stick with which to beat the government of the day.

'Imperial debate' in national politics usually connoted criticism of past government failure rather than consideration of future plans. But what of the millions of visitors that came through the turnstiles of the Vincennes colonial exhibition? A commercial success and a publicity festival, the *exposition coloniale* did not achieve its central objective. There was little sign after 1931 of a more deeply rooted popular imperialism in France. Far from bringing the empire to France as a tangible reality, colonial exhibitions highlighted the gulf separating imperial enthusiasts from the public at large. The Vincennes *exposition* was less a celebration of Third Republic imperialism than a desperate attempt to persuade the home population to take the empire seriously. On the rare occasions when a government – specifically, Léon Blum's first Popular Front Ministry in 1936 – proposed major colonial reform, opposition in the Chamber of Deputies and, even more so, in the Senate, undermined the government's programme. Popular Frontism in the empire unleashed social changes and political forces that colonial authorities struggled to contain for years afterward. Herein lies its importance, regardless of the frustration of reformist initiatives.

The apparatus of the French colonial state never lived up to the lofty ideals set for it by republican imperialists. The cultural universalism of assimilationists fell foul of reluctance to jeopardise existing colonial hierarchies. Citizenship rights were withheld from all but a fraction of the most francophile indigenous elite. Targeted at a favoured few, associationist policies never appealed to the majority of colonial subjects. John Ruedy's telling verdict on the 1919 Jonnart Law holds true for administrative reforms enacted in the inter-war period: 'The Jonnart legislation can be viewed in one sense as France's final rejection of the doctrine of assmiliation and in another as a fateful step in the direction of political instability'.[3] Associationism traded on the value of 'tradition', understood as popular respect for indigenous hierarchies, as a stabilising force in colonial societies. Official respect for cultural difference thus became the watertight justification for the restriction of power to the French and their allies among local elites. Nowhere was this more apparent than in the vocational bent of colonial education policy for rural *indigènes*. A French-style academic programme was inappropriate for pupils destined to remain colonial subjects rather than French citizens.

In the 1920s colonial modernisation became synonymous with the selective importation of French policies and practices. Urban planning shows this process in operation. Lauded by the imperial lobby as concrete proof of imperial achievement, the inter-war transformation of colonial cities had mixed results. Urban social change in the Maghreb drew greatest comment because more Europeans were directly involved. Increased urban segregation, the concentration of economic resources and state services in settler-dominated communities, and the general characterisation of

Muslim cities as traditional and unchanging confirmed two important points. First, in the eyes of the colonial authorities, French leadership was essential to modernise the North African territories. Second, the institutions and cultural practices of Muslim society were considered antithetical to socio-economic development.[4]

Colonial economies in the inter-war years were characterised by their extreme market sensitivity to changes in international commodity prices. Relatively short-lived boom conditions in the mid to late 1920s were followed by acute economic contraction in the depression years of 1931–35 and slow recovery thereafter. Colonial reforms attempted at the height of the 1920s booms – by Maurice Viollette in Algiers and by Alexandre Varenne in Hanoi – fell foul of settler commercial interests that had tightened their grip on the colonial export economy.[5] During the depression the financial orthodoxy of centre-right governments was replicated in the colonies through the reduction of state expenditure, cutbacks in public sector employment and a contraction of the money supply. Metropolitan deflationary policies and the structural problems of imperial trade were compounded by French currency adjustments. Between 1930 and 1936, the franc's high convertibility rate delayed colonial export recovery. The decline in French exports in the depression years 1931–35 was amplified in the colonies, many of which relied on sales of primary products that could be purchased cheaper from other non-European markets such as the British and Dutch empires (coal, plantation rubber, ores, tropical hardwoods, groundnuts and fruits), East Asia (rice, silk) and the United States (cereal crops).

The absence of state welfare provision for colonial populations set them apart from French society, helping to perpetuate stereotypical racial images of modern and primitive, civilised and uncivilised, progressive and backward. Few colonial officials who witnessed colonial conditions at first hand were unmoved by them. In December 1928 Raphaël Antonetti, governor-general of AEF, and not one easily swayed by scenes of colonial poverty, conceded that a long administrative career spanning seven colonies had not prepared him for the abject poverty he encountered in Equatorial Africa. The French colonial state had failed. For thirty years it permitted trading companies to exploit the indigenous population without restraint.[6] The Kongo Wara revolt was one direct consequence of this failure, but the litany of brutality, high mortality rates and endemic disease among forced labourers in AEF stands among the most damning evidence of colonial exploitation in the inter-war period. By the time the Popular Front took office in 1936 social deprivation throughout French Africa and elsewhere in the empire was especially acute. Over the preceding five years labour exactions increased, as did the net tax burden on colonial subjects. All this at a time when the colonies were expected to purchase a greater share of French manufactured goods despite the collapse in the export value of most colonial commodities. In 1929 the French empire absorbed 18.6 per cent of French exports. Five years later this figure had risen to 30.8 per cent. Salvation for hard-pressed French manufacturers, this rise in the empire's share of French exports conceals the immense hardship of colonial consumers taxed to the hilt, exploited as cheap labour and compelled to buy overpriced French goods.[7]

Colonial discrimination was starkest in areas of high European settlement. Take Morocco for instance. A 1932 French governmental loan, contracted to finance schools and hospitals, was repaid by Moroccan taxpayers and profits from the protectorate's phosphate industry. At this point only four per cent of the total Moroccan population was French. Yet the settler population received the lion's share of state support. In the predominantly Muslim cities of Marrakech, Fez and Meknès hospitals for the majority population received 500,000, 800,000 and 500,000 francs in loan capital, while the three cities' European hospitals were each allocated between four and five million francs. Put another way, although the Muslim population of Marrakech, Fez and Meknès constituted over ninety per cent of the combined total, it received an eighth of state hospital funding.[8]

Gender discrimination was also acute in the colonies. Among subject populations, men were more likely to die in the service of empire, whether as soldiers, forced labourers or junior auxiliaries of the colonial state. But women suffered the greater disadvantages in daily life. The spread of wage labour and more widespread use of cash often diminished women's economic power relative to that of their husbands and male relatives. The quest for cash-paid work led to increased economic migration, particularly in those colonies where seasonal agricultural employment, plantation farming and labour camps were common. Women in the inter-war empire were systematically marginalised. They were denied political rights more thoroughly than men, excluded from much of the colonial labour market as well as the rudimentary educational system, and prone to the double discrimination of a colonial system that privileged masculine control and indigenous societies that privileged domestic roles. Yet women were far from silent witnesses to colonial politics and anti-colonial protest. New women's movements, street protests and popular committees, involvement in anti-colonial nationalism, and adaptation to fast-changing economic roles marked out women's colonial experience after 1919. Siân Reynolds's comment regarding French women in inter-war France holds good for the colonies: 'women were not outside politics, even politics as formally defined, let alone the politics of workplace, family and culture'.[9]

The Popular Front government was not especially sensitive to gender issues, Denise Moran Savineau's enquiry into women's lives in AOF notwithstanding. Moran's meticulous catalogue of injustice against women in AOF bore no immediate fruit. By the time she completed her survey work in May 1938 the Popular Front had collapsed. Her investigation, like most of those initiated during 1936–37, was left to gather dust. Blum's government was more concerned with the empire's industrial work force than its women labourers and planned to extend to the colonies labour reforms introduced in France in June 1936. These included a labour code codifying worker entitlements, paid annual holidays and a forty-hour working week in industrial and commercial enterprises. It failed to meet these objectives. Conscious of the administrative and settler opposition he would face, Marius Moutet opted for a lengthy consultation process prior to phasing in labour reforms. The rue Oudinot sought advice from corporate managers, employers, chambers of commerce, the colonial labour inspectorate and municipal councils. These consultations revealed deep-seated opposition to the wholesale application of metropolitan labour reform.

Historians of inter-war France agree that one reason for the abiding fascination of the Popular Front years is that they anticipated the societal divisions later exposed by the four years of Vichy rule. Some political analysts have gone further, arguing that without the Popular Front there would have been no Vichy. In its espousal of racial and gender hierarchy the Vichy state capitalised on the reactionary conservatism already rooted among elements of the French right, the Catholic church, pro-natalist organisations and colonial settler groups, as well as the less clearly articulated hostility among the wider French public to colonial immigration and greater democratic rights for women. The more profound societal divisions and the class and racial prejudice laid bare by the perceived threat of Popular Front government between 1934 and 1938 were in many ways an ideological forcing ground for Vichy's authoritarian, anti-republican agenda. There was nothing new in Vichy's construction of policies towards women, racial minorities in France and indigenous peoples in the empire in accordance with pseudo-scientific concepts of race theory. In particular, societal division, gender inequality and racial hierarchy were all ascribed to common biological roots. In this sense, Vichy's subjugation of women, its policies of racial exclusion and its identification of degenerate races within the empire were of a piece with a longer-running discourse of the anti-republican right. The embrace of Vichy's National Revolution was the logical progression from inter-war rightist antagonism to the individualist, egalitarian and democratic values of Jacobin republicanism.[10]

The most virulent opposition to colonial rule developed in territories whose ethnic identity and societal values were actively undermined by the French presence. *Algérie française* and *l'Indochine française* were imaginary constructions. But their representation as new societies was also instrumental to official propaganda. In republican imperialist rhetoric French Algeria meant just that: a country fashioned from chaos by military effort, pioneering settlement, French legal norms and cultural values. There was a right-wing dimension to this. Comparison between the vigour of *colon* society and the corrupt, unhealthy lifestyle of French industrial workers was calculated to appeal to those settlers for whom inter-war France seemed an alien, decadent place. By 1936 *colon* societies in North Africa increasingly defined themselves in opposition to 'the nauseating filthiness of the so-called civilised life of the Metropole'.[11] French Indochina was a less ambitious project in terms of societal transformation and French colonisation. Yet the edifice of French colonial rule in South East Asia, the federal administration and the very nomenclature of 'Indochina' subsumed the identities of its subject peoples – the Vietnamese, the Cambodians and the Laotians. By the mid-1930s the anti-colonial struggle of the ICP dominated federation politics. The conflict between the French authorities and the ICP over the impact of colonialism on the populations of Cochin-China, Annam and Tonkin was also a struggle over the concept of a Vietnamese nation. French administrators scrupulously avoided the terms 'Vietnam' and 'Vietnamese'. A federation of the three *Ky*, distinct from the wider Indochina federation, was obviously inimical to French efforts to prevent Vietnamese unification. The chasm between rulers and ruled was not just cultural and political, it was social. Settlers in Indochina often characterised the rural interior as a closed and forbidding environment. Even suburban *quartiers* built for administrators and their families were designed to keep a disease-bearing, seditious population at a safe distance.[12] Hardly surprising that the extent of poverty and dissent was poorly understood. In the depression years Tonkin's principal port of Haiphong remained a showcase of French commercial investment. Yet from 1931 to 1935 the city's population shrank from 168,000 to 73,000 as Vietnamese returned to the countryside in search of food and work.[13]

Algérie française and *l'Indochine française* stood apart because, by accident or design, their socio-political complexion was refashioned to suit differing French images of model colonies. The impact of colonialism in these territories was by no means unique. Governance in the other large colonial federations – AOF and AEF – subverted social organisation locally and nationally. Recall the frequent redrawing of boundaries, the administrative separation from Senegal of the Four Communes of Dakar, Gorée, Saint-Louis and Rufisque in 1924, the 'abolition' of Upper Volta in 1932. In Madagascar, too, the establishment of all-island government after 1895 had an ulterior motive – to weaken the power base of the Merina dynasty in and around Tananarive.[14] One lesson of the anti-colonial uprisings of the years 1925–31 was that colonial rule catalysed the development of national consciousness among marginalised populations. Better roads and improved communications, combined with limited economic opportunities and inadequate social provision, proved a potent mixture. Opponents of colonial rule spread their message more easily, finding a receptive audience among peasant farmers, urban workers and migrant labourers that identified French imperialism with the grinding poverty of their daily existence.[15] The development of a federal transport system undermined the separatism at the heart of French policy in the Vietnamese territories. In 1936 the completion of the Annam coastal rail line between Nha Trang and Tourane marked the last major stage of the trans-Indochina railway project started some forty years earlier. This 'imperial corridor', albeit largely confined to a coastal rail system, strengthened the economic and human bonds between Cochin-China in the south, Annam and Tonkin in the north. So, too, did the *route intercoloniale* road-building programme, federally funded from 1911.[16] Urban electrification schemes and telephone communications shortened distances and broke down the internal frontiers of colonial states.[17]

Differing degrees of colonisation, economic potential and infrastructure development also shaped the cumbersome apparatus of imperial defence. The demarcation of civil–military responsibilities, clear enough on paper, was muddied in practice by the overlapping responsibilities of ministries, regional army commands and colonial governments. In general terms, the colonial authorities produced the funds for local defence, the Ministry of Colonies regulated deployments of troops between territories and the service ministries devised the overall strategy of empire protection. The result was the atomisation of colonial defence policy as government and general staff inevitably focused on the coming war with Nazi Germany.

The Second World War, a struggle between competing ideological systems, placed the spotlight on colonial injustice. Metropolitan demand for men and materials, and heightened police control of the colonial state, nourished popular hostility to French rule. Frantic initial efforts to improvise colonial defences, raise additional regiments, increase economic output and suppress local dissent gave way to more methodical government planning, military preparation and police repression in the winter of 1939–40. The lost liberties and harsher restrictions that attended defeat and occupation in metropolitan France were facets of day-to-day colonial life for subject peoples. Colonial nationalism was sure to emerge stronger whatever the war's outcome. If France was victorious, colonial subjects could justifiably expect reward for their individual and collective contribution. Wartime promises made, and promises broken, of constitutional reform, improved living standards, even independence, were sure to rebound on France's post-war governments. If France was defeated, the edifice of colonial control was bound to crack. Above all, the Second World War threatened to expose the myth of the French empire as a coherent imperial power system. Sure enough, by July 1940 the empire fractured. The June 1940 defeat was not the sole cause. When the armistice agreements were signed on 22 and 25 June 1940, there were virtually no German, Italian or

Japanese forces in any colonial territory. Most of the empire escaped enemy occupation. Tunisia was completely overrun by Axis forces in early 1943; French Indochina eventually came under full Japanese control in March 1945. The French colonial system was instead broken apart by external pressure, by internal dissent among rulers and ruled, and, uniquely so in the French case, by the rivalries of competing colonial elites. But French reluctance to decolonise built on myths, some Gaullist, others more broadly based, of past imperial unity and popular imperialist commitment.[18] The empire of the inter-war years displayed few of the qualities the French attached to it after 1945.

Notes

1 Gershovich, *French Military Rule*, 177–81; R. Reinders, 'Racialism on the left. E. D. Morel and the 'black horror on the Rhine', *International Review of Social History*, 12:1 (1968), 1–28; Neilson, 'The "black horror" ', 606–27.
2 Melzer, 'Spectacles and sexualities', 228–9.
3 Ruedy, *Modern Algeria*, 112.
4 King, 'Writing colonial space', 551, 555–6.
5 ADA, Sarraut papers, 12J259: Algérie, démission de Maurice Viollette.
6 Antonetti quote, 28 December 1928, cited in Coquery-Vidrovitch, *Le Congo*, 528.
7 Oloruntimehin, 'The economy of French West Africa', 69–70.
8 Abu-Lughod, *Rabat. Urban Apartheid*, 194–5.
9 Reynolds, *France between the Wars*, 206.
10 Francine Muel-Dreyfus, *Vichy and the Eternal Feminine. A Contribution to the Political Sociology of Gender* (Durham: Duke University Press, 2001), 6–7, 311.
11 1936 Fez press quote cited in Hoisington, Jnr, *The Casablanca Connection*, 115.
12 Nicola Cooper, *France in Indochina*, chapter 8, and her earlier 'Urban planning and architecture in colonial Indochina', *French Cultural Studies*, 11:1 (2000), 75–99.
13 Brocheux, 'The state and the 1930s depression in French Indochina', 256.
14 Ellis, 'The political elite of Imerina', 219–34.
15 A point reluctantly acknowledged by Governor-general Pierre Pasquier: ADA, Sarraut papers, 12J307/Dossier: événements de Yen Bay, 6 June 1930.
16 Brocheux and Hémery, *Indochine, la colonisation ambiguë*, 127–8. By 1943 the Indochina federation had 32,000 km of metalled roads.
17 *Ibid.*, 133. An official inquiry in 1937 calculated that industrial production generated only 19.6 per cent of federal revenue in Indochina.
18 On the 'colonial myth' idea see D. Bruce Marshall, *The French Colonial Myth and Constitution Making in the Fourth Republic* (New Haven CT: Yale University Press, 1973); Andrew Shennan, *Rethinking France. Plans for Renewal, 1940–46* (Oxford: Oxford University Press, 1989), chapter 6; Charles-Robert Ageron, 'La survivance d'un mythe : la puissance par l'empire colonial (1944–1947)', *Revue Française d'Histoire d'Outre-Mer*, 77 (1985), 388–97; Tony Smith, 'The French colonial consensus and people's war, 1946–1958', *Journal of Contemporary History*, 9 (1974), 217–47.

[355]

BIBLIOGRAPHY

Primary sources

Centre des Archives d'Outre-Mer (CAOM), Aix-en-Provence

Ministère des Colonies Fonds de la Direction des affaires politiques (affpol).
Afrique Occidentale Française Fonds Moderne, série 17G Affaires politiques; série 19G Affaires musulmanes; série 21G Police et sûreté.
Gouvernement Général de l'Afrique Equatoriale Française (GGAEF), série D Politique et administration générale: sous-série 1D Corréspondance générale du Bureau des affaires politiques, 1923–57.
Gouvernement Général d'Algérie (GGA), série H Affaires indigènes: sous-série 8H Organisation administrative; sous-série 9H Surveillance des indigènes; sous-série 11H Rapports politiques périodiques.
Département d'Alger, série F Police et maintien de l'ordre.
Gouvernement Général de l'Indochine (GGI), série D Administration générale; série F Affaires politiques; nouveau fonds.
Gouvernement Général de Madagascar (GGM), série D Politique et administration générale: sous-série B Corréspondance; sous-série 4D Rapports d'ensemble au Ministère sur la situation générale de Madagascar; sous-série 6D Dossiers divers de la Direction des affaires politiques.
Iconographie, matières 1/affiches
Papiers d'Agents, série PA: Jean Decoux papers (PA14), Robert Delavignette papers (PA19), Hubert Deschamps papers (PA36), Georges Mandel papers (PA18), Marius Moutet papers (PA28), Maurice Prouteaux papers (PA50), Albert Sarraut papers (PA9).

Ministère des Affaires Etrangères (MAE), Paris

Série E Syrie-Liban, 1918–29/1930–40.
Série E Asie, 1918–29.
Série M Maroc, 1917–40.
Série P Tunisie, 1917–40.
Papiers d'Agents: Joseph Avenol papers (PA 036), Henry de Jouvenel papers (PA 092), Georges Leygues papers (PA 110), Gabriel Puaux papers (PA 252).

BIBLIOGRAPHY

Service Historique de l'Armée (SHA), Vincennes

Série H Outre-Mer: sous-série 4H Levant; sous-série 5H Afrique Occidentale Française; sous-série 6H Afrique Equatoriale Française; sous-série 8H Madagascar et ses dépendances; sous-série 9H Inde française; sous-série 10H Indochine française.
Série 1N Conseil Supérieur de la Guerre (CSG).
Série 2N Comité Permanent de la Défense Nationale (CPDN).
Série 6N Evénements d'Indochine, 1930–31.
Série 7N Etat-Major de l'Armée (EMA).
Série 9N Direction de l'infanterie 9N268–9N270: Direction des troupes coloniales.
Fonds privés: General Fernand Gambiez papers (1K540), General Goislard de Monsabert papers (1K380), General Maxime Weygand papers (1K130).

Service Historique de l'Armée de l'Air (SHAA), Vincennes

Série C Présence aérienne française hors métropole.
Sous-série 1C Forces aériennes françaises au Levant.
Sous-série 2C Forces aériennes françaises au Maroc.
Guy La Chambre papers.

Service Historique de la Marine (SHM), Vincennes

Série 1BB Etat-major Général, deuxième bureau: Levant files.

Centre des Archives Diplomatiques, Nantes (CADN)

Fonds Protectorat du Maroc, sous-série: Direction des affaires chérifiennes, 1912–56.
Fonds Beyrouth, série: Cabinet politique.

Archives Nationales (AN), Paris

Série F[7] Interior Ministry, Police files.
Série F[60] Prime Minister's Office files.
Fonds privés: Louis-Hubert Lyautey papers, Paul Painlevé papers, Joseph Paul-Boncour papers.

Services des Archives de la Préfecture de Police (APP), Paris

Série BA Police surveillance of colonial immigrants; files on colonial nationalist parties.

Archives Départementales de l'Aude (ADA), Carcassonne, Fonds Albert Sarraut: Sous-Série 12J

Rôle politique sous la Troisième République

BIBLIOGRAPHY

12J43 Surveillance du Communisme, 1921–28.
12J44 L'action Communiste en Orient et en Afrique, 1924–28.
12J55 Comité parlementaire français du commerce, 1932.
12J69 Ministère de l'Intérieur, Cabinet Doumergue, 1934.
12J117 Constitution du Cabinet Chautemps, 1937.
12J118 Ministère d'état chargé des affaires de l'Afrique du Nord, Cabinet Chautemps, 1937–38.
Politique coloniale
12J162 Politique coloniale, 1920–35.
12J163 Mise en valeur des colonies, 1920–26.
12J174 L'économie des colonies, 1926–33.
12J191 Fêtes, cérémonies, conférences, 1920–38.
12J253 Afrique Occidentale Française, 1918–56.
12J254 Afrique Occidentale Française, rapports, 1918–57.
12J258 Afrique du Nord, généralités, 1925–55.
12J259 Algérie, 1925–57.
12J270 La Guyane, 1922–23.
12J277 Indochine, Autres gouverneurs-généraux, 1920–38.
12J280 Indochine, Situation politique, 1918–36.
12J281 Indochine, Politique indigène, 1917–20.
12J303 Indochine, Partis politiques, rapports, 1918–33.
12J304 Indochine, Assassinats, 1917–1919.
12J305 Indochine, Attentats, 1918.
12J307 Indochine, rébellion de la garnison de Yen Bay, 1930.

Public Record Office (PRO), London

FO 371 Foreign Office general correspondence.
WO 33 War Office reports/miscellaneous papers.
WO 106 Directorate of Military Operations and Intelligence.
WO 193 Directorate of Military Operations collation files.

Hoover Institution on War, Revolution and Peace, Stanford University

Banque de France: Assemblée Générale des actionnaires, 1938.
Gaston Bergery papers.
Robert Delavignette papers.
Louis Loucheur papers.

Official publications

Journal Officiel de la République Française.
Documents Diplomatiques Français. 3 août–31 décembre 1914; 1920 (volumes I and II) (Paris: Imprimerie Nationale, 1997 ff.); *1915* (volume I) (Brussels: Peter Lang, 2002).

BIBLIOGRAPHY

Newspapers and periodicals

Action Coloniale
L'Afrique Française
Les Continents
La Dépêche coloniale et maritime
La Dépêche de Toulouse
L'Écho de Paris
L'Entente Franco-Musulmane
L'Humanité
Le Monde Colonial illustré
La Nation Annamite
L'Océanie Française
L'Oeuvre
Outré-Mer Revue générale de colonisation
Le Paria Tribune des populations des colonies
Le Petit Parisien
Le Peuple
Le Populaire
Revue Africaine
Revue Française d'Outre-Mer
Revue Indigène
Revue Indochinoise
Le Temps

Memoirs, diaries, contemporary writings

Andréa, C. J. E., *La Révolte druze et l'insurrection de Damas* Paris: Payot, 1937.

Chivas-Baron, Clotilde, *La Femme française aux colonies* Paris: Larose Editeurs, 1929.

Cohen, William B., *Robert Delavignette on the French Empire. Selected Writings* Chicago: University of Chicago Press, 1977.

Corréard, Jules, *France algérienne* Paris: Larose Editeurs, 1938.

Coutou-Bégarie, Hervé, and Claude Huan (eds), *Lettres et notes de l'Amiral Darlan* Paris: Economica, 1992.

Delavignette, Robert, *Freedom and Authority in French West Africa* Oxford: Oxford University Press, 1950.

D'Esperey, Maréchal Franchet, *Une Oeuvre française: l'Algérie. Conférences organisés par la Société des anciens élèves de l'Ecole libre des sciences politiques* Paris: Alcan, 1929.

Faye, Stéphane, *Le Nouveau Monde français. Maroc, Algérie, Tunisie* Paris: Plon, 1924.

Feraoun, Mouloud, *Journal 1955–1962. Reflections on the French–Algerian War* James D. Le Sueur (ed.), Lincoln NE: University of Nebraska Press, 2000.

Gide, André, *Voyages au Congo. Carnets de route* Paris: Gallimard, 1927.

Guérin, Daniel, *Front populaire, révolution manquée* Paris: Maspero, 1970.

Gwynn, Sir Charles W., *Imperial Policing* London: Macmillan, 1936.

Hadj, Messali, *Les Mémoires de Messali Hadj* Paris: J. C. Lattès, 1982.

Lavergne, Bernard, *Le Principe des nationalités et les guerres, son application au problème colonial* Paris: Alcan, 1921.

Le Révérend, André (ed.), *Un Lyautey inconnu. Corréspondance et journal inédits 1874–1934* Paris: Perrin, 1980.

Mandouze, André, *Mémoires d'Outre-siècle I, D'une résistance à l'autre* Paris: Viviane Hamy, 1998.

Mérat, Louis, *L'Heure de l'économie dirigée d'intérêt général aux colonies* Paris: Sirey, 1936.

Mercier, Gustave, *Le Centenaire de l'Algérie. Exposé d'ensemble* Algiers: Soubiron, 1931.

Messimy, Adolpe, *Mes souvenirs* Paris: Plon, 1937.

Peyrouton, Bernard Marcel, *Du service public à la prison commune. Souvenirs: Tunis, Rabat, Buenos Aires, Vichy, Alger, Frèsnes* Paris: Plon, 1950.

Sarraut, Albert, *La Mise en valeur des colonies françaises* Paris: Payot, 1923.

—— *Grandeur et servitude coloniales* (10th rpt) Paris: Sagittaire, 1931.

Sartre, Jean-Paul, *War Diaries. Notes from a Phoney War, 1939–1940* English translation, London: Verso, 1984.

Simon, Jacques (ed.), *Messali Hadj par les texts* Paris: Editions Bouchèns, 2000.

Secondary sources

Books

Abenon, Lucien, Danielle Bégot and Jean-Pierre Sainton (eds), *Construire l'histoire antillais* Paris: Editions du CTHS, 2002.

Abu-Lughod, Janet L., *Rabat. Urban Apartheid in Morocco* Princeton NJ: Princeton University Press, 1980.

Adamthwaite, Anthony, *France and the Coming of the Second World War* London: Frank Cass, 1977.

—— *Grandeur and Misery. France's Bid for Power in Europe, 1914–1940* London: Arnold, 1995.

Ageron, Charles-Robert, *Histoire de l'Algérie contemporaine* Paris: Presses Universitaires de France, 1964.

—— *Les Musulmans algériens et la France 1871–1919* II, Paris: Presses Universitaires de France, 1968.

—— *France coloniale ou parti colonial* Paris: Presses Universitaires de France, 1978.

—— (ed.), *Le Chemins de la décolonisation de l'empire française 1936–1956* Paris: Editions CNRS, 1986.

Albord, Maurice, *L'Armée française et les états du Levant 1936–1946* Paris: CNRS, 2000.

Aldrich, Robert, *The French Presence in the South Pacific, 1842–1940* London: Macmillan, 1990.

—— *Greater France. A History of French Overseas Expansion* London: Macmillan, 1996.

—— and Martyn Lyons (eds), *The Sphinx in the Tuileries and other Essays in Modern French History* Sydney: University of Sydney Press, 1999.

—— *Colonialism and Homosexuality* London: Routledge, 2003.

Alexander, Martin S., *The Republic in Danger. General Maurice Gamelin and the Politics of French Defence, 1933–1940* Cambridge: Cambridge University Press, 1992.

—— and Helen Graham (eds), *The French and Spanish Popular Fronts. Comparative Perspectives* Cambridge: Cambridge University Press, 1989.

—— and William J. Philpott (eds), *Anglo-French Defence Relations between the Wars* London: Palgrave, 2002.

Allen, Philip M., *Madagascar. Conflicts of Authority in the Great Island* Boulder CO: Westview Press, 1995.

Allman, Jean, Susan Geiger and Nakanike Musisi (eds), *Women in African Colonial Histories* Bloomington IN: Indiana University Press, 2002.

Al Sayyad, Nezar (ed.), *Forms of Dominance. On the Architecture and Urbanism of the Colonial Enterprise* Aldershot: Ashgate, 1992.

Altbach, Phillip G., and Gail P. Kelly (eds), *Education and Colonialism* London: Longman, 1978.

Àlvarez, José E., *The Betrothed of Death. The Spanish Foreign Legion during the Rif Rebellion, 1920–1927* Westport CT: Greenwood Press, 2001.

Amar, Marianne, and Pierre Milza, *L'Immigration en France au XXe siècle* Paris: Armand Colin, 1990.

Amselle, Jean-Loup, and Emmanuelle Sibeud (eds), *Maurice Delafosse. Entre orientalisme et ethnographie : l'itinéraire d'un africaniste 1870–1926* Paris: Maisonneuve & Larose, 1998.

Anderson, Lisa, *The State and Social Transformation in Tunisia and Libya, 1830–1980* Princeton NJ: Princeton University Press, 1986.

Andrew, Christopher M., and A. S. Kanya-Forstner, *France Overseas. The Great War and the Climax of French Imperial Expansion* London: Thames & Hudson, 1981.

Atkin, Nicholas, and Frank Tallett (eds), *The Right in France, 1789–1997* London: I. B. Tauris, 1997.

Attal, Michel, *Les Émeutes de Constantine, 5 août 1934* Paris: Editions Romillot, 2002.

Bakalti, Souad, *La Femme tunisienne au temps de la colonisation 1881–1956* Paris: Editions l'Harmattan, 1996.

Balfour, Sebastian, *Deadly Embrace. Morocco and the Road to the Spanish Civil War* Oxford: Oxford University Press, 2002.

Baron, Beth, *The Women's Awakening in Egypt. Culture, Society, and the Press* New Haven CT: Yale University Press, 1994.

Becker, Annette, *War and Faith. The Religious Imagination in France, 1914–1930* Oxford: Berg, 1998.

Becker, Charles, Saliou Mbaye and Ibrahima Thioub (eds), *AOF : réalités et heritages. Sociétés ouest-africaines et ordre colonial 1895–1960* (2 vols) Dakar: Direction des Archives du Sénégal, 1997.

Becker, Jean-Jacques, and Serge Berstein, *Histoire de l'anti-communisme* Paris: Olivier Orban, 1987.

Becker, Josef, and Franz Knipping (eds), *Power in Europe? Great Britain, France, Italy and Germany in a Postwar World, 1945–1950* Berlin: Walter de Gruyter, 1986.

Belamri, Rabah, *L'Oeuvre de Louis Bertrand. Miroir de l'idéologie colonialiste* Algiers: OPU, 1980.

Bernard-Duquenet, N., *Le Sénégal et le Front populaire* Paris: Editions l'Harmattan, 1985.

Bernardini, Jean-Marc, *Le Darwinisme social en France 1859–1918. Fascination et rejet d'une idéologie* Paris: Editions CNRS, 1997.

Betts, Raymond, *Assimilation and Association in French Colonial Theory, 1890–1914* New York: Columbia University Press, 1961.

—— *France and Decolonisation, 1900–1960* London: Macmillan, 1991.

Bezançon, Pascale, *Une Colonisation éducatrice? L'expérience indochinoise 1860–1945*, Paris: Editions l'Harmattan, 2002.

Bidwell, Robin, *Morocco under Colonial Rule. French Administration of Tribal Areas, 1912–1956* London: Frank Cass, 1973.

Biondi, Jean-Pierre, *Les Anticolonialistes 1881–1962* Paris: Robert Laffont, 1992.

Blanchard, Pascal, and Armelle Chatelier (eds), *Images et Colonies. Actes du colloque* Paris: ACHAC, 1993.

Blanchard, Pascal, and Sandrine Lemaire (eds), *Culture coloniale. La France conquise par son empire 1871–1931* Paris: Editions autrement, 2003.

Bokova, Lenka, *La Confrontation franco-syrienne à l'époque du Mandat 1925–1927* Paris: Editions l'Harmattan, 1990.

Boomgaard, Peter, and Ian Brown (eds), *Weathering the Storm. The Economies of South East Asia in the 1930s Depression* Singapore: ISEAS, 2000.

Bouche, Denise, *L'Enseignement dans les territoires français de l'Afrique occidentale de 1817 à 1920. Mission civilisatrice ou formation d'une élite?* (2 vols) Paris: Honoré Champion, 1975.

—— *Histoire de la colonisation française II, Flux et reflux 1815–1962* Paris: Fayard, 1991.

Bouguessa, Kamel, *Aux sources du nationalisme algérien. Les pionniers de populisme révolutionnaire en marche* Algiers: Casbah Editions, 2000.

Bourse de Beyrouth, *Le Bourse de Beyrouth 1920–1970* Beirut: Bourse de Beyrouth, brochure cinquantenaire, 1970.

Boyce, Robert (ed.), *French Foreign and Defence Policy, 1918–1940. The Decline and Fall of a Great Power* London: Routledge, 1998.

Brocheux, Pierre, and Daniel Hémery, *Indochine : la colonisation ambiguë 1858–1954* (2nd edn) Paris: Editions la Découverte, 2001.

Brown, Ian (ed.), *The Economies of Africa and Asia in the Inter-war Depression* London: Routledge, 1989.

Brown, Judith, and Wm Roger Louis (eds), *The Oxford History of the British Empire. The Twentieth Century* Oxford: Oxford University Press, 1999.

Brown, Kenneth, Bernard Hourcade, Michèle Jolé, Claude Liauzu, Peter Sluglett and Sami Zubaida (eds), *Etat, ville et mouvements sociaux au Maghreb et en Moyen Orient* Paris: Editions l'Harmattan, 1989.

Brunet, J-P., *Jacques Doriot. Du communisme au fascisme* Paris: Balland, 1986.

Burke III, Edmund (ed.), *Struggle and Survival in the Modern Middle East* London: I. B. Tauris, 1993.

Burrin, Philippe, *La Dérive fasciste. Doriot, Déat, Bergery 1933–1945* Paris: Editions du Seuil, 1986.

Bush, Barbara, *Imperialism, Race and Resistance. Africa and Britain, 1919–1945* London: Routledge, 1999.

Callahan, Michael D., *Mandates and Empire. The League of Nations and Africa, 1914–1931* Brighton: Sussex Academic Press, 1999.

Cantier, Jacques, *L'Algérie sous le régime de Vichy*, Paris: Odile Jacob, 2002.

Carlier, Claude, and Guy Pedroncini (eds), *Les Troupes coloniales dans la Grande Guerre* Paris: Economica, 1997.

Caron, Vicki, *Uneasy Asylum. France and the Jewish Refugee Crisis, 1933–1942* Stanford CA: Stanford University Press, 1999.

Çelik, Zeynep, *Urban Forms and Colonial Confrontations. Algiers under French Rule* Berkeley CA: University of California Press, 1997.

Chadwick, Kay (ed.), *Catholicism, Politics and Society in Twentieth Century France* Liverpool: Liverpool University Press, 2000.

Chafer, Tony, *The End of Empire in West Africa. France's Successful Decolonization?* Oxford: Berg, 2002.

—— and Amanda Sackur (eds), *The French Colonial Empire and the Popular Front. Hope and Disillusion* London: Macmillan, 1999.

—— and Amanda Sackur (eds), *Promoting the Colonial Idea. Propaganda and Visions of Empire in France* London: Palgrave, 2002.

Charle, Christophe, *La Crise des sociétés impériales 1900–1940 : Allemagne, France, Grande-Bretagne. Essai d'histoire comparée* Paris: Editions du Seuil, 2001.

Chickering, Roger, and Stig Forster (eds), *The Shadows of Total War. Europe, East Asia and the United States, 1919–1939* Cambridge: Cambridge University Press, 2003.

Clancy-Smith, Julia, and Frances Gouda (eds), *Domesticating the Empire. Race, Gender, and Family Life in French and Dutch Colonialism*, Charlottesville VA: University of Virginia Press, 1998.

Clayton, Anthony, *France, Soldiers and Africa* London: Brassey's, 1988.

Cloarec, Vincent, *La France et la question de Syrie* Paris: CNRS, 1998.

Cohen, William B., *Rulers of Empire. The French Colonial Service in Africa* Stanford CA: Stanford University Press, 1971.

Cole, Jennifer, *Forget Colonialism? Sacrifice and the Art of Memory in Madagascar* Berkeley CA: University of California Press, 2001.

Collot, Claude, and Jean-Robert Henry (eds), *Le Mouvement national algérien. Textes 1912–1954* Paris: Editions l'Harmattan, 1978.

Colonna, Fanny, *Instituteurs algériens 1883–1939* Paris: Presses de la FNSP, 1975.

Confer, Vincent, *France and Algeria. The Problem of Civil and Political Reform* Syracuse NY: Syracuse University Press, 1966.

Conklin, Alice L., *A Mission to Civilize. The Republican Idea of Empire in France and West Africa, 1895–1930* Stanford CA: Stanford University Press, 1997.

Constantine, Stephen, *The Making of British Colonial Development Policy, 1914–1940* London: 1984.

Cook, James J., *New French Imperialism, 1880–1910. The Third Republic and Colonial Expansion* Hamden NH: Archon Books, 1973.

Cooper, Frederick, *Decolonization and African Society. The Labour Question in French and British Africa* Cambridge: Cambridge University Press, 1996.

Cooper, Frederick, and Ann Laura Stoler (eds), *Tensions of Empire. Colonial Cultures in a Bourgeois World* Berkeley CA: University of California Press, 1997.

Cooper, Frederick, Thomas C. Holt and Rebecca J. Scott (eds), *Beyond Slavery. Explorations of Race, Labour and Citizenship in Postemancipation Societies* Chapel Hill NC: University of North Carolina Press, 2000.

Cooper, Nicola, *France in Indochina. Colonial Encounters* Oxford: Berg, 2001.

Coquery-Vidrovitch, Catherine, *Le Congo au temps des grands compagnies concessionaires 1898–1930* Paris: Mouton, 1972 (rpt 2002).

—— (ed.), *Entreprises et entrepreneurs en Afrique au XIXe et XXe siècles* I Paris: Editions l'Harmattan, 1983.

—— *Africa. Endurance and Change South of the Sahara* Berkeley CA: University of California Press, 1988. (English translation of *Afrique noire. Permanences et ruptures* Paris: Payot, 1985.)

—— and Odile Georg (eds), *L'Afrique occidentale au temps des Français. Colonisateurs et colonisés c. 1860–1960* Paris: Editions de la Découverte, 1992.

Couland, Jacques, *Le Mouvement syndical au Liban 1919–1946* Paris: Editions Sociales, 1970.

Crozier, Andrew J., *Appeasement and Germany's Last Bid for Colonies* London: Macmillan, 1988.

Dann, Uriel (ed.), *The Great Powers in the Middle East, 1919–1939* New York: Holmes & Meier, 1988.

Degeorge, Gérard, *Damas des Ottomans à nos jours* Paris: Editions l'Harmattan, 1994.

Di Leonardo, Micaela (ed.), *Gender at the Crossroads of Knowledge. Feminist Anthropology in the Postmodern Era* Berkeley CA: University of California Press, 1991.

Dockrill, Michael, *British Establishment Perspectives on France, 1936–1940* London: Macmillan, 1999.

Dreifort, John E., Myopic Grandeur: *The Ambivalence of French Foreign Policy toward the Far East, 1919–1945* Kent OH: Kent State University Press, 1991.

Driver, Felix, and David Gilbert (eds), *Imperial Cities. Landscape, Display and Identity* Manchester: Manchester University Press, 1999.

Duiker, William J., *The Rise of Nationalism in Vietnam, 1900–1941* Ithaca NY: Cornell University Press, 1976.

Dunwoodie, Peter, *Writing French Algeria*, Oxford: Clarendon Press, 1998.

Duroselle, Jean-Baptiste, *La Décadence. Politique étrangère de la France 1932–1939* Paris: Imprimerie Nationale, 1979.

Echenberg, Myron, *Colonial Conscripts. The Tirailleurs Sénégalais in French West Africa, 1857–1960* Portsmouth NH: Heinemann, 1990.

—— *Black Death, White Medicine. Bubonic Plague and the Politics of Public Health in Colonial Senegal, 1914–1945* Oxford: James Currey, 2002.

Ezra, Elizabeth, *The Colonial Unconscious. Race and Culture in Interwar France* Ithaca NY: Cornell University Press, 2000.

Fall, Bouboucar, *Le Travail forcé en Afrique occidentale française 1900–1946* Paris: Editions Karthala, 1993.

Falola, T., and P. E. Lovejoy (eds), *Pawnship in Africa. Debt Bondage in Historical Perspective* Boulder CO: Westview Press, 1994.

Favreau, Bertrand, *Georges Mandel ou la passion de la République 1885–1944* Paris: Fayard, 1996.

Ferro, Marc, (ed.), *Le Livre noir de la colonialisme* Paris: Robert Laffont, 2003.

Fieldhouse, D. K. *Merchant Capital and Economic Decolonization. The United Africa Company, 1929–1987* Oxford: Clarendon Press, 1994.

Forcade, Olivier, Eric Duhamel and Philippe Vial (eds), *Militaires en république 1870–1962. Les officiers, le pouvoir et la vie publique en France* Paris: Publications de la Sorbonne, 1999.

Frankenstein, Robert, *Le Prix du réarmement français 1935–1939* Paris: Publications de la Sorbonne, 1982.

Freedman, Jane, and Carrie Tarr (eds), *Women, Immigration and Identities in France* Oxford: Berg, 2000.

Frémeaux, Jacques, *Les Empires coloniaux dans le processus de mondialisation*, Paris: Maisonneuve & Larose, 2002.

—— *La France et l'Algérie en guerre 1830–1870, 1954–1962* Paris: Economica, 2002.

Fry, Michael G., and Itamar Rabinovitch (eds), *Despatches from Damascus. Gilbert MacKereth and British Policy in the Levant, 1933–1939* Tel Aviv: Dayan Centre, 1985.

Gadant, Monique, *Le Nationalisme algérien et les femmes* Paris: Editions l'Harmattan, 1995.

Gelvin, James L., *Divided Loyalties. Nationalism and Mass Politics in Syria at the Close of Empire* Berkeley CA: University of California Press, 1998.

Genova, James E., *Colonial Ambivalence, Cultural Authenticity, and the Limitations of Mimicry in French-Ruled West Africa, 1914–1956* New York: Peter Lang, 2004.

Gershovich, Moshe, *French Military Rule in Morocco. Colonialism and its Consequences* London: Frank Cass, 2000.

Gifford, Prosser, and Wm Roger Louis (eds), *France and Britain in Africa* New Haven CT: Yale University Press, 1971.

Gilbert, David, *Chroniques secrètes d'Indochine 1928–1946* I, *Le Gabon* Paris: Editions l'Harmattan, 1994.

Girardet, Raoul, *L'Idée coloniale en France de 1871 à 1962* Paris: Table Ronde, 1972.

Godlewska, Anne, and Neil Smith (eds), *Geography and Empire*, Oxford: Blackwell, 1994.

Graham, B. D., *Choice and Democratic Order. The French Socialist Party, 1937–1950* Cambridge: Cambridge University Press, 1994.

Groupe Afrique noire, *L'Histoire des femmes en Afrique* Cahier no. 11, Paris: Editions l'Harmattan, 1987.

Gruner, Roger, *Du Maroc traditionnel au Maroc moderne. Le contrôle civil au Maroc 1912–1956* Paris: Nouvelles Editions Latines, 1984.

Güçlü, Yücel, *The Question of the Sanjak of Alexandretta. A Study of French–Turkish–Syrian Relations* Ankara: Turkish Historical Society, 2001.

Guelmami, Abdelmajid, *La Politique sociale en Tunisie de 1881 à nos jours* Paris: Editions l'Harmattan, 1996.

Guillaume, Jean-François, *Les Myths fondateurs de l'Algérie française* Paris: Editions l'Harmattan, 1992.

Hagemann, Karen, and Stefanie Schüler-Springorum (eds), *Home/Front. The Military, War and Gender in Twentieth Century Germany* Oxford: Berg, 2002.

Halstead, John P., *Rebirth of a Nation. The Origins and Rise of Moroccan Nationalism, 1912–1944* Cambridge MA: Harvard University Press, 1967.

Hamed-Touati, M'Barka, *Immigration maghrébine et activités politiques en France de la première guerre mondiale à la veille du Front populaire* Tunis: Publications de la Faculté des Sciences Humaines et Sociales de l'Université de Tunis, 1994.

Hargreaves, Alec G., *The Colonial Experience in French Fiction. A Study of Pierre Loti, Ernest Psichari and Pierre Mille*, London: Macmillan, 1981.

—— and Michael J. Heffernan (eds), *French and Algerian Identities from Colonial Times to the Present.* Lewiston NY: Edwin Mellen Press, 1993.

—— and Mark McKinney (eds), *Post-colonial Cultures in France* London: Routledge, 1997.

Harp, Stephen L., *Marketing Michelin. A Cultural History of Twentieth Century France* Baltimore MD: Johns Hopkins University Press, 2001.

Hart, David M., *Tribe and Society in Rural Morocco* London: Frank Cass, 2000.

Hazareesingh, Sudhir, *Political Traditions in Modern France* Oxford: Oxford University Press, 1994.

Hémery, Daniel, *Révolutionnaires viétnamiens et pouvoir colonial en Indochine* Paris: Maspero, 1975.

Heydemann, Stephen (ed.), *War, Institutions, and Social Change in the Middle East* Berkeley CA: University of California Press, 2000.

Hoisington Jr, William A., *The Casablanca Connection. French Colonial Policy, 1936–1943* Chapel Hill NC: University of North Carolina Press, 1984.

—— *Lyautey and the French Conquest of Morocco* London: Macmillan, 1995.

Horn, Martin, *Britain, France, and the Financing of the First World War* Montreal: McGill, 2002.

Hughes, Matthew, *Allenby and British Strategy in the Middle East, 1917–1919* London: Frank Cass, 1999.

Hyam, Ronald, *Empire and Sexuality* Manchester: Manchester University Press, 1990.

Imlay, Talbot, *Facing the Second World War. Strategy, Politics, and Economics in Britain and France, 1938–1940* Oxford: Oxford University Press, 2003.

Ingram, Norman, *The Politics of Dissent. Pacifism in France, 1919–1939* Oxford: Clarendon Press, 1991.

Isaacman, Allen, and Richard R. Roberts (eds), *Cotton, Colonialism and Social History in Sub-Saharan Africa* Portsmouth NH: Heinemann, 1995.

Jackson, Julian, *The Politics of Depression in France, 1932–1936* Cambridge: Cambridge University Press, 1985.

—— *The Popular Front in France. Defending Democracy, 1934–1938* Cambridge: Cambridge University Press, 1988.

—— *France. The Dark Years, 1940–1944* Oxford: Oxford University Press, 2001.

Jackson, Peter, *France and the Nazi Menace. Intelligence and Policy Making, 1933–1939* Oxford: Oxford University Press, 2000.

Jankowski, James, and Israel Gershoni (eds), *Rethinking Nationalism in the Arab Middle East* New York: Columbia University Press, 1997.

Jeanneney, Jean-Noël, *Leçon d'histoire pour une gauche au pouvoir. La faillite du Cartel 1924–1926* Paris: Editions du Seuil, 1977.

Jennings, Eric T., *Vichy in the Tropics. Pétain's National Revolution in Madagascar, Guadeloupe, and Indochina, 1940–1944* Stanford CA: Stanford University Press, 2001.

Johnson, G. Wesley, *The Emergence of Black Politics in Senegal. The Struggle for Power in the Four Communes, 1900–1920* Stanford CA: Stanford University Press, 1971.

—— (ed.), *Double Impact. France and Africa in the Age of Imperialism* Westport CT: Greenwood Press, 1985.

Julien, Charles-André, *L'Afrique du Nord en marche. Algérie–Tunisie–Maroc 1880–1952*, Paris: Julliard, 1952. (Rpt. Paris: Omnibus, 2002.)

Kaddache, Mahfoud, *Le Parti du peuple algérien 1937–1939. Documents et témoignages pour servir à l'étude du nationalisme algérien* Algiers: Office des Publications Universitaires, 1985.

—— *L'Emir Khaled. Documents et témoignages pour servir à l'étude du nationalisme algérien* Algiers: Office des Publications Universitaires, 1987.

—— *Histoire du nationalisme algérien* I, *Question nationale et politique algérienne 1919–1951* (2nd edn) Algiers: Entreprise Nationale du Livre, 1993.

Kateb, Kamel, *Européens, 'indigènes' et Juifs en Algérie 1830–1962*, Paris: Editions de l'Institut national d'études démographiques, 2001.

Kayali, Hasan, *Arabs and Young Turks. Ottomanism, Arabism and Islamism in the Ottoman Empire, 1908–1918* Berkeley CA: University of California Press, 1997.

Khalidi, Rashid, Lisa Anderson, Muhammad Muslih and Reeva S. Somon (eds), *The Origins of Arab Nationalism* New York: Columbia University Press, 1991.

Khánh, Hunyh Kim, *Vietnamese Communism, 1925–1945* Ithaca NY: Cornell University Press, 1982.

Khoury, Gérard D., *La France et l'Orient arabe. Naissance du Liban moderne* Paris: Armand Colin, 1993.

Khoury, Philip S., *Syria and the French Mandate. The Politics of Arab Nationalism, 1920–1945* London: I. B. Tauris, 1987.

Klein, Martin, *Slavery and Colonial Rule in French West Africa* Cambridge: Cambridge University Press, 1998.

Knibiehler, Y., and R. Goutalier, *La Femme au temps des colonies* Paris: Editions Stock, 1985.

Koerner, Francis, *Madagascar. Colonisation française et nationalisme malgache XXe siècle* Paris: Editions l'Harmattan, 1994.

Kolboom, Ingo, *La Revanche des patrons. Le patronat français face au Front populaire* Paris: Flammarion, 1986.

Koulakssis, Ahmed, and Gilbert Meynier, *L'Emir Khaled premier za'im? Identité algérienne et colonialisme français* Paris: Editions l'Harmattan, 1987.

Lafuente, Gilles, *La Politique berbère de la France et le nationalisme marocain* Paris: Editions l'Harmattan, 1999.

Landau, Paul S., and Deborah D. Kaspin (eds), *Images and Empires. Visuality in Colonial and Postcolonial Africa* Berkeley CA: University of California Press, 2002.

Lazreg, Marnia, *The Eloquence of Silence. Algerian Women in Question* London: Routledge, 1994.

Lebovics, Herman, *True France. The Wars over Cultural Identity, 1900–1945* Ithaca NY: Cornell University Press, 1992.

Lefeuvre, Daniel, *Chère Algérie. Comptes et mécomptes de la tutelle coloniale 1930–1962* Paris: Société Française d'Histoire d'Outre-Mer, 1997.

Lefranc, Georges, *Histoire du Front populaire* Paris: Payot, 1974.

Le Naour, Jean-Yves, *La Honte noire. L'Allemagne et les troupes coloniales françaises 1914–1945* Paris: Hachette, 2003.

Le Révérend, André, *Lyautey* Paris: Fayard, 1983.

Lerner, Henri, *Catroux* Paris: Albin Michel, 1990.

Lewis, Joanna, *Empire State-building. War and Welfare in Kenya, 1925–1952* Oxford: James Currey, 2000.

Lockman, Zachary, *Comrades and Enemies. Arab and Jewish Workers in Palestine, 1906–1948* Berkeley CA: University of California Press, 1996.

Lomo Myazhiom and Aggée Célestin, *Mariages et domination française en Afrique noire 1916–1958* Paris: Editions l'Harmattan, 2001.

Lorcin, Patricia M. E., *Imperial Identities. Stereotyping, Prejudice and Race in Colonial Algeria* London: I. B. Tauris, 1999.

Lowry, Donal (ed.), *The South African War Reappraised* Manchester: Manchester University Press, 2000.

Lunn, Joe, *Memoirs of the Maelstrom. A Senegalese Oral History of the First World War* Portsmouth NH: Heinemann, 1999.

Lynch, Frances M. B., *France and the International Economy. From Vichy to the Treaty of Rome* London: Routledge, 1997.

MacKenzie, John M., *Propaganda and Empire* Manchester: Manchester University Press, 1984.

—— (ed.), *Imperialism and Popular Culture* Manchester: Manchester University Press, 1986.

Macleod, Roy, and Milton Lewis (eds), *Disease, Medicine, and Empire. Perspectives on Western Medicine and the Experience of European Expansion* London: Routledge, 1988.

MacMaster, Neil, *Colonial Migrants and Racism. Algerians in France, 1900–1962* London: Macmillan, 1997.

Mamdani, Mahmood, *Citizen and Subject. Contemporary Africa and the Legacy of late Colonialism* Princeton NJ: Princeton University Press, 1996.

Manchuelle, François, *Willing Migrants. Soninke Labor Diasporas, 1848–1960* London: James Currey, 1997.

Manning, Patrick, *Francophone Sub-Saharan Africa, 1880–1985* Cambridge: Cambridge University Press, 1988.

Marr, David G., *Vietnamese Anticolonialism, 1885–1925* Berkeley CA: University of California Press, 1971.

—— *Vietnamese Tradition on Trial, 1920–1945* Berkeley CA: University of California Press, 1981.

Marseille, Jacques, *Empire colonial et capitalisme français. Histoire d'un divorce* Paris: Albin Michel, 1984.

—— (ed.), *Les Performances des enterprises françaises au vingtième siècle* Paris: Editions Le Monde, 1995.

Marshall, D. Bruce, *The French Colonial Myth and Constitution Making in the Fourth Republic* New Haven CT: Yale University Press, 1973.

Marzouki, Ilhem, *Le Mouvement des femmes en Tunisie au XXème siècle. Feminisme et politique* Tunis: Cérès productions, 1993.

Mbembe, Achille, *La Naissance du maquis dans le Sud-Cameroun 1920–1960* Paris: Karthala, 1996.

McLintock, Anne, *Imperial Leather. Race, Gender and Sexuality in a Colonial Context* London: Routledge, 1995.

Mechat, Samya El, *Le Nationalisme tunisien. Scission et conflits*, Paris: Editions l'Harmattan, 2002.

Melman, B. (ed.), *Borderlines. Gender and Identities in War and Peace, 1870–1930* London: Routledge, 1998.

Meriwether, Margaret L., and Judith E. Tucker (eds), *Women and Gender in the Modern Middle East* Boulder CO: Westview Press, 1999.

Merrick, Jeffery, and Michael Sibalis (eds), *Homosexuality in French History and Culture* New York: Hawarth Press, 2001.

Metzger, Chantal, *L'Empire colonial français dans la stratégie du Troisième Reich 1936–1945* Brussels: Peter Lang, 2002.

Meynier, Gilbert, *Histoire Intérieure du FLN 1954–1962* Paris: Fayard, 2002.

Michel, Marc, *L'Appel à l'Afrique. Contributions et réactions à l'effort de guerre en AOF 1914–1919* Paris: Publications de la Sorbonne, 1982.

—— *Gallieni* Paris: Fayard, 1989.

Miller, Michael B., *Shanghai on the Métro. Spies, Intrigue, and the French between the Wars* Berkeley CA: University of California Press, 1994.

Milza, Pierre, and Raymond Poidevin (eds), *La Puissance française à la 'Belle Epoque'. Mythe ou réalité?* Paris: Editions Complèxe, 1992.

Moghadam, Valentine M. (ed.), *Gender and National Identity. Women and Politics in Muslim Societies* London: Zed Books, 1994.

Morlat, Patrice, *La Répression coloniale au Vietnam 1908–1940* Paris: Editions l'Harmattan, 1990.

—— *Les Affaires politiques de l'Indochine 1895–1923. Les grands commis du savoir au pouvoir* Paris: Editions l'Harmattan, 1995.

—— *Indochine: années vingt. Le balcon de la France sur le Pacifique* Paris: Les Indes Savants, 2001.

Mouilleau, Elisabeth, *Fonctionnaires de la République et artisans de l'empire. Le cas des contrôleurs civils en Tunisie 1881–1956* Paris: Editions l'Harmattan, 2000.

Mouré, Kenneth, *Managing the Franc Poincaré. Economic Understanding and Political Constraint in French Monetary Policy, 1928–1936* Cambridge: Cambridge University Press, 1991.

—— *The Gold Standard Illusion. France, the Bank of France, and the International Gold Standard, 1914–1939* Oxford: Oxford University Press, 2002.

Mueleman, Johan H., *Les Constantinois entre les deux guerres. L'évolution économique et sociale de la population rurale* Assen: Van Gorcum, 1985.

Nafi, Basheer M., *Arabism, Nationalism and the Palestine Question, 1908–1941* Reading MA: Ithaca Press, 1998.

N'Dumbre, K. A., *Hitler voulait l'Afrique. Le projet Troisième Reich sur le continent africain* Paris: Editions l'Harmattan, 1980.

Ngando, Blaise Alfred, *La France au Cameroun 1916–1939. Colonialisme ou mission civilisatrice?* Paris: Editions l'Harmattan, 2002.

Nicolas, Armand, *Histoire de la Martinique de 1848 à 1939* Paris: Editions l'Harmattan, 1996.

Noiriel, Gérard, *Les Origines républicaines de Vichy* Paris: Hachette, 1999.

Nora, Pierre, *Realms of Memory. Rethinking the French Past* New York: Columbia University Press, 2001.

Norindr, Panivong, *Phantasmaic Indochina. French Colonial Ideology in Architecture, Film and Literature* Durham NC: Duke University Press, 1996.

Nouschi, André, *L'Algérie amère 1914–1994*, Paris: Editions de la Maison des Sciences de l'Homme, 1995.

Nye, Robert A., *Crime, Madness, and Politics in Modern France. The Medical Concept of National Decline* Princeton NJ: Princeton University Press, 1985.

—— *Masculinity and Male Codes of Honour in Modern France* Oxford: Oxford University Press, 1993.

Omissi, David, and Andrew Thompson (eds), *The Impact of the South African War* London: Palgrave, 2002.

Osborne, Michael A., *Nature, the Exotic, and the Science of French Colonialism* Bloomington IN: Indiana University Press, 1994.

Oved, Georges, *La Gauche française et le nationalisme marocain 1905–1954* I Paris: Editions l'Harmattan, 1984.

Passmore, Kevin, *From Liberalism to Fascism. The Right in a French Province, 1928–1939* Cambridge: Cambridge University Press, 1997.

Peabody, Sue, and Tyler Stovall (eds), *The Color of Liberty. Histories of Race in France* Durham NC: Duke University Press, 2003.

Peer, Shanny, *France on Display. Peasants, Provincials and Folklore in the 1937 Paris World's Fair* Albany NY: State University of New York Press, 1998.

Pennell, C. R., *A Country with a Government and a Flag. The Rif War in Morocco* Wisbech: Middle East and North African Studies Press, 1986.

—— *Morocco since 1830. A History* London: Hurst, 2000.

Persell, Stuart Michael, *The French Colonial Lobby, 1889–1938* Stanford CA: Stanford University Press, 1983

Pervillé, Guy, *Les Etudiants algériens de l'université française 1880–1962* Paris: CNRS, 1984.

Power, Thomas F., *Jules Ferry and the Renaissance of French Imperialism* New York: Octagon Books, 1977.

—— *De l'empire français à la décolonisation* Paris: Hachette, 1991.

Prévotat, Jacques, *Les Catholiques et l'Action française 1988–1939* Paris: Fayard, 2001.

Prochaska, David, *Making Algeria French. Colonialism in Bône, 1870–1920* Cambridge, Cambridge University Press, 1990.

Prost, Antoine, *Republican Identities in War and Peace. Representations of France in the 19th and 20th Centuries* Oxford: Berg, 2002.

Quinn, Frederick, *The French Overseas Empire* Westport CT: Praeger, 2000.

Rabinow, Paul, *French Modern. Norms and Forms of the Social Environment* Chicago: University of Chicago Press, 1989.

Randrianja, Solofo, *Société et luttes anticoloniales à Madagascar 1896 à 1946* Paris: Karthala, 2001.

Recham, Belkacem, *Les Musulmans algériens dans l'armée française 1919–1945* Paris: Editions l'Harmattan, 1996.

Renouvin, Pierre, and René Rémond (eds), *Léon Blum. Chef de gouvernement 1936–1937* Paris: FNSP, 1967.

Reynolds, Siân, *France between the Wars. Gender and Politics* London: Routledge, 1996.

Rivet, Daniel, *Lyautey et l'institution du protectorat français au Maroc 1912–1925* (3 vols) Paris: Editions l'Harmattan, 1988.

—— *Le Maroc de Lyautey à Mohammed V. Le double visage du protectorat* Paris: Editions Denoël, 1999.

—— *Le Maghreb à l'épreuve de la colonisation* Paris: Hachette, 2002.

Roberts, Mary Louise, *Civilization without Sexes. Reconstructing Gender in Postwar France, 1917–1927* Chicago: University of Chicago Press, 1994.

Roberts, Richard L., *Two Worlds of Cotton. Colonialism and the Regional Economy in the French Soudan, 1800–1946* Stanford CA: Stanford University Press, 1996.

Robinson, David, *Paths of Accommodation. Muslim Societies and French Colonial Authorities in Senegal and Mauritania, 1880–1920* Athens OH: Ohio University Press, 2000.

Roche, Christian, *Le Sénégal à la conquête de son indépendance 1939–1960* Paris: Karthala, 2001.

Ross, Kristin, *Fast Cars, Clean Bodies. Decolonization and the Reordering of French Culture* Cambridge MA: MIT Press, 1995.

Ruedy, John, *Modern Algeria. The Origins and Development of a Nation* Bloomington IN: Indiana University Press, 1992.

Ruscio, Alain (ed.), *Viet Nam. L'histoire, la terre, les hommes* Paris: Editions l'Harmattan, 1989.

—— *Que le temps était belle au temps des colonies* Paris: Larose, 2000.

Russell, Malcolm, *The First Modern Arab State. Syria under Faysal, 1918–1920* Minneapolis MN: Bibliotheca Islamica, 1985.

Savarese, Eric, *L'Ordre colonial et sa légitimation en France métropolitaine* Paris: Editions l'Harmattan, 1998.

Schneider, William H., *Quality and Quantity. The Quest for Biological Regeneration in Twentieth Century France* Cambridge: Cambridge University Press, 1990.

Schuker, Stephen, *The End of French Predominance in Europe. The Ruhr Occupation and the Dawes Plan, 1923–1924* Chapel Hill NC: University of North Carolina Press, 1976.

Shambrook, Peter, *French Imperialism in Syria, 1927–1936* Reading MA: Ithaca Press, 1998.

Shennan, Andrew, *Rethinking France. Plans for Renewal, 1940–1946* Oxford: Oxford University Press, 1989.

Sherman, Daniel J., *The Construction of Memory in Interwar France* Chicago: University of Chicago Press, 1999.

Shorrock, William I., *From Ally to Enemy. The Enigma of Fascist Italy in French Diplomacy, 1920–1940* Kent OH: Kent State University Press, 1988.

Short, K. R. M. (ed.), *Film and Radio Propaganda in World War II* London: Croom Helm, 1983.

Silverman, Maxim, *Deconstructing the Nation. Immigration, Racism and Citizenship in Modern France* London: Routledge, 1992.

Sivan, Emmanuel, *Communisme et nationalisme en Algérie 1920–1962* Paris: FNSP, 1976.

Slavin, David Henry, *Colonial Cinema and Imperial France, 1919–1939. White*

Blind Spots, Male Fantasies, Settler Myths Baltimore MD: Johns Hopkins University Press, 2001.

Slyomovics, Susan (ed.), *The Walled Arab City in Literature, Architecture and History. The Living Medina in the Maghrib* London: Frank Cass, 2001.

Smith, Leonard V., Stéphane Audoin-Ruzeau and Annette Becker, *France and the Great War 1914–1918* Cambridge: Cambridge University Press, 2003.

Smith, Paul, *Feminism and the Third Republic. Women's Political and Civil Rights in France, 1918–1945* Oxford: Oxford University Press, 1996.

Sorum, Paul Clay, *Intellectuals and Decolonization in France* Chapel Hill NC: University of North Carolina Press, 1977.

Soucy, Robert, *French Fascism. The Second Wave, 1933–1939* New Haven CT: Yale University Press, 1995.

Sowerine, Charles, *France since 1870. Culture, Politics and Society* London: Palgrave, 2001.

Spagnolo, John (ed.), *Problems of the Modern Middle East in Historical Perspective* Reading MA: Ithaca Press, 1992.

Sternhell, Zeev, *Ni droite, ni gauche. L'Idéologie fasciste en France* Paris: Editions du Seuil, 1983.

Stoler, Ann Laura, *Carnal Knowledge and Imperial Power. Race and the Intimate in Colonial Rule* Berkeley CA: University of California Press, 2002.

Stora, Benjamin, *Nationalistes algériens et révolutionnaires français au temps du Front populaire* Paris: Editions l'Harmattan, 1987.

—— and Zakya Daoud, *Ferhat Abbas, une utopie algérienne* Paris: Editions Denoël, 1995.

Stovall, Tyler, *The Rise of the Paris Red Belt* Berkeley CA: University of California Press, 1990.

—— and Georges Van Den Abbeele (eds), *French Civilization and its Discontents. Nationalism, Colonialism, Race* Oxford: Lexington Books, 2003.

Strobel, Margaret, *European Women and the Second British Empire* Bloomington IN: Indiana University Press, 1991.

Le Sueur, James D., *Uncivil War. Intellectuals and Identity Politics during the Decolonization of Algeria* Philadelphia: Pennsylvania University Press, 2001.

Tai, Hue-Tam Ho, *Radicalism and the Origins of the Vietnamese Revolution* Cambridge MA: Harvard University Press, 1992.

Tanenbaum, Jan Karl *General Maurice Sarrail, 1856–1929. The French Army and Left-wing Politics* Chapel Hill NC: University of North Carolina Press, 1974.

Tauber, Eliezer, *The Formation of Modern Syria and Iraq* London: Frank Cass, 1995.

Thobie, Jacques, Gilbert Meynier, Catherine Coquery-Vidrovitch and Charles-Robert Ageron, *Histoire de la France coloniale 1914–1990* Paris: Armand Colin, 1990.

Thomas, Martin, *Britain, France and Appeasement. Anglo-French Relations in the Popular Front Era* Oxford: Berg, 1996.

—— *The French Empire at War, 1940–45* Manchester: Manchester University Press, 1998.

Thompson, Elizabeth, *Colonial Citizens. Republican Rights, Paternal Privilege and Gender in French Syria and Lebanon* New York: Columbia University Press, 2000.

Ungar, Steven, and Tom Conley (eds), *Identity Papers. Contested Nationhood in Twentieth Century France* Minneapolis MN: University of Minnesota Press, 1996.

Venier, Pascal, *Lyautey avant Lyautey* Paris: Editions l'Harmattan, 1997.

Verdès-Leroux, Jeannine, *Les Français d'Algérie de 1830 à aujourd-hui* Paris: Fayard, 2001.

Vermeren, Pierre, *La Formation des élites marocaines et tunisiennes. Des nationalistes aux islamistes 1920–2000* Paris: Editions la Découverte, 2002.

Vinen, Richard, *The Politics of French Business, 1936–1945* Cambridge: Cambridge University Press, 1992.

Weber, Eugen, *Action Française. Royalism and Reaction in Twentieth Century France* Stanford CA: Stanford University Press, 1962.

Weber, Jacques, *Pondichéry et les comptoirs de l'Inde française après Dupleix* Paris: Editions Denoël, 1996.

Westerlund, David, and Eva Evers Rosander (eds), *African Islam and Islam in Africa. Encounters between Sufis and Islamists* London: Hurst, 1997.

White, Owen, *Children of the French Empire. Misegenation and Colonial Society in French West Africa 1895–1960* Oxford: Clarendon Press, 1999.

Windebank, Jan, and Renate Gunther (eds), *Violence and Conflict in the Politics and Society of Modern France* Lampeter: Edwin Mellen Press, 1995.

Winock, Michel, *Nationalism, Antisemitism and Fascism in France* Stanford CA: Stanford University Press, 1998.

Winter, Jay, Geoffrey Parker and Mary R. Hubeck (eds), *The Great War and the Twentieth Century* New Haven CT: Yale University Press, 2000.

Woolman, David S., *Rebels in the Rif. Abd-el-Krim and the Rif Rebellion* Stanford CA: Stanford University Press, 1968.

Wright, Gwendolyn, *The Politics of Design in French Colonial Urbanism*, Chicago: University of Chicago Press, 1991.

Young, Robert J., *In Command of France. French Foreign Policy and Military Planning, 1933–1939* Cambridge MA: Harvard University Press, 1978.

Zamir, Meir, *The Formation of Modern Lebanon* London: Croom Helm, 1985.

—— *Lebanon's Quest. The Road to Statehood, 1926–1939* London: I. B. Tauris, 1997.

Zinoman, P., *The Colonial Bastille. A History of Imprisonment in Vietnam, 1862–1940* Berkeley CA: University Press of California, 2001.

Articles

Abrams, L., and D. J. Miller, 'Who were the French colonialists? A reassessment of the Parti colonial, 1890–1914', *Historical Journal*, 19:3 (1976), 685–725.

Abu-Lughod, Janet 'The Islamic city. Historic myth, Islamic essence, and contemporary relevance', *International Journal of Middle East Studies*, 19:2 (1987), 155–76.

Ageron, Charles-Robert, 'Enquête sur les origines du nationalisme algérien. L'emir Khâled, petit-fils d'Abd El-Kader, fut-il le premier nationaliste algérien?' *Revue de l'Occident Musulman*, 2 (1967), 9–49.

—— 'La politique berbère du protectorat marocain de 1913 à 1934', *Revue d'Histoire Moderne et Contemporaine*, 18:1 (1971), 50–90.

—— 'Une émeute anti-juive à Constantine (août 1934)', *Revue de l'Occident Musulman et de la Méditerranée* 3 (1973), 23–40.

—— 'L'idée d'Eurafrique et le débat colonial franco-allemand de l'entre-deux-guerres', *Revue d'Histoire Moderne et Contemporaine*, 22:3 (1975), 446–75.

—— 'La presse parisienne devant la guerre du Rif (avril 1925–mai 1926)', *Revue de l'Occident Musulman et de la Méditerranée* 24 (1977), 7–27.

—— 'A propos d'une prétendue politique de "répli imperial" dans la France des années 1938–1939', *Revue d'Histoire Maghrébine*, 12 (1978), 228–37.

—— 'L'association des étudiants musulmans nord-africains en France durant l'entre-deux-guerres. Contribution à l'étude des nationalismes maghrébins', *Revue Française d'Histoire d'Outre-Mer* 70:258 (1983), 25–56.

—— 'Les colonies devant l'opinion publique française (1919–1939)', *Revue Française d'Histoire d'Outre-Mer*, 77:286 (1990), 31–73.

Ahmad, Eqbal, and Stuart Schaar, 'M'hamed Ali: Tunisian labor organizer', in Burke III, *Struggle and Survival in the Modern Middle East*, 191–204.

Aissaoui, Rabah, ' "Nous voulons déchirer le baillon et briser nos chaînes". Racism, colonialism and universalism in the discourse of Algerian nationalists in France between the wars', *French History*, 17:2 (2003), 186–209.

Akpo, Catherine, 'Solidarités et rivalités franco-britanniques en Afrique de l'Ouest (1936–1946)', *Relations Internationales*, 77 (1994), 21–35.

Aldrich, Robert, 'Vestiges of the colonial empire. The Jardin Colonial in Paris', in Aldrich and Lyons, *The Sphinx in the Tuileries*, 194–204.

—— 'Putting the colonies on the map. Colonial names in Paris streets', in Chafer and Sackur, *Promoting the Colonial Idea*, 211–23.

Alexandre, François, 'Le PCA de 1919 à 1939. Données en vue d'éclaircir son action et son rôle', *Revue Algérienne des Sciences Juridiques, Economiques et Politiques*, 11:4 (1974), 175–214.

Allain, Jean-Claude, 'Les emprunts d'état marocains avant 1939', in Ageron, *Les Chemins de la décolonisation*, 131–45.

Andrew, C. M., and A. S. Kanya-Forstner, 'The French "Colonial Party". Its composition, aims and influence, 1885–1914', *Historical Journal*, 14:1 (1971), 99–128.

—— 'The French Colonial Party and French colonial war aims, 1914–1918', *Historical Journal*, 17:1 (1974), 79–106.

—— 'France, Africa, and the First World War', *Journal of African History*, 19:1 (1978), 11–23.

—— 'Centre and periphery in the making of the second French colonial empire, 1815–1920', *Journal of Imperial and Commonwealth History*, 16:3 (1988), 9–34.

Aouimeur, Mouloud, 'Contribution à l'étude de la propagande socialiste en Algérie dans les années 1920 et 1930', *Revue Française d'Histoire d'Outre-Mer*, 89:324 (1999), 151–71.

Arcidiacono, B., 'Aux racines du nationalisme en terrain colonisé. Quelques cas de l'entre-deux-guerres (Maghreb, Indochine, Indonesie, Inde et Nigeria)', *Relations Internationales*, 18 (1979), 149–88.

Arnoulet, François, 'Les Tunisiens et la première guerre mondiale (1914–1918)', *Revue de l'Occident Musulman et de la Méditerranée* 38 (1985), 47–61.

Asiwaju, A. I., 'Migrations as revolt. The example of the Ivory Coast and the Upper Volta before 1945', *Journal of African History*, 17:4 (1976), 577–94.

Audigier, François, 'L'Alliance Démocratique de 1933 à 1937 ou l'anachronisme en politique', *Vingtième Siècle*, 47:3 (1995), 147–57.

Ayo Langley, J., 'Pan-Africanism in Paris, 1924–1936', *Journal of Modern African Studies*, 7:1 (1969), 69–94.

Azzou, El Mustafa, 'Les hommes d'affaires américains au Maroc avant 1956', *Guerres Mondiales et Conflits Contemporains*, 180 (1995), 131–45.

Baron, Beth, 'Unveiling in early twentieth century Egypt. Practical and symbolic considerations', *Middle Eastern Studies*, 25:3 (1989), 370–86.

—— 'The construction of national honour in Egypt', *Gender and History*, 5:2 (1993), 244–55.

—— 'The politics of female notables in postwar Egypt', in Melman, *Borderlines*, 329–50.

Bassett, Thomas, 'The development of cotton in northern Ivory Coast, 1910–1965', *Journal of African History*, 19:2 (1978), 267–84.

Bayly, Susan, 'French anthropology and the Durkheimians in colonial Indochina', *Modern Asian Studies*, 34:3 (2000), 581–622.

Becker, Jean-Jacques, 'La perception de la puissance par le Parti Communiste', *Revue d'Histoire Moderne et Contemporaine*, 31:4 (1984), 636–42.

Becker, Laurence C., 'An experiment in the reorganisation of agricultural production in the French Soudan (Mali), 1920–40', *Africa*, 64:3 (1994), 373–90.

Belanus, René, 'Félix Éboué, gouverneur nègre du Front populaire à la Guadeloupe', in Lucien Abenon, Danielle Bégot and Jean-Pierre Sainton (eds), *Construire l'histoire antillais* (Paris: Editions du CTHS, 2002), 173–95.

Benadada, Assia, 'Les femmes dans le mouvement nationaliste marocain', *Clio. Histoire, Femmes et Sociétés*, 9 (1999), 67–73.

Bennoune, Mahfoud, 'Socio-economic changes in rural Algeria, 1830–1954', *Peasant Studies Newsletter*, 11:2 (1973), 11–18.

—— 'The introduction of nationalism into rural Algeria, 1919–1954', *Maghreb Review*, 2:3 (1977), 1–12.

Berliner, Brett A., 'Dancing dangerously. Colonizing the exotic at the Bal Nègre in the inter-war years', *French Cultural Studies*, 12:1 (2001), 59–75.

Berman, Bruce, and John Lonsdale, 'Coping with the contradictions: The development of the colonial state, 1895–1914', *Journal of African History*, 20:4 (1979), 487–505.

Bernard-Duquenot, Nicole, 'Le Front populaire et le problème des prestations en AOF', *Cahiers d'Etudes Africaines*, 61 (1976), 159–72.

Berry, David, ' "Fascism or revolution!" Anarchism and antifascism in France, 1933–1939', *Contemporary European History*, 8:1 (1999), 51–71.

Berstein, Serge, 'La perception de la puissance par le Parti Radical-Socialiste', *Revue d'Histoire Moderne et Contemporaine*, 31:4 (1984), 619–35.

Bessis, Juliette, 'Le mouvement ouvrier tunisien. De ses origines à l'indépendance', *Le Mouvement Social*, 89 (1974), 85–108.

Betts, Raymond F., 'Imperial designs. French colonial architecture and urban planning in sub-Saharan Africa', in Wesley Johnson, *Double Impact*, 191–207.

Binoche, Jacques, 'La politique extrême-orientale française et les relations franco-japonaises 1919–1939', *Revue Française d'Histoire d'Outre-Mer* 86 (1989), 531–43.

Binoche-Guedra, Jacques-W., 'La réprésentation parlementaire coloniale (1871–1940)', *Revue Historique*, 280:2 (1988), 522–33.

Blatt, Joel, 'The parity that meant superiority. French naval policy toward Italy at the Washington Naval Conference and inter-war French foreign policy', *French Historical Studies*, 12:2 (1981), 223–48.

—— 'France and the Washington Conference', *Diplomacy and Statecaft*, 4:3 (1993), 192–219.

Bokova, Lenka, 'Le traité du 4 mars 1921 et la formation de l'état du Djebel Druze sous le mandat français', *Revue de l'Occident Musulman et de la Méditerranée* 49 (1989), 213–22.

Booth, Anne, 'Four colonies and a kingdom. A comparison of fiscal, trade, and exchange rate policies in South East Asia in the 1930s', *Modern Asian Studies*, 37:2 (2003), 429–60.

Bouatta, Cherifa, 'Feminine militancy. *Moudjahidates* during and after the Algerian war', in Moghadam, *Gender and National Identity*, 18–39.

Bouche, Denise, 'Quatorze millions de Français dans la fédération de l'Afrique Occidentale Française?' *Revue Française d'Histoire d'Outre-Mer*, 69:255 (1982), 97–113.

Boulan, Jeanne, 'Polygamists need not apply. Becoming a French citizen in colonial Algeria, 1918–1938', *Proceedings of the Western Society for French History* 24 (1997), 110–19.

Bou-Nacklie, N. E., 'Les troupes spéciales. Religious and ethnic recruitment, 1916–1946', *International Journal of Middle East Studies*, 25:4 (1993), 645–60.

—— 'Tumult in Syria's Hama in 1925. The failure of a revolt', *Journal of Contemporary History*, 33:2 (1998), 273–89.

Braibant, Patrick, 'L'administration coloniale et le profit commercial en Côte d'Ivoire pendant la crise de 1929', *Revue Française d'Histoire d'Outre-Mer*, 63:3–4 (1976), 555–74.

Bretelle-Establet, Florence, 'Resistance and reciprocity. French colonial medicine in southwest China, 1898–1930', *Modern China*, 25:2 (1999), 171–203.

Brett, Michael, 'The colonial period in the Maghrib and its aftermath. The present state of historical writing', *Journal of African History*, 17:2 (1976), 291–305.

Brocheux, Pierre, 'Le prolétariat des plantations d'hévéas au Vietnam méridional. Aspects sociaux et politiques (1927–1937)', *Le Mouvement Social*, 90:1 (1975), 55–86.

—— 'Crise économique et société en Indochine française', *Revue Française d'Histoire d'Outre-Mer*, 63: 232 (1976), 655–67.

—— 'L'implantation du mouvement communiste en Indochine française. Le cas du Nghe-Tinh (1930–1931)', *Revue d'Histoire Moderne et Contemporaine*, 24:1 (1977), 49–74.

—— 'The state and the 1930s depression in French Indochina', in Boomgaard and Brown, *Weathering the Storm*, 251–70.

Brunschwig, Henri, 'Politique et économie dans l'empire français d'Afrique noire 1870–1914', *Journal of African History*, 11:3 (1970), 401–17.

Bryder, Linda, 'Sex, race, and colonialism. An historiographical review', *International History Review*, 20:4 (1998), 806–54.

—— 'L'impérialisme en Afrique noire', *Revue Historique*, 249:1 (1973), 129–42.

Burke III, Edmund, 'Pan-Islam and Moroccan resistance to French colonial penetration, 1900–1912', *Journal of African History*, 13:1 (1972), 97–118.

—— 'Moroccan resistance, pan-Islam and German war strategy, 1914–18', *Francia* 3 (1975), 434–64.

—— 'A comparative view of French native policy in Morocco and Syria, 1912–1925', *Middle Eastern Studies*, 9 (1973), 175–86.

—— 'Fez, the setting sun of Islam. A study of the politics of colonial ethnography', *Maghreb Review*, 2:4 (1977), 1–7.

Burrows, Matthew, ' "*Mission Civilisatrice*": French cultural policy in the Middle East, 1860–1914', *Historical Journal*, 29:1 (1986), 109–35.

Camiscioli, Elisa, 'Intermarriage, independent nationality, and the individual rights of French women. The law of 10 August 1927', *French Politics, Culture and Society*, 17:3–4 (1999), 52–73.

—— 'Producing citizens, reproducing the "French race". Immigration, demography, and pronatalism in early twentieth-century France', *Gender and History*, 13:3 (2001), 593–621.

Cannon, Byron D., 'Irreconciliability of reconciliation. Employment of Algerian veterans under the Plan Jonnart, 1919–1926', *Maghreb Review*, 24:1–2 (1999), 42–50.

Cantier, Jacques, 'Les gouverneurs Viollette et Bordes et la politique algérienne de la France à la fin des années 1920', *Revue Française d'Histoire d'Outre-Mer*, 84:314 (1997), 25–49.

Carroll, David, 'Camus's Algeria. Birthrights, colonial injustice, the fiction of a French-Algerian people', *Modern Language Notes*, 112 (1997), 517–49.

Chachoua, Kamel, 'Religion, cité et identité en Kabylie', *Les Cahiers de l'Orient* 61:1 (2001), 87–98.

Chonchirdson, Sud, 'The Indochinese Congress (May 1936–March 1937). False hope of Vietnamese nationalists', *Journal of Southeast Asian Studies*, 30:2 (1999), 338–46.

Chopra, Preeti, 'Pondicherry. A French enclave in India', in Al Sayyad, *Forms of Dominance*, 107–37.

Christelow, Allan, 'The Muslim judge and municipal politics in colonial Algeria and Senegal', *Comparative Studies in Society and History*, 24:1 (1982), 3–24.

—— 'Algerian interpreters and the French colonial adventure in sub-Saharan Africa', *Maghreb Review*, 10:4–6 (1985), 101–8.

—— 'Ritual, culture and the politics of Islamic reformism in Algeria', *Middle Eastern Studies*, 23:3 (1987), 255–73.

—— 'The mosque at the edge of the plaza. Islam in the Algerian colonial city', *Maghreb Review*, 25:3–4 (2000), 289–308.

Clancy-Smith, Julia, 'A women without her distaff. Gender, work, and handicraft production in colonial North Africa', in Meriwether and Tucker, *Women and Gender in the Modern Middle East*, 25–62.

Clark, Andrew F., 'Slavery and its demise in the Upper Senegal valley, West Africa, 1890–1920', *Slavery and Abolition*, 15:1 (1994), 51–71.

—— 'Internal migrations and population movements in the Upper Senegal valley (West Africa), 1890–1920', *Canadian Journal of African Studies*, 28:3 (1994), 399–420.

Clay, Christopher, 'The origins of modern banking in the Levant. The branch network of the Imperial Ottoman Bank, 1890–1914', *International Journal of Middle East Studies*, 26 (1994), 589–614.

Cleaveland, Timothy, 'Islam and the construction of social identity in the nineteenth-century Sahara', *Journal of African History*, 39 (1998), 365–88.

Codo, Bellarmin C., and Sylvian C. Anignikin, 'Pouvoir colonial et tentatives d'intégration africaines dans le système capitaliste : le cas du Dahomey entre les deux guerres', *Canadian Journal of African Studies*, 16:2 (1982), 331–42.

Cohen, William B., 'The lure of empire. Why Frenchmen entered the colonial service', *Journal of Contemporary History*, 4:1 (1969), 103–16.

—— 'The colonial policy of the Popular Front', *French Historical Studies*, 7:3 (1972), 368–93.

—— 'Malaria and French imperialism', *Journal of African History*, 24:1 (1983), 23–36.

Cole, Jennifer, and Karen Middleton, 'Rethinking ancestors and colonial power in Madagascar', *Africa*, 71:1 (2001), 5–13.

Collomp, Catherine, 'Immigrants, labor markets, and the state. A comparative approach: France and the United States, 1880–1930', *Journal of American History*, 86:1 (1999), 41–66.

Commins, David Dean, 'Religious reformers and Arabists in Damascus, 1885–1915', *International Journal of Middle East Studies*, 18 (1986), 405–25.

Conklin, Alice L., 'A force for civilization. Republican discourse and French administration in West Africa, 1895–1930', in Becker *et al.*, *AOF: réalités et heritages* I, 283–302.

—— ' "Democracy" rediscovered. Civilization through association in French West Africa (1914–1930)', *Cahiers d'Etudes Africaines*, 145:37 (1997), 59–84.

—— 'Colonialism and human rights: a contradiction in terms? The case of France and West Africa, 1895–1914', *American Historical Review*, 103:2 (1998), 419–42.

—— 'Boundaries unbound. Teaching French history as colonial history and colonial history as French history', *French Historical Studies*, 23:2 (2000), 215–38.

Cooper, Nicola, 'Urban planning and architecture in colonial Indochina', *French Cultural Studies*, 11:1 (2000), 75–99.

Cooper, Sandi E., 'Pacifism, feminism, and fascism in inter-war France', *International History Review*, 19:1 (1997), 103–14.

Coquery-Vidrovitch, Catherine, 'L'impact des intérêts coloniaux. SCOA et CFAO dans l'ouest africain 1910–1965', *Journal of African History*, 16:4 (1975), 595–621.

—— 'L'Afrique coloniale française et la crise de 1930 : crise structurelle et genèse du sous-développement', *Revue Française d'Histoire d'Outre-Mer*, 63: 232 (1976), 386–424.

—— 'L'impérialisme français en Afrique noire : idéologie impériale et politique d'équipement, 1924–1935', *Relations Internationales*, 7 (1976), 261–82.

—— 'Mutation de l'impérialisme colonial français dans les années 1930', *African Economic History*, 4:4 (1977), 103–52.

—— 'Colonisation ou impérialisme : la politique africaine de la France entre les deux guerres', *Le Mouvement Social*, 107:2 (1979), 51–76.

—— 'Nationalité et citoyenneté en Afrique occidentale française : originaires et citoyens dans le Sénégal colonial', *Journal of African History*, 42 (2001), 285–305.

Cordell, Dennis D., and Joel W. Gregory, 'Historical demography and demographic history', *Canadian Journal of African Studies*, 14:3 (1980), 389–416.

—— 'Labour reservoirs and population. French colonial strategies in Koudougou, Upper Volta, 1914 to 1939', *Journal of African History*, 23 (1982), 205–24.

Dalloz, Jacques, 'Les Vietnamiens dans le franc-maconnerie coloniale', *Revue Française d'Histoire d'Outre-Mer*, 85:320 (1998), 103–18.

Damis, John, 'The origins and significance of the Free School Movement in Morocco, 1919–1931', *Revue de l'Occident Musulman et de la Méditerranée* 19 (1975), 75–99.

Daouda, Kadidiatoul'Kouboura, and Jacques Thobie, '*Ouest-éclair* (Rennes) et l'empire colonial français de 1936 à 1939', *Revue Française d'Histoire d'Outre-Mer*, 69:255 (1982), 115–27.

Dawn, C. Ernest, 'The formation of pan-Arab ideology in the inter-war years', *International Journal of Middle East Studies*, 20 (1988), 67–91.

Delafosse, Louise, 'Comment prit fin la carrière coloniale de Maurice Delafosse', *Revue Française d'Histoire d'Outre-Mer*, 61:222 (1974), 74–115.

Denzer, LaRay, 'Towards a study of the history of West African women's participation in nationalist politics. The early phase, 1935–1960', *Africana Research Bulletin*, 6:4 (1976), 65–85.

Derrick, Jonathan, 'The dissenters. Anti-colonialism in France, *c.* 1900–40', in Chafer and Sackur, *Promoting the Colonial Idea*, 53–68.

Dillemann, Louis, 'Les Druzes et la révolte syriénne de 1925', *Revue Française d'Histoire d'Outre-Mer*, 69:254 (1982), 49–54.

Dine, Philip, 'Un héroïsme problématique : le sport, la littérature et la guerre d'Algérie', *Europe* 806 (June/July 1996), 177–85.

—— 'France, Algeria and sport. From colonisation to globalisation', *Modern and Contemporary France*, 10:4 (2002), 498.

Domenichini, J-P., 'Jean Ralaimongo (1884–1943)', *Revue Française d'Histoire d'Outre-Mer*, 204 (1969), 236–87.

Donadey, Anne, ' "Y'a bon Banania" : ethics and cultural criticism in the colonial context', *French Cultural Studies*, 11:1 (2000), 9–29.

Drew, Allison, 'Bolshevizing Communist Parties. The Algerian and South African experiences', *International Review of Social History*, 48 (2003), 167–201.

Dreyfus, Michel, 'Pacifistes, socialistes et humanistes dans les années trente', *Revue d'Histoire Moderne et Contemporaine*, 35 (1988), 452–69.

Duiker, William J., 'The Revolutionary Youth League, cradle of Communism in Vietnam', *China Quarterly*, 51 (July–September 1972), 475–99.

Echenberg, Myron, 'Paying the blood tax. Military conscription in French West Africa, 1914–1929', *Revue Canadienne des Etudes Africaines*, 10:2 (1975), 171–92.

—— 'Les migrations militaires en Afrique Occidentale Française 1900–1945', *Canadian Journal of African Studies*, 14:3 (1980), 429–50.

—— ' "Morts pour la France". The African soldier in France during the Second World War', *Journal of African History*, 26 (1985), 363–80.

—— and Jean Filipovich, 'African military labour and the building of the Office du Niger installations, 1925–1950', *Journal of African History*, 27 (1986), 533–51.

Eckert, Andreas, 'African rural entrepreneurs and labor in the Cameroon littoral', *Journal of African History*, 40:1 (1999), 109–26.

Edwards, Penny, ' "Propagender". Marianne, Joan or Arc and the export of French gender ideology to colonial Cambodia, 1863–1954', in Chafer and Sackur, *Promoting the Colonial Idea*, 116–30.

Eldar, Dan, 'France in Syria. The abolition of the Sharifian government, April–July 1920', *Middle Eastern Studies*, 29:3 (1993), 487–504.

Ellis, Stephen, 'The political elite of Imerina and the revolt of the Menalamba. The creation of a colonial myth in Madagascar, 1895–1898', *Journal of African History*, 21:2 (1980), 219–34.

Enders, Armelle, 'L'Ecole Nationale de la France d'Outre-Mer et la formation des administrateurs coloniaux', *Revue d'Histoire Moderne et Contemporaine*, 40:2 (1993), 272–88.

Eppel, Michael, 'The elite, the *effendiyya*, and the growth of nationalism and pan-Arabism in Hashemite Iraq, 1921–1958', *International Journal of Middle East Studies*, 30:2 (1998), 227–50.

Fieldhouse, D. K., 'The economic exploitation of Africa. Some British and French comparisons', in Gifford and Louis, *France and Britain in Africa*, 593–662.

—— 'Review article. The economics of French empire', *Journal of African History*, 27 (1986), 169–72.

Filipovich, Jean, 'Destined to fail. Forced Settlement at the Office du Niger, 1926–1945', *Journal of African History*, 42:2 (2001), 239–60.

Fine, Martin, 'Albert Thomas. A reformer's vision of modernization, 1914–32', *Journal of Contemporary History*, 12:3 (1977), 545–64.

Fitzgerald, Edward P., 'France's Middle East ambitions, the Sykes–Picot negotiations, and the oilfields of Mosul, 1915–1918', *Journal of Modern History*, 66:4 (1994), 697–725.

Fleischmann, Ellen L., 'The emergence of the Palestinian women's movement, 1929–39', *Journal of Palestine Studies*, 29:3 (2000), 16–32.

Fleming, Shannon E., and Ann K. Fleming, 'Primo de Rivera and Spain's Moroccan problem, 1923–27', *Journal of Contemporary History*, 12 (1977), 85–99.

Fletcher, Yaël Simpson, ' "A more perfect equality?" Colonial workers and French communists in Marseilles, 1936–1938', *Proceedings of the Western Society for French History*, 24 (1997), 506–15.

—— ' "Capital of the colonies". Real and imagined boundaries between metropole and empire in 1920s Marseilles', in Driver and Gilbert, *Imperial Cities*, 136–54.

—— ' "Irresistible seductions". Gendered representations of colonial Algeria around 1930', in Clancy-Smith and Gouda, *Domesticating the Empire*, 193–210.

Formes, Malia B., 'Beyond complicity versus resistance. Recent work on gender and European imperialism', *Journal of Social History*, 23:3 (1995), 629–41.

Fraser, Cary, 'The twilight of colonial rule in the British West Indies. Nationalist assertion versus imperial hubris in the 1930s', *Journal of Caribbean History*, 30:1–2 (1996), 1–27.

Furlough, Ellen, '*Une leçon des choses*. Tourism, empire, and the nation in inter-war France', *French Historical Studies*, 25:3 (2002), 441–73.

Gelvin, James L. 'The social origins of popular nationalism in Syria. Evidence for a new framework', *International Journal of Middle East Studies*, 26 (1994), 645–61.

—— 'Demonstrating communities in post-Ottoman Syria', *Journal of Interdisciplinary History*, 25:1 (1994), 23–44.

Gemie, Sharif, 'Loti, orientalism and the French colonial experience', *Journal of European Area Studies*, 8:2 (2000), 149–65.

Georg, Odile, 'The French provinces and "Greater France"', in Chafer and Sackur, *Promoting the Colonial Idea*, 82–101.

Gervais, Raymond, 'La plus riche des colonies pauvres : la politique monétaire et fiscale de la France au Tchad 1900–1920', *Canadian Journal of African Studies*, 16:1 (1982), 93–112.

Geschière, Peter, 'European planters, African peasants, and the colonial state. Alternatives in the *mise en valeur* of Makaland, south-east Cameroon, during the interbellum', *African Economic History*, 12 (1983), 83–108.

Glover, John, ' "The Mosque is one thing, the administration is another". Murid *marabouts* and Wolof aristocrats in colonial Senegal', *International Journal of African Historical Studies*, 33:2 (2001), 351–65.

Goff, David H., 'Carrots, sticks, and cocoa pods. African and administrative initiatives in the spread of cocoa cultivation in Assikasso, Ivory Coast, 1908–1920', *International Journal of African Historical Studies*, 20:3 (1987), 401–16.

Goscha, Christopher E., 'L'Indochine repensée par les "Indochinois" : Pham Qùynh et les deux débats de 1931 sur l'immigration, le fédéralisme et la réalité de l'Indochine', *Revue Française d'Histoire d'Outre-Mer*, 82:309 (1995), 421–53.

Gouda, Frances, '*Nyonyas* on the colonial divide. White women in the Dutch East Indies, 1900–1942', *Gender and History*, 5:3 (1993), 318–42.

Gras, Yves, 'L'Indochine française et le nationalisme vietnamien (de la conquête à 1939)', *Revue Historique des Armées*, 4 (1984), 31–41.

Gray, Christopher, 'Lambaréné, Okoumé and the transformation of labor along the Middle Ogooué (Gabon), 1870–1945', *Journal of African History*, 40:1 (1999), 87–107.

Greenhalgh, Michael, 'The new centurians. French reliance on the Roman past during the conquest of Algeria', *War and Society*, 16:1 (1998), 1–28.

Guyer, Jane, 'Head tax, social structure and rural incomes in Cameroon, 1922–1937', *Cahiers d'Etudes Africaines*, 20 (1980), 305–22.

Haddad, Mahmoud, 'The origins of Arab nationalism reconsidered', *International Journal of Middle East Studies*, 26 (1994), 201–22.

Halstead, John P., 'The changing character of Moroccan reformism, 1921–1934', *Journal of African History*, 5:3 (1964), 435–47.

Hamadeh, Shirine, 'Creating the traditional city. A French project', in Al Sayyad, *Forms of Dominance*, 241–59.

Hardy, Andrew, 'The economics of French rule in Indochina. A biography of Paul Bernard (1892–1960)', *Modern Asian Studies*, 32:4 (1998), 807–48.

Hargreaves, John D., 'Assimilation in eighteenth-century Senegal', *Journal of African History*, 6:2 (1965), 177–84.

Hay, Margaret Jean, 'Queens, prostitutes and peasants. Historical perspectives on African women, 1971–1986', *Canadian Journal of African Studies*, 22:3 (1988), 431–47.

Hecht, Robert M., 'Immigration, land transfer and tenure changes in Divo, Ivory Coast, 1940–80', *Africa*, 55:3 (1985), 319–36.

Heffernan, Michael J., 'The Parisian poor and the colonization of Algeria during the Second Republic', *French History*, 3:4 (1989), 377–403.

—— 'The science of empire. The French geographical movement and the forms of French imperialism, 1870–1920', in Godlewska and Smith, *Geography and Empire*, 92–114.

—— 'The French right and the overseas empire', in Atkin and Tallett, *The Right in France*, 89–113.

Hémery, Daniel, 'Du patriotisme au marxisme : l'immigration vietnamienne en France de 1926 à 1930', *Le Mouvement Social*, 90:1 (1975), 3–54.

—— 'Aux origines des guerres d'indépendance vietnamiennes : pouvoir colonial et phénomène communiste en Indochine avant le seconde guerre mondiale', *Le Mouvement Social*, 101 (1977), 3–35.

—— 'L'Indochine, les droits humains entre colonisateurs et colonises, la Ligue des Droits de l'Homme (1898–1954)', *Outre-Mers*, 88:330 (2001), 223–39.

Henley, David E. F., 'Ethnogeographic integration and exclusion in anticolonial nationalism. Indonesia and Indochina', *Comparative Studies in Society and History*, 37:2 (1995), 286–324.

Henni, Ahmed, 'La naissance d'une classe moyenne paysanne musulmane après la première guerre mondiale', *Revue Française d'Histoire d'Outre-Mer*, 83:311 (1996), 47–64.

Hodgson, Dorothy L., and Sheryl McCurdy, 'Wayward wives, misfit mothers, and disobedient daughters. "Wicked" women and the reconfiguration of gender in Africa', *Canadian Journal of African Studies*, 30:1 (1996), 1–9.

Hoisington Jr, William A., 'Cities in revolt. The Berber Dahir (1930) and France's urban strategy in Morocco', *Journal of Contemporary History*, 13:4 (1978), 433–48.

—— 'In search of a native elite. Casablanca and French urban policy, 1914–24', *Maghreb Review*, 12:5–6 (1987), 160–5.

—— 'The Mediterranean Committee and French North Africa, 1935–1940', *Historian*, 53:2 (1991), 255–66.

—— 'French rule and the Moroccan elite', *Maghreb Review*, 22:1 (1997), 138–45.

Horne, John, 'Immigrant workers in France during World War I', *French Historical Studies*, 16:1 (1985), 57–88.

Hunt, Nancy Rose, 'Placing African women's history and locating gender', *Social History*, 14:3 (1989), 359–79.

Hunwick, John, 'Sub-Saharan Africa and the wider world of Islam. Historical and contemporary perspectives', in Westerlund and Rosander, *African Islam and Islam in Africa*, 28–54.

Huss, Marie-Monique, 'Pro-natalism in inter-war France', *Journal of Contemporary History*, 25:1 (1990), 39–68.

Hyam, Ronald, 'Concubinage and the colonial service. The Crewe circular (1909)', *Journal of Imperial and Commonwealth History*, 14 (1986), 170–86.

Ibhawoh, Bonny, 'Stronger than the Maxim gun. Law, human rights and British colonial hegemony in Nigeria', *Africa*, 72:1 (2002), 55–83.

Idowu, H. O., 'The establishment of elective institutions in Senegal, 1869–1880', *Journal of African History*, 9:2 (1968), 261–77.

Ihrai-Aouchar, Amina, 'La presse nationaliste et le régime du protectorat au Maroc dans l'entre-deux-guerres', *Revue de l'Occident Musulman et de la Méditerranée*, 34 (1983), 91–104.

Irbouh, Hamid, 'French colonial art education and the Moroccan feminine milieu. A case study from Fez, 1927–30', *Maghreb Review*, 25:3–4 (2000), 275–88.

Irvine, William D., 'Fascism in France and the strange case of the Croix de Feu', *Journal of Modern History* 63:2 (1991), 271–95.

Jackson, Jeffrey H., 'Making jazz French. The reception of jazz music in Paris, 1927–1934', *French Historical Studies*, 25:1 (2002), 149–70.

Jacobson, Jon, 'Strategies of French foreign policy after World War I', *Journal of Modern History*, 55:1 (1983), 78–95.

Jankowski, James, 'Egyptian responses to the Palestine problem in the inter-war period', *International Journal of Middle East Studies* 12:1 (1980), 1–38.

Jauffret, Jean-Charles, 'La loi du 7 juillet 1900 sur l'organisation des troupes coloniales : un accroissement de la puissance?' in Milza and Poidevin, *La Puissance française à la 'Belle Epoque'*, 51–62.

Jennings, Eric T., 'Monuments to Frenchness? The memory of the Great War and the politics of Guadeloupe's identity, 1914–1945', *French Historical Studies*, 21:4 (1998), 561–92.

—— 'From Indochine to Indochic. The Lang-Bian/Dalat Palace Hotel and French colonial leisure, power and culture', *Modern Asian Studies*, 37:1 (2003), 159–94.

Jensen, Geoffrey, 'Toward the "moral conquest" of Morocco. Hispano-Arabic education in early twentieth-century North Africa', *Journal of Contemporary History*, 31:2 (2001), 205–29.

Joarder, Safiuddin, 'The Syrian nationalist uprising (1925–1927) and Henri de Jouvenel', *Muslim World*, 68 (July 1977), 185–204.

Joffé, E. G. H., 'The Moroccan nationalist movement. Istiqlal, the Sultan and the country', *Journal of African History*, 26 (1985), 289–307.

—— 'Maghribi Islam and Islam in the Maghrib. The eternal dichotomy', in Westerlund and Rosander, *African Islam and Islam in Africa*, 55–71.

Johnson, George Wesley, 'The rivalry between Diagne and Merlin for political mastery of French West Africa', in Becker *et al.*, *AOF: réalités et heritages* I, 303–14.

Jones, D. H., 'The Catholic mission and some aspects of assimilation in Senegal, 1817–1852', *Journal of African History*, 21 (1980), 323–40.

Kaddache, Mahfoud, 'L'opinion politique musulmane en Algérie et l'administration française (1939–1942)', *Revue d'Histoire de la Deuxième Guerre Mondiale*, 114 (1979), 95–115.

Kanya-Forstner, A. S., 'The war, imperialism and decolonization', in Winter *et al.*, *The Great War and the Twentieth Century*, 231–62.

Keiger, John F. V., 'Raymond Poincaré and the Ruhr crisis', in Boyce, *French Foreign and Defence Policy*, 49–70.

Keller, Richard, 'Madness and colonization. Psychiatry in the British and French empires, 1800–1962', *Journal of Social History*, 35:2 (2001), 295–326.

Kelly, Gail P., 'Colonial schools in Vietnam. Policy and practice', in Altbach and Kelly, *Education and Colonialism*, 96–121.

—— 'Interwar schools and the development of African history in French West Africa', *History in Africa*, 10 (1983), 163–85.

—— 'The presentation of indigenous society in the schools of French West Africa and Indochina, 1918 to 1938', *Comparative Studies in Society and History*, 26:3 (1984), 523–42.

Khoury, Philip S., 'Factionalism among Syrian nationalists during the French Mandate', *International Journal of Middle East Studies*, 13 (November 1981), 441–69.

—— 'The tribal shaykh, French tribal policy, and the nationalist movement in Syria between two world wars', *International Journal of Middle East Studies*, 18:2 (1982), 180–93.

—— 'Syrian urban politics in transition. The quarters of Damascus during the French mandate', *International Journal of Middle East Studies*, 16:4 (1984), 507–40.

—— 'Divided loyalties? Syria and the question of Palestine, 1919–39', *Middle Eastern Studies*, 21:3 (1985), 324–48.

—— 'The Syrian independence movement and the growth of economic nationalism in Damascus', *British Society for Middle Eastern Studies Bulletin*, 14:1 (1988), 25–37.

—— 'The urban notables paradigm revisited', *Revue de l'Occident Musulman et de la Méditerranée* 56 (1990), 215–28.

Killingray, David, 'The idea of a British imperial African army', *Journal of African History*, 20:3 (1979), 421–36.

King, Anthony D., 'Writing colonial space. A review article', *Comparative Studies in Society and History*, 37:4 (1995), 541–54.

Koerner, Francis, 'Les répercussions de la guerre d'Espagne en Oranie (1936–1939)', *Revue d'Histoire Moderne et Contemporaine*, 22:3 (1975), 476–87.

—— 'Un Socialiste auvergnat Gouverneur Général d'Indochine. Le cas d'Alexandre Varenne (1925–1928)', *Revue Historique*, 285:1 (1991), 133–45.

Koller, Christian, 'Race and gender stereotypes in the discussion on colonial troops. A Franco-German comparison, 1914–1923', in Hagemann and Schüler-Springorum, *Home/Front*, 134–57.

Koos, Cheryl, 'Gender, anti-individualism, and nationalism. The Alliance Nationale and the pronatalist backlash against the *femme moderne*, 1933–1940', *French Historical Studies*, 19:4 (1996), 699–723.

Laffey, John F., 'Municipal imperialism in decline. The Lyon Chamber of Commerce, 1925–1938', *French Historical Studies*, 9:3–4 (1975), 329–53.

—— 'Lyonnais imperialism in the Far East, 1900–1938', *Modern Asian Studies*, 10:2 (1976), 225–48.

—— 'Imperialists divided. The views of Tonkin's colons before 1914', *Histoire Sociale/Social History*, 92 (1977), 92–113.

—— 'French Far Eastern policy in the 1930s', *Modern Asian Studies*, 23:1 (1989), 117–49.

Lafuente, Gilles, 'Dossier marocain sur le dahir berbère de 1930', *Revue de l'Occident Musulman et de la Méditerranée* 38 (1985), 83–116.

Lagana, Marc, 'L'échec de la commission d'enquête coloniale du Front populaire', *Historical Reflections*, 16:1 (1989), 79–97.

Lambert, Michael C., 'From citizenship to *négritude*. "Making a difference" in elite ideologies of colonized francophone West Africa', *Comparative Studies in Society and History*, 35:2 (1993), 239–62.

Lamprakos, Michele, 'Le Corbusier and Algiers. The Plan Obus as colonial urbanism', in Al Sayyad, *Forms of Dominance*, 183–210.

Larcher, Agathe, 'La voie étroite des réformes coloniales et la "collaboration franco-annamite" (1917–1928)', *Revue Française d'Histoire d'Outre-Mer*, 82:309 (1995), 387–420.

Lawrence, Paul, ' "Un flot d'agitateurs politiques, de fauteurs de désordre et de criminels". Adverse perceptions of immigrants in France between the wars', *French History*, 14:2 (2000), 201–21.

Le Guenac, Nicole, 'Le PCF et la guerre du Rif', *Le Mouvement Social*, 78:1 (1972), 48–63.

Levisse-Touzé, Christine, 'La préparation économique, industrielle et militaire de l'Afrique du Nord à la veille de la guerre', *Revue d'Histoire de la Deuxième Guerre Mondiale*, 142 (1986), 1–18.

Lewis, Mary Dewhurst, 'The strangeness of foreigners. Policing migration and nation in inter-war Marseille', *French Politics, Culture and Society*, 20:3 (2002), 65–96.

Lockman, Zachary, 'British policy towards Egyptian labour activism, 1882–1936', *International Journal of Middle East Studies*, 20 (1988), 265–85.

Lonsdale, John, 'States and social processes in Africa. A historiographical survey', *African Studies Review*, 24:2/3 (1981), 139–225.

Lorcin, Patricia M. E., 'Rome and France in Africa. Recovering colonial Algeria's Latin past', *French Historical Studies*, 25:2 (2002), 295–329.

Louis, O., 'De Bizerte à Mers el-Kebir : les bases navales d'Afrique du Nord dans l'entre-deux-guerres', *Revue Historique des Armées*, 4 (1999), 31–45.

Lowry, Donal, ' "The Boers were the beginning of the end"? The wider impact of the South African war', in Lowry, *The South African War Reappraised*, 203–46.

Lunn, Joe, ' "Les races guerrières". Racial preconceptions in the French military about West African soldiers during the First World War', *Journal of Contemporary History*, 34:4 (1999), 517–36.

Lydon, Ghislaine, 'The unravelling of a neglected source. A report on women in francophone Africa in the 1930s', *Cahiers d'Etudes Africaines*, 147 (1997), 555–84.

MacDougall, James, ' "Soi-même" comme un "autre". Les histories coloniales d'Ahmad Tawfiq al-Madani (1899–1983)', *Revue des Mondes Musulmans et de la Méditerrannée*, 95–98 (2002), 95–110.

MacMaster, Neil, 'Patterns of Emigration, 1905–1954. "Kabyles" and "Arabs" ', in Hargreaves and Heffernan, *French and Algerian Identities*, 21–31.

—— 'The Rue Fondary murders of 1923 and the origins of anti-Arab racism', in Windebank and Gunther, *Violence and Conflict*, 149–60.

—— 'Writing French Algeria', *French Cultural Studies*, 11 (2000), 149–55.

—— 'Imperial façades. Muslim institutions and propaganda in inter-war Paris', in Chafer and Sackur, *Promoting the Colonial Idea*, 71–81.

Mahafzah, A., 'La France et le mouvement nationaliste arabe de 1914 à 1950', *Relations Internationales*, 19 (1979), 295–312.

Makdisi, Ussama, 'After 1860. Debating religion, reform, and nationalism in the Ottoman Empire', *International Journal of Middle East Studies*, 33:3 (2002), 601–17.

Maktabi, Rania, 'The Lebanese census of 1932 revisited. Who are the Lebanese?' *British Journal of Middle Eastern Studies*, 26:2 (1999), 219–41.

Manchuelle, François, 'Origines républicaines de la politique d'expansion coloniale de Jules Ferry 1838–1865', *Revue Française d'Histoire d'Outre-Mer*, 75:279 (1988), 185–206.

—— 'Slavery, emancipation and labour migration in West Africa. The case of the Soninke', *Journal of African History*, 30:1 (1989), 89–106.

Manigand, Christine, 'Henry de Jouvenel, Haut-commissaire de la République française en Syrie et au Liban (1925–1926)', *Guerres Mondiales et Conflits Contemporains*, 192 (1998), 101–12.

Marchal, Jean-Yves, 'L'Office du Niger : îlot de prospérité paysanne ou pôle de production agricole', *Canadian Journal of African Studies*, 8:1 (1974), 73–90.

Marcovich, Anne, 'French colonial medicine and colonial rule. Algeria and Indochina', in Macleod and Lewis, *Disease, Medicine, and Empire*, 103–17.

Marseille, Jacques, 'L'industrie cotonnière française et l'impérialisme colonial', *Revue d'Histoire Economique et Sociale*, 53:2–3 (1975), 386–412.

—— 'La conférence des gouverneurs-généraux des colonies (novembre 1936)', *Le Mouvement Social*, 101 (1977), 61–84.

—— 'L'industrialisation des colonies. Affaiblissement ou renforcement de la puissance française?' *Revue Française d'Histoire d'Outre-Mer*, 69:254 (1982), 23–34.

—— 'Les relations commerciales entre la France et son empire colonial de 1880 à 1914', *Revue d'Histoire Moderne et Contemporaine*, 31:2 (1984), 286–307.

—— 'The phases of French colonial imperialism. Towards a new periodization', *Journal of Imperial and Commonwealth History*, 13:3 (1985), 127–41.

—— 'Les images de l'Afrique en France (des années 1880 aux années 1930)', *Canadian Journal of African Studies*, 22:1 (1988), 121–30.

Martin, Phyllis M., 'Contesting clothes in colonial Brazzaville', *Journal of African History*, 35:3 (1994), 401–26.

M'Bokolo, Elikia, 'Forces sociales et idéologies dans la décolonisation de l'AEF', *Journal of African History*, 22 (1981), 393–407.

McKesson, John A., 'French colonialism revisited', *French Politics and Society*, 13:1 (1995), 92–103.

McKinney, Mark, ' "Tout cela, je ne voulais pas le laisser perdre". Colonial *lieux de mémoire* in the comic books of Jacques Ferrandez', *Modern and Contemporary France*, 9:1 (2001), 43–53.

Méouchy, Nadine, 'La presse de Syrie et du Liban entre les deux guerres (1918–1939)', *Revue des Mondes Musulmans et de la Méditerranée*, 95–98 (2002), 55–70.

Melzer, Annabelle, 'Spectacles and sexualities. The *mise en scène* of the Tirailleur Sénégalais on the western front, 1914–1920', in Melman, *Borderlines*, 213–44.

Metzger, Chantal, 'L'empire colonial français dans la stratégie du Troisième Reich (1936–1945)', *Relations Internationales*, 101:1 (2000), 41–55.

Meynier, Gilbert, 'Volonté de propagande ou inconscient affiche? Images et imaginaire coloniaux français dans l'entre-deux-guerres', in Blanchard and Chatelier, *Images et Colonies*, 41–8.

Michel, Marc, 'La genèse du recrutement de 1918 en Afrique noire française', *Revue Française d'Histoire d'Outre-Mer*, 58 (1971).

—— 'Un programme réformiste en 1919. Maurice Delafosse et la politique indigene en AOF', *Cahiers d'Etudes Africaines*, 5:58 (1975), 313–27.

—— 'La puissance par l'empire. Note sur la perception du facteur imperial dans l'élaboration de la défense nationale (1936–1938)', *Revue Française d'Histoire d'Outre-Mer*, 69:254 (1982), 35–46.

—— 'Colonisation et défense nationale : le général Mangin et la Force Noire', *Guerres Mondiales et Conflits Contemporains*, 145 (1987), 27–44.

—— ' "Mémoire officielle", discours et pratique coloniale. Le 14 juillet et le 11 novembre au Sénégal entre les deux guerres', *Revue Française d'Histoire d'Outre-Mer*, 77:287 (1990), 145–58.

Moitt, Bernard, 'Slavery, flight and redemption in Senegal, 1819–1905', *Slavery and Abolition*, 14:2 (1993), 70–86.

Mouré, Kenneth, ' "Une éventualité absolument exclue". French reluctance to devalue, 1933–1936', *French Historical Studies*, 15:3 (1988), 479–505.

Munholland, Kim, 'Rival approaches to Morocco. Delcassé, Lyautey, and the Algerian–Moroccan border, 1903–1905', *French Historical Studies*, 5 (1968), 328–43.

—— 'The French response to the Vietnamese nationalist movement, 1905–1914', *Journal of Modern History*, 47:4 (1975), 655–75.

Murray, Alison, 'Documentary fiction. Images of sub-Saharan Africa in colonial film between the wars', *Proceedings of the Western Society for French History*, 25 (1998), 186–95.

—— 'Le tourisme Citroën au Sahara (1924–1925)', *Vingtième Siècle*, 68 (2000), 95–107.

—— 'Teaching colonial history through film', *French Historical Studies*, 25:1 (2002), 41–52.

Nelson, Keith L., 'The "black horror on the Rhine". Race as a factor in post-World War I diplomacy', *Journal of Modern History*, 42:4 (1970), 606–27.

Norindr, Panivong, 'Representing Indochina. The French colonial fantasmatic and the Exposition Coloniale de Paris', *French Cultural Studies*, 6:1 (1995), 35–60.

Nørlund, Irene, 'The French Empire, the colonial state in Vietnam and economic policy, 1885–1940', *Australian Economic History Review*, 31:1 (1991), 72–89.

—— 'Rice and the colonial lobby. The economic crisis in French Indochina in the 1920s and 1930s', in Boomgaard and Brown, *Weathering the Storm*, 198–226.

Nouschi, André, 'Pipelines et politiques au Proche-Orient dans les années 1930', *Relations Internationales*, 19 (1979), 279–94.

Offen, Karen, 'The second sex and the *baccalauréat* in republican France, 1880–1924', *French Historical Studies*, 13:2 (1983), 252–86.

—— 'Depopulation, nationalism and feminism in *fin-de-siècle* France', *American Historical Review*, 89:4 (1984), 655–75.

Olmert, Yossi, 'A false dilemma? Syria and Lebanon's independence during the mandatory period', *Middle Eastern Studies*, 32:3 (1996), 41–73.

Oloruntimehin, Olatunji, 'Education for colonial dominance in French West Africa from 1900 to the Second World War', *Journal of the Historical Society of Nigeria*, 7:2 (1974), 347–56.

—— 'The economy of French West Africa between the two World Wars', *Journal of African Studies*, 4:1 (1977), 51–76.

Osborn, Emily Lynn, ' "Circle of iron". African colonial employees and the interpretation of colonial rule in French West Africa', *Journal of African History*, 44:1 (2003), 29–50.

Osterhaus, André, and Claude Sissau, 'Les révoltes de femmes en Afrique durant la période coloniale', in Groupe Afrique noire, *L'Histoire des femmes en Afrique*, Cahier no. 11, (Paris: Editions l'Harmattan, 1987), 36–41.

O'Toole, Thomas, 'The 1928–1931 Gbaya insurrection in Ubangui-Shari. Messianic movement or village self-defense?' *Canadian Journal of African Studies*, 18:2 (1984), 329–44.

Oved, Georges, 'Contribution à l'étude de l'endettement de la colonisation agricole au Maroc', *Revue Française d'Histoire d'Outre-Mer*, 63:232 (1976), 492–505.

Palermo, Lucy E., 'Mixed messages. *L'Illustration* on the Exposition Coloniale of 1931', *Proceedings of the Western Society for French History*, 25 (1998), 425–50.

Paxton, Robert, 'The five stages of fascism', *Journal of Modern History*, 70:1 (1998), 1–23.

Pederson, Jean Elizabeth, ' "Special customs". Paternity suits and citizenship in France and the colonies, 1870–1912', in Clancy-Smith and Gouda, *Domesticating the Empire*, 43–64.

Pederson, Susan, 'National bodies, unspeakable acts. The sexual politics of colonial policy making', *Journal of Modern History*, 63:4 (1991), 647–80.

Pennell, C. R., 'Ideology and practical politics. A case study of the Rif war in Morocco, 1921–1926', *International Journal of Middle East Studies*, 14 (1982), 19–33.

—— 'Women and resistance to colonialism in Morocco. The Rif, 1916–1926', *Journal of African History*, 28 (1987), 107–18.

Person, Yves, 'Le Front populaire au Sénégal (mai 1936–octobre 1938)', *Le Mouvement Social*, 107:2 (1979), 77–102.

Pervillé, Guy, 'Le sentiment national des étudiants algériens de culture français de 1912 à 1942', *Relations Internationales*, 2 (1974), 233–59.

Picciola, André, 'Quelques aspects de la Côte d'Ivoire en 1919', *Cahiers d'Etudes Africaines*, 13:2 (1973), 239–74.

Pithon, Rémy, 'Opinions publiques et réprésentations culturelles face aux problèmes de la puissance. Le témoignage du cinéma français (1938–1939)', *Relations Internationales*, 33 (1983), 91–102.

—— 'French film propaganda, July 1939–June 1940', in Short, *Film and Radio Propaganda*, 78–93.

Powers, David S., 'Orientalism, colonialism, and legal history. The attack on Muslim family endowments in Algeria and India', *Comparative Studies in Society and History*, 31:3 (1989), 535–71.

Prochaska, David, 'The political culture of settler colonialism in Algeria. Politics in Bône (1870–1920)', *Revue de l'Occident Musulman et de la Méditerranée* 49 (1989), 293–311.

—— 'Approaches to the economy of colonial Annaba, 1870–1920', *Africa*, 60:4 (1990), 497–524.

—— 'History as literature, literature as history. Cagayous of Algiers', *American Historical Review*, 101:3 (1996), 671–711.

Qadéry, Mustapha El, 'Les Berbères entre le mythe colonial et la négation nationale.

Le cas du Maroc', *Revue d'Histoire Moderne et Contemporaine*, 45:2 (1998), 425–50.

Rabearimanana, Lucile, 'Changements et persistence de la domination française à Madagascar de 1930 à 1972', *Relations Internationales*, 77 (1994), 99–114.

Rabinovitch, Itamar, 'The compact minorities and the Syrian state, 1918–45', *Journal of Contemporary History*, 14:4 (1979), 693–712.

—— 'Oil and local politics. The French–Iraqi negotiations of the early 1930s', in Dann, *The Great Powers in the Middle East*, 172–82.

Rabut, Elisabeth, 'Le mythe parisien de la mise en valeur des colonies africaines à l'aube du XXe siècle : la commission des concessions coloniales, 1898–1912', *Journal of African History*, 20:2 (1979), 271–87.

Rainero, Romain, 'La politique fasciste à l'égard de l'Afrique du Nord : l'épée de l'Islam et la revendication sur la Tunisie', *Revue Française d'Histoire d'Outre-Mer*, 64:237 (1977), 498–515.

Regad-Pellagru, Claudette, 'La conception de la politique française des grands travaux et l'évolution de l'Indochine de 1936 à 1947', in Ageron, *Les Chemins de la décolonisation*, 147–55.

Reggiani, Andrés Horacio, 'Procreating France. The politics of demography, 1919–1945', *French Historical Studies*, 19:3 (1996), 75–56.

Reinders, R., 'Racialism on the left. E. D. Morel and the "black horror on the Rhine" ', *International Review of Social History*, 12:1 (1968), 1–28.

Rey-Goldzeiguer, Annie, 'Réflexions sur l'image et la perception du Maghreb et des Maghrébins dans la France du XIXe et XXe siècles', in Blanchard and Chatelier, *Images et Colonies*, 33–40.

Reynolds, Siân, 'Women and the Popular Front. The case of the three women Ministers', *French History*, 8:2 (1994), 196–224.

Rioux, Jean-Pierre, 'Les socialistes dans l'entreprise au temps du Front populaire. Quelques remarques sur les Amicales socialistes (1936–1939)', *Le Mouvement Social*, 16:1 (1979), 3–24.

Rivet, Daniel, 'Reformer le protectorat français au Maroc?' *Revue des Mondes Musulmans et de la Méditerranée*, 83 (1998), 75–92.

Roberts, Mary Louise, ' "This civilization no longer has sexes". *La Garçonne* and cultural crisis in France after World War I', *Gender and History*, 4:1 (1992), 49–69.

Roberts, Richard, and Martin A. Klein, 'The Banamba slave exodus of 1905 and the decline of slavery in the western Sudan', *Journal of African History*, 21 (1980), 375–94.

Robinson, David Robinson, 'French "Islamic" policy and practice in late nineteenth century Senegal', *Journal of African History*, 29 (1988), 415–35.

Rosenberg, Clifford, 'Albert Sarraut and republican racial thought', *French Politics, Culture and Society* 20:3 (2002), 97–114.

—— 'The politics of healthcare provision in interwar Paris', *French Historical Studies*, 27:3 (2004), 637–68.

Roshwald, Aviel, 'Colonial dreams of the French right wing, 1881–1914', *Historian*, 57:1 (1994), 59–74.

Sabatier, Peggy R., ' "Elite" education in French West Africa. The era of limits, 1903–1945', *International Journal of African Historical Studies*, 11:2 (1978), 247–66.

[389]

Sah, Léonard I., 'Activités allemandes et germanophilie au Cameroun (1936–1939)', *Revue Française d'Histoire d'Outre-Mer*, 69:255 (1982), 129–44.

Salerno, Reynolds M., 'Britain, France and the emerging Italian threat, 1935–1938', in Alexander and Philpott, *Anglo-French Defence Relations*, 72–91.

Salvaing, Bernard, 'La femme dahoméenne vue par les missionaires. Arrogance culturelle ou antiféminisme clerical?' *Cahiers d'Etudes Africaines*, 84 (1981), 507–22.

Sanson, Rosemonde, 'La perception de la puissance par l'Alliance démocratique', *Revue d'Histoire Moderne et Contemporaine*, 31:4 (1984), 636–57.

Sari, Djilali, 'The role of the medinas in the reconstruction of Algerian culture and identity', in Slyomovics, *The Walled Arab City*, 69–79.

Sauvy, Alfred, 'The economic crisis of the 1930s in France', *Journal of Contemporary History*, 4:4 (1969), 21–35.

Schilcher, Linda Schatkowski, 'The famine of 1915–1918 in Greater Syria', in Spagnolo, *Problems of the Modern Middle East*, 229–58.

Schler, Lynn, 'Ambiguous spaces. The struggle over African identities and urban communities in colonial Douala, 1914–45', *Journal of African History*, 44:1 (2003), 51–72.

Schlesinger, Mildred, 'The Cartel des gauches: precursor to the Front populaire', *European Studies Review*, 8:2 (1978), 211–34.

Schor, Ralph, 'Immigration familiale et assimilation : l'opinion de spécialistes', *Revue de l'Occident Musulman et de la Méditerranée* 43 (1987), 67–71.

Schweitzer, T-A., 'Le Parti communiste français, le Comintern et l'Algérie dans les années 1930', *Le Mouvement Social*, 78 (1972), 115–36.

Searing, James F., 'Conversion to Islam. Military recruitment and generational conflict in a Sereer-Safèn village (Bandia), 1920–38', *Journal of African History*, 44:1 (2003), 73–94.

Segalen, Martine, 'Here but invisible. The presentation of women in French ethnography museums', *Gender and History*, 6:3 (1994), 334–44.

Semidei, Manuela, 'Les Socialistes français et le problème colonial entre les deux guerres (1919–1939)', *Revue Française de Science Politique*, 18:6 (1968), 1115–53.

Serre, J., 'Vie et morts des entreprises en Indochine française (1875–1944)', *Revue Française d'Histoire d'Outre-Mer*, 87 (2000), 159–76.

Sherman, Daniel J., 'Bodies and names. The emergence of commemoration in interwar France', *American Historical Review*, 103:2 (1998), 443–66.

—— ' "People's Ethnographic": Objects, Museums, and the Colonical Inheritance of French Ethnography', *French Historical Studies*, 27:3 (2004), 674–86.

Shmuelevitz, Aryeh, 'Atatürk's policy toward the great powers. Principles and guide-lines', in Dann, *The Great Powers in the Middle East*, 311–16.

Shorrock, William I., 'The Tunisian question in French policy toward Italy', *International Journal of African Historical Studies*, 16:4 (1983), 631–51.

Showalter, Dennis E., 'Plans, weapons, doctrines. The strategic cultures of inter-war Europe', in Chickering and Forster, *The Shadows of Total War*, 55–81.

Singer, Barnett, 'From patriots to pacifists. The French primary school teachers, 1880–1940', *Journal of Contemporary History*, 12:3 (1977), 413–34.

—— 'Lyautey. An interpretation of the man and French imperialism', *Journal of Contemporary History*, 26:1 (1991), 131–58.

Sirot, Stéphane, 'Les conditions de travail et les grèves des ouvriers coloniaux à Paris des lendemains de la première guerre mondiale à la veille de la Front populaire', *Revue Française d'Histoire d'Outre-Mer*, 83:311 (1996), 65–92.

Slavin, David H., 'The French left and the Rif war, 1924–1925. Racism and the limits of internationalism', *Journal of Contemporary History*, 26:1 (1991), 5–32.

—— 'French colonial film before and after *Itto*. From Berber myth to race war', *French Historical Studies*, 21:1 (1998), 125–55.

Slim, Souad, and Anne-Laure Dupont, 'La vie intellectuelle des femmes à Beyrouth dans les années 1920 à travers la revue *Minerva*', *Revue des Mondes Musulmans et de la Méditerranée*, 95–98 (2002), 381–406.

Sluglett, Peter, 'Urban dissidence in mandatory Syria. Aleppo, 1918–1936', in Brown *et al.*, *Etat, ville et mouvements sociaux*, 301–16.

Smith, Paul, 'Political parties, parliament and women's suffrage in France, 1919–1939', *French History*, 11:3 (1997), 338–55.

Smith, R. B., 'Bui Quang Chieu and the Constitutionalist Party in French Cochinchina, 1917–1930', *Modern Asian Studies*, 3:2 (1969), 131–50.

—— 'The foundation of the Indochinese Communist Party, 1929–1930', *Modern Asian Studies*, 32:4 (1998), 769–805.

Smith, Tony, 'Muslim impoverishment in colonial Algeria', *Revue de l'Occident Musulman*, 156 (1974), 139–72.

—— 'The French colonial consensus and people's war, 1946–1958', *Journal of Contemporary History*, 9 (1974), 217–47.

—— 'A comparative study of French and British decolonization', *Comparative Studies in Society and History*, 20:1 (1978), 70–102.

Smyth, Rosaleen, 'The development of British colonial film policy, 1927–1939, with special reference to East and Central Africa', *Journal of African History*, 20:3 (1979), 437–50.

Sohn, Ann-Marie, 'The Golden Age of male adultery. The Third Republic', *Journal of Social History*, 28:3 (1995), 469–90.

Sorlin, Pierre, 'The fanciful empire. French feature films and the colonies in the 1930s', *French Cultural Studies*, 2 (1991), 135–51.

Sorlot, Marc, 'Les entourages militaires d'André Maginot dans les années 1920', in Forcade *et al.*, *Militaires en République*, 143–51.

Spagnolo, John, 'The definition of a style of internal politics of the French educational investment in Ottoman Beirut', *French Historical Studies*, 8:4 (1974), 563–84.

Sraieb, Noureddine, 'Islam, réformisme et condition féminine en Tunisie : Tahar Haddad (1898–1935)', *Clio: Histoire, Femmes et Sociétés*, 9 (1999), 75–92.

Stoler, Ann Laura, 'Rethinking colonial categories. European communities and the boundaries of rule', *Comparative Studies in Society and History*, 31:1 (1989), 134–61.

—— 'Making empire respectable. The politics of race and sexual morality in twentieth-century colonial cultures', *American Ethnologist* 16:4 (1989), 634–60.

—— 'Carnal knowledge and imperial power. Gender, race and morality in colonial Asia', in Di Leonardo, *Gender at the Crossroads of Knowledge*, 51–101.

—— 'Sexual affronts and racial frontiers. European identities and the cultural politics of exclusion in colonial South East Asia', *Comparative Studies in Society and History*, 34:3 (1992), 514–51.

Stora, Benjamin, 'La gauche socialiste révolutionnaire, et la question du Maghreb au moment du Front populaire (1935–1938)', *Revue Française d'Histoire d'Outre-Mer*, 70: 258 (1983), 57–79.

—— 'Les mémoires de Messali Hadj. Aspects du manuscrit original', *Revue de l'Occident et de la Méditerranée*, 36 (1985), 75–101.

—— 'Les juifs d'Algérie dans le regard des militaires et des juifs de France à l'époque de la conquête (1830–1855)', *Revue Historique*, 284:4 (1990), 333–9.

—— 'La construction d'un imaginaire politique dans l'espace migratoire. Les algériens en France 1920–1954', *Maghreb Review*, 16:3–4 (1991), 196–9.

Stovall, Tyler, 'Colour-blind France? Colonial workers during the First World War', *Race and Class*, 35:2 (1993), 35–55.

—— 'The color line behind the lines. Racial violence in France during the First World War', *American Historical Review*, 103:3 (1998), 739–69.

Strebel, Elizabeth Grottle, 'French social cinema and the Popular Front', *Journal of Contemporary History*, 12:3 (1977), 499–520.

Stuart-Fox, Martin, 'The French in Laos, 1887–1945', *Modern Asian Studies*, 29:1 (1995), 111–39.

Summers, Anne, and R. W. Johnson, 'World War I conscription and social change in Guinea', *Journal of African History*, 19:1 (1978), 25–38.

Swearingen, Will D., 'In pursuit of the granary of Rome. France's wheat policy in Morocco, 1915–1931', *International Journal of Middle East Studies*, 17 (185), 347–63.

Taboulet, Georges, 'La France et l'Angleterre face au conflit sino-japonais (1937–1939)', *Revue d'Histoire Diplomatique*, 88 (January–June 1974), 112–44.

Taguieff, Pierre-André, 'Face à l'immigration : mixophobie, xénophobie ou selection. Un débat français dans l'entre-deux-guerres', *Vingtième Siècle*, 47:3 (1995), 103–31.

Tai, Hue-Tam Ho, 'The politics of compromise. The Constitutionalist Party and the electoral reforms of 1922 in French Cochin-china', *Modern Asian Studies*, 18:3 (1984), 371–91.

Thébaud, Françoise, 'Le mouvement nataliste dans la France d'entre-deux-guerres : l'Alliance national pour l'accroissement de la population française', *Revue d'Histoire Moderne et Contemporaine* 32 (1985), 276–301.

Thobie, Jacques, 'Le nouveau cours des relations franco-turques et l'affaire du sandjak d'Alexandrette, 1921–1939', *Relations Internationales*, 19 (autumn 1979), 355–74.

—— 'La France a-t-elle une politique culturelle dans l'empire ottoman à la veille de la première guerre mondiale?' *Relations Internationales*, 25:1 (1981), 21–40.

Thomas, Martin, 'At the heart of things? French imperial defense planning in the late 1930s', *French Historical Studies*, 21:2 (1998), 325–61.

—— 'France and the Czechoslovak crisis', *Diplomacy and Statecraft*, 10:2–3 (1999), 122–59.

—— 'The Vichy government and French colonial prisoners of war, 1940–1944', *French Historical Studies*, 25:4 (2002), 657–92.

—— 'Imperial defence or diversionary attack? Anglo-French strategic planning in the Near East, 1936–1940', in Alexander and Philpott, *Anglo-French Defence Relations*, 157–85.

'Bedouin tribes and the imperial intelligence services in Syria, Iraq and Transjordan in the 1920s', *Journal of Contemporary History*, 38:4 (2003), 539–62.

Thompson, Andrew, 'Publicity, philanthropy and commemoration. British society and the war', in Omissi and Thompson, *The Impact of the South African War*, 99–123.

Thompson, Elizabeth, 'The climax and crisis of the colonial welfare state in Syria and Lebanon during World War II', in Heydemann, *War, Institutions, and Social Change*, 59–99.

Thioub, Ibrahima, 'Economie coloniale et rémunération de la force de travail : le salaire de manoeuvre à Dakar de 1930 à 1954', *Revue Française d'Histoire d'Outre-Mer*, 81:305 (1994), 427–53.

—— 'Sénégal : la santé des détenus dans les prisons coloniales', *Revue Française d'Histoire d'Outre-Mer*, 89:324 (1999), 65–78.

Tumblety, Joan, ' "Civil wars of the mind". The commemoration of the 1789 revolution in the Parisian press of the radical right, 1939', *Journal of Contemporary History*, 30:3 (2000), 389–429.

Vann, Michael G., 'The good, the bad, and the ugly. Variation and difference in French racism in colonial Indochina', *Proceedings of the Western Society for French History*, 25 (1998), 11–23.

Venier, Pascal, 'A campaign of colonial propaganda. Gallieni, Lyautey and the defence of the military regime in Madagascar, May 1899 to July 1900', in Chafer and Sackur, *Promoting the Colonial Idea*, 29–39.

Wall, Irwin M., 'Socialists and bureaucrats. The Blum government and the French administration, 1936–37', *International Review of Social History*, 19:3 (1974), 325–46.

White, Owen, 'Miscegenation and the popular imagination', in Chafer and Sackur, *Promoting the Colonial Idea*, 133–42.

Wilder, Gary, 'Framing Greater France between the wars', *Journal of Historical Sociology*, 14:2 (2001), 198–225.

Woodside, Alexander B., 'The development of social organizations in Vietnamese cities in the late colonial period', *Pacific Affairs*, 44:1 (1971), 39–64.

Wright, Gwendolyn, 'Tradition in the service of modernity. Architecture and urbanism in French colonial policy, 1900–1930', *Journal of Modern History*, 59:2 (1987), 291–316.

Yearwood, Peter, 'Great Britain and the repartition of Africa, 1914–19', *Journal of Imperial and Commonwealth History*, 18:1 (1990), 316–41.

—— ' "In a casual way with a blue pencil". British policy and the partition of Kamerun, 1914–1919', *Canadian Journal of African Studies*, 27:2 (1993), 218–44.

Zamir, Meir, 'Faisal and the Lebanese question, 1918–1920', *Middle Eastern Studies*, 27:3 (1991), 404–26.

Zaretsky, Robert D., 'Neither left, nor right, nor straight ahead. Recent books on fascism in France'. *Journal of Modern History*, 73:1 (2001), 118–32.

Zeraffa, Danièle, 'La perception de la puissance dans la formation Démocrate chrétienne', *Revue d'Histoire Moderne et Contemporaine*, 31:4 (1984), 658–65.

Zinoman, Peter, 'Colonial prisons and anti-colonial resistance in French Indochina. The Thai Nguyen rebellion, 1917', *Modern Asian Studies*, 34:1 (2000), 57–98.

PhD theses

Gallup, Dorothea M., 'The French image of Algeria. Its origin, its place in colonial ideology, its effect on Algerian acculturation', University of California Los Angeles, PhD, 1973.

Gates, Caroline L., 'The historical role of political economy in the development of modern Lebanon. The state and the economy from colonialism to independence, 1939–1952', Oxford University DPhil, 1985.

Kerr, David H., 'The temporal authority of the Maronite patriarchate, 1920–1958. A study in the relationship of religious and secular power', Oxford University DPhil, 1973.

Miller, Carol, 'Lobbying the League. Women's international organizations and the League of Nations', Oxford University DPhil, 1992.

Rosenberg, Clifford, 'Republican surveillance. Immigration, citizenship and the police in interwar Paris', Princeton University PhD, 2000.

Solh, Raghid, 'Lebanon and Arab nationalism, 1935–1945', Oxford University DPhil, 1985.

INDEX